American Women Activists' Writings

American Women Activists' Writings

An Anthology, 1637–2002

Edited by
Kathryn Cullen-DuPont

Cooper Square Press

First Cooper Square Press edition 2002

This Cooper Square Press hardcover edition of *American Women Activists' Writings* is an original publication. It is published by arrangement with the editor.

Published by Cooper Square Press,
An Imprint of Rowman & Littlefield Publishing Group, Inc.
150 Fifth Avenue, Suite 817
New York, NY 10011

Distributed by National Book Network

Library of Congress Cataloging-in-Publication Data
American women activists' writings: an anthology, 1637–2002 / edited by Kathryn Cullen-DuPont.— 1st Cooper Square Press ed.
    p. cm.
  Includes bibliographical references.
  ISBN 0-8154-1185-5 (cloth : alk. paper)
    1. Women—United States—History—Sources.   2. Women social reformers—United States—History—Sources.   3. Women civic leaders—United States—History—Sources.   I. Cullen-DuPont, Kathryn.

HQ1410 .A45   2002
305.4'0973—dc21   2001053728

⊗™ The paper used in this publication meets the minimum requirements of American National Standard for Information Sciences—Permanence of Paper for Printed Library Materials, ANSI/NISO Z.39.48-1992.
Manufactured in the United States of America

For my mother-in-law,
Barbara DuPont

and in memory of my father-in-law,
Joseph G. DuPont

Acknowledgments

~

I would like to thank my editor, Michael Dorr; assistant editor Ross Plotkin; production editor Julie Kirsch; my literary agent, Elizabeth Frost-Knappman; the staffs of the New York Public Library, the Bancroft Library at the University of California, Berkeley, and the Sophia Smith Collection at Smith College; and all those who so generously granted permission to include their writings in this anthology. I would also like to thank my husband, Joseph DuPont; my children, Melissa and Jesse Cullen-DuPont; and my parents, Martin and Arlene Cullen, for their continued interest and support.

Contents

~

Pg.10

Chronology of Events

1637   Anne Hutchinson is tried by the civil court of the Massachusetts Bay colony and convicted of "traducing the ministers and their ministry."

1638   Anne Hutchinson is tried before the clergy and the church of Boston; she is convicted of heresy and excommunicated.

1775   Abigail Adams writes to her husband, John Adams, to request that he and the Continental Congress include women's rights in the new nation's code of laws.

1821   Lucretia Mott is recorded as a Quaker minister.

1823   Catharine Beecher, with her sister Mary, opens what becomes the Hartford Female Seminary.

1826   Sojourner Truth escapes slavery.

1832   Maria W. Stewart delivers her first speech, at Franklin Hall, Boston.

1833   Maria W. Stewart gives her "Farewell Address."

1836   Angelina Grimké writes "An Appeal to the Christian Women of the South" and Sarah Grimké writes an "Epistle to the Clergy of the Southern States."

1837   The Massachusetts clergy reads from the orthodox church's pulpits a *Pastoral Letter* denouncing the Grimké sisters for speaking to "mixed" audiences of men and women. Catharine Beecher adds her own criticism in "An Essay on Slavery and Abolitionism, with Reference to the Duty of American Women."

Mount Holyoke Seminary, founded by Mary Lyon, opens its doors. It will become Mount Holyoke College.

1840   Elizabeth Cady Stanton accompanies her husband to the World Anti-Slavery Convention in London, England. When female delegates are refused participation on grounds of gender, Stanton, Lucretia Mott, and other women speak of beginning a women's rights movement upon their return to the United States.

1845   Margaret Fuller's *Woman in the Nineteenth Century* is published.

1847   Elizabeth Blackwell begins her medical training at Geneva University.

Lucy Stone graduates from Oberlin College. The college's policy calls for the graduation speeches of female students to be read aloud on their behalf by male students. Refused permission to read her own speech, Stone insists that it remain unread.

1848   Elizabeth Cady Stanton, Lucretia Mott, and others organize the Seneca Falls Convention, and the women's movement in the United States officially begins.

1851   Sojourner Truth delivers her speech "Ain't I a Woman."

The True Remedies for the Wrongs of Woman by Catharine Beecher is published.

1855   Lucy Stone and Henry Blackwell marry. They use the occasion to protest the inequities in marriage law, and Lucy Stone retains her surname.

1859   Frances Ellen Watkins Harper's "The Two Officers" appears in the *Anglo-African Magazine*. It is believed to be the first short story published by an African American.

1860   The Reverend Theophilus Packard, exercising his discretion as a husband, has his wife, Elizabeth Packard, committed to the Illinois State Hospital for the Insane.

1864   At the conclusion of *Packard v. Packard*, Elizabeth Packard is found sane and given her liberty. She begins her campaign for legislative reform.

1869   The women's movement splits into two factions, represented by the National Woman American Suffrage Association, headed by Elizabeth Cady Stanton and Susan B. Anthony, and the American Woman Suffrage Association, headed by Lucy Stone.

1870   Henry Blackwell reads Catharine Beecher's statement in opposition to women's suffrage to those attending a convention of the American Woman Suffrage Association.

Victoria Woodhull becomes the first woman to run for election to the U.S. presidency.

1871   Anna Howard Shaw receives her license to preach in the Methodist Protestant Church.

Abigail Scott Dunniway begins publication of her suffrage newspaper *The New Northwest*.

1872   Victoria Woodhull exposes the affair of abolitionist clergy-man Henry Ward Beecher and Elizabeth Tilden in her newspaper, *Woodhull & Claflin's Weekly*, explaining that her goal is to expose the hypocrisy of those who criticize her stand on "free love."

Susan B. Anthony is arrested for voting.

1873   Susan B. Anthony is convicted of illegal voting.

1879   Frances Willard becomes president of the National Woman's Christian Temperance Union.

1880   Anna Howard Shaw becomes the first ordained woman minister in the Methodist Protestant Church.

1881   Clara Barton addresses the U.S. Congress to urge the United States to sign the 1864 Geneva convention.

1882   The United States signs the 1864 Geneva Convention and becomes a member of the International Red Cross.

1884   Zitkala-Sa leaves her home at the Yankon Sioux Agency to attend a Quaker-run boarding school for Native American children.

1889   Jane Addams and Ellen Starr found Hull House in Chicago.

Carry Nation begins wrecking damage on Kansas saloons.

1892   In response to the Homestead Strike, Emma Goldman helps her lover to procure a gun for his attempted assas-sination of steel mill owner Henry Clay Frick.

1895   Ida B. Wells-Barnett publishes *A Red Record*, a study of lynching in America.

Lillian Wald founds what becomes the Visiting Nurse Service of New York.

Liliuokalani, queen of Hawaii, is placed under house arrest and forced to abdicate her throne.

1900   The American Red Cross is established, and Clara Barton becomes its first president.

Carrie Chapman Catt is elected president of the National American Woman Suffrage Association.

Helen Keller enters Radcliffe College.

1901   Anna Julia Cooper becomes principal of the M Street High School in Washington, D.C.

1903   "Mother" Mary Jones conducts a march of child mill workers from Pennsylvania to President Theodore Roosevelt's home in Oyster Bay, New York, to denounce child labor and demand reform.

1904   Ida Tarbell's book, *The History of the Standard Oil Company*, is published.

Mary McLeod Bethune founds what becomes the Bethune-Cookman College.

1906   Elizabeth Gurley Flynn gives her first speech. Later that year, she is arrested for the first time.

Emma Goldman advises poor families to steal bread. She is arrested and jailed for one year.

Anna Julia Cooper is dismissed as principal of the M Street High School.

1908   The U.S. government strips Emma Goldman's former husband of his citizenship, thereby stripping Goldman of her citizenship as well.

1909   Ida B. Wells-Barnett travels to Cairo, Illinois, to protest the reinstatement of a sheriff who had failed to protect his prisoner from a lynch mob.

1912   Margaret Sanger nurses Sadie Sachs through the aftereffects of a self-induced abortion and, three months later, attends her as she dies following another self-induced abortion.

1915   Emma Goldman is arrested for instructing an audience in the use of contraceptives. She spends fifteen days in jail.

1916   Carrie Chapman Catt outlines her "Winning Plan" for what becomes the final phase of the suffrage struggle.

        Jeannette Rankin becomes the first woman elected to serve in the U.S. House of Representatives.

1917   Carrie Chapman Catt addresses the U.S. Congress to urge passage of the Nineteenth Amendment.

        Jeannette Rankin votes against the United States' entry into World War I.

        Alice Paul, while picketing the White House to demand women's suffrage, is arrested on charges of obstructing a sidewalk. She is convicted and sentenced to seven months' imprisonment.

1919   Congress passes the Nineteenth Amendment and submits it to the states for ratification.

1920   The Nineteenth Amendment, enfranchising women, is ratified.

1923   Alice Paul drafts the Equal Rights Amendment.

1927   Dorothy Day converts to Roman Catholicism.

1928   Amelia Earhart becomes the first woman to fly across the Atlantic Ocean, as a log keeper on the *Friendship*.

1930   Babe Didrikson Zaharias is chosen for the women's All-American basketball team for the first time.

1931   Jane Addams is awarded the Nobel Prize for Peace.

1932   Amelia Earhart becomes the first woman to fly solo across the Atlantic Ocean.

1933   Dorothy Day and Peter Maurin found the *Catholic Worker* newspaper.

1935   President Franklin D. Roosevelt appoints Mary McLeod Bethune administrator of the Office of Minority Affairs. Her title is later changed to Director of the Division of Negro Affairs.

1937   Amelia Earhart disappears while attempting to fly around the world.

1941   Jeanette Rankin is the only member of Congress to vote against entry into World War II.

       Rachel Carson's first book, *Under the Sea Wind*, is published.

1948   The Universal Declaration of Human Rights, crafted largely by Eleanor Roosevelt, passes the General Assembly of the United Nations.

1959   On her seventy-fifth birthday, Eleanor Roosevelt reflects upon her life in the essay "Milestones."

1961   Helen Gurley Flynn becomes the first female national chair of the Communist Party.

Rachel Carson's *The Silent Spring* is published.

Eleanor Roosevelt is appointed by President John F. Kennedy to head the Commission on the Status of Women.

1962   Members of Women Strike for Peace appear before the House Un-American Activities Committee.

Jessie Lopez De La Cruz joins Cesar Chavez in his effort to unionize migrant farm workers.

1963   Anne Moody helps to end segregation at the Woolworth's lunch counter in Mississippi.

Betty Friedan's *The Feminine Mystique* is published.

1965   The Supreme Court's decision in *Griswold v. Connecticut* invalidates all state laws restricting married persons' access to contraception.

1969   The Abortion Counseling Service of Women's Liberation is formed in Chicago. It begins to operate under the code name "Jane."

1971   The Supreme Court decision in *Reed v. Reed* finds sex discrimination to be a violation of the Fourteenth Amendment's equal protection clause. Ruth Bader Ginsburg is part of the victorious legal team.

1972   The Equal Rights Amendment is passed by Congress and sent to the states for ratification.

Gloria Steinem and Patricia Carbine found *Ms.* magazine.

The Supreme Court rules, in *Eisenstadt v. Baird*, that states may not restrict unmarried persons' access to contraception.

1973   The Supreme Court's decision in *Roe v. Wade* legalizes abortion in the United States.

1975   Susan Brownmiller's *Against Our Will: Men, Women and Rape* is published.

Phyllis Schlafly founds Stop ERA to work for the defeat of the Equal Rights Amendment.

1980   Merle Woo writes her "Letter to Ma."

1981   Sandra Day O'Connor becomes the first woman to serve on the U.S. Supreme Court.

1982   The Equal Rights Amendment fails, three states short of ratification.

Alice Walker's *The Color Purple* is published.

1984   Geraldine Ferraro receives the Democratic Party's nomination for election to vice president.

1985   Wilma Mankiller becomes Principal Chief of the Cherokee Nation.

1986   Mary Cunningham Agee founds the Nurturing Network to help women find alternatives to abortion in the event of an unwanted pregnancy.

1992   Margarethe Cammermeyer becomes the highest-ranking military official discharged for homosexuality.

         Alice Walker's *Possessing the Secret of Joy* is published.

1993   Ruth Bader Ginsburg becomes the second woman to serve on the U.S. Supreme Court.

1995   Hillary Rodham Clinton travels to Beijing, China, as the honorary chairperson of the U.S. delegation to the United Nations' fourth international conference on women.

         Eileen Collins becomes the first woman to pilot a U.S. space shuttle.

1996   Ruth Bader Ginsburg writes the majority opinion in *United States v. Commonwealth of Virginia*, which prohibits the exclusion of women from state-supported schools.

1998   Cardinal John O'Connor of New York proposes Dorothy Day for sainthood.

1999   Eileen Collins becomes the first woman to command a space mission.

2000   Hillary Rodham Clinton becomes the only First Lady to win elective office when she is elected to represent New York State in the U.S. Senate.

Introduction

~

America's women activists have striven bravely and tirelessly to affect the course of American history and the welfare of those whose days, in the end, comprise that history. They labored at times with the barest of tools, with hands that were sometimes deemed the property of others and with voices that were counted at no polling booth. Working to win justice and rights for themselves—rights to their own person, to education, to suffrage— they worked simultaneously for the benefit of others. They have been the valiant champions of our wounded soldiers, our child laborers, our urban poor, and other of our distressed communities. Their story, as told in their letters, memoirs, diaries, and speeches, is as wide and varied as America itself.

This anthology begins with the then-government's attempt to silence a woman. Anne Hutchinson's problems were twofold. First, she was a woman and thus not permitted to address mixed audiences of men and women in the Massachusetts Bay colony. Second (and perhaps of greater import to colony officials and clergy), her religious beliefs differed from the norm. Anne Hutchinson lost her legal bid to expound her religious views to her neighbors, and she was ultimately exiled from the Massachusetts Bay colony. She was not, however, the last woman to insist upon the right to preach. Before the end of the nineteenth century, Sojourner Truth, Lucretia Mott, and Anna Howard Shaw would all succeed where Hutchinson failed.

Until the mid-nineteenth century, women's voices were disregarded in the country's secular debates as well. Abigail Adams, in the course of offering her thoughts on the progress of the American Revolution to her husband, John Adams, asked that women's rights be recognized in the nation's founding documents. John replied to her in dismissive jest and shared his more serious thoughts on the subject with a male colleague. Maria Stewart made only four public speeches on race relations in the early 1830s before she concluded she "made myself contemptible in the eyes of many" and returned to silence. The Grimke sisters, lecturing under the auspices of the American Anti-Slavery Society in the later 1830s, were condemned in print by educator Catharine Beecher and from the pulpit by Massachusetts's orthodox clergy for abandoning "woman's sphere." Thereafter, their time was, of necessity, divided between the abolition cause and their defense of women's right to speak of it in public. The issue erupted on an international stage in 1840, when Lucretia Mott and other abolitionist women traveled to London to attend the World Anti-Slavery Convention. After a full day's argument as to their fitness to attend, they were separated from the men and seated behind a curtain. There, they were expected to listen silently to the proceedings; instead, they whispered plans for a women's rights movement upon their return to the United States.

That movement began in organized earnest at the Seneca Falls Convention in 1848 and continues still. Along the way, women working to better the lot of women have sometimes disagreed as to what that might mean. Elizabeth Cady Stanton, Susan B. Anthony, Lucretia Mott, Sojourner Truth, and others demanded suffrage; Catharine Beecher believed it would undermine women's traditional role in the family and steadfastly opposed it. Decades later, Carry Nation viewed herself as defending traditional ideals when she destroyed saloons that lured men from their families; Frances Willard, just as dedicated to the temperance cause, urged the women in her organization to support suffrage in order to better effect change. After suffrage was won, Alice Paul drafted the Equal Rights Amendment; years later, Phyllis Schlafly would become a leader in the fight to defeat it.

Perhaps no question has been more divisive than that of abortion. I have included a voice from both sides of the argument, each offering a unique perspective on the issue. Laura Kaplan of "Jane" holds a pro-choice viewpoint, Mary Cunningham Agee a pro-life one. Each woman began work with the belief that women seeking abortions were vulnerable to victimization. The members of Jane sought to empower women by transforming the abortion procedure into something women performed for each other, outside the reach of the legal or medical establishments. In contrast, Mary Cunningham Agee works to make financial and other resources available to unhappily pregnant women, in order to ensure that neither neediness nor the coercion of families or partners becomes a factor in that decision.

One of the most important questions of justice in this country has been the pursuit of equality for African Americans. African-American women have been active in every aspect of this long-sustained battle, and they have left eloquent testimony. I have included an excerpt from Sojourner Truth's dictated autobiography, in which she describes her escape from slavery and her successful lawsuit for the return of one of her children; one of Maria W. Stewart's speeches, in which she protests the colonization movement's plan to expatriate American blacks to Liberia; Frances Ellen Watkins Harper's letters about her work for the Underground Railroad and selections of her poetry in support of abolitionism and women's rights; Anna Julia Cooper's essay in support of classical education for all qualified students, at a time when Booker T. Washington was successfully urging vocational training for African Americans; Mary McLeod Bethune's recollection of founding what became Bethune-Cookman College; Ida B. Wells-Barnett's chronicle of her anti-lynching work; Anne Moody's memory of integrating the Woolworth lunch counter in Mississippi; and Alice Walker's assessment of her work to end female genital mutilation.

On other issues of justice and need, women have also played an enormous role. Within these pages, Clara Barton recalls her Civil War work and urges Congress to join the International Red Cross; Lillian Wald creates a health care system to serve New York City's poor; Mother Jones marches with child laborers to protest on the lawn of a president's mansion; Rachel Carson draws attention to the earth's fragility; Jessie Lopez De La Cruz organizes migrant workers; and Margarethe Cammermeyer attempts to end the military's discharge of homosexuals. There are a number of "firsts" in this anthology as well: Elizabeth Blackwell, entering medical school; Lucy Stone, retaining her surname upon marriage; Victoria Woodhull, running for election as president of the United States; Jeannette Rankin, serving in Congress; Wilma Mankiller, becoming principal chief of the Cherokee Nation; and First Lady Hillary Rodham Clinton, winning election to the U.S. Senate.

All told, this anthology chronicles a very long journey. In its last pages, we find Ruth Bader Ginsburg sitting on the highest court in America, taking part in decisions that are as final in the twenty-first century as Governor John Winthrop's was in the seventeenth century. It is a picture that contrasts sharply with the silencing of Anne Hutchinson in that earlier courtroom, for Ginsburg, sitting in a position of power Hutchinson could only have imagined, writes for Hutchinson's successors a majority opinion. "Sex classifications . . . may not be used, as they once were, to create or perpetuate the legal, social and economic inferiority of women." The opinion ends with the traditional and weighty phrase, "It is so ordered."

And so it has been. And yet, the need for activism remains. For women on their own behalf, certainly. As Ginsburg herself explained in her confirmation hearings, the step-by-step legislative and courtroom acknowledgment of women's rights in America doesn't offer the satisfaction of one written, iron-clad guarantee. "I remain an advocate of the equal rights amendment, I will tell you," Ginsburg explained, "for this reason: because I have a daughter and a granddaughter, and I would like the legislature of this country and of all the states to stand up and say, 'We know what that history was in the *nineteenth* century, and we want to make a clarion call that women and men are equal before the law, just as every modern human rights document in the world does since 1970.' I'd like to see that statement made just that way in the United States Constitution," she concluded. Abigail Adams's early plea for mention in what were then new documents still has resonance.

As do other pleas found in these long-ago pages: pleas for fair wages; an end to racial discrimination; better stewardship of our planet; food, homes, and health care for all. Certainly, women will continue to be among the activists addressing these needs.

In the meantime, I hope I've left the reader with both a thorough sampling of the hard work undertaken to date and an indication of what that work has meant to the women in question. For while I have tried to present the varied viewpoints and wide impact of American women activists, I have not intended this anthology as simply a collection of position papers. Rather, I have intended it as a collection of private reflections upon public action: an exploration of how the difficult choice was made, what in childhood or later life propelled one to action, an occasional tallying of the costs and sacrifices. Thus, I have not excerpted from any of Helen Keller's fund-raising speeches, but from a section of her autobiography that illustrates just what it is to overcome a handicap to succeed in college; not from Gloria Steinem's editorials at *Ms.* magazine, but from an essay in appreciation of her mother's life; not from Betty Friedan's *Feminine Mystique*, but from her autobiographical account of its writing; and not from any of Merle Woo's essays or lectures, but from her "Letter to Ma." I hope the reader will be inspired by the example of these women, as I have been. It has been a privilege and a pleasure to spend the last few years in the company of their words.

KATHRYN CULLEN-DUPONT
Brooklyn, New York
January 2002

Anne Hutchinson

~

ANNE HUTCHINSON (ca. 1591–1643) was put on trial and convicted by the civil and religious authorities of the Massachusetts Bay colony in 1637 and 1638, respectively. While theological matters were at the center of her judges' inquiry, behavior "not fitting for your sex" was an issue as well, as evidenced by the first pages of the civil record. In addition to Governor John Winthrop, she is questioned by Deputy Governor Thomas Dudley and two assistants to the General Court, Simon Bradstreet and John Endicott.

~

November 1637

The Examination of Mrs. Ann Hutchinson at the court at Newtown.

Mr. Winthrop, governor. Mrs. Hutchinson, you are called here as one of those that have troubled the peace of the commonwealth and the churches here; you are known to be a woman that hath had a great share in the promoting and divulging of those opinions that are causes of this trouble, and to be nearly joined not only in affinity and affection with some of those the court had taken notice of and passed censure upon, but you have spoken divers things as we have been informed very prejudicial to the honour of the churches and ministers thereof, and you have maintained a meeting and an assembly in your house that hath been condemned by the general assembly as a thing not tolerable nor comely in the sight of God nor fitting for your sex, and

---

Hall, David D. *The Antinomian Controversy, 1636–1638: A Documentary History.* Durham: Duke University Press, 1990, pp. 312–318.

1

notwithstanding that was cried down you have continued the same, therefore we have thought good to send for you to understand how things are, that if you be in an erroneous way we may reduce you that so you may become a profitable member here among us, otherwise if you be obstinate in your course that then the court may take such course that you may trouble us no further, therefore I would intreat you to express whether you do not hold and assent in practice to those opinions and factions that have been handled in court already, that is to say, whether you do not justify Mr. Wheelwright's sermon and the petition.

Mrs. Hutchinson. I am called here to answer before you but I hear no things laid to my charge.

Gov. I have told you some already and more I can tell you.

Mrs. H. Name one Sir.

Gov. Have I not named some already?

Mrs. H. What have I said or done?

Gov. Why for your doings, this you did harbour and countenance those that are parties in this faction that you have heard of.

Mrs H. That's matter of conscience, Sir.

Gov. Your conscience you must keep or it must be kept for you.

Mrs. H. Must not I then entertain the saints because I must keep my conscience.

Gov. Say that one brother should commit felony or treason and come to his other brother's house, if he knows him guilty and conceals him he is guilty of the same. It is his conscience to entertain him, but if his conscience come into act in giving countenance and entertainment to him that hath broken the law he is guilty too. So if you do countenance those that are transgressors of the law you are in the same fact.

Mrs. H. What law do they transgress?

Gov. The law of God and of the state.

Mrs. H. In what particular?

Gov. Why in this among the rest, whereas the Lord doth say honour thy father and thy mother.

Mrs. H. Ey Sir in the Lord.

Gov. This honour you have broke in giving countenance to them.

Mrs. H. In entertaining those did I entertain them against any act (for there is the thing) or what God hath appointed?

Gov. You knew that Mr. Wheelwright did preach this sermon and those that countenance him in this do break a law.

Mrs. H. What law have I broken?

Gov. Why the fifth commandment.

Mrs. H. I deny that for he saith in the Lord.

Gov. You have joined with them in the faction.

Mrs. H. In what faction have I joined with them?

Gov. In presenting the [Antinomian party] petition [to the General Court].

Mrs. H. Suppose I had set my hand to the petition what then?

Gov. You saw that case tried before.

Mrs. H. But I had not my hand to the petition.

Gov. You have councelled them.

Mrs. H. Wherein?

Gov. Why in entertaining them.

Mrs. H. What breach of law is that Sir?

Gov. Why dishonouring of parents.

Mrs. H. But put the case Sir that I do fear the Lord and my parents, may not I entertain them that fear the Lord because my parents will not give me leave?

Gov. If they be the fathers of the commonwealth, and they of another religion, if you entertain them then you dishonour your parents and are justly punishable.

Mrs. H. If I entertain them, as they have dishonoured their parents I do.

Gov. No but you by countenancing them above others put honour upon them.

Mrs. H. I may put honor upon them as the children of God and as they do honor the Lord.

Gov. We do not mean to discourse with those of your sex but only this; you do adhere unto them and do endeavor to set forward this faction and so you do dishonour us.

Mrs. H. I do acknowledge no such thing neither do I think that I ever put any dishonour upon you.

Gov. Why do you keep such a meeting at your house as you do every week upon a set day?

Mrs. H. It is lawful for me so to do, as it is all your practices and can you find a warrant for yourself and condemn me for the same thing? The ground of my taking it up was, when I first came to this land because I did not go to such meetings as those were, it was presently reported that I did not allow of such meetings but held them unlawful and therefore in that regard they said I was proud and did despise all ordinances, upon that a friend came unto me and told me of it and I to prevent such aspersions took it up, but it was in practice before I came therefore I was not the first.

Gov. For this, that you appeal to our practice you need no confutation. If your meeting had answered to the former it had not been offensive, but I will say that there was no meeting of women alone, but your meeting is of another sort for there are sometimes men among you.

Mrs. H. There was never any man with us.

Gov. Well, admit there was no man at your meeting and that you was sorry for it, there is no warrant for your doings, and by what warrant do you continue such a course?

Mrs. H. I conceive there lyes a clear rule in Titus,* that the elder women should instruct the younger and then I must have a time wherein I must do it.

Gov. All this I grant you, I grant you a time for it, but what is this to the purpose that you Mrs. Hutchinson must call a company together from their callings to come to be taught of you?

Mrs. H. Will it please you to answer me this and to give me a rule for then I will willingly submit to any truth. If any come to my house to be instructed in the ways of God what rule have I to put them away?

Gov. But suppose that a hundred men come unto you to be instructed will you forbear to instruct them?

---

*Titus 2.3, 4, 5.

Mrs. H. As far as I conceive I cross a rule in it.

Gov. Very well and do you not so here?

Mrs. H. No Sir for my ground is they are men.

Gov. Men and women all is one for that, but suppose that a man should come and say Mrs. Hutchinson I hear that you are a woman that God hath given his grace unto and you have knowledge in the word of God I pray instruct me a little, ought you not to instruct this man?

Mrs. H. I think I may.—Do you think it not lawful for me to teach women and why do you call me to teach the court?

Gov. We do not call you to teach the court but to lay open yourself.

Mrs. H. I desire you that you would then set me down a rule by which I may put them away that come unto me and so have peace in so doing.

Gov. You must shew your rule to receive them.

Mrs. H. I have done it.

Gov. I deny it because I have brought more arguments than you have.

Mrs. H. I say, to me it is a rule.

Mr. Endicot. You say there are some rules unto you. I think there is a contradiction in your own words. What rule for your practice do you bring, only a custom in Boston.

Mrs. H. No Sir that was no rule to me but if you look upon the rule in Titus it is a rule to me. If you convince me that it is no rule I shall yield.

Gov. You know that there is no rule that crosses another, but this rule crosses that in the Corinthians.* But you must take it in this sense that elder women must instruct the younger about their business, and to love their husbands and not to make them to clash.

Mrs. H. I do not conceive but that it is meant for some publick times.

Gov. Well, have you no more to say but this?

Mrs. H. I have said sufficient for my practice.

---

*1 Corinthians 14.34, 35.

Gov. Your course is not to be suffered for, besides that we find such a course as this to be greatly prejudicial to the state, besides the occasion that it is to seduce many honest persons that are called to those meetings and your opinions being known to be different from the word of God may seduce many simple souls that resort unto you, besides that the occasion which hath come of late hath come from none but such as have frequented your meetings, so that now they are flown off from magistrates and ministers and this since they have come to you, and besides that it will not well stand with the commonwealth that families should be neglected for so many neighbours and dames and so much time spent, we see no rule of God for this, we see not that any should have authority to set up any other exercises besides what authority hath already set up and so what hurt comes of this you will be guilty of and we for suffering you.

Mrs. H. Sir I do not believe that to be so.

Gov. Well, we see how it is we must therefore put it away from you, or restrain you from maintaining this course.

Mrs. H. If you have a rule for it from God's word you may.

Gov. We are your judges, and not you ours and we must compel you to it.

Mrs. H. If it please you by authority to put it down I will freely let you for I am subject to your authority.

Mr. Bradstreet. I would ask this question of Mrs. Hutchinson, whether you do think this is lawful? For then this will follow that all other women that do not are in a sin.

Mrs. H. I conceive this is a free will offering.

Bradst. If it be a free will offering you ought to forbear it because it gives offence.

Mrs. H. Sir, in regard of myself I could, but for others I do not yet see light but shall further consider of it.

Bradst. I am not against all women's meetings but do think them to be lawful.

Mr. Dudley, dep. gov. Here hath been much spoken concerning Mrs. Hutchinson's meetings and among other answers she saith that men come not there, I would ask you this one question then, whether never any man was at your meeting?

Gov.   There are two meetings kept at their house.

Dep. Gov.   How; is there two meetings?

Mrs. H.   Ey Sir, I shall not equivocate, there is a meeting of men and women and there is a meeting only for women.

Dep. Gov.   Are they both constant?

Mrs. H.   No, but upon occasions they are deferred.

Mr. Endicot.   Who teaches in the men's meetings none but men, do not women sometimes?

Mrs. H.   Never as I heard, not one.

Dep. Gov.   I would go a little higher with Mrs. Hutchinson. About three years ago we were all in peace. Mrs. Hutchinson from that time she came hath made a disturbance, and some that came over with her in the ship did inform me what she was as soon as she was landed. I being then in place dealt with the pastor and teacher of Boston and desired them to enquire of her, and then I was satisfied that she held nothing different from us, but within half a year after, she had vented divers of her strange opinions and had made parties in the country, and at length it comes that Mr. Cotton and Mr. Vane were of her judgment, but Mr. Cotton hath cleared himself that he was not of that mind, but now it appears by this woman's meeting that Mrs. Hutchinson hath so forestalled the minds of many by their resort to her meeting that now she hath a potent party in the country. Now if all these things have endangered us as from that foundation and if she in particular hath disparaged all our ministers in the land that they have preached a covenant of works, and only Mr. Cotton a covenant of grace, why this is not to be suffered, and therefore being driven to the foundation and it being found that Mrs. Hutchinson is she that hath depraved all the ministers and hath been the cause of what is fallen out, why we must take away the foundation and the building will fall.

Mrs. H.   I pray Sir prove it that I said they preached nothing but a covenant of works.

Abigail Adams

~

ABIGAIL ADAMS (1744–1818), America's second First Lady, sent her husband, John Adams, a now-famous demand for women's rights during his participation in the Continental Congress. Perhaps less well known is John Adams's dismissive reply to his wife and his subsequent letter to James Sullivan, in which he more seriously explores the status of women and other disenfranchised people. Abigail Adams's retort to her husband is lighthearted, but her own letter to a friend, Mercy Otis Warren, displays frustration. Women's independence was not the only political issue Abigail and John Adams discussed; as will be seen in the first letter, the day's political events were a routine part of the couple's correspondence.

~

Abigail Adams to John Adams
November 27, 1775

'Tis a fortnight tonight since I wrote you a line, during which I have been confined with the jaundice, rheumatism and a most violent

Rogers, Katharine M. *Early American Women Writers: From Anne Bradstreet to Louisa May Alcott, 1650–1865*. New York: Meridian, 1991, pp. 158–160, 162–164 (letters dated November 27, 1775, and April 27, 1776).

Baron, Robert C. *Soul of America: Documenting Our Past, 1492–1974*. Golden, CO: Fulcrum, Inc., 1989, pp. 39–42 (letters dated March 31 and April 14, 1776).

Rossi, Alice S. *The Feminist Papers: From Adams to de Beauvoir*. Boston: Northeastern University Press, 1988, pp. 13–15 (letters dated May 7 and 26, 1776).

cold; I yesterday took a puke, which has relieved me, and I feel much better today. Many, very many people who have had the dysentery are now afflicted both with the jaundice and rheumatism; some it has left in hectics, some in dropsies.

The great and incessant rains we have had this fall (the like cannot be recollected) may have occasioned some of the present disorders. The jaundice is very prevalent in the [Army] camp. We have lately had a week of very cold weather, as cold as January, and a flight of snow, which I hope will purify the air of some of the noxious vapors. It has spoiled many hundreds of bushels of apples, which were designed for cider, and which the great rains had prevented people from making up. Suppose we have lost five barrels by it.

Col. Warren returned last week to Plymouth, so that I shall not hear anything from you till he goes back again, which will not be till the last of this month.

He damped my spirits greatly by telling me that the court had prolonged your stay [at the Continental Congress] another month. I was pleasing myself with the thoughts that you would soon be upon your return. 'Tis in vain to repine. I hope the public will reap what I sacrifice.

I wish I knew what mighty things were fabricating. If a form of government is to be established here, what one will be assumed? Will it be left to our assemblies to choose one? and will not many men have many minds? and shall we not run into dissensions among ourselves?

I am more and more convinced that man is a dangerous creature, and that power, whether vested in many or a few, is ever grasping and like the grave cries give, give. The great fish swallow up the small, and he who is most strenuous for the rights of the people, when vested with power, is as eager after the prerogatives of government. You tell me of degrees of perfection to which human nature is capable of arriving, and I believe it, but at the same time lament that our admiration should arise from the scarcity of the instances.

The building up a great empire, which was only hinted at by my correspondent, may now, I suppose, be realized even by the unbelievers. Yet will not ten thousand difficulties arise in the formation of it? The reins of government have been so long slackened that I fear the people will not quietly submit to those restraints which are necessary for the peace and security of the community; if we separate from Britain, what code of laws will be established? How shall we be governed so as to retain our liberties? Can any government be free which is not administered by general stated laws? Who shall frame these laws? Who will give them force and energy? 'Tis true your resolutions as a body have hitherto had the force of laws. But will they continue to have?

When I consider these things and the prejudices of people in favor of ancient customs and regulations, I feel anxious for the fate of our monarchy or democracy or whatever is to take place. I soon get lost in a labyrinth of perplexities, but whatever occurs, may justice and righteousness be the stability of our times, and order arise out of confusion. Great difficulties may be surmounted by patience and perseverance.

I believe I have tired you with politics. As to news, we have not any at all. I shudder at the approach of winter when I think I am to remain desolate. Suppose your weather is warm yet. . . .

I have with me now the only daughter of your brother; I feel a tenderer affection for her as she has lost a kind parent. Though too young to be sensible of her own loss, I can pity her. She appears to be a child of a very good disposition—only wants to be a little used to company.

Our little ones send duty to Papa and want much to see him. Tom says he won't come home till the battle is over—some strange notion he has got into his head. He has got a political creed to say to him when he returns.

I must bid you good night. 'Tis late for one who am much of an invalid. I was disappointed last week in receiving a packet by the post, and upon unsealing it found only four newspapers. I think you are more cautious than you need be. All letters, I believe, have come safe to hand. I have sixteen from you, and wish I had as many more. Adieu. Yours.

Abigail Adams to John Adams
March 31, 1776

I wish you would ever write me a Letter half as long as I write you; and tell me if you may where your Fleet are gone? What sort of Defence Virginia can make against our common Enemy? Whether it is so situated as to make an able Defence? Are not the Gentry Lords and the common people vassals, are they not like the uncivilized Natives Brittain represents us to be? I hope their Riffel Men who have shewen themselves very savage and even Blood thirsty; are not a specimen of the Generality of the people.

I am willing to allow the Colony great merrit for having produced a Washington but they have been shamefully duped by a Dunmore.

I have sometimes been ready to think that the passion for Liberty cannot be Equally Strong in the Breasts of those who have been accustomed to deprive their fellow Creatures of theirs. Of this I am certain that it is not founded upon that generous and christian principal of doing to others as we would that others should do unto us.

Do not you want to see Boston; I am fearfull of the small pox, or I should have been in before this time. I got Mr. Crane to go to our House and see what state it was in. I find it has been occupied by one of the Doctors of a Regiment, very dirty, but no other damage has been done to it. The few things which were left in it are all gone. Cranch has the key which he never delivered up. I have wrote to him for it and am determined to get it cleand as soon as possible and shut it up. I look upon it a new acquisition of property, a property which one month ago I did not value at a single Shilling, and could with pleasure have seen it in flames.

The Town in General is left in a better state that we expected, more oweing to a percipitate flight than any Regard to the inhabitants, tho some individuals discoverd a sense of honour and justice and have left the rent of the Houses in which they were, for the owners and the furniture unhurt, or if damaged sufficient to make it good.

Others have committed abominable Ravages. The Mansion House of your President is safe and the furniture unhurt whilst both the House and Furniture of the Solisiter General have fallen a prey to their own merciless party. Surely the very Fiends feel a Reverential awe for Virtue and patriotism, whilst they Detest the paricide and traitor.

I feel very differently at the approach of spring to what I did a month ago. We knew not then whether we could plant or sow with safety, whether when we had toiled we could reap the fruits of our own industry, whether we could rest in our own Cottages, or whether we should not be driven from the sea coasts to seek shelter in the wilderness, but now we feel as if we might sit under our own vine and eat the good of the land.

I feel *a gaieti de Coar* to which before I was a stranger. I think the Sun looks brighter, the Birds sing more melodiously, and Nature puts on a more chearfull countanance. We feel a temporary peace, and the poor fugitives are returning to their deserted habitations.

Tho we felicitate ourselves, we sympathize with those who are trembling least the Lot of Boston should be theirs. But they cannot be in similar circumstances unless pusilanimity and cowardise should take possession of them. They have time and warning given them to see the Evil and shun it.—I long to hear that you have declared an independancy—and by the way in the new Code of Laws which I suppose it will be necessary for you to make, I desire you would Remember the Ladies, and be more generous and favourable to them than your ancestors. Do not put such unlimited power into the hands of the Husbands. Remember all Men would be tyrants if they could. If perticuliar care and attention is not paid to the Ladies we are determined to foment a Rebelion, and will not hold ourselves bound by any Laws in which we have no voice, or Representation.

That your Sex are naturally Tyrannical is a Truth so thoroughly established as to admit of no dispute, but such of you as wish to be happy willingly give up the harsh title of Master for the more tender and endearing one of Friend. Why then, not put it out of the power of the vicious and the Lawless to use us with cruelty and indignity with impunity. Men of Sense in all Ages abhor those customs which treat us only as the vassals of your Sex. Regard us then as Beings placed by providence under your protection and in imitation of the Supreem Being make use of that power only for our happiness.

John Adams to Abigail Adams
April 14, 1776

You justly complain of my short Letters, but the critical State of Things and the Multiplicity of Avocations must plead my Excuse.—You ask where the Fleet is. The inclosed Papers will inform you. You ask what Sort of Defence Virginia can make. I believe they will make an able Defence. Their Militia and minute Men have been some time employed in training themselves, and they have Nine Battallions of regulars as they call them, maintained among them, under good Officers, at the Continental Expence. They have set up a Number of Manufactories of Fire Arms, which are busily employed. They are tolerably supplied with Powder, and are successfull and assiduous, in making Salt Petre. Their neighbouring Sister or rather Daughter Colony of North Carolina, which is a warlike Colony, and has several Battallions at the Continental Expence, as well as a pretty good Militia, are ready to assist them, and they are in very good Spirits, and seem determined to make a brave Resistance.—The Gentry are very rich, and the common People very poor. This Inequality of Property, gives an Aristocratical Turn to all their Proceedings, and occasions a strong Aversion in their Patricians, to Common Sense. But the Spirit of these Barons, is coming down, and it must submit.

It is very true, as you observe they have duped by Dunmore. But this is a Common Case. All the Colonies are duped, more or less, at one Time and another. A more egregious Bubble was never blown up, than the Story of Commissioners coming to treat with the Congress. Yet is has gained Credit like a Charm, not only without but against the clearest Evidence. I never shall forget the Delusion, which seized our best and most sagacious Friends the dear Inhabitants of Boston, the Winter before last. Credulity and the Want of Foresight, are Imperfections in the human Character, that no Politicians can sufficiently guard against.

You have given me some Pleasure, by your Account of a certain House in Queen Street. I had burned it, long ago, in Imagination. It rises now to my View like a Phoenix.—What shall I say of the Solicitor General? I pity his pretty Children, I pity his Father, and his sisters. I wish I could be clear that it is no moral Evil to pity him and his Lady. Upon Repentance they will certainly have a large Share in the Compassions of many. But let Us take Warning and give it to our Children. Whenever Vanity, and Gaiety, a Love of Pomp and Dress, Furniture, Equipage, Buildings, great Company, expensive Diversions, and elegant Entertainments get the better of the Principles and Judgments of Men or Women there is no knowing where they will stop, nor into what Evils, natural, moral, or political, they will lead us.

Your Description of your own *Gaiety de Coeur*, charms me. Thanks be to God you have just Cause to rejoice—and may the bright prospect be obscured by no Cloud.

As to Declarations of Independency, be patient. Read our Privateering Laws, and our Commercial Laws. What signifies a Word.

As to your extraordinary Code of Laws, I cannot but laugh. We have been told that our Struggle has loosened the bands of Government every where. That Children and Apprentices were disobedient—that schools and Colledges were grown turbulent—that Indians slighted their Guardians and Negroes grew insolent to their Masters. But your Letter was the first Intimation that another Tribe more numerous and powerfull than all the rest were grown discontented.—This is rather too coarse a Compliment but you are so saucy, I wont blot it out.

Depend upon it, We know better than to repeal our Masculine systems. Altho they are in full Force, you know they are little more than Theory. We dare not exert our Power in its full Latitude. We are obliged to go fair, and softly, and in Practice you know We are the subjects. We have only the Name of Masters, and rather than give up this, which would compleatly subject Us to the Despotism of the Peticoat, I hope General Washington, and all our brave Heroes would fight. I am sure every good Politician would plot, as long as he would against Despotism, Empire, Monarchy, Aristocracy, Oligarchy, or Ochlocracy.—A fine Story indeed. I begin to think the Ministry as deep as they are wicked. After stirring up Tories, Landjobbers, Trimmers, Bigots, Canadians, Indians, Negroes, Hanoverians, Hessians, Russians, Irish Roman Catholicks, Scotch Renegadoes, at last they have stimulated them to demand new Priviledges and threaten to rebell.

Abigail Adams to Mercy Otis Warren
Braintree, April 27, 1776

I set myself down to comply with my friend's request, who I think seems rather low spirited.

I did write last week, but not meeting with an early conveyance, I thought the letter of but little importance and tossed it away. I acknowledge my thanks due to my friend for the entertainment she so kindly afforded me in the characters drawn in her last letter, and if coveting my neighbor's goods was not prohibited by the sacred law, I should be most certainly tempted to envy her the happy talent she possesses above the rest of her sex, by adorning with her pen even trivial occurrences, as well as dignifying the most important. Cannot you communicate some of those graces to your friend and suffer her to pass them upon the world for her own that she may feel a little more upon an equality with you?—'Tis true I often receive large packages from Philadelphia. They contain, as I said before, more newspapers than letters, though they are not forgotten. It would be hard indeed if absence had not some alleviations.

I dare say he writes to no one unless to [me] oftener than to your [husband], because I know there is no one besides in whom he has an equal confidence. His letters to me have been generally short, but he pleads in excuse the critical state of affairs and the multiplicity of avocations and says further that he has been very busy, and writ near ten sheets of paper about some affairs which he does not choose to mention for fear of accident.

He is very saucy to me in return for a list of female grievances which I transmitted to him. I think I will get you to join me in a petition to Congress. I thought it was very probable our wise statesmen would erect a new government and form a new Code of Laws. I ventured to speak a word in behalf of our sex, who are rather hardly dealt with by the laws of England, which give such unlimited power to the husband to use his wife ill.

I requested that our legislators would consider our case, and as all men of delicacy and sentiment are averse to exercising the power they possess, yet as there is a natural propensity in human nature to domination, I thought the most generous plan was to put it out of the power of the arbitrary and tyrannic to injure us with impunity by establishing some laws in our favor upon just and liberal principles.

I believe I even threatened fomenting a rebellion in case we were not considered, and assured him we would not hold ourselves bound by any laws in which we had neither a voice, nor representation.

In return he tells me he cannot but laugh at my extraordinary Code of Laws. That he had heard their struggle had loosened the bands of government, that children and apprentices were disobedient, that schools and colleges were grown turbulent, that Indians slighted their guardians, and Negroes grew insolent to their masters. But my letter was the first intimation that another tribe more numerous and powerful than all the rest were grown discontented. This is rather too coarse a compliment, he adds, but that I am so saucy he won't blot it out.

So I have helped the sex abundantly, but I will tell him I have only been making trial of the disinterestedness of his virtue, and when weighed in the balance have found it wanting.

It would be bad policy to grant us greater power, say they, since under all the disadvantages we labor, we have the ascendancy over their hearts.

And charm by accepting, by submitting sway.

I wonder Apollo and the Muses could not have indulged me with a poetical genius. I have always been a votary to her charms, but never could ascend Parnassus myself.

I am very sorry to hear of the indisposition of your [husband]. I am afraid it will hasten his return, and I do not think he can be spared.

Though certain pains attend the cares of State
A good man owes his country to be great,
Should act abroad the high distinguished part
Or show at least the purpose of his heart.

Good night, my friend. You will be so good as to remember me to our worthy Friend Mrs. Winthrop when you see her and write soon. . . .

Abigail Adams to John Adams
Braintree, May 7, 1776

I can not say that I think you very generous to the Ladies, for whilst you are proclaiming peace and good will to Men, Emancipating all Nations, you insist upon retaining an absolute power over Wives. But you must remember that Arbitrary power is like most other things which are very hard, very liable to be broken—and notwithstanding all your wise Laws and Maxims we have it in our power not only to free ourselves but to subdue our Masters, and without violence throw both your natural and legal authority at our feet—

"Charm by accepting, by submitting sway
Yet have our Humour most when we obey."

John Adams to James Sullivan
Philadelphia, 26 May, 1776

It is certain, in theory, that the only moral foundation of government is, the consent of the people. But to what an extent shall we carry this principle? Shall we say that every individual of the community, old and young, male and female, as well as rich and poor, must consent, expressly, to every act of legislation? No, you will say, this is impossible. How, then, does the right arise in the majority to govern the minority, against their will? Whence arises the right of the men to govern the women, without their consent? Whence the right of the old to bind the young, without theirs?

But let us first suppose that the whole community, of every age, rank, sex, and condition, has a right to vote. This community is assembled. A motion is made, and carried by a majority of one voice. The minority will not agree to this. Whence arises the right of the majority to govern, and the obligation of the minority to obey?

From necessity, you will say, because there can be no other rule.

But why exclude women?

You will say, because their delicacy renders them unfit for practice and experience in the great businesses of life, and the hardy enterprises of war, as well as the arduous cares of state. Besides, their attention is so much engaged with the necessary nurture of their children, that nature has made them fittest for domestic cares. And children have not judgment or will of their own. True. But will not these reasons apply to others? Is it not equally true, that men in general, in every society, who are wholly destitute of property, are also too little acquainted with public affairs to form a right judgment, and too dependent upon other men to have a will of their own? If this is a fact, if you give to every man who has no property, a vote, will you not make a fine encouraging provision for corruption, by your fundamental law? Such is the frailty of the human heart, that very few men who have no property, have any judgment of their own. They talk and vote as they are directed by some man of property, who has attached their minds to his interest.

Upon my word, Sir, I have long thought an army a piece of clockwork and to be governed only by principles and maxims, as fixed as any in mechanics; and, by all that I have read in the history of mankind, and in authors who have speculated upon society and government, I am much inclined to think a government must manage a society in the same manner; and that this is machinery too. . . .

Your idea that those laws which affect the lives and personal liberty of all, or which inflict corporal punishment, affect those who are not qualified to vote, as well as those who are, is just. But so they do women, as well as men; children, as well as adults. What reason should there be for excluding a man of twenty years eleven months and twenty-seven days old, from a vote, when you admit one who is twenty-one? The reason is, you must fix upon some period in life, when the understanding and will of men in general, is fit to be trusted by the public. Will not the same reason justify the state in fixing upon some certain quantity of property, as a qualification?

The same reasoning which will induce you to admit all men who have no property, to vote, with those who have, for those laws which affect the person, will prove that you ought to admit women and children; for, generally speaking, women and children have as good judgments, and as independent minds, as those men who are wholly destitute of property; these last being to all intents and purposes as much dependent upon others, who will please to feed, clothe, and employ them, as women are upon their husbands, or children on their parents. . . .

Depend upon it, Sir, it is dangerous to open so fruitful a source of controversy and altercation as would be opened by attempting to alter the qualifications of voters; there will be no end of it. New claims will arise; women will demand a vote; lads from twelve to twenty-one will think their rights not enough attended to; and every man who has not a farthing, will demand an equal voice with any other, in all acts of state. It tends to confound and destroy all distinctions, and prostrate all ranks to one common level.

Margaret Fuller

~

MARGARET FULLER (1810–1850), who would write one of the most important works of early American feminism, *Woman in the Nineteenth Century* (1845), received a wider-ranging and more rigorous education than perhaps any of her female contemporaries. In this excerpt from her *Autobiographical Romance*, she recollects her studies and other childhood experiences.

~

My father was a lawyer and a politician. He was a man largely endowed with that sagacious energy, which the state of New England society, for the last half century, has been so well fitted to develop. His father was a clergyman, settled as pastor in Princeton, Massachusetts, within the bounds of whose parish-farm was Wachuset. His means were small, and the great object of his ambition was to send his sons to college. As a boy, my father was taught to think only of preparing himself for Harvard University, and when there of preparing himself for the profession of Law. As a Lawyer, again, the ends constantly presented were to work for distinction in the community, and for the means of supporting a family. To be an honored citizen, and to have a home on earth, were made the great aims of existence. To open the deeper fountains of the soul, to regard life here as the prophetic entrance to immortality, to develop his spirit to perfection,—motives like these had never been suggested to him, either by fellow-beings

---

Fuller, Margaret. *The Essential Margaret Fuller.* Jeffrey Steele, ed. New Brunswick, NJ: Rutgers University Press, 1992, pp. 24–37.

or by outward circumstances. The result was a character, in its social aspect, of quite the common sort. A good son and brother, a kind neighbor, an active man of business—in all these outward relations he was but one of a class, which surrounding conditions have made the majority among us. In the more delicate and individual relations, he never approached but two mortals, my mother and myself.

His love for my mother was the green spot on which he stood apart from the common-places of a mere bread-winning, bread-bestowing existence. She was one of those fair and flower-like natures, which sometimes spring up even beside the most dusty highways of life—a creature not to be shaped into a merely useful instrument, but bound by one law with the blue sky, the dew, and the frolic birds. Of all persons whom I have known, she had in her most of the angelic,—of that spontaneous love for every living thing, for man, and beast, and tree, which restores the golden age.

My earliest recollection is of a death,—the death of a sister, two years younger than myself. Probably there is a sense of childish endearments, such as belong to this tie, mingled with that of loss, of wonder, and mystery; but these last are prominent in memory. I remember coming home and meeting our nursery-maid, her face streaming with tears. . . .

She took me by the hand and led me into a still and dark chamber,—then drew aside the curtain and showed me my sister. I see yet that beauty of death! The highest achievements of sculpture are only the reminder of its severe sweetness. Then I remember the house all still and dark,—the people in their black clothes and dreary faces,—the scent of the newly-made coffin,—my being set up in a chair and detained by a gentle hand to hear the clergyman,—the carriages slowly going, the procession slowly doling out their steps to the grave. But I have no remembrance of what I have since been told I did,—insisting, with loud cries, that they should not put the body in the ground. I suppose that my emotion was spent at the time, and so there was nothing to fix that moment in my memory.

I did not then, nor do I now, find any beauty in these cere-monies. What had they to do with the sweet playful child? Her life and death were alike beautiful, but all this sad parade was not. Thus my first experience of life was one of death. She who would have been the companion of my life was severed from me, and I was left alone. This has made a vast difference in my lot. Her char-acter, if that fair face promised right, would have been soft, grace-ful and lively; it would have tempered mine to a gentler and more gradual course.

My father,—all of whose feelings were now concentred on me,—in-structed me himself. The effect of this was so far good that, not passing through the hands of many ignorant and weak persons as so many do at preparatory schools, I was put at once under disci-pline of considerable severity, and, at the same time, had a more than ordinarily high standard presented to me. My father was a man of business, even in literature; he had been a high scholar at college, and was warmly attached to all he had learned there, both from the pleasure he had derived in the exercise of his faculties and the associated memories of success and good repute. He was, be-side, well read in French literature, and in English, a Queen Anne's man. He hoped to make me the heir of all he knew, and of as much more as the income of his profession enabled him to give me means of acquiring. At the very beginning, he made one great mistake, more common, it is to be hoped, in the last generation, than the warnings of physiologists will permit it to be with the next. He thought to gain time, by bringing forward the intellect as early as possible. Thus I had tasks given me, as many and various as the hours would allow, and on subjects beyond my age; with the addi-tional disadvantage of reciting to him in the evening, after he re-turned from his office. As he was subject to many interruptions, I was often kept up till very late; and as he was a severe teacher, both from his habits of mind and his ambition for me, my feelings were kept on the stretch till the recitations were over. Thus frequently, I was sent to bed several hours too late, with nerves unnaturally stimulated. The consequence was a premature development of the brain, that made me a "youthful prodigy" by day, and by night a victim of spectral illusions, nightmare, and somnambulism, which at the time prevented the harmonious development of my bodily powers and checked my growth, while, later, they induced continual headache, weakness and nervous affectations, of all kinds. As these again re-acted on the brain, giving undue force to every thought and every feeling, there was finally produced a state of being both too active and too intense, which wasted my constitution, and will bring me,—even although I have learned to understand and regulate my now morbid temperament,—to a premature grave.

No one understood this subject of health then. No one knew why this child, already kept up so late, was still unwilling to retire. . . . They did not know that, so soon as the light was taken away, she seemed to see colossal faces advancing slowly towards her, the eyes dilating, and each feature swelling loathsomely as they came, till at last, when they were about to close upon her, she started up with a shriek which drove them away, but only to return when she lay down again. They did not know that, when at last she went to sleep, it was to dream of horses trampling over her, and to awake once more in fright, or, as she had just read in her Virgil, of being among trees that dripped with blood, where she walked and walked and could not get out, while the blood became a pool and plashed over her feet, and rose higher and higher, till soon she dreamed it would reach her lips. No wonder the child arose and walked in her sleep, moaning all over the house, till once, when they heard her, and came and waked her, and she told what she had dreamed, her father sharply bid her "leave off thinking of such nonsense, or she would be crazy,"—never knowing that he was himself the cause of all these horrors of the night. Often she dreamed of following to the grave the body of her mother, as she had done that of her sister, and woke to find the pillow drenched in tears. These dreams softened her heart too much, and cast a deep shadow over her young days; for then, and later, the life of dreams,—probably because there was in it less to distract the mind from its own earnestness,—has often seemed to her more real, and been remembered with more interest, than that of waking hours.

Poor child! Far remote in time, in thought, from that period, I look back on these glooms and terrors, wherein I was enveloped, and perceive that I had no natural childhood!

Thus passed my first years. My mother was in delicate health, and much absorbed in the care of her younger children. In the house was neither dog nor bird, nor any graceful animated form of existence. I saw no persons who took my fancy, and real life offered no attraction. Thus my already over-excited mind found no relief from without, and was driven for refuge from itself to the world of books. I was taught Latin and English grammar at the same time, and began to read Latin at six years old, after which, for some years, I read it daily. In this branch of study, first by my father, and afterwards by a tutor, I was trained to quite a high degree of precision. I was expected to understand the mechanism of the language thoroughly, and in translating to give the thoughts in as few well-arranged words as possible, and without breaks or hesitation,—for with these my father had absolutely no patience.

Indeed, he demanded accuracy and clearness in everything: you must not speak, unless you can make your meaning perfectly intelligible to the person addressed; must not express a though, unless you can give a reason for it, if required; must not make a statement, unless sure of all particulars—such were his rules. "But," "if," "unless," "I am mistaken," and "it may be so," were words and phrases excluded from the province where he held sway. Trained to great dexterity in artificial methods, accurate, ready, with entire command of his resources, he had no belief in minds that listen, wait, and receive. He had no conception of the subtle and indirect motions of imagination and feeling. His influence on me was great, and opposed to the natural unfolding of my character, which was fervent, of strong grasp, and disposed to infatuation, and self-forgetfulness. He made the common prose world so present to me, that my natural bias was controlled. I did not go mad, as many would do, at being continually roused from my dreams. I had too much strength to be crushed,—and since I must put on the fetters, could not submit to let them impede my motions. My own world sank deep within, away from the surface of my life; in what I did and said I learned to have reference to other minds. But my true life was only the dearer that it was secluded and veiled over by a thick curtain of available intellect, and that coarse, but wearable stuff woven by the ages,—Common Sense.

In accordance with this discipline in heroic common sense, was the influence of those great Romans, whose thoughts and lives were my daily food during those plastic years. The genius of Rome displayed itself in Character, and scarcely needed an occasional wave of the torch of thought to show its lineaments, so marble strong they gleamed in every light. Who, that has lived with those men, but admires the plain force of fact, of thought passed into action? They take up things with their naked hands. There is just the man, and the block he casts before you,—no divinity, no demon, no unfulfilled aim, but just the man and Rome, and what he did for Rome. Everything turns your attention to what a man can become. . . .

I steadily loved this ideal in my childhood, and this is the cause, probably, why I have always felt that man must know how to stand firm on the ground, before he can fly. . . .

Ovid gave me not Rome, nor himself, but a view into the enchanted gardens of the Greek mythology. This path I followed, have been following ever since; and now, life half over, it seems to me, as in my childhood, that every thought of which man is susceptible, is intimated there. In those young years, indeed, I did not see what I now see, but loved to creep from amid the Roman pikes to lie beneath this great vine, and see the smiling and serene shapes go by, woven from the finest fibres of all the elements. I knew not why, at that time,—but I loved to get away from the hum of the forum, and the mailed clang of Roman speech, to these shifting shows of nature, these Gods and Nymphs born of the sunbeam, the wave, the shadows on the hill.

As with Rome I antedated the world of deeds, so I lived in those Greek forms the true faith of a refined and intense childhood. So great was the force of reality with which these forms impressed me, that I prayed earnestly for a sign,—that it would lighten in some particular region of the heavens, or that I might find a bunch of grapes in the path, when I went forth in the morning. But no sign was given, and I was left a waif stranded upon the shores of modern life!

Of the Greek language, I knew only enough to feel that the sounds told the same story as the mythology;—that the law of life in that land was beauty, as in Rome it was a stern composure. I wish I had learned as much of Greece as of Rome,—so freely does the mind play in her sunny waters, where there is no chill, and the restraint is from within out; for these Greeks, in an atmosphere of ample grace, could not be impetuous, or stern, but loved moderation as equable life always must, for it is the law of beauty.

With these books I passed my days. The great amount of study exacted of me soon ceased to be a burden, and reading became a habit and a passion. The force of feeling, which, under other circumstances, might have ripened thought, was turned to learn the thoughts of others. This was not a tame state, for the energies brought out by rapid acquisition gave glow enough. I thought with rapture of the all-accomplished man, him of the many talents, wide resources, clear sight, and omnipotent will. A Caesar seemed great enough. I did not then know that such men impoverish the treasury to build the palace. I kept their statues as belonging to the hall of my ancestors, and loved to conquer obstacles, and fed my youth and strength for their sake.

Still, though the bias was so great that in earliest years I learned, in these ways, how the world takes hold of a powerful nature, I had yet other experiences. None of these were deeper than what I found in the happiest haunt of my childish years,—our little garden. Our house, though comfortable, was very ugly, and in a neighborhood which I detested,—every dwelling and its appurtenances having a *mesquin* [shabby] and huddled look. I liked nothing about us except the tall graceful elms before the house, and the dear little garden behind. Our back door opened on a high flight of steps, by which I went down to a green plot, much injured in my ambitious eyes by the presence of the pump and tool-house. This opened into a little garden, full of choice flowers and fruit-trees, which was my mother's delight, and was carefully kept. Here I felt at home. A gate opened thence into the fields,—a wooden gate made of boards, in a high, unpainted board wall, and embowered in the clematis creeper. This gate I used to open to see the sunset heaven; beyond this black frame I did not step, for I liked to look at the deep gold behind it. How exquisitely happy I was in its beauty, and how I loved the silvery wreaths of my protecting vine! I never would pluck one of its flowers at that time, I was so jealous of its beauty, but often since I carry off wreaths of it from the wild-wood, and it stands in nature to my mind as the emblem of domestic love.

Of late I have thankfully felt what I owe to that garden, where the best hours of my lonely childhood were spent. Within the house everything was socially utilitarian; my books told of a proud world, but in another temper were the teachings of the little garden. There my thoughts could lie callow in the nest, and only be fed and kept warm, not called to fly or sing before the time. I loved to gaze on the roses, the violets, the lilies, the pinks; my mother's hand had planted them, and they bloomed for me. I culled the most beautiful. I looked at them on every side. I kissed them, I pressed them to my bosom with passionate emotions, such as I have never dared express to any human being. An ambition swelled my heart to be as beautiful, as perfect as they. I have not kept my vow. Yet, forgive, ye wild asters, which gleam so sadly amid the fading grass; forgive me, ye golden autumn flowers, which so strive to reflect the glories of the departing distant sun; and ye silvery flowers, whose moonlight eyes I knew so well, forgive! Living and blooming in your unchecked law, ye know nothing of the blights, the distortions, which beset the human being; and which at such hours it would seem that no glories of free agency could ever repay!

There was, in the house, no apartment appropriated to the purpose of a library, but there was in my father's room a large closet filled with books, and to these I had free access when the task-work of the day was done. Its window overlooked wide fields, gentle slopes, a rich and smiling country, whose aspect pleased without much occupying the eye, while a range of blue hills, rising at about twelve miles distance, allured to reverie. "Distant mountains," says Tieck, "excite the fancy, for beyond them we place the scene of our Paradise." Thus, in the poems of fairy adventure, we climb the rocky barrier, pass fearless its dragon caves, and dark pine forests, and find the scene of enchantment in the vale behind. My hopes were never so definite, but my eye was constantly allured to that distant blue range, and I would sit, lost in fancies, till tears fell on my cheek. I loved this sadness; but only in later years, when the realities of life had taught me moderation, did the passionate emotions excited by seeing them again teach how glorious were the hopes that swelled my heart while gazing on them in those early days.

Melancholy attends on the best joys of a merely ideal life, else I should call most happy the hours in the garden, the hours in the book closet. . . .

Three great authors it was my fortune to meet at this important period. . . .

Ever memorable is the day on which I first took a volume of SHAKESPEARE in my hand to read. It was on a Sunday.

—This day was punctiliously set apart in our house. We had family prayers, for which there was no time on other days. Our dinners were different, and our clothes. We went to church. My father put some limitations on my reading, but—bless him for the gentleness which has left me a pleasant feeling for the day!— he did not prescribe what was, but only what was *not*, to be done. And the liberty this left was a large one. "You must not read a novel, or a play;" but all other books, the worst, or the best, were open to me. . . .

This Sunday—I was only eight years old—I took from the bookshelf a volume lettered SHAKSPEARE. It was not the first time I had looked at it, but before I had been deterred from attempting to read, by the broken appearance along the page, and preferred smooth narrative. But this time I held in my hand "Romeo and Juliet" long enough to get my eye fastened to the page. It was a cold winter afternoon. I took the book to the parlor fire, and had there been seated an hour or two, when my father looked up and asked me what I was reading so intently. "Shakspeare," replied the child, merely raising her eye from the page. "Shakspeare,—that won't do; that's no book for Sunday; go put it away and take another." I went as I was bid, but took no other. Returning to my seat, the unfinished story, the personages to whom I was but just introduced, thronged and burnt my brain. I could not bear it long; such a lure it was impossible to resist. I went and brought the book again. There were several guests present, and I had got half through the play before I again attracted attention. "What is that child about that she don't hear a word that's said to her?" quoth my aunt. "What are you reading?" said my father. "Shakspeare" was again the reply, in a clear, though somewhat impatient, tone. "How?" said my father angrily,—then restraining himself before his guests,—"Give me the book and go directly to bed."

Into my little room no care of his anger followed me. Alone, in the dark, I thought only of the scene placed by the poet before my eye, where the free flow of life, sudden and graceful dialogue, and forms, whether grotesque or fair, seen in the broad lustre of his imagination, gave just what I wanted, and brought home the life I seemed born to live. My fancies swarmed like bees, as I contrived the rest of the story;—what all would do, what say, where go. . . . Thus was I absorbed when my father entered. He felt it right, before going to rest, to reason with me about my disobedience, shown in a way, as he considered, so insolent. I listened, but could not feel interested in what he said, nor turn my mind from what engaged it. He went away really grieved at my impenitence, and quite at a loss to understand conduct in me so unusual.

—Often since I have seen the same misunderstanding between parent and child,—the parent thrusting the morale, the discipline, of life upon the child, when just engrossed by some game of real importance and great leadings to it. That is only a wooden horse to the father,—the child was careering to distant scenes of conquest and crusade, through a country of elsewhere unimagined beauty. None but poets remember their youth; but the father who does not retain poetical apprehension of the world . . . must be a tyrant in his home. . . .

My attention thus fixed on Shakspeare, I returned to him at every hour I could command. Here was a counterpoise to my Romans, still more forcible than the little garden. My author could read the Roman nature too,—read it in the sternness of Coriolanus, and in the varied wealth of Caesar. But he viewed these men of will as only one kind of men; he kept them in their place, and I found that he, who could understand the Roman, yet expressed in Hamlet a deeper thought.

In CERVANTES, I found far less productive talent,—indeed, a far less powerful genius,—but the same wide wisdom, a discernment piercing the shows and symbols of existence, yet rejoicing in them all, both for their own life, and as signs of the unseen reality. . . .

[W]ho is not conscious of a sincere reverence for the Don, prancing forth on his gaunt steed? Who would not rather be he than any of the persons who laugh at him? . . .

My third friend was MOLIÉRE, one very much lower, both in range and depth, than the others, but, as far as he goes, of the same character. . . . It was . . . only the poor social world of Paris that he saw, but he viewed it from the firm foundations of his manhood, and every lightest laugh rings from a clear perception, and teaches life anew.

These men were all alike in this,—they loved the *natural history* of man. Not what he should be, but what he is, was the favorite subject of their thought. . . .

It will be seen that my youth was not unfriended, since those great minds came to me in kindness. A moment of action in one's self, however, is worth an age of apprehension through others; not that our deeds are better, but that they produce a renewal of our being. I have had more productive moments and of deeper joy, but never hours of more tranquil pleasure than those in which these demi-gods visited me,—and with a smile so familiar, that I imagined the world to be full of such. They did me good, for by them a standard was early given of sight and thought, from which I could never go back, and beneath which I cannot suffer patiently my own life or that of any friend to fall. They did me harm, too, for the child fed with meat instead of milk becomes too soon mature. Expectations and desires were thus early raised, after which I must long toil before they can be realized. How poor the scene around, how tame one's own existence, how meagre and faint every power, with these beings in my mind! Often I must cast them quite aside in order to grow in my small way, and not sink into despair. Certainly I do not wish that instead of these masters I had read baby books, written down to children, and with such ignorant dulness that they blunt the senses and corrupt the tastes of the still plastic human being. But I do wish that I had read no books at all till later,—that I had lived with toys, and played in the open air. Children should not cull the fruits of reflection and observation early, but expand in the sun, and let thoughts come to them. They should not through books antedate their actual experiences, but should take them gradually, as sympathy and interpretation are needed. With me, much of life was devoured in the bud.

Sojourner Truth

~

SOJOURNER TRUTH (1791–1883; originally named Isabella) escaped slavery in 1826, one year before the New York State legislature mandated freedom for all adults held as slaves. She later became famous as a traveling preacher and for her work in the
abolitionist and women's rights movements. Her speech, "Ain't I a
Woman," which refuted a white male's assertion that women were
too delicate to enjoy suffrage, is particularly well known. In this excerpt from her autobiography, *Narrative of Sojourner Truth*, she recounts her escape from slavery and the legal battle to regain custody of one of her children. (Since Truth was illiterate, she dictated
her autobiography to Olive Gilbert, and Gilbert's voice does in-
trude on occasion.)

~

Slaveholder's Promises

After emancipation had been decreed by the State, some years before the time fixed for its consummation, Isabella's master told her
if she would do well, and be faithful, he would give her 'free papers,' one year before she was legally free by statute. In the year
1826, she had a badly diseased hand, which greatly diminished her
usefulness; but on the arrival of July 4, 1827, the time specified
for her receiving her 'free papers,' she claimed the fulfilment of
her master's promise; but he refused granting it, on account (as he

Truth, Sojourner. *Narrative of Sojourner Truth*. Written for Sojourner Truth
by Olive Gilbert, 1850. Rpt., New York: Penguin Books, 1998, pp. 26–37.

alleged) of the loss he had sustained by her hand. She plead that she had worked all the time, and done many things she was not wholly able to do, although she knew she had been less useful than formerly; but her master remained inflexible. Her very faithfulness probably operated against her now, and he found it less easy than he thought to give up the profits of his faithful Bell, who had so long done him efficient service.

But Isabella inwardly determined that she would remain quietly with him only until she had spun his wool—about one hundred pounds—and then she would leave him, taking the rest of the time to herself. 'Ah!' she says, with emphasis that cannot be written, 'the slaveholders are TERRIBLE for promising to give you this or that, or such and such a privilege, if you will do thus and so; and when the time of fulfilment comes, and one claims the promise, they, forsooth, recollect nothing of the kind; and you are, like as not, taunted with being a LIAR; or, at best, the slave is accused of not having performed *his* part or condition of the contract.' 'Oh!' said she, 'I have felt as if I could not live through the *operation* sometimes. Just think of us! *so* eager for our pleasures, and just foolish enough to keep feeding and feeding ourselves up with the idea that we should get what had been thus fairly promised; and when we think it is almost in our hands, find ourselves flatly denied! Just think! how *could* we bear it? Why, there was Charles Brodhead promised his slave Ned, that when harvesting was over, he might go and see his wife, who lived some twenty or thirty miles off. So Ned worked early and late, and as soon as the harvest was all in, he claimed the promised boon. His master said, he had merely told him he "would *see* if he could go, when the harvest was over; but now he saw that he *could not go*." But Ned, who still claimed a positive promise, on which he had fully depended, went on cleaning his shoes. His master asked him if he intended going, and on his replying "yes," took up a sled-stick that lay near him, and gave him such a blow on the head as broke his skull, killing him dead on the spot. The poor colored people all felt struck down by the blow.' Ah! and well they might. Yet it was but one of a long series of bloody, and other most effectual blows, struck against their liberty and their lives. But to return from our digression.

The subject of this narrative was to have been free July 4, 1827, but she continued with her master till the wool was spun, and the heaviest of the 'fall's work' closed up, when she concluded to take her freedom into her own hands, and seek her fortune in some other place.

Her Escape

The question in her mind, and one not easily solved, now was, 'How can I get away?' So, as was her usual custom, she 'told God she was afraid to go in the night, and in the day every body would see her.' At length, the thought came to her that she could leave just before the day dawned, and get out of the neighborhood where she was known before the people were much astir. 'Yes,' said she, fervently, 'that's a good thought! Thank you, God, for *that* thought!' So, receiving it as coming direct from God, she acted upon it, and one fine morning, a little before day-break, she might have been seen stepping stealthily away from the rear of Master Dumont's house, her infant on one arm and her wardrobe on the other; the bulk and weight of which, probably, she never found so convenient as on the present occasion, a cotton handkerchief containing both her clothes and her provisions.

As she gained the summit of a high hill, a considerable distance from her master's, the sun offended her by coming forth in all his pristine splendor. She thought it never was so light before; indeed, she thought it much too light. She stopped to look about her, and ascertain if her pursuers were yet in sight. No one appeared, and, for the first time, the question came up for settlement, 'Where, and to whom, shall I go?' In all her thoughts of getting away, she had not once asked herself whither she should direct her steps. She sat down, fed her infant, and again turning her thoughts to God, her only help, she prayed him to direct her to some safe asylum. And soon it occurred to her, that there was a man living somewhere in the direction she had been pursuing, by the name of Levi Rowe, whom she had known, and who, she thought, would be likely to befriend her. She accordingly pursued her way to his house, where she found him ready to entertain and assist her, though he was then on his death-bed. He bade her partake of the hospitalities of his house, said he knew of two good places where she might get in, and requested his wife to show her where they were to be found. As soon as she came in sight of the first house, she recollected having seen it and its inhabitants before, and instantly exclaimed, 'That's the place for me; I shall stop there.' She went there, and found the good people of the house, Mr. and Mrs. Van Wagener, absent, but was kindly received and hospitably entertained by their excellent mother, till the return of her children. When they arrived, she made her case known to them. They listened to her story, assuring her they never turned the needy away, and willingly gave her employment.

She had not been there long before her old master, Dumont, appeared, as she had anticipated; for when she took French leave of him, she resolved not to go too far from him, and not put him to as much trouble in looking her up—for the latter he was sure to do—as Tom and Jack had done when they ran away from him, a short time before. This was very considerate in her, to say the least. . . .

When her master saw her, he said, 'Well, Bell, so you've run away from me.' 'No, I did not *run* away; I walked away by daylight, and all because you had promised me a year of my time.' His reply was, 'You must go back with me.' Her decisive answer was, 'No, I *won't* go back with you.' He said, 'Well, I shall take the *child*.' *This* also was as stoutly negatived.

Mr. Isaac S. Van Wagener then interposed, saying, he had never been in the practice of buying and selling slaves; he did not believe in slavery; but, rather than have Isabella taken back by force, he would buy her services for the balance of the year—for which her master charged twenty dollars, and five in addition for the child. The sum was paid, and her master Dumont departed; but not till he had heard Mr. Van Wagener tell her not to call him master,—

adding, 'there is but *one* master; and he who is *your* master is *my* master.' Isabella inquired what she *should* call him? He answered, 'Call me Isaac Van Wagener, and my wife is Maria Van Wagener.' Isabella could not understand this, and thought it a *mighty change*, as it most truly was from a master whose word was law, to simple Isaac S. Van Wagener, who was master to *no* one. With these noble people, who, though they could not be the masters of slaves, were undoubtedly a portion of God's nobility, she resided one year, and from them she derived the name of Van Wagener; he being her last master in the eye of the law, and a slave's surname is ever the same as his master. . . .

Illegal Sale of Her Son

A little previous to Isabel's leaving her old master, he had sold her child, a boy of five years, to a Dr. Gedney, who took him with him as far as New York city, on his way to England; but finding the boy too small for his service, he sent him back to his brother, Solomon Gedney. This man disposed of him to his sister's husband, a wealthy planter, by the name of Fowler, who took him to his own home in Alabama.

This illegal and fraudulent transaction had been perpetrated some months before Isabella knew of it, as she was now living at Mr. Van Wagener's. The law expressly prohibited the sale of any slave out of the State,—and all minors were to be free at twenty-one years of age; and Mr. Dumont had sold Peter with the express understanding, that he was soon to return to the State of New York, and be emancipated at the specified time.

When Isabel heard that her son had been sold South, she immediately started on foot and alone, to find the man who had thus dared, in the face of all law, human and divine, to sell her child out of the State; and if possible, to bring him to account for the deed.

Arriving at New Paltz, she went directly to her former mistress, Dumont, complaining bitterly of the removal of her son. Her mistress heard her through, and then replied—'*Ugh!* a *fine* fuss to make about a little *nigger*! Why, have n't you as many of 'em left as you can see to and take care of? A pity 'tis, the niggers are not all in Guinea!! Making such a halloo-balloo about the neighborhood; and all for a paltry nigger!!!' Isabella heard her through, and after a moment's hesitation, answered, in tones of deep determination—'*I'll have my child again.*' 'Have *your child* again!' repeated her mistress— her tones big with contempt, and scorning the absurd idea of her getting him. 'How can you get him? And what have you to support him with, if you could? Have you any money?' 'No,' answered Bell, 'I have no money, but God has enough, or what's better! And I'll have my child again.' These words were pronounced in the most slow, solemn and determined measure and manner. And in speaking of it, she says, 'Oh, my God! I know'd I'd have him again. I was sure God would help me to get him. Why, I felt so *tall within*—I felt as if the power of a nation was with me!'

The impressions made by Isabella on her auditors, when moved by lofty or deep feeling, can never be transmitted to paper, (to use the words of another,) till by some Daguerrian art, we are enabled to transfer the look, the gesture, the tones of voice, in connection with the quaint, yet fit expressions used, and the spirit-stirring animation that, at such a time, pervades all she says.

After leaving her mistress, she called on Mrs. Gedney, mother of him who had sold her boy; who, after listening to her lamentations, her grief being mingled with indignation at the sale of her son, and her declaration that she would have him again—said, 'Dear me! What a disturbance to make about your child! What, is *your* child better than *my* child? My child is gone out there, and yours is gone to live with her, to have enough of everything, and to be treated like a gentleman!' And here she laughed at Isabel's absurd fears, as she would represent them to be. 'Yes,' said Isabel, '*your* child has gone there, but she is *married* and my boy has gone as a *slave*, and he is too little to go so far from his mother. Oh, I must have my child.' And here the continued laugh of Mrs. G. seemed to Isabel, in this time of anguish and distress, almost demoniacal. . . .

It Is Often Darkest Just Before Dawn

This homely proverb was illustrated in the case of our sufferer; for, at the period at which we have arrived in our narrative, to her the darkness seemed palpable, and the waters of affliction covered her soul; yet light was about to break in upon her.

Soon after the scenes related in our last chapter, which had harrowed up her very soul to agony, she met a man, (we would like to tell you *who*, dear reader, but it would be doing him no kindness, even at the present day, to do so,) who evidently sympathized with her, and counselled her to go to the Quakers, telling her they were already feeling very indignant at the fraudulent sale of her son, and assuring her that they would readily assist her, and direct her what to do. He pointed out to her two houses, where lived some of those people, who formerly, more than any other sect, perhaps, lived out the principles of the gospel of Christ. She wended her way to their dwellings, was listened to, unknown as she personally was to them, with patience, and soon gained their sympathies and active co-operation.

They gave her lodgings for the night; and it is very amusing to hear her tell of the 'nice, high, clean, white, *beautiful* bed' assigned her to sleep in, which contrasted so strangely with her former pallets, that she sat down and contemplated it, perfectly absorbed in wonder that *such* a bed should have been appropriated to one like herself. For some time she thought that she would lie down beneath it, on her usual bedstead, the floor. 'I did, indeed,' says she, laughing heartily at her former self. However, she finally concluded to make use of the bed, for fear that not to do so might injure the feelings of her good hostess. In the morning, the Quaker saw that she was taken and set down near Kingston, with directions to go to the Court House, and enter complaint to the Grand Jury.

. . . [S]he found the Grand Jurors indeed sitting, and . . . commenced to relate her injuries. After holding some conversation among themselves, one of them rose, and bidding her follow him, led the way to a side office, where he heard her story, and asked her 'if she could *swear* that the child she spoke of was her son?' 'Yes,' she answered, 'I *swear* it's my son.' 'Stop, stop!' said the lawyer, 'you must swear by this book'—giving her a book, which she thinks must have been the Bible. She took it, and putting it to her lips, began again to swear it was her child. The clerks, unable to preserved their gravity any longer, burst into an uproarious laugh; and one of them inquired of lawyer Chip of what use it could be to make *her* swear. 'It will answer the law,' replied the officer. He then made her comprehend just what he wished her to do, and she took a lawful oath, as far as the outward ceremony could make it one. All can judge how far she understood its spirit and meaning.

He now gave her a writ, directing her to take it to the constable of New Paltz, and have him serve it on Solomon Gedney. She obeyed, walking, or rather *trotting*, in her haste, some eight or nine miles.

But while the constable, through mistake, served the writ on a brother of the real culprit, Solomon Gedney slipped into a boat, and was nearly across the North River, on whose banks they were standing, before the dull Dutch constable was aware of his mistake. Solomon Gedney, meanwhile, consulted a lawyer, who advised him to go to Alabama and bring back the boy, otherwise it might cost him fourteen years' imprisonment, and a thousand dollars in cash. By this time, it is hoped he began to feel that selling slaves unlawfully was not so good a business as he had wished to find it. He secreted himself till due preparations could be made, and soon set sail for Alabama. Steamboats and railroads had not then annihilated distance to the extent they now have, and although he left in the fall of the year, spring came ere he returned, bringing the boy with him—but holding on to him as his property. It had ever been Isabella's prayer, not only that her son might be returned, but that he should be delivered from bondage, and into her own hands, lest he should be punished out of mere spite to her, who was so greatly annoying and irritating to her oppressors; and if her suit was gained, her very triumph would add vastly to their irritation.

She again sought advice of Esquire Chip, whose counsel was, that the aforesaid constable serve the before-mentioned writ upon the right person. This being done, soon brought Solomon Gedney up to Kingston, where he gave bonds for his appearance at court, in the sum of $600.

Esquire Chip next informed his client, that her case must now lie over till the next session of the court, some months in the future. 'The law must take its course,' said he.

'What! wait another court! wait *months*!' said the persevering mother. 'Why, long before that time, he can go clear off, and take my child with him—no one knows where. I *cannot* wait; I *must* have him *now*, whilst he is to be had.' 'Well,' said the lawyer, very coolly, 'if he puts the boy out of the way, he must pay the $600— one half of which will be yours;' supposing, perhaps, that $300 would pay for a 'heap of children,' in the eye of a slave who never, in all her life, called a dollar her own. But in this instance, he was mistaken in his reckoning. She assured him, that she had not been seeking money, neither would money satisfy her; it was her son, and her son alone she wanted, and her son she must have. Neither could she wait court, not she. The lawyer used his every argument to convince her, that she ought to be very thankful for what they had done for her; that it was a great deal, and it was but reasonable that she should now wait patiently the time of the court.

Yet she never felt, for a moment, like being influenced by these suggestions. She felt confident she was to receive a full and literal answer to her prayer, the burden of which had been—'O Lord, give my son into my hands, and that speedily! Let not the spoilers have him any longer,' Notwithstanding, she very distinctly saw that those who had thus far helped her on so kindly were *wearied* of her, and she feared God was wearied also. She had a short time previous learned that Jesus was a Saviour, and an intercessor; and she thought that if Jesus could but be induced to plead for her in the present trial, God would listen to *him*, though he were wearied of *her* importunities. To him, of course, she applied. As she was walking about, scarcely knowing whither she went, asking within herself, 'Who will show me any good, and lend a helping hand in this matter,' she was accosted by a perfect stranger, and one whose name she has never learned, in the following terms: 'Halloo, there; how do you get along with your boy? do they give him up to you?' She told him all, adding that now every body was tired, and she had none to help her. He said, 'Look here! I'll tell you what you'd better do. Do you see that stone house yonder?' pointing in a particular direction. 'Well, lawyer Demain lives there, and do you go to him, and lay your case before him; I think he'll help you. *Stick to him.* Don't give him peace till he does. I feel sure if you press him, he'll do it for you,' She needed no further urging, but trotted off at her peculiar gait in the direction of his house, as fast as possible,— and she was not encumbered with stockings, shoes, or any other heavy article of dress. When she had told him her story, in her impassioned manner, he looked at her a few moments, as if to ascertain if he were contemplating a new variety of the genus homo, and then told her, if she would give him five dollars, he would get her sone for her, in twenty-four hours. 'Why,' she replied, '*I* have no *money*, and never had a dollar in my life!' Said he, 'If you will go to those Quakers in Poppletown, who carried you to court, they will help you to five dollars in cash, I have no doubt; and you shall have your son in twenty-four hours, from the time you bring me that sum.' She performed the journey to Poppletown, a distance of some ten miles, very expeditiously; collected considerable more than the sum specified by the barrister; then, shutting the money tightly in her hand, she trotted back, and paid the lawyer a larger fee than he had demanded. . . .

The lawyer now renewed his promise, that she should have her son in twenty-four hours. But Isabella, having no idea of this space of time, went several times in a day, to ascertain if her son had come. Once, when the servant opened the door and saw her, she said, in a tone expressive of much surprise, 'Why, this woman's come again!' She then wondered if she went too often. When the lawyer appeared, he told her the twenty-four hours would not expire till the next morning; if she would call then, she would see her son. The next morning saw Isabel at the lawyer's door, while he was yet in his bed. He now assured he it was morning till noon; and that before noon her son would be there, for he had sent the famous 'Matty Styles' after him, who would not fail to have the boy and his master on hand in due season, either dead or alive; of that he was sure. Telling her she need not come again; he would himself inform her of their arrival.

After dinner, he appeared to Mr. Rutzer's, (a place the lawyer had procured for her, while she awaited the arrival of her boy,) assuring her, her son had come; but that he stoutly denied having any mother, or any relatives in that place; and said, 'she must go over and identify him.' She went to the office, but at sight of her the boy cried aloud, and regarded her as some terrible being, who was about to take him away from a kind and loving friend. He knelt, even, and begged them, with tears, not to take him away from his dear master, who had brought him from the dreadful South, and been so kind to him.

When he was questioned relative to the bad scar on his forehead, he said, 'Fowler's horse hove him.' And of the one on his cheek, 'That was done by running against the carriage.' In answering these questions he looked imploringly at his master, as much as to say, 'If they are falsehoods, you bade me say them; may they be satisfactory to you, at least.'

The justice, noting his appearance, bade him forget his master and attend only to him. But the boy persisted in denying his mother, and clinging to his master, saying his mother did not live in such a place as that. However, they allowed the mother to identify her son; and Esquire Demain pleaded that he claimed the boy for her, on the ground that he had been sold out of the State, contrary to the laws in such cases made and provided— spoke of the penalties annexed to said crime, and of the sum of money the delinquent was to pay, in case any one chose to prosecute him for the offence he had committed. . . . When the pleading was at an end, Isabella understood the Judge to declare, as the sentence of the Court, that the 'boy be delivered into the hands of the mother—having no other master, no other con-troller, no other conductor, but his mother.' This sentence was obeyed; he was delivered into her hands, the boy meanwhile begging, most piteously, *not* to be taken from his dear master, saying she was not his mother, and that his mother did not live in such a place as that. And it was some time before lawyer De-main, the clerks, and Isabella, could collectively succeed in calm-ing the child's fears, and in convincing him that Isabella was not some terrible monster, as he had for the last months, probably, been trained to believe; and who, in taking him away from his master, was taking him from all good, and consigning him to all evil.

When at last kind words and *bon bons* had quieted his fears, and he could listen to their explanations, he said to Isabella—'Well, you *do* look like my mother *used* to;' and she was soon able to make him comprehend some of the obligations he was under, and the relation he stood in, both to herself and his master. She commenced as soon as practicable to examine the boy, and found, to her utter astonish-ment, that from the crown of his head to the sole of his foot, the cal-losities and indurations on his entire body were most frightful to be-hold. His back she described as being like her fingers, as she laid them side by side.

'Heavens! what is all *this*?' said Isabel. He answered, 'It is where Fowler whipped, kicked, and beat me.' She exclaimed, 'Oh, Lord Jesus, look! see my poor child! Oh Lord, "render unto them double" for all this! Oh my God! Pete, how *did* you bear it?'

'Oh, this is nothing, mammy—if you should see Phillis, I guess you'd *scare*! She had a little baby, and Fowler cut her till the milk as well as blood ran down *her* body. You would *scare* to see Phillis, mammy.'

Maria W. Stewart

~

MARIA W. STEWART (1803–1879), the first American-born woman known to lecture in public about political issues, was an ardent abolitionist and supporter of increased rights and opportunities for free blacks and women. Born free in Connecticut herself, she called on white Northerners to end their employment and educational discrimination against her people and implored free people of African descent to use all means within their power to gain an education. In this 1833 speech, she, among other things, criticizes the colonization movement's plant to expatriate African Americans to Liberia.

~

African rights and liberty is a subject that ought to fire the breast of every free man of color in these United States, and excite in his bosom a lively, deep, decided and heart-felt interest. When I cast my eyes on the long list of illustrious names that are enrolled on the bright annals of fame among the whites, I turn my eyes within, and ask my thoughts, "Where are the names of our illustrious ones?" It must certainly have been for the want of energy on the part of the free people of color, that they have been long willing to bear the yoke of oppression. It must have been the want of ambition and force that has given the whites occasion to say that our natural abilities are not as good, and our capacities by nature inferior to theirs. They boldly assert that did we possess a natural independence of soul, and feel a love for liberty within our breasts, some one of our

Stewart, Maria W. *Maria W. Stewart, America's First Black Woman Political Writer: Essays and Speeches.* Marilyn Richardson, ed. Bloomington and Indianapolis: Indiana University Press, 1987, pp. 56–64.

sable race, long before this, would have testified it, notwithstanding the disadvantages under which we labor. We have made ourselves appear altogether unqualified to speak in our own defence, and are therefore looked upon as objects of pity and commiseration. We have been imposed upon, insulted and derided on every side; and now, if we complain, it is considered as the height of impertinence. We have suffered ourselves to be considered as dastards, cowards, mean, faint-hearted wretches; and on this account (not because of our complexion) many despise us, and would gladly spurn us from their presence.

These things have fired my soul with a holy indignation, and compelled me thus to come forward, and endeavor to turn their attention to knowledge and improvement; for knowledge is power. I would ask, is it blindness of mind, or stupidity of soul, or the want of education that has caused our men who are 60 or 70 years of age, never to let their voices be heard, nor their hands be raised in behalf of their color? Or has it been for the fear of offending the whites? If it has, O ye fearful ones, throw off your fearfulness, and come forth in the name of the Lord, and in the strength of the God of Justice, and make yourselves useful and active members in society; for they admire a noble and patriotic spirit in others; and should they not admire it in us? If you are men, convince them that you possess the spirit of men; and as your day, so shall your strength be. Have the sons of Africa no souls? Feel they no ambitious desires? Shall the chains of ignorance forever confine them? Shall the insipid appellation of "clever negroes," or "good creatures," any longer content them? Where can we find among ourselves the man of science, or a philosopher, or an able statesman, or a counsellor at law? Show me our fearless and brave, our noble and gallant ones. Where are our lecturers in natural history, and our critics in useful knowledge? There may be a few such men among us, but they are rare. It is true our fathers bled and died in the revolutionary war, and others fought bravely under the command of Jackson, in defence of liberty. But where is the man that has distinguished himself in these modern days by acting wholly in the defence of African rights and liberty? There was one, although he sleeps, his memory lives.

I am sensible that there are many highly intelligent men of color in these United States, in the force of whose arguments, doubtless, I should discover my inferiority; but if they are blessed with wit and talent, friends and fortune, why have they not made themselves men of eminence, by striving to take all the reproach that is cast upon the people of color, and in endeavoring to alleviate the woes of their brethren in bondage? Talk, without effort, is nothing; you are abundantly capable, gentlemen, of making yourselves men of distinction; and this gross neglect, on your part, causes my blood to boil within me. Here is the grand cause which hinders the rise and progress of people of color. It is their want of laudable ambition and requisite courage.

Individuals have been distinguished according to their genius and talents, ever since the first formation of man, and will continue to be while the world stands. The different grades rise to honor and respectability as their merits may deserve. History informs us that we sprung from one of the most learned nations of the whole earth; from the seat, if not the parent, of science. Yes, poor despised Africa was once the resort of sages and legislators of other nations, was esteemed the school for learning, and the most illustrious men in Greece flocked thither for instruction. But it was our gross sins and abominations that provoked the Almighty to frown thus heavily upon us, and give our glory unto others. Sin and prodigality have caused the downfall of nations, kings and emperors; and were it not that God in wrath remembers mercy, we might indeed despair; but a promise is left us; "Ethiopia shall again stretch forth her hands unto God."

But it is no use for us to boast that we sprung from this learned and enlightened nation, for this day a thick mist of moral gloom hangs over millions of our race. Our condition as a people has been low for hundreds of years, and it will continue to be so, unless by true piety and virtue, we strive to regain that which we have lost. White Americans, by their prudence, economy, and exertions, have sprung up and become one of the most flourishing nations in the world, distinguished for their knowledge of the arts and sciences, for their polite literature. While our minds are vacant and starve for want of knowledge, theirs are filled to overflowing. Most of our color have been taught to stand in fear of the white man from their earliest infancy, to work as soon as they could walk, and to call "master" before they could scarce lisp the name of mother. Continual fear and laborious servitude have in some degree lessened in us that natural force and energy which belong to man; or else, in defiance of opposition, our men, before this, would have nobly and boldly contended for their rights. But give the man of color an equal opportunity with the white from the cradle to manhood, and from manhood to the grave, and you would discover the dignified statesman, the man of science, and the philosopher. But there is no such opportunity for the sons of Africa, and I fear that our powerful ones are fully determined that there never shall be. Forbid, ye Powers on high, that it should any longer be said that our men possess no force. O ye sons of Africa, when will your voices be heard in our legislative halls, in defiance of your enemies, contending for equal rights and liberty? How can you, when you reflect from what you have fallen, refrain from crying mightily unto God, to turn away from us the fierceness of his anger, and remember our transgressions against us no more forever? But a god of infinite purity will not regard the prayers of those who hold religion in one hand, and prejudice, sin and pollution in the other; he will not regard the prayers of self-righteousness and hypocrisy. Is it possible, I exclaim, that for the want of knowledge we have labored for hundreds of years to support others, and been content to receive what they chose to give us in return? Cast your eyes about, look as far as you can see; all, all is owned by the lordly white, except here and there a lowly dwelling which the man of color, midst deprivations, fraud, and opposition has been scarce able to procure. Like King Solomon, who put neither nail nor hammer to the temple, yet received the praise; so also have the white Americans gained themselves a name, like the names of the great men that are in the earth, while in reality we have been their principal foundation and support. We have pursued the shadow, they have obtained the substance; we have performed the labor, they have received the profits; we have planted the vines, they have eaten the fruits of them.

I would implore our men, and especially our rising youth, to flee from the gambling board and the dance-hall; for we are poor, and have no money to throw away. I do not consider dancing as criminal in itself, but it is astonishing to me that our fine young men are so blind to their own interest and the future welfare of their children as to spend their hard earnings for this frivolous amusement; for it has been carried on among us to such an unbecoming extent that it has become absolutely disgusting. "Faithful are the wounds of a friend, but the kisses of an enemy are deceitful [Proverbs 27:6]." Had those men among us who had an opportunity, turned their attention as assiduously to mental and moral improvement as they have to gambling and dancing, I might have remained quietly at home and they stood contending in my place. These polite accomplishments will never enroll your names on the bright annals of fame who admire the belle void of intellectual knowledge, or applaud the dandy that talks largely on politics, without striving to assist his fellow in the revolution, when the nerves and muscles of every other man forced him into the field of action. You have a right to rejoice, and to let your hearts cheer you in the days of your youth; yet remember that for all these things God will bring you into judgment. Then, O ye sons of Africa, turn your mind from these perishable objects, and contend for the cause of God and the rights of man. Form yourselves into temperance societies. There are temperate men among you; then why will you any longer neglect to strive, by your example, to suppress vice in all its abhorrent forms? You have been told repeatedly of the glorious results arising from temperance, and can you bear to see the whites arising in honor and respectability without endeavoring to grasp after that honor and respectability also?

But I forbear. Let our money, instead of being thrown away as heretofore, be appropriated for schools and seminaries of learning for our children and youth. We ought to follow the example of the whites in this respect. Nothing would raise our respectability, add to our peace and happiness, and reflect so much honor upon us, as to be ourselves the promoters of temperance, and the supporters, as far as we are able, of useful and scientific knowledge. The rays of light and knowledge have been hid from our view; we have been taught to consider ourselves as scarce superior to the brute creation; and have performed the most laborious part of American drudgery. Had we as a people received one-half the early advantages the whites have received, I would defy the government of these United States to deprive us any longer of our rights.

I am informed that the agent of the Colonization Society has recently formed an association of young men for the purpose of influencing those of us to go to Liberia who may feel disposed. The colonizationists are blind to their own interest, for should the nations of the earth make war with America, they would find their forces much weakened by our absence; or should we remain here, can our "brave soldiers" and "fellow citizens," as they were termed in time of calamity, condescend to defend the rights of whites and be again deprived of their own, or sent to Liberia in return? Or, if the colonizationists are the real friends to Africa, let them expend the money which they collect in erecting a college to educate her injured sons in this land of gospel, light, and liberty; for it would be most thankfully received on our part, and convince us of the truth of their professions, and save time, expense, and anxiety. Let them place before us noble objects worthy of pursuit, and see if we prove ourselves to be those unambitious negroes they term us. But, ah, methinks their hearts are so frozen toward us they had rather their money should be sunk in the ocean than to administer it to our relief: and I fear, if they dared, like Pharaoh, king of Egypt, they would order every male child among us to be drowned. But the most high God is still as able to subdue the lofty pride of these white Americans as He was the heart of that ancient rebel. They say, though we are looked upon as things, yet we sprang from a scientific people. Had our men the requisite force and energy they would soon convince them by their efforts, both in public and private, that they were men, or things in the shape of men. Well may the colonizationists laugh us to scorn for our negligence; well may they cry: "Shame to the sons of Africa." As the burden of the Israelites was too great for Moses to bear, so also is our burden too great for our noble advocate to bear. You must feel interested, my brethren, in what he undertakes, and hold up his hands by your good works, or in spite of himself his soul will become discouraged and his heart will die within him; for he has, as it were, the strong bulls of Bashan [Psalms 22:12] to contend with.

It is of no use for us to wait any longer for a generation of well educated men to arise. We have slumbered and slept too long already; the day is far spent; the night of death approaches; and you have sound sense and good judgment sufficient to begin with, if you feel disposed to make a right use of it. Let every man of color throughout the United States, who possesses the spirit and principles of a man, sign a petition to Congress to abolish slavery in the District of Columbia, and grant you the rights and privileges of common free citizens; for if you had had faith as a grain of mustard seed [Matthew 13:31], long before this the mountain of prejudice might have been removed. We are all sensible that the Anti-Slavery Society has taken hold of the arm of our whole population, in order to raise them out of the mire. Now all we have to do is, by a spirit of virtuous ambition, to strive to raise ourselves; and I am happy to have it in my power thus publicly to say that the colored inhabitants of this city, in some respects, are beginning to improve. Had the free people of color in these United States nobly and freely contended for their rights, and showed a natural genius and talent, although not so brilliant as some; had they held up, encouraged and patronized each other, nothing could have hindered us from being a thriving and flourishing people. There has been a fault among us. The reason why our distinguished men have not made themselves more influential, is because they fear that the strong current of opposition through which they must pass would cause their downfall and prove their overthrow. And what gives rise to this opposition? Envy. And what has it amounted to? Nothing. And who are the cause of it? Our whited sepulchres [Matthew 23:27], who want to be great, and don't know how; who love to be called of men "Rabbi, Rabbi;" who put on false sanctity, and humble themselves to their brethren for the sake of acquiring the highest place in the synagogue and the uppermost seat at the feast. You, dearly beloved, who are the genuine followers of our Lord Jesus Christ—the salt of the earth, and the light of the world—are not so culpable. As I told you in the very first of my writing, I will tell you again, I am but as a drop in the bucket—as one particle of the small dust of the earth [Isaiah 40:15]. God will surely raise up those among us who will plead the cause of virtue and the pure principles of morality more eloquently than I am able to do.

It appears to me that America has become like the great city of Babylon, for she has boasted in her heart: "I sit a queen and am no widow, and shall see no sorrow [Revelation 18:7]!" She is, indeed, a seller of slaves and the souls of men; she has made the Africans drunk with the wine of her fornication; she has put them completely beneath her feet, and she means to keep them there; her right hand supports the reins of government and her left hand the wheel of power, and she is determined not to let go her grasp. But many powerful sons and daughters of Africa will shortly arise, who will put down vice and immorality among us, and declare by Him that sitteth upon the throne that they will have their rights; and if refused, I am afraid they will spread horror and devastation around. I believe that the oppression of injured Africa has come up before the majesty of Heaven; and when our cries shall have reached the ears of the Most High, it will be a tremendous day for the people of this land; for strong is the hand of the Lord God Almighty.

Life has almost lost its charms for me; death has lost its sting, and the grave its terrors [I Corinthians 15:55]; and at times I have a strong desire to depart and dwell with Christ, which is far better. Let me entreat my white brethren to awake and save our sons from dissipation and our daughters from ruin. Lend the hand of assistance to feeble merit; plead the cause of virtue among our sable race; so shall our curses upon you be turned into blessings; and though you should endeavor to drive us from these shores, still we will cling to you the more firmly; nor will we attempt to rise above you; we will presume to be called your equals only.

The unfriendly whites first drove the native American from his much loved home. Then they stole our fathers from their peaceful and quiet dwellings, and brought them hither, and made bond-men and bond-women of them and their little ones. They have obliged our brethren to labor; kept them in utter ignorance; nourished them in vice, and raised them in degradation; and now that we have enriched their soil, and filled their coffers, they say that we are not capable of becoming like white men, and that we can never rise to respectability in this country. They would drive us to a strange land. But before I go, the bayonet shall pierce me through. African rights and liberty is a subject that ought to fire the breast of every free man of color in these United States, and excite in his bosom a lively, deep, decided, and heartfelt interest.

Mary Lyon

~

MARY LYON (1797–1849), founder of what became Mount Holyoke College, struggled for four years to secure funding for Mount Holyoke Seminary and was criticized for traveling throughout the countryside to do so. She persisted, however, and raised $27,000, with some large donations and many contributions of $5.00 or less. Because she provided Mount Holyoke with a sound financial foundation, the school, unlike most other female seminaries at the time, was able to outlive its founder and provide educational opportunity to young women of varied financial backgrounds. Mount Holyoke opened on November 8, 1837, and is today one of America's finest liberal arts colleges. Mary Lyon wrote the first of these letters while a teacher at Zilpah Grant's Ipswich (Mass.) Female Seminary and the last while awaiting Mount Holyoke's opening day.

~

To Rev. Edward Hitchcock
February 4, 1832

Rev. and Dear Sir:
Knowing that you are interested to learn anything about the proposed plan for a permanent female seminary, which has been agitated by some of its friends for more than a year, I make no apology for this communication. Local, private, and personal views, I

Lyon, Mary. *The Inception of Mount Holyoke College; portions of letters written by Mary Lyon between 1831 and 1837.* Springfield, MA: Springfield Printing and Binding Co. [n.d.], pp. 6–26.

think, should be far removed from this object. Could I be permitted to labor in the portico, and spend my days in clearing the ground for that which is destined to continue, and to exert an extensive and salutary influence on female education, and on religion from generation to generation, it would be the height of my ambition. What permanent female seminaries are now in existence? What one in New England of a high character is necessarily, from its plan, destined to outlive its present teachers? Ought this so to be? Are not a few permanent female seminaries needed? Could there be one or two of this character designed for older young ladies preparing to teach, and soon to go forth and exert an influence in a variety of ways on the cause of education and religion, would not great good result? The prospect now is that this subject will be presented to the public in some form or other. The attempt may be fruitless.

It is generally understood that the location should be in Ipswich but it is not absolutely necessary. Feeling that a genial soil would be of vast importance in this first attempt, I have been exceedingly desirous that the location on Connecticut river should receive, at least, a little attention before it is finally settled in Essex county.

If you think this a vain and impracticable scheme, my only request is, that you would commit this sheet to the flames, and bury the whole in oblivion.

To Miss Zilpah Grant,
Principal of Ipswich (Mass.) Female Seminary
January 10, 1833

When I consider the apparent expectations of those who are ready to say, "It is a good plan," it does not appear to me probable that you or I shall live to see a female seminary in New England, such as we desire, so endowed as to become permanent.

I am not, however, disheartened. I am ready to attempt anything which seems pointed out by Providence, even without any surety of success. I have never known such an overwhelming interest in the great plan as I have for a few weeks past. It does appear to me that it is a good plan, and one which God in his own time will own and bless. I know of nothing which I should not be ready to do, nor any sacrifice which I should not be ready to make, to promote the object.

To Miss Zilpah Grant
February 4, 1833

I feel more and more that the whole business must, in name, devolve on benevolent gentlemen, and not on yourself or myself. I do not feel so much afraid as I did that they will not take the right steps, but I feel much more afraid that they will not act at all. If anything at all should be done, the less you and I have to do with the business part of the affair, the better. If the object should excite attention, there is danger that many good men will fear the effect on society of so much female influence, and what they will call female greatness. I imagine I have seen a little of this already, and if more interest were to be felt in the cause, more jealousy might be excited.

To Miss Zilpah Grant
March 1, 1833

Yesterday was my birthday. Thirty-six years of my life are gone, and now I am one year more than middle aged. To look back step by step, it seems a long life, and the remaining years in prospect seem few and short. But my life and strength may be prolonged for many years to come. I would that it might be so, if it is the will of the Lord. But in one thing I can rejoice—that as long as the Lord of the vineyard has need of my feeble service, he will allow me the unspeakable privilege of living and laboring. . . .

One thing I have for several weeks wanted to propose to you. It is this: If Providence should ever make it plainly our duty to occupy different fields of labor, and to dissolve our legal connection, I should deem it one of the greatest earthly blessings which I could possibly enjoy, to keep as many of the cords which now bind us together unbroken as could be done under existing circumstances; that we should assist each other in forming plans; that we should visit each other often, write to each other often. A union somewhat like this would be to me an unspeakable satisfaction; it would seem to save my bleeding heart from sinking under the stroke of a separation; and my judgment says, that such a union would be suited to advance the great cause to which we have consecrated our lives. . . .

I will dwell a moment on the main argument: The hope of founding a permanent seminary. This is so great an object that it would be right to sacrifice considerable good for the sake of a small probability of success. If it must be delayed entirely for several years, I have thought that there was nothing that we could do together that we could not do separately. . . .

To Thomas White, Esq., Ashfield
March 5, 1834

My Dear Sir:

In your old age, would you not be glad, with a few other kindred souls, to be the means of commencing a great work, which, in importance to the welfare of our country, of the church, and of the world, shall not fall behind the home missionary, or any other of our leading benevolent societies? Would you not gladly see such a work begun and advancing? And how would your heart rejoice, if, before you sleep in the dust, you could see it rise and spread as our foreign missionary operations have done? This I believe may be accomplished, and he who, first putting his hand to the work, shall say to others, "Come and do likewise," will deserve a place with Mills, with Robert Raikes, and others of like eminence.

I have long had a secret hope that the time would arrive, when I could consistently give up my present sphere of labor, and in some way devote my life, my strength, and all my powers to this object. The time has now arrived and I expect to close my connection with this seminary after laboring a half year longer.

To Her Mother, Jemima Shepard Lyon
May 12, 1834

My very dear Mother:

I do not expect to continue my connection with Miss Grant after this summer. I have for a great while been thinking about those young ladies who find it necessary to make such an effort for their education as I made.

In one respect from year to year, I have not felt quite satisfied with my present field of labor. I have desired to be in a school, the expenses of which would be so small, that many who are now discouraged from endeavoring to enjoy the privileges of this, might be favored with those which are similar at less expense.

I have had the pleasure of seeing many who have enjoyed these privileges occupying the place of mothers. I have noticed with peculiar interest the cultivated and good common sense, the correct reasoning, the industry, and perseverance, the patience, meekness, and gentleness of many of them.

Since I have lived to see so many of these ladies in their own families, I have felt more than ever before, that my field of labor was among the most desirable. I have felt that I could thank Him who has given me my work to do. While I have enjoyed much, I have not been quite satisfied.

Sometimes my heart has burned within me; and again I have bid it be quiet. I have sometimes speculated and built airy castles, and again I have bid my mind dwell on sober realities. I have though that there might be a plan devised by which something could be done. I have further thought, that if I could be entirely released from all engagements and all encumbrances, perhaps I might in time find some way opened before me, for promoting this good object. With this view, I decided some time since to propose a separation. Perhaps you may inquire what course I expect to take, and where is to be my future scene of labor. This I do not know. The present path of duty is plain. The future I leave with Him who doeth all things well.

To Miss W.
August 1, 1834

I wish the same public interest could be excited to extend female education to the common walks of life that exists with regard to the education of young men. Oh that the church would take our highest female seminaries under her direct control, protection, and support! And do you not believe that this will be done at some future time? If any institution should ask for public support, would it not be desirable that in some particulars it should present certain marked features which would be approved by common Christians? On this account, I have thought that in the proposed seminary it would be well to have the domestic work done by the members, not as an essential feature of the institution, but as a mere appendage.

I have the greatest confidence that a system might be formed by which all the domestic work of a family of one hundred could be performed by the young ladies themselves, and in the most perfect order, without any sacrifice of improvement in knowledge, or of refinement. Might not this simple feature do away with much of the prejudice against female education among common people? If this prejudice could by any means be removed, how much would it do for the cause!

April 2, 1835

My very dear Mother:
I often feel that my life is far advanced, and that I can do but little more myself. But this great work is all to be done through human instrumentality. How small a portion of it has yet been done! O that

I might do a little more before I depart hence! But my greatest hope is that I may have the privilege of encouraging, stimulating, and strengthening some who may continue to labor when I am laid in the grave.

Will you, my dear mother, pray for this new institution, that God will open the hearts of his children in its behalf, and that the Spirit of God may rest on its future teachers and pupils, that it may be a spot where souls may be born to God, and saints quickened in the Lord's service? It is my heart's desire that holiness to the Lord may be inscribed upon all connected with it, and that a succession of teachers may be raised up, who shall there continue to labor for Christ long after we are laid in our graves.

To Her Sister
October 24, 1835

You will doubtless be glad to know something about the Mount Holyoke Seminary. The work goes on slowly. I hope they will be able to commence building next spring. We have much to try our faith and much to excite our hopes. The work of endeavoring to found and build up this seminary is one which I trust the Lord will own and bless; but I do not expect it will be carried forward as on flowery beds of ease, I only ask that it may receive the smile of Providence in that way which shall best promote the interest of the great cause to which it is consecrated.

To Miss Catharine E. Beecher,
July 1, 1836

The terms high, low, and moderate tuition mean very different things in different parts of the country. Our plan is to place tuition at what will be regarded by the New England community, including the wealthy and the educated with farmers and mechanics, as moderate tuition.

Here I would have you distinctly understand that we do not adopt this standard because we consider ourselves under any obligation to *man* so to do. Neither do we consider it necessary that other institutions should adopt the same standard, or that this institution should certainly abide by it evermore, though at present it is essential to our success. I have not been alone in considering it of great importance to establish a permanent seminary in New England for educating female teachers. Honorably to do this, from twenty to forty thousand dollars must be raised; and such a sum for such an object would form almost an era in female education. I have regarded it as a work for life. In laying our plans we examined carefully every step.

I am convinced that to give the first impulse to this work, something must be presented which is more tangible, and of real, though of less value, and be made to stand out in bold relief. For this purpose we have chosen the reduction of expenses, as compared with other large seminaries not aided by the public. Every step we take proves it a good selection. We carefully avoid all extravagant statements; indeed we usually state only general facts, leaving each to make his own estimate and draw his own conclusions. There is an expectation that economy will be practiced in the establishment, and that the funds, gathered by little and little, will be reserved for the good of the institution, and not for private emolument.

You speak of the importance of raising the compensation of teachers. In a list of motives for teaching, I should place first, the great motive, which cannot be understood by the natural heart, "Love thy neighbor as thyself." On this list, though not second in rank, I have been accustomed to place pecuniary considerations.

To Miss Catharine E. Beecher
October 7, 1836

We had a fine day for the laying of the corner stone. It was a day of deep interest. This is an affecting spot to me. The stones and brick and mortar speak a language which vibrates through my very soul. I have indeed lived to see the time when a body of gentlemen have ventured to lay the corner stone of an edifice which will cost about $15,000, and will be an institution for the education of females. Surely the Lord hath remembered our low estate. This will be an era in female education.

From a Circular Addressed to Ladies of Her Acquaintance, 1836

The enterprise of founding this institution was commenced about two years ago. The work has since been going forward slowly. The first edifice is now erecting. It is ninety-four by fifty feet, and of four stories, besides the basement. It will furnish good public accommodations for the school and the family, private chambers for the teachers, and for eighty young ladies. Additions are to be made hereafter, as the liberality of the Christian public shall furnish the means. The time has now come when we must make our arrangements for furniture. The business needs immediate attention. The sum necessary for one chamber will be from fifty to sixty dollars. Dear Madam, would not the ladies in your place consider it a privilege to furnish one of these chambers? Would you not consider it a privilege to bring the subject before them so fairly that they will do it with promptness?

Had I a thousand lives I could sacrifice them all in suffering and hardship for the sake of Mount Holyoke Seminary. Did I possess the greatest fortune, I could readily relinquish it all, and become poor, and more than poor, if its prosperity should demand it. Its grand object is, to furnish the greatest possible number of female teachers, of high literary qualifications, and of benevolent, self-denying zeal; and every other good must, if need be, be sacrificed to this great object. . . .

To Miss Zilpah Grant
September 14, 1837

When I look through to [opening day] November 8 it seems like looking down a precipice of many hundred feet, which I must descend. I can only avoid looking at the bottom, and fix my eye on the nearest stone, till I have safely reached it.

Sarah Grimké and Angelina Grimké Weld

~

SARAH GRIMKÉ (1792–1873) and **ANGELINA GRIMKÉ WELD** (1805–1879), sisters born and raised on a Southern slave-holding plantation, grew to despise slavery and moved to Philadelphia to join the fight against it. As two of the earliest women to speak publicly to "promiscuous" audiences, that is, audiences comprised of both men and women, they found themselves at the center of a controversy unrelated to abolition. The Massachusetts clergy denounced them in a pastoral letter that was read from every one of the state's orthodox pulpits, and Catharine Beecher, a prominent advocate of women's education, published an essay warning Angelina in particular that she had stepped outside "woman's sphere." The following letters, written separately and jointly by the sisters, explore their work within the abolitionist movement, the impact of this work on their familial relationships, and their growing realization that women confined to "woman's sphere" are unable to assist others in escaping their own assigned places.

~

Angelina Grimké to Theodore D. Weld and John Greenleaf Whittier
Brookline, Massachusetts, August 20, 1837

To Theodore D. Weld and J. G. Whittier
Brethren beloved in the Lord.

Weld, Theodore Dwight, Angelina Grimké Weld, and Sarah Grimké. *Letters of Theodore Dwight Weld, Angelina Grimké Weld and Sarah Weld, 1822–1844*. 2 vols. Gilbert H. Barnes and Dwight L. Dumond, eds. New York: D. Appleton-Century Company, Inc., 1934, pp. 427–430, 471–472, 678–679, 781–782, 787–790.

As your letters came to hand at the same time and both are devoted mainly to the same subject we have concluded to answer them on one sheet and jointly. You seem greatly alarmed at the idea of our advocating the *rights of woman*. Now we will first tell you *how* we came to begin those letters in the Spectator. Whilst we were at Newburyport we received a note from Mary Parker telling us that Wm. S. Porter [editor of the *Spectator*] had requested her to try to obtain some one to write for his paper in order that it might be better sustained. She asked him whether *she* might choose the subject and named the *province of woman*: he said yes, he would be glad to have such pieces to publish. Just at this time the Pastoral Letter came out, and Mary requested us to write something every week about *Woman* for the Spectator. We consulted together and viewed this unexpected opportunity of throwing our views before the public as providential. As I was writing to C. [Catherine] E. B[eecher], S. M. G. [Sarah] undertook it and as this paper was not an abolition paper we could not see any impropriety in embracing this opening. These letters have not been the means of *arousing* the public attention to the subject of Womans rights, it was the Pastoral Letter which did the mischief. The ministers seemed panic struck at once and commenced a most violent attack upon us. I do not say *absurd* for in truth if it can be fairly established that women *can lecture*, then why may they not preach and if *they* can preach, then woe! woe be unto that Clerical Domination which now rules the world under the various names of Gen'l Assemblies, Congregational Associations, etc. *This Letter* then roused the attention of the whole country to enquire what *right* we had to open our mouths for the dumb; the people were continually told "it is a *shame* for a *woman* to speak in the churches." Paul suffered not a *woman* to *teach* but commanded *her* to be in silence. The pulpit is too *sacred a place* for *woman's* foot etc. Now my dear brothers *this invasion of our rights* was just such an attack upon *us*, as that made upon Abolitionists generally when they were told a few years ago that *they had no right* to discuss the subject of Slavery. Did *you* take no notice of this assertion? Why no! With one heart and one voice you said,

We will settle *this right before* we go one step further. *The time* to assert a right is *the* time when *that* right is denied. *We must establish this right* for if we do not, it will be impossible for *us* to go *on with the work of Emancipation*. But you will say that not-withstand[ing] the denial of your right you still had crowded audiences—*curiosity*, it was a new thing under the sun to see a *woman* occupy the place of a lecturer and the people were very anxious to *hear* and *see* for themselves: but you certainly *must* know that the leaven which the ministers are so assiduously working into the minds of the people *must* take effect in process of time, and *will close every church to us*, if we give the community no reasons to counteract the sophistry of priests and levities. In this State particularly there is an utter ignorance on the subject. Some few noble minds bursting thro' the trammels of educational prejudice FEEL that woman does stand on the same platform of human rights with man, but even these cannot sustain their ground by argument, and as soon as they open their lips to assert her *rights*, their opponents throw perverted scripture into their faces and call O yea, clamor for *proof*, PROOF, PROOF! and this *they cannot* give and are beaten off the field in disgrace. Now we are confident that there are scores of such minds panting after light on this subject: "the children *ask* bread and no MAN giveth it unto them." There is an eagerness to understand our views. Now is it wrong to give those views in a series of letters in a paper NOT devoted to Abolition?

And can you not see that women *could* do, and *would* do a hundred times more for the slave if she were not fettered? Why! we are gravely told that we are out of our sphere even when we circulate petitions; out of our "appropriate sphere" when we speak to women only; and out of them when we *sing* in the churches. Silence is *our* province, submission *our* duty. If then we "give *no reason* for the hope that is in us," that we have *equal rights* with our brethren, how can we expect to be permitted *much longer to exercise those rights*? IF I know my own heart, I am NOT actuated by any selfish considerations (but I do sincerely thank our dear brother J. G. W[hittier] for the suggestion) but we are actuated by the full conviction that if we are to do any good in the Anti Slavery cause, our *right* to labor in it *must* be firmly established; *not* on the ground of Quakerism, but on the only firm bases of human rights, the Bible. Indeed I contend brethren that *this* is not *Quaker* doctrine, it is no more like *their* doctrine on Women than our Anti Slavery is like their Abolition, just about the same difference. I will explain myself. Women are regarded as equal to men on the ground of *spiritual gifts*, *not* on the broad ground of *humanity*. Woman may *preach*; this is a *gift*; but woman must *not* make the discipline by which *she herself* is to be governed. O that you were here that we might have a good long, *long* talk over matters and things, then I could explain myself far better. And I think we could convince you that *we* cannot push Abolitionism forward with all our might *until* we take up the stumbling block out of the road. We cannot see with brother Weld in this matter. We acknowledge the excellence of his reasons for urging us to labor in this cause of the Slave, our being Southerners, etc., but then we say how can we expect to be able to hold meetings much longer when people are so diligently taught to *despise us* for thus stepping out of the sphere of woman! Look at this instance: after we had left Groton the *Abolition* minister there, at a Lyceum meeting poured out his sarcasm and ridicule upon our heads and among other things said, he would as soon be caught robbing a hen roost as encouraging a woman to lecture. Now brethren if the leaders of the people thus speak of our labors, *how long* will we be allowed to prosecute them? Answer me this question. You may depend upon it, tho' to meet *this* question *may appear* to be turning out of our road, that *it is not*. IT IS NOT: we *must* meet it, and meet it *now* and meet it like *women* in the fear of the Lord. Why the language of the priests and levites to us women is that of Davids brother to him. "Why camest thou down hither? and with whom hast thou left those few sheep in the wilderness? I know thy pride and the naughtiness of thy heart; for thou art come down that thou mightest see the battle." They utterly deny *our right* to interfere with this or any other moral reform except in the particular way *they* choose to mark out for us to walk in. If we dare to stand upright and do our duty according to the dictates of *our own* consciences, why then we are compared to Fanny Wright and so on. Why, my dear brothers can you not see the deep laid scheme of the clergy against us as lecturers? They know full well that if they can persuade the people it is a *shame* for us to speak in public, and that every time we open our mouths for the dumb we are breaking a divine command, that even if we spoke with the tongues of *men* or of angels, we should have *no hearers*. They are springing a deep mine beneath our feet, and we shall *very* soon be compelled to retreat for we shall have *no* ground to stand on. If we surrender the right to *speak* to the public this year, we must surrender the right to petition next year and the right to *write* the year after and so on. What *then* can *woman* do for the slave when she is herself under the feet of man and shamed into *silence*? Now we entreat *you* to weigh candidly the *whole subject*, and then we are sure you will see, this is no more than an abandonment of our first love than the effort made by Anti Slavery men to establish the *right* of free discussion. . . .

Sarah and Angelina Grimké
to the Editor of the *National Enquirer*.*

S. M. and A. E. Grimké's former Connexion with slavery

As we are frequently asked, what relation we have in past years sustained to the system of slavery, and as we feel that individuals have a *perfect right to know*, we have thought it best to publish the following facts.

When S. M. G. [Sarah Grimké] was quite young, her father gave her a little African girl to wait upon her; but after a few years, she died. This was the only slave she ever owned. It must have been 30 years ago.

In the year 1827, our mother gave A. E. G. [Angelina Grimké] a young woman. She soon became uneasy with holding her a slave,

---

*From the *National Enquirer*, October 26, 1837.

and in a few months returned her to the donor. NO money transactions ever passed about it—NONE was paid, and NONE was received. S[t]ill, she at that time only saw men as trees walking, and was not sensible of the sin she was committing in returning a fellow creature into bondage. She only felt that she did not want the responsibility of such an ownership, but had no clear conception of the intrinsic principles of slavery.

In 1835, she began to read anti-slavery publications, and for the first time saw that slavery, under all circumstances, was sinful; she had always mourned over the ignorance, degradation, and cruelty, of slavery, but never understood the chattel principle, out of which all these abominations grew as naturally as the trunk and branches from the root of the tree. During the eight years which had elapsed since the time of her being a slaveholder, the slave had been sold, and had become the mother of three or four children. A. E. G. felt conscience-stricken at what she had done, and wrote to the then owner of the woman and her children, offering to *redeem* them from slavery at any price that might be named; and at the same time stating the change in her views, and the reasons why she could not offer to *buy* them, as that would be a recognition of the right of one man to hold another as property. The owner would not accede to this proposition, so that this slave is still in bondage. This is the only slave she ever owned.

We have been induced to state these facts because many persons have heard that we had slaves and liberated them; and we do not wish the credit of doing that which we had no opportunity of doing.

S. M. and A. E. GRIMKÉ.
East Boyleston, 2d inst.

Sarah Grimké to Elizabeth Pease
Manlius, New York [May 20?, 1838]

. . . I must now give thee some account of my dear sister's marriage, which probably thou hast already heard of. Her precious husband is emphatically a man of God, a member of the Presbyterian

Church. Of course Angelina will be disowned for forming this connection, and I shall be for attending the marriage. We feel no regret at this circumstance, believing that the discipline which cuts us off from membership for an act so strictly in conformity with the will of God, and so sanctioned by His word as is the marriage of the righteous, must be anti-Christian, and I am thankful for the opportunity to testify against it. The marriage was solemnized at the house of our sister, Anna R. Frost, in Philadelphia, on the 14th instant. By the law of Pennsylvania a marriage is legal if witnessed by twelve persons. Neither clergyman nor magistrate is required to be present. Angelina could not conscientiously consent to be married by a clergyman, and Theodore D. Weld cheerfully consented to have the marriage solemnized in such a manner as comparted with her views. We all felt that the presence of a magistrate, a stranger, would be unpleasant to us at such a time, and we therefore concluded to invite such of our friends as we desired, and have the marriage solemnized as a religious act, in a religious and social meeting. Neither Theodore nor Angelina felt as if they could bind themselves to any preconceived form of words, and accordingly uttered such as the Lord gave them at the moment. Theodore addressed Angelina in a solemn and tender manner. He alluded to the unrighteous power vested in a husband by the laws of the United States over the person and property of his wife, and he abjured all authority, all government, save the influence which love would give to them over each other as moral and immortal beings. I would give much to recall his words, but I cannot. Angelina's address to him was brief but comprehensive, containing a promise to honor him, to prefer him above herself, to love him with a pure heart fervently. Immediately after this we knelt, and dear Theodore poured out his soul in solemn supplication for the blessing of God on their union, that it might be productive of enlarged usefulness, and increased sympathy for the slave. Angelina followed in a melting appeal to our Heavenly Father, for a blessing on them, and that their union might glorify Him, and then asked His guidance and overshadowing love through the rest of their pilgrimage. A colored

Presbyterian minister then prayed, and was followed by a white one, and then I felt as if I could not restrain the language of praise and thanksgiving to Him who had condescended to be in the midst of this marriage feast, and to pour forth abundantly the oil and wine of consolation and rejoicing. The Lord Jesus was the first guest invited to be present, and He condescended to bless us with His presence, and to sanction and sanctify the union which was thus consummated. The certificate was then read by William Lloyd Garrison, and was signed by the company. The evening was spent in pleasant social intercourse. Several colored persons were present, among them two liberated slaves, who formerly belonged to our father, had come by inheritance to sister Anna, and had been freed by her. They were our invited guests, and we thus had an opportunity to bear our testimony against the horrible prejudice which prevails against colored persons, and the equally awful prejudice against the poor. . . .

[Sarah M. Grimké]

Angelina G. Weld to Elizabeth Pease
Fort Lee, New Jersey, August 14, 1839

My dear Friend

Thy long and very interesting favor of 4th Mo. 19th came duly to hand and should have been answered before, but for the feebleness of my health at the time of its reception, and my subsequent absence from home, first at Philadelphia and recently at Manlius in the Western part of the state of New York, whither we went to see my husband's parents—now my only surviving parents; for within the last two weeks we have received intelligence of our dear Mother's decease which occurred on the 21st of last month. She took a violent cold which fell on her bowels, and in 14 days terminated her useful life, for altho' in her 76th year, yet her health was uniformly so vigorous and her mind so active, that for the last 25 years she has been preeminently the promoter of every benevolent enterprize in Charleston, and was indefatigable in her labors of love among the poor. She suffered but little pain and her mind was kept in a calm and peaceful frame, giving the sweet assurance to those around her that she now sleeps in Jesus. But O! my sister *thou* canst estimate the bitterness of our sorrow, when I tell thee she died a *slaveholder*. For many years Sister S. and myself have done all we could to induce our beloved Mother to regard Slavery as a great sin and to wash her hands of all its pollutions, but our labors were vain; and now that she has been taken from us, and we were not permitted to gather around her dying bed. . . .

Angelina G. Weld to Anna R. Frost
Fort Lee, New Jersey, August 18, 1839

My Dear Sister—

    We felt very much obliged to thee for thy letter of the 31 ult: peculiarly so, as it contains the only particulars of our beloved Mother's removal from time to eternity. Brother Henry very kindly wrote immediately after the solemn event, but as Fort Lee is so small a place, I suppose we did not get our letter until two or three days after thou hadst received thine. E. Bascom also wrote and her's was directed to thee as well as to ourselves: I enclose it. Our Sisters have not yet written to us, and this has added another bitter ingredient to the cup of sorrow we have had to drink; but I feel in this, as I have done in other deep trials, that the Great Physician of my soul knows so thoroughly the diseases of my heart that the medicines he administers are just *right*. I still *hope* they will write and tell us *all* that is in their hearts. I suppose the "bitter cup" wh'h Sister E. says was preparing for Mother was our testimonies in "American Slavery as it is." She is mistaken, if she supposes Mother knew nothing of them. Sister wrote to her on the subject sometime before they were published, tho' I did not. Those are what thou callest "our last *infamous* publication." Dear Sister, we can most fully adopt thy language and call, not only our testimonies, but the whole book "an *infamous* publication" inasmuch as it does develope beyond all contradiction the secrets of our Southern prisonhouse. Yes, "thank heaven," it is assuredly doing more to open blind eyes and unstop the deaf ears than any book that has ever been published in this Country. Neither life nor death can obliterate from our memories nor from *God's book of remembrance*, the bloody abominations of *our own household*, and the time has come when the command has gone forth into many hearts to "bring to light the hidden things of darkness." Too long, too long have we hidden these things, prompted by a stronger feeling of sympathy for the OPPRESSOR than for the helpless and the dumb, who have been drinking the bitter waters of Marah for 400 years. From the style of thy letter, dear Sister, thou seemest to think it far more *infamous* in us to have *told* what our eyes have seen of the horrors of slavery, even tho' we have mentioned *no names*, than that others should actually have committed such outrages upon this peeled and plundered poor. Is this judging *righteous* judgment? Suppose thou or thy child should, by some mysterious providence of God, be reduced to slavery to-morrow, to be carried to the South and trodden in the dust by the hoof of oppression, mingling YOUR blood and sweat in the "bitter cups" *you* had to drink on a plantation or under the power of a cruel and heartless owner, how *then* my sister wouldst *thou* feel about the exposure of the horrors of the system which threw *you* beyond the protection of law and down to the level with the brute creation? Ponder these things on thy knees before that God who is no respecter of persons, but who lets loose the thunderbolts of his wrath against the Pharoas on their thrones of earthly glory, as well as against the cringing vassals who bow before him. We know that it was the *exposure* of FACTS with regard to the African Slave trade which first roused the heart of Clarkson to *feel*, and nerved his arm to do battle in the holy cause of human rights, and that *facts*, FACTS, have set in motion all that machinery in England which has at last worked out a *peaceful* and glorious deliverance for 800,000 slaves in the B. W. Indies, and so filled England with horror and indignation at the SYSTEM, that she has actually sent agents into all cotton growing Countries to ascertain whether she cannot procure this article *free* from the stain of Slavery, that she may no longer strike hands with the slave-holders of America by purchasing their stolen goods. What we have written we have written from a deep and solemn sense of duty, and neither life nor *death* can shake the rock of principle upon which we stand. It cost us more *agony of soul* to write those testimonies than any thing we ever did; but the Lord required it and gave us strength to do it, leaving *all* the consequences in HIS holy hands.

Thou askest, my sister, why *we* do not examine whether we have not committed sins of as great magnitude, and mentionest two things of which I know *nothing at all*, and then goest on to say thou mightest *"enumerate* other circumstances." Now if thou knowest of any act of cruelty I ever perpetrated upon, or was the *means* of having perpetrated upon any of our slaves, at any time, I beg as a favor thou wilt tell me of it, for I assure thee I will PUBLISH it without the least hesitation, for I have NO wish to cover up my own sins, but will make use of it as an additional evidence of the horrible effects of the system. Please *"enumerate these other circumstances"* and help us dear Sister to do the work of repentance by bringing to our remembrance the sins of bygone years.

I am indeed sorry for thee if thou canst for one moment believe that in writing those testimonies we aimed any "envenomed shafts" at the Mother who bore us—No! No! We wrote them to show the awful havock which arbitrary power makes in human hearts, and to excite a holy indignation against an *institution* which degrades the *oppressor* as well as the oppressed. These shafts are now sharp in the hearts of the king's enemies. These shafts have not been aimed *in vain*, but are now doing the work on the SYSTEM of SLAVERY which they were designed to do. As to *personal* feeling we had NONE.

Thou sayest we had better write and say what is to be done with Stephen. Now the fact is, we have nothing to say about him. We never have regarded him as a piece of property which might be moved about at our pleasure. Whenever he wishes to come to the North our house shall be open to receive him; whilst he chooses to remain in Charleston with his wife, it is impossible for us to have the care of him. All we can do is to contribute to his support when he is sick or insane, and this may be for many years. The $15 which he paid to dear Mother had better be used, I should think, to defray his expenses as far as it will go.

I am very glad to hear Mother left me her watch, and hope Sisters will be careful to send it to me by some *safe* opportunity. I knew she intended doing so, for *she knew* I loved and honored her as a parent, tho' I felt bound in christian and filial faithfulness to pursue the course I have, and to rebuke, exhort and entreat her on account of her sins; and surely *she knew* and *all* her children *knew* that there was none who would do or suffer more for her than my precious Sister Sarah. We know not to what thou alludest about Lleuwellyn. Farewell, my dear Sister; for the Lord, in his mercy, has given me a heart to *love* and pity not "them that are in bonds" only, but their oppressors and *all* who sympathize with their oppressors more than with them. Farewell—in a Sister's *love*.

A. G. Weld

Elizabeth Cady Stanton

~

ELIZABETH CADY STANTON (1815–1902), founder of the organized women's movement in the United States, eloped with abolitionist Henry B. Stanton in 1840 just before he set sail to the World Anti-Slavery Convention in London, England. Attending that convention as Henry's guest, she was shocked when the duly elected women delegates were refused their seats on grounds of gender and angered when she and the female delegates were seated behind a curtain "to listen." Behind that curtain, the women envisioned a women's rights movement; eight years later, at the Seneca Falls Convention, that movement was officially born. In her autobiography, *Eighty Years & More*, Elizabeth Cady Stanton recalls the World Anti-Slavery Convention of 1840, the Seneca Falls Convention of 1848, and what she learned in between.

~

Our chief object in visiting England at this time was to attend the World's Anti-slavery Convention, to meet June 12, 1840, in Freemasons' Hall, London. Delegates from all the anti-slavery societies of civilized nations were invited, yet, when they arrived, those representing associations of women were rejected. Though women were members of the National Anti-slavery Society, accustomed to speak and vote in all its conventions, and to take an equally active part with men in the whole anti-slavery struggle, and were there as del-

---

Stanton, Elizabeth Cady. *Eighty Years and More: Reminiscences, 1815–1897*. 1898. Rpt., New York: Schocken Books, 1971, pp. 79–83, 144, 145–151.

egates from associations of men and women, as well as those dis-
tinctively of their own sex, yet all alike were rejected because they
were women. Women, according to English prejudices at that time,
were excluded by Scriptural texts from sharing equal dignity and
authority with men in all reform associations; hence it was to English minds pre-eminently unfitting that women should be admitted
as equal members to a World's Convention. The question was hotly
debated through an entire day. My husband made a very eloquent
speech in favor of admitting the women delegates.

When we consider that Lady Byron, Anna Jameson, Mary
Howitt, Mrs. Hugo Reid, Elizabeth Fry, Amelia Opie, Ann Green
Phillips, Lucretia Mott, and many remarkable women, speakers
and leaders in the Society of Friends, were all compelled to listen
in silence to the masculine platitudes on woman's sphere, one may
form some idea of the indignation of unprejudiced friends, and especially that of such women as Lydia Maria Child, Maria Chapman, Deborah Weston, Angelina and Sarah Grimké, and Abby
Kelly, who were impatiently waiting and watching on this side, in
painful suspense, to hear how their delegates were received. Judging from my own feelings, the women on both sides of the Atlantic
must have been humiliated and chagrined, except as these feelings
were outweighed by contempt for the shallow reasoning of their
opponents and their comical pose and gestures in some of the intensely earnest flights of their imagination.

The clerical portion of the convention was most violent in its
opposition. The clergymen seemed to have God and his angels especially in their care and keeping, and were in agony lest the
women should do or say something to shock the heavenly hosts.
Their all-sustaining conceit gave them abundant assurance that
their movements must necessarily be all-pleasing to the celestials
whose ears were open to the proceedings of the World's Convention. Deborah, Huldah, Vashti, and Esther might have questioned
the propriety of calling it a World's Convention, when only half of
humanity was represented there; but what were their opinions
worth compared with those of the Rev. A. Harvey, the Rev. C. Stout,

or the Rev. J. Burnet, who, Bible in hand, argued woman's subjection, divinely decreed when Eve was created.

One of our champions in the convention, George Bradburn, a tall thick-set man with a voice like thunder, standing head and shoulders above the clerical representatives, swept all their arguments aside by declaring with tremendous emphasis that, if they cold prove to him that the Bible taught the entire subjection of one-half of the race to the other, he should consider that the best thing he could do for humanity would be to bring together every Bible in the universe and make a grand bonfire of them.

It was really pitiful to hear narrow-minded bigots, pretending to be teachers and leaders of men, so cruelly remanding their own mothers, with the rest of woman-kind, to absolute subjection to the ordinary masculine type of humanity. I always regretted that the women themselves had not taken part in the debate before the convention was fully organized and the question of delegates settled. It seemed to me then, and does now, that all delegates with credentials from recognized societies should have had a voice in the organization of the convention, though subject to exclusion afterward. However, the women sat in a low curtained seat like a church choir, and modestly listened to the French, British, and American Solons for twelve for the longest days in June, as did, also, our grand [William Lloyd] Garrison and [Nathaniel P.] Rogers in the gallery. They scorned a convention that ignored the rights of the very women who had fought, side by side, with them in the anti-slavery conflict. "After battling so many long years," said Garrison, "for the liberties of African slaves, I can take no part in a convention that strikes down the most sacred rights of all women." After coming three thousand miles to speak on the subject nearest his heart, he nobly shared the enforced silence of the rejected delegates. It was a great act of self-sacrifice that should never be forgotten by women.

Thomas Clarkson was chosen president of the convention and made a few remarks in opening, but he soon retired, as his age and many infirmities made all public occasions too burdensome, and

Joseph Sturge, a Quaker, was made chairman. Sitting next to Mrs. Mott, I said:

"As there is a Quaker in the chair now, what could he do if the spirit should move you to speak?"

"Ah," she replied, evidently not believing such a contingency possible, "where the spirit of the Lord is, there is liberty."

She had not much faith in the sincerity of abolitionists who, while eloquently defending the natural rights of slaves, denied freedom of speech to one-half the people of their own race. Such was the consistency of an assemblage of philanthropists! They would have been horrified at the idea of burning the flesh of the distinguished women present with red-hot irons, but the crucifixion of their pride and self-respect, the humiliation of the spirit, seemed to them a most trifling matter. The action of this convention was the topic of discussion, in public and private, for a long time, and stung many women into new thought and action and gave rise to the movement for women's political equality both in England and the United States.

As the convention adjourned, the remark was heard on all sides, "It is about time some demand was made for new liberties for women." As Mrs. Mott and I walked home, arm in arm, commenting on the incidents of the day, we resolved to hold a convention as soon as we returned home, and form a society to advocate the rights of women. . . .

These were the first women I had ever met who believed in the equality of the sexes and who did not believe in the popular orthodox religion. The acquaintance of Lucretia Mott, who was a broad, liberal thinker on politics, religion, and all questions of reform, opened to me a new world of thought. As we walked about to see the sights of London, I embraced every opportunity to talk with her. It was intensely gratifying to hear all that, through years of doubt, I had dimly thought, so freely discussed by other women, some of them no older than myself—women, too, of rare intelligence, cultivation, and refinement. After six weeks' sojourn under the same roof with Lucretia Mott, whose conversation was uniformly on a high plane, I felt that I knew her too well to sympathize with the orthodox Friends, who denounced her as a dangerous woman because she doubted certain dogmas they fully believed. . . .

The First Woman's Rights Convention

In the spring of 1847 we moved to Seneca Falls. . . .

[M]y life was comparatively solitary, and the change from Boston was somewhat depressing. There, all my immediate friends were reformers, I had near neighbors, a new home with all the modern conveniences, and well-trained servants. Here our residence was on the outskirts of the town, roads very often muddy and no sidewalks most of the way, Mr. Stanton was frequently from home, I had poor servants, and an increasing number of children. To keep a house and grounds in good order, purchase every article for daily use, keep the wardrobes of half a dozen human beings in proper trim, take the children to dentists, shoemakers, and different schools, or find teachers at home, altogether made sufficient work to keep one brain busy, as well as all the hands I could impress into the service. Then, too, the novelty of housekeeping had passed away, and much that was once attractive in domestic life was now irksome. . . .

Up to this time life had glided by with comparative ease, but now the real struggle was upon me. My duties were too numerous and varied, and none sufficiently exhilarating or intellectual to bring into play my higher faculties. I suffered with mental hunger, which, like an empty stomach, is very depressing. I had books, but no stimulating companionship. To add to my general dissatisfaction at the change from Boston, I found that Seneca Falls was a malarial region, and in due time all the children were attacked with chills and fever which, under homeopathic treatment in those days, lasted three months. The servants were afflicted in the same way. Cleanliness, order, the love of the beautiful and artistic, all faded away in the struggle to accomplish what was absolutely necessary from hour to hour. Now I understood, as I never had before, how women could sit down and rest in the midst of general disorder. Housekeeping, under such conditions, was impossible, so I packed our clothes, locked up the house, and went to that harbor of safety, home, as I did ever after in stress of weather.

I now fully understood the practical difficulties most women had to contend with in the isolated household, and the impossibility of woman's best development if in contact, the chief part of her life, with servants and children. Fourier's phalansterie community life and co-operative households had a new significance for me. Emerson says, "A healthy discontent is the first step to progress." The general discontent I felt with woman's portion as wife, mother, housekeeper, physician, and spiritual guide, the chaotic conditions into which everything fell without her constant supervision, and the wearied, anxious look of the majority of women impressed me with a strong feeling that some active measures should be taken to remedy the wrongs of society in general, and of women in particular. My experience at the World's Anti-slavery Convention, all I had read of the legal status of women, and the oppression I saw everywhere, together swept across my soul, intensified now by many personal experiences. It seemed as if all the elements had conspired to impel me to some onward step. I could not see what to do or where to begin—my only thought was a public meeting for protest and discussion.

In this tempest-tossed condition of mind I received an invitation to spend the day with Lucretia Mott, at Richard Hunt's, in Waterloo. There I met several members of different families of Friends, earnest, thoughtful women. I poured out, that day, the torrent of my long-accumulating discontent, with such vehemence and indignation that I stirred myself, as well as the rest of the party, to do and dare anything. My discontent, according to Emerson, must have been healthy, for it moved us all to prompt action, and we decided, then and there, to call a "Woman's Rights Convention." We wrote the call that evening and published it in the *Seneca County Courier* the next day, the 14th of July, 1848, giving only five days' notice, as the convention was to be held on the 19th and 20th. The call was inserted without signatures,—in fact it was a mere announcement of a meeting,—but the chief movers and managers were Lucretia Mott, Mary Ann McClintock, Jane Hunt, Martha C. Wright, and myself. The convention, which was held two days in the Methodist Church, was in every way a grand success. The house was crowded at every session, the speaking good, and a religious earnestness dignified all the proceedings.

These were the hasty initiative steps of "the most momentous reform that had yet been launched on the world—the first organized protest against the injustice which had brooded for ages over the character and destiny of one-half the race." No words could express our astonishment on finding, a few days afterward, that what seemed to us so timely, so rational, and so sacred, should be a subject for sarcasm and ridicule to the entire press of the nation. With our Declaration of Rights and Resolutions for a text, it seemed as if every man who could wield a pen prepared a homily on "woman's sphere." All the journals from Maine to Texas seemed to strive with each other to see which could make our movement appear the most ridiculous. The anti-slavery papers stood by us manfully and so did Frederick Douglass, both in the convention and in his paper, *The North Star*, but so pronounced was the popular voice against us, in the parlor, press, and pulpit, that most of the ladies who had attended the convention and signed the declaration, one by one, withdrew their names and influence and joined our persecutors. Our friends gave us the cold shoulder and felt themselves disgraced by the whole proceeding.

If I had had the slightest premonition of all that was to follow that convention, I fear I should not have had the courage to risk it, and I must confess that it was with fear and trembling that I consented to attend another, one month afterward, in Rochester. Fortunately, the first one seemed to have drawn all the fire, and of the second but little was said. But we had set the ball in motion, and now, in quick succession, conventions were held in Ohio, Indiana, Massachusetts, Pennsylvania, and in the City of New York, and have been kept up nearly every year since. . . .

The same year of the convention, the Married Woman's Property Bill, which had given rise to some discussion on woman's rights in New York, had passed the legislature. This encouraged action on the part of women, as the reflection naturally arose that, if the men who make the laws were ready for some onward step, surely the women themselves should express some interest in the legislation. Ernestine L. Rose, Paulina Wright (Davis), and I had spoken before committees of the legislature years before, demanding equal property rights for women. We had circulated petitions for the Married Woman's Property Bill for many years, and so also had the leaders of the Dutch aristocracy, who desired to see their life-long accumulations descend to their daughters and grandchildren rather than pass into the hands of dissipated, thriftless sons-in-law. Judge Hertell, Judge Fine, and Mr. Geddes of Syracuse prepared and championed the several bills, at different times, before the legislature. Hence the demands made in the convention were not entirely new to the reading and thinking public of New York—the first State to take any action on the question. As New York was the first State to put the word "male" in her constitution in 1778, it was fitting that she should be first in more liberal legislation. The effect of the convention on my own mind was most salutary. The discussions had cleared my ideas as to the primal steps to be taken for woman's enfranchisement, and the opportunity of expressing myself fully and freely on a subject I felt so deeply about was a great relief. I think all women who attended the convention felt better for the statement of their wrongs, believing that the first step had been taken to right them.

Elizabeth Blackwell

~

ELIZABETH BLACKWELL (1821–1910), America's first female physician, did not have an easy time gaining admission to medical school. She was denied admission to Bowdoin, Yale, Harvard, and every medical school in the cities of New York and Philadelphia, before she finally began her studies at Geneva College in 1847. She recounts these experiences in her autobiography, *Pioneer Work in Opening the Medical Profession to Women*.

~

In the summer of 1847, with my carefully hoarded earnings, I resolved to seek an entrance into a medical school. Philadelphia was then considered the chief seat of medical learning in America, so to Philadelphia I went; taking passage in a sailing vessel from Charleston for the sake of economy.

In Philadelphia I boarded in the family of Dr. William Elder. He and his admirable wife soon became warm and steadfast friends. Dr. Elder (author of the life of Dr. Kane, the Arctic voyager) was a remarkable man, of brilliant talent and genial nature. He took a generous interest in my plans, helping by his advice and encouragement through the months of effort and refusals which were now encountered.

Applications were cautiously but persistently made to the four medical colleges of Philadelphia for admission as a regular student. The interviews with their various professors were by turns hopeful

---

Blackwell, Elizabeth. *Pioneer Work in Opening the Medical Profession to Women*. Hastings, U.K.: K. Barry, 1895, pp. 58–69.

and disappointing. Whilst pursuing these inquiries I commenced my anatomical studies in the private school of Dr. Allen. This gentleman by his thoughtful arrangements enabled me to overcome the natural repulsion to these studies generally felt at the outset. With a tact and delicacy for which I have always felt grateful, he gave me as my first lesson in practical anatomy a demonstration of the human wrist. The beauty of the tendons and exquisite arrangements of this part of the body struck my artistic sense, and appealed to the sentiment of reverence with which this anatomical branch of study was ever afterwards invested in my mind.

During the following months, whilst making applications to the different medical colleges of Philadelphia for admission as a regular student, I enlisted the services of my friends in the search for an Alma Mater. The interviews with the various professors, though disappointing, were often amusing.

Extracts from the Journal of 1847

May 27.—Called on Dr. Jackson (one of the oldest professors in Philadelphia), a small, bright-faced, grey-haired man, who looked up from his newspaper and saluted me with, 'Well, what is it? What do you want?' I told him I wanted to study medicine. He began to laugh, and asked me why. Then I detailed my plans. He became interested; said he would not give me an answer then; that there were great difficulties, but he did not know that they were insurmountable; he would let me know on Monday. I came home with a lighter heart, though I can hardly say I hope. On Monday Dr. Jackson said he had done his best for me, but the professors were all opposed to my entrance. Dr. Horner advised me to try the Filbert Street and Franklin schools. A professor of Jefferson College thought it would be impossible to study there, and advised the New England schools.

June 2.—Felt gloomy as thunder, trudging round to Dr. Darrach. He is the most non-committal man I ever saw. I harangued him, and he sat full five minutes without a word. I asked at last if he could give me any encouragement. 'The subject is a novel one, madam, I have nothing to say either for or against it; you have awakened trains of thought upon which my mind is taking action, but I cannot express my opinion to you either one way or another.' 'Your opinion, I fear, is unfavourable.' 'I did not say so. I beg you, madam, distinctly to understand that I express no opinion one way or another; the way in which my mind acts in this matter I do not feel at liberty to unfold.' 'Shall I call on the other professors of your college?' 'I cannot take the responsibility of advising you to pursue such a course.' 'Can you not grant me admittance to your lectures, as you do not feel unfavourable to my scheme?' 'I have said no such thing; whether favourable or unfavourable, I have not expressed any opinion; and I beg leave to state clearly that the operation of my mind in regard to this matter I do not feel at liberty to unfold.' I got up in despair, leaving his mind to take action on the subject at his leisure.

Dr. Warrington told me that he had seen his friend Dr. Ashmead, who had told him that Paris was such a horrible place that I must give up my wish for a medical education—indeed, his communication would be so unfavourable that he would rather not meet me in person. I told the Doctor that if the path of duty led me to hell I would go there; and I did not think that by being with devils I should become a devil myself—at which the good Doctor stared.

Nevertheless, I shrink extremely from the idea of giving up the attempt in America and going to France, although the suggestion is often urged on me.

The fear of successful rivalry which at that time often existed in the medical mind was expressed by the dean of one of the smaller schools, who frankly replied to the application, 'You cannot expect us to furnish you with a stick to break our heads with;' so revolutionary seemed the attempt of a woman to leave a subordinate position and seek to obtain a complete medical education. A similarly mistaken notion of the rapid practical success which would attend a lady doctor was shown later by one of the professors of my medical college, who was desirous of entering into partnership with me on condition of sharing profits over 5,000 dollars on my first year's practice.

During these fruitless efforts my kindly Quaker adviser, whose private lectures I attended, said to me: 'Elizabeth, it is of no use trying. Thee cannot gain admission to these schools. Thee must go to Paris and don masculine attire to gain the necessary knowledge,' Curiously enough, this suggestion of disguise made by good Dr. Warrington was also given me by Doctor Pankhurst, the Professor of Surgery in the largest college in Philadelphia. He thoroughly approved of a woman's gaining complete medical knowledge; told me that although my public entrance into the classes was out of the question, yet if I would assume masculine attire and enter the college he could entirely rely on two or three of his students to whom he should communicate my disguise, who would watch the class and give me timely notice to withdraw should my disguise be suspected.

But neither the advice to go to Paris nor the suggestion of disguise tempted me for a moment. It was to my mind a moral crusade on which I had entered, a course of justice and common sense, and it must be pursued in the light of day, and with public sanction, in order to accomplish its end.

The following letter to Mrs. Willard of Troy, the well-known educationalist, describes the difficulties through which the young student had to walk warily:—

Philadelphia: May 24

I cannot refrain from expressing my obligations to you for directing me to the excellent Dr. Warrington. He has allowed me to visit his patients, attend his lectures, and make use of his library, and has spoken to more than one medical friend concerning my wishes; but with deep regret I am obliged to say that all the information hitherto obtained serves to show me the impossibility of accomplishing my purpose in America. I find myself rigidly excluded from the regular college routine, and there is no thorough course of lectures that can supply its place. The general sentiment of the physicians is strongly opposed to a woman's intruding herself into the profession; consequently it would be perhaps impossible to obtain private instruction, but if that were possible, the enormous expense would render it impracticable, and where the feelings of the profession are strongly enlisted against such a scheme, the museums, libraries, hospitals, and all similar aids would be closed against me. In view of these and numerous other difficulties Dr. Warrington is discouraged, and joins with his medical brethren in advising me to give up the scheme. But a strong idea, long cherished till it has taken deep root in the soul and become an all-absorbing duty, cannot thus be laid aside. I must accomplish my end. I consider it the noblest and most useful path that I can tread, and if one country rejects me I will go to another.

Through Dr. Warrington and other sources I am informed that my plan can be carried out in Paris, though the free Government lectures, delivered by the faculty, are confined to men, and a diploma is strictly denied to a woman, even when (as in one instance, as it is said) she has gone through the course in male attire; yet every year thorough courses of lectures are delivered by able physicians on every branch of medical knowledge, to which I should be admitted without hesitation and treated with becoming respect. The true place for study, then, seems open to me; but here, again, some friendly physicians raise stronger objections than ever. 'You, a young unmarried lady,' they say, 'go to Paris, that city of fearful immorality, where every feeling will be outraged and insult attend you at every step; where vice is the natural atmosphere, and no young man can breathe it without being contaminated! Impossible, you are lost if you go!'

Now, dear madam, I appeal to you, who have had the opportunity of studying the French in their native land, is not this a false view, a greatly exaggerated fear? Is it not perfectly true everywhere that a woman who respects herself will be respected by others; that where the life is directed by a strong, pure motive to a noble object, in a quiet, dignified, but determined manner, the better feelings of mankind are enlisted, and the woman excites esteem and respectful sympathy? To my mind this is perfectly clear, and I trust that your more experienced judgment will confirm my opinion. Probably, then, if all the information which I am still collecting agree with what I have already received, I may sail for France in the course of the summer, that I may familarise myself with a rapid French delivery before the commencement of the winter lectures.

I have tried to look every difficulty steadily in the face. I find none which seem to me unconquerable, and with the blessing of Providence I trust to accomplish my design.

After a short, refreshing trip with my family to the seaside, the search was again renewed in Philadelphia. But applications made for admission to the medical schools both of Philadelphia and of New York were met with similarly unsuccessful results.

I therefore obtained a complete list of all the smaller schools of the Northern States, 'country schools,' as they were called. I examine their prospectuses, and quite at a venture sent in applications for admission to twelve of the most promising institutions, where full courses of instruction were given under able professors. The result was awaited with much anxiety, as the time for the commencement of the winter sessions was rapidly approaching. No answer came for some time. At last, to my immense relief (though not surprise, for failure never seemed possible), I received the following letter from the medical department of a small university town in the western part of the State of New York:—

Geneva: October 20, 1847

To Elizabeth Blackwell, Philadelphia.

I am instructed by the faculty of the medical department of Geneva University of acknowledge receipt of yours of 3rd inst. A quorum of the faculty assembled last evening for the first time during the session, and it was thought important to submit your proposal to the class (of students), who have had a meeting this day, and acted entirely on their own behalf, without any interference on the part of the faculty. I send you the result of their deliberations and need only add that there are no fears but that you can by judicious management, not only 'disarm criticism,' but elevate yourself without detracting in the least from the dignity of the profession.

Wishing you success in your undertaking, which some may deem bold in the present state of society, I subscribe myself,

Yours respectfully,
Charles A. Lee,
Dean of the Faculty.
15 Geneva Hotel.

This letter enclosed the following unique and manly letter, which I had afterwards copied on parchment, and esteem one of my most valued possessions:—

At a meeting of the entire medical class of Geneva Medical College, held this day, October 20, 1847, the following resolutions were unanimously adopted:—

1. *Resolved*—That one of the radical principles of a Republican Government is the universal education of both sexes; that to every branch of scientific education the door should be open equally to all; that the application of Elizabeth Blackwell to become a member of our class meets our entire approbation; and in extending our unanimous invitation we pledge ourselves that no conduct of ours shall cause her to regret her attendance at this institution.
2. *Resolved*—That a copy of these proceedings be signed by the chairman and transmitted to Elizabeth Blackwell.

T. J. Stratton, *Chairman*.

With an immense sigh of relief and aspiration of profound gratitude to Providence I instantly accepted the invitation, and prepared for the journey to Western New York State.

Leaving Philadelphia on November 4, I hastened through New York, travelled all night, and reached the little town of Geneva at 11 P.M. on November 6.

The next day, after a refreshing sleep, I sallied forth for an interview with the dean of the college, enjoying the view of the beautiful lake on which Geneva is situated, notwithstanding the cold, drizzling, windy day. After an interview with the authorities of the college I was duly inscribed on the list as student No. 130, in the medical department of the Geneva University.

I at once established myself in a comfortable boarding-house, in the same street as my college, and three minutes' walk from it— a beautiful walk along the high bank overlooking the lake. I hung my room with dear mementoes of absent friends, and soon with hope and zeal and thankful feelings of rest I settled down to study.

Naturally, some little time was required to adjust the relations of the new student to her unusual surroundings. My first experiences are thus given in a letter to a sister:—

Geneva: November 9, 1847

I've just finished copying the notes of my last lecture. Business is over for to-day; I throw a fresh stick into my 'air-tight,' and now for refreshment by a talk with my own dear sister. Your letter containing E.'s was the first to welcome me in my new residence; right welcome, I assure you, it was, for I was gloomy—very. It was on Monday evening your letter came—my first work-day in Geneva. It had rained incessantly; I was in an upper room of a large boarding-house without a soul to speak to. I had attended five lectures, but nevertheless I did not know whether I could do what I ought to, for the Professor of Anatomy was absent, and had been spoken of as a queer man. The demonstrator hesitated as to my dissecting; I had no books, and didn't know where to get any; and my head was bewildered with running about the great college building—never going out of the same door I went in at.

This evening, however, I have finished my second day's lectures; the weather is still gloomy, but I feel sunshiny and happy, strongly encouraged, with a grand future before me, and all owing to a fat little fairy in the shape of the Professor of Anatomy! This morning, on repairing to the college, I was introduced to Dr. Webster, the Professor of Anatomy, a little plump man, blunt in manner and very voluble. He shook me warmly by the hand, said my plan was capital; he had some fun too about a lady pupil, for he never lost a joke; the class had acted manfully; their resolutions were as good as a political meeting, &c.

He asked me what branches I had studied. I told him all but surgery. 'Well,' said Dr. Lee, 'do you mean to practise surgery?' 'Why, of course she does,' broke in Dr. Webster. 'Think of the cases of femoral hernia; only think what a well-educated woman would do in a city like New York. Why, my dear sir, she'd have her hands full in no time; her success would be immense. Yes, yes, you'll go through the course, and get your diploma with great *éclat* too; we'll give you the opportunities. You'll make a stir, I can tell you.'

I handed him a note of introduction from Dr. Warrington, and then he told me to wait in the ante-room while he read it to the medical class, who were assembled in the amphitheatre for his lecture, which was to be preparatory to one of the most delicate operations in surgery, and I suppose he wanted to remind them of their promise of good behaviour. I could hear him reading it. When his age and experience were spoken of there was a shout of laughter, for he can't be more than forty-five and not much of dignity about him; but at the conclusion there was a round of applause, after which I quietly entered, and certainly have no reason to complain of medical students, for though they eye me curiously, it is also in a very friendly manner. After the lecture was over, the demonstrator, who now shows the utmost friendliness, explained to me at the Doctor's request a very important subject which I had lost. It was admirably done, illustrated on the subject, and if to-day's lessons were a fair specimen, I certainly shall have no cause to complain of my anatomical instructors. The plan pursued here is admirable, and New York and Philadelphia may learn more than one lesson from Geneva. Dr. Webster came to me laughing after the first lecture, saying: 'You attract too much attention, Miss Blackwell; there was a very large number of strangers present this afternoon—I shall guard against this in future.' 'Yes,' said Dr. Lee; 'we were saying to-day that this step might prove quite a good advertisement for the college; if there were no other advantage to be gained, it will attract so much notice. I shall bring the matter into the medical journals; why, I'll venture to say in ten years' time one-third the classes in our colleges will consist of women. After the precedent you will have established, people's eyes will be opened.'

Now, all this kind feeling encourages me greatly, and I need it; for though my purpose has never wavered, a flat, heavy feeling was growing upon me from constant disappointment. I was fast losing that spring of hope that is so pleasant; consequently praise cannot make me vain, and the notice I attract is a matter of perfect indifference. I sit quietly in this large assemblage of young men, and they might be women or mummies for aught I care. I sometimes think I'm too much disciplined, but it is certainly necessary for the position I occupy. I believe the professors don't exactly know in what species of the human family to place me, and the students are a little bewildered. The other people at first regarded me with suspicion, but I am so quiet and gentle that suspicion turns to astonishment, and even the little boys in the street stand still and stare as I pass. 'Tis droll; sometimes I laugh, sometimes I feel a little sad, but in Geneva the nine days' wonder soon will cease, and I cannot but congratulate myself on having found at last the right place for my beginning.

Lucretia Mott

~

LUCRETIA MOTT (1793–1880), a Quaker minister who was central to both the abolitionist and women's rights movements, was a founder of the Philadelphia Female Anti-Slavery Society and an organizer of the Seneca Falls Convention. In these 1856 remarks to the Seventh National Woman's Rights Convention, she implores religious women to use their own judgment when evaluating the Bible's teachings.

~

At this late hour it will not be proper for me to add many words, even were it necessary. You have heard all, it seems to me, that can be said upon the subject, and if I would add anything it would be rather to offer an encouraging view as to what has already been effected, and to inspire the hope that the time is not far distant when those wrongs and evils, under which woman is suffering—so clearly depicted at this and at former Conventions—will be so obvious to the thinking men of the American People, that they will be ready to redress them. And although woman may not yet be so awakened to the consideration of the subjects as to be sensible of the blessing of entire freedom, she will, I doubt not, as she comes to reflect on the subject more and more, see herself in her true light. It only needs that we should look back a few years to see the progress that has been made. Even in England, in 1840, when a few women went over as delegates to the World's Anti-Slavery

Mott, Lucretia. *Lucretia Mott: Her Complete Speeches and Sermons*. Dana Green, ed. New York: The Edwin Mellen Press, 1980, pp. 227–232.

Convention, although the call had been made so universal, yet they were afraid to welcome women to a seat in that Convention, lest they should be ridiculed in the morning papers. Daniel O'Connell, Dr. Bowring, William Howitt, and some able and strong men of that time, it is true, came forth and approved the claim of women to a seat; and O'Connell showed that, even then, women exercised the right to vote as holders of bank-stock, and as members of the East India Company, and some other institutions of that country. Their youthful queen, too, had just then ascended the throne, thus showing how very inconsistent it was to make objections to the claim of equal rights for women. Dr. Bowring at that time, or soon after, wrote a letter to the friends in this country, saying that he had feared that the women question was launched among them without sufficient preparation; but the coming of these women would form an era in the history of philanthropic bravery; that they had left a deep if not a wide impression; that they had created apostles, if as yet they had not many followers. Well, the result, as shown from the facts presented to you this evening, the petitions to Parliament, for the redress of the wrongs of women, the willingness to receive, to so great an extent, such a memorial, all go to show a change that has taken place in the minds of many there. Some of you must know that among the English authors, when Maria Edgeworth wrote, within the day and generation of some of the older ones of us, she was not willing to let her own name appear as an author, but her first works, and those of her sister, were put forth in the name of her father, because it was not considered decorous then for a woman to appear as an author. It was supposed to be without the sphere of woman. And you know how since that time woman has advanced in the literary field. You know that when the work entitled "Jane Eyre" appeared, with a fictitious name, it was said to be a work of too great power for any woman—that it must have been written by a man. It proved, however, to have been written by a woman.

So we have seen already, in the few years' efforts that have been made in this Woman's Rights Reform how colleges for women, schools of design, and other institutions, heretofore unknown, have sprung up, opening to woman new fields, and extending and elevating her sphere.

I was glad this morning when that young man came forth with his objections against our claim, based upon the Bible; and although it would not be proper to go into a theological discussion of the question, it is of the greatest importance that religiously-minded women, those who have been accustomed to regard this volume as their rule of faith and practice, should be led to examine these Scriptures, and see whether these things are as our opponents claim. And if they will read that book intelligently, not with the eye of the theologian, nor with a blind faith in what their ministers have taught them, but with a reliance upon their own judgment, they will discover that the Scriptures cannot be wielded against us. They will find that from the earliest days of which the Scriptures gave account, honorable women have risen, notwithstanding the obstacles of the times in which they lived, to a high degree of eminence. They were the Deborahs, the Huldahs, the Annas, and others, in olden times, who filled conspicuous places, and to whom the honorable men of the age resorted for counsel in times of exigency. Deborah assured one of the captains of the host that he was not to succeed, for the honor of the battle was to be given to a woman. She was a prophetess; and if you will read you will find that prophetesses were recognized as well as prophets from the earliest days. And in later time, Anna and the woman of Samaria, and others were employed to speak to the men of the city, to all those who looked for redemption in Jerusalem. And women were recognized in the very first noble act that was brought to view after the disciples came together, which was a realization of the old prophecy, that the time should come when women as well as men should prophesy. And even Paul, though he is quoted so much as an authority for bringing women under subjection, even he gave special directions to woman how she should attire herself when she did publically pray or prophesy; and in the seeming prohibition of woman's speaking in church, there is no mention of preaching, of praying, or of prophesying. There is something said, to be sure, about the subjection to the husband, but it was also said that it was spoken in a mystery in reference to the Church, evidently not intending thereby to apply it literally. In the metaphors of that age you know there is great liberty taken on other subjects; why not on that? Even though Paul should approve of many things, being himself under the influence of the Jewish customs of that age, with regard to woman, I would ask of those who most religiously bind themselves to the authority of Scripture, whether they find any Scripture text from the beginning to the end of the Bible that makes it incumbent upon them to receive any recommendation given by Paul to the women of the Church of this day, unless it be in the great principles of virtue, of justice and of love, which are unvarying in all ages of the world? No; when theologians quote Paul as against us, they should be careful lest they prove too much; for, if the recommendations of Paul were to be applied now, no woman would be allowed to enter into a second marriage after having lost her first husband. Paul says he thinks they should not marry again, and at the same time says, he thinks he has the Spirit of the Lord. But this prohibition of Paul is not applied now, and hence theologians do not bring it up against us, as they do some other prohibitions in regard to women.

And I would ask that young theologian, who quoted the Bible against us, what he thinks of the direction concerning holding his peace when he is in his pulpit, when anything is revealed to him that sitteth by, allowing that person to utter his thoughts, so that all may speak, and all be edified? With the exception of the Quakers, and perhaps the Methodists, there is always one singled out as the "oracle of God" to the congregation; and this recommendation of Paul is entirely ignored. So also with the direction to wash one another's feet, and many other things.

It would be well for people to remember that this readiness to bring up the Bible against this reform has been equally manifested in regard to every other reform. I would not undervalue the efficacy of these Scriptures to any that may profit thereby, but I would ask that all should read them so intelligently as to discriminate between that which belonged to the age exclusively in which it was written, and that which is applicable to the time in which we live. Very great changes occur in history, very great advances are made, and we must make this discrimination in everything.

The young man who spoke here this morning asked whether it was not a new idea this claim of equality for women, this claim in her behalf of the inalienable right to life, liberty and the pursuit of happiness. Strange as it may appear, the great statesman and politicians of the age do not seem to be aware of the application of the principles they are constantly upholding. The very men who signed the Declaration of Independence, many of them educated under English aristocratic institutions, did not seem to know how far those principles would carry them. Some of them at that time were very much opposed to educating the working-classes, for fear it would raise them above their proper level. And more recently, many who professed so great a reverence for these republican principles, were strongly opposed to a universal popular education, in place of the charity schools that disgraced the age.

There has been a great advance as regards the education of women. Many of our grandmothers did not know how to write their own names, it being then regarded as unnecessary for woman to learn to write. Now she has so far come up to the level of the intelligence of society as to rise above the mere drudgery of life, and demand something more.

Catharine Beecher in her first public work expressed the belief that time was coming when woman would not be satisfied with her present low aims; and when she returned from the precincts of education she would no longer be satisfied with seeking a little reading, and working devices on muslin and lace, but, her powers being called out, she would be seeking immortal minds, wherever she could fasten impressions that should never be effaced. She did not anticipate the fastening of impressions on immortal minds in public conventions. No; she revolted at such an idea, because she had been educated by her father to believe that the pulpit and the public platform was no place for woman. But a few months ago I received a note from her, inviting me to attend at a large public school, where she was going to deliver an address to men and women; showing that her own mind has undergone a change upon the subject, in the general advancement of public opinion.

The religious veneration of woman has been so misdirected by her religious training, that she needs to be taught to judge for herself. She will find, when she does so, that the Scriptures have been perverted, and that the customs of society are not always founded in truth and justice. Nor will her veneration for the good, the true, and the divine, be lessened when she learns to respect the divinity of her own nature; nor will she be ashamed of this new Gospel of truth, or afraid to declare it before the people. She will behold a vision of a new heaven and a new earth, wherein dwelleth righteousness; and entering in, she will find all that will supply the wants of her spiritual nature. She will find the inspiration that was in Paul, and in all the servants of the Most High, in olden times, is not withheld now, even from woman, but that she will be prepared to go forth upon the mission whereunto she may be called.

Believe me, my sisters, the time is come for you to avail yourselves of all the avenues that are opened to you. I would that woman would wake up to a sense of the long-continued degradation and wrong that has been heaped upon her! Like the poor slave at the South, too many of our sex are insensible of their wrongs, and incapable of fully appreciating the blessings of freedom. I therefore submit, in reference to this subject, the following resolution:

> Resolved, That as the poor slave's alleged contentment with his servile and cruel bondage, only proves the depth of his degradation; so the assertion of woman that she has all the rights she wants, only proves how far the restrictions and disabilities to which she has been subjected have rendered her insensible to the blessings of true liberty.

Elizabeth Packard

~

ELIZABETH PACKARD (1816–1897) espoused religious beliefs that differed from those of her Calvinist clergyman husband. These beliefs caused strife between the couple and, it seems, the dismissal of Reverend Packard by three successive church congregations. In 1860, Reverend Packard—under an Illinois law that permitted husbands to institutionalize wives "without the evidence of insanity required in other cases"—committed Elizabeth to the Illinois State Hospital for the Insane. When she returned home three years later, he locked her away in her children's former nursery and went so far as to nail the windows shut from the outside. It was this change of locale that entitled Elizabeth to a trial, since the law made no mention of a wife being "put away" in her own home. Elizabeth Packard was declared sane and restored to liberty in 1864. Thereafter, she campaigned for the reform of laws governing the mentally ill and won legislative changes in four states. She recounts her experiences in this excerpt from *Marital Power Exemplified: Mrs. Packard's Trial*.

~

A brief narrative of the events which occasioned [my] Trial . . . [is] here presented for the kind reader's candid consideration. It was in a Bible-class in Manteno, Kankakee County, Illinois, that I

Packard, Mrs. E. P. W. *Marital Power Exemplified in Mrs. Packard's Trial and Self-Defense from the Charge of Insanity; Three Years' Imprisonment for Religious Belief, by the Arbitrary Will of a Husband with an Appeal to the Government to so Change the Laws as to Protect the Rights of Married Women.* Hartford: Published by the Authoress, 1866, pp. 3–11.

defended some religious opinions which conflicted with the Creed of the Presbyterian Church in that place, which brought upon me the charge of insanity. It was at the invitation of Deacon Dole, the teacher of that Bible-class, that I consented to become his pupil, and it was at his special request that I brought forward my views to the consideration of the class. The class numbered six when I entered it, and forty-six when I left it. I was about four months a member of it. I had not the least suspicion of danger or harm arising in any way, either to myself or others, from thus complying with his wishes, and thus uttering some of my honestly cherished opinions. I regarded the principle of religious tolerance as the vital principle on which our government was based, and I in my ignorance supposed this right was protected to all American citizens, even to the wives of clergymen. But, alas! my own sad experience has taught me the danger of believing a lie on so vital a question. The result was, I was legally kidnapped and imprisoned three years simply for uttering these opinions under these circumstances.

I was kidnapped in the following manner.—Early on the morning of the 18th of June, 1860, as I arose from my bed, preparing to take my morning bath, I saw my husband approaching my door with our two physicians, both members of his church and of our Bible-class,—and a stranger gentleman, sheriff Burgess. Fearing exposure I hastily locked my door, and proceeded with the greatest dispatch to dress myself. But before I had hardly commenced, my husband forced an entrance into my room through the window with an axe! And I, for shelter and protection against an exposure in a state of almost entire nudity, sprang into bed, just in time to receive my unexpected guests. The trio approached my bed, and each doctor felt my pulse, and without asking a single question both pronounced me insane. So it seems that in the estimation of these two M. D's, Dr. Merrick and Newkirk, insanity is indicated by the action of the pulse instead of the mind! Of course, my pulse was bounding at the time from excessive fright; and I ask, what lady of refinement and fine and tender sensibilities would not have a quickened pulse by such an untimely, unexpected, unmanly, and even outrageous entrance into her private sleeping room? I say it would be impossible for any woman, unless she was either insane or insensible to her surroundings, not to be agitated under such circumstances. This was the only medical examination I had. This was the only trial of *any kind* that I was allowed to have, to prove the charge of insanity brought against me by my husband. I had no chance of *self defence* whatever. My husband then informed me that the "forms of law" were all complied with, and he therefore requested me to dress myself for a ride to Jacksonville, to enter the Insane Asylum as an inmate. I objected, and protested against being imprisoned *without any trial*. But to no purpose. My husband insisted upon it that I had no protection in the law, but himself, and that he was doing by me just as the laws of the State allowed him to do. I could not then credit this statement, but now *know* it to be too sadly true; for the Statue of Illinois expressly states that a man may put his wife into an Insane Asylum without evidence of insanity. This law now stands on the 26th page, section 10, of the Illinois statute book, under the general head of "charities"! The law was passed February 15, 1851.

I told my husband I should not go voluntarily into the Asylum, and leave my six children and my precious babe of eighteen months, without some kind of trial; and that the law of force, brute force, would be the only power that should thus put me there. I then begged of him to handle me gently, if he was determined to force me, as I was easily hurt, and should make no physical resistance. I was soon in the hands of the sheriff; who forced me from my home by ordering two men to carry me to the wagon which took me to the depot. Esquire Labrie, our nearest neighbor, who witnessed this scene, said he was willing to testify before any court under oath, that "Mrs. Packard was literally kidnapped." I was carried to the cars from the depot in the arms of two strong men, whom my husband appointed for this purpose, amid the silent and almost speechless gaze of a large crowd of citizens who had collected for the purpose of rescuing me from the hands of my persecutors. But they were prevented from executing their purpose by the lie Deacon Dole was requested by my husband to tell the "excited crowd," viz: that "The Sheriff has legal papers to defend this proceeding," and they well knew that for them to resist the Sheriff, the laws would expose themselves to imprisonment. The Sheriff confessed afterwards to persons who are now willing to testify under oath, that he told them that he did not have a sign of a legal paper with him, simply because the probate court refused to give him any, because, as they affirmed, he had not given them one evidence of insanity in the case. Sheriff Burgess died while I was incarcerated.

When once in the Asylum I was beyond the reach of all human aid, except what could come through my husband, since the law allows no one to take them out, except the one who put them in, or by his consent; and my husband determined never to take me out, until I recanted my new opinions, claiming that I was incurably insane so long as I could not return to my old standpoint of religious belief. Of course, I could not believe at my option, but only as light and evidence was presented to my own mind, and I was too conscientious to act the hypocrite, by professing to believe what I could not believe. I was therefore pronounced "hopelessly insane," and in about six weeks from the date of my imprisonment, my husband made his arrangements to have me, henceforth, legally regarded as hopelessly insane. In this defenceless, deplorable condition I lay closely imprisoned three years, being never allowed to step my foot on the ground after the first four months. At the expiration of three years, my oldest son, Theophilus, became of age, when he immediately availed himself of his manhood, by a legal compromise with his father and the trustees, wherein he volunteered to hold himself wholly responsible for my support for life, if his father would only consent to take me out of my prison. This proposition was accepted by Mr. Packard, with this proviso: that if ever I returned to my own home and children he should put me in again for life. The Trustees had previously notified Mr.

Packard that I must be removed, as they should keep me no longer. Had not this been the case, my son's proposition would doubtless have been rejected by him.

The reasons why the Trustees took this position was, because they became satisfied that I was not a fit subject for that institution, in the following manner: On one of their official visits to the institution, I coaxed Dr. McFarland, superintendent of the Asylum, to let me go before them and "fire a few guns at Calvinism," as I expressed myself, that they might know and judge for themselves whether I deserved a life-long imprisonment for indulging such opinions. Dr. McFarland replied to my request, that the Trustees were Calvinists, and the chairman a member of the Presbyterian Synod of the United States.

"Never mind," said I, "I don't care if they are, I am not afraid to defend my opinions even before the Synod itself. I don't want to be locked up here all my lifetime without doing something. But if they are Calvinists," I added, "you may be sure they will call me insane, and then you will have them to back you up in your opinion and position respecting me." This argument secured his consent to let me go before them. He also let me have two sheets of paper to write my opinions upon. With my document prepared, "or gun loaded," as I called it, and examined by the Doctor to see that all was right, that is, that it contained no exposures of himself, I entered the Trustees' room, arm in arm with the Doctor, dressed in as attractive and tasteful a style as my own wardrobe and that of my attendant's would permit. Mr. Packard was present, and he said to my friends afterwards that he never saw his wife look so "sweet and attractive" as I then did. After being politely and formally introduced to the Trustees, individually, I was seated by the chairman, to receive his permission to speak, in the following words: "Mrs. Packard, we have heard Mr. Packard's statement, and the Doctor said you would like to speak for yourself. We will allow you ten minutes for that purpose."

I then took out my gold watch, (which was my constant companion in my prison,) and looking at it, said to the Doctor, "please tell me if I overgo my limits, will you?" And then commenced reading my document in a quiet, calm, clear, tone of voice. It commenced with these words: "Gentlemen, I am accused of teaching my children doctrines ruinous in their tendency, and such as alienate them from their father. I reply, that my teachings and practice both, are ruinous to Satan's cause, and do alienate my children from Satanic influences, I teach Christianity, my husband teaches Calvinism. They are antagonistic systems and uphold antagonistic authorities. Christianity upholds God's authority; Calvinism the devil's authority," &c., &c.

Thus I went on, most dauntlessly and fearlessly contrasting the two systems, as I viewed them, until my entire document was read, without being interrupted, although my time had more than expired. Confident I had secured their interest as well as attention, I ventured to ask if I might be allowed to read another document I held in my hand, which the Doctor had not seen. The request was voted upon and met not only with an unanimous response in the affirmative, but several cried out: "Let her go on! Let us hear the whole!" This document bore heavily upon Mr. Packard and the Doctor both. Still I was tolerated. The room was so still I could have heard a clock tick. When I had finished, instead of then dismissing me, they commenced questioning me, and I only rejoiced to answer their questions, being carful however not to let slip any chance I found to expose the darkest parts of this foul conspiracy, wherein Mr. Packard and their Superintendent were the chief actors. Packard and McFarland both sat silent and speechless, while I fearlessly exposed their wicked plot against my personal liberty and my rights. They did not deny or contradict one statement I made, although so very hard upon them both.

Thus nearly one hour was passed, when Mr. Packard was requested to leave the room. The Doctor left also, leaving me alone with the Trustees. These intelligent men at once endorsed my statements, and became my friends. They offered me my liberty at once, and said that anything I wanted they stood ready to do for me. Mr. Brown, the Chairman, said he saw it was of no use for me to go to my husband; but said they would send me to my children if I wished to go, or to my father in Massachusetts, or they would board me up in Jacksonville. I thanked them for their kind and generous offers; "but," said I, "it is of no use for me to accept of any one of them, for I am still Mr. Packard's wife, and there is no law in America to protect a wife from her husband. I am not safe from him outside these walls, on this continent, unless I flee to Canada; and there, I don't know as a fugitive wife is safe from her husband. The truth is, he is determined to keep me in an Asylum prison as long as I live, if it can be done; and since no law prevents his doing so, I see no way for me but to live and die in this prison. I may as well die here as in any other prison."

These manly gentlemen apprehended my sad condition and expressed their real sympathy for me, but did not know what to advise me to do. Therefore they left it to me and the Doctor to do as we might think best. I suggested to the Doctor that I write a book, and in this manner lay my case before the People—the government of the United States—and ask for the protection of the laws. The Doctor fell in with this suggestion, and I accordingly wrote my great book of seven hundred pages, entitled "The Great Drama,—An Allegory," the first installment of which is already in print and six thousand copies in circulation. This occupied me nine months, which completed my three years of prison life.

The Trustees now ordered Mr. Packard to take me away, as no one else could legally remove me. I protested against being put into his hands without some protection, knowing, as I did, that he intended to incarcerate me for life in Northampton Asylum, if he ever removed me from this. But, like as I entered the Asylum against my will, and in spite of my protest, so I was put out of it into the absolute power of my persecutor again, against my will, and in spite of my protest to the contrary.

I was accordingly removed to Granville, Putnam County, Illinois, and placed in the family of Mr. David Field, who married my adopted sister, where my son paid my board for about four months. During this time, Granville community became acquainted with me and the facts in the case, and after holding a meeting of the citizens on the subject the result was, that Sheriff Leaper was appointed to communicate to me their decision, which was, that I go home to my children taking their voluntary pledge as my protection; that, should Mr. Packard again attempt to imprison me without a trial, that they would use their influence to get him imprisoned in a penitentiary, where they thought the laws of this Commonwealth would place him. They presented me thirty dollars also to defray the expenses of my journey home to Manteno. I returned to my husband and little ones, only to be again treated as a lunatic. He cut me off from communication with this community, and my other friends, by intercepting my mail; made me a close prisoner in my own house; refused me interviews with friends who called to see me, so that he might meet with no interference in carrying out the plan he had devised to get me incarcerated again for life. This plan was providentially disclosed to me, by some letters he accidentally left in my room one night, wherein I saw that I was to be entered, in a few days, into Northampton Insane Asylum for life; as one of these letters from Doctor Prince, Superintendent of that Asylum, assured me of this fact. Another from his sister, Mrs. Marian Severance, of Massachusetts, revealed the mode in which she advised her brother to transfer me from my home prison to my Asylum prison. She advised him to let me go to New York, under the pretence of getting my book published, and have him follow in a train behind, assuring the conductors that I must be treated as an insane person, although I should deny the charge, as all insane persons did, and thus make sure of their aid as accomplices in this conspiracy against my personal liberty. The conductor must be directed to switch me off to Northampton, Mass., instead of taking me to New York, and as my through ticket would indicate to me that all was right, she thought this could be done without arousing my suspicions; then engage a carriage to transport me to the Asylum under pretext of a hotel, and then lock me up for life as a state's pauper! Then, said she, you will have her out of the way, and can do as you please with her property, her children, and even her wardrobe; don't, says she, be even responsible this time for her clothing. (Mr. Packard was responsible for my body clothing in Jacksonville prison, but for nothing else. I was supported there three years as a state pauper. This fact, Mr. Packard most adroitly concealed from my rich father and family relatives, so that he could persuade my deluded father to place more of my patrimony in his hands, under the false pretense that he needed it to make his daughter more comfortable in the Asylum. My father sent him money for this purpose, supposing Mr. Packard was paying my board at the Asylum.)

Another letter was from Dr. McFarland, wherein I saw that Mr. Packard had made application for my readmission there, and Dr. McFarland had consented to receive me again as an insane patient! But the Trustees put their veto upon it, and would not consent to his plea that I be admitted there again. Here is his own statement, which I copied from his own letter: "Jacksonville, December 18, 1863. Rev. Mr. Packard, Dear Sir: The Secretary of the Trustees has probably before this communicated to you the result of their action in the case of Mrs. Packard. It is proper enough to state that I favored her readmission"! Then follows his injunction to Mr. Packard to be sure not to publish any thing respecting the matter. Why is this? Does an upright course seek or desire concealment? Nay, verily: It is conscious guilt alone that seeks concealment, and dreads agitation lest his crimes be exposed. Mine is only one of a large class of cases, where he has consented to readmit a sane person, particularly the wives of men, whose influence he was desirous of securing for the support of himself in his present lucrative position.

Yes, many intelligent wives and mothers did I leave in that awful prison, whose only hope of liberty lies in the death of their lawful husbands, or in a change of the laws, or in a thorough ventilation of that institution. Such a ventilation is needed, in order that justice be done to that class of miserable inmates who are now unjustly confined there.

When I had read these letters over three or four times, to make it sure I had not mistaken their import, and even took copies of some of them, I determined upon the following expedient as my last and only resort, as a self defensive act.

There was a stranger man who passed my window daily to get water from our pump. One day as he passed I beckoned to him to take a note which I had pushed down through where the windows come together, (my windows were firmly nailed down and screwed together, so that I could not open them,) directed to Mrs. A. C. Haslett, the most efficient friend I knew of in Manteno, wherein I informed her of my imminent danger, and begged of her if it was possible in any way to rescue me to do so, forthwith, for in a few days I should be beyond the reach of all human help. She communi-- nicated these facts to the citizens, when mob law was suggested as the only available means of rescue which lay in their power to use, as no law existed which defended a wife from a husband's power, and no man dared to take the responsibility of protecting me against my husband. And one hint was communicated to me clandestinely that if I would only break through my window, a company was formed who would defend me when once outside our house. This rather unlady like mode of self defence I did not like to resort to, knowing as I did, if I should not finally succeed in this attempt, my persecutors would gain advantage over me, in that I had once injured property, as a reason why I should be locked up. As yet, none of my persecutors had not the shadow of capital to make out the charge of insanity upon outside, of my opinions; for my conduct and deportment had uniformly been kind, lady-like and Christian; and even to this date, January, 1866, I challenge any individual to prove me guilty of one unreasonable or insane act. The lady-like Mrs. Haslett sympathized with me in these views; therefore she sought council of Judge Starr of Kankakee City, to know if any law could reach my case so as to give me the justice of a trial of any kind, before another incarceration. The Judge told her that if I was a prisoner in my own house, and any were willing to take oath upon it, a writ of habeas corpus might reach my case and thus secure me a trial. Witnesses were easily found who could take oath to this fact, as many had called at our house to see that my windows were screwed together on the outside, and our front outside door firmly fastened on the outside, and our back outside door most vigilantly guarded by day and locked by night. In a few days this writ was accordingly executed by the Sheriff of the county, and just two days before Mr. Packard was intending to start with me for Massachusetts to imprison me for life in Northampton Lunatic Asylum, he was required by this writ to bring me before the court and give his reasons to the court why he kept his wife a prisoner. The reason he gave for so doing was, that I was Insane. The Judge replied, "Prove it!" The Judge then empannelled a jury of twelve men, and [a] Trial ensued as the result. This trial continued five days. Thus my being made a prisoner at my own home was the only hinge on which my personal liberty for life hung, independent of mob law, as there is no law in the State that will allow a married woman the right of a trial against the charge of insanity brought against her by her husband; and God only knows how many innocent wives and mothers my case represents, who have thus lost their liberty for life, by this arbitrary power, unchecked as it is by no law on the Statute book of Illinois.

Lucy Stone

~

LUCY STONE (1818–1893), abolitionist and woman's rights leader, gave fully of herself to both movements. While still a student at Oberlin College, she made plans to become a public lecturer for the abolitionist movement, in defiance of the then-prevailing notion that women should not engage in such activity. (So strong was this notion that Oberlin College, progressive enough to admit women, had the graduation speeches of its female students read aloud on their behalf by male students; Lucy Stone, refusing to comply with this tradition on her own graduation day, let her speech remain unread.) She married abolitionist Henry Blackwell in 1855, protesting inequalities in marriage law as she did so and retaining her surname, to nationwide surprise. She quickly became

Blackwell, Alice Stone. *Lucy Stone: Pioneer of Woman's Rights*. Boston: Little, Brown, and Company, 1930, pp. 65–67.

Stanton, Elizabeth Cady, Susan B. Anthony, and Matilda Joslyn Gage. *History of Woman Suffrage*. Vol. 1, 1881. Rpt., Salem, NH: Ayer Company, 1985, pp. 260–261 (marriage protest), 165–167 (remarks at the 1855 National Woman's Rights Convention, Cincinnati, Ohio).

Stanton, Elizabeth Cady, Susan B. Anthony, and Matilda Joslyn Gage. *History of Woman Suffrage*. Vol. 2, 1882. Rpt., Salem, NH: Ayer Company, 1985, pp. 383–384 (remarks at 1869 meeting of the American Equal Rights Association, New York City).

Frost, Elizabeth, and Kathryn Cullen-DuPont. *Women's Suffrage in America: An Eyewitness History*. New York: Facts On File, 1992, p. 202 (letter to Elizabeth Cady Stanton dated October 19, 1869).

one of the most important leaders of the early women's suffrage movement. Stone supported the Fourteenth and Fifteenth Amendments, which addressed the voting rights of African American men but not of women. Her comment from a contentious 1869 meeting of abolitionists and women's rights workers, which many people attended in both capacities, is frequently quoted: "There are two great oceans; in the one is the black man, and in the other is the woman. . . . I will be thankful in my soul if *any* body can get out . . ." The longer excerpt below gives a sense of her anguish as women's suffrage was left behind. Elizabeth Cady Stanton and Susan B. Anthony, the other two most prominent women's rights leaders, opposed passage of the Fourteenth and Fifteenth Amendments. In 1869, prompted by this and other disagreements, Lucy Stone wrote to Stanton to say that she was founding the American Woman Suffrage Association to work separately for suffrage.

～

Lucy Stone to Her Mother, Hannah Stone, in 1846

I know, Mother, you feel badly about the plan I have proposed to myself, and that you would prefer to have me take some other course, if I could in conscience. Yet, Mother, I know you too well to suppose that you would wish me to turn away from what I think is my duty, and go all my days in opposition to my convictions of right, lashed by a reproaching conscience.

I surely would not be a public speaker if I sought a life of ease, for it will be a most laborious one; nor would I do it for the sake of honor, for I know that I shall be disesteemed, nay, even hated, by some who are now my friends, or who profess to be. Neither would I do it if I sought wealth, because I could secure it with far more ease and worldly honor by being a teacher. But, Mother, the gold that perishes in the using, the honor that comes from men, the ease or indolence which eats out the energy of the soul, are not the objects at which I aim. If I would be true to myself, true to my

Heavenly Father, I must be actuated by high and holy principles, and pursue that course of conduct which, to me, appears best calculated to promote the highest good of the world. Because I know I shall suffer, shall I, for this, like Lot's wife, turn back? No, Mother, if in this hour of the world's need I should refuse to lend my aid, however small it may be, I should have no right to think of myself as a Christian, and I should forever despise Lucy Stone. If, while I hear the wild shriek of the slave mother robbed of her little ones, or the muffled groan of the daughter spoiled of her virtue, I do not open my mouth for the dumb, am I not guilty? Or should I go, as you said, from house to house to do it, when I could tell so many more in less time, if they should be gathered in one place? You would not object, or think it wrong, for a man to plead the cause of the suffering and the outcast; and surely the moral character of the act is not changed because it is done by a woman.

I received a letter the other day from a friend saying: "I regret for the sake of others that your mother refuses her consent for you to become a public speaker. I regret it less on your own account. The position of a woman advocating the right is so painful that I feel as though I did not wish you to be subject to all the trials that will be heaped upon you."

But, Mother, there are no trials so great as they suffer who neglect or refuse to do what they believe is their duty. I expect to plead not for the slave only, but for suffering humanity everywhere. ESPECIALLY DO I MEAN TO LABOR FOR THE ELEVATION OF MY SEX. The little pamphlet that I sent to you, written by S. J. May, gives a faint outline of what is to be done, and the changes that are to be wrought. But I will not speak further upon this subject at this time, only to ask that you will not withhold your consent from my doing anything that I think it my duty to do. You will not, will you, Mother?

I am not boarding at the public hall this spring, because I could not room alone there, and I can improve so much faster alone that I choose to board in a private family, though I have to pay twelve and a half cents more a week. The family are perfect haters of Disunionism. They berate [abolitionists William Lloyd] Garrison, Stephen and Abby Foster most unmercifully; but I have to bear it patiently, so it does me good, though it is not very pleasant.

We are trying to get the faculty to let the ladies of our class read their own pieces when they graduate. They have never been allowed to do it, but we expect to read for ourselves, or not to write.

Marriage of Lucy Stone under Protest, May 1, 1855

It was my privilege to celebrate May day by officiating at a wedding in a farm-house among the hills of West Brookfield. The bridegroom was a man of tried worth, a leader in the Western Anti-Slavery Movement; and the bride was one whose fair name is known throughout the nation; one whose rare intellectual qualities are excelled by the private beauty of her heart and life.

I never perform the marriage ceremony without a renewed sense of the iniquity of our present system of laws in respect to marriage; a system by which "man and wife are one, and that one is the husband." It was with my hearty concurrence, therefore, that the following protest was read and signed, as a part of the nuptial ceremony; and I send it to you, that others may be induced to do likewise.

Rev. Thomas Wentworth Higginson

Protest

While acknowledging our mutual affection by publicly assuming the relationship of husband and wife, yet in justice to ourselves and a great principle, we deem it a duty to declare that this act on our part implies no sanction of, nor promise of voluntary obedience to such of the present laws of marriage, as refuse to recognize the wife as an independent, rational being, while they confer upon the husband an injurious and unnatural superiority, investing him with legal powers which no honorable man would exercise, and which no man should possess. We protest especially against the laws which give to the husband:

1. The custody of the wife's person.
2. The exclusive control and guardianship of their children.
3. The sole ownership of her personal, and use of her real estate, unless previously settled upon her, or placed in the hands of trustees, as in the case of minors, lunatics, and idiots.
4. The absolute right to the product of her industry.
5. Also against laws which give to the widower so much larger and more permanent an interest in the property of his deceased wife, than they give to the widow in that of the deceased husband.
6. Finally, against the whole system by which "the legal existence of the wife is suspended during marriage," so that in most States, she neither has a legal part in the choice of her residence, nor can she make a will, nor sue or be sued in her own name, nor inherit property.

We believe that personal independence and equal human rights can never be forfeited, except for crime; that marriage should be an equal and permanent partnership, and so recognized by law; that until it is so recognized, married partners should provide against the radical injustice of present laws, by every means in their power.

We believe that where domestic difficulties arise, no appeal should be made to legal tribunals under existing laws, but that all difficulties should be submitted to the equitable adjustment of arbitrators mutually chosen.

Thus reverencing law, we enter our protest against rules and customs which are unworthy of the name, since they violate justice, the essence of law.

Henry B. Blackwell,
Lucy Stone

Remarks at the 1855 National
Women's Rights Convention, Cincinnati, Ohio

The last speaker alluded to this movement as being that of a few disappointed women. From the first years to which my memory stretches, I have been a disappointed woman. When, with my brothers, I reached forth after the sources of knowledge, I was reproved with "It isn't fit for you; it doesn't belong to women." Then there was but one college in the world where women were admitted, and that was in Brazil. I would have found my way there, but by the time I was prepared to go, one was opened in the young State of Ohio—the first in the United States where women and negroes could enjoy opportunities with white men. I was disappointed when I came to seek a profession worthy an immortal being—every employment was closed to me, except those of the teacher, the seamstress, and the housekeeper. In education, in marriage, in religion, in everything, disappointment is the lot of woman. It shall be the business of my life to deepen this disappointment in every woman's heart until she bows down to it no longer. I wish that women, instead of being walking show-cases, instead of begging of their fathers and brothers the latest and gayest new bonnet, would ask of them their rights.

The question of Woman's Rights is a practical one. The notion has prevailed that it was only an ephemeral idea; that it was but women claiming the right to smoke cigars in the streets, and to frequent bar-rooms. Others have supposed it a question of comparative intellect; others still, of sphere. Too much has already been said and written about woman's sphere. Trace all the doctrines to their source and they will be found to have no basis except in the usages and prejudices of the age. This is seen in the fact that what is tolerated in woman in one country is not tolerated in another. In this country women may hold prayer-meetings, etc., but in Mohammedan countries it is written upon their mosques, "Women and dogs, and other impure animals, are not permitted to enter." Wendell Phillips says, "The best and greatest thing one is capable

of doing, that is his sphere." I have confidence in the Father to believe that when He gives us the capacity to do anything He does
not make a blunder. Leave women, then, to find their sphere. And
do not tell us before we are born even, that our province is to cook
dinners, darn stockings, and sew on buttons. We are told woman
has all the rights she wants; and even women, I am ashamed to say,
tell us so. They mistake the politeness of men for rights—seats
while men stand in this hall to-night, and their adulations; but
these are mere courtesies. We want rights. The flour-merchant, the
house-builder, and the postman charge us no less on account of our
sex; but when we endeavor to earn money to pay all these, then,
indeed, we find the difference. Man, if he have energy, may hew
out for himself a path where no mortal has ever trod, held back by
nothing but what is in himself; the world is all before him, where
to choose; and we are glad for you, brothers, men, that it is so. But
the same society that drives forth the young man, keeps woman at
home—a dependent—working little cats on worsted, and little
dogs on punctured paper; but if she goes heartily and bravely to
give herself to some worthy purpose, she is out of her sphere and
she loses caste. Women working in tailor-shops are paid one-third
as much as men. Some one in Philadelphia has stated that women
make fine shirts for twelve and a half cents apiece; that no woman
can make more than nine a week, and the sum thus earned, after
deducting rent, fuel, etc., leaves her just three and a half cents a day
for bread. Is it a wonder that women are driven to prostitution? Female teachers in New York are paid fifty dollars a year, and for every
such situation there are five hundred applicants. I know not what
you believe of God, but I believe He gave yearnings and longings to
be filled, and that He did not mean all our time should be devoted
to feeding and clothing the body. The present condition of woman
causes a horrible perversion of the marriage relation. It is asked of a
lady, "Has she married well?" "Oh, yes, her husband is rich."
Woman must marry for a home, and you men are the sufferers by
this; for a woman who loathes you may marry you because you have
the means to get money which she can not have. But when woman

can enter the lists with you and make money for herself, she will marry you only for deep and earnest affection.

I am detaining you too long, many of you standing, that I ought to apologize, but women have been wronged so long that I may wrong you a little. [*Applause.*] A woman undertook in Lowell to sell shoes to ladies. Men laughed at her, but in six years she has run them all out, and has a monopoly of the trade. Sarah Tyndale, whose husband was an importer of china, and died bankrupt, continued his business, paid off his debts, and has made a fortune and built the largest china warehouse in the world. (Mrs. Mott here corrected Lucy. Mrs. Tyndale has not the largest china warehouse, but the largest assortment of china in the world.) Mrs. Tyndale, herself, drew the plans of her warehouse, and it is the best plan ever drawn. A laborer to whom the architect showed it, said: "Don't she know e'en as much as some men?" I have seen a woman at manual labor turning out chair-legs in a cabinet-shop, with a dress short enough not to drag in the shavings. I wish other women would imitate her in this. It made her hands harder and broader, it is true, but I think a hand with a dollar and a quarter a day in it, better than one with a crossed ninepence. The men in the shop didn't use tobacco, nor swear—they can't do those things where there are women, and we owe it to our brothers to go wherever they work to keep them decent. The widening of woman's sphere is to improve her lot. Let us do it, and if the world scoff, let it scoff—if it sneer, let it sneer—but we will go on emulating the example of the sisters Grimke and Abby Kelly. When they first lectured against slavery they were not listened to as respectfully as you listen to us. So the first female physician meets many difficulties, but to the next the path will be made easy.

Lucretia Mott has been a preacher for years; her right to do so is not questioned among Friends. But when Antoinette Brown felt that she was commanded to preach, and to arrest the progress of thousands that were on the road to hell; why, when she applied for ordination they acted as though they had rather the whole world should go to hell, than that Antoinette Brown should be allowed to tell them how to keep out of it. She is now ordained over a parish in the State of New York, but when she meets on the Temperance platform the Rev. John Chambers, or your own Gen. Carey [*applause*] they greet her with hisses. Theodore Parker said: "The acorn that the school-boy carries in his pocket and the squirrel stows in his cheek, has in it the possibility of an oak, able to withstand, for ages, the cold winter and the driving blast." I have seen the acorn men and women, but never the perfect oak; all are but abortions. The young mother, when first the new-born babe nestles in her bosom, and a heretofore unknown love springs up in her heart, finds herself unprepared for this new relation in life, and she sends forth the child scarred and dwarfed by her own weakness and imbecility, as no stream can rise higher than its fountain.

Remarks at the 1869 Meeting of the American Equal Rights Association, New York City

Mrs. Stanton will, of course, advocate the precedence for her sex, and Mr. Douglass will strive for the first position for his, and both are perhaps right. If it be true that the government derives its authority from the consent of the governed, we are safe in trusting that principle to the uttermost. If one has a right to say that you can not read and therefore can not vote, then it may be said that you are a woman and therefore can not vote. We are lost if we turn away from the middle principle and argue for one class. I was once a teacher among fugitive slaves. There was one old man, and every tooth was gone, his hair was white, and his face was full of wrinkles, yet, day after day and hour after hour, he came up to the school-house and tried with patience to learn to read, and by-and-by, when he had spelled out the first few verses of the first chapter of the Gospel of St. John, he said to me, "Now, I want to learn to write." I tried to make him satisfied with what he had acquired, but the old man said, "Mrs. Stone, somewhere in the wide world I have a son; I have not heard from him in twenty years; if I should hear from him, I want to write to him, so take hold of my hand and teach me." I did, but before he had proceeded in many lessons, the angels came and gathered him up and bore him to his Father. Let no man speak of an educated suffrage. The gentleman who addressed you claimed that the negroes had the first right to the suffrage, and drew a picture which only his great word-power can do. He again in Massachusetts, when it had cast a majority in favor of Grant and negro suffrage, stood upon the platform and said that woman had better wait for the negro; that is, that both could not be carried, and that the negro had better be the one. But I freely forgave him because he felt as he spoke. But woman suffrage is more imperative than his own; and I want to remind the audience that when he says what the Ku-Kluxes did all over the South, the Ku-Kluxes here in the North in the shape of men, take away the children from the mother, and separate them as completely as if done on the block of the auctioneer. Over in New Jersey they have a law which says that *any* father—he might be the most brutal man that ever existed—*any* father, it says, whether he be under age or not, may by his last will and testament dispose of the custody of his child, born or to be born, and that such disposition shall be good against all persons, and that the mother may not recover her child; and that law modified in form exists over every State in the Union except in Kansas. Woman has an ocean of wrongs too deep for any plummet, and the negro, too, has an ocean of wrongs that can not be fathomed. There are two great oceans; in the one is the black man, and in the other is the woman. But I thank God for that XV. Amendment, and hope that it will be adopted in every State. I will be thankful in my soul if *any* body can get out of the terrible pit. But I believe that the safety of the government would be more promoted by the admission of woman as an element of restoration and harmony than the negro. I believe that the influence of woman will save the country before every other power. [*Applause.*] I see the signs of the times pointing to this consummation, and I believe that in some parts of the country women will vote for the President of these United States in 1872. [*Applause*]

Letter to Elizabeth Cady Stanton, October 19, 1869

Enclosed I send you a copy of the call for a convention to form an American Woman Suffrage association. I wish I could have had a quiet hour with you, to talk about it. I *hope* you will see it as I do, that with two societies each, in harmony with itself, each having the benefit of national names, each attracting those who naturally belong to it, we shall secure the hearty active cooperation of *all* the friends of the cause, better than either could do alone. People will differ, as to what they consider the best methods & means. The true wisdom is not to ignore, but to provide for the fact. So far as I have influence, this soc. shall never be an enemy or antagonist of yours in any way. It will simply fill a field and combine forces, which yours does not. I shall rejoice when any of the onerous works are carried, no matter who does it.

Your little girls, and mine will reap the easy harvest which it costs so much to sow.

Catharine Beecher

~

CATHARINE BEECHER (1800–1879), an advocate for women's education, was also a leading guardian of women's traditional role. She opposed women's suffrage, believing that women already wielded indirect influence upon public policy through their influence on men and that the entrance of women into public life would irreparably damage American families and homes. What Beecher sought for women was an increased public respect for their work within the home and within professions such as teaching, which she considered a natural extension of that sphere.

~

From *The True Remedy for the Wrongs of Woman*, 1851

My Dear Sister:

. . . On the subject of woman's rights and duties, I regard the Bible view of the case as not only the common-sense aspect, but that it is far *more favorable* to woman's increased influence and high

Boydston, Jeanne, Mary Kelly, and Anne Margolis. *The Limits of Sisterhood: The Beecher Sisters on Women's Rights and Woman's Sphere*. Chapel Hill: University of North Carolina Press, 1988, pp. 140–142 (*True Remedy for the Wrongs of Woman*).

Beecher, Catharine E., and Harriet Beecher Stowe. *The American Woman's Home*. New York: J. B. Ford & Co., 1869, pp. 463–468 ("An Appeal to American Women").

Frost, Elizabeth, and Kathryn Cullen-DuPont. *Women's Suffrage in America: An Eyewitness History*. New York: Facts On File, 1992, pp. 216–218.

position in social and domestic life than that of those who dissent from it.

What, then, is the *general principle* which the Bible inculcates? It is simply the common-sense rule that where there is *power*, and power that can not be successfully resisted, there men and women both, are to submit without contest. . . .

But there is another side to this subject. For while it is our duty when subject to power not to resist, it is equally taught that whenever this power passes into our hands, we may lawfully *use* it. . . . The general principle . . . is this: If you are not able to resist successfully, or to escape from any power that oppresses you, do not attempt it, but submit without repining, for it is the will of God. But as soon as you have the power, *use it.* . . .

But how is it with man and woman in the relation of the family? If there is anything to which a man has a right, it is his own earnings; and when a woman consents to be supported by him, she can not take away this right. As the general rule, therefore, man must hold the power of *physical strength* and the *power of the purse*. The Bible, then, gives this very wise and common-sense advice: If a woman chooses to put herself into the power of a man by becoming his wife, let her submit to that power and obey her husband. . . .

No woman is under obligations to marry unless she chooses to do so. . . .

[W]hat is the law of the Bible to the husband? In the first place, he is to love his wife as he does himself; that is, he is to regard her wishes, enjoyment, and interests as of the same value as his own. Next, he is to *honor* his wife; and, what is better, he is to honor her "*as the weaker vessel*"—that is, he is to treat her more tenderly and guard her from evil more carefully than he would if she were his equal in position and strength. Thus, he is to give her the precedence of himself in all the enjoyments, comforts, and conveniences, of life. . . .

Neither men nor women, when talking and writing on this subject, have fully recognized what are the *Bible rights* of woman. . . .

And owing to this, some women . . . write and talk as if the great end and aim of woman was to conform to the will and wishes of husbands, to soothe all their ill humors, and to make the most of a bad bargain. . . .

The true attitude to be assumed by woman, not only in the domestic but in all our social relations, is that of an intelligent, immortal being, whose interests and rights are *every way* equal in value to that of the other sex. . . . And every woman is to *claim* this, as the right which God has conferred upon her. . . .

It is my full conviction that there is no *real* social evil to which woman is now subjected which is not fully in her power to remedy.

Is it claimed that there are civil laws which are unjust and unequal, and contrary to the Bible rights of our sex? Let every intelligent woman use her influence with the lawmakers, and in *an acceptable manner*, and these laws would speedily be changed.

Is it claimed that, in social customs, the guilty woman is treated with overbearing cruelty, and the guilty man with shameful leniency? Let all virtuous women decide that they will treat both sexes alike, and the unjust custom will speedily pass away.

Is it claimed that woman is deprived of the means of education, and of honorable and remunerative employ? There is wealth and power enough in the hands of women alone, to rectify all the evils that spring from this source.

Is it claimed that women are excluded from all offices of honor and emolument? Instead of rushing into the political arena to join in the scramble for office, or attempting to wedge into the overcrowded learned professions of man, let woman raise and dignify her own profession, and endow posts of honor and emolument in it, that are suited to the character and duties of her sex. . . .

From "An Appeal to American Women," Included as the Appendix to the 1869 Edition of *The American Woman's Home*

My Honored Countrywomen:

It is now over forty years that I have been seeking to elevate the character and condition of our sex, relying, as to earthly aid, chiefly on your counsel and coöperation. I am sorrowful at results that have followed these and similar efforts, and ask your sympathy and aid.

Let me commence with a brief outline of the past. I commenced as an educator in the city of Hartford, Ct., when only the primary branches and one or two imperfect accomplishments were the ordinary school education, and was among the first pioneers in seeking to introduce some of the higher branches. The staid, conservative citizens queried of what use to women were Latin, Geometry, and Algebra, and wondered at a request for six recitation rooms and a study-hall for a school of nearly a hundred, who had as yet only one room. The appeal was then made to benevolent, intelligent women, and by their influence all that was sought was liberally bestowed.

But the course of study then attempted was scarcely half of what is now pursued in most of our colleges for young women, while there has been added a round and extent of accomplishments then unknown. Yet this moderate amount so stimulated brain and nerves, and so excited competition, that it became needful to enforce a rule, requiring a daily report, that only two hours a day had been devoted to study out of school hours. Even this did not avail to save from injured health both the teacher who projected these improvements and many of her pupils. This example and that of similar institutions spread all over the nation, with constantly increasing demand for more studies, and decreasing value and respect for domestic pursuits and duties.

Ten years of such intellectual excitement exhausted the nervous fountain, and my profession as a school-teacher was ended.

The next attempt was to introduce Domestic Economy as *a science to be studied* in schools for girls. For a while it seemed to succeed; but ere long was crowded out by Political Economy and many other economies, except those most needed to prepare a woman for her difficult and sacred duties.

In the progress of years, it came to pass that the older States teemed with educated women, qualified for no other department of woman's profession but that of a school-teacher, while the newer States abounded in children without schools.

I again appealed to my countrywomen for help, addressing them through the press and also by the assistance of a brother (in assemblies in many chief cities) in order to raise funds to support an agent. The funds were bestowed, and thus the services of Governor Slade were secured, and, mainly by these agencies, nearly one thousand teachers were provided with schools, chiefly in the West.

Meantime, the intellectual taxation in both private and public schools, the want of proper ventilation in both families and schools, the want of domestic exercise which is so valuable to the feminine constitution, the pernicious modes of dress, and the prevailing neglect of the laws of health, resulted in the general decay of health among women. At the same time, the overworking of the brain and nerves, and the "cramming" system of study, resulted in a deficiency of mental development which is very marked. It is now a subject of general observation that young women, at this day, are decidedly inferior in mental power to those of an earlier period, notwithstanding their increased advantages. For the mind, crowded with undigested matter, is debilitated the same as is the body by over-feeding.

Recent scientific investigations give the philosophy of these results. For example, Professor Houghton, of Trinity College, Dublin, gives as one item of protracted experiments in animal chemistry, that two hours of severe study abstracts as much vital strength as is demanded by a whole day of manual labor. The reports of the Massachusetts Board of Education add other facts that, in this connection, should be deeply pondered. For example, in one public school of eighty-five pupils only fifty-four had refreshing sleep; fifty-nine had headaches or constant weariness, and only fifteen were perfectly well. In this school it was found, and similar facts are common in all our public and high schools, that, in addition to six school-hours, thirty-one studied three hours and a half; thirty-five, four hours; and twelve, from four to seven hours. And yet the most learned medical men maintain that the time devoted to brain labor, daily, should not exceed six hours for healthy men, and three hours for growing children.

Alarmed at the dangerous tendencies of female education, I made another appeal to my sex, which resulted in the organization of the American Woman's Education Association, the object being to establish *endowed* professional schools, in connection with literary institutions, in which woman's profession should be honored and taught as are the professions of men, and where woman should be trained for some self-supporting business. From this effort several institutions of a high literary character have come into existence at the West, but the organization and endowment of the professional schools is yet incomplete from many combining impediments, the chief being a want of appreciation of woman's profession, and of the *science* and *training* which its high and sacred duties require. But the reports of the Association will show that never before were such superior intellectual advantages secured to a new country by so economical an outlay.

Let us now look at the dangers which are impending. And first, in regard to the welfare of the family state, the decay of the female constitution and health has involved such terrific sufferings, in addition to former cares and pains of maternity; that multitudes of both sexes so dread the risks of marriage as either to avoid it, or meet them by methods *always* injurious and often criminal. Not only so, multitudes of intelligent and conscientious persons, in private and by the press, unaware of the penalties of violating nature, openly impugn the inspired declaration, "Children are a heritage of the Lord."

Add to these, other influences that are robbing home of its safe and peaceful enjoyments. Of such, the condition of domestic service is not the least. We abound in domestic helpers from foreign shores, but they are to a large extent thriftless, ignorant, and unscrupulous, while as thriftless and inexperienced housekeepers, from boarding-school life, have no ability to train or to control. Hence come antagonism and ceaseless "worries" in the parlor, nursery, and kitchen, while the husband is wearied with endless complaints of breakage, waste of fuel and food, neglect, dishonesty, and deception, and home is any thing but a harbor of comfort and peace. Thus come clubs to draw men from comfortless homes, and, next, clubs for the deserted women.

Meantime, domestic service—disgraced, on one side, by the stigma of our late slavery, and, on the other, by the influx into our kitchens of the uncleanly and ignorant—is shunned by the self-respecting and well educated, many of whom prefer either a miserable pittance or the career of vice to this fancied degradation. Thus comes the overcrowding in all avenues for woman's work, and the consequent lowering of wages to starvation prices for long protracted toils.

From this come diseases to the operatives, bequeathed often to their offspring. Factory girls must stand ten hours or more, and consequently in a few years debility and disease ensue, so that they never can rear healthy children, while the foreigners who supplant them in kitchen labor are almost the only strong and healthy women to rear large families. The sewing-machine, hailed as a blessing, has proved a curse to the poor; for it takes away profits from needlewomen, while employers testify that women who use this machine for steady work, in two years or less become hopelessly diseased and can rear no children. Thus it is that the controlling political majority of New England is passing from the educated to the children of ignorant foreigners.

Add to these disastrous influences, the teachings of "free love;" the baneful influence of spiritualism, so called; the fascinations of the *demi-monde*; the poverty of thousands of women who, but for desperate temptations, would be pure—all these malign influences are sapping the foundations of the family state.

Meantime, many intelligent and benevolent persons imagine that the grand remedy for the heavy evils that oppress our sex is to introduce woman to political power and office, to make her a party in primary political meetings, in political caucuses, and in the scramble and fight for political offices; thus bringing into this dangerous *melée* the distinctive tempting power of her sex. Who can look at this new danger without dismay?

But it is neither generous nor wise to join in the calumny and ridicule that are directed toward philanthropic and conscientious laborers for the good of our sex, because we fear their methods are not safe. It would be far wiser to show by example a better way.

Let us suppose that our friends have gained the ballot and the powers of office: are there any real beneficent measures for our sex, which they would enforce by law and penalties, that fathers, brothers, and husbands would not grant to a united petition of our sex, or even to a majority of the wise and good? Would these not confer what the wives, mothers, and sisters deemed best for themselves and the children they are to train, very much sooner than they would give power and office to our sex to enforce these advantages by law? Would it not be a wiser thing to *ask* for what we need, before trying so circuitous and dangerous a method? God has given to man the physical power, so that all that woman may gain, either by petitions or by ballot, will be the gift of love or of duty; and the ballot never will be accorded till benevolent and conscientious men are the majority— a millennial point far beyond our present ken.

The American Woman's Education Association aims at a plan which its members believe, in its full development, will more effectually remedy the "wrongs of woman" than any other urged on public notice. Its general aim has been stated; its details will appear at another time and place. . . .

Statement of Catharine Beecher
in Opposition to Women's Suffrage, Read to the
American Woman Suffrage Association Convention
May 11, 1870

[Although Beecher had dropped her former opposition to women's public speaking (she had disapproved of the Grimké sisters' public lectures in the 1830s), she asked Henry Blackwell to read aloud this letter on her behalf.]

I will first state to what I am not opposed. And, first, I am not opposed to women speaking in public to any who are willing to hear, nor do I object to women's preaching, sanctioned as it is by a prophetic apostle—as one of the millennial results. It is true that no women were appointed among the first twelve, or the seventy disciples sent out by the Lord, nor were women appointed to be apostles or bishops or elders. But they were not forbidden to teach or preach, except in places where it violated a custom that made a woman appear as one of a base and degraded class if she thus violated custom.

Nor am I opposed to a woman earning her own independence in any lawful calling, and wish many more were open to her which are now closed.

Nor am I opposed to the agitation and organization of women, as women, to set forth the wrongs suffered by great multitudes of our sex, which are multiform and most humiliating. Nor am I opposed to women's undertaking to govern both boys and men—they always have done it, and always will. The most absolute and cruel tyrants I have ever known were selfish, obstinate, unreasonable women to whom were chained men of delicacy, honor, and piety, whose only alternatives were helpless submission, or ceaseless and disgraceful broils.

Nor am I opposed to the claim that women have equal rights with men. I rather claim that they have the sacred, superior rights that God and good men accord to the weak and defenseless, by which they have the easiest work, the most safe and comfortable places, and the largest share of all the most agreeable and desirable enjoyments of this life. My main objection to the woman suffrage organizations is mainly this, that a wrong mode is employed to gain a right object.

The "right object" sought is to remedy the wrongs and relieve the sufferings of great multitudes of our sex. The "wrong mode" is that which aims to enforce by law instead of by love. It is one which assumes that man is the author and abetter of all these wrongs, and that he must be restrained and regulated by constitutions and laws, as the chief and most trustworthy method.

In opposition to this, I hold that the fault is as much, or more, with women than with men, inasmuch as that we have all the power we need to remedy all wrongs and sufferings complained of, and yet we do not use it for that end. It is my deep conviction that all reasonable and conscientious men of our age, and especially of our country, are not only willing, but anxious to provide for the best good of our sex, and that they will gladly bestow all that is just, reasonable, and kind, whenever we unite in asking in the proper spirit and manner. It is because we do not ask, or "because we ask amiss," that we do not receive all we need both from God and men. Let me illustrate my meaning by a brief narrative of my own experience. To begin with my earliest: I can not remember a time when I did not find a father's heart so tender that it was always easier for him to give anything I asked than to deny me. Of my seven brothers, I know not one who would not take as much or more care of my interests than I should myself. The brother who presides is here because it is so hard for him to say "No" to any woman seeking his aid.

It is half a century this very spring since I began to work for the education and relief of my sex, and I have succeeded so largely by first convincing intelligent and benevolent women that what I aimed at was right and desirable, and then securing their influence with their fathers, brothers, and husbands; and always with success. American women have only to unite in asking for whatever is just and reasonable, in a proper spirit and manner, in order to secure all that they need.

Here, then, I urge my greatest objections to the plan of female suffrage; for my countrywomen are seeking it only as an instrument for redressing wrongs and relieving wants by laws and civil influences. Now, I ask, why not take a shorter course, and ask to have the men do for us what we might do for ourselves if we had the ballot? Suppose we point out to our State Legislatures and to Congress the evils that it is supposed the ballot would remedy, and draw up petitions for these remedial measures, would not these petitions be granted much sooner and with far less irritation and conflict than must ensue before we gain the ballot? And in such petitions thousands of women would unite who now deem that female suffrage would prove a curse rather than a benefit.

And here I will close with my final objection to woman suffrage, and that is that it will prove a measure of injustice and oppression to the women who oppose it. Most of such women believe that the greatest cause of the evils suffered by our sex is that the true profession of woman, in many of its most important departments, is not respected; that women are not trained either to the science or the practice of domestic duties as they need to be, and that, as the consequence, the chief labors of the family state pass to ignorant foreigners, and by cultivated women are avoided as disgraceful.

They believe the true remedy is to make woman's work honorable and remunerative, and that the suffrage agitation does not tend to this, but rather to drain off the higher classes of cultivated women from those more important duties to take charge of political and civil affairs that are more suitable for men.

Now if women are all made voters, it will be their duty to vote, and also to qualify themselves for this duty. But already women have more than they can do well in all that appropriately belongs to women, and to add the civil and political duties of men would be deemed a measure of injustice and oppression.

Frances Ellen
Watkins Harper

~

FRANCES ELLEN WATKINS HARPER (1854–1885), the author of what is believed to be the first short story published by an African American, used her talents in service of the abolitionist and women's rights movements. Believing "it may be that God himself has written upon both my heart and brain a commission to use time, talent and energy in the cause of freedom," she lectured for the Maine Anti-Slavery Society, wrote poems illustrating slavery's injustices, and sent her work's proceeds to fund the Underground Railroad. Grateful to John Brown for his attempted insurrection, she also sent a donation to Brown's wife. Later, when women's rights workers were divided in their response to the Fourteenth and Fifteenth Amendments, Harper was one of the African-American women who sided with Lucy Stone to support the enfranchisement of African-American men without the enfranchisement of any women. (Other African-American women, such as Sojourner Truth and Harriet Tubman, joined Elizabeth Cady Stanton and Susan B. Anthony, who withheld support.) After passage and ratification of these amendments, she worked to gain support, especially from the newly enfranchised African-American men, for women's suffrage.

Still, William. *The Underground Railroad*. 1872. Rpt., New York: Arno Press, 1968, pp. 758, 760–763, 766–767 (letters).

Rogers, Katharine M. *Early American Women Writers: From Anne Bradstreet to Louisa May Alcott, 1650–1895*. New York: Meridian, 1991, pp. 498–500 ("The Slave Auction" and "The Slave Mother").

Sterling, Dorothy. *We Are Your Sisters: Black Women in the Nineteenth Century*. New York: W. W. Norton & Company, 1984 ("Dialogue on Woman's Rights").

~

Letter to William Still,
Chairman and Corresponding Secretary of
the Philadelphia Branch of the Underground Railroad,
August 1854

Well, I am out lecturing. I have lectured every night this week; besides addressed a Sunday-school, and I shall speak, if nothing prevent, to-night. My lectures have met with success. Last night I lectured in a white church in Providence. Mr. Gardener was present, and made the estimate of about six hundred persons. Never, perhaps, was a speaker, old or young, favored with a more attentive audience. [. . .] My voice is not wanting in strength, as I am aware of, to reach pretty well over the house. The church was the Roger Williams; the pastor, a Mr. Furnell, who appeared to be a kind and Christian man. [. . .] My maiden lecture was Monday night in New Bedford on the Elevation and Education of our People. Perhaps as intellectual a place as any I was ever at of its size.

Letter to William Still,
Niagara Falls, Canada,* September 12, 1856

Well, I have gazed for the first time upon Free Land, and, would you believe it, tears sprang to my eyes, and I wept. Oh, it was a glorious sight to gaze for the first time on a land where a poor slave flying from our glorious land of liberty would in a moment find his fetters broken, his shackles loosed, and whatever he was in the land of Washington, beneath the shadow of Bunker Hill Monument or even Plymouth Rock, here he becomes a man and

---

*Harper had traveled to Canada to visit former slaves who had been helped by the Underground Railroad.

a brother. I have gazed on Harper's Ferry, or rather the rock at the Ferry; I have seen it towering up in simple grandeur, with the gentle Potomac gliding peacefully at its feet, and felt that that was God's masonry, and my soul had expanded in gazing on its sublimity. I have seen the ocean singing its wild chorus of sounding waves, and ecstacy has thrilled upon the living chords of my heart. I have since then seen the rainbow-crowned Niagara chanting the choral hymn of Omnipotence, girdled with grandeur, and robed with glory; but none of these things have melted me as the first sight of Free Land. Towering mountains lifting their hoary summits to catch the first faint flush of day when the sunbeams kiss the shadows from morning's drowsy face may expand and exalt your soul. The first view of the ocean may fill you with strange delight. Niagara—the great, the glorious Niagara—may hush your spirit with its ceaseless thunder; it may charm you with its robe of crested spray and rainbow crown; but the land of Freedom was a lesson of deeper significance than foaming waves or towering mounts.

The Slave Mother

Heard you that shriek? It rose
  So wildly on the air,
It seemed as if a burdened heart
  Was breaking in despair.

Saw you those hands so sadly clasped—
  The bowed and feeble head—
The shuddering of that fragile form—
  That look of grief and dread?

Saw you the sad, imploring eye?
  Its every glance was paid,
As if a storm of agony
  Were sweeping through the brain.

She is a mother, pale with fear,
  Her boy clings to her side,
And in her kirtle vainly tries
  His trembling form to hide.

He is not hers, although she bore
  For him a mother's pains;
He is not hers, although her blood
  Is coursing through his veins!

He is not hers, for cruel hands
  May rudely tear apart
The only wreath of household love
  That binds her breaking heart.

His love has been a joyous light
  That o'er her pathway smiled,
A fountain gushing ever new,
  Amid life's desert wild.

His lightest word has been a tone
  Of music round her heart,
Their lives a streamlet blent in one—
  Oh, Father! must they part?

They tear him from her circling arms,
  Her last and fond embrace.
Oh! never more may her sad eyes
  Gaze on his mournful face.

No marvel, then, these bitter shrieks
  Disturb the listening air;
She is a mother, and her heart
  Is breaking in despair.

—1857

Letter to William Still, December 15, 185[9]?

I send you to-day two dollars for the Underground Rail Road. It is only a part of what I subscribed at your meeting. May God speed the flight of the slave as he speeds through our Republic to gain his liberty in a monarchical land. I am still in the lecturing field, though not very strong physically. [. . .] Send me word what I can do for the fugitive.

Letter to Mary Brown, November 14, 1859

My Dear Madam:
In an hour like this the common words of sympathy may seem like idle words, and yet I want to say something to you, the noble wife of the hero of the nineteenth century. Belonging to the race your dear husband reached forth his hand to assist, I need not tell you that my sympathies are with you. I thank you for the brave words you have spoken. A republic that produces such a wife and mother may hope for better days. Our heart may grow more hopeful for humanity when it sees the sublime sacrifice it is about to receive from his hands. Not in vain has your dear husband periled all, if the martyrdom of one hero is worth more than the life of a million cowards. From the prison comes forth a shout of triumph over that power whose ethics are robbery of the feeble and oppression of the weak, the trophies of whose chivalry are a plundered cradle and a scourged and bleeding woman. Dear sister, I thank you for the brave and noble words that you have spoken. Enclosed I send you a few dollars as a token of my gratitude, reverence and love.

Undated Letter to William Still

How fared the girl who came robed in male attire? Do write me every time you write how many come to your house; and, my dear friend, if you have that much in hand of mine from my books, will you please pay the Vigilance Committee two or three dollars for me to help carry on the glorious enterprise. Now, please do not write back that you are not going to do any such thing. Let me explain a few matters to you. In the first place, I am able to give something. In the second place, I am willing to do so.

Another Undated Letter to William Still

My health is not very strong, and I may have to give up before long. I may have to yield on account of my voice, which I think, has become somewhat affected. I might be so glad if it was only so that I could go home among my own kindred and people, but slavery comes up like a dark shadow between me and the home of my childhood. Well, perhaps it is my lot to die from home and be buried among strangers; and yet I do not regret that I have espoused this cause; perhaps I have been of some service to the cause of human rights, and I hope the consciousness that I have not lived in vain, will be a halo of peace around my dying bed; a heavenly sunshine lighting up the dark valley and shadow of death.

Letter to William Still,
Following the Emancipation Proclamation, 1863

I spoke in Columbus on the President's Proclamation. [. . .] But was not such an event worthy the awakening of every power— the congratulation of every faculty? What hath God wrought! We may well exclaim how event after event has paved the way for freedom. In the crucible of disaster and defeat God has stirred the nation, and permitted no permanent victory to crown her banners while she kept her hand upon the trembling slave and held him back from freedom. And even now the scale may still seem to oscillate between the contending parties, and some may say,

Why does not God give us full and quick victory? My friend, do not despair if even deeper shadows gather around the fate of the nation, that truth will not ultimately triumph, and the right be established and vindicated; but the deadly gangrene has taken such deep and almost fatal hold upon the nation that the very centres of its life seem to be involved in its eradication. Just look, after all the trials deep and fiery through which the nation has waded, how mournfully suggestive was the response the proclamation received from the democratic triumphs which followed so close upon its footsteps. Well, thank God that the President did not fail us, that the fierce rumbling of democratic thunder did not shake from his hand the bolt he leveled against slavery. Oh, it would have been so sad if, after all the desolation and carnage that have dyed our plains with blood and crimsoned our borders with warfare, the pale young corpses trodden down by the hoofs of war, the dim eyes that have looked their last upon the loved and lost, and the arm of Executive power failed us in the nation's fearful crisis! For how mournful it is when the unrighted wrongs and fearful agonies of ages reach their culminating point, and events solemn, terrible and sublime marshal themselves in dread array to mould the destiny of nations, the hands appointed to hold the helm of affairs, instead of grasping the mighty occasions and stamping them with the great seals of duty and right, permit them to float along the current of circumstances without comprehending the hour of visitation or the momentous day of opportunity. Yes, we may thank God that in the hour when the nation's life was convulsed, and fearful gloom had shed its shadows over the land, the President reached out his hand through the darkness to break the chains on which the rust of centuries had gathered. Well, did you ever expect to see this day? I know that all is not accomplished; but we may rejoice in what has been already wrought,—the wondrous change in so short a time. Just a little while since the American flag to the flying bondman was an ensign of bondage; now it has become a symbol of protection and freedom. Once the slave was a despised and trampled on pariah;

now he has become a useful ally to the American government. From the crimson sods of war springs the white flower of freedom, and songs of deliverance mingle with the crash and roar of war. The shadow of the American army becomes a covert for the slave, and beneath the American Eagle he grasps the key of knowledge and is lifted to a higher destiny.

Letter to William Still, Following the Assassination of President Abraham Lincoln, April 19, 1865

Sorrow treads on the footsteps of the nation's joy. A few days since the telegraph thrilled and throbbed with a nation's joy. To-day a nation sits down beneath the shadow of its mournful grief. Oh, what a terrible lesson does this event read to us! A few years since slavery tortured, burned, hung and outraged us, and the nation passed by and said, they had nothing to do with slavery where it was, slavery would have something to do with them where they were. Oh, how fearfully the judgments of Ichabod have pressed upon the nation's life! Well, it may be in the providence of God this blow was needed to intensify the nation's hatred of slavery, to show the utter fallacy of basing national reconstruction upon the votes of returned rebels, and rejecting loyal black men; making (after all the blood poured out like water, and wealth scattered like chaff) a return to the old idea that a white rebel is better or of more account in the body politic than a loyal black man. [. . .] Moses, the meekest man on earth, led the children of Israel over the Red Sea, but was not permitted to see them settled in Canaan. Mr. Lincoln has led up through another Red Sea to the table land of triumphant victory, and God has seen fit to summon for the new era another man. It is ours then to bow to the Chastener and let our honored and loved chieftain go. Surely the everlasting arms that have hushed him so strangely to sleep are able to guide the nation through its untrod future; but in vain should be this fearful baptism of blood if from the dark bosom of slavery springs such terrible crimes. Let the whole nation resolve that the whole virus shall be eliminated from its body; that in the future slavery shall only be remembered as a thing of the past that shall never have the faintest hope of a resurrection.

Dialogue on Woman's Rights

JACOB
I don't believe a single bit
In those new-fangled ways
Of women running to the polls
And voting nowadays.
Now there's my Betsy, just as good
As any wife need be
Who sits and tells me day by day
That women are not free;
And then I smile and say to her,
"You surely make me laff;
This talk about your rights and wrongs
Is nothing else but chaff."

JOHN
Now, Jacob, I don't think like you;
I think that Betsy Ann
Has just as good a right to vote
As you or any man

JACOB
Now, John, do you believe for true
In women running round,
And when you come to look for them
They are not to be found?

Pray, who would stay at home to nurse,
To cook, to wash and sew,
While women marched unto the polls?
That's what I want to know.

JOHN
Who stays at home when Betsy Ann
Goes out day after day
To wash and iron, cook and sew,
Because she gets her pay?
I'm sure she wouldn't take quite so long
To vote and go her way,
As when she leaves her little ones
And works out day by day

JACOB
Well, I declare, that is the truth!
To vote, it don't take long,
But, then, I kind of think somehow
That women's voting's wrong.

JOHN
The masters thought before the war
That slavery was right;
But we who felt the heavy yoke
Didn't see it in that light.
Some thought that it would never do
For us in Southern lands,
To change the fetters on our wrists
For the ballot in our hands.
Now if you don't believe 'twas right
To crowd us from the track
How can you push your wife aside
And try to hold her back?

JACOB
Well, wrong is wrong and right is right,
For woman as for man
I almost think that I will go
And vote with Betsy Ann.

JOHN
I hope you will and show the world
You can be brave and strong
A noble man, who scorns to do
The feeblest woman wrong.

—1885

Anna Howard Shaw

~

ANNA HOWARD SHAW (1847–1919), suffragist and president of the National American Woman Suffrage Association from 1904–1915, was also the first ordained woman minister in the Methodist Protestant Church. In her autobiography, *Anna Howard Shaw: The Story of a Pioneer*, she recalls her pursuit of a license to preach, which she was awarded in 1871. (She would be ordained in 1880.)

~

I was fourteen. For once, I had been in the woods all day, buried in my books; and when I returned at night, still in the dream world these books had opened to me, father was awaiting my coming with a brow dark with disapproval. As it happened, mother had felt that day some special need of me, and father reproached me bitterly for being beyond reach—an idler who wasted time while mother labored. He ended a long arraignment by predicting gloomily that with such tendencies I would make nothing of my life.

The injustice of the criticism cut deep; I knew I had done and was doing my share for the family, and already, too, I had begun to feel the call of my career. For some reason I wanted to preach—to talk to people, to tell them things. Just why, just what, I did not yet know—but I had begun to preach in the silent woods, to stand up on stumps and address the unresponsive trees, to feel the stir of aspiration within me.

Shaw, Anna Howard. *Anna Howard Shaw: The Story of a Pioneer*. 1915. Rpt., Cleveland, OH: The Pilgrim Press, 1994, pp. 44–45, 54–64.

When my father had finished all he wished to say, I looked at him and answered, quietly, "Father, some day I am going to college."

I can still see his slight, ironical smile. It drove me to a second prediction. I was young enough to measure success by material results, so I added, recklessly:

"And before I die I shall be worth ten thousand dollars!"

The amount staggered me even as it dropped from my lips. It was the largest fortune my imagination could conceive, and in my heart I believed that no woman ever had possessed or would possess so much. So far as I knew, too, no woman had gone to college. But now that I had put my secret hopes into words, I was desperately determined to make those hopes come true. After I became a wage-earner I lost my desire to make a fortune, but the college dream grew with the years. . . .

When I was fifteen years old I was offered a situation as school-teacher. By this time the community was growing around us with the rapidity characteristic of these Western settlements, and we had nearer neighbors whose children needed instruction. I passed an examination before a school-board consisting of three nervous and self-conscious men whose certificate I still hold, and I at once began my professional career. . . . The school was four miles from my home, so I "boarded round" with the families of my pupils, staying two weeks in each place, and often walking from three to six miles a day to and from my little log school-house in every kind of weather. During the first year I had about fourteen pupils, of varying ages, sizes, and temperaments, and there was hardly a book in the school-room except those I owned. One little girl, I remember, read from an almanac, while a second used a hymn-book. . . .

The largest salary I could earn by teaching in our Northern woods was one hundred and fifty-six dollars a year, for two terms of thirteen weeks each; and from this, of course, I had to deduct the cost of my board and clothing—the sole expenditure I allowed myself. The dollars for an education accumulated very, very slowly, until at last, in desperation, weary of seeing the years of my youth rush past, bearing my hopes with them, I took a sudden and radical step. I gave up teaching, left our cabin in the woods, and went to Big Rapids to live with my sister Mary, who had married a successful man and who generously offered me a home. There, I had decided, I would learn a trade of some kind, of any kind; it did not greatly matter what it was. The sole essential was that it should be a money-making trade, offering wages which would make it possible to add more rapidly to my savings. In those days, almost fifty years ago, and in a small pioneer town, the fields open to women were few and unfruitful. The needle at once presented itself, but at first I turned with loathing from it. I would have preferred the digging of ditches or the shoveling of coal; but the needle alone persistently pointed out my way, and I was finally forced to take it.

Fate, however, as if weary at last of seeing me between her paws, suddenly let me escape. Before I had been working a month at my uncongenial trade Big Rapids was favored by a visit from a Universalist woman minister, the Reverend Marianna Thompson, who came there to preach. Her sermon was delivered on Sunday morning, and I was, I think, almost the earliest arrival of the great congregation which filled the church. It was a wonderful moment when I saw my first woman minister enter her pulpit; and as I listened to her sermon, thrilled to the soul, all my early aspirations to become a minister myself stirred in me with cumulative force. After the services I hung for a time on the fringe of the group that surrounded her, and at last, when she was alone and about to leave, I found courage to introduce myself and pour forth the tale of my ambition. Her advice was as prompt as if she had studied my problem for years.

"My child," she said, "give up your foolish idea of learning a trade, and go to school. You can't do anything until you have an education. Get it, and get it *now*."

Her suggestion was much to my liking, and I paid her the compliment of acting on it promptly, for the next morning I entered the Big Rapids High School, which was also a preparatory school for college. There I would study, I determined, as long as my money held out, and with the optimism of youth I succeeded in confining my imagination to this side of that crisis. . . .

The preceptress of the high school was Lucy Foot, a college graduate and a remarkable woman. I had heard much of her sympathy and understanding; and on the evening following my first day in school I went to her and repeated the confidences I had reposed in the Reverend Marianna Thompson. My trust in her was justified. She took an immediate interest in me, and proved it at once by putting me into the speaking and debating classes, where I was given every opportunity to hold forth to helpless classmates when the spirit of eloquence moved me. . . .

From that night Miss Foot lost no opportunity of putting me into the foreground of our school affairs. I took part in all our debates, recited yards of poetry to any audience we could attract, and even shone mildly in our amateur theatricals. It was probably owing to all this activity that I attracted the interest of the presiding elder of our district—Dr. Peck, a man of progressive ideas. There was at that time a movement on foot to license women to preach in the Methodist Church, and Dr. Peck was ambitious to be the first presiding elder to have a woman ordained for the Methodist ministry. He had urged Miss Foot to be this pioneer, but her ambitions did not turn in that direction. Though she was a very devout Methodist, she had no wish to be the shepherd of a religious flock. She loved her school-work, and asked nothing better than to remain in it. Gently but persistently she directed the attention of Dr. Peck to me, and immediately things began to happen.

Without telling me to what it might lead, Miss Foot finally arranged a meeting at her home by inviting Dr. Peck and me to dinner. Being unconscious of any significance in the occasion, I chatted light-heartedly about the large issues of life and probably settled most of them to my personal satisfaction. Dr. Peck drew me out and led me on, listened and smiled. When the evening was over and we rose to go, he turned to me with sudden seriousness:

"My quarterly meeting will be held at Ashton," he remarked, casually. "I would like you to preach the quarterly sermon."

For a moment the earth seemed to slip away from my feet. I stared at him in utter stupefaction. Then slowly I realized that, incredible as it seemed, the man was in earnest.

"Why," I stammered, "*I* can't preach a sermon!"

Dr. Peck smiled at me. "Have you ever tried?" he asked.

I started to assure him vehemently that I never had. Then, as if Time had thrown a picture on a screen before me, I saw myself as a little girl preaching alone in the forest, as I had so often preached to a congregation of listening trees. I qualified my answer.

"Never," I said, "to human beings."

Dr. Peck smiled again. "Well," he told me, "the door is open. Enter or not, as you wish."

He left the house, but I remained to discuss his overwhelming proposition with Miss Foot. A sudden sobering thought had come to me.

"But," I exclaimed, "I've never been converted. How can I preach to any one?"

We both had the old-time idea of conversion, which now seems so mistaken. We thought one had to struggle with sin and with the Lord until at last the heart opened, doubts were dispersed, and the light poured in. Miss Foot could only advise me to put the matter before the Lord, to wrestle and to pray; and thereafter, for hours at a time, she worked and prayed with me, alternately urging, pleading, instructing, and sending up petitions in my behalf. Our last session was a dramatic one, which took up the entire night. Long before it was over we were both worn out; but toward morning, either from exhaustion of body or exaltation of soul, I seemed to see the light, and it made me very happy. With all my heart I wanted to preach, and I believed that now at last I had my call. The following day we sent word to Dr. Peck that I would preach the sermon at Ashton as he had asked, but we urged him to say nothing of the matter for the present, and Miss Foot and I also kept the secret locked in our breasts. I knew only too well what view my family and my friends would take of such a step and of me. To them it would mean nothing short of personal disgrace and a blotted page in the Shaw record.

I had six weeks in which to prepare my sermon, and I gave it most of my waking hours as well as those in which I should have been asleep. I took for my text: "And as Moses lifted up the serpent in the wilderness, even so must the Son of Man be lifted up; that whosoever believeth in Him should not perish, but have eternal life."

It was not until three days before I preached the sermon that I found courage to confide my purpose to my sister Mary, and if I had confessed my intention to commit a capital crime she could not have been more disturbed. We two had always been very close, and the death of Eleanor, to whom we were both devoted, had drawn us even nearer to each other. Now Mary's tears and prayers wrung my heart and shook my resolution. But, after all, she was asking me to give up my whole future, to close my ears to my call, and I felt that I could not do it. My decision caused an estrangement between us which lasted for years. On the day preceding the delivery of my sermon I left for Ashton on the afternoon train; and in the same car, but as far away from me as she could get, Mary sat alone and wept throughout the journey. She was going to my mother, but she did not speak to me; and I, for my part, facing both alienation from her and the ordeal before me, found my one comfort in Lucy Foot's presence and understanding sympathy.

There was no church in Ashton, so I preached my sermon in its one little school-house, which was filled with a curious crowd, eager to look at and hear the girl who was defying all conventions by getting out of the pew and into the pulpit. There was much whispering and suppressed excitement before I began, but when I gave out my text silence fell upon the room, and from that moment until I had finished my hearers listened quietly. A kerosene-lamp stood on a stand at my elbow, and as I preached I trembled so violently that the oil shook in its glass globe; but I finished without breaking down, and at the end Dr. Peck, who had his own reasons for nervousness, handsomely assured me that my first sermon was better than his maiden effort had been. It was evidently not a failure, for the next day he invited me to follow him around in his circuit, which included thirty-six appointments; he wished me to preach in each of the thirty-six places, as it was desirable to let the various ministers hear and know me before I applied for my license as a local preacher.

The sermon also had another result, less gratifying. It brought out, on the following morning, the first notice of me ever printed in a newspaper. This was instigated by my brother-in-law, and it was brief but pointed. It read:

> A young girl named Anna Shaw, seventeen years old,* preached at Ashton yesterday. Her real friends deprecate the course she is pursuing.

The little notice had something of the effect of a lighted match applied to gunpowder. An explosion of public sentiment followed it, the entire community arose in consternation, and I became a bone of contention over which friends and strangers alike wrangled until they wore themselves out. The members of my family, meeting in solemn council, sent for me, and I responded. They had a proposition to make, and they lost no time in putting it before me. If I gave up my preaching they would send me to college and pay for my entire course. They suggested Ann Arbor, and Ann Arbor tempted me sorely; but to descend from the pulpit I had at last entered—the pulpit I had visualized in all my childish dreams—was not to be considered. We had a long evening together, and it was a very unhappy one. At the end of it I was given twenty-four hours in which to decide whether I would choose my people and college, or my pulpit and the arctic loneliness of a life that held no family circle. It did not require twenty-four hours of reflection to convince me that I must go my solitary way.

That year I preached thirty-six times, at each of the presiding elder's appointments; and the following spring, at the annual Methodist Conference of our district, held at Big Rapids, my name

---

*She was actually twenty-three.

was presented to the assembled ministers as that of a candidate for a license to preach. There was unusual interest in the result, and my father was among those who came to the Conference to see the vote taken. During these Conferences a minister voted affirmatively on a question by holding up his hand, and negatively by failing to do so. When the question of my license came up the majority of the ministers voted by raising both hands, and in the pleasant excitement which followed my father slipped away. Those who saw him told me he looked pleased; but he sent me no message showing a change of viewpoint, and the gulf between the family and its black sheep remained unabridged. Though the warmth of Mary's love for me had become a memory, the warmth of her hearthstone was still offered me. I accepted it, perforce, and we lived together like shadows of what we had been.

Victoria Woodhull

∽

VICTORIA WOODHULL (1838–1927), the first woman to run for election as president of the United States, was a controversial woman's rights crusader. In addition to women's suffrage, a cause Woodhull aided with the delivery of a well-researched and force-ful argument delivered before the Judiciary Committee of the House of Representatives in 1871, Woodhull embraced the cause of "free love," as sex without marriage was referred to in the nine-teenth century. Attacked for these views in the press and from the pulpit, Woodhull decided to expose the extra-marital affair of one of the clergy, famed abolitionist Henry Ward Beecher. Woodhull told the tale and set forth her reasons in the November 2, 1872, is-sue of her newspaper, *Woodhull & Claflin's Weekly*.

∽

The Great Scandal Case
Detailed Statement of the Whole Matter by Mrs. Woodhull
From *Woodhull & Claflin's Weekly*, November 2, 1872.

I propose, as the commencement of a series of aggressive moral warfare on the social question, to begin in this article with venti-lating one of the most stupendous scandals which has ever oc-curred in any community. I refer to that which has been whispered broad-cast for the last two or three years through the cities of New

---

Woodhull, Victoria. "The Beecher-Tilton Scandal: A Complete History of the Case, from November 1872 to the Present Time, with Mrs. Wood-hull's Statement, as Published in *Woodhull & Claflin's Weekly*, November 2, 1972," New York: F. A. Bancker, 1874, pp. 3–17.

York and Brooklyn, touching the character and conduct of the Rev. * * * * * * in his relations with the family of Mr. T * * * I intend that this article shall burst like a bombshell into the ranks of the moralistic social camp.

I am engaged in officering, and in some sense conducting, a social revolution on the marriage question. I have strong convictions to the effect that this institution, as a *bond* or *promise* to love another to the end of life, and forego all other loves or passional gratifications, has outlived its day of usefulness; that the most intelligent and really virtuous of our citizens, especially in the large cities of Christendom, have outgrown it; are constantly and systematically unfaithful to it; despise and revolt against it, as a slavery in their hearts; and only submit to the semblance of fidelity to it from the dread of a sham public opinion, based on the ideas of the past, and which no longer really represent the convictions of any body. The doctrines of scientific socialism have profoundly penetrated and permeated public opinion. No thought has so rapidly and completely carried the convictions of the thinking portions of the community as stirpiculture. The absurdity is too palpable, when it is pointed out, that we give a hundred times more attention to the laws of breeding as applied to horses and cattle and pigs, and even to our barnyard fowls, than we do to the same laws as applied to human beings. It is equally obvious, on a little reflection, that stirpiculture, or the scientific propagation and cultivation of the human animal, demands free love or freedom of the varied union of the sexes under the dictates of the highest and best knowledge on the subject, as an essential and precedent condition. These considerations are too palpable to be ignored, and they look to the complete and early supersedure of the old and traditional institution of marriage, by the substitution of some better system for the maintenance of women as mothers, and of children as progeny. All intelligent people know these facts and look for the coming of some wiser and better system of social life. The supersedure of marriage in the near future, by some kind of socialistic arrangement, is as much a foregone conclusion with all the best thinkers of to-day as was the approaching dissolution of slavery no more than five or ten years before its actual abolition in the late war.

But, in the meantime, men and women tremble on the brink of the revolution, and hesitate to avow their convictions, while yet partly aware of their rights, and urged by the legitimate impulses of nature, they act upon the new doctrines while they profess obedience to the old. In this manner an organized hypocrisy has become the tone of our modern society. Poltroony, cowardice and deception rule the hour. The continuance, for generations, of such utter falsity, touching one of the most sacred interests of humanity, will almost eradicate the sense of honesty from the human soul. Every consideration of sound expediency demands that these days be shortened; that somebody lead the van in announcement of the higher order of life.

Impelled by such views, I entered the combat with old errors, as I believe them to be, and brought forward, in addition to the wise and powerful words which others have uttered on the subject, the arguments which my own inspiration and reflections suggested. No sooner had I done so than the howl of persecution sounded in my ears. Instead of replying to my arguments, I was assaulted with shameful abuse. I was young and inexperienced in the business of reform, and astounded to find what, as I have since learned from the veterans in the cause, is the usual fact, that the most persistant and slanderous and foul-mouthed accusations came from precisely those who, as I often happened to know, stood nearest to me in their convictions, and whose lives, privately, were a protest against the very repression which I denounce. It was a paradox which I could not understand, that I was denounced as utterly bad for affirming the right of others to do as they did; denounced by the very persons whom my doctrines could alone justify, and who claimed, at the same time, to be conscientious and good men. My position led, nevertheless, to continuous confidences relating to people's own opinions and lives and the opinions and lives of others. My mind became charged with a whole literature of astonishing disclosures. The lives of almost the whole army of spiritualistic and social reformers, of all the schools, were laid open before me. But the matter did not stop there. I found that, to a great extent, the social revolution was as far advanced among leading lights of the business and wealthy circles, and of the various professions, not excluding the clergy and the churches, as among technical reformers.

It was, nevertheless, from these very quarters that I was most severely assailed. It was vexatious and trying, I confess, for one of my temper, to stand under the galling fire of personalities from parties who should have been my warmest advocates, or who should, else, have reformed their lives in accordance with a morality which they wished the public to understand they professed. I was sorely and repeatedly tempted to retort, in personalities, to these attacks. But simply as personality or personal defense, or spiteful retort, I have almost wholly abstained during these years of sharp conflict from making any use of the rich resources at my command for that kind of attack.

But, in the meantime, the question came to press itself upon my consideration: Had I any right, having assumed the championship of social freedom, to forego the use of half the weapons which the facts no less than the philosophy of the subject placed at my command for conducting the war, through any mere tenderness to those who were virtual traitors to the truth which they knew and were surreptitiously acting upon? Had not the sacred cause of human rights and human well being a paramount claim over one's own conduct? Was I not, in withholding the facts and conniving at a putrid mass of seething falsehood and hypocrisy, in some sense a partaker in these crimes; and was I not, in fact, shrinking from the responsibility of making the exposure more through regard for my own sensitiveness and dislike to be hurt than from any true sympathy with those who would be called upon to suffer?

These questions once before my mind would never be disposed of until they were fairly settled upon their own merits, and apart, so far as I could separate them from my own feelings or the feelings of those who were more directly involved. I have come slowly, deliberately, and I may add reluctantly, to my conclusions. I went back to and studied the history of other reforms. I found that Garrison not only denounced slavery in the abstract, but that he attacked it in the concrete. It was not only "the sum of all villainies," but it was the particular villainy of this and that and the other great and influential man, North and South, in the community. Reputations had to suffer. He bravely and persistently called things by their right names. He pointed out and depicted the individual instances of cruelty. He dragged to the light and scathed and stigmatized the individual offenders. He made them a hissing and a by word, so far as in him lay. He shocked the public sensibilities by actual and vivid pictures of slaveholding atrocities, and sent spies into the enemies' camp to search out the instances. The world cried shame! and said it was scandalous, and stopped their ears and blinded their eyes, that their own sensibilities might not be hurt by these horrid revelations. They cast the blanket of their charities and sympathies around the real offenders for their misfortune in being thought to the light and denounced the informer as a malignant and cruel wretch for not covering up scenes too dreadful to be thought upon; as if it were not a thousand times more dreadful that they should be enacted. But the brave old Cyclops ignored alike their criticisms, their protests, and their real and their mock sensibilities, and hammered away at his anvil, forging thunderbolts of the gods; and nobody now says he was wrong. A new public opinion had to be created, and he knew that people had to be shocked, and that individual personal feelings had to be hurt. As Bismarck is reported to have said: "If an omelet has to be made some eggs have to be broken." Every revolution has its terrific cost, if not in blood and treasure, then still in the less tangible but alike real sentimental injury of thousands of sufferers. The preliminary and paramount question is: Ought the revolution to be made, cost what it may? Is the cost to humanity greater of permitting the standing evil to exist? and, if so, then let the cost be incurred, fall where it must. If justice to humanity demand the given expenditure, then accepting the particular enterprise of reform, we accept all its necessary consequences, and enter upon our work, fraught, it may be, with repugnance to ourselves, as it is necessarily with repugnance to others.

I have said that I came slowly, deliberately and reluctantly to the adoption of this method of warfare. I was also hindered and delayed by the fact that if I entered upon it at all I saw no way to avoid making the first onslaught in the most distinguished quarters. It would be cowardice in me to unearth the peccadilloes of little men, and to leave untouched the derelictions and offences of the magnates of social and intellectual power and position. How slowly I have moved in this matter, and how reluctantly it may be inferred, will appear from these little points of history.

More than two years ago these two cities—New York and Brooklyn—were rife with rumors of an awful scandal in * * * Church. These rumors were whispered and covertly alluded to in almost every circle. But the very enormity of the facts, as the world views such matters, hushed the agitation and prevented exposure. The press, warned by the laws of libel, and by a tacit and in the main honorable *consensus* to ignore all such rumors until they enter the courts, or become otherwise matters of irrepressible notoriety, abstained from any direct notice of the subject, and the rumors themselves were finally stifled or forgotten. A few persons only knew something directly of the facts, but among them, situated as I was, I happened to be one. Already the question pressed on me whether I ought not to use the event to forward the cause of social freedom, but I only saw clear in the matter to the limited extent of throwing out some feelers to the public on the subject. It was often a matter of long and anxious consultation between me and my cabinet of confidential advisers.

In June, 1870, *Woodhull & Claflin's Weekly* published an article in reply to Mr. H. C. B's attack on myself in the columns of the *Independent*, the editorship of which had just been vacated by Mr. T * * * In this article the following paragraph occurred: "At this very moment awful and herculean efforts are being made in a neighboring city to suppress the most terrific scandal which has ever astonished and convulsed my community. Clergy, congregation and community will be alike hurled into more than all the consternation which the great explosion in Paris carried to that unfortunate city, if this effort at suppression fail."

Subsequently I published a letter in both *World* and *Times*, in which was the following sentence: "I know a clergyman of eminence in Brooklyn who lives in concubinage with the wife of another clergyman of equal eminence."

It was generally and well understood, among the people of the press especially, than both of these references were to this case of Mr. * * * * * * * and it came to be generally suspected that I was better informed regarding the facts of the case than others, and was reserving publicity of my knowledge for a more convenient season. This suspicion was heightened nearly into conviction when it transpired that Mr. T * * * was an earnest and apparently conscientious advocate of many of my radical theories, as appeared in his far-famed biography of me, and in numerous other publications in the *Golden Age* and elsewhere. Mr. T * * *'s warmest friends were shocked at his course, and when he added to his remarkable proceedings, his brilliant advocacy of my Fourteenth Amendment theory, in his letters to Horace Greeley, Charles Summer and Maj. Carpenter, they considered him irremediably committed to the most radical of all radicals. Assurance was made doubly sure when he presided at Steinway Hall, when I, for the first time, fully and boldly advanced my free-love doctrines. It was noted, however, that this man who stood before the world so fully committed to the broadest principles of liberty, made it convenient to be conspicuously absent from the convention of the Woman Suffragists at Washington last January. All sort of rumors were thereupon rife. Some said he had "gone back" on his advocacy of free-love; some said that a rupture had taken place between him and the leaders of the suffrage movement, and many were the theories brought forward to explain the facts. But the real cause did not transpire until Mr. T * * * was found at Cincinnati urging as a candidate the very man whom he had recently so severely castigated with his most caustic pen. It was then wisely surmised that political ambition, and the editorial chair of the *Tribune*, and his life-long personal devotion to Mr. Greeley, were the inducements which had sufficed to turn his head and heart away, temporarily at least, from our movement.

About this time, rumors floated out that Mrs. Woodhull, disgusted at the recent conduct of Mr. T * * * and the advice given him by certain of his friends, was animadverting in not very measured terms upon their conduct. An article specifying matters involving several of these persons obtained considerable circulation, and with other circumstances, such as the definite statement of facts, with names and places, indicated that the time was at hand, nigh even unto the door, when the things that had remained hidden should be brought to light, and the whole affair be made public.

Some time in August last there appeared in the *Evening Telegram* a paragraph which hinted broadly at the nature of the impending *exposé*. About this time a gentleman from abroad, to whom I had related some of the facts in my possession, repeated them to a member of Rev. * * * church, who denounced the whole story as an infamous libel; but some days later he acknowledged both to his friend and me that he had inquired into the matter and had learned that it was "a damning fact." This gentleman occupies a responsible position, and his word is good for all that he utters. Such was the facility with which confirmations were obtained when sought for. When, therefore, those who were conversant with the case, saw in the *Boston Herald* and other papers that I had made a public statement regarding the whole matter, they were not in the least surprised. It shows that the press had concluded that it was time to recognize the sensation which, whether they would or not, was destined soon to shake the social structure from its foundation.

A reporter was then specially detailed to interview me in order, as he said, that the matter might be published in certain of the New York papers. Why that interview has been suppressed is not possible to affirm with certainty, but it is easy to guess. An impecunious reporter can be bought off with a few hundred dollars. And there are those who would readily pay thousands to shut the columns of the press against this exposure. Fortunately I have a nearly verbatim copy of the report, as the interviewer prepared it, and in this shape I shall now present it to the public. . . .

The following is the re-statement from notes, aided by my recollection, of the interviewing upon this subject by the press reporter already alluded to:

Reporter:—"Mrs. Woodhull, I have called to ask if you are prepared and willing to furnish a full statement of the Beecher-Tilton scandal for publication in the city papers?"

Mrs. Woodhull:—"I do not know that I ought to object to repeating whatever I know in relation to it. You understand, of course, that I take a different view of such matters from those usually avowed by other people. Still I have good reason to think that far more people entertain views corresponding to mine than dare to assert them or openly live up to them."

Reporter:—"How, Mrs. Woodhull, would you state in the most condensed way your opinions on this subject, as they differ from those avowed and ostensibly lived by the public at large?"

Mrs. Woodhull:—"I believe that the marriage institution, like slavery and monarchy, and many other things which have been good or necessary in their day, is now *effete*, and in a general sense injurious, instead of being beneficial to the community, although of course it must continue to linger until better institutions can be formed. I mean by marriage, in this connection, any *forced* or *obligatory tie* between the sexes, *any legal intervention* or *constraint* to prevent people from adjusting their love relations precisely as they do their religious affairs in this country, in complete personal freedom; changing and improving them from time to time, and according circumstances."

Reporter:—"I confess, then, I cannot understand why you of all persons should have any fault to find with Mr. Beecher, even assuming everything to be true of him which I have hitherto heard only vaguely hinted at."

Mrs. Woodhull:—"*I* have no fault to find with him in any such sense as you mean, nor in any such sense as that in which the world will condemn him. I have no doubt that he has done the very best which he could do under all the circumstances—with his demanding physical nature, and with the terrible restrictions upon a clergyman's life, imposed by that ignorant public opinion about physiological laws, which they, nevertheless, more, perhaps, than any other class, do their best to perpetuate. The fault I find with Mr. Beecher is of a wholly different character, as I have told him repeatedly and frankly, and as he knows very well. It is, indeed, the exact opposite to that for which the world will condemn him. I condemn him because I know, and have had every opportunity to know, that he entertains, on conviction, substantially the same views which I entertain on the social question; that, under the influence of these convictions, he has lived for many years, perhaps for his whole adult life, in a manner which the religious and moralist public ostensibly, and to some extent really, condemn; that he has permitted himself, nevertheless, to be over-awed by public opinion, to profess to believe otherwise than as he does believe, to have helped to maintain for these many years that very social slavery under which he was chafing, and against which he was secretly revolting both in thought and practice; and that he has, in a word, consented, and still consents to be a hypocrite. The fault with which I, therefore, charge him, is not infidelity to the old ideas, but unfaithfulness to the new. He is in heart, in conviction and in life, an ultra socialist reformer; while in seeming and pretension he is the upholder of the old social slavery, and, therefore, does what he can to crush out and oppose me and those who act and believe with me in forwarding the great social revolution. I know, myself, so little of the sentiment of fear, I have so little respect for an ignorant and prejudiced public opinion, I am so accustomed to say the thing that I think and do the thing that I believe to be right, that I doubt not I am in danger of having far too little sympathy with the real difficulties of a man situated as Mr. Beecher has been, and is, when he contemplates the idea of facing social opprobrium. Speaking from my feelings, I am prone to denounce him as a poltroon, a coward and a sneak; not, as I tell you, for anything that he has done, and for which the world would condemn him, but for failing to do what it seems to me so clear he ought to do; for failing, in a word, to stand shoulder to shoulder with me and others who are endeavoring to hasten a social regeneration which he believes in. . . . Let it be once understood *that whosoever is true to himself or herself is thereby, and necessarily, true to all others,* and the whole social question will be solved. *The barter and sale of wives stands on the same moral footing as the barter and sale of slaves.* The god-implanted human affections cannot, and will not, be any longer subordinated to these external, legal restrictions and conventional engagements. *Every human being belongs to himself or herself by a higher title than any which, by surrenders or arrangements or promises, he or she can confer upon any other human being. Self-ownership is inalienable.* These truths are the latest and greatest discoveries in true science. . . ."

So much for the interviewing which was to have been published some months ago; but when it failed or was suppressed, I was still so far undecided that I took no steps in the matter, and had no definite plan for the future in respect to it, until the events as I have recited then, which occurred at Boston. Since then I have not doubted that I must make up my mind definitely to act aggressarily in this matter, and to use the facts in my knowledge to compel a more wide-spread discussion of the social question. I take the step deliberately, as an agitator and social revolutionist, which is my profession. . . .

I believe, as the law of peace, *in the right of privacy,* in the sanctity of individual relations. It is nobody's business but their own, in the absolute view, what Mr. Beecher and Mrs. Tilton have done, or may choose at any time to do, as between themselves. And the world needs, too, to be taught just that lesson. . . . It is not, therefore, Mr. Beecher as the individual that I pursue, but Mr. Beecher as the representative man: Mr. Beecher as a power in the world; and Mr. Beecher as my auxiliary in a great war for freedom, or Mr. Beecher as a violent enemy and a powerful hindrance to all that I am bent on accomplishing.

To Mr. Beecher, as the individual citizen, I tender, therefore, my humble apology, meaning and deeply feeling what I say, for this or any interference on my part, with his private conduct. I hold that Mr. Tilton himself, that Mrs. Beecher herself, have no more right to inquire, or to know or spy over, with a view to knowing, what has transpired between Mr. Beecher and Mrs. Tilton than they have to know what I ate for breakfast, or where I shall spend my next evening; and that Mr. Beecher's congregation and the public at large have just as little right to know or to inquire. I hold that the so-called morality of society is a complicated mass of sheer impertinence and a scandal on the civilization of this advanced century, that the system of social espionage under which we live is damnable, and that the very first axiom of a true morality is for the people *to mind their own business*, and learn to respect, religiously, the social freedom and the sacred social privacy of all others; but it was the paradox of Christ, that as the Prince of Peace, he still brought on earth, *not peace* but *a sword*. It is the paradox of life that, in order to have peace, we must first have war; and it is the paradox of my position that, believing in the right of privacy and in the perfect right of Mr. Beecher socially, morally and divinely to have sought the embraces of Mrs. Tilton, or of any other woman or women whom he loved and who loved him, and being a promulgator and public champion of those very rights, I still invade the most secret and sacred affairs of his life, and drag them to the light and expose him to the opprobrium and vilification of the public. I do again, and with deep sincerity, ask his forgiveness. But the case is exceptional, and what I do I do for a great purpose. The social world is in the very agony of its new birth, or, to resume the warlike simile, the leaders of progress are in the very act of storming the last fortress of bigotry and error. Somebody must be hurled forward into the gap. I have the power, I think, to compel Mr. Beecher to go forward and to do the duty for humanity from which he shrinks; and I should, myself, be false to the truth if I were to shrink from compelling him. . . . I believe I see clearly and prophetically for him in the future a work a hundred times greater than all he has accomplished in the past. I believe, as I have said, a wise Providence, or, as I term it, and believe it to be, the conscious and well calculated interference of the spirit world, has forecast and prepared these very events as a part of the drama of this great social revolution. . . .

So again, it was not the coming together of these two loving natures in the most intimate embrace, nor was it that nature blessed that embrace with the natural fruits of love which was the bad element in this whole transaction. They, on the contrary, were good elements, beautiful and divine elements, and among God's best things for man.

The evil and the whole evil in this whole matter, then, lies elsewhere. It lies in a false and artificial or manufactured opinion, in respect to this very question of what is good or what is evil in such matters. It lies in the belief that society has the right to prohibit, to prescribe and regulate, or in any manner to interfere with the private love manifestations of its members, any more than it has to prescribe their food and their drink. It lies in the belief consequent upon this, that lovers own their lovers, husbands their wives and wives their husbands, and that they have the right to complain of, to spy over, and to interfere, even to the extent of murder, with every other or outside manifestation of love. It lies in the *compulsory hypocrisy and systematic falsehood* which is thus enforced and inwrought into the very structure of society, and in the consequent and wide-spread injury to the whole community.

Susan B. Anthony

~

SUSAN B. ANTHONY (1820–1906), one of the foremost leaders of the woman's suffrage movement, agreed with Missouri lawyer Francis Minor when he suggested that women could claim suffrage under the Fourteenth Amendment. Minor pointed out that the Fourteenth Amendment, before specifically addressing the voting rights of African-American males, stated that "All persons born or naturalized in the United States . . . are citizens of the United States and of the State wherein they reside. No State shall make or enforce any law which shall abridge the privileges or immunities of citizens of the United States. . . ." He reasoned that, since women were clearly citizens according to the Amendment and voting was a privilege of citizenship, no state could bar women from voting.

Susan B. Anthony voted in 1872 and was promptly arrested. Since she would not be able to speak in her own defense at trial due to gender, Anthony toured the countryside to plead her case in the months beforehand. At the 1873 trial itself, she was forced to sit in silence until a verdict was rendered. Convicted of illegal voting and fined $100, she was asked by U.S. Associate Justice Ward Hunt, "Has the prisoner anything to say why sentence should not be pronounced?" Anthony used the opportunity to speak her mind. (The judge's repeated attempts to silence her have been retained.)

Stanton, Elizabeth Cady, Susan B. Anthony, and Matilda Joslyn Gage. *History of Woman Suffrage*. Vol. 2, 1882. Rpt., Salem, NH: Ayer Company, 1985, pp. 630–646, 687–689.

～

Friends and Fellow-citizens:
I stand before you to-night, under indictment for the alleged crime of having voted illegally at the last Presidential election. I shall endeavor this evening to prove to you that in voting, I not only committed no crime, but simply exercised my "citizen's right," guaranteed to me and all United States citizens by the National Constitution, beyond the power of any State to deny.

Our democratic republican government is based on the idea of the natural right of every individual member thereof to a voice and a vote in making and executing the laws. We assert the province of government to be to secure the people in the enjoyment of their inalienable rights. We throw to the winds the old dogma that governments can give rights. Before governments were organized, no one denies that each individual possessed the right to protect his own life, liberty, and property. And when 100 or 1,000,000 people enter into a free government, they do not barter away their natural rights; they simply pledge themselves to protect each other in the enjoyment of them, through prescribed judicial and legislative tribunals. They agree to abandon the methods of brute force in the adjustment of their differences, and adopt those of civilization. The Declaration of Independence, the National and State Constitutions, and the organic laws of the Territories, all alike propose to protect the people in the exercise of their God-given rights. Not one of them pretends to bestow rights.

> All men are created equal, and endowed by their Creator with certain inalienable rights. Among these are life, liberty, and the pursuit of happiness. That to secure these, governments are instituted among men, deriving their just powers from the consent of the governed.

Here is no shadow of government authority over rights, nor exclusion of any class from their full and equal enjoyment. Here is pronounced the rights of all men, and "consequently," as the Quaker preacher said, "of all women," to a voice in the government. And here, in this very first paragraph of the Declaration, is the assertion of the natural right of all to the ballot; for, how can "the consent of the governed" be given, if the right to vote be denied. Again:

> That whenever any form of government becomes destructive of these ends, it is the right of the people to alter or abolish it, and to institute a new government, laying its foundations on such principles, and organizing its powers in such forms as to them shall seem most likely to effect their safety and happiness.

Surely, the right of the whole people to vote is here clearly implied. For, however destructive to their happiness this government might become, a disfranchised class could neither alter nor abolish it, nor institute a new one, except by the old brute force method of insurrection and rebellion. One half of the people of this Nation today are utterly powerless to blot from the statute books an unjust law, or to write there a new and a just one. The women, dissatisfied as they are with this form of government, that enforces taxation without representation,—that compels them to obey laws to which they have never given their consent—that imprisons and hangs them without a trial by a jury of their peers—that robs them, in marriage, of the custody of their own persons, wages, and children—are this half of the people left wholly at the mercy of the other half, in direct violation of the spirit and letter of the declarations of the framers of this government, every one of which was based on the immutable principle of equal rights to all. By those declarations, kings, priests, popes, aristocrats, were all alike dethroned, and placed on a common level, politically, with the lowliest born subject or serf. By them, too, men, as such, were deprived of their divine right to rule, and placed on a political level with women. By the practice of those declarations all class and caste distinction will be abolished; and slave, serf, plebeian, wife, woman, all alike, will bound from their subject position to the proud platform of equality.

The preamble of the Federal Constitution says:

> We, the people of the United States, in order to form a more perfect union, establish justice, insure domestic tranquility, provide for the common defense, promote the general welfare, and secure

the blessings of liberty to ourselves and our posterity, do ordain and establish this Constitution for the United States of America.

It was we, the people, not we, the white male citizens, nor yet we, the male citizens, but we, the whole people, who formed this Union. And we formed it, not to give the blessings of liberty, but to secure them; not to the half of ourselves and the half of our posterity, but to the whole people—women as well as men. And it is downright mockery to talk to women of their enjoyment of the blessings of liberty while they are denied the use of the only means of securing them provided by this democratic republican government—the ballot. . . .

What, I ask you, is the distinctive difference between the inhabitants of a Monarchical and those of a Republican form of government, save that in the Monarchical the people are subjects, helpless, powerless, bound to obey laws made by superiors—while in the Republican, the people are citizens, individual sovereigns, all clothed with equal power, to make and unmake both their laws and their law makers. And the moment you deprive a person of his right to a voice in the government, you degrade him from the status of a citizen to that of a subject, and it matters very little to him whether his monarch be an individual tyrant, as is the Czar of Russia, or a 15,000,000 headed monster, as here in the United States.

But, it is urged, the use of the masculine pronouns he, his, and him, in all the constitutions and laws, is proof that only men were meant to be included in their provisions. If you insist on this version of the letter of the law, we shall insist that you be consistent, and accept the other horn of the dilemma, which would compel you to exempt women from taxation for the support of the government, and from penalties for the violation of laws.

A year and a half ago I was at Walla Walla, Washington Territory. I saw there a theatrical company, the "Pixley Sisters," playing before crowded houses every night of the whole week of the Territorial fair. The eldest of those three fatherless girls was scarce eighteen. Yet every night a United States officer stretched out his long fingers, and clutched six dollars of the proceeds of the exhibitions of those orphan girls, who, but a few years before, were starvelings in the streets of Olympia, the capital of that far-off north-west territory. So the poor widow, who keeps a boarding-house, manufactures shirts, or sell apples and peanuts on the street corners of our cities, is compelled to pay taxes from her scanty pittance. I would that the women of this republic at once resolve, never again to submit to taxation until their right to vote be recognized. Miss Sarah E. Wall, of Worcester, Mass., twenty years ago, took this position. For several years, the officers of the law distrained her property and sold it to meet the necessary amount; still she persisted, and would not yield an iota, though every foot of her lands should be struck off under the hammer. And now, for several years, the assessor has left her name off the tax list, and the collector passed her by without a call. Mrs. J. S. Weeden, of Viroqua, Wis., for the past six years has refused to pay her taxes, though the annual assessment is $75. Mrs. Ellen Van Valkenburg, of Santa Cruz, Cal., who sued the County Clerk for refusing the register her name, declares she will never pay another dollar of tax until allowed to vote; and all over the country, women property holders are waking up to the injustice of taxation without representation, and ere long will refuse, *en masse*, to submit to the imposition.

There is no she, or her, or hers, in the tax laws. . . .

The same is true of all the criminal laws:

No person shall be compelled to be a witness against himself, etc.

In the law of May 31, 1870, the 19th section of which I am charged with having violated; not only are all the pronouns masculine, but everybody knows that that particular section was intended expressly to hinder the rebels from voting. It reads:

If any person shall knowingly vote without his having a lawful right, etc.

Precisely so with all the papers served on me—the U.S. Marshal's warrant, the bail-bond, the petition for habeas corpus, the bill of indictment—not one of them had a feminine pronoun printed in it; but, to make them applicable to me, the Clerk of the Court made a little carat at the left of "he" and placed an "s" over it, thus making she out of he. Then the letters "is" were scratched out, the little carat placed under and "er" over, to make her out of his, and I insist if government officials may thus manipulate the pronouns to tax, fine, imprison, and hang women, women may take the same liberty with them to secure to themselves their right to a voice in the government.

So long as any classes of men were denied their right to vote, the government made a show of consistency, by exempting them from taxation. When a property qualification of $250 was required of black men in New York, they were not compelled to pay taxes, so long as they were content to report themselves worth less than that sum; but the moment the black man died, and his property fell to his widow, the black woman's name would be put on the assessor's list, and she be compelled to pay taxes on the same property exempted to her husband. The same is true of ministers in New York. So long as the minister lives, he is exempted from taxation on $1,500 of property, but the moment the breath goes out of his body, his widow's name will go down on the assessor's list, and she will have to pay taxes on the $1,500. So much for the special legislation in favor of women. In all the penalties and burdens of the government (except the military), women are reckoned as citizens, equally with men. Also, in all the privileges and immunities, save those of the jury-box and ballot-box, the two fundamental privileges on which rest all the others. The United States government not only taxes, fines, imprisons, and hangs women, but it allows them to pre-empt lands, register ships, and take out passport and naturalization papers. . . .

If a foreign-born woman, by becoming a naturalized citizen, is entitled all rights and privileges of citizenship, is not a native-born woman by her National citizenship, possessed of equal rights and privileges? . . .

Though the words persons, people, inhabitants, electors, citizens, are all used indiscriminately in the National and State constitutions, there was always a conflict of opinion, prior to the war, as to whether they were synonymous terms, as for instance:

No *person* shall be a representative who shall not have been seven years a *citizen*, and who shall not, when elected, be an *inhabitant* of that State in which he is chosen. No *person* shall be a senator who shall not have been a *citizen* of the United States, and an *inhabitant* of that State in which he is chosen.

But, whatever room there was for a doubt, under the old regime, the adoption of the XIV. Amendment settled that question forever, in its first sentence:

All persons born or naturalized in the United States and subject to the jurisdiction thereof, are citizens of the United States and of the State wherein they reside.

And the second settles the equal status of all persons—all citizens:

No State shall make or enforce any law which shall abridge the privileges or immunities of citizens; nor shall any State deprive any person of life, liberty or property, without due process of law, nor deny to any person within its jurisdiction the equal protection of the laws.

The only question left to be settled now, is: Are women persons? And I hardly believe any of our opponents will have the hardihood to say they are not. Being persons, then, women are citizens, and no State has a right to make any new law, or to enforce any old law, that shall abridge their privileges or immunities. Hence, every discrimination against women in the constitutions and laws of the several States, is to-day null and void, precisely as is every one against negroes. Is the right to vote one of the privileges or immunities of citizens? I think the disfranchised ex-rebels, and the ex-state prisoners will all agree with me, that it is not only one of them, *but the one without which all the others are nothing.* Seek first the kingdom of the ballot, and all things else shall be given thee, is the political injunction. . . .

But if you will insist that the XV. Amendment's emphatic interdiction against robbing United States citizens of their right to vote, "on account of race, color, or previous condition of servitude," is a recognition of the right, either of the United States or any State, to rob citizens of that right for any or all other reasons, I will prove to you that the class of citizens for which I now plead, and to which I belong, may be, and are, by all the principles of our Government, and many of the laws of the States, included under the term "previous condition of servitude."

First.—The married women and their legal status. What is servitude? "The condition of a slave." What is a slave? "A person who is robbed of the proceeds of his labor; a person who is subject to the will of another."

By the law of Georgia, South Carolina, and all the States of the South, the negro had no right to the custody and control of his person. He belonged to his master. If he was disobedient, the master had the right to use correction. If the negro didn't like the correction, and attempted to run away, the master had a right to use coercion to bring him back. By the law of every State in this Union to-day, North as well as South, the married woman has no right to the custody and control of her person. The wife belongs to her husband; and if she refuses obedience to his will, he may use moderate correction, and if she doesn't like his moderate correction, and attempts to leave his "bed and board," the husband may use moderate coercion to bring her back. The little word "moderate," you see, is the saving clause for the wife, and would doubtless be overstepped should her offended husband administer his correction with the "cat-o'-nine-tails," or accomplish his coercion with blood-hounds.

Again, the slave had no right to the earnings of his hands, they belonged to his master; no right to the custody of his children, they belonged to his master; no right to sue or be sued, or testify in the courts. If he committed a crime, it was the master who must sue or be sued. In many of the States there has been special legislation, giving to married women the right to property inherited, or received by bequest, or earned by the pursuit of any avocation outside of the home; also, giving her the right to sue and be sued in matters pertaining to such separate property; *but not a single State of this Union has ever secured the wife in the enjoyment of her right to the joint ownership of the joint earnings of the marriage copartnership.* And since, in the nature of things, the vast majority of married women never earn a dollar by work outside of their families, nor inherit a dollar from their fathers, it follows that from the day of their marriage to the day of the death of their husbands, not one of them ever has a dollar, except it shall please her husband to let her have it. In some of the States, also, there have been laws passed giving to the mother a joint right with the father in the guardianship of the children. But twenty years ago, when our woman's rights movement commenced, by the laws of the State of New York, and all the States, the father had the sole custody and control of the children. No matter if he were a brutal, drunken libertine, he had the legal right, without the mother's consent, to apprentice her sons to rumsellers, or her daughters to brothel keepers. He could even will away an unborn child, to some other person than the mother. And in many of the States the law still prevails, and legal mothers are still utterly powerless under the common law.

I doubt if there is, to-day, a State in this Union where a married woman can sue or be sued for slander of character, and until quite recently there was not one in which she could sue or be sued for injury of person. However damaging to the wife's reputation any slander may be, she is wholly powerless to institute legal proceedings against her accuser, unless her husband shall join with her; and how often have we heard of the husband conspiring with some outside barbarian to blast the good name of his wife. A married woman can not testify in the courts in cases of joint interest with her husband. A good farmer's wife near Earlville, Ill., who had all the rights she wanted, went to the dentist of the village, who made her a full set of false teeth, both upper and under. The dentist pronounced them an admirable fit, and the wife declared they gave her fits to wear them; that she could neither chew nor talk with them in her mouth. The dentist sued the husband; his counsel brought the wife as witness; the judge ruled her off the stand, saying:

> A married woman can not be a witness in matters of joint interest between herself and her husband.

Think of it, ye good wives, the false teeth in your mouths a joint interest with your husbands, about which you are legally incompetent to speak! If in our frequent and shocking railroad accidents a married woman is injured in her person, in nearly all of the States, it is her husband who must sue the company, and it is to her husband that the damages, if there are any, will be awarded. In Ashfield, Mass., supposed to be the most advanced of any State in the Union in all things, humanitarian as well as intellectual, a married woman was severely injured by a defective sidewalk. Her husband sued the corporation and recovered $13,000 damages. And those $13,000 belong to him *bona fide*; and whenever that unfortunate wife wishes a dollar of it to supply her needs she must ask her husband for it; and if the man be of a narrow, selfish, niggardly nature, she will have to hear him say, every time:

> "What have you done, my dear, with the twenty-five cents I gave you yesterday?"

Isn't such a position, I ask you, humiliating enough to be called "servitude"? That husband, as would any other husband, in nearly every State of this Union, sued and obtained damages for the loss of the services of his wife, precisely as the master, under the old slave regime, would have done, had his slave been thus injured, and precisely as he himself would have done had it been his ox, cow, or horse instead of his wife. There is an old saying that "a rose by any other name would smell as sweet," and I submit if the deprivation by law of the ownership of one's own person, wages, property, children, the denial of the right as an individual, to sue and be sued, and to testify in the courts, is not a condition of servitude most bitter and absolute, though under the sacred name of marriage?

Does any lawyer doubt my statement of the legal status of married women? I will remind him of the fact that the old common law of England prevails in every State in this Union, except where the Legislature has enacted special laws annulling it. And I am ashamed that not one State has yet blotted from its statute books the old common law of marriage, by which Blackstone, summed up in the fewest words possible, is made to say: "Husband and wife are one, and that one is the husband."

Thus may all married women, wives, and widows, by the laws of the several States, be technically included in the XV. Amendment's specification of "condition of servitude," present or previous. And not only married women, but I will also prove to you that by all the great fundamental principles of our free government, the entire womanhood of the nation is in a "condition of servitude" as surely as were our revolutionary fathers, when they rebelled against old King George. Women are taxed without representation, governed without their consent, tried, convicted, and punished without a jury of their peers. And is all this tyranny any less humiliating and degrading to women under our democratic-republican government to-day than it was to men under their aristocratic, monarchical government one hundred years ago? There is not an utterance of old John Adams, John Hancock, or Patrick Henry, but finds a living response in the soul of every intelligent, patriotic woman of the nation. Bring to me a common-sense woman property holder, and I will show you one whose soul is fired with all the indignation of 1776, every time the tax-gatherer presents himself at her door. . . .

Is anything further needed to prove woman's condition of servitude sufficiently orthodox to entitle her to the guarantees of the XV. Amendment? Is there a man who will not agree with me, that to talk of freedom without the ballot, is mockery—is slavery—to the women of this Republic? . . .

And it is upon this just interpretation of the United States Constitution that our National Woman Suffrage Association, which celebrates the twenty-fifth anniversary of the woman's right movement, in New York on the 6th of May next, has based all its arguments and action the past three years. We no longer petition Legislature or Congress to give us the right to vote. We appeal to the women everywhere to exercise their too long neglected "citizen's right to vote." We appeal to the inspectors of election everywhere to receive the votes of all United States citizens, as it is their duty to do. We appeal to United States commissioners and marshals to arrest the inspectors who reject the names and votes of United States citizens, as it is their duty to do, and leave those alone who, like our eighth ward inspectors, perform their duties faithfully and well. We ask the juries to fail to return verdicts of "guilty" against honest, law-abiding, tax-paying United States citizens for offering their votes at our elections; or against intelligent, worthy young men, inspectors of election, for receiving and counting such citizens' votes. We ask the judges to render true and unprejudiced opinions of the law, and wherever there is room for a doubt to give its benefit on the side of liberty and equality to women. . . .

Susan B. Anthony's Comments
Upon Her Conviction for Illegal Voting, 1873

The Court: The prisoner will stand up. Has the prisoner anything to say why sentence shall not be pronounced?

Miss Anthony: Yes, your honor, I have many things to say; for in your ordered verdict of guilty, you have trampled underfoot every vital principle of our government. My natural rights, my civil rights, my political rights, are all alike ignored. Robbed of the fundamental privilege of citizenship, I am degraded from the status of a citizen to that of a subject; and not only myself individually, but all of my sex, are, by your honor's verdict, doomed to political subjection under this so-called Republican government.

Judge Hunt: The Court can not listen to a rehearsal of arguments the prisoner's counsel has already consumed three hours in presenting.

Miss Anthony: May it please your honor, I am not arguing the question, but simply stating the reasons why sentence can not, in justice, be pronounced against me. Your denial of my citizen's right to vote is the denial of my right of consent as one of the governed, the denial of my right of representation as one of the taxed, the denial of my right to a trial by a jury of my peers as an offender against law, therefore, the denial of my sacred rights to life, liberty, property, and—

Judge Hunt: The Court can not allow the prisoner to go on.

Miss Anthony: But your honor will not deny me this one and only poor privilege of protest against this high-handed outrage upon my citizen's rights. May it please the Court to remember that since the day of my arrest last November, this is the first time that either myself or any person of my disfranchised class has been allowed a word of defense before judge or jury—

Judge Hunt: The prisoner must sit down; the Court can not allow it.

Miss Anthony: All my prosecutors, from the 8th Ward corner grocery politician, who entered the complaint, to the United States Marshal, Commissioner, District Attorney, District Judge, your honor on the bench, not one is my peer, but each and all are my political sovereigns; and had you honor submitted my case to the jury, as was clearly your duty, even then I should have had just cause of protest, for not one of those men was my peer; but, native or foreign, white or black, rich or poor, educated or ignorant, awake or asleep, sober or drunk, each and every man of them was my political superior; hence, in no sense, my peer. Even, under such circumstances, a commoner of England, tried before a jury of lords, would have far less cause to complain than should I, a woman, tried before a jury of men. Even my counsel, the Hon. Henry R. Selden, who has argued my cause so ably, so earnestly, so unanswerably before your honor, is my political sovereign. Precisely as no disfranchised person is entitled to sit upon a jury, and no woman is entitled to the franchise, so, none but a regularly admitted lawyer is allowed to practice in the courts, and no woman can gain admission to the bar—hence, jury, judge, counsel, must all be of the superior class.

Judge Hunt: The Court must insist—the prisoner has been tried according to the established forms of law.

Miss Anthony: Yes, your honor, but by forms of law all made by men, interpreted by men, administered by men, in favor of men, and against women; and hence, your honor's ordered verdict of guilty, against a United States citizen for the exercise of "that citizen's right to vote," simply because that citizen was a woman and not a man. But, yesterday, the same man-made forms of law declared it a crime punishable with $1,000 fine and six months' imprisonment, for you, or me, or any of us, to give a cup of cold water, a crust of bread, or a night's shelter to a panting fugitive as he was tracking his way to Canada. And every man or woman in whose veins coursed a drop of human sympathy violated that wicked law, reckless of consequences, and was justified in so doing. As then the slaves who got their freedom must take it over, or under, or through the unjust forms of law, precisely so now must women, to get their right to a voice in this Government, take it; and I have taken mine, and mean to take it at every possible opportunity.

Judge Hunt: The Court orders the prisoner to sit down. It will not allow another word.

Miss Anthony: When I was brought before your honor for trial, I hoped for a broad and liberal interpretation of the Constitution and its recent amendments, that should declare all United States citizens under its protecting ægis—that should declare equality of rights the national guarantee to all persons born or naturalized in the United States. But failing to get this justice—failing, even, to get a trial by a jury *not* of my peers—I ask not leniency at your hands—but rather the full rigors of the law.

Judge Hunt: The Court must insist—*(Here the prisoner sat down.)*

Judge Hunt: The prisoner will stand up. *(Here Miss Anthony arose again.)* The sentence of the Court is that you pay a fine of one hundred dollars and the costs of the prosecution.

Miss Anthony: May it please your honor, I shall never pay a dollar of your unjust penalty. All the stock in trade I possess is a $10,000 debt, incurred by publishing my paper—*The Revolution*—four years ago, the sole object of which was to educate all women to do precisely as I have done, rebel against your man-made, unjust, unconstitutional forms of law, that tax, fine, imprison, and hang women, while they deny them the right of representation in the Government; and I shall work on with might and main to pay every dollar of that honest debt, but not a penny shall go to this unjust claim. And I shall earnestly and persistently continue to urge all women to the practical recognition of the old revolutionary maxim, that "Resistance to tyranny is obedience to God."

Judge Hunt: Madam, the Court will not order you committed until the fine is paid.

Frances E. Willard

FRANCES E. WILLARD (1839–1898) was dean of women at Northwestern University from 1873–1874 and president of the National Woman's Christian Temperance Union from 1879 until her death in 1898. In her autobiography, *Glimpses of Fifty Years*, she recalls her conversion to the temperance cause and her assumption of a leadership role in that struggle.

From my earliest recollection there hung on the dining-room wall at our house, a pretty steel engraving. It was my father's certificate of membership in the Washingtonian Society, and was dated about 1835. He had never been a drinking man, was a reputable young husband, father, business man and church member, but when the movement reached Churchville, near Rochester, N.Y., he joined it. The little picture represented a bright, happy temperance home with a sweet woman at the center, and over against it a dismal, squalid house with a drunken man staggering in, bottle in hand. Unconsciously and ineffaceably I learned from that one object-lesson what the precepts and practice of my parents steadily enforced, that we were to let strong drink alone.

In 1855 I cut from my favorite *Youth's Cabinet*, the chief juvenile paper of that day, the following pledge, and pasting it in our family Bible, insisted on its being signed by every member of the family—parents, brother, sister and self.

Willard, Frances E. *Glimpses of Fifty Years: The Autobiography of an American Woman.* Chicago: Women's Temperance Publication Association, 1889, pp. 331–341.

"A pledge we make no wine to take,
Nor brandy red that turns the head,
Nor fiery rum that ruins home,
Nor brewers' beer, for that we fear,
And cider, too, will never do.
To quench our thirst, we'll always bring
Cold water from the well or spring;
So here we pledge perpetual hate
To all that can intoxicate."

It is still there, thus signed, and represents the first bit of temperance work I ever did. Its object was simply to enshrine in the most sacred place our home afforded a pledge that I considered uniquely sacred. Nobody asked me to sign it, nor was there a demand because of exterior temptation, for we were living in much isolation on a farm three miles from Janesville, Wis., where my childhood was invested—not "spent."

Coming to Evanston, Ill., in 1858, we found a prohibition village, the charter of the University forbidding the sale of any intoxicating liquor as a beverage.

Temperance was a matter of course in this "Methodist heaven" where we have lived from that day to this, from the time it had but a few hundred, until now when it claims seven thousand inhabitants.

About 1863–'65 a "Temperance Alliance" was organized here by L. L. Greenleaf, then our leading citizen, the Chicago representative of the Fairbanks' firm, who have made St. Johnsbury, Vt., a model temperance town. Before that Alliance I read one temperance essay when I was a quiet school teacher amid these shady groves, and one evening at the "Alliance sociable" I offered the pledge for the first time and was rebuffed by a now distinguished literary man, then a paster and editor in our village. This was my first attempt and his brusque and almost angry negative hurt me to the heart. We are excellent friends all the same, and I do not believe he dreams how much he pained me, so little do we know what touches us, and what we touch, as we wend our way along life's crowded street.

In all my teaching, in Sunday-school, public school and semi-nary, I never mentioned total abstinence until the winter of the Cru-sade, taking it always as a matter of course that my pupils didn't drink, nor did they as a rule.

I never in my life saw wine offered in my own country but once, when Mrs. Will Knox, of Pittsburgh, a former Sunday-school scholar of my sister Mary, brought cake and wine to a young lady of high family in our church, and to me, when we went to call on her after her wedding. "Not to be singular" we touched it to our lips—but that was twenty-five years ago, before the great examples burnt into the Nation's memory and conscience by Lucy Webb Hayes, Rose Cleveland and Frances Folsom Cleveland.

That was truly a prophetic innovation at the White House when our gracious Mrs. Hayes replaced the dinner with its wine-glasses by the stately and elegant reception. Perhaps while men rule the state in their government "of the minority, by the minority, for the minority," its highest expression will still be the dinner-table with its clinking glasses and plenty of tobacco-smoke afterward, but when men and women both come into the kingdom for the glad new times that hasten to be here, the gustatory nerve will be dethroned once and for evermore. For there are so many more wor-thy and delightful ways of investing (not "spending") one's time; there are so many better things to do. The blossoming of women into deeds of philanthropy gives us a hint of the truer forms of so-ciety that are to come. Emerson said, "We descend to meet," be-cause he claims that we are on a higher plane when alone with God and nature. But this need not be so. Doubtless in the outworn and stereotyped forms of society where material pleasures still hold sway, we do "descend to meet," but when a philanthropic purpose determines our companionships, and leads to our convenings, then we climb together into purer and more vital air. The "coming women," nay, the women who have come, have learned the loveli-est meanings of the word "society." Indeed, some of us like to call it "comradeship," instead, this interchange of highest thought and tenderest aspiration, in which the sense of selfhood is diminished and the sense of otherhood increased. We make no "formal calls," but the informal ones are a hundred-fold more pleasant. If a new woman's face appear in church we wonder if she won't "come with us" in . . . the W. C. T. U., or some other dear "ring-around-a-rosy" circle, formed "for others' sake." If new children sit beside her in the church pew, we plan to win them for our Band of Hope or other philanthropic guild where they will learn to find "society" in nobler forms than this poor old world has ever known before. The emptiness of conventional forms of speech and action is never so patent as when contrasted with the "fullness of life" that crowns those hearts banded together to bring the day when all men's weal shall be each man's care. Wordsworth wrote wearily of

"The greetings where no kindness is."

From 1868 to 1870 I studied and traveled abroad, not tasting wine until in Denmark, after three months' absence, I was taken suddenly and violently ill with something resembling cholera, and the kind-faced physician in Copenhagen bending above my weakness said in broken French: "Mademoiselle, you must put wine in the water you drink or you will never live to see your home." This prescription I then faithfully followed for two years with a gradual tendency so to amend as to make it read, "You may put water in your wine," and a leaning toward the "pure article," especially when some rich friend sent for a costly bottle of "Rudesheimer," or treated me to such a luxury as "Grand Chartreuse." At a London dinner where I was the guest of English friends, and seven wineglasses stood around my plate, I did not protest or abstain—so easily does poor human nature fall away, especially when backed up by a medical prescription. But beyond a flushing of the cheek, an unwonted readiness at repartee and an anticipation of the dinner hour, unknown to me before or since, I came under no thralldom, and returning to this blessed "land of the wineless dinner table," my natural environments were such that I do not recall the use of intoxicants by me, "as a beverage," from that day to this.

Thus much do I owe to a Methodist training and the social usages of my grand old mother church. Five years in Oberlin, Ohio, in my childhood, also did much to ground me in the faith of total abstinence and the general laws of hygiene.

In 1873 came that wonderful Christmas gift to the world—the woman's temperance crusade, beginning in Hillsboro, Ohio, December 23, and led by that loyal Methodist woman, Mrs. Judge Thompson, daughter of Gov. Trimble and sister of Dr. Trimble, the oldest member of the last M. E. General Conference. All through that famous battle winter of Home *versus* Saloon, I read every word that I could get about the movement, and my brother Oliver A. Willard, then editor of the *Chicago Evening Mail*, gave favorable and full reports, saying privately to me, "I shall speak just as well of the women as I dare to"—a most characteristic editorial remark, I have since thought, though more frequently acted out than uttered! Meanwhile it occurred to me, strange to say, for the *first time*, that I ought to work for the good cause *just where I was*—that everybody ought. Thus I first received "the arrest of thought" concerning which in a thousand different towns I have since then tried to speak, and I believe that in this simple change of personal attitude from passive to aggressive lies the only force that can free this land from the drink habit and the liquor traffic. It would be like dynamite under the saloon if, *just where he is*, the minister would begin active work against it; if, just where he is, the teacher would instruct his pupils; if, just where he is, the voter would dedicate his ballot to this movement, and so on through the shining ranks of the great powers that make for righteousness from father and mother to Kindergarten toddler, if each were this day doing what each could, *just where he is*.

I was teaching rhetoric and composition to several hundred students of the Northwestern University and my eyes were opened to perceive that in their essays they would be as well pleased and would gain more good if such themes were assigned as "John B. Gough" and "Neal Dow" [temperance reformers; Dow ran for president of the United States in 1880 as the candidate of the Prohibition Party] rather than "Alexander the Great" and "Plato the Philosopher," and that in their debates they would be at least as much enlisted by the question "Is Prohibition a Success?" as by the question, "Was Napoleon a blessing or a curse?" So I quietly sandwiched in these practical themes to the great edification of my pupils and with a notable increase in their enthusiasm and punctuality. Never in my fifteen years as teacher did I have exercises so interesting as in the Crusade winter—1874.

Meanwhile in Chicago the women of the Churches were mightily aroused. They gathered up in ten days fourteen thousand signatures to a petition asking that the Sunday closing ordinance might be no longer a dead letter, and while some remained in old Clark Street Church to pray, a procession of them led by Mrs. Rev. Moses Smith, moved across the street to the Court House and going in before the Common Council (the first and last time that women have ever ventured into that uncanny presence), they offered their petition and made their plea. Their petition was promptly tabled and the ordinance for whose enforcement they had pleaded, was abrogated then and there at the dictate of the liquor power while a frightful mob collected threatening them violence; the police disappeared and only by the prompt action of such men as Rev. Dr. Arthur Edwards in finding a side exit for them, was Chicago saved the indelible disgrace of seeing some of its chief Christian women mobbed on the streets by the minions of saloon, gambling den and haunt of infamy. All these things we read at Evanston next morning and "while we were musing the fire burned."

Events moved rapidly. Meetings were held in Chicago to protest against the great indignity and to organize for further work. There were fewer writers and speakers among women then than now. Some missionary and educational addresses of mine made within the two years past caused certain Methodist friends to name me as a possible speaker; and so to my quiet home eleven miles up the lake-shore came Mrs. Charles H. Case, a leading Congregational lady of the city, asking me to go and try.

It is my nature to give myself utterly to whatever work I have in hand, hence nothing less than my new-born enthusiasm for the Crusade and its heroines would have extorted from me a promise to enter on this untried field, but I agreed to attend a noon meeting in Clark Street Church a few days later and when the time came went from the recitation room to the rostrum, finding the place so packed with people that Mrs. Dr. Jutkins who was waiting for me at the door had much ado to get a passage made for us. Ministers were on the platform in greater numbers than I had ever seen before or have seen since in that or any other city. They spoke, they sang, they prayed with the fervor of a Methodist camp. Philip Bliss was at the organ and sang one of his sweetest songs. For myself, I was frightened by the crowd and overwhelmed by a sense of my own emptiness and inadequacy. What I said I do not know except that I was with the women heart, hand and soul, in this wonderful new "Everybody's War."

Soon after, I spoke in Robert Collyer's Church with Mrs. Mary H. B. Hitt, now president of the Northwestern Branch of the Woman's Foreign Missionary Society. Here, for the first and last time, I read my speech. I believe it was Rev. Dr. L. T. Chamberlain, who called it a "school-girl essay"—and served it right. Robert Collyer took up the collection himself, I remember, rattling the box and cracking jokes along the aisle as he moved among his aristocratic "Northsiders." I went home blue enough and registered a vow as yet well nigh unbroken, that I would never again appear before a popular audience manuscript in hand.

My next attempt was in Union Park Congregational Church a few weeks later. Here I had my "heads" on paper, but from that time forward I "swung clear" of the manuscript crutch and the "outline" walking-stick. In June I resigned my position as Dean in the Woman's College and Professor of Æsthetics in the Northwestern University. It has been often said in my praise that I did this for the explicit purpose of enlisting in the temperance army, but it is my painful duty in this plain, unvarnished tale to admit that the reasons upon which I based that act, so revolutionary of all my most cherished plans and purposes, related wholly to the local situation in the University itself. However, having resigned, my strongest impulses were toward the Crusade movement as is sufficiently proved by the fact that, going East immediately, I sought the leaders of the newly formed societies of temperance women, Dr. and Mrs. W. H. Boole, Mrs. Helen E. Brown, Mrs. Rebecca Collins, Mrs. M. F. Hascall and others of New York, Mrs. Mary C. Johnson, Mrs. Mary E. Hartt, H. W. Adams, and others of Brooklyn, and these were the first persons who befriended and advised me in the unknown field of "Gospel temperance." With them I went to Jerry McAuley's Mission, and to "Kit Burns's Rat-Pit," and saw the great unwashed, unkempt, ungospeled and sin-scarred multitude for the first time in my life as they gathered in a dingy down-town square to hear Dr. Boole preach on Sabbath afternoon.

With several of these new friends I went to Old Orchard Beach, Me., where Francis Murphy, a drinking man and saloon-keeper recently reformed, had called the first "Gospel Temperance Camp Meeting" known to our annals. Here I met Neal Dow and heard the story of Prohibitory Law. Here I saw that strong, sweet woman, Mrs. L. M. N. Stevens, our white ribbon leader in Maine, almost from then till now; and here in a Portland hotel, where I stayed with Mary Hartt, of Brooklyn, and wondered "where the money was to come from" as I had none, and had mother's expenses and my own to meet, I opened the Bible lying on the hotel bureau and lighted on this memorable verse: Psalm 37:3, *"Trust in the Lord, and do good; so shall thou dwell in the land, and verily thou shalt be fed."*

That was a turning-point in life with me. Great spiritual illumination, unequaled in all my history before, had been vouchsafed me in the sorrowful last days at Evanston, but here came clinching faith for what was to me a most difficult emergency.

Going to Boston I now sought Dr. Dio Lewis, for, naturally enough, I wished to see and counsel with the man whose words had been the match that fired the powder mine. He was a considerate and kind old gentleman who could only tell me o'er and o'er that "if the women would go to the saloons they could soon close them up forever." But we had already passed beyond that stage, so I went on to broader counsels. Convinced that I must make my own experience and determine my own destiny, I now bent all my forces to find what Archimedes wanted, "where to stand" within the charmed circle of the temperance reform. Chicago must be my field, for home was there and the sacred past with its graves of the living and dead. But nobody had asked me to work there and I was specially in mood to wait and watch for providential intimations. Meanwhile many and varied offers came from the educational field, tempting in respect of their wide outlook and large promise of financial relief. In this dilemma I consulted my friends as to their sense of my duty, every one of them, including my dear mother and my revered counselor, Bishop Simpson, uniting in the decision that he thus expressed: "If you were not dependent on your own exertions for the supply of current needs, I would say, be a philanthropist, but of all work, the temperance work pays least and you cannot afford to take it up. I therefore counsel you to remain in your chosen and successful field of the higher education."

No one stood by me in the preference I freely expressed to join the Crusade women except Mrs. Mary A. Livermore, who sent me a letter full of enthusiasm for the new line of work and predicted success for me therein. It is said that Napoleon was wont to consult his marshals and then do as he pleased, but I have found this method equally characteristic of ordinary mortals and certainly it was the one I followed in the greatest decision of my life. While visiting in Cambridge, Mass., at the home of Mr. and Mrs. John S. Paine, with whom I had traveled in Egypt and Palestine, I received two letters on the same day. The first was from Rev. Dr. Van Norman, of New York, inviting me to become "Lady Principal" of his elegant school for young women, adjoining Central Park, where I was to have just what and just a few classes as I chose, and a salary of twenty-four hundred dollars per year. The other was from Mrs. Louise S. Rounds of Centenary M. E. Church, Chicago, one of the women who had gone to the City Council on that memorable night of March, 1874, and she wrote in substance as follows:

"I was sitting at my sewing work to-day, pondering the future of our young temperance association. Mrs. O. B. Wilson, our president, does all she can and had shown a really heroic spirit, coming to Lower Farwell Hall for a prayer-meeting every day in the week, though she lives a long distance from there and is old and feeble, and the heat has been intense. She can not go on much longer and it has come to me, as I believe from the Lord, that you ought to be our President. We are a little band without money or experience, but with strong faith. I went right out to see some of our leading women and they all say that if you will agree to come, there will be no trouble about your election. Please let me hear at once."

I can not express the delight with which I greeted this announcement. Here was my "open door" all unknown and unsought—a place prepared for me in one true temperance woman's heart and a chance to work for the cause that had in so short a time become so dear to me. I at once declined the New York offer and very soon after started for the West.

The first saloon I ever entered was Sheffner's, on Market Street, Pittsburgh, on my way home. In fact, that was the only glimpse I ever personally had of the Crusade. It had lingered in this dun-colored city well nigh a year and when I visited my old friends at the Pittsburgh Female College I spoke with enthusiasm of the Crusade, and of the women who were, as I judged from a morning paper, still engaged in it here. They looked upon me with astonishment when I proposed to seek out those women and go with them to the saloons, for in the two years that I had taught in Pittsburgh these friends associated me with the recitation room, the Shakspeare Club, the lecture course, the opera, indeed, all the haunts open to me that a literary-minded woman would care to enter. However, they were too polite to desire to disappoint me, and so they had me piloted by some of the factotums of the place to the headquarters of the Crusade, where I was warmly welcomed, and soon found myself walking down street arm in arm with a young teacher from the public school, who said she had a habit of coming in to add one to the procession when her day's duties were over.

We paused in front of the saloon that I have mentioned. The ladies ranged themselves along the curbstone, for they had been forbidden in anywise to incommode the passers-by, being dealt with much more strictly than a drunken man or a heap of dry-goods boxes would be. At a signal from our gray-haired leader, a sweet-voiced woman began to sing, "Jesus the water of life will give," all our voices soon blending in that sweet song. I think it was the most novel spectacle that I recall. There stood women of undoubted religious devotion and the highest character, most of them crowned with the glory of gray hairs. Along the stony pavement of that stoniest of cities rumbled the heavy wagons, many of them carriers of beer; between us and the saloon in front of which we were drawn up in line, passed the motley throng, almost every man lifting his hat and even the little newsboys doing the same. It was American manhood's tribute to Christianity, and to womanhood, and it was significant and full of pathos. The leader had already asked the saloon-keeper if we might enter, and he had declined, else the prayer-meeting would have occurred inside his door. A sorrowful old lady whose only son had gone to ruin through that very death-trap, knelt on the cold, moist pavement and offered a broken-hearted prayer, while all our heads were bowed. At a signal we moved on and the next saloon-keeper permitted us to enter. I had no more idea of the inward appearance of a saloon than if there had been no such place on earth. I knew nothing of its high, heavily-corniced bar, its barrels with the ends all pointed towards the looker-on, each barrel being furnished with a faucet; its shelves glittering with decanters and cut glass, its floors thickly strewn with saw-dust, and here and there a round table with chairs—nor of its abundant fumes, sickening to healthful nostrils. The tall, stately lady who led us, placed her Bible on the bar and read a psalm, whether hortatory or imprecatory, I do not remember, but the spirit of these crusaders was so gentle, I think it must have been the former. Then we sang "Rock of Ages" as I thought I had never heard it sung before, with a tender confidence to the height of which one does not rise in the easy-going, regulation prayer-meeting, and then one of the older women whispered to me softly that the leader wished to know if I would pray. It was strange, perhaps, but I felt not the least reluctance, and kneeling on that sawdust floor, with a group of earnest hearts around me, and behind them, filling every corner and extending out into the street, a crowd of unwashed, unkempt, hard-looking drinking men, I was conscious that perhaps never in my life, save beside my sister Mary's dying bed, had I prayed as truly as I did then. This was my Crusade baptism. The next day I went on to the West and within a week had been made president of the Chicago W. C. T. U.

Clara Barton

~

CLARA BARTON (1821–1912), famous for nursing both Confederate and Union soldiers during the Civil War, traveled to Switzerland in 1869 and became acquainted with the International Red Cross, founded five years prior. She returned to the United States, determined that her country should sign the 1864 Geneva Convention and thus become a member of the International Red Cross. She gave the following speech before Congress in 1881 and was gratified when the treaty was finally signed the following year. When the American Red Cross was established in 1900, Clara Barton was named its first president.

~

I had borne some part in the operations of field hospitals in actual service in the battles of the Rebellion, and some public notice had been taken of that work. But, broken in health, I was directed by my physicians to go to Europe prepared to remain three years.

In September, 1869, I arrived at Geneva, Switzerland. In October I was visited by the president and members of the "International Committee for the relief of the wounded in war." They wished to learn if possible why the United States had declined to sign the [Geneva] treaty. Our position was incomprehensible to them. They had thought the people of America, with their grand

Barton, Clara. *The Red Cross: A History of This Remarkable Movement in the Interest of Humanity.* Washington, D.C.: American National Red Cross, 1898, pp. 60–72.

sanitary record,* would be the first to appreciate and accept it. I listened in silent wonder to all this recital, and when I did reply it was to say that I had never in America heard of the Convention of Geneva nor of the treaty, and was sure that as a country America did not know she had declined; that she would be the last to withhold recognition of a humane movement; that it had doubtless been referred to and declined by some one department of the government, or some one official, and had never been submitted to the people; and as its literature was in languages foreign to our English-speaking population, it had no way of reaching us.

You will naturally infer that I examined it. I became all the time more deeply impressed with the wisdom of its principles, the good practical sense of its details, and its extreme usefulness in practice. Humane intelligence had devised its provisions and peculiarly adapted it to win popular favor. The absurdity of our own position in relation to it was simply marvelous. As I counted up its roll of twenty-two nations—not a civilized people in the world but ourselves missing, and saw Greece, Spain, and Turkey there, I began to fear that in the eyes of the "rest of mankind" we could not be far from barbarians. This reflection did not furnish a stimulating food for national pride. I grew more and more ashamed. But the winter wore on as winters do with invalids abroad. The summer found me at Berne in quest of strength among its mountain views and baths.

On the fifteenth of July, 1870, France declared war against Prussia. Within three days a band of agents from the "International Committee of Geneva," headed by Dr. Louis Appia (one of the prime movers of the convention), equipped for work and *en route* for the seat of war, stood at the door of my villa inviting me to go with them and take such part as I had taken in our own war. I had not strength to trust for that, and declined with thanks, promising to follow in my own time and way, and I did

---

*The U.S. Sanitary Commission provided medical care to the troops during the Civil War.

follow within a week. No shot had then been fired—no man had fallen—yet this organized, powerful commission was on its way, with its skilled agents, ready to receive, direct and dispense the charities and accumulations which the generous sympathies of twenty-two nations, if applied to, might place at its disposal. These men had treaty power to go directly on to any field, and work unmolested in full co-operation with the military and commanders-in-chief; their supplies held sacred and their efforts recognized in seconded in every direction by either belligerent army. Not a man could lie uncared for nor unfed. I thought of the Peninsula in McClellan's campaign—of Pittsburg Landing, Cedar Mountain and second Bull Run, Antietam, Old Fredericksburg with its acres of snow-covered and gun-covered *glacee*, and its fourth-day flag of truce; of its dead, and starving wounded, frozen to the ground, and our commissions and their supplies in Washington, with no effective organization to go beyond; of the Petersburg mine, with its four thousand dead and wounded and no flag of truce, the wounded broiling in a July sun—died and rotted where they fell. I remembered our prisons, crowded with starving men whom all the powers and pities of the world could not reach even with a bit of bread. I thought of the widows' weeds still fresh and dark through all the land, north and south, from the pine to the palm; the shadows on the hearths and hearts over all my country. Sore, broken hearts, ruined, desolate homes! Was this people to decline a humanity in war? Was this a country to reject a treaty for the help of wounded soldiers? Were these the women and men to stand aloof and consider? I believed if these people knew that the last cloud of war had forever passed from their horizon, the tender, painful, deathless memories of what had been would bring them in with a force no power could resist. They needed only to know.

As I journeyed on and saw the work of these Red Cross societies in the field, accomplishing in four months under their systematic organization what we failed to accomplish in four years without it—no mistakes, no needless suffering, no starving, no lack of care, no waste, no confusion, but order, plenty, cleanliness and comfort wherever that little flag made its way—a whole continent marshaled under the banner of the Red Cross—as I saw all this, and joined and worked on it, you will not wonder that I said to my- self "If I live to return to my country I will try to make my people understand the Red Cross and that treaty." But I did more than re- solve, I promised other nations I would do it, and other reasons pressed me to remember my promise. The Franco-Prussian war and the war of the commune were both enormous in the extent of their operations and in the suffering of individuals. This great modern international impulse of charity went out everywhere to meet and alleviate its miseries. The small, poor countries gave of their poverty and the rich nations poured out abundantly of their vast resources. The contributions of those under the Red Cross went quietly, promptly through international responsible channels, were thoughtfully and carefully distributed through well-known agents, returns, accurate to a franc, were made and duly published to the credit of the contributing nations, and *the object aimed at was accomplished*.

America, filled with German and French people, with people humane and universal in their instincts of citizenship and brother- hood, freighted ships with supplies and contributions in money prodigal and vast. They arrived in Europe, but they were not un- der the treaty regulations. No sign of the Red Cross authorized any one to receive and distribute them. The poor baffled agents, honest, well meaning and indefatigable, did all that individuals without system or organization could do. But for the most part the magnif- icent charity of America was misapplied and went as unsystem- atized charity always tends to go, to ruin and to utter waste. *The ob- ject aimed at was not accomplished*.

At the end of the report of the international organization of the Red Cross occurs something like this: "It is said that the United States of America also contributed something for the sick and wounded, but what, or how much, or to whom, or when or where, it is impossible to tell."

In the autumn of 1873, I returned to America more broken in health than when I left in 1869. Then followed years of suffering in which I forgot how to walk, but I remembered my resolve and my promise. After almost five years I was able to go to Washington with a letter from Monsieur Moynier, president of the International Committee of Geneva, to the President of the United States, asking once more that our government accede to the articles of the convention. Having been made the official bearer of this letter, I presented it in 1877 to President Hayes, who received it kindly, referring it to his Secretary of State, Mr. Evarts, who in his turn referred it to his assistant secretary as the person who would know all about it, examine and report for decision. I then saw how it was made to depend not alone upon one department, but one man, who had been the assistant secretary of state in 1864 and also in 1868, when the treaty had been on the two previous occasions presented to our government. It was a settled thing. There was nothing to hope for from that administration. The matter had been officially referred and would be decided accordingly. It would be declined because it had been declined. If I pressed it to a decision, it would only weight it down with a third refusal. I waited. My next thought was to refer it to Congress. That step would be irregular, and discourteous to the administration. I did not like to take it, still I attempted it, but could not get it considered, for it promised neither political influence, patronage, nor votes.

The next year I returned to Washington to try Congress again. I published a little pamphlet of two leaves addressed to the members and senators, to be laid upon their desks in the hope they would take the trouble to read so little as that, and be by so much the better prepared to consider and act upon a bill if I could get one before them. My strength failed before I could get that bill presented, and I went home again in midwinter. There then remained but a portion of the term of that administration, and I determined, if possible, to outlive it, hoping another would be more responsive. Meanwhile I wrote, talked, and did whatever I could to spread the idea among the people, and March, 1881, when the administration of President Garfield came in, I went again to Washington. The subject was very cordially received by the President and carefully referred by him to Secretary Blaine, who considered it himself, conferred fully with me, and finally laid it before the President and the cabinet. . . . [T]he letter Mr. Blaine addressed to me, . . . gives the assurance that President Garfield would recommend the adoption of the treaty in his message to Congress.

What were the provisions of that treaty . . . ? It was merely the proposed adoption of a treaty by this government with other nations for the purpose of ameliorating the conditions incident to warfare, humanizing its regulations, softening its barbarities, and so far as possible, lessening the sufferings of the wounded and sick who fall by it. . . .

The articles of this treaty provide, as its first and most important feature, for the entire and strict neutrality of all material and supplies contributed by any nation for the use of the sick and wounded in war; also that persons engaged in the distribution of them, shall not be subject to capture; that all hospitals, general or field, shall be neutral, respected and protected by all belligerents; that all persons comprising the medical service, surgeons, chaplains, superintendents, shall be neutral, continuing their work after the occupation of a field or post the same as before, and when no longer needed be free to retire; that they may send a representative to their own headquarters if needful; that field hospitals shall retain their own equipments; that inhabitants of a country who entertain and care for the wounded of either side, in their houses, shall be protected; that the generals of an army shall so inform the people; that commanders-in-chief shall have the power to deliver immediately to the outposts of the enemy soldiers who have been wounded in an engagement, both parties consenting to the same; that the wounded, incapable of serving, shall be returned when healed; that all transports of wounded and all evacuations of posts or towns shall be protected by absolute neutrality. That the sick and wounded shall be entertained regardless of nationality; and that commanders-in-chief shall act in accordance with the instructions of their respective governments, and in conformity to the treaty. In order that all may understand, and no mistake be possible, it also provides that one uniform international flag shall mark all hospitals, all posts of sick and wounded, and one uniform badge or sign shall mark all hospital material, and be worn by all persons properly engaged in the hospital service of any nation included within the treaty; that this international flag and sign shall be a red cross on a white ground, and that the nations within the compact shall not cease their endeavors until every other nation capable of making war shall have signed this treaty, and thus acceded to the general principles of humanity in warfare recognized by other peoples.

Thirty-one governments have already signed this treaty, thirty-one nations are in this humane compact. The United States of America is not in it, and the work to which your attention is called, and which has occupied me for the last several years, is to induce her to place herself there.

This is what the Red Cross means, not an order of knighthood, not a commandery, not a secret society, not a society at all by itself, but the powerful, peaceful sign and the reducing to practical usefulness of one of the broadest and most needed humanities the world has ever known.

These articles, it will be observed, constitute at once a treaty governing our relations with foreign nations, and additional articles of war governing the conduct of our military forces in the field. As a treaty under the constitution, the President and Senate are competent to deal with them; as additional articles of war, Congress must sanction and adopt them before they can become effective and binding upon the government and the people. For this reason I have appealed to Congress as well as to the Executive Department. . . .

In attempting to present to the people of this country the plan of the Red Cross societies, it is proper to explain that originally and as operating in other countries they recognize only the miseries arising from war. Their humanities, although immense, are confined to this war centre. The treaty does not cover more than this, but the resolutions for the establishment of societies under the treaty, permit them to organize in accordance with the spirit and needs of their nationalities. By our geographical position and isolation we are far less liable to the disturbances of war than the nations of Europe, which are so frequently called upon that they do well to keep in readiness for the exigencies of war alone. But no country is more liable than our own to great overmastering calamities, various, widespread and terrible. Seldom a year passes that the nation from sea to sea is not, by the shock of some sudden, unforeseen disaster, brought to utter consternation, and stands shivering like a ship in a gale, powerless, horrified and despairing. Plagues, cholera, fires, flood, famine, all bear upon us with terrible force. Like war these events are entirely out of the common course of woes and necessities. Like death they are sure to come in some form and at some time, and like it no mortal knows where, how or when.

What have we in readiness to meet these emergencies save the good heart of our people and their impulsive, generous gifts? Certainly no organized system for collection, reception nor distribution; no agents, nurses nor material, and, worst of all, no funds; nowhere any resources in *reserve* for use in such an hour of peril and national woe; every movement crude, confused and unsystematized, every thing as unprepared as if we had never known a calamity before and had no reason to expect one again.

Meanwhile the suffering victims wait! True, in the shock we bestow most generously, lavishly even. Men "on Change" plunge their hands into their pockets and throw their gold to strangers, who may have neither preparation nor fitness for the work they undertake, and often no guaranty for honesty. Women, in the terror and excitement of the moment and their eagerness to aid, beg in the streets and rush into fairs, working day and night, to the neglect of other duties in the present, and at the peril of all health in the future—often an enormous outlay for very meagre returns. Thus our gifts fall far short of their best, being hastily bestowed, irresponsibly received and wastefully applied. . . .

Charity bears an open palm, to give is her mission. But I have never classed these Red Cross societies with charities. I have rather considered them as a wise national provision which seeks to garner and store up something against an hour of sudden need. In all our land we have not one organization of this nature and which acts upon the system of conserved resources. Our people have been more wise and thoughtful in the establishment of means for preventing and arresting the destruction of property than the destruction of human life and the lessening of consequent suffering. They have provided and maintain at an immense cost, in the aggregate, a system of fire departments with their expensive buildings and apparatus, with their fine horses and strong men kept constantly in readiness to dash to the rescue at the first dread clang of the fire bell. Still, while the electric current may flash upon us at any moment its ill tidings of some great human distress, we have no means of relief in readiness such as these Red Cross societies would furnish.

I beg you will not feel that in the presentation of this plan of action I seek to add to the labors of the people. On the contrary, I am striving to lessen them by making previous, calm preparation do away with the strain and confusion of unexpected necessities and haste. I am providing not weariness, but rest.

And, again, I would not be understood as suggesting the raising of more moneys for charitable purposes; rather I am trying to save the people's means, to economize their charities, to make their gifts do more by the prevention of needless waste and extravagance. If I thought that the formation of these societies would add a burden to our people I would be the last to advocate it. I would not, however, yield the fact of the treaty. For patriotism, for national honor, I would stand by that at all cost. My first and greatest endeavor has been to wipe from the scroll of my country's fame the stain of imputed lack of common humanity, to take her out of the roll of barbarism. . . .

It may be said that this treaty jeopardizes our traditional policy, which jealously guards against entangling alliances abroad; that as we are exempt by our geographical position from occasions for war this treaty must bring us not benefits but only burdens from other people's calamities and wars—calamities and wars which we do not create and of which we may properly reap the incidental advantages. But this treaty binds none to bear burdens, but only to refrain from cruelties; it binds not to give but to allow others to give wisely and to work humanely if they will, while all shall guarantee to them undisturbed activity in deeds of charity. . . .

[D]eplore it as we may, war *is the great fact* of all history and its most pitiable feature is not after all so much the great numbers slain, wounded and captured in battle, as their cruel after treatment as wounded and prisoners, no adequate provision being made for their necessities, no humane care even permitted, except at the risk of death or imprisonment as spies, of those moved by wise pity or a simple religious zeal.

Among these hard facts appears a conscientious theorist and asks, Is not war a great sin and wrong? Ought we to provide for it, to make it easy, to lessen its horrors, to mitigate its sufferings? Shall we not in this way encourage rulers and peoples to engage in war for slight and fancied grievances?

We provide for the victims of the great wrong and sin of intemperance. These are for the most part voluntary victims, each in a measure the arbiter of his own fate. The soldier has generally no part, no voice, in creating the war in which he fights. He simply obeys as he must his superiors and the laws of his country. Yes, it is a great wrong and sin, and for that reason I would provide not only for, but against it.

But here comes the speculative theorist! Isn't it encouraging a bad principle; wouldn't it be better to do away with all war? Wouldn't peace societies be better? Oh, yes, my friend, as much better as the millennium would be better than this, but it is not here. Hard facts are here; war is here; war is the outgrowth, indicator and relic of barbarism. Civilization alone will do away with it, and scarcely a quarter of the earth is yet civilized, and that quarter not beyond the possibilities of war. It is a long step yet to permanent peace. We cannot cross a stream until we reach it. The sober truth is, we are called to deal with facts, not theories; we must practice if we would teach. And be assured, my friends, there is not a peace society on the face of the earth to-day, nor ever will be, so potent, so effectual against war as the Red Cross of Geneva.

The sooner the world learns that the halo of glory which surrounds a field of battle and its tortured, thirsting, starving, pain-racked, dying victims exists only in imagination; that it is all sentiment, delusion, falsehood, given for effect; that soldiers do not die painless deaths; that the sum of all human agony finds its equivalent on the battlefield in the hospital, by the weary wayside and in the prison; that, deck it as you will, it is agony; the sooner and more thoroughly the people of the earth are brought to realize and appreciate these facts, the more slow and considerate they will be about rushing into hasty and needless wars, and the less popular war will become.

Death by the bullet painless! What did this nation do during eighty agonizing and memorable days but to watch the effects of one bullet wound? Was it painless? Painless either to the victim or the nation? Though canopied by a fortitude, patience, faith and courage scarce exceeded in the annals of history, still was it agony. And when in his delirious dreams the dying President [Garfield] murmured, "The great heart of the nation will not let the soldier die," I prayed God to hasten the time when every wounded soldier would be sustained by this sweet assurance; that in the combined sympathies, wisdom, enlightenment and power of the nations, he should indeed feel that the great heart of the people would not let the soldier die.

Friends, was it accident, or was it providence which made it one of the last acts of James A. Garfield in health to pledge himself to urge upon the representatives of his people in Congress assembled, this great national step for the relief and care of wounded men? Living or dying it was his act and his wish, and no member in that honored, considerate and humane body but will feel himself in some manner holden to see it carried out.

Jane Addams

~

JANE ADDAMS (1860–1935), Nobel Peace Prize recipient, suffragist, and friend to the immigrant poor, began her public career by becoming a founder of Hull House in Chicago. By the time she founded that now-famous settlement house in 1889, Addams was certain that her life would be one of concrete service. As this section of her memoir, *Twenty Years at Hull House,* illustrates, however, the leap from intellectual outrage to physical action was a difficult one for her to make. This excerpted chapter is entitled, "The Snare of Preparation."

~

The winter after I left school was spent in the Woman's Medical College of Philadelphia, but the development of the spinal difficulty which had shadowed me from childhood forced me into Dr. Weir Mitchell's hospital for the late spring, and the next winter I was literally bound to a bed in my sister's house for six months. . . . The long illness inevitably put aside the immediate prosecution of a medical course, and though I had passed my examinations creditably enough in the required subjects for the first year, I was very glad to have a physician's sanction for giving up clinics and dissecting rooms and to follow his prescription of spending the next two years in Europe.

Before I returned to America I had discovered that there were other genuine reasons for living among the poor than that of practicing medicine upon them, and my brief foray into the profession was never resumed.

Addams, Jane. *Twenty Years at Hull House.* 1910. Rpt., New York: NAL Penguin, 1981, pp. 60–74.

The long illness left me in a state of nervous exhaustion with which I struggled for years, traces of it remaining long after Hull-House was opened in 1889. At the best it allowed me but a limited amount of energy, so that doubtless there was much nervous depression at the foundation of the spiritual struggles which this chapter is forced to record. However, it could not have been all due to my health, for as my wise little notebook sententiously remarked, "In his own way each man must struggle, lest the moral law become a far-off abstraction utterly separated from his active life."

It would, of course, be impossible to remember that some of these struggles ever took place at all, were it not for these selfsame notebooks, in which, however, I no longer wrote in moments of high resolve, but judging from the internal evidence afforded by the books themselves, only in moments of deep depression when overwhelmed by a sense of failure.

One of the most poignant of these experiences, which occurred during the first few months after our landing upon the other side of the Atlantic, was on a Saturday night, when I received an ineradicable impression of the wretchedness of East London, and also saw for the first time the overcrowded quarters of a great city at midnight. A small party of tourists were taken to the East End by a city missionary to witness the Saturday night sale of decaying vegetables and fruit, which, owing to the Sunday laws in London, could not be sold until Monday, and, as they were beyond safe keeping, were disposed of at auction as late as possible on Saturday night. On Mile End Road, from the top of an omnibus which paused at the end of a dingy street lighted by only occasional flares of gas, we saw two huge masses of ill-clad people clamoring around two hucksters' carts. They were bidding their farthings and ha'pennies for a vegetable held up by the auctioneer, which he at last scornfully flung, with a gibe for its cheapness, to the successful bidder. In the momentary pause only one man detached himself from the groups. He had bidden on a cabbage, and when it struck his hand, he instantly sat down on the curb, tore it with his teeth, and hastily devoured it, unwashed and uncooked as it was. He and his fellows were types of the "submerged tenth," as our missionary guide told us, with some little satisfaction in the then new phrase, and he further added that so many of them could scarcely be seen in one spot save at this Saturday night auction, the desire for cheap food being apparently the one thing which could move them simultaneously. They were huddled into ill-fitting, cast-off clothing, the ragged finery which one sees only in East London. Their pale faces were dominated by that most unlovely of human expressions, the cunning and shrewdness of the bargain-hunter who starves if he cannot make a successful trade, and yet the final impression was not of ragged, tawdry clothing nor of pinched and sallow faces, but of myriads of hands, empty, pathetic, nerveless and workworn, showing white in the uncertain light of the street, and clutching forward for food which was already unfit to eat.

Perhaps nothing is so fraught with significance as the human hand, this oldest tool with which man has dug his way from savagery, and with which he is constantly groping forward. I have never since been able to see a number of hands held upward, even when they are moving rhythmically in a callisthenic exercise, or when they belong to a class of chubby children who wave them in eager response to a teacher's query, without a certain revival of this memory, a clutching at the heart reminiscent of the despair and resentment which seized me then.

For the following weeks I went about London almost furtively, afraid to look down narrow streets and alleys lest they disclose again this hideous human need and suffering. I carried with me for days at a time that curious surprise we experience when we first come back into the streets after days given over to sorrow and death; we are bewildered that the world should be going on as usual and unable to determine which is real, the inner pang or the outward seeming. In time all huge London came to seem unreal save the poverty in its East End. . . .

[T]he painful impression was increased because at the very moment of looking down the East London street from the top of the omnibus, I had been sharply and painfully reminded of "The Vision of Sudden Death" which had confronted De Quincey one summer's night as he was being driven through rural England on a high mail coach. Two absorbed lovers suddenly appear between the narrow, blossoming hedgerows in the direct path of the huge vehicle which is sure to crush them to their death. De Quincey tries to send them a warning shout, but finds himself unable to make a sound because his mind is hopelessly entangled in an endeavor to recall the exact lines from the *Iliad* which describe the great cry with which Achilles alarmed all Asia militant. Only after his memory responds is his will released from its momentary paralysis, and he rides on through the fragrant night with the horror of the escaped calamity thick upon him, but he also bears with him the consciousness that he had given himself over so many years to classic learning—that when suddenly called upon for a quick decision in the world of life and death, he had been able to act only through a literary suggestion.

This is what we were all doing, lumbering our minds with literature that only served to cloud the really vital situation spread before our eyes. It seemed to me too preposterous that in my first view of the horror of East London I should have recalled De Quincey's literary description of the literary suggestion which had once paralyzed him. In my disgust it all appeared a hateful, vicious circle which even the apostles of culture themselves admitted, for had not one of the greatest among the moderns plainly said that "conduct, and not culture is three fourths of human life."

For two years in the midst of my distress over the poverty which, thus suddenly driven into my consciousness, had become to me the "Weltschmerz," there was mingled a sense of futility, of misdirected energy, the belief that the pursuit of cultivation would not in the end bring either solace or relief. I gradually reached a conviction that the first generation of college women had taken their learning too quickly, had departed too suddenly from the active, emotional life led by their grandmothers and great-grandmothers, that the contemporary education of young women had developed too exclusively the power of acquiring knowledge and of merely receiving impressions; that somewhere in the process of "being educated" they had lost that simple and almost automatic response to the human appeal, that old healthful reaction resulting in activity from the mere presence of suffering or of helplessness; that they are so sheltered and pampered they have no chance even to make "the great refusal."

In the German and French *pensions*, which twenty-five years ago were crowded with American mothers and their daughters who had crossed the seas in search of culture, one often found the mother making real connection with the life about her, using her inadequate German with great fluency, gaily measuring the enormous sheets or exchanging recipes with the German Hausfrau, visiting impartially the nearest kindergarten and market, making an atmosphere of her own, hearty and genuine as far as it went, in the house and on the street. On the other hand, her daughter was critical and uncertain of her linguistic acquirements, and only at ease when in the familiar receptive attitude afforded by the art gallery and the opera house. In the latter she was swayed and moved, appreciative of the power and charm of the music, intelligent as to the legend and poetry of the plot, finding use for her trained and developed powers as she sat "being cultivated" in the familiar atmosphere of the classroom which had, as it were, become sublimated and romanticized.

I remember a happy busy mother who, complacent with the knowledge that her daughter daily devoted four hours to her music, looked up from her knitting to say, "If I had had your opportunities when I was young, my dear, I should have been a very happy girl. I always had musical talent, but such training as I had, foolish little songs and waltzes and not time for half an hour's practice a day."

The mother did not dream of the sting her words left and that the sensitive girl appreciated only too well that her opportunities were fine and unusual, but she also knew that in spite of some facility and much good teaching she had no genuine talent and never would fulfill the expectations of her friends. She looked back upon her mother's girlhood with positive envy because it was so full of happy industry and extenuating obstacles, with undisturbed opportunity to believe that her talents were unusual. The girl looked wistfully at her mother, but had not the courage to cry out what was in her heart: "I might believe I had unusual talent if I did not know what good music was; I might enjoy half an hour's practice a day if I were busy and happy the rest of the time. You do not know what life means when all the difficulties are removed! I am simply smothered and sickened with advantages. It is like eating a sweet dessert the first thing in the morning."

This, then, was the difficulty, this sweet dessert in the morning and the assumption that the sheltered, educated girl has nothing to do with the bitter poverty and the social maladjustment which is all about her, and which, after all, cannot be concealed, for it breaks through poetry and literature in the burning tide which overwhelms her; it peers at her in the form of heavy-laden market women and underpaid street laborers, gibing her with a sense of her uselessness.

I recall one snowy morning in Saxe-Coburg, looking from the window of our little hotel upon the town square, that we saw crossing and recrossing it a single file of women with semicircular, heavy, wooden tanks fastened upon their backs. They were carrying in this primitive fashion to a remote cooling room these tanks filled with a hot brew incident to one stage of beer making. The women were bent forward, not only under the weight which they were bearing, but because the tanks were so high that it would have been impossible for them to have lifted their heads. Their faces and hands, reddened in the cold morning air, showed clearly the white scars where they had previously been scalded by the hot stuff which splashed if they stumbled ever so little on their way. Stung into action by one of those sudden indignations against cruel conditions which at times fill the young with unexpected energy, I found myself across the square, in company with mine host, interviewing the phlegmatic owner of the brewery who received us with exasperating indifference, or rather received me, for the innkeeper mysteriously slunk away as soon as the great magnate of the town began to speak. I went back to a breakfast for which I had lost my appetite, as I had for Gray's *Life of Prince Albert* and his wonderful tutor, Baron Stockmar, which I had been reading late the night before. The book had lost its fascination; how could a good man, feeling so keenly his obligation "to make princely the mind of his prince," ignore such conditions of life for the multitude of humble, hard-working folk. We were spending two months in Dresden that winter, given over to much reading of *The History of Art* and to much visiting of its art gallery and opera house, and after such an experience I would invariably suffer a moral revulsion against this feverish search after culture. . . .

The wonder and beauty of Italy later brought healing and some relief to the paralyzing sense of the futility of all artistic and intellectual effort when disconnected from the ultimate test of the conduct it inspired. The serene and soothing touch of history also aroused old enthusiasms, although some of their manifestations were such as one smiles over more easily in retrospection than at the moment. I fancy that it was no smiling matter to several people in our party, whom I induced to walk for three miles in the hot sunshine beating down upon the Roman Campagna, that we might enter the Eternal City on foot through the Porta del Popolo, as pilgrims had done for centuries. . . . This melodramatic entrance into Rome . . . was the prelude to days of enchantment, and I returned to Europe two years later in order to spend a winter there and to carry out a great desire to systematically study the Catacombs. In spite of my distrust of "advantages" I was apparently not yet so cured but that I wanted more of them.

[T]wo years . . . elapsed before I again found myself in Europe. . . .

In one of the intervening summers between these European journeys I visited a western state where I had formerly invested a sum of money in mortgages. I was much horrified by the wretched conditions among the farmers, which had resulted from a long period of drought, and one forlorn picture was fairly burned into my mind. A number of starved hogs—collateral for a promissory note—were huddled into an open pen. Their backs were humped in a curious, camel-like fashion, and they were devouring one of their own number, the latest victim of absolute starvation or possibly merely the one least able to defend himself against their voracious hunger. The farmer's wife looked on indifferently, a picture of despair as she stood in the door of the bare, crude house, and the two children behind her, whom she vainly tried to keep out of sight, continually thrust forward their faces almost covered by masses of coarse, sunburned hair, and their little bare feet so black, so hard, the great cracks so filled with dust that they looked like flattened hoofs. The children could not be compared to anything so joyous as satyrs, although they appeared but half-human. It seemed to me quite impossible to receive interest from mortgages placed upon farms which might at any season be reduced to such conditions, and with great inconvenience to my agent and doubtless with hardship to the farmers, as speedily as possible I withdrew all my investment. But something had to be done with the money, and in my reaction against unseen horrors I bought a farm near my native village and also a flock of innocent-looking sheep. My partner in the enterprise had not chosen the shepherd's lot as a permanent occupation, but hoped to speedily finish his college course upon half the proceeds of our venture. This pastoral enterprise still seems to me to have been essentially sound, both economically and morally, but perhaps one partner depended too much upon the impeccability of her motives and the other found himself too preoccupied with study to know that it is not a real kindness to bed a sheepfold with straw, for certainly the venture ended in a spectacle scarcely less harrowing than the memory it was designed to obliterate. At least the sight of two hundred sheep with four rotting hoofs each, was not reassuring to one whose conscience craved economic peace. A fortunate series of sales of mutton, wool, and farm enabled the partners to end the enterprise without loss, and they passed on, one to college and the other to Europe, if not wiser, certainly sadder for the experience.

It was during this second journey to Europe that I attended a meeting of the London match girls who were on strike and who met daily under the leadership of well-known labor men of London. The low wages that were reported at the meetings, the phossy jaw which was described and occasionally exhibited, the appearance of the girls themselves I did not, curiously enough, in any wise connect with what was called the labor movement. . . . But of course this impression of human misery was added to the others which were already making me so wretched. . . .

The beginning of 1887 found our little party of three in very picturesque lodgings in Rome, and settled into a certain student's routine. But my study of the Catacombs was brought to an abrupt end in a fortnight by a severe attack of sciatic rheumatism, which kept me in Rome with a trained nurse during many weeks, and later sent me to the Riviera to lead an invalid's life once more. . . .

It is hard to tell just when the very simple plan which afterward developed into the Settlement began to form itself in my mind. It may have been even before I went to Europe for the second time, but I gradually became convinced that it would be a good thing to rent a house in a part of the city where many primitive and actual needs are found, in which young women who had been given over too exclusively to study might restore a balance of activity along traditional lines and learn of life from life itself; where they might try out some of the things they had been taught and put truth to "the ultimate test of the conduct it dictates or inspires." I do not remember to have mentioned this plan to anyone until we reached Madrid in April 1888.

We had been to see a bullfight rendered in the most magnificent Spanish style, where greatly to my surprise and horror, I found that I had seen, with comparative indifference, five bulls and many more horses killed. The sense that this was the last survival of all the glories of the amphitheater, the illusion that the riders on the caparisoned horses might have been knights of a tournament, or the matador a slightly armed gladiator facing his martyrdom, and all the rest of the obscure yet vivid associations of an historic survival, had carried me beyond the endurance of any of the rest of the party. I finally met them in the foyer, stern and pale with disapproval of my brutal endurance, and but partially recovered from the faintness and disgust which the spectacle itself had produced upon them. I had no defense to offer to their reproaches save that I had not thought much about the bloodshed; but in the evening the natural and inevitable reaction came, and in deep chagrin I felt myself tried and condemned, not only by this disgusting experience but by the entire moral situation which it revealed. It was suddenly made quite clear to me that I was lulling my conscience by a dreamer's scheme, that a mere paper reform had become a defense for continued idleness, and that I was making it a *raison d'être* for going on indefinitely with study and travel. It is easy to become the dupe of a deferred purpose, of the promise the future can never keep, and I had fallen into the meanest type of self-deception in making myself believe that all this was in preparation for great things to come. Nothing less than the moral reaction following the experience at a bullfight had been able to reveal to me that so far from following in the wake of a chariot of philanthropic fire, I had been tied to the tail of the veriest ox-cart of self-seeking.

I had made up my mind that next day, whatever happened, I would begin to carry out the plan, if only by talking about it. I can well recall the stumbling and uncertainty with which I finally set it forth to Miss Starr, my old-time school friend, who was one of our party. I even dared to hope that she might join in carrying out the plan, but nevertheless I told it in the fear of that disheartening experience which is so apt to afflict our most cherished plans when they are at last divulged, when we suddenly feel that there is nothing there to talk about, and as the golden dream slips through our fingers we are left to wonder at our own fatuous belief. But gradually the comfort of Miss Starr's companionship, the vigor and enthusiasm which she brought to bear upon it, told both in the growth of the plan and upon the sense of its validity, so that by the time we had reached the enchantment of the Alhambra, the scheme had become convincing and tangible although still most hazy in detail.

A month later we parted in Paris, Miss Starr to go back to Italy, and I to journey on to London to secure as many suggestions as possible from those wonderful places of which we had heard, Toynbee Hall and the People's Palace. So that it finally came about that in June, 1888, years after my first visit in East London, I found myself at Toynbee Hall equipped not only with a letter of introduction from Canon Fremantle, but with high expectations and a certain belief that whatever perplexities and discouragement concerning the life of the poor were in store for me, I should at least know something at firsthand and have the solace of daily activity. I had confidence that although life itself might contain many difficulties, the period of mere passive receptivity had come to an end, and I had at last finished with the ever-lasting "preparation for life," however ill-prepared I might be.

It was not until years afterward that I came upon Tolstoy's phrase "the snare of preparation," which he insists we spread before the feet of young people, hopelessly entangling them in a curious inactivity at the very period of life when they are longing to construct the world anew and to conform it to their own ideals.

Anna Julia Cooper

~

ANNA JULIA COOPER (c. 1858–1964), freed from slavery by the
Emancipation Proclamation during her early childhood, became a
teacher of Latin in 1887 and principal of the M Street High School
in Washington, D.C., in 1901. At the time, Booker T. Washington at
the Tuskegee Institute and many national policymakers recom-
mended vocational training rather than classical education for
black students, believing that such training would more quickly
lead to African American advancement. Cooper disagreed. She
published *A Voice from the South by a Black Woman of the South* (1892),
demanding that higher education be made available regardless of
race or sex. As principal of M Street High School, she provided qualified African Americans with a college preparatory curriculum.
Cooper's students were admitted to top colleges, including Brown,
Harvard, and Yale, and she organized her staff into an effective scholarship search committee to make college attendance possible for even
her neediest students. Despite her success Cooper was dismissed
from her position as principal in 1906—a removal that seems to have
been specifically requested by officials at Tuskegee. The following is
an excerpt from *A Voice from the South by a Black Woman of the South.*

~

Matthew Arnold during his last visit to America in '82 or '83,
lectured before a certain co-educational college in the West. After
the lecture he remarked, with some surprise, to a lady professor,
that the young women in his audience, he noticed, paid as close

Cooper, Anna Julia. *A Voice from the South by a Black Woman of the South.*
1892. Rpt., New York: Negro Universities Press, 1969, pp. 67–79.

attention as the men, *all the way through*. This led, of course, to a spirited discussion of the higher education for women, during which he said to his enthusiastic interlocutor, eyeing her philosophically through his English eyeglass: "But—eh—don't you think it—eh—spoils their chawnces, you know!"

Now, as to the result to women, this is the most serious argument ever used against the higher education. If it interferes with marriage, classical training has a grave objection to weigh and answer.

For I agree with Mr. [Grant] Allen [author of *Plain Words on the Woman Question*] at least on this one point, that there must be marrying and giving in marriage even till the end of time.

I grant you that intellectual development, with the self-reliance and capacity for earning a livelihood which it gives, renders woman less dependent on the marriage relation for physical support (which, by the way, does not always accompany it). Neither is she compelled to look to sexual love as the one sensation capable of giving tone and relish, movement and vim to the life she leads. Her horizon is extended. Her sympathies are broadened and deepened and multiplied. She is in closer touch with nature. Not a bud that opens, not a dew drop, not a ray of light, not a cloud-burst or a thunderbolt, but adds to the expansiveness and zest of her soul. And if the sun of an absorbing passion be gone down, still 'tis night that brings the stars. She has remaining the mellow, less obtrusive, but none the less enchanting and inspiring light of friendship, and into its charmed circle she may gather the best the world has known. She can commune with Socrates about the *daimon* he knew and to which she too can bear witness; she can revel in the majesty of Dante, the sweetness of Virgil, the simplicity of Homer, the strength of Milton. She can listen to the pulsing heart throbs of passionate Sappho's encaged soul, as she beats her bruised wings against her prison bars and struggles to flutter out into Heaven's æther, and the fires of her own soul cry back as she listens. "Yes; Sappho, I know it all; I know it all." Here, at last, can be communion without suspicion; friendship without misunderstanding; love without jealousy.

We must admit then that Byron's picture, whether a thing of beauty or not, has faded from the canvas of to-day.

"Man's love," he wrote, "is of man's life a thing apart,
'Tis woman's whole existence.
Man may range the court, camp, church, the vessel and the mart,
Sword, gown, gain, glory offer in exchange.
Price, fame, ambition, to fill up his heart—
And few there are whom these cannot estrange.
Men have all these resources, we *but one*—
To love again and be again undone."

This may have been true when written. *It is not true to-day*. The old, subjective, stagnant, indolent and wretched life for woman has gone. She has as many resources as men, as many activities beckon her on. As large possibilities swell and inspire her heart.

Now, then, does it destroy or diminish her capacity for loving?

Her standards have undoubtedly gone up. The necessity of speculating in 'chawnces' has probably shifted. The question is not now with the woman "How shall I so cramp, stunt, simplify and nullify myself as to make me eligible to the honor of being swallowed up into some little man?" but the problem, I trow, now rests with the man as to how he can so develop his God-given powers as to reach the ideal of a generation of women who demand the noblest, grandest and best achievements of which he is capable; and this surely is the only fair and natural adjustment of the chances. Nature never meant that the ideals and standards of the world should be dwarfing and minimizing ones, and the men should thank us for requiring of them the richest fruits which they can grow. If it makes them work, all the better for them.

As to the adaptability of the educated woman to the marriage relation, I shall simply quote from that excellent symposium of learned women that appeared recently under Mrs. Armstrong's signature. . . . "Admitting no longer any question as to their intellectual equality with the men whom they meet, with the simplicity of conscious strength, they take their place beside the men who challenge them, and fearlessly face the result of their actions. They deny that their education in any way unfits them for the duty of wifehood and maternity or primarily renders these conditions any less attractive to them than to the domestic type of woman. On the contrary, they hold that their knowledge of physiology makes them better mothers and housekeepers; their knowledge of chemistry makes them better cooks; while from their training in other natural sciences and in mathematics, they obtain an accuracy and fair-mindedness which is of great value to them in dealing with their children or employees."

So much for their willingness. Now the apple may be good for food and pleasant to the eyes, and a fruit to be desired to make one wise. Nay, it may even assure you that it has no aversion whatever to being tasted. Still, if you do not like the flavor all these recommendations are nothing. Is the intellectual woman *desirable* in the matrimonial market?

This I cannot answer. I confess my ignorance. I am no judge of such things. I have been told that strong-minded women could be, when they thought it worth their while, quite endurable, and, judging from the number of female names I find in college catalogues among the alumnae with double patronymics, I surmise that quite a number of men are willing to put up with them.

Now I would that my task ended here. Having shown that a great want of the world in the past has been a feminine force; that that force can have its full effect only through the untrammelled development of woman; that such development, while it gives her to the world and to civilization, does not necessarily remove her from the home and fireside; finally, that while past centuries have witnessed sporadic instances of this higher growth, still it was reserved for the latter half of the nineteenth century to render it common and general enough to be effective; I might close with a glowing prediction of what the twentieth century may expect from this heritage of twin forces—the masculine battered and toil-worn as a grim veteran after centuries of warfare, but still strong, active, and vigorous, ready to help with his hard-won experience the young recruit rejoicing in her newly found freedom, who so confidently places her hand in his with mutual pledges to redeem the ages.

> "And so the twain upon the skirts of Time,
> Sit side by side, full-summed in all their powers,
> Dispensing harvest, sowing the To-be,
> Self-reverent each and reverencing each."

Fain would I follow them, but duty is nearer home. The high ground of generalities is alluring but my pen is devoted to a special cause: and with a view to further enlightenment on the achievements of the century for THE HIGHER EDUCATION OF COLORED WOMEN, I wrote a few days ago to the colleges which admit women and asked how many colored women had completed the B. A. course in each during its entire history. These are the figures returned: Fisk leads the way with twelve; Oberlin next with five; Wilberforce, four; Ann Arbor and Wellesley three each, Livingstone two, Atlanta one, Howard, as yet, none.

I then asked the principal of the Washington High School how many out of a large number of female graduates from his school had chosen to go forward and take a collegiate course. He replied that but one had ever done so, and she was then in Cornell.*

Others ask questions too, sometimes, and I was asked a few years ago by a white friend, "How is it that the men of your race seem to outstrip the women in mental attainment?" "Oh," I said, "so far as it is true, the men, I suppose, from the life they lead, gain more by contact; and so far as it is only apparent, I think the women are more quiet. They don't feel called to mount a barrel and harangue by the hour every time they imagine they have produced an idea."

But I am sure there is another reason which I did not at that time see fit to give. The atmosphere, the standards, the

---

*Graduated from Scientific Course, June, 1890, the first colored woman to graduate from Cornell.

requirements of our little world do not afford any special stimulus to female development.

It seems hardly a gracious thing to say, but it strikes me as true, that while our men seem thoroughly abreast of the times on almost every other subject, when they strike the woman question they drop back into sixteenth century logic. They leave nothing to be desired generally in regard to gallantry and chivalry, but they actually do not seem sometimes to have outgrown that old contemporary of chivalry—the idea that women may stand on pedestals or live in doll houses, (if they happen to have them) but they must not furrow their brows with thought or attempt to help men tug at the great questions of the world. I fear the majority of colored men do Not yet think it worth while that women aspire to higher education. Not many will subscribe to the "advanced" ideas. . . . The three R's, a little music and a good deal of dancing, a first rate dress-maker and a bottle of magnolia balm, are quite enough generally to render charming any woman possessed of tact and the capacity for worshipping masculinity.

My readers will pardon my illustrating my point and also giving a reason for the fear that is in me, by a little bit of personal experience. When a child I was put into a school near home that professed to be normal and collegiate, i.e. to prepare teachers for colored youth, furnish candidates for the ministry, and offer collegiate training for those who should be ready for it. Well, I found after a while that I had a good deal of time on my hands. I had devoured what was put before me, and, like Oliver Twist, was looking around to ask for more. I constantly felt (as I suppose many an ambitious girl has felt) a thumping from within unanswered by any beckoning from without. Class after class was organized for these ministerial candidates (many of them men who had been preaching before I was born). Into every one of these classes I was expected to go, with the sole intent, I thought at the time, of enabling the dear old principal, as he looked from the vacant countenances of his sleepy old class over to where I sat, to get off his solitary pun—his never-failing pleasantry, especially in hot weather—which was, as he called out "Any one!" to the effect that "*any* one" then meant "*Annie* one."

Finally a Greek class was to be formed. My inspiring preceptor informed me that Greek had never been taught in the school, but that he was going to form a class *for the candidates for the ministry*, and if I liked I might join it. I replied—humbly I hope, as became a female of the human species—that I would like very much to study Greek, and that I was thankful for the opportunity, and so it went on. A boy, however meager his equipment and shallow his pretentions, had only to declare a floating intention to study theology and he could get all the support, encouragement and stimulus he needed, be absolved from work and invested beforehand with all the dignity of his far away office. While a self-supporting girl had to struggle on by teaching in the summer and working after school hours to keep up with her board bills, and actually to fight her way against positive discouragements to the higher education; till one such girl one day flared out and told the principal "the only mission opening before a girl in his school was to marry one of those candidates." He said he didn't know but it was. And when at last that same girl announced her desire and intention to go to college it was received with about the same incredulity and dismay as if a brass button on one of those candidate's coats had propounded a new method for squaring the circle or trisecting the arc.

Now this is not fancy. It is a simple unvarnished photograph, and what I believe was not in those days exceptional in colored schools, and I ask the men and women who are teachers and co-workers for the highest interests of the race, that they give the girls a chance! We might as well expect to grow trees from leaves as hope to build up a civilization or a manhood without taking into consideration our women and the home life made by them, which must be the root and ground of the whole matter. Let us insist then on special encouragement for the education of our women and special care in their training. Let our girls feel that we expect something more of them than that they merely look pretty and appear well in society. Teach them that there is a race with special needs which they and only they can help; that the world needs and is already asking for their trained, efficient forces. Finally, if there is an ambitious girl with pluck and brain to take the higher education, encourage her to make the most of it. Let there be the same flourish of trumpets and clapping of hands as when a boy announces his determination to enter the lists; and then, as you know that she is physically the weaker of the two, don't stand from under and leave her to buffet the waves alone. Let her know that your heart is following her, that your hand, though she sees it not, is ready to support her. To be plain, I mean let money be raised and scholarships be founded in our colleges and universities for self-supporting, worthy young women, to offset and balance the aid that can always be found for boys who will take theology.

The earnest well trained Christian young woman, as a teacher, as a home-maker, as wife, mother, or silent influence even, is as potent a missionary agency among our people as is the theologian; and I claim that at the present stage of our development in the South she is even more important and necessary.

Let us then, here and now, recognize this force and resolve to make the most of it—not the boys less, but the girls more.

Lillian Wald

~

LILLIAN WALD (1867–1940), founder of the Visiting Nurse Service and, indeed, a founder of public health nursing, began her nursing service on the lower East Side of Manhattan in 1895 with one other nurse, Mary Brewster. Today the Visiting Nurse Service of New York serves approximately 17,000 New Yorkers in their homes each week, and various other cities are served by Visiting Nurse Services of their own. In her memoir, *The House on Henry Street*, Lillian Wald describes the early days of the institution.

~

A sick woman in a squalid rear tenement, so wretched and so pitiful that, in all the years since, I have not seen anything more appealing, determined me, within half an hour, to live on the East Side.

I had spent two years in a New York training-school for nurses; strenuous years for an undisciplined, untrained girl, but a wonderful human experience. After graduation, I supplemented the theoretical instruction, which was casual and inconsequential in the hospital classes twenty-five years ago, by a period of study at a medical college. It was while at the college that a great opportunity came to me.

I had little more than an inspiration to be of use in some way or somehow, and going to the hospital seemed the readiest means of realizing my desire. While there, the long hours "on duty" and the

Wald, Lillian. *The House on Henry Street*. 1915. Rpt., New Brunswick, NJ: Transaction Publishers, 1991, pp. 1–11, 17, 26–28.

exhausting demands of the ward work scarcely admitted freedom for keeping informed as to what was happening in the world out-side. The nurses had no time for general reading; visits to and from friends were brief; we were out of the current and saw little of life save as it flowed into the hospital wards. It is not strange, therefore, that I should have been ignorant of the various movements which reflected the awakening of the social conscience at the time, or of the birth of the "settlement," which twenty-five years ago was giving form to a social protest in England and America. Indeed, it was not until the plan of our work on the East Side was well developed that knowledge came to me of other groups of people who, reacting to a humane or an academic appeal, were adopting this mode of expres-sion and calling it a "settlement."

Two decades ago the words "East Side" called up a vague and alarming picture of something strange and alien: a vast crowded area, a foreign city within our own, for whose conditions we had no concern. Aside from its exploiters, political and economic, few people had any definite knowledge of it, and its literary "discov-ery" had but just begun.

The lower East Side then reflected the popular indifference— it almost seemed contempt—for the living conditions of a huge population. And the possibility of improvement seemed, when my inexperience was startled into thought, the more remote be-cause of the dumb acceptance of these conditions by the East Side itself. Like the rest of the world I had known little of it, when friends of a philanthropic institution asked me to do some-thing for that quarter.

Remembering the families who came to visit patients in the wards, I outlined a course of instruction in home nursing adapted to their needs, and gave it in an old building in Henry Street, then used as a technical school and now part of the settlement. Henry Street then as now was the center of a dense industrial population.

From the schoolroom where I had been giving a lesson in bed-making, a little girl led me one drizzling March morning. She had told me of her sick mother, and gathering from her incoherent account that a child had been born, I caught up the paraphernalia of the bed-making lesson and carried it with me.

The child led me over broken roadways,—there was no asphalt, although its use was well established in other parts of the city,—over dirty mattresses and heaps of refuse,—it was before Colonel Waring had shown the possibility of clean streets even in that quarter,—between tall, reeking houses whose laden fire-escapes, useless for their appointed purpose, bulged with household goods of every description. The rain added to the dismal appearance of the streets and to the discomfort of the crowds which thronged them, intensifying the odors which assailed me from every side. Through Hester and Division streets we went to the end of Ludlow; past odorous fish-stands, for the streets were a market-place, un-regulated, unsupervised, unclean; past evil-smelling, uncovered garbage-cans; and—perhaps worst of all, where so many little chil-dren played—past the trucks brought down from more fastidious quarters and stalled on these already overcrowded streets, lending themselves inevitably to many forms of indecency.

The child led me on through a tenement hallway, across a court where open and unscreened closets were promiscuously used by men and women, up into a rear tenement, by slimy steps whose ac-cumulated dirt was augmented that day by the mud of the streets, and finally into the sickroom.

All the maladjustments of our social and economic relations seemed epitomized in this brief journey and what was found at the end of it. The family to which the child led me was neither criminal nor vicious. Although the husband was a cripple, one of those who stand on street corners exhibiting deformities to enlist compassion, and masking the begging of alms by a pretense at selling; although the family of seven shared their two rooms with boarders,—who were literally boarders, since a piece of timber was placed over the floor for them to sleep on,—and although the sick woman lay on a wretched, unclean bed, soiled with a hemorrhage two days old, they were not degraded human beings, judged by any measure of moral values.

In fact, it was very plain that they were sensitive to their condition, and when, at the end of my ministrations, they kissed my hands (those who have undergone similar experiences will, I am sure, understand), it would have been some solace if by any conviction of the moral unworthiness of the family I could have defended myself as a part of a society which permitted such conditions to exist. Indeed, my subsequent acquaintance with them revealed the fact that, miserable as their state was, they were not without ideals for the family life, and for society, of which they were so unloved and unlovely a part.

That morning's experience was a baptism of fire. Deserted were the laboratory and the academic work of the college. I never returned to them. On my way from the sickroom to my comfortable student quarters my mind was intent on my own responsibility. To my inexperience it seemed certain that conditions such as these were allowed because people did not *know*, and for me there was a challenge to know and to tell. When early morning found me still awake, my naive conviction remained that, if people knew things,—and "things" meant everything implied in the condition of this family,— such horrors would cease to exist, and I rejoiced that I had had a training in the care of the sick that in itself would give me an organic relationship to the neighborhood in which this awakening had come.

To the first sympathetic friend to whom I poured forth my story, I found myself presenting a plan which had been developing almost without conscious mental direction on my part. It was doubtless the accumulation of many reflections inspired by acquaintance with the patients in the hospital wards, and now, with the Ludlow Street experience, resistlessly impelling me to action.

Within a day or two a comrade from the training-school, Mary Brewster, agreed to share in the venture. We were to live in the neighborhood as nurses, identify ourselves with it socially, and, in brief, contribute to it our citizenship. That plan contained in embryo all the extended and diversified social interests of our settlement group to-day.

We set to work immediately to find quarters—no easy task, as we clung to the civilization of a bathroom, and according to a legend current at the time there were only two bathrooms in tenement houses below Fourteenth Street. . . .

Before September of the year 1893 we found a house on Jefferson Street, the only one in which our careful search disclosed the desired bathtub. . . .

Naturally, objections to two young women living alone in New York under these conditions had to be met, and some assurance as to our material comfort was given to anxious, though at heart sympathetic, families by compromising on good furniture, a Baltimore heater for cheer, and simple but adequate household appurtenances. Painted floors with easily removed rugs, windows curtained with spotless but inexpensive scrim, a sitting-room with pictures, books, and restful chairs, a tiny bedroom which we two shared, a small dining-room in which the family mahogany did not look out of place, and a kitchen, constituted our home for two full years. . . .

Times were hard that year. In the summer the miseries due to unemployment and rising rents and prices began to be apparent, but the pinch came with the cold weather. Perhaps it was an advantage that we were so early exposed to the extraordinary sufferings and the variety of pain and poverty in that winter of 1893–94, memorable because of extreme economic depression. The impact of strain, physical and emotional, left neither place nor time for self-analysis and consequent self-consciousness, so prone to hinder and to dwarf wholesome instincts, and so likely to have proved an impediment to the simple relationship which we established with our neighbors. . . .

As our plan crystallized my friend and I were certain that a system for nursing the sick in their homes could not be firmly established unless certain fundamental social facts were recognized. We tried to imagine how loved ones for whom we might be solicitous would react were they in the place of the patients whom we hoped to serve. With time, experience, and the stimulus of creative minds our technique and administrative methods have naturally improved, but this test gave us vision to establish certain principles, whose soundness has been proved during the growth of the service.

We perceived that it was undesirable to condition the nurse's service upon the actual or potential connection of the patient with a religious institution or free dispensary, or to have the nurse assigned to the exclusive use of one physician, and we planned to create a service on terms most considerate of the dignity and independence of the patients. We felt that the nursing of the sick in their homes should be undertaken seriously and adequately; that instruction should be incidental and not the primary consideration; that the etiquette, so far as doctor and patient were concerned, should be analogous to the established system of private nursing; that the nurse should be as ready to respond to calls from the people themselves as to calls from physicians; that she should accept calls from all physicians, and with no more red-tape or formality than if she were to remain with one patient continuously.

The new basis of the visiting-nurse service which we thus inaugurated reacted almost immediately upon the relationship of the nurse to the patient, reversing the position the nurse had formerly held. Chagrin at having the neighbors see in her an agent whose presence proclaimed the family's poverty or its failure to give adequate care to its sick member was changed to the gratifying consciousness that her presence, in conjunction with that of the doctor, . . . proclaimed the family's liberality and anxiety to do everything possible for the sufferer.

Liliuokalani,
Queen of Hawaii

~

LILIUOKALANI (1838–1917), queen of Hawaii, was placed under house arrest and forced to abdicate her throne in 1895, in order that Hawaii might be annexed to the United States. That annexation was accomplished by joint congressional resolution in 1898, and Hawaii became the fiftieth state 1959. Liliuokalani's account of her overthrow appears in her memoir, *Hawaii's Story by Hawaii's Queen*.

~

It has been my endeavor, in these recollections, to avoid speaking evil of any person, unless absolutely demanded by the exigencies of my case before the public. I simply state facts, and let others form their own judgment of the individuals. But of [American] Minister John L. Stevens it must be said that he was either mentally incapable of recognizing what is to be expected of a gentleman, to say nothing of a diplomatist, or he was decidedly in league with those persons who had conspired against the peace of Hawaii from the date of the "Queen's Jubilee" in 1887. Several times in my presence, to which he had access by virtue of his official position, he conducted himself with such a disregard of good manners as to excite the comment of my friends.

His official despatches to his own government, from the very first days of his landing, abound in statements to prove (according to his view) the great advantage of an overthrow of the monarchy, and a cession of my domains to the rule of the United States. His own daughter went as a messenger to the largest one of the islands

Liliuokalani. *Hawaii's Story by Hawaii's Queen*. 1898. Rpt., Honolulu, HI: Mutual Publishing, 1990, pp. 243–244, 267–277.

of my kingdom to secure names for a petition for the annexation of the Hawaiian Islands to the American Union, and by an accident lost her life, with the roll containing the few names she had secured. All this took place while he was presumed to be a friendly minister to a friendly power, and when my minister was under the same relation to his government. Of his remarks regarding myself personally I will take no notice. . . .

⌒

On the sixteenth day of January, 1895, Deputy Marshal Arthur Brown and Captain Robert Waipa Parker were seen coming up the walk which leads from Beretania Street to my residence. Mrs. Wilson told me that they were approaching. I directed her to show them into the parlor, where I soon joined them. Mr. Brown informed me that he had come to serve a warrant for my arrest; he would not permit me to take the paper which he held, nor to examine its contents.

It was evident they expected me to accompany them; so I made preparations to comply, supposing that I was to be taken at once to the station-house to undergo some kind of a trial. I was informed that I could bring Mrs. Clark with me if I wished, so she went for my hand-bag; and followed by her, I entered the carriage of the deputy marshal, and was driven through the crowd that by this time had accumulated at the gates of my residence at Washington Place. As I turned the corner of the block on which is built the Central Congregational church, I noticed the approach from another direction of Chief Justice Albert F. Judd; he was on the sidewalk, and was going toward my house, which he entered. In the mean time the marshal's carriage continued on its way, and we arrived at the gates of Iolani Palace, the residence of the Hawaiian sovereigns.

We drove up the front steps, and I remember noticing that troops of soldiers were scattered all over the yard. The men looked as though they had been on the watch all night. They were resting on the green grass, as though wearied by their vigils; and their arms were stacked near their tents, these latter having been pitched at intervals all over the palace grounds. Staring directly at us were the muzzles of two brass field-pieces, which looked warlike and formidable as they pointed out toward the gate from their positions on the lower veranda. Colonel J. H. Fisher came down the steps to receive me; I dismounted, and he led the way up the staircase to a large room in the corner of the palace. Here Mr. Brown made a formal delivery of my person into the custody of Colonel Fisher, and having done this, withdrew.

Then I had an opportunity to take a survey of my apartments. There was a large, airy, uncarpeted room with a single bed in one corner. The other furniture consisted of one sofa, a small square table, one single common chair, an iron safe, a bureau, a chiffonier, and a cupboard, intended for eatables, made of wood with wire screening to allow the circulation of the air through the food. Some of these articles may have been added during the days of my imprisonment. I have portrayed the room as it appears to me in memory. There was, adjoining the principal apartment, a bath-room, and also a corner room and a little boudoir, the windows of which were large, and gave access to the veranda.

Colonel Fisher spoke very kindly as he left me there, telling me that he supposed this was to be my future abode; and if there was anything I wanted I had only to mention it to the officer, and that it should be provided. In reply, I informed him that there were one or two of my attendants whom I would like to have near me, and that I preferred to have my meals sent from my own house. As a result of this expression of my wishes, permission was granted to my steward to bring me my meals three times each day.

That first night of my imprisonment was the longest night I have ever passed in my life; it seemed as though the dawn of day would never come. I found in my bag a small Book of Common Prayer according to the ritual of the Episcopal Church. It was a great comfort to me, and before retiring to rest Mrs. Clark and I spend a few minutes in the devotions appropriate to the evening. . . .

Outside of the rooms occupied by myself and my companion there were guards stationed by day and by night, whose duty it was to pace backward and forward through the hall, before my door, and up and down the front veranda. The sound of their never-ceasing footsteps as they tramped on their beat fell incessantly on my ears. One officer was in charge, and two soldiers were always detailed to watch our rooms. I could not but be reminded every instant that I was a prisoner, and did not fail to realize my position. My companion could not have slept at all that night; her sighs were audible to me without cessation; so I told her the morning following that, as her husband was in prison, it was her duty to return to her children. Mr. Wilson came in after I had breakfasted, accompanied by the Attorney-general, Mr. W. O. Smith; and in conference it was agreed between us that Mrs. Clark could return home, and that Mrs. Wilson should remain as my attendant; that Mr. Wilson would be the person to inform the government of any request to be made by me, and that any business transactions might be made through him.

On the morning after my arrest all my retainers residing on my estates were arrested, and to the number of about forty persons were taken to the station-house, and then committed to jail. Amongst these was the agent and manager of my property, Mr. Joseph Heleluhe. . . .

Mr. Heleluhe was taken by the government officers, stripped of all clothing, placed in a dark cell without light, food, air, or water, and was kept there for hours in hopes that the discomfort of his position would induce him to disclose something of my affairs. After this was found to be fruitless, he was imprisoned for about six weeks; when, finding their efforts in vain, his tormentors released him. No charge was ever brought against him in any way, which is true of about two hundred persons who were similarly confined.

On the very day I left the house, so I was informed by Mr. Wilson, Mr. A. F. Judd had gone to my private residence without search-warrant; and that all the papers in my desk, or in my safe, my diaries, the petitions I had received from my people,—all things of that nature which could be found were swept into a bag, and carried off by the chief justice in person. My husband's private papers were also included in those taken from me.

To this day, the only document which has been returned to me is my will. Never since have I been able to find the private papers of my husband nor those of mine that had been kept by me for use or reference, and which had no relation to political events. . . .

After Mr. Judd had left my house, it was turned over to the Portuguese military company under the command of Captain Good. These militiamen ransacked it again from garret to cellar. Not an article was left undisturbed. Before Mr. Judd had finished they had begun their work, and there was no trifle left unturned to see what might be hidden beneath. Every drawer of desk, table, or bureau was wrenched out, turned upside down, the contents pulled over on the floors, and left in confusion there. . . .

The place was then seized, and the government assumed possession; guards were placed on the premises, and no one was allowed to enter.

For the first few days nothing occurred to disturb the quiet of my apartments save the tread of the sentry. On the fourth day I received a visit from Mr. Paul Neumann, who asked me if, in the event that it should be decided that all the principal parties to the revolt must pay for it with their lives, I was prepared to die? I replied to this in the affirmative, telling him I had no anxiety for myself, and felt no dread of death. He then told me that six others besides myself had been selected to be shot for treason, but that he would call again, and let me know further about our fate. I was in a state of nervous prostration, as I have said, at the time of the outbreak, and naturally the strain upon my mind had much aggravated my physical troubles; yet it was with much difficulty that I obtained permission to have visits from my own medical attendant.

About the 22d of January a paper was handed to me by Mr. Wilson, which, on examination, proved to be a purported act of abdication for me to sign. It had been drawn out for the men in power by their own lawyer, Mr. A. S. Hartwell, whom I had not seen until he came with others to see me sign it. The idea of abdicating never originated with me. I knew nothing at all about such a transaction until they sent to me, by the hands of Mr. Wilson, the insulting proposition written in abject terms. For myself, I would have chosen death rather than to have signed it; but it was represented to me that by my signing this paper all the persons who had been arrested, all my people now in trouble by reason of their love and loyalty towards me, would be immediately released. Think of my position,—sick, a lone woman in prison, scarcely knowing who was my friend, or who listened to my words only to betray me, without legal advice or friendly counsel, and the stream of blood ready to flow unless it was stayed by my pen.

My persecutors have stated, and at that time compelled me to state, that this paper was signed and acknowledged by me after consultation with my friends whose names appear at the foot of it as witnesses. Not the least opportunity was given to me to confer with any one; but for the purpose of making it appear to the outside world that I was under the guidance of others, friends who had known me well in better days were brought into the place of my imprisonment, and stood around to see a signature affixed by me.

When it was sent to me to read, it was only a rough draft. After I had examined it, Mr. Wilson called, and asked me if I were willing to sign it. I simply answered that I would see when the formal or official copy was shown me. On the morning of the 24th of January the official document was handed to me, Mr. Wilson making the remark, as he gave it, that he hoped I would not retract, that is, he hoped that I would sign the official copy.

Then the following individuals witnessed my subscription of the signature which was demanded of me: William G. Irwin, H. A. Widemann, Samuel Parker, S. Kalua Kookano, Charles B. Wilson, and Paul Neumann. The form of acknowledgment was taken by W. L. Stanley, Notary Public.

So far from the presence of these persons being evidence of a voluntary act on my part, was it not an assurance to me that they, too, knew that, unless I did the will of my jailers, what Mr. Neumann had threatened would be performed, and six prominent citizens immediately put to death. I so regarded it then, and I still believe that murder was the alternative. Be this as it may, it is certainly happier for me to reflect to-day that there is not a drop of the blood of my subjects, friends or foes, upon my soul.

When it came to the act of writing, I asked what would be the form of signature; to which I was told to sign, "Liliuokalani Dominis." This sounding strange to me, I repeated the question, and was given the same reply. At this I wrote what they dictated without further demur, and more readily for the following reasons.

Before ascending the throne, for fourteen years, or since the date of my proclamation as heir apparent, my official title has been simply Liliuokalani. Thus I was proclaimed both Princess Royal and Queen. Thus it is recorded in the archives of the government to this day. The Provisional Government nor any other had enacted any change in my name. All my official acts, as well as my private letters, were issued over the signature of Liliuokalani. But when my jailers required me to sign "Liliuokalani Dominis," I did as they commanded. Their motive in this as in other actions was plainly to humiliate me before my people and before the world. I saw in a moment, what they did not, that, even were I not complying under the most severe and exacting duress, by this demand they had overreached themselves. There is not, and never was, within the range of my knowledge, any such a person as Liliuokalani Dominis.

It is a rule of common law that the acts of any person deprived of civil rights have no force nor weight, either at law or in equity; and that was my situation. Although it was written in the document that it was my free act and deed, circumstances prove that it was not; it had been impressed upon me that only by its execution could the lives of those dear to me, those beloved by the people of Hawaii, be saved, and the shedding of blood be averted. I have never expected the revolutionists of 1887 and 1893 to willingly restore the rights notoriously taken by force or intimidation; but this act, obtained under duress, should have no weight with the authorities of the United States, to whom I appealed. But it may be asked, why did I not make some protest at the time, or at least shortly thereafter, when I found my friends sentenced to death and imprisonment? I did. There are those now living who have seen my written statement of all that I have recalled here. It was made in my own handwriting, on such paper as I could get, and sent outside of the prison walls and into the hands of those to whom I wished to state the circumstances under which that fraudulent act of abdication was procured from me. This I did for my own satisfaction at the time.

After those in my place of imprisonment had all affixed their signatures, they left, with the single exception of Mr. A. S. Hartwell. As he prepared to go, he came forward, shook me by the hand, and the tears streamed down his cheeks. This was a matter of great surprise to me. After this he left the room. If he had been engaged in a righteous and honorable action, why should he be affected? Was it the consciousness of a mean act which overcame him so? Mrs. Wilson, who stood behind my chair throughout the ceremony, made the remark that those were crocodile's tears. I leave it to the reader to say what were his actual feelings in the case.

Zitkala-Sa

~

ZITKALA-SA (also known as Gertrude Simmons Bonnin or Red Bird, 1876–1938), author and activist in the pan-Indian movement, spent her early childhood with her mother at the Yankton Sioux Agency in South Dakota before enrolling in White's Manual Institute, an Indiana boarding school for Native Americans. Although she valued her education, continuing on to college in 1895 and becoming a teacher herself in 1897, her immersion into the world of the "paleface missionaries," as she referred to her teachers, was fraught with conflict. In these excerpts from four autobiographical articles originally published in the *Atlantic Monthly*, Zitkala-Sa assesses what was gained—and what was irretrievably lost—during her boarding-school days.

~

The first turning away from the easy, natural flow of my life occurred in an early spring. It was in my eighth year; in the month of March, I afterward learned. At this age I knew but one language, and that was my mother's native tongue.

From some of my playmates I heard that two paleface missionaries were in our village. They were from that class of white men who wore big hats and carried large hearts, they said. Running direct to my mother, I began to question her why these two strangers were among us. She told me, after I had teased much, that they had come to take away Indian boys and girls to the East. My mother

Andrews, William L. *Classic American Autobiographies*. New York: Penguin Books, 1992, pp. 429–438, 443–447, 450, 457–459.

did not seem to want me to talk about them. But in a day or two, I gleaned many wonderful stories from my playfellows concerning the strangers.

"Mother, my friend Jedéwin is going home with the missionaries. She is going to a more beautiful country than ours; the palefaces told her so!" I said wistfully, wishing in my heart that I too might go.

Mother sat in a chair, and I was hanging on her knee. Within the last two seasons my big brother Dawée had returned from a three years' education in the East, and his coming back influenced my mother to take a farther step from her native way of living. First it was a change from the buffalo skin to the white man's canvas that covered our wigwam. Now she had given up her wigwam of slender poles, to live, a foreigner, in a home of clumsy logs.

"Yes, my child, several others besides Judéwin are going away with the palefaces. Your brother said the missionaries had inquired about his little sister," she said, watching my face very closely.

My heart thumped so hard against my breast, I wondered if she could hear it.

"Did he tell them to take me, mother?" I asked, fearing lest Dawée had forbidden the palefaces to see me, and that my hope of going to the Wonderland would be entirely blighted.

With a sad, slow smile, she answered: "There! I knew you were wishing to go, because Judéwin has filled you ears with the white men's lies. Don't believe a word they say! Their words are sweet, but, my child, their deeds are bitter. You will cry for me, but they will not even soothe you. Stay with me, my little one! Your brother Dawée says that going East, away from your mother, is too hard an experience for his baby sister."

Thus my mother discouraged my curiosity about the lands beyond our eastern horizon; for it was not yet an ambition for Letters that was stirring me. But on the following day the missionaries did come to our very house. I spied them coming up the footpath leading to our cottage. A third man was with them, but he was not my brother Dawée. It was another, a young interpreter, a paleface who had a smattering of the Indian language. I was ready to run out to meet them, but I did not dare to displease my mother. With great glee, I jumped up and down on our ground floor. I begged my mother to open the door, that they would be sure to come to us. Alas! They came, they saw, and they conquered!

Judéwin had told me of the great tree where grew red, red apples; and how we could reach out our hands and pick all the red apples we could eat. I had never seen apple trees. I had never tasted more than a dozen red apples in my life; and when I heard of the orchards of the East, I was eager to roam among them. The missionaries smiled into my eyes, and patted my head. I wondered how mother could say such hard words against them.

"Mother, ask them if little girls may have all the red apples they want, when they go East," I whispered aloud, in my excitement.

The interpreter heard me, and answered: "Yes, little girl, the nice red apples are for those who pick them; and you will have a ride on the iron horse if you go with these good people."

I had never seen a train, and he knew it.

"Mother, I'm going East! I like big red apples, and I want to ride on the iron horse! Mother, say yes!" I pleaded.

My mother said nothing. The missionaries waited in silence; and my eyes began to blur with tears, though I struggled to choke them back. The corners of my mouth twitched, and my mother saw me.

"I am not ready to give you any word," she said to them. "Tomorrow I shall send you my answer by my son."

With this they left us. Alone with my mother, I yielded to my tears, and cried aloud, shaking my head so as not to hear what she was saying to me. This was the first time I had ever been so unwilling to give up my own desire that I refused to hearken to my mother's voice.

There was a solemn silence in our home that night. Before I went to bed I begged the Great Spirit to make my mother willing I should go with the missionaries.

The next morning came, and my mother called me to her side. "My daughter, do you still persist in wishing to leave your mother?" she asked.

"Oh, mother, it is not that I wish to leave you, but I want to see the wonderful Eastern land," I answered.

My dear old aunt came to our house that morning, and I heard her say, "Let her try it."

I hoped that, as usual, my aunt was pleading on my side. My brother Dawée came for mother's decision. I dropped my play, and crept close to my aunt.

"Yes, Dawée, my daughter, though she does not understand what it all means, is anxious to go. She will need an education when she is grown, for then there will be fewer real Dakotas, and many more palefaces. This tearing her away, so young, from her mother is necessary, if I would have her an educated woman. The palefaces, who owe us a large debt for stolen lands, have begun to pay a tardy justice in offering some education to our children. But I know my daughter must suffer keenly in this experiment. For her sake, I dread to tell you my reply to the missionaries. Go, tell them that they may take my little daughter, and that the Great Spirit shall not fail to reward them according to their hearts."

Wrapped in my heavy blanket, I walked with my mother to the carriage that was soon to take us to the iron horse. I was happy. I met my playmates, who were also wearing their best thick blankets. We showed one another our new beaded moccasins, and the width of the belts that girdled our new dresses. Soon we were being drawn rapidly away by the white man's horses. When I saw the lonely figure of my mother vanish in the distance, a sense of regret settled heavily upon me. I felt suddenly weak, as if I might fall limp to the ground. I was in the hands of strangers whom my mother did not fully trust. I no longer felt free to be myself, or to voice my own feelings. The tears trickled down my cheeks, and I buried my face in the folds of my blanket. Now the first step, parting me from my mother, was taken, and all my belated tears availed nothing. . . .

∽

The first day in the land of apples was a bitter-cold one; for the snow still covered the ground, and the trees were bare. A large bell rang for breakfast, its loud metallic voice crashing through the belfry overhead and into our sensitive ears. The annoying clatter of shoes on bare floors gave us no peace. The constant clash of harsh noises, with an undercurrent of many voices murmuring an unknown tongue, made a bedlam within which I was securely tied. And though my spirit tore itself in struggling for its lost freedom, all was useless.

A paleface woman, with white hair, came up after us. We were placed in a line of girls who were marching into the dining room. These were Indian girls, in stiff shoes and closely clinging dresses. The small girls wore sleeved aprons and shingled hair. As I walked noiselessly in my soft moccasins, I felt like sinking to the floor, for my blanket had been stripped from my shoulders. I looked hard at the Indian girls, who seemed not to care that they were even more immodestly dressed than I, in their tightly fitting clothes. While we marched in, the boys entered at an opposite door. I watched for the three young braves who came in our party. I spied them in the rear ranks, looking as uncomfortable as I felt.

A small bell was tapped, and each of the pupils drew a chair from under the table. Supposing this act meant they were to be seated, I pulled out mine and at once slipped into it from one side. But when I turned my head, I saw that I was the only one seated, and all the rest at our table remained standing. Just as I began to rise, looking shyly around to see how our chairs were to be used, a second bell was sounded. All were seated at last, and I had to crawl back into my chair again. I heard a man's voice at one end of the hall, and I looked around to see him. But all the others hung their heads over their plates. As I glanced at the long chain of tables, I caught the eyes of a paleface woman upon me. Immediately I dropped my eyes, wondering why I was so keenly watched by the strange woman. The man ceased his mutterings, and then a third bell was tapped. Every one picked up his knife and fork and began eating. I began crying instead, for by this time I was afraid to venture anything more.

But this eating by formula was not the hardest trial in that first day. Late in the morning, my friend Judéwin gave me a terrible warning. Judéwin knew a few words of English; and she had overheard the paleface woman talk about cutting our long, heavy hair. Our mothers had taught us that only unskilled warriors who were captured had their hair shingled by the enemy. Among our people, short hair was worn by mourners, and shingled hair by cowards!

We discussed our fate some moments, and when Judéwin said, "We have to submit, because they are strong," I rebelled.

"No, I will not submit! I will struggle first!" I answered.

I watched my chance, and when no one noticed I disappeared. I crept up the stairs as quietly as I could in my squeaking shoes,— my moccasins had been exchanged for shoes. Along the hall I passed, without knowing whither I was going. Turning aside to an open door, I found a large room with three white beds in it. The windows were covered with dark green curtains, which made the room very dim. Thankful that no one was there, I directed my steps toward the corner farthest from the door. On my hands and knees I crawled under the bed, and cuddled myself in the dark corner.

From my hiding place I peered out, shuddering with fear whenever I heard footsteps near by. Though in the hall loud voices were calling my name, and I knew that even Judéwin was searching for me, I did not open my mouth to answer. Then the steps were quickened and the voices became excited. The sounds came nearer and nearer. Women and girls entered the room. I held my breath, and watched them open closet doors and peep behind large trunks. Some one threw up the curtains, and the room was filled with sudden light. What caused them to stoop and look under the bed I do not know. I remember being dragged out, though I resisted by kicking and scratching wildly. In spite of myself, I was carried downstairs and tied fast in a chair.

I cried aloud, shaking my head all the while until I felt the cold blades of the scissors against my neck, and heard then gnaw off one of my thick braids. Then I lost my spirit. Since the day I was taken from my mother I had suffered extreme indignities. People had stared at me. I had been tossed about in the air like a wooden puppet. And now my long hair was shingled like a coward's! In my anguish I moaned for my mother, but no one came to comfort me. Not a soul reasoned quietly with me, as my own mother used to do; for now I was only one of many little animals driven by a herder. . . .

∿

After my first three years of school, I roamed again in the Western country through four strange summers.

During this time I seemed to hang in the heart of chaos, beyond the touch or voice of human aid. My brother, being almost ten years my senior, did not quite understand my feelings. My mother had never gone inside of a schoolhouse, and so she was not capable of comforting her daughter who could read and write. Even nature seemed to have no place for me. I was neither a wee girl nor a tall one; neither a wild Indian nor a tame one. This deplorable situation was the effect of my brief course in the East, and the unsatisfactory "teenth" in a girl's years. . . .

My mother was troubled by my unhappiness. Coming to my side, she offered me the only printed matter we had in our home. It was an Indian Bible, given her some years ago by a missionary. She tried to console me. "Here, my child, are the white man's papers. Read a little from them," she said most piously.

I took it from her hand, for her sake; but my enraged spirit felt more like burning the book, which afforded me no help, and was a perfect delusion to my mother. I did not read it, but laid it unopened on the floor, where I sat on my feet. The dim yellow light of the braided muslin burning in a small vessel of oil flickered and sizzled in the awful silent storm which followed my rejection of the Bible.

Now my wrath against the fates consumed my tears before they reached my eyes. I sat stony, with a bowed head. My mother threw a shawl over her head and shoulders, and stepped out into the night.

After an uncertain solitude, I was suddenly aroused by a loud cry piercing the night. It was my mother's voice wailing among the barren hills which held the bones of buried warriors. She called aloud for her brothers' spirits to support her in her helpless misery. My fingers grew icy cold, as I realized that my unrestrained tears had betrayed my suffering to her, and she was grieving for me.

Before she returned, though I knew she was on her way, for she had ceased her weeping, I extinguished the light, and leaned my head on the window sill.

Many schemes of running away from my surroundings hovered about in my mind. A few more moons of such a turmoil drove me away to the Eastern school. I rode on the white man's iron steed, thinking it would bring me back to my mother in a few winters, when I should be grown tall, and there would be congenial friends awaiting me. . . .

At the close of this second term of three years I was the proud owner of my first diploma. The following autumn I ventured upon a college career against my mother's will.

～

Though an illness left me unable to continue my college course, my pride kept me from returning to my mother. Had she known of my worn condition, she would have said the white man's papers were not worth the freedom and health I had lost by them. Such a rebuke from my mother would have been unbearable, and as I felt then it would be far too true to be comfortable.

Since the winter when I had my first dreams about red apples I had been traveling slowly toward the morning horizon. There had been no doubt about the direction in which I wished to go to spend my energies in a work for the Indian race. Thus I had written my mother briefly, saying my plan for the year was to teach in an Eastern Indian school. Sending this message to her in the West, I started at once eastward.

Thus I found myself, tired and hot, in a black veiling of car smoke, as I stood wearily on a street corner of an old-fashioned town, waiting for a car. In a few moment more I should be on the school grounds, where a new work was ready for my inexperienced hands.

～

As months passed over me, I slowly comprehended that the large army of white teachers in Indian schools had a larger missionary creed than I had suspected.

It was one which included self-preservation quite as much as Indian education. When I saw an opium-eater holding a position as teacher of Indians, I did not understand what good was expected, until a Christian in power replied that this pumpkin-colored creature had a feeble mother to support. An inebriate paleface sat stupid in a doctor's chair, while Indian patients carried their ailments to untimely graves, because his fair wife was dependent upon him for her daily food.

I find it hard to count that white man a teacher who tortured an ambitious Indian youth by frequently reminding the brave changeling that he was nothing but a "government pauper."

Though I burned with indignation upon discovering on every side instances no less shameful than those I have mentioned, there was no present help. Even the few rare ones who have worked nobly for my race were powerless to choose workmen like themselves. To be sure, a man was sent from the Great Father to inspect Indian schools, but what he saw was usually the students' sample work *made* for exhibition. I was nettled by this sly cunning of the workmen who hoodwinked the Indian's pale Father at Washington.

My illness, which prevented the conclusion of my college course, together with my mother's stories of the encroaching frontier settlers, left me in no mood to strain my eyes in searching for latent good in my white co-workers.

At this stage of my own evolution, I was ready to curse men of small capacity for being the dwarfs their God had made them. In the process of my education I had lost all consciousness of the nature world about me. Thus, when a hidden rage took me to the small white-walled prison which I then called my room, I unknowingly turned away from my one salvation.

Alone in my room, I sat like the petrified Indian woman of whom my mother used to tell me. I wished my heart's burdens would turn me to unfeeling stone. But alive, in my tomb, I was destitute!

For the white man's papers I had given up my faith in the Great Spirit. For these same papers I had forgotten the healing in trees and brooks. On account of my mother's simple view of life, and my lack of any, I gave her up, also. I made no friends among the race of people I loathed. Like a slender tree, I had been uprooted from my mother, nature, and God. I was shorn of my branches, which had waved in sympathy and love for home and friends. The natural coat of bark which had protected my oversensitive nature was scraped off to the very quick.

Now a cold bare pole I seemed to be, planted in a strange earth. Still, I seemed to hope a day would come when my mute aching head, reared upward to the sky, would flash a zigzag lightning across the heavens. With this dream of vent for a long-pent consciousness, I walked again amid the crowds.

At last, one weary day in the schoolroom, a new idea presented itself to me. It was a new way of solving the problem of my inner self. I liked it. Thus I resigned my position as teacher; and now I am in an Eastern city, following the long course of study I have set for myself. Now, as I look back upon the recent past, I see it from a distance, as a whole. I remember how, from morning till evening, many specimens of civilized peoples visited the Indian school. The city folks with canes and eyeglasses, the countrymen with sunburnt cheeks and clumsy feet, forgot their relative social ranks in an ignorant curiosity. Both sorts of these Christian palefaces were alike astounded at seeing the children of savage warriors so docile and industrious.

As answers to their shallow inquiries they received the students' sample work to look upon. Examining the neatly figured pages, and gazing upon the Indian girls and boys bending over their books, the white visitors walked out of the schoolhouse well satisfied: they were educating the children of the red man! They were paying a liberal fee to the government employees in whose able hands lay the small forest of Indian timber.

In this fashion many have passed idly through the Indian schools during the last decade, afterward to boast of their charity to the North American Indian. But few there are who have paused to question whether real life or long-lasting death lies beneath this semblance of civilization.

Carry A. Nation

~

CARRY A. NATION (1846–1911), a temperance leader famed for destroying saloons during her "Hatchetation" missions, considered herself a "Home Defender." In her autobiography, *The Use and Need of the Life of Carry A. Nation*, she remembers life in her own, undefended, marital home.

~

In the fall of 1865, Dr. Gloyd, a young physician, called to see my father to secure the country school, saying he wished to locate in our section of the country, and wanted to take a school that winter, and then he could decide where he would like to practice his profession.

This man was a thorough student, spoke, and read, several different languages. He boarded with us. I liked him, and stood in awe of him because of his superior education, never thinking that he loved me, until he astonished me one evening by kissing me. I had never had a gentleman to take such a privilege and felt shocked, threw up my hands to my face, saying several times: "I am ruined." My aunt and mother had instilled great reserve in my actions, when in company of gentlemen, so much so that I had never allowed one to sit near or hold my hand. This was not because I did not like their society, but I had been taught that to inspire respect or love from a man, you must keep him at a distance. This often made me awkward and reserved, but it did me no harm. When I learned that Dr. Gloyd loved me, I began to

Nation, Carry A. *The Use and Need of the Life of Carry A. Nation*. Topeka, KS: F. M. Steves & Sons, 1909, pp. 61–74.

love him. He was an only child. His parents had but a modest living. My mother was not pleased with seeing a growing attachment between us, for there was another match she had planned for me. When she saw this she would not allow me to sit alone in the room with him, so our communication was mostly by writing letters. I never knew Shakespeare until he read it to me, and I became an ardent admirer of the greatest poet. The volume of Shakespeare on his table was our postoffice. In the morning at breakfast he would manage to call the name "Shakespeare;" then I would know there was a letter for me in its leaves. After teaching three months he went to Holden, Missouri, and located; sent for his father and mother and in two years we were married.

My father and mother warned me that the doctor was addicted to drink, but I had no idea of the curse of rum. I did not fear anything, for I was in love, and doubted in him nothing. When Dr. Gloyd came up to marry me the 21st of November, 1867, I noticed with pain, that his countenance was not bright, he was changed. The day was one of the gloomiest I ever saw, a mist fell, and not a ray of sunshine. I felt a foreboding on the day I had looked forward to, as being one of the happiest. I did not find Dr. Gloyd the lover I expected. He was kind but seemed to want to be away from me; used to sit and read, when I was so hungry for his caresses and love. I have heard that this is the experience of many other young married women. They are so disappointed that their husbands change so after marriage. With my observation and experience I believe that men have it in their power to keep the love of ninety-nine women out of a hundred. Why do women lose love for their husbands? I find it is mostly due to indifference on the part of the husband. I often hear the experience of those poor abandoned sisters. I ask, Why are you in this house of sin and death? When I can get their confidence, many of them say: "I married a man; he drank, and went with other women. I got discouraged or spiteful, and went to the bad also." I find that drink causes so much enmity between the sexes. Drinking men neglect their wives. Their wives become jealous. Men often go with abandoned women under the influence of that drink that animates the animal passions and asks not for the association of love, but the gratification of lust. Men do not go to the houses of ill-fame to meet women they love but oftener those they almost hate. The drink habit destroys in men the appreciation of a home life, and when a women leaves all others for one man, she does, and should, expect his companionship, and is not satisfied without it. Libertines, taking advantage of this, select women whose husbands are neglectful, and he wins victims by his attentions, and poor woman, as at the first, is beguiled. Marriage, while it is the blissful consummation of pure love, is the most serious of all relations, and girls and boys should early be instructed about the secrets of their own natures, the object of marriage, and the serious results of any marriage where true love is not the object. I confess myself that I was not fit to marry with the ignorance of its holy purpose. . . .

About five days after we were married, Dr. Gloyd came in, threw himself on the bed and fell asleep. I was in the next room and saw his mother bow down over his face. She did not know I saw her. When she left, I did the same thing, and the fumes of liquor came in my face. I was terror stricken, and from that time on, I knew why he was so changed. Not one happy moment did I see! I cried most all the time. My husband seemed to understand that I knew his condition. Twice, with tears in his eyes, he remarked: "Oh! Pet, I would give my right arm to make you happy." He would be out until late every night. I never closed my eyes. His sign in front of the door on the street would creak in the wind, and I would sit by the window waiting to hear his footsteps. I never saw him stagger. . . . People would call for him in case of sickness, but he could not be found.

My anguish was unspeakable, I was comparatively a child. I wanted some one to help me. . . . The world was all at once changed to me, it was like a place of torture. I thought certainly, there must be a way to prevent this suicide and murder. I now know, that the impulse was born in me then to combat to the death this inhumanity to man. . . .

I was so ignorant I did not know that I owed a duty to myself to avoid gloomy thoughts; did not know that a mother could entail a curse on her offspring before it was born. Oh, the curse that comes through heredity, and this liquor evil, a disease that entails more depravity on children unborn, than all else, unless it be tobacco. There is an object lesson taught in the Bible. The mother of Samson was told by an angel to "drink neither wine nor strong drink," Judges 13:4, before her child was born. God shows by this, that these things are injurious. Mothers often make drunkards of their own children, before they are born. My parents heard that Dr. Gloyd was drinking. My father came down to visit us, and I went home with him. My mother told me I must never go back to my husband again. I knew time was near at hand, when I would be helpless, with a drunken husband, and no means of support. What could I do? I kept writing to "Charlie," as I called him. He came to see me once; my mother treated him as a stranger. He expressed much anxiety about my confinement in September; got a party to agree to come for him at the time; but my mother would not allow it. In six weeks after my little girl was born, my mother sent my brother with me to Holden to get my trunk and other things to bring them home. Her words to me were: "If you stay in Holden, never return home again." My husband begged me to stay with him; he said: "Pet, if you leave me, I will be a dead man in six months." I wanted stay with him, but dared not disobey my mother and be thrown out of shelter, for I saw I could not depend on my husband. . . . In a little less than six months from the day my child was born, I got a telegram telling of his death. His father died a few months before he did, and mother Gloyd was left entirely alone.

Mother Gloyd was a true type of a New England housewife, and I had always lived in the south. I could not say at this time that I loved her, although I respected her very highly. But I wanted to be with the mother of the man I loved more than my own life; I wanted to supply his place if possible. My father gave me several lots; by selling one of these and Dr. Gloyd's library and instruments, I built a house of three rooms on one of the lots and rented the house we lived in, which brought us in a little income, but not sufficient to support us. I wanted to prepare myself to teach, and I attended the Normal Institute of Warrensburg. I was not able to pay my board and Mr. Archie Gilkerson and wife charged me nothing and were as kind to me as parents. God bless them! I got a certificate and was given the primary room in the Public School at Holden. Mother Gloyd kept house and took care of Charlien, my little girl, and I made the living. This continued for four years. I lost my position as teacher in that school this way: A Dr. Moore was a member of the board, he criticised me for the way I had the little ones read; for instance, in the sentence, "I saw a man," I had them use the short a instead of the long a, and so with the article a; having them read it as we would speak it naturally. He made this serious objection, and I lost my place and Dr. Moore's niece got my room as teacher. This was a severe blow to me, for I could not leave mother Gloyd and Charlien to teach in another place, and I knew of no other way of making a living except by teaching. I resolved then to get married. I made it a subject of prayer and went to the Lord explaining things about this way. I said: "My Lord, you see the situation I cannot take care of mother and Charlien. I want you to help me. If it be best for me to marry I will do so. I have no one picked out, but I want you to select the one that you think best. I want to give you my life, and I want by marrying to glorify and serve you, as well as to take care of mother and Charlien and be a good wife." . . .

In about ten days from that time I made this a subject of prayer, I was walking down the street in Holden and passed a place where Mr. Nation was standing, who had come up from Warrensburg, where he was then editing the "Warrensburg Journal." He was standing in the door with his back to me, but turned and spoke. There was a peculiar thrill which passed through my heart which made me start. The next day I got a letter from him, asking me to correspond with him. I was not surprised; had been expecting something like it. I knew that this was in answer to my prayer, and David Nation was to be the husband God selected for me. He was nineteen years older than I, was very good looking, and was a well-informed, successful lawyer, also a minister in the Christian Church. My friends in Holden opposed this because of the difference in our ages and of his large family. I gave him the loving confidence of a true wife and he was often very kind to me. We were married within six weeks from the time I got the letter from him. Mother Gloyd went to live with us and continued to do so for fifteen years, until she died. My married life with Mr. Nation was not a happy one. I found out that he deceived me in so many things. I can remember the first time I found this out. I felt that something was broken that could never be mended. What a shattered thing is betrayed confidence! Oh, husbands and wives, do not lie to each other, even though you should do a vile act; confess to the truth of the matter! There will be some trouble over it, but you can never lose your love for a truthful person. I hated lying because I loved the truth. . . .

I shall not in this book give to the public the details of my life as a wife of David Nation any more than possible. He and I agreed in but few things, and still we did not have the outbreaks many husbands and wives have. The most serious trouble that ever rose between us was in regard to Christianity. My Christian life was an offence unto him, and I found out if I yielded to his ideas and views that I would be false to every true motive. He saw that I resented this influence and it caused him to be suspicious and jealous. I think my combative nature was largely developed by living with him, for I had to fight for everything that I kept. About two years after we were married we exchanged our mutual properties for seventeen hundred acres of land on the San Bernard river in Texas, part of which was a cotton plantation. We knew nothing of the cultivation of cotton or of plantation life. . . .

We were as helpless on the plantation as little children. The cultivation of cotton was very different from anything we had been used to. A bad neighbor threw all of our plows in the Bernard river and everything seemed to go wrong. We had eight horses die in the pasture the spring after we moved there. Soon the money we took with us was gone and Mr. Nation became discouraged. He went to Brazoria, the county seat, and stayed six weeks during court, for the purpose of entering the practice of law again.

The cotton had been lanted before he left. A neighbor named Martin Hanks came over and told me not to allow the cotton to go to waste, said he would lend me his plows, and advised me to get a colored man named Edmond, who was his master's overseer in slave time, to manage this crop for me. I hired five other negroes, paying them with things I had in the house, for I had not a cent of money. The result was a fine crop of cotton. Mr. Nation's daughter Lola, was then eleven years old, and Charlien was three years younger. We lived six miles from a school, and just at a time when the girls needed school most. I began to see what a disastrous move we had made. I became very despondent and sick at heart. I was young and did not know then how to contend with disappointments on every hand. . . .

I was in Columbia one day and stopped at the Old Columbia Hotel, owned by the Messrs. Park, two brothers. Mrs. Ballenger a widow was renting it from Messrs. Park. I said to them: "If you ever need a tenant, send for me." In a few months Mrs. Ballenger's daughter died and she left. Mr. Park sent for me to come. We had a carload of good plain furniture and bedding, some handsome tableware, but no money to buy provisions.

Dear old mother Gloyd was a great help to me. She had once kept hotel herself. I did not ask credit, at the store and this is how I got the money to begin keeping hotel: There was an Irish ditcher named Dunn, whose wife did my work. She was a good cook. I borrowed of Mr. Dunn three dollars and fifty cents, and with this money began the hotel business. The house was a rattle trap, plastering off, and a regular bed-bug nest. I fumigated, pasted the walls over with cloth and newspapers, where the plastering was off, and made curtains out of old sheets. My purchases were about like this for the first day: Fifty cents worth of meat, coffee ten cents, rice ten cents and sugar twenty-five, potatoes five, etc. The transients at one meal would give me something to spend for the next. I assisted about the cooking and helped in the dining-room. Mother Gloyd and Lola attended to the chamber work, and little Charlien was the one who did the buying for the house. I would often wash out my tablecloths at night myself and iron them in the morning before breakfast. . . . For several months my little children and I ate nothing but broken food. I can never put on paper the struggles of this life. I would not know one day how we would get along the next.

The bitterest sorrows of my life have come from not having the love of a husband. I must here say that I have had, at times, in the society of those I love, a foretaste of what this could be. For years I never saw a loving husband that I did not envy the wife; it was a cry of my heart for love. I used to ask God why He denied me this. I can see now why it was. I know it was God's will for me to marry Mr. Nation. Had I married a man I could have loved, God could never have used me. Phrenologists who have examined my head have said: "How can you, who are such a lover of home be without one?" The very things that I was denied caused me to have a desire to secure it for others.

Helen Keller

~

HELEN KELLER (1880–1968), feminist, socialist, a founder of the American Civil Liberties Union, and crusader for the handicapped, lost both her sight and hearing at nineteen months of age. Taught by Anne Sullivan (1866–1936) to use Braille for reading and writing and to communicate with others by spelling words into their hands, Keller excelled at her studies and entered Radcliffe College in 1900. In her autobiography, *The Story of My Life*, she recalls her years of study.

~

In October, 1896, I entered the Cambridge School for Young Ladies, to be prepared for Radcliffe.

When I was a little girl, I visited Wellesley and surprised my friends by the announcement, "Some day I shall go to college—but I shall go to Harvard!" When asked why I would not go to Wellesley, I replied that there were only girls there. The thought of going to college took root in my heart and became an earnest desire, which impelled me to enter into competition for a degree with seeing and hearing girls, in the face of the strong opposition of many true and wise friends. When I left New York the idea had become a fixed purpose; and it was decided that I should go to Cambridge. This was the nearest approach I could get to Harvard and to the fulfillment of my childish declaration.

At the Cambridge School the plan was to have Miss Sullivan attend the classes with me and interpret to me the instruction given.

Keller, Helen. *The Story of My Life*. 1902. Rpt., New York: Penguin Books USA, 1988, pp. 63–75.

Of course my instructors had had no experience in teaching any but normal pupils, and my only means of conversing with them was reading their lips. My studies for the first year were English history, English literature, German, Latin, arithmetic, Latin composition and occasional themes. Until then I had never taken a course of study with the idea of preparing for college; but I had been well drilled in English by Miss Sullivan, and it soon became evident to my teachers that I needed no special instruction in this subject beyond a critical study of the books prescribed by the college. I had had, moreover, a good start in French, and received six months' instruction in Latin; but German was the subject with which I was most familiar.

In spite, however, of these advantages, there were serious drawbacks to my progress. Miss Sullivan could not spell out in my hand all that the books required, and it was very difficult to have text-books embossed in time to be of use to me, although my friends in London and Philadelphia were willing to hasten the work. For a while, indeed, I had to copy my Latin in braille, so that I could recite with the other girls. My instructors soon became sufficiently familiar with my imperfect speech to answer my questions readily and correct mistakes. I could not make notes in class or write exercises; but I wrote all my compositions and translations at home on my typewriter.

Each day Miss Sullivan went to the classes with me and spelled into my hand with infinite patience all that the teachers said. In study hours she had to look up new words for me and read and reread notes and books I did not have in raised print. The tedium of that work is hard to conceive. Frau Gröte, my German teacher, and Mr. Gilman, the principal, were the only teachers in the school who learned the finger alphabet to give me instruction. No one realized more fully than dear Frau Gröte how slow and inadequate her spelling was. Nevertheless, in the goodness of her heart she laboriously spelled out her instructions to me in special lessons twice a week, to give Miss Sullivan a little rest. But, though everybody was kind and ready to help us, there was only one hand that could turn drudgery into pleasure.

That year I finished arithmetic, reviewed my Latin grammar, and read three chapters of Caesar's "Gallic War." In German I read, partly with my fingers and partly with Miss Sullivan's assistance, Schiller's "Lied von der Glocke" and "Taucher," Heine's "Harzreise," Freytag's "Aus dem Staat Friedrichs des Grossen," Riehl's "Fluch Der Schönheit," Lessing's "Minna von Barnhelm," and Goethe's "Aus meinem Leben." I took the greatest delight in these German books, especially Schiller's wonderful lyrics, the history of Frederick the Great's magnificent achievements and the account of Goethe's life. . . .

At the Cambridge school, for the first time in my life, I enjoyed the companionship of seeing and hearing girls of my own age. I lived with several others in one of the pleasant houses connected with the school, the house where Mr. Howells used to live, and we all had the advantage of home life. I joined them in many of their games, even blind man's bluff and frolics in the snow; I took long walks with them; we discussed our studies and read aloud the things that interested us. Some of the girls learned to speak to me, so that Miss Sullivan did not have to repeat their conversation.

At Christmas, my mother and little sister spent the holidays with me, and Mr. Gilman kindly offered to let Mildred study in his school. So Mildred stayed with me in Cambridge, and for six happy months we were hardly ever apart. It makes me most happy to remember the hours we spent helping each other in study and sharing our recreation together.

I took my preliminary examinations for Radcliffe from the 29th of June to the 3rd of July in 1897. The subjects I offered were Elementary and Advanced German, French, Latin, English, and Greek and Roman history, making nine hours in all. I passed in everything, and received "honours" in German and English.

Perhaps an explanation of the method that was in use when I took my examinations will not be amiss here. The student was required to pass in sixteen hours—twelve hours being called elementary and four advanced. He had to pass five hours at a time to have them counted. The examination papers were given out at nine o'clock at Harvard and brought to Radcliffe by a special messenger. Each candidate was known, not by his name, but by a number. I was No. 233, but, as I had to use a typewriter, my identity could not be concealed.

It was thought advisable for me to have my examinations in a room by myself, because the noise of the typewriter might disturb the other girls. Mr. Gilman read all the papers to me by means of the manual alphabet. A man was placed on guard at the door to prevent interruption.

The first day I had German. Mr. Gilman sat beside me and read the paper through first, then sentence by sentence, while I repeated the words aloud, to make sure that I understood him perfectly. The papers were difficult, and I felt very anxious as I wrote out my answers on the typewriter. Mr. Gilman spelled to me what I had written, and I made such changes as I thought necessary, and he inserted them. I wish to say here that I have not had this advantage since in any of my examinations. At Radcliffe no one reads the papers to me after they are written, and I have no opportunity to correct errors unless I finish before the time is up. In that case I correct only such mistakes as I can recall in the few minutes allowed, and make notes of these corrections at the end of my paper. If I passed with higher credit in the preliminaries than in the finals, there are two reasons. In the finals, no one read my work over to me, and in the preliminaries I offered subjects with some of which I was in a measure familiar before my work in the Cambridge school; for at the beginning of the year I had passed examinations in English, History, French and German, which Mr. Gilman gave me from previous Harvard papers.

Mr. Gilman sent my written work to the examiners with a certificate that I, candidate No. 233, had written the papers.

All the other preliminary examinations were conducted in the same manner. None of them was so difficult as the first. I remember that the day the Latin paper was brought to us, Professor Schilling came in and informed me I had passed satisfactorily in German. This encouraged me greatly, and I sped on to the end of the ordeal with a light heart and a steady hand.

~

When I began my second year at the Gilman school, I was full of hope and determination to succeed. But during the first few weeks I was confronted with unforeseen difficulties. Mr. Gilman had agreed that that year I should study mathematics principally. I had physics, algebra, geometry, astronomy, Greek and Latin. Unfortunately, many of the books I needed had not been embossed in time for me to begin with the classes, and I lacked important apparatus for some of my studies. The classes I was in were very large and it was impossible for the teachers to give me special instruction. Miss Sullivan was obliged to read all the books to me, and interpret for the instructors, and for the first time in eleven years it seemed as if her dear hand would not be equal to the task.

It was necessary for me to write algebra and geometry in class and solve problems in physics, and this I could not do until we bought a braille writer, by means of which I could put down the steps and processes of my work. I could not follow with my eyes the geometrical figures drawn on the blackboard, and my only means of getting a clear idea of them was to make them on a cushion with straight and curved wires, which had bent and pointed ends. I had to carry in my mind, as Mr. Keith says in his report, the lettering of the figures, the hypothesis and conclusion, the construction and the process of the proof. In a word, every study had its obstacles. Sometimes I lost all courage and betrayed my feelings in a way I am ashamed to remember, especially as the signs of my trouble were afterward used against Miss Sullivan, the only person of all the kind friends I had there, who could make the crooked straight and the rough places smooth.

Little by little, however, my difficulties began to disappear. The embossed books and other apparatus arrived, and I threw myself into the work with renewed confidence. Algebra and geometry were the only studies that continued to defy my efforts to comprehend them. As I have said before, I had no aptitude for mathematics; the different points were not explained to me as fully as I wished. The geometrical diagrams were particularly vexing because I could not see the relation of the different parts to one another, even on the cushion. It was not until Mr. Keith taught me that I had a clear idea of mathematics.

I was beginning to overcome these difficulties when an event occurred which changed everything.

Just before the books came, Mr. Gilman had begun to remonstrate with Miss Sullivan on the ground that I was working too hard, and in spite of my earnest protestations, he reduced the number of my recitations. At the beginning we had agreed that I should, if necessary, take five years to prepare for college, but at the end of the first year the success of my examinations showed Miss Sullivan, Miss Harbaugh (Mr. Gilman's head teacher), and one other, that I could without too much effort complete my preparation in two years more. Mr. Gilman at first agreed to this; but when my tasks had become somewhat perplexing, he insisted that I was overworked, and that I should remain at his school three years longer. I did not like his plan, for I wished to enter college with my class.

On the seventeenth of November I was not very well, and did not go to school. Although Miss Sullivan knew that my indisposition was not serious, yet Mr. Gilman, on hearing of it, declared that I was breaking down and made changes in my studies which would have rendered it impossible for me to take my final examinations with my class. In the end the difference of opinion between Mr. Gilman and Miss Sullivan resulted in my mother's withdrawing my sister Mildred and me from the Cambridge School.

After some delay it was arranged that I should continue my studies under a tutor, Mr. Merton S. Keith, of Cambridge. Miss Sullivan and I spent the rest of the winter with our friends, the Chamberlins in Wrentham, twenty-five miles from Boston.

From February to July, 1898, Mr. Keith came out to Wrentham twice a week, and taught me algebra, geometry, Greek and Latin. Miss Sullivan interpreted his instruction.

In October, 1898, we returned to Boston. For eight months Mr. Keith gave me lessons five times a week, in periods of about an hour. He explained each time what I did not understand in the previous lesson, assigned new work, and took home with him the Greek exercises which I had written during the week on my typewriter, corrected them fully, and returned them to me.

In this way my preparation for college went on without interruption. I found it much easier and pleasanter to be taught by myself than to receive instruction in class. There was no hurry, no confusion. My tutor had plenty of time to explain what I did not understand, so I got on faster and did better work than I ever did in school. I still found more difficulty in mastering problems in mathematics than I did in any other of my studies. I wish algebra and geometry had been half as easy as the languages and literature. But even mathematics Mr. Keith made interesting; he succeeded in whittling problems small enough to get through my brain. He kept my mind alert and eager, and trained it to reason clearly, and to seek conclusions calmly and logically, instead of jumping wildly into space and arriving nowhere. He was always gentle and forbearing, no matter how dull I might be, and believe me, my stupidity would often have exhausted the patience of Job.

On the 29th and 30th of June, 1899, I took my final examinations for Radcliffe College. The first day I had Elementary Greek and Advanced Latin, and the second day Geometry, Algebra and Advanced Greek.

The college authorities did not allow Miss Sullivan to read the examination papers to me; so Mr. Eugene C. Vining, one of the instructors at the Perkins Institution for the Blind, was employed to copy the papers for me in American braille. Mr. Vining was a stranger to me, and could not communicate with me, except by writing braille. The proctor was also a stranger, and did not attempt to communicate with me in any way.

The braille worked well enough in the languages, but when it came to geometry and algebra, difficulties rose. I was sorely perplexed, and felt discouraged wasting much precious time, especially in algebra. It is true that I was familiar with all literary braille in common use in this country—English, American, and New York

Point; but the various signs and symbols in geometry and algebra in the three systems are very different, and I had used only the English braille in my algebra.

Two days before the examinations, Mr. Vining sent me a braille copy of one of the old Harvard papers in algebra. To my dismay I found that it was in the American notation. I sat down immediately and wrote to Mr. Vining, asking him to explain the signs. I received another paper and a table of signs by return mail, and I set to work to learn the notation. But on the night before the algebra examination, while I was struggling over some very complicated examples, I could not tell the combinations of bracket, brace and radical. Both Mr. Keith and I were distressed and full of forebodings for the morrow; but we went over to the college a little before the examination began, and had Mr. Vining explain more fully the American symbols.

In geometry my chief difficulty was that I had always been accustomed to read the propositions in line print, or to have them spelled into my hand; and somehow, although the propositions were right before me, I found the braille confusing, and could not fix clearly in my mind what I was reading. But when I took up algebra I had a harder time still. The signs, which I had so lately learned, and which I thought I knew, perplexed me. Besides, I could not see what I wrote on my typewriter. I had always done my work in braille or in my head. Mr. Keith had relied too much on my ability to solve problems mentally, and had not trained me to write examination papers. Consequently my work was painfully slow, and I had to read the examples over and over before I could form any idea of what I was required to do. Indeed, I am not sure now that I read all the signs correctly. I found it very hard to keep my wits about me.

But I do not blame any one. The administrative board of Radcliffe did not realize how difficult they were making my examinations, nor did they understand the peculiar difficulties I had to surmount. But if they unintentionally placed obstacles in my way, I have the consolation of knowing that I overcame them all.

〜

The struggle for admission to college was ended, and I could now enter Radcliffe whenever I pleased. Before I entered college, however, it was thought best that I should study another year under Mr. Keith. It was not, therefore, until the fall of 1900 that my dream of going to college was realized.

I remember my first day at Radcliffe. It was a day full of interest for me. I had looked forward to it for years. A potent force within me, stronger than the persuasion of my friends, stronger even than the pleadings of my heart, had impelled me to try my strength by the standards of those who see and hear. I knew that there were obstacles in the way; but I was eager to overcome them. I had taken to heart the words of the wise Roman who said, "To be banished from Rome is but to live outside of Rome." Debarred from the great highways of knowledge, I was compelled to make the journey across country by unfrequented roads—that was all; and I knew that in college there were many bypaths where I could touch hands with girls who were thinking, loving and struggling like me.

I began my studies with eagerness. Before me I saw a new world opening in beauty and light, and I felt within me the capacity to know all things. In the wonderland of Mind I should be as free as another. Its people, scenery, manners, joys, tragedies should be living, tangible interpreters of the real world. The lecture-halls seemed filled with the spirit of the great and the wise, and I thought the professors were the embodiment of wisdom. If I have since learned differently, I am not going to tell anybody. . . .

I am frequently asked how I overcome the peculiar conditions under which I work in college. In the classroom I am of course practically alone. The professor is as remote as if he were speaking through a telephone. The lectures are spelled into my hand as rapidly as possible, and much of the individuality of the lecturer is lost to me in the effort to keep in the race. The words rush through my hand like hounds in pursuit of a hare which they often miss. But in this respect I do not think I am much worse off than the girls who take notes. If the mind is occupied with the mechanical process of hearing and putting words on paper at pell-mell speed, I should not think one could pay much attention to the subject under consideration or the manner in which it is presented. I cannot make notes during the lectures, because my hands are busy listening. Usually I jot down what I can remember of them when I get home. I write the exercises, daily themes, criticisms and hour-tests, the mid-year and final examinations, on my typewriter, so that the professors have no difficulty in finding out how little I know. When I began the study of Latin prosody, I devised and explained to my professor a system of signs indicating the different meters and quantities.

I use the Hammond typewriter. I have tried many machines, and I find the Hammond is the best adapted to the peculiar needs of my work. With this machine movable type shuttles can be used, and one can have several shuttles, each with a different set of characters—Greek, French, or mathematical, according to the kind of writing one wishes to do on the typewriter. Without it, I doubt if I could go to college.

Very few of the books required in the various courses are printed for the blind, and I am obliged to have them spelled into my hand. Consequently I need more time to prepare my lessons than other girls. The manual part takes longer, and I have perplexities which they have not. There are days when the close attention I must give to details chafes my spirit, and the thought that I must spend hours reading a few chapters, while in the world without other girls are laughing and singing and dancing, makes me rebellious; but I soon recover my buoyancy and laugh the discontent out of my heart. For, after all, every one who wishes to gain true knowledge must climb the Hill Difficulty alone, and since there is no royal road to the summit, I must zigzag it in my own way. I slip back many times, I fall, I stand still, I run against the edge of hidden obstacles, I lose my temper and find it again and keep it better. I trudge on, I gain a little, I feel encouraged, I get more eager and climb higher and begin to see the widening horizon.

"Mother" Mary Jones

~

"MOTHER" MARY JONES (1830–1930), a labor agitator and organizer of the late nineteenth and early twentieth centuries, was involved in many of each century's most important strikes. She also had other methods of bringing the workers' plight to national attention. In *The Autobiography of Mother Jones*, she remembers her 1903 march of child mill workers from Kensington, Pennsylvania, to the home of President Theodore Roosevelt in Oyster Bay, New York.

~

The March of the Mill Children

In the spring of 1903 I went to Kensington, Pennsylvania, where seventy-five thousand textile workers were on strike. Of this number at least ten thousand were little children. The workers were striking for more pay and shorter hours. Every day little children came into Union Headquarters, some with their hands off, some with the thumb missing, some with their fingers off at the knuckle. They were stooped little things, round shouldered and skinny. Many of them were not over ten years of age, although the state law prohibited their working before they were twelve years of age.

The law was poorly enforced and the mothers of these children often swore falsely as to their children's age. In a single block in Kensington, fourteen women, mothers of twenty-two children all under twelve, explained it was a question of starvation or perjury. That the fathers had been killed or maimed at the mines.

Jones, Mary Harris. *The Autobiography of Mother Jones*. Mary Field Parton, ed. Chicago: Charles H. Kerr & Company, 1925, pp. 71–83.

I asked the newspaper men why they didn't publish the facts about child labor in Pennsylvania. They said they couldn't because the mill owners had stock in the papers.

"Well, I've got stock in these little children," said I, "and I'll arrange a little publicity."

We assembled a number of boys and girls one morning in Independence Park and from there we arranged to parade with banners to the court house where we would hold a meeting.

A great crowd gathered in the public square in front of the city hall. I put the little boys with their fingers off and hands crushed and maimed on a platform. I held up their mutilated hands and showed them to the crowd and made the statement that Philadelphia's mansions were built on the broken bones, the quivering hearts and drooping heads of these children. That their little lives went out to make wealth for others. That neither state or city officials paid any attention to these wrongs. That they did not care that these children were to be the future citizens of the nation.

The officials of the city hall were standing in the open windows. I held the little ones of the mills high up above the heads of the crowd and pointed to their puny arms and legs and hollow chests. They were light to lift.

I called upon the millionaire manufacturers to cease their moral murders, and I cried to the officials in the open windows opposite, "Some day the workers will take possession of your city hall, and when we do, no child will be sacrificed on the alter of profit."

The officials quickly closed the windows, just as they had closed their eyes and hearts.

The reporters quoted my statement that Philadelphia mansions were built on the broken bones and quivering hearts of children. The Philadelphia papers and the New York papers got into a squabble with each other over the question. The universities discussed it. Preachers began talking. That was what I wanted. Public attention on the subject of child labor.

The matter quieted down for a while and I concluded the people needed stirring up again. The Liberty Bell that a century ago rang out for freedom against tyranny was touring the country and crowds were coming to see it everywhere. That gave me an idea. These little children were striking for some of the freedom that childhood ought to have, and I decided that the children and I would go on a tour.

I asked some of the parents if they would let me have their little boys and girls for a week or ten days, promising to bring them back safe and sound. They consented. A man named Sweeny was marshal for our "army." A few men and women went with me to help with the children. They were on strike and I thought they might as well have a little recreation.

The children carried knapsacks on their backs in which was a knife and fork, a tin cup and plate. We took along a wash boiler in which to cook the food on the road. One little fellow had a drum and another had a fife. That was our band. We carried banners that said, "We want more schools and less hospitals." "We want time to play." "Prosperity is here. Where is ours?"

We started from Philadelphia where we held a great mass meeting. I decided to go with the children to see President Roosevelt to ask him to have Congress pass a law prohibiting the exploitation of childhood. I though that President Roosevelt might see these mill children and compare them with his own little ones who were spending the summer on the seashore at Oyster Bay. I thought, too, out of politeness, we might call on [J. P.] Morgan in Wall Street who owned the mines where many of these children's fathers worked.

The children were very happy, having plenty to eat, taking baths in the brooks and rivers every day. I thought when the strike is over and they go back to the mills, they will never have another holiday like this. All along the line of march the farmers drove out to meet us with wagon loads of fruit and vegetables. Their wives brought the children clothes and money. The interurban trainmen would stop their trains and give us free rides.

Marshal Sweeny and I would go ahead to the towns and arrange sleeping quarters for the children, and secure meeting halls. As we marched on, it grew terribly hot. There was no rain and the roads were heavy with dust. From time to time we had to send some of the children back to their homes. They were too weak to stand the march.

We were on the outskirts of New Trenton, New Jersey, cooking our lunch in the wash boiler, when the conductor on the interurban car stopped and told us the police were coming down to notify us that we could not enter the town. There were mills in the town and the mill owners didn't like our coming.

I said, "All right, the police will be just in time for lunch."

Sure enough, the police came and we invited them to dine with us. They looked at the little gathering of children with their tin plates and cups around the wash boiler. They just smiled and spoke kindly to the children, and said nothing at all about not going into the city.

We went in, held our meeting, and it was the wives of the police who took the little children and cared for them that night, sending them back in the morning with a nice lunch rolled up in paper napkins.

Everywhere we had meetings, showing up with living children, the horrors of child labor.

At one town the mayor said we could not hold a meeting because he did not have sufficient police protection. "These little children have never known any sort of protection, your honor," I said, "and they are used to going without it." He let us have our meeting.

One night in Princeton, New Jersey, we slept in the big cool barn on Grover Cleveland's great estate. The heat became intense. There was much suffering in our ranks, for our little ones were not robust. The proprietor of the leading hotel sent for me. "Mother," he said, "order what you want and all you want for your army, and there's nothing to pay."

I called on the mayor of Princeton and asked for permission to speak opposite the campus of the University. I said I wanted to speak on higher education. The mayor gave me permission. A great crowd gathered, professors and students and the people; and I told them that the rich robbed these little children of any education of the lowest order that they might send their sons and daughters to places of higher education. That they used the hands and feet of little children that they might buy automobiles for their wives and police dogs for their daughters to talk French to. I said the mill owners take babies almost from the cradle. And I showed those professors children in our army who could scarcely read or write because they were working ten hours a day in the silk mills of Pennsylvania.

"Here's a text book on economics," I said, pointing to a little chap, James Ashworth, who was ten years old and who was stooped over like an old man from carrying bundles of yarn that weighted seventy-five pounds. "He gets three dollars a week and his sister who is fourteen gets six dollars. They work in a carpet factory ten hours a day while the children of the rich are getting their higher education.". . .

[In New York City,] we marched to Twentieth Street. I told an immense crowd of the horrors of child labor in the mills around the anthracite region and I showed them some of the children. I showed them Eddie Dunphy, a little fellow of twelve, whose job it was to sit all day on a high stool, handing in the right thread to another worker. Eleven hours a day he sat on the high stool with dangerous machinery all about him. All day long, winter and summer, spring and fall, for three dollars a week.

And then I showed them Gussie Rangnew, a little girl from whom all the childhood had gone. Her face was like an old woman's. Gussie packed stockings in a factory, eleven hours a day for a few cents a day.

We raised a lot of money for the strikers and hundreds of friends offered their homes to the little ones while we were in the city.

The next day we went to Coney Island at the invitation of Mr. Bostick who owned the wild animal show. The children had a wonderful day such as they never had in all their lives. After the exhibition of the trained animals, Mr. Bostick let me speak to the audience. There was a back drop to the tiny stage of the Roman Colosseum with the audience painted in and two Roman emperors down in front with their thumbs down. Right in front of the emperors were the empty iron cages of the animals. I put my little children in the cages and they clung to the iron bars while I talked.

I told the crowd that the scene was typical of the aristocracy of employers with their thumbs down to the little ones of the mills and factories, and people sitting dumbly by.

"We want President Roosevelt to hear the wail of the children who never have a chance to go to school but work eleven and twelve hours a day in the textile mills of Pennsylvania; who weave the carpets that he and you walk upon; and the lace curtains in your windows, and the clothes of the people. Fifty years ago there was a cry against slavery and men gave up their lives to stop the selling of black children on the block. Today the white child is sold for two dollars a week to the manufacturers. Fifty years ago the black babies were sold C.O.D. Today the white baby is sold on the installment plan.

"In Georgia where children work day and night in the cotton mills they have just passed a bill to protect song birds. What about the little children from whom all song is gone?

"I shall ask the president in the name of the aching hearts of these little ones that he emancipate them from slavery. I will tell the president that the prosperity he boasts of is the prosperity of the rich wrung from the poor and the helpless. . . .

"We are told that every American boy has the chance of being president. I tell you that these little boys in the iron cages would sell their chance any day for good square meals and a chance to play. These little toilers whom I have taken from the mills—deformed, dwarfed in body and soul, with nothing but toil before them—have never heard that they have a chance, the chance of every American male citizen, to become the president. . . .

I saw a stylishly dressed young man down in the front of the audience. Several times he grinned. I stopped speaking and pointing to him I said, 'Stop your smiling, young man! Leave this place! Go home and beg the mother who bore you in pain, as the mothers of these little children bore them, go home and beg her to give you brains and a heart."

He rose and slunk out, followed by the eyes of the children in the cage. The people sat stone still and out in the rear a lion roared.

The next day we left Coney Island for Manhattan Beach to visit Senator Platt, who had made an appointment to see me at nine o'-clock in the morning. The children got stuck in the sand banks and I had a time cleaning the sand off the littlest ones. So we started to walk on the railroad track. I was told it was private property and we had to get off. Finally a saloon keeper showed us a short cut into the sacred grounds of the hotel and suddenly the army appeared in the lobby. The little fellows played "Hail, hail, the gang's all here" on their fifes and drums, and Senator Platt[,] when he saw the little army ran away through the back door to New York.

I asked the manager if he would give the children breakfast and charge it up to the Senator as we had an invitation to breakfast that morning with him. He gave us a private room and he gave those children such a breakfast as they had never had in all their lives. I had breakfast too, and a reporter from one of the Hearst papers and I charged it all up to Senator Platt.

We marched down to Oyster Bay but the president refused to see us and he would not answer my letters. But our march had done its work. We had drawn the attention of the nation to the crime of child labor. And while the strike of the textile workers in Kensington was lost and the children driven back to work, not long afterward the Pennsylvania legislature passed a child labor law that sent thousands of children home from the mills, and kept thousands of others from entering the factory until they were fourteen years of age.

Ida M. Tarbell

~

IDA M. TARBELL (1857–1944), author and journalist, exposed the predatory business practices of John D. Rockefeller and his company when she wrote *The History of the Standard Oil Company* (1904). In her autobiography, *All in the Day's Work*, she recalls the writing of that book and her subsequent reception as a "muckraker."

~

Not a few of the personal experiences in gathering my materials left me with unhappy impressions, more unhappy in retrospect perhaps than they were at the moment. They were part of the day's work, sometimes very exciting parts. There was the two hours I spent in studying Mr. John D. Rockefeller. As the work had gone on, it became more and more clear to me that the Standard Oil Company was his creation. "An institution is the lengthened shadow of one man," says Emerson. I found it so.

Everybody in the office interested in the work began to say, "After the book is done you must do a character sketch of Mr. Rockefeller." I was not keen for it. It would have to be done like the books, from documents; that is, I had no inclination to use the extraordinary gossip which came to me from many sources. If I were to do it I wanted only that of which I felt I had sure proof, only those things which seemed to me to help explain the public life of this powerful, patient, secretive, calculating man of so peculiar and special a genius.

Tarbell, Ida M. *All in the Day's Work*. New York: Macmillan Company, 1939, pp. 234–242.

"You must at least look at Mr. Rockefeller," my associates insisted. "But how?" . . . It was John Siddall [an assistant hired from the Cleveland *Chautauquan*] who then took the matter in hand.

"You must see him," was Siddall's judgment.

To arrange it became almost an obsession. And then what seemed to him like a providential opening came. It was announced that on a certain Sunday of October 1903 Mr. Rockefeller before leaving Cleveland, where he had spent his summer, for his home in New York would say good-bye in a little talk to the Sunday school of his church—a rally, it was called. As soon as Siddall learned of this he begged me to come on. "We can go to Sunday school; we can stay to church. I will see that we have seats where we will have full view of the man. You will get him in action."

Of course I went, feeling a little mean about it too. He had not wanted to be seen apparently. It was taking him unaware.

Siddall's plan worked to perfection, worked so well from the start that again and again he seemed ready to burst from excitement in the two hours we spent in the church.

We had gone early to the Sunday-school room where the rally was to open—a dismal room with a barbaric dark green paper with big gold designs, cheap stained-glass windows, awkward gas fixtures. Comfortable, of course, but so stupidly ugly. We were sitting meekly at one side when I was suddenly aware of a striking figure standing in the doorway. There was an awful age in his face—the oldest man I had ever seen, I thought, but what power! At that moment Siddall poked me violently in the ribs and hissed, "There he is."

The impression of power deepened when Mr. Rockefeller took off his coat and hat, put on a skullcap, and took a seat commanding the entire room, his back to the wall. It was the head which riveted attention. It was big, great breadth from back to front, high broad forehead, big bumps behind the ears, not a shiny head but with a wet look. The skin was as fresh as that of any healthy man about us. The thin sharp nose was like a thorn. There were no lips; the mouth looked as if the teeth were all shut hard. Deep furrows ran down each side of the mouth from the nose. There were puffs under the little colorless eyes with creases running from them.

Wonder over the head was almost at once diverted to wonder over the man's uneasiness. His eyes were never quiet but darted from face to face, even peering around the jog at the audience close to the wall.

When he rose to speak, the impression of power that the first look at him had given increased, and the impression of age passed. I expected a quavering voice, but the voice was not even old, if a little fatigued, a little thin. It was clear and utterly sincere. He meant what he was saying. He was on his own ground talking about dividends, dividends of righteousness. "If you would take something out," he said, clenching the hand of his outstretched right arm, "you must put something in"—emphasizing "put something in" with a long outstretched forefinger.

The talk over, we slipped out to get a good seat in the gallery, a seat where we could look full on what we knew to be the Rockefeller pew.

Mr. Rockefeller came into the auditorium of the church as soon as Sunday school was out. He sat a little bent in his pew, pitifully uneasy, his head constantly turning to the farthest right or left, his eyes searching the faces almost invariably turned towards him. It was plain that he, and not the minister, was the pivot on which that audience swung. Probably he knew practically everybody in the congregation; but now and then he lingered on a face, peering at it intently as if he were seeking what was in the mind behind it. He looked frequently at the gallery. Was it at Siddall and me?

The services over, he became the friendly patron saint of the flock. Coming down the aisle where people were passing out, he shook hands with everyone who stopped, saying, "A good sermon." "The Doctor gave us a good sermon." "It was a very good sermon, wasn't it?"

My two hours' study of Mr. Rockefeller aroused a feeling I had not expected, which time has intensified. I was sorry for him. I know no companion so terrible as fear. Mr. Rockefeller, for all the conscious power written in face and voice and figure, was afraid, I told myself, afraid of his own kind. My friend Lewis Emery, Jr. [an independent oil refiner], priding himself on being a victim, was free and happy. Not gold enough in the world to tempt him to exchange his love of defiance for a power which carried with it a head as uneasy as that on Mr. Rockefeller's shoulders.

My unhappiness was increased as the months went by with the multiplying of tales of grievances coming from every direction. I made a practice of looking into them all, as far as I could; and while frequently I found solid reasons for the complaints, frequently I found the basic motives behind them—suspicion, hunger for notoriety, blackmail, revenge.

The most unhappy and most unnatural of these grievances came to me from literally the last person in the world to whom I should have looked for information—Frank Rockefeller—brother of John D. Rockefeller.

Frank Rockefeller sent word to me by a circuitous route that he had documents in a case which he thought ought to be made public, and that if I would secretly come to him in his office in Cleveland he would give them to me. I knew that there had been a quarrel over property between the two men. It made much noise at the time—1893—had gone to the courts, had caused bitterness inside the family itself; but because it was a family affair I had not felt that I wanted to touch it. But here it was laid on my desk.

So I went to Cleveland, where John Siddall had a grand opportunity to play the role of sleuth which he so enjoyed, his problem being to get me into Mr. Rockefeller's office without anybody suspecting my identity. He succeeded.

I found Mr. Rockefeller excited and vindictive. He accused his brother of robbing (his word) him and his partner James Corrigan of all their considerable holdings of stock in the Standard Oil Company. The bare facts were that Frank Rockefeller and James Corrigan had been interested in the early Standard Oil operations in Cleveland and had each acquired then a substantial block of stock. Later they had developed a shipping business on the Lakes, iron and steel furnaces in Cleveland. In the eighties they had borrowed money from John D. Rockefeller, putting up their Standard Oil stock as collateral. Then came the panic of '93, and they could not meet their obligations. In the middle of their distress John Rockefeller had foreclosed, taking over their stocks, leaving them, so they charged, no time in which to turn around although they felt certain that they would be able a little later, out of the substantial business they claimed they had built up, to pay their debt to him. Their future success proved they could have done so.

I could see John Rockefeller's point as I talked with his brother Frank. Frank Rockefeller was an open-handed, generous trader—more interested in the game than in the money to be made. He loved good horses—raised them, I believe, on a farm out in Kansas; he liked gaiety, free spending. From his brother John's point of view he was not a safe man to handle money. He did not reverence it; he used it in frivolous ways of which his brother did not approve. So it was as a kind of obligation to the sacredness of money that John Rockefeller had foreclosed on his own brother and his early friend James Corrigan. He was strictly within his legal rights and within what I suppose he called his moral right.

But the transaction left a bitterness in Frank Rockefeller's heart and mind which was one of the ugliest things I have ever seen. "I have taken up my children from the Rockefeller family lot. [Or "shall take up"—I do not know now which it was.] They shall not lie in the same enclosure with John D. Rockefeller."

The documents in this case, which I later analyzed for the character sketch on which we had decided, present a fair example of what were popularly called "Standard Oil methods" as well as what they could do to the minds and hearts of victims.

The more intimately I went into my subject, the more hateful it became to me. No achievement on earth could justify those methods, I felt. I had a great desire to end my task, hear no more of it. No doubt part of my revulsion was due to a fagged brain. The work had turned out to be much longer and more laborious than I had had reason to expect.

The plan I had taken to Mr. McClure in the fall of 1890, which we had talked over in Salsomaggiore, Italy—I still have notes of our talk on a yellow piece of the stationery of the Hôtel des Thermes—called for three papers, possibly twenty-five thousand words. But before we actually began publication Mr. Phillips and Mr. McClure decided we might venture on six. We went through the six, and the series was stretched to twelve. Before we were through we had nineteen articles, and when the nineteen were off my hands I asked nothing in the world but to get them into a book and escape into the safe retreat of a library where I could study people long dead, and if they did things of which I did not approve it would be all between me and the books. There would be none of these harrowing human beings confronting me, tearing me between contempt and pity, admiration and anger, baffling me with their futile and misdirected power or their equally futile and misdirected weakness. I was willing to study human beings in the library but no longer, for a time at least, in flesh and blood, so I thought.

The book was published in the fall of 1904—two fat volumes with generous appendices of what I considered essential documents. I was curious about the reception it would have from the Standard Oil Company. I had been told repeatedly they were preparing an answer to flatten me out; but if this was under way it was not with Mr. Rockefeller's consent, I imagined. To a mutual friend who had told him the articles should be answered Mr. Rockefeller was said to have replied: "Not a word. Not a word about that misguided woman." To another who asked him about my charges he was reported as answering: "All without foundation. The idea of the Standard forcing anyone to sell his refinery is absurd. The refineries wanted to sell to us, and nobody that was sold or worked with us but has made money, is glad he did so.

"I thought once of having an answer made to the McClure articles but you know it has always been the policy of the Standard to keep silent under attack and let their acts speak for themselves." . . .

But I wanted an answer from Mr. Rockefeller. What I got was neither direct nor, from my point of view, serious. It consisted of wide and what must have been a rather expensive anonymous distribution of various critical comments. The first of these was a review of the book which appeared in the *Nation* soon after its publication. The writer—one of the *Nation's* staff reviewers, I later learned—sneered at the idea that there was anything unusual in the competitive practices which I called illegal and immoral. "They are a necessary part of competition," he said. "The practices are odious it is true, competition is necessarily odious." Was it necessarily odious?

I did not think so. The practices I believed I had proved, I continued to consider much more dangerous to economic stability than airing them, even if I aired them in the excited and irrational fashion the review charged. As I saw it, the struggle was between Commercial Machiavellism and the Christian Code. . . .

I had hoped that the book might be received as a legitimate historical study, but to my chagrin I found myself included in a new school, that of the muckrakers. Theodore Roosevelt, then President of the United States, had become uneasy at the effect on the public of the periodical press's increasing criticisms and investigations of business and political abuses. He was afraid that they were adding to the not inconsiderable revolutionary fever abroad, driving people into socialism. Something must be done, and in a typically violent speech he accused the school of being concerned only with the "vile and debasing." Its members were like the man in John Bunyan's "Pilgrim's Progress" who with eyes on the ground raked incessantly "the straws, the small sticks, and dust of the floor." They were muckrakers. The conservative public joyfully seized the name.

Roosevelt had of course misread his Bunyan. The man to whom the Interpreter called the attention of the Pilgrim was raking riches which the Interpreter contemptuously called "straws" and "sticks" and "dust." The president would have been nearer Bunyan's meaning if he had named the rich sinners of the times who in his effort to keep his political balance he called "malefactors of great wealth"—if he had called them, "muckrakers of great wealth" and applied the word "malefactors" to the noisy and persistent writers who so disturbed him.

Mary McLeod Bethune

~

MARY McLEOD BETHUNE (1875–1955), educator, civil rights leader, and presidential advisor, was the first child in her family to be born free of slavery in her parents' own home. In 1904, with $1.50, she founded what later became the Bethune-Cookman College. She recounts the college's founding, its growth, and her appointment as Director of the Division of Negro Affairs in her essay "Faith That Moved a Dump Heap."

~

I was first stirred to serious thinking as a child by the custom of holding family prayers every morning and evening. In the corner, by our huge clay fireplace, sat my old grandmother, Sophia, a red bandanna around her head, nodding, and smoking a long-stemmed pipe. All day she talked to God as if He were a person actually present: "Dear God, I am so happy to be living in this loving family circle, where I can get hot biscuits and butter, and coffee with cream, sitting at my own fireside." Mother, more restrained, would thank God for giving her freedom, shelter, and the privilege of having her children with her.

On Sundays, Mother always took us to church and Sunday school. The minister used to visit us on occasion, his pockets full of books. He would read and preach to us, and we would all sing hymns and spirituals.

I was born in Maysville, South Carolina, a country town in the midst of rice and cotton fields. My mother, father, and older

Bethune, Mary McLeod. "Faith That Moved a Dump Heap," *Who* magazine, vol. 1, no. 3, June 1941, pp. 32–35, 54. Reprinted by permission of the Sophia Smith Collection, Smith College, Northampton, Massachusetts.

brothers and sisters had been slaves until the Emancipation Proclamation. My mother, Patsy McIntosh, belonged to the McIntosh family of South Carolina; my father, Samuel McLeod, to the McLeods. Like all the slaves of that period, they took the family names of their masters. After Mother was freed she continued in the McIntosh employ until she had earned enough to buy five acres of her own from her former master. Then my parents built our cabin, cutting and burning the logs with their own hands. I was the last of seventeen children, ten girls and seven boys. When I was born, the first free child in their own home, my mother exulted; "Thank God, Mary came under our own vine and fig tree."

Mother was of royal African blood, of a tribe ruled by matriarchs. She had dark, soft skin, thin lips, a delicately molded nose, and very bright eyes. Throughout all her bitter years of slavery she had managed to preserve a queenlike dignity. She supervised all the business of the family. Over the course of years, by the combined work and thrift of the family, and Mother's foresight, Father was able to enlarge our home site to thirty-five acres.

Most of my brothers and sisters had married and left home when I was growing up—there were only seven or eight children still around. Mother worked in the fields at Father's side, cutting rice and cotton, and chopping fodder. Each of us children had tasks to perform, according to our aptitudes. Some milked the cows, others helped with the washing, ironing, cooking, and housecleaning. I was my father's champion cotton picker. When I was only nine, I could pick 250 pounds of cotton a day.

But my great joy was in those moments of spontaneous prayer and song which relieved our days of ceaseless toil. Young as I was, I would gather a crowd around me, and like a little evangelist, I would preach, teach, or lead the singing.

Both Grandmother and Mother had taught me Bible stories. I would sit at their feet, picturing myself as the hero or the heroine of every tale. Then, as we were sitting around the fireplace one evening, it flashed through my mind with the intensity of flame that if my favorite, Queen Esther, had been willing to risk her life

and plead with the king for her people, I could and would risk
mine to do the same for my people.

"Whosoever Believeth"

But my mind dwelt on earthly, as well as on heavenly, subjects. On
market days, when my father let me walk to town with him, I noticed the contrast between the lives of the masters and their servants. I looked at the white people around me who were living in
homes with real glass windows. Their little girls wore white silk
dresses and soft shoes, and rode in carriages, with piles of books on
the seats beside them. I glanced down at my own brogue shoes,
with brass tips, and my neat but tattered clothes. I had no books. I
could not even read!

Dimly it began to permeate my mind that these things came
with education. I saw my people still in darkness; unable, in spite
of their being free, in spite of all their heart-breaking toil, to experience the good things of life.

But how was I to help them? I could not even help myself. For
it was almost impossible for a Negro child, especially in the South,
to get education. There were hundreds of square miles, sometimes
entire states, without a single Negro school, and colored children
were not allowed in public schools with white children. Mr. Lincoln had told our race we were free, but mentally we were still enslaved.

A knock on our door changed my life overnight. There stood a
young woman, a colored missionary sent by the Northern Presbyterian Church to start a school near by. She asked my parents to
send me. Every morning I picked up a little pail of milk and bread,
and walked five miles to school; every afternoon, five miles home.
But I walked always on winged feet.

The whole world opened to me when I learned to read. As soon
as I understood something, I rushed back and taught it to the others at home. My teacher had a box of Bibles and texts, and she gave

me one of each for my very own. That same day the teacher opened the Bible to John 3:16, and read: "For God so loved the world, that He gave His only begotten Son, that whosoever believeth in Him should not perish, but have everlasting life."

With these words the scales fell from my eyes and the light came flooding in. My sense of inferiority, my fear of handicaps, dropped away. "Whosoever," it said. No Jew nor Gentile, no Catholic nor Protestant, no black nor white: just "whosoever." It meant that I, a humble Negro girl, had just as much chance as anybody in the sight and love of God. These words stored up a battery of faith and confidence and determination in my heart, which has not failed me to this day.

I could scarcely wait to run home and tell my mother. For the first time, I gathered the family in a circle around me and read aloud to them from the Good Book. "Praise the Lord," cried my mother. "Halleluiah." That night I drove the first nail of my life work.

By the time I was fifteen I had taken every subject taught at our little school and could go no farther. Dissatisfied, because this taste of learning had aroused my appetite, I was forced to stay at home. Father's mule died—a major calamity—and he had to mortgage the farm to buy another. In those days, when a Negro mortgaged his property they never let him get out of debt.

I used to kneel in the cotton fields and pray that the door of opportunity should be opened to me once more, so that I might give to others whatever I might attain.

The Way Opens

My prayers were answered. A white dressmaker, way off in Denver, Colorado, had become interested in the work of our little neighborhood school and had offered to pay for the higher education of some worthy girl. My teacher selected me, and I was sent to Scotia Seminary in Concord, North Carolina. There I studied English, Latin, higher mathematics, and science, and after classes I worked in the Scotia laundry and kitchen to earn as much extra money as I could.

Scotia broadened my horizon and gave me my first intellectual contacts with white people, for the school had a mixed faculty. The white teachers taught that the color of a person's skin has nothing to do with his brains, and that color, caste, or class distinctions are an evil thing.

When I was graduated I offered myself eagerly for missionary service in Africa, but the church authorities felt I was not sufficiently mature. Instead, they gave me another scholarship, and I spent two years at the Moody Bible School, in Chicago. Again I offered myself for missionary service, and again I was refused. Cruelly disappointed, I got a position at Haines Institute, in Augusta, Georgia, presided over by dynamic Lucy C. Laly, a pioneer Negro educator. From her I got a new vision: my life work lay, not in Africa but in my own country. And with the first money I earned I began to save in order to pay off Father's mortgage, which had hung over his head for ten years!

Seven Years' Service

During my early teaching days I met my future husband. He too was then a teacher, but to him teaching was only a job. Following our marriage, he entered upon a business career. When our baby son was born, I gave up my work temporarily, so that I could be all mother for one precious year. After that I got restless again to be back at my beloved work, for having a child made me more than ever determined to build better lives for my people.

Like Jacob, who served seven years for Rachel, I was to serve seven years, going as an instructor from one small mission school to another, before I could locate a hearthstone to call my own. Whenever I accumulated a bit of money I was off on an exploring trip, seeking a location where a new school would do the greatest good for the greatest number. I would leave my son with relatives or with his father, who was not altogether sympathetic. He would chide me: "You are foolish to make sacrifices and build for nothing. Why not stop chasing around and stay put in a good job?" Common sense whispered he was right. But I was inspired by the noble life and work of Booker T. Washington, whose writings had become a second bible to me and now urged me on.

In 1904 I heard rumors which sent me off on another of my many pilgrimages. Henry Flagler was building the Florida East Coast Railroad, and hundreds of Negroes had gathered in Florida for construction work. I found there dense ignorance and meager educational facilities, racial prejudice of the most violent type—crime and violence.

Creating a College

Finally I arrived at Daytona Beach, a beautiful little village, shaded by great oaks and giant pines. A wondrous light filled my mind—this seemed the place and time to plant my seed!

Next morning I combed the town, hunting for a location. I found a shabby four-room cottage, for which the owner wanted a rental of eleven dollars a month. My total capital was a dollar and a half, but I talked him into trusting me until the end of the month for the rest. This was in September. A friend let me stay at her home, and I plunged into the job of creating something from nothing.

I spoke at churches, and the ministers let me take up collections. I buttonholed every woman who would listen to me, told people I was going to open a new type of school, to give more than mere reading or book learning. I told them I proposed to teach the essentials of homemaking, the arts, the skilled trades—and good citizenship.

On October 3, 1904, I opened the doors of my school, with an enrollment of five little girls, aged from eight to twelve, whose parents paid me fifty cents' weekly tuition. My own child was the only boy in the school. Thought I hadn't a penny left, I considered cash money as the smallest part of my resources. I had faith in a loving God, faith in myself, and a desire to serve. Although I saw my work would have to be done on a day-to-day basis, I built a fence of trust around each day.

We burned logs and used the charred splinters as pencils, and mashed elderberries for ink. I begged strangers for a broom, a lamp, a bit of cretonne to put around the packing case which served as my desk. I haunted the city dump and the trash piles behind hotels, retrieving discarded linen and kitchenware, cracked dishes, broken chairs, pieces of old lumber. Everything was scoured and mended. This was part of the training to salvage, to reconstruct, to make bricks without straw. As parents began gradually to leave their children overnight, I had to provide sleeping accommodations. I took corn sacks for mattresses. Then I picked Spanish moss from trees, dried and cured it, and used it as a substitute for mattress hair.

The school expanded fast. In less than two years I had 250 pupils. In desperation I hired a large hall next to my original little cottage, and used it as a combined dormitory and classroom. I concentrated more and more on girls, as I felt that they especially were hampered by lack of educational opportunities. And besides, they are the mothers of the race, the homemakers and spiritual guides.

I had many volunteer workers and a few regular teachers, who were paid from fifteen to twenty-five dollars a month and board. I was supposed to keep the balance of the funds for my own pocket, but there was never any balance—only a yawning hole. I wore old clothes sent me by mission boards, recut and redesigned for me in our dressmaking classes. At last I saw that our only solution was to stop renting space, and to buy and build our own college.

Five Dollars Down

Near by was a field, popularly called Hell's Hole, which was used as a dumping ground. I approached the owner, determined to buy it. The price was $250. In a daze, he finally agreed to take five dollars down, and the balance in two years. I promised to be back in a few days with the initial payment. He never knew it, but I didn't have five dollars. I raised this sum selling ice cream and sweet-potato pies to the workmen on construction jobs, and I took the owner his money in small change wrapped in my handkerchief.

That's how the Bethune-Cookman college campus started.

We at once discovered the need of an artesian well. The estimate was two hundred dollars. Here again we started with an insignificant payment, the balance remaining on trust. But what use was a plot without a building? I hung on to contractors' coat-tails, begging for loads of sand and secondhand bricks. I went to all the carpenters, mechanics, and plasterers in town, pleading with them to contribute a few hours' work in the evening in exchange for sandwiches and tuition for their children and themselves.

Slowly the building rose from its foundations. The name over the entrance still reads Faith Hall.

I had learned already that one of my most important jobs was to be a good beggar! I rang doorbells and tackled cold prospects without a lead. I wrote articles for whoever would print them, distributed leaflets, rode interminable miles of dusty roads on my old bicycle; invaded churches, clubs, lodges, chambers of commerce. If a prospect refused to make a contribution I would say, "Thank you for your time." No matter how deep my hurt, I always smiled. I refused to be discouraged, for neither God nor man can use a discouraged person.

Strongly interracial in my ideas, I looked forward to an advisory board of trustees composed of both white and colored people. I did my best missionary work among the prominent winter visitors to Florida. I would pick out names of "newly arrived guests," from the newspapers, and write letters asking whether I could call.

One of these letters went to James N. Gamble, of Procter & Gamble. He invited me to call at noon the next day. I borrowed a watch from a friend, jumped on my trusty old bicycle, and arrived early. I hid behind some bushes until the clock hands pointed to exactly twelve. Then I pressed the bell.

Mr. Gamble himself opened the door, and when I gave my name he looked at me in astonishment. "Are you the woman trying to build a school here? Why, I thought you were a white woman."

I laughed. "Well, you see how white I am." Then I told my story. "I'd like you to visit my school and, if it pleases you, to stand behind what I have in my mind," I finished.

He consented. I scurried around town and persuaded the mayor and the leading real estate dealer to act as a reception committee. When Mr. Gamble arrived the next day, everything had been scrubbed with soap and water until it glistened—including the pupils. He made a careful tour of inspection, agreed to be a trustee, and gave me a check for $150—although I hadn't mentioned money. For many years he was one of our most generous friends.

Another experience with an unexpected ending was my first meeting with J. S. Peabody, of Columbia City, Indiana. After I had made an eloquent appeal for funds he gave me exactly twenty-five cents. I swallowed hard, thanked him smilingly, and later entered the contribution in my account book.

A White Lie

Two years later he reappeared. "Do you remember me?" he asked. "I'm one of your contributors." I greeted him cordially. He went on: "I wonder if you recall how much I gave you when I was here last?"

Not wishing to embarrass him, I told a white lie: "I'll have to look it up in my account book." Then after finding the entry, I said, "Oh, yes, Mr. Peabody, you gave us twenty-five cents."

Instead of being insulted, he was delighted that we kept account of such minute gifts. He immediately handed me a check for a hundred dollars and made arrangements to furnish the building. When he died, a few years later, he left the school $10,000.

Experiences like these taught me that an apparent disappointment may be the prelude to glorious success. One evening I arranged a meeting at an exclusive hotel, expecting to talk to a large audience of wealthy people. But so many social functions were taking place that same night that I was greeted by an audience of exactly six. I was sick at heart—but I threw all my enthusiasm into my talk. At the end a gentleman dropped a twenty-dollar bill in the hat.

The next day he unexpectedly appeared at the school. He said his name was Thomas H. White, but it meant nothing to me. He looked around, asked where the shabby but immaculate straw matting on the floor came from. I said, "The city dump." He saw a large box of corn meal, and inquired what else there was to eat. I replied, "That's all we have at the moment." Then he walked about the grounds and saw an unfinished building, on which construction work had been temporarily abandoned for lack of funds. That was nothing new—there were always unfinished buildings cluttering up the landscape of our school. But I think the crowning touch was when he saw our dressmaking class working with a broken-down Singer sewing machine.

He turned to me, saying, "I believe you are on the right track. This is the most promising thing I've seen in Florida." He pressed a check in my hand, and left. The check was for $250. The following day he returned again, with a new sewing machine. Only then did I learn that Mr. White was the Singer people's principal competitor.

Mr. White brought plasterers, carpenters, and materials to finish our new building. Week after week he reappeared, with blankets for the children, shoes and a coat for me, everything we had dreamed of getting. When I thanked him, with tears in my eyes, for his generosity, he waved me aside.

"I've never invested a dollar that has brought greater returns than the dollars I have given you," he told me. And when this great soul died, he left a trust of $67,000, the interest to be paid us "as long as there is a school."

Do you wonder I have faith?

I never stop to plan. I take things step by step. For thirty-five years we have never had to close our doors for lack of food or fuel, although often we had to live from day to day.

Once, in our early days of struggle, we had no dishes. I knew a cook at a near-by hotel, whose husband was a traveling salesman. Since she never ate at home, I borrowed her china. On Christmas Eve she called on me.

"I'm awfully sorry," she said. "But my husband just telegraphed me that he's coming home tomorrow and wants to give a dinner for his Lodge. I'll have to ask you for my dishes."

As I started to gather them together, one of my little girls piped up, "But Mrs. Bethune, what are we going to do for dishes?"

"I don't know," I answered with a strange confidence, "but the Lord will provide. Let's hurry and pack these dishes nicely—"

Just then someone rang the bell. It was the chauffeur of Mrs. Lawrence Thompson, a dear friend of mine, with a huge basket, and a note which read: "Since my son has just given me a beautiful new set of china for Christmas, I want you to have my old set of dishes to use for your school."

The Lord Provides

On another occasion one of our buildings had to have a new roof. I tried to raise funds without success. I waited and waited. Then I acted. Calling together a few carpenters and roofers, who knew my true financial state, I instructed them, "We have enough old lumber lying around. Put up the scaffolds!"

"But Mrs. Bethune," they protested, "what's the use? You can't buy rafters or shingles."

"Go ahead and build the scaffold, anyhow," I commanded. "When the time comes to put on the roof the money will be there." Grumblingly they went to work. A few hours later, as the scaffolding was in process of construction, the postman arrived. I slit open the letters—bills, bills, bills! The last envelope, however, held a cheering message from a friend in Tarrytown, New York—and a check for $1,000.

As the school expanded, whenever I saw a need for some training or service we did not supply, I schemed to add it to our curriculum. Sometimes that took years. When I came to Florida, there were no hospitals where a Negro could go. A student became critically ill with appendicitis, so I went to a local hospital and begged a white physician to take her in and operate. My pleas were so desperate he finally agreed. A few days after the operation, I visited my pupil.

When I appeared at the front door of the hospital, the nurse ordered me around to the back way. I thrust her aside—and found my little girl segregated in a corner of the porch behind the kitchen. Even my toes clenched with rage.

That decided me. I called on three of my faithful friends, asking them to buy a little cottage behind our school as a hospital. They agreed, and we started with two beds.

From this humble start grew a fully equipped twenty-bed hospital—our college infirmary and a refuge for the needy throughout the state. It was staffed by white and black physicians and by our own student nurses. We ran this hospital for twenty years as part of our contribution to community life; but a short time ago, to ease our financial burden, the city took it over.

Gradually, as educational facilities expanded and there were other places where small children could go, we put the emphasis on high-school and junior-college training. In 1922, Cookman College, a men's school, the first in the state for the higher education of Negroes, amalgamated with us. The combined coeducational college, now run under the auspices of the Methodist Episcopal Church, is called Bethune-Cookman College. We have fourteen modern buildings, a beautiful campus of thirty-two acres, an enrollment in regular and summer sessions of 600 students, a faculty and staff of thirty-two, and 1,800 graduates. The college property, now valued at more than $800,000, is entirely unencumbered.

When I walk through the campus, with its stately palms and well-kept lawns, and think back to the dump-heap foundation, I rub my eyes and pinch myself. And I remember my childish visions in the cotton fields.

But values cannot be calculated in ledger figures and property. More than all else the college has fulfilled my ideals of distinctive training and service. Extending far beyond the immediate sphere of its graduates and students, it has already enriched the lives of 100,000 Negroes.

In 1934, President Franklin D. Roosevelt appointed me director of the division of Negro affairs of the National Youth Administration. My main task now is to supervise the training provided for 600,000 Negro children, and I have to run the college by remote control. Every few weeks, however, I snatch a day or so and return to my beloved home.

This is a strenuous program. The doctor shakes his head and says, "Mrs. Bethune, slow down a little. Relax! Take it just a little easier." I promise to reform, but in an hour the promise is forgotten.

For I am my mother's daughter, and the drums of Africa still beat in my heart. They will not let me rest while there is a single Negro boy or girl without a chance to prove his worth.

Elizabeth Gurley Flynn

~

ELIZABETH GURLEY FLYNN (1890–1964), agitator and organizer for the Industrial Workers of the World and the first female national chairperson of the Communist Party in America, was a superb orator known as "the Rebel Girl." In the autobiography that bears her nickname as its title, the Rebel Girl describes her first speeches and first arrests.

~

First Speech, 1906

In 1906 the Bronx Socialist Forum, which our family attended regularly, closed. We shifted our allegiance to the Harlem Socialist Club, at 250 West 125th Street. In good weather, open-air meetings were held on the corners of 7th Avenue and 125th Street—with women speaking for suffrage—and Socialist meetings arranged by this club. In winter the Socialist meetings were held in their headquarters, up two flights of stairs. We used to walk over from the South Bronx—carfares for a whole family were more than we could afford. Events took a sudden turn during my second year in Morris High School. I had lost a few months in school during that winter due to an infected jaw from an abscessed tooth. During that period I had studied two more books, which helped to catapult me

Flynn, Elizabeth Gurley. *The Rebel Girl*. New York: International Publishers, 1973, pp. 53–58, 61–64, 122–124. Excerpt reprinted by permission of International Publishers Co., New York.

into socialists activities. One was the *Vindication of the Rights of Women* by Mary Wollstonecraft; the other was *Women and Socialism* by August Bebel. (Forty-six years later in 1951 this book was listed as a Government's exhibit in Federal Judge Dimock's court in a trial under the Smith Act. It is now out of print, practically a collector's item.)

Someone at the Harlem Socialist Club, hearing of my debating experience and knowing of my reading and intense interest in socialism, asked me to make a speech. My father was not much impressed with the idea. He thought they should have asked *him* to expound Marxism, on which he now considered himself an expert. I'm afraid my father would be labeled a "male-supremacist" these days. Once I stood up at a meeting and asked the speaker a question. He frowned upon such a performance. Couldn't I have asked him to explain on our way home? But my mother encouraged me and I accepted the offer to speak. I tried to select a subject upon which my father would not interfere too much, something he did not consider too important. It was "What Socialism Will Do For Women."

Wednesday, January 31, 1906, is a date engraved on my memory, the occasion of my first public speech. It was a small place, holding not more than 75 people, but like the Mayflower, legends grew around it. That little boat would have rivalled the gigantic Queen Mary if she had carried all the ancestors now claimed as passengers. And my little hall would have been of Carnegie Hall proportions to accommodate all who have told me, "I heard your first speech!" . . .

I was a slender serious girl, not yet 16, with my black hair loose to my waist, tied with a ribbon. I wore a long full skirt down to my ankles, as was proper in 1906, a white shirt waist and a red tie. I had labored to write my speech and had stubbornly resisted all attempts of . . . my father and others to tell me what to say or to actually write it for me. Good or bad, I felt it had to be my own. I began to quake inwardly at the start, facing an adult audience for the first time. But they were sympathetic and I was soon sailing along serenely. When I concluded, I asked for questions, as I had heard other speakers do. None were forthcoming. The audience apparently sensed that I was nervous. How they laughed when I said resentfully: "Just because I'm young and a girl, is no reason you shouldn't ask me questions!"

My speech was compounded of my limited personal experience, which I felt very acutely, however, and my rather wide reading. It was in the spirit of the Wollstonecraft book, which advocated the rights of women in 1792—economic, political, educational and social. That was a period of ferment over "the rights of man" in America and Europe. The substance of my speech was based on the more modern book, by Bebel[,] a German Socialist leader who was a member of the Reichstag for 50 years. Bebel was tried in 1872 with Wilhelm Liebknecht, charged with "high treason" by the Bismarck government, and sentenced to two years in the fortress, Hubertusburg. While there, he worked on this, his most famous book.

It was translated into English by Daniel de Leon, editor of the *Daily People*, organ of the Socialist Labor Party, and published in 1904 by Kerr. I was interested to hear from Steve Nelson, on his return from fighting in Spain in the late 1930s, that the first Socialist book he had read was Bebel's *Women and Socialism*. Lenin well described it as "written strongly, aggressively, against bourgeois society." So great is the author's sympathy with woman, his indignation at the indignities and injustices she has endured, and so strong was his faith in her abilities and capacities as a human being, that one could well believe a woman wrote it.

My advent as a speaker caused no comment outside of the weekly Socialist paper, *The Worker*, which said: "In view of her youth, although knowing she was very bright, the comrades were prepared to judge her lecture indulgently; they found that no indulgence was called for, that she had a surprising grasp of the subject and handled it with skill." With this blessing I was launched on my career as a public speaker.

"Woman's Place"

The first socialist speech in 1906 dealt with the status of women, who were then considered inferior and treated as such in every walk of life. "Woman's place" was a subject of considerable debate 50 years ago. Women were denied the right to vote and deprived of all legal rights over their children, homes or property. Many schools, leading colleges and professions were practically closed to them. Only a few succeeded in overcoming these barriers and they were denied appointments and advancement in their chosen field. The "career girl" was discouraged. Women in industry were overworked and miserably underpaid in the jobs open to them—and always paid less than men on the same level. They were denied opportunities to enter skilled trades and had little protection from labor organizations.

The unionization of women, even in occupations like the needle trades where they predominated, had scarcely yet begun. Equal opportunities, equal pay, and the right to be organized, were the crying needs of women wage-earners then and unfortunately these demands remain with us today. Many union leaders, like Samuel Gompers, president of the American Federation of Labor, did not consider women workers organizable or dependable. "They only work for pin money!" was the usual complaint. An outside job was considered by the woman worker herself as a temporary necessary evil—a stop-gap between her father's home and her husband's home. Fathers and husbands collected women's wages, sometimes right at the company office. Women did not have a legal right to their own earnings. There was no consideration for the special needs and problems of working mothers, though they were numerous and pressing. Even the clothes of women hampered them—the long skirts that touched the ground, the big unwieldy sleeves, the enormous hats. You were still "a girl" if your skirt was above your shoe tops.

The struggle for the right of women to vote was nationwide and growing. It had started with the first Equal Rights Convention, at

Seneca Falls, New York, in 1848, led by Elizabeth Cady Stanton and Susan B. Anthony,* which was addressed by Frederick Douglass, the great Negro leader. The suffragists had been ridiculed, assaulted by mobs, refused halls, arrested for attempting to vote, disowned by their families. By 1904, groups of working women, especially Socialist women, were banding together to join in the demand for the vote. Two years later, International Women's Day was born on the East Side of New York, at the initiative of these women demonstrating for suffrage. It spread around the world and is universally celebrated today, while here it is deprecated as "a foreign holiday."

The suffrage movement was growing more militant and figures like Maude Malone appeared. She organized the Harlem Equal Rights League in 1905. She interrupted Theodore Roosevelt at a meeting of 3,000 people to demand where he stood on woman suffrage. She walked up and down Broadway, at the same time we were holding our street meetings there, with signs front and back, like a sandwich man, demanding "Votes for Women," and lost her post as a librarian in consequence. Once she was speaking at 125th Street and a heckler asked: "How would you like to be a man?" She answered: "Not much. How would you?" (Maude Malone died at 78 in 1951. She had been librarian at the *Daily Worker* for four and a half years.)

Suffragist speakers on streetcorners were invariably told: "Go home and wash your dishes," or, regardless of their age: "Who's taking care of your children?" Others said: "Imagine a pregnant woman running for office," or "How could women serve on juries and be locked up with men jurors?" I recall an experience at Guffanti's restaurant over 40 years ago, when I was with Margaret Sanger and a woman doctor friend, who started to smoke cigarettes. We were ordered by the management to desist or leave. The doctor asked a man smoking a big cigar: "Do you object to my smoking?" He replied: "Hell, no, lady, go right ahead." Finally, the manager ordered a screen placed around our table to shut the "hussies" from view.

---

*Flynn is mistaken here. Susan B. Anthony did not attend the Seneca Falls Convention.

There was a prevalent concept that "woman's work" was confined to the domestic scene. "Woman's place is in the home," was the cry. Women were constantly accused of taking "men's jobs." I spoke in my first speech of the drudgery and monotony of women's unpaid labor in the millions of American kitchens, of primitive handicraft jobs done by women at home, a hangover from times when the home was the center of hand manufacture. With the advent of power-operated machinery many tasks which traditionally belonged to women had been taken out of the home into mass production industry, such as spinning, weaving, sewing, baking, soap-making, food-preserving, making dairy products. Women were forced to follow their jobs into the outside world, there to be accused of taking away "men's jobs." I stressed the possibility, at least under socialism, of industrializing all the domestic tasks by collective kitchens and dining places, nurseries, laundries, and the like.

I said then and am still convinced that the full opportunity for women to become free and equal citizens with access to all spheres of human endeavor cannot come under capitalism, although many demands have been won by organized struggle. I referred to August Bebel's views of a socialist society, like those of all of us, as speculative and prophetic—"the personal opinion of the author himself," he said. He foresaw the abolition of prostitution and of loveless, arranged marriages, the establishment of economic independence of women and the freedom of mothers from dependence on individual men, the social care of children, the right of every woman to an education, to work and to participate in government; to be a wife, mother, worker and citizen; to enter the arts and sciences and all the professions. I was fired with determination to fight for all this. . . .

I Mount the Soap Box and Get Arrested

My advent as a speaker at the Harlem Socialist Club in 1906 brought me invitations to speak elsewhere. There were many progressive forums held at that time in practically every section of the city and in nearby cities. I visited Newark, Philadelphia, Providence and Boston. One such gathering was extremely popular with "radicals" of all descriptions. It was called the "Unity Congregation" and was conducted like a church, with readings, songs, and a main speech or sermon. Hugh O. Pentecost, an ex-minister then a lawyer, conducted this assemblage. . . . It was held at Lyric Hall on 6th Avenue between 41st and 42nd Streets opposite Bryant Park, where the Automat now is. It was a famous old meeting place, originally called Apollo Hall. A life-sized statue of a Greek god adorned a niche in the side wall. It was here, in 1872, that the Equal Rights Convention had nominated Victoria C. Woodhull for President and Frederick Douglass for Vice-President of the United States.

My friend Fred Robinson and I attended this forum and we gave out circulars at the door advertising a series of printed mottoes by Fred's older brother, Victor, who later became a professor. The only one I recall is: "Progress is written in one word—disobedience." Mr. Pentecost spoke every Sunday and did not ordinarily invite others to share his platform. Imagine how highly honored I felt when he asked me to speak there! I chose for my subject "Education," in which I voiced all my criticism of the school system—too much homework, not sufficient manual work, not enough subjects of practical value to students, especially those who could not go to college. This is remembered by many as my "first speech."

In the summer of 1906 I began to speak on the street. I took to it like a duck to water. So many of our street meetings were held at 125th Street and 7th Avenue that an enthusiast tacked a metal marker on one of the trees, "Liberty Tree." Needless to say, there were no amplifiers or loudspeakers in those days. Tom Lewis, pioneer soapboxer, who could be heard for blocks, taught me to speak, especially how to project my voice outdoors. "Breathe deep, use your diaphragm as a bellows; don't talk on your vocal chords or you'll get hoarse in no time. Throw your voice out." His advice was effective.

I often wonder how modern audiences would receive the fervid oratory popular then. Styles of speech have changed with the radio and public speaking systems, which have compelled modulation of the voice, eliminated action, and calmed down the approach. Then we gesticulated, we paced the platform, we appealed to the emotions. We provoked arguments and questions. We spoke loudly, passionately, swiftly. We used invectives and vituperation, we were certainly not "objective" in our attacks on capitalism and all its works. Even when newly-arrived immigrants did not understand our words they shared our spirit. At all our indoor mass meetings there were speakers in many languages—Jewish, Russian, Polish, Italian, German and others. Our foreign-born comrades, like Pedro Estove in Spanish, Arturo Giovannitti in Italian, and Bill Shatoff in Russian, were magnificent orators. They inspired us to more beautiful and moving language in English.

In August 1906, I was arrested with my father and several others for "speaking without a permit" and "blocking traffic" at 38th Street and Broadway, then the heart of the theatrical district. The chairman was a little old man with a derby hat—Michael Cody, who sold the *Weekly People* for years at all Socialist meetings. The auspices of our meeting was the Unity Club, an attempt to unite Socialist Party and Socialist Labor Party speakers on one platform. One of our number had a flair for showmanship and had devised a striking unity banner, topped by a whirling contraption with the flags of all nations, flanked by red flares for illumination. Someone in the audience objected to the flags and insisted that only the American flag should be displayed. Naturally our colorful caravan, rivaling a circus, caused a sensation, even on Broadway, and the argument increased the crowd to huge proportions. When the police officer ordered us to stop, we refused and the reserves were called. Our arrests followed.

We were released on bail at 2 a.m. and appeared before Magistrate Walsh in Jefferson Market Court the next day. Our trial was something of a disappointment to Pop, who wanted to tell the judge off, but Mr. Pentecost, who appeared as our lawyer, hushed him up. He spoke of my extreme youth to my great embarrassment, although I did feel a little better when he said I was "the coming Socialist woman orator of America."

We were all discharged, with the judge advising me to go back to school that Fall and be a student a while longer before I become a teacher. He said to the prosecutor: "Better some socialism than a suspicion of oppression!" He said I was wasting my time trying to convert "the tenderloin riffraff" and the idle curiosity seekers of Broadway. Seldom is judicial advice of this sort taken, and we returned forthwith to bigger and better meetings, although the working class districts would have been more appropriate for our purposes. The newspapers featured my arrest as "Mere Child Talks Bitterly of Life." *The New York Times* editorialized in a humorous, patronizing style about "the ferocious Socialist haranguer, Miss Flynn, who will graduate at school in two years and whose shoe tops at present show below her skirts, [who] tells us what to think, which is just what she thinks." Pop never forgave Mr. Pentecost. "That damned lawyer wouldn't let me talk!" he'd rave.

Strangely enough, when I returned to Morris High School in the Fall, no comment was made on the arrest. But attending school by day and meetings by night was a heavy toll, not conducive to proper rest or study. I had an excellent scholastic record in grammar school with all A marks, but it had now declined alarmingly. Mr. Denbigh, the principal, tried to convince me that I should concentrate on my studies and give up the outside activities, of which he expressed no criticism. He said if I finished my education I would be better equipped for work in the labor movement a few years later. My mother agreed with Mr. Denbigh. But I was impatient. It did not seem to me that anything I was learning there had relationship to life or would be helpful to me. With the Revolution on my mind I found it difficult to concentrate on Latin or geometry. And I smarted under the "too young" attitude of adults. So within the next few months I left school, an action I deeply regretted in later years. . . .

I Get Arrested Some More

While I was in the anthracite area in the Spring of 1911, the IWW local of Philadelphia sent for me. A critical situation had arisen among the workers in the plant of the Baldwin Locomotive Works, occupying a large area in the center of the city. It has long since moved to Chester, Pennsylvania. Twelve hundred employees, among whom were some IWW members, had been suddenly laid off by the company without reason. They were gathered around the plant in protest. It was our plan to try to organize them all into the IWW and fight for reinstatement. So we held a street meeting at the corner of 15th and Buttonwood Streets. The first few speakers were not molested, but when I spoke, I was arrested. The cops said officials of the company had telephoned a complaint. I was taken by car downtown and lodged in the jail in City Hall, under the statue of William Penn.

The police magistrate before whom I appeared was a squat politician who growled at me: "These people don't want you there!"—meaning the bosses, of course. The workers had hooted and booed the cops for arresting me and demonstrated that they *did* want to hear me. He sneered at our efforts to organize the men and called it "a money-making scheme." He was the first to call me "an outside agitator," a name I heard often in the next few years. I was fined $10 for "disturbing the peace."

The next week, after passing the word quietly around the plant, we returned to the widest streets bordering on it—Broad and Spring Garden, where we attempted to hold another meeting. Again no one else was arrested until I spoke. I was ordered to stop and "move on" and when I refused I was arrested. The police said they "had orders from higher up," though they acted reluctantly in face of the angry workers. Again the charge was "obstructing the highway and breach of the peace." I was taken before the same irate Irish judge who again fined me $10. We held a protest meeting on City Hall Plaza, which was generally used as a forum for Sunday meetings in those days, and enlisted much popular support.

On the occasion of one of these arrests, I believe it was the first, a very provocative act was committed by the police. A Negro policeman, and there were very few at that time, was thrust forward by the white cops to make the arrest and face the jeers and catcalls of over a thousand workers, predominantly Irish. The contemptible meanness of forcing him to arrest a white woman—and an Irish one at that—was clear to me. I felt the man trembling when he grasped my arm. "Don't worry, I'll see that they don't hurt you!" I assured him. He smiled down at me, at my naïveté and size, too, I presume. I was greatly relieved when we reached the local police station, followed by hundreds of workers. I felt I had delivered him safely. Usually I had scant sympathy for a policeman, but from this instance I began to realize that a special persecution of the Negro people extended to all walks of life, and no Negro was exempt, not even a policeman.

My mother and the whole family took care of my son while I was away. I had previously received $19 a week salary from the IWW plus railroad fares and expenses, which were very little. This was raised to $21 after Fred was born. Our rent at home was $18 a month. Anyone of the family who worked chipped in to help out. My sister Kathie worked in Macy's in the summer vacation months to keep herself in college. She was determined to be a teacher. It was hard sailing, but we were no different from hundreds of families around us in the South Bronx and those whom I met in my travels. I stayed in homes wherever I went. I knew the lives of working people at first hand. In those days no traveling Socialist or IWW speaker went to a hotel. It was customary to stay at a local comrade's house. This was partly a matter of economy, to save expenses for the local people, and partly a matter of security for the speaker in many outright strongholds of reaction, like one-plant company towns.

But, more than all else, it was a comradeship, even if you slept with one of the children or on a couch in the dining room. It would have been considered cold and unfriendly to allow a speaker to go off alone to a hotel. It was a great event when a speaker came to town. They wanted to see you as much as possible. People came from all around to socialize at the house where the speaker stayed. They heard about other parts of the country while the speaker could learn all about the conditions in that area. It was hard on the older speakers, but while I was young and vigorous I did not mind. Only many years later did it become customary for speakers to be put up in hotels. By then, I enjoyed it.

Emma Goldman

~

EMMA GOLDMAN (1869–1940), anarchist author and lecturer, feminist, and birth control advocate, attracted the U.S. government's attention on various occasions. During the 1892 Homestead strike, she helped her lover procure a gun for his attempted assassination of steel mill owner and millionaire, Henry Clay Frick. (She later denounced violence as a means of social change.) In 1894, she advised poor families to steal bread if necessary and was consequently jailed for one year. In 1915, she spent fifteen days in jail after instructing a New York City audience in the use of contraceptives. Since Goldman had become a United States citizen upon marriage to Jacob Kershner, from whom she was later divorced, that citizenship, under the laws then applying to women, was dependent upon her former husband remaining a U.S. citizen. In 1908, the U.S. government stripped Kershner of his citizenship; that move, U.S. Secretary of Commerce and Labor Oscar S. Straus later wrote, was undertaken to "quietly strip Goldman of her own citizenship." In her autobiography, *Living My Life*, Goldman describe lectures, arrests, and the loss of her American citizenship.

~

In planning our tour to take place during the presidential campaign we had overlooked the interest of the American masses in the political circus. The result was failure of the initial part of our trip. In Indianapolis, the first city to bring out a large attendance,

---

Goldman, Emma. *Living My Life*. Vol. 1, 1931. Rpt., New York: Dover Publications, 1970, pp. 442–450.

my lecture was suppressed in the usual manner. The Mayor expressed regret that the police had overstepped their powers, but of course he could not act against the department. The Chief said that stopping the meeting might have been bad law, but that it was good common sense.

We were more fortunate in St. Louis, where we experienced no interference. There I met William Marion Reedy, the editor of the St. Louis *Mirror*. He and his paper were an oasis in the desert of American intellectuality. Reedy, a man of ability, broad culture, and rich humour, also possessed a courageous spirit. His fellowship made our stay in St. Louis a pleasant event and brought me large and varied audiences. After my departure he published in his weekly an article that he called "The Daughter of the Dream." No finer appreciation of my ideas and no greater tribute to me had ever been written by a non-anarchist before.

In Seattle Ben [Reitman] and I were arrested. His offence consisted in putting his weight too heavily against the door of the hall, which he had found barred; mine was in protesting against his arrest. At the station-house it developed that the price of my manager's offence was a dollar and a half, representing the amount the landlord demanded for his broken lock. After we paid for this injury to the sanctity of property, we were both released. Of course, there were no further meetings in Seattle and no redress for the loss we had sustained.

In Everett no hall was open to us. In Bellingham our train was met by detectives. They followed us to the hotel, and when we went out to find a restaurant, they put us under arrest. "Would you please wait until we have dined?" Ben asked with an engaging smile. "Sure," said our protectors, "we will wait." It was bright and warm in the restaurant, drizzling and chilly outside, but we took no pity on our watchdogs. We lingered long over our meal, well aware that we should have the whole night before us in a place neither warm nor bright. In the station-house we were presented with the warrant. It was a document worthy of immortality. "Emma Goldman and Dr. Ben L. Reitman," it read, "anarchists and outlaws, having conspired to hold an unlawful assembly," and so forth in the same spirit. We were given the choice between leaving Bellingham at once or going to the city jail. It being the first hospitality offered us in the State of Washington, we decided in favour of the jail. At midnight the offer to get out of town was repeated, but having already made myself at home in the cell, I refused to leave. Ben did likewise.

In the morning we were taken before a magistrate, who placed us under five-thousand-dollar bail. It was only too apparent that the judge knew that the police had undertaken more than they would be able to carry through. We could not be tried for merely "attempting" to hold a meeting, but we were at their mercy, just the same. We knew no one in town likely to bail us out, and we had no means of getting in touch with a lawyer. I was interested, however, to find out how far legalized stupidity could go.

In the afternoon two strangers arrived. They introduced themselves as Mr. Schamel, attorney, and Mr. Lynch. The former volunteered his services gratis; the latter offered to be our bondsman.

"But you don't know us," I said in astonishment. "How can you risk so much money?"

"Oh, yes," said Mr. Schamel, "we do know you. We are not anarchists, but we feel that anyone who will stand up for an ideal as you have done is worthy of trust."

If I had not been afraid of shocking them, I should have embraced them in open court. The old fossil on the bench, who had blustered when we appeared friendless before him in the morning, was personified politeness now. We were quickly bailed out, entertained at a restaurant by our new friends, and accompanied to the train.

When we reached Blaine, on the Canadian border, a man came into our car, walked straight up to me, and inquired: "You are Emma Goldman, are you not?"—"And who are you?"—"I am a Canadian immigration inspector. I have orders to invite you to leave the train." What could one do but comply with such a gentlemanly request? At the office the inspector in charge seemed very much surprised that I looked like a lady and had no bombs about me. He assured us that he had gathered from the stories in the American press that I was a very dangerous person. He had therefore decided to hold up my entry into Canada until he could receive instructions from Ottawa. Meanwhile, he asked me, as his guest, to make myself at home in his hut. I could have anything I wanted in the way of food and drink. In case of delay we would be given the best rooms in the local hotel. He spoke in a polite manner, his tone more friendly than I had ever heard from an American official. While the result was the same, I did not feel quite so indignant over the new interference.

The next morning our jovial inspector informed us that Ottawa had wired to let Emma Goldman proceed. There was no law in monarchical Canada to forbid my entry into the country. American democracy, with its anti-anarchist laws, was made to appear rather ludicrous.

San Francisco held a special attraction. The ex-soldier William Buwalda, as a result of our agitation on his behalf, had been pardoned by President Roosevelt. He was released after ten months' imprisonment, two weeks before our arrival in the city.

Owing to a terrific rain-storm my first meeting, in the Victory Theatre, was poorly attended. We were not discouraged, however, because of the wide publicity given my series of eight lectures and two debates. The following afternoon William Buwalda called on me, a very different man in his civilian clothes from the soldier whose hand I had clasped for a fleeting moment that memorable afternoon on the platform of Walton's Pavilion. His fine, open face, intelligent eyes, and firm mouth were indicative of an independent character. I wondered how he had stood fifteen years of military service without becoming warped. Buwalda related that he had joined the Army mainly because of tradition. American-born, he was of Dutch stock and nearly all the men of his family had done military service in Holland. He had believed in American freedom and he had considered its army forces a necessary protection. On several occasions he had come across my name in the papers. He had thought Emma Goldman a crank and had paid little attention to articles about me. "That is not very flattering," I interrupted: "how could you be so rude to a lady?" "It is true, though," he replied with a smile. Military people live in a world of their own, he explained, and he had been particularly occupied for several years past. He had taken up a course of veterinary surgery because he was passionately fond of horses, and he had also studied short-hand. Added to his duties in the barracks, it had kept him too busy for other interests.

He had come upon my meeting accidentally, while out for a walk. He had seen the large crowd and the police before the Walton Pavilion. It had made him curious and he thought it a good opportunity to practise his stenography by taking down the speech. "Then you appeared," he continued, "a little, unassuming figure in black, and you started to talk. I began to feel disturbed. I thought at first it was the heat in the hall and the tense atmosphere. I did not forget the purpose that had brought me. For a while I was able to follow you; then I became distracted by your voice. I felt myself carried along by your sledge-hammer arraignment of all I held high. I was filled with resentment. I wanted to raise my voice in protest, to challenge your statements before the whole assembly. But the more I resisted your influence, the more I fell under its sway. Your eloquence held me breathless to the end of your speech. I felt confused and eager to escape. Instead I was caught by the crowd and found myself standing on the platform holding out my hand to you."

"And then?" I asked. "Did you see the detectives following you? Did you realize that they would cause you trouble?"

"I don't remember how I got out of the hall, and I did not feel that I had done anything wrong. I was upset by what I had heard and in the grip of the turmoil you had caused in me. All the way to the Presidio I kept thinking: 'She's wrong, she's entirely wrong! Patriotism is not the last resort of scoundrels. Militarism isn't only murder and destruction!' After the plain-clothes men had reported me to my superior officer, I was put under arrest. I thought it was all a mistake, that I had been taken for someone else and that I should be freed in the morning. To think otherwise would have meant that you were right, and my whole being rebelled against that. For several days I clung to the belief that you had misrepresented the Government which I had served for fifteen years; that my country was too fair and too just to be guilty of your unreasonable charges. But when I was brought before the military tribunal, I began to see that you had spoken the truth. I was asked what you had done for me that I should mix with such a dangerous person, and I replied: 'She has made me think.' Yes, you had made me think, Emma Goldman, for the first time in all my forty years."

I held out my hand to him and said: "Now that you are free from your military shackles, we can shake hands without fear. Let us be friends."

He took my hand eagerly. "Friends for life and comrades as well, dear, big, little Emma."

I was so carried away by his story that I had forgotten it was time to prepare for my meeting. Never being able to eat before a lecture, I did not mind going without dinner. But for my guest I had proved a poor hostess. My new comrade gallantly assured me that he did not care for food.

When we came within a block of the hall, we saw the streets filled with people. I thought it was our announcements that had brought out the vast crowd, but when we reached the Victory Theatre, I was received with open arms by detectives and put under arrest. Buwalda protested and was also arrested. We were hustled into the patrol wagon to find that Ben, too, had met with the same fate. As the wagon rattled through the streets, he hurriedly related that the police had ordered everyone out of the theatre, freely using their clubs. He had objected to their methods, of course, and was put under arrest. He had sent someone with a warning to me, but evidently the comrade had found me gone.

At police headquarters William Buwalda was discharged with a severe reprimand for associating with "dangerous criminals." Ben and I were charged with "conspiracy, making unlawful threats, using force and violence, and disturbing the public peace." In the morning we were taken before a judge, who held us for trial under sixteen-thousand-dollar bail each. The same day Alexander Horr was arrested for distributing a handbill protesting against the action of the authorities. The task of raising our bond and arranging for counsel and publicity fell to Cassius V. Cook, a man I had met only casually a few years before. But he proved to be a tower of strength.

Within a few days Sasha and other New York friends telegraphed that five thousand dollars would be sent towards our bail and that money was being raised for our defence. From all over the country protests and contributions began pouring in. Charles T. Sprading, of Los Angeles, whom I had first met in Denver on my maiden tour to the Coast in 1897, our buoyant Charlie, of ready wit and merry pranks, wired two thousand dollars as bail. The Forresters, and other friends, helped in a similar way. What did our trouble matter with such good comradeship to aid us?

Our lawyers, Messrs. Kirk and King, intelligent and brave men, exerted themselves in our behalf, and within a few days Mr. Kirk succeeded in having our bail released. We were to be liberated and placed in his custody. But unexpectedly another indictment came, charging us with "unlawful assemblage, denouncing as unnecessary all organized government," and—horror of horrors—with "preaching anarchist doctrines." Bail was set at two thousand dollars each. I was to be tried first, Ben to follow.

Among the sensational reports in the San Francisco press regarding the raid of our meeting and our arrest was one enlarging upon "Emma Goldman's lack of sentiment and feeling." While in jail, she had been given a telegram announcing her father's death, the paper stated, which she received without the least sign of emotion. As a matter of fact, my father's end, though not unexpected, had affected me deeply and had recalled to me the details of his wasted life. An invalid for over thirty years, he had of late been more frequently ill than usually. When I had seen him on my last visit to Rochester, in October, I had been shocked to find him so near death. The giant he had once been was now shattered by the storms of life.

With the passing years had come to me better understanding of Father, and mutual sympathy had drawn us gradually closer. My beloved Helena had had much to do with my change towards him. It was helped also by my awakening to the complexities of sex as a force dominating our feelings. I had learned to understand better my own turbulent nature, and my experiences had made me see what had been obscure to me so long in the character of my father. His violence and hardness had only been symptoms of an intensely sexual nature that had failed to find adequate expression.

My parents had been brought together in the traditional Jewish orthodox fashion, without love. They were mismated from the first. Mother had been left a widow at twenty-three, with two children, a little store her only earthly possession. Whatever love she had had died with the young man to whom she had been married at the age of fifteen. Father had brought into the match a fire of passionate youth. His wife was only one year his senior and radiantly beautiful. The impelling need of his nature drove him to her and made him more insistent in proportion as Mother fought back his insatiable hunger. My coming had marked her fourth childbirth, each one nearly bringing her to the grave. I recalled some remarks I had heard her make when I was too young to understand their meaning. They illuminated much that had been dark to me and caused me to realize what a purgatory my parents' intimacy must have been for them both. No doubt they would have been shocked had anyone called to their attention the true source of the struggle between them and of Father's uncontrollable temper. With the decline of health came also a lessening of his erotic vitality and a resultant psychic change. Father grew more mellow, patient, and kindly. The affection he had rarely shown his own children he now lavished on those of my two sisters. When I once referred to the harsh methods he had used towards us, he assured me that it could not be true. The tenderness that had come into his nature blotted out even the remembrance of past severity. The best in him, formerly hidden by emotional stress, by the struggle for existence and years of physical suffering, came into its own at last. He now felt and gave us a newly born affection, which in its turn awakened our love for him.

The court farce in San Francisco, ending in our acquittal, did more for anarchism than months of our propaganda might have accomplished. But the most significant event was William Buwalda's letter to the military authorities and his entry into our ranks. The historic document, published in the May 1909 issue of *Mother Earth*, read as follows:

Hudsonville, Michigan
April 6, 1909

Hon. Joseph M. Dickinson,
Secretary of War,
Washington, D.C.

Sir:—

After thinking the matter over for some time I have decided to send back this trinket* to your Department, having no further use for such baubles, and enable you to give it to some one who will appreciate it more than I do.

It speaks to me of faithful service, of duty well done, of friendships inseparable, friendships cemented by dangers and hardships and sufferings shared in common in camp and in the field. But, sir, it also speaks to me of bloodshed—possibly some of it unavoidably innocent—in defence of loved ones, of homes; homes in many cases but huts of grass, yet cherished none the less.

It speaks of raids and burnings, of many prisoners taken and, like vile beasts, thrown in the foulest of prisons. And for what? For fighting for their homes and loved ones.

It speaks to me of . . . horrors and cruelties and sufferings; of a country laid waste with fire and sword; of animals useful to

---

*The medal awarded William Buwalda for faithful service in the Philippines.

man wantonly killed; of men, women, and children hunted like wild beasts, and all this in the name of Liberty, Humanity, and Civilization.

In short, it speaks to me of War—legalized murder, if you will—upon a weak and defenceless people. We have not even the excuse of self-defence.

Yours sincerely,
Wm. Buwalda
R. R. No. 3
Hudsonville, Michigan

Our departure for Australia had been set for January. The arrest and subsequent free-speech fight in San Francisco forced us to postpone it until April. At last we were ready, our trunks packed, a grand farewell party arranged for us. We were about to secure passage when a telegram from Rochester [concerning Emma Goldman's ex-husband] demolished our plans. "Washington revoked Kershner's citizenship papers," it read; "dangerous to leave country."

My sister had written me months before that two suspicious-looking individuals had been snooping about to secure data on Kershner. He had left the city years previously and nothing had been heard from him since then. Not finding Kershner, the men had pestered his parents and tried to get information from them. I had dismissed the matter from my mind at the time as of no consequence. But now the blow came. I was deprived of my citizenship without even an opportunity to contest the action of the Federal authorities.* I knew that if I should leave the country, I should not be permitted to re-enter it. My Australian tour had to be abandoned at a great financial loss, not to mention the expenditures invested by our Australian friends in preparing for my activities there. It was a bitter disappointment, much mitigated, fortunately,

---

*Until 1922, women lost their American citizenship upon marriage to foreign nationals or upon their husband's loss of or renunciation of American citizenship.

by the undaunted optimism of my hobo manager. His zeal merely increased with the obstacles we encountered. His energy was dynamic and tireless.

Australia eliminated from our itinerary, we went to Texas instead. El Paso, San Antonio, and Houston were new ground. I was cautioned to avoid the Negro question, but though I made no concessions to the prejudices of the South, I was in no way molested, nor was there any police interference. I even walked with Ben from El Paso to Mexico and back again before the United States immigration inspector had time to realize the chance he had missed to save his Government from the Emma Goldman menace.

Ida B. Wells-Barnett

~

IDA B. WELLS-BARNETT (1862–1931), journalist, suffragist, and African-American rights leader, began what was essentially a one-woman anti-lynching campaign after three of her friends were lynched. She raised the issue in the *Memphis Free Press*, a newspaper of which she was part owner; published a statistical study of three years of lynchings in America, entitled *A Red Record* (1895); and founded anti-lynching societies in Boston, New York, and several other cities. In her autobiography, *Crusade for Justice: The Autobiography of Ida B. Wells*, she describes the aftermath of a 1909 lynching in Cairo, Illinois.

~

Directly after the Springfield riot, at the next session of the legislature, a law was enacted which provided that any sheriff who permitted a prisoner to be taken from him and lynched should be removed from office. . . .

    In due course of time the daily press announced that a lynching had taken place in Cairo, Illinois. The body of a white woman had been found in an alley in the residential district and, following the usual custom, the police immediately looked for a Negro. Finding a shiftless, penniless colored man known as "Frog" James, who seemed unable to give a good account of himself, according to

Wells-Barnett, Ida B. *Crusade for Justice: The Autobiography of Ida B. Wells*. Alfreda M. Duster, ed. Chicago: University of Chicago Press, 1970, pp. 309–320. Excerpt from *Crusade for Justice* reprinted by permission of the University of Chicago Press.

police, this man was locked up in the police station and according to the newspapers a crowd began to gather around the station and the sheriff was sent for.

Mr. Frank Davis, the sheriff, after a brief conversation with the prisoner, took him to the railroad station, got on the train, and took him up into the woods accompanied by a single deputy. They remained there overnight. Next morning, when a mob had grown to great proportions, they too went up into the country and had no trouble in locating the sheriff and his prisoner. He was placed on a train and brought back to town, accompanied by the sheriff. The newspapers announced that as the train came to a standstill, some of the mob put a rope around "Frog's" neck and dragged him out of the train and to the most prominent corner of the town, where the rope was thrown over an electric light arch and the body hauled up above the heads of the crowd.

Five hundred bullets were fired into it, some of which cut the rope, and the body dropped to the ground. Members of the mob seized hold of the rope and dragged the body up Washington Street, followed by men, women, and children, some of the women pushing baby carriages. The body was taken near to the place where the corpse of the white girl had been found. Here they cut off his head, stuck it on a fence post, built a fire around the body and burned it to a crisp.

When the news of this horrible thing appeared in the papers, immediately a meeting was called and a telegram sent to Governor Deneen demanding that the sheriff of Alexander County be dispossessed. The newspapers had already quoted the governor as saying that he did not think it mandatory on him to displace the sheriff. But when our telegram reached him calling attention to the law, he immediately ousted him by telegram.

This same law provided that after the expiration of a short time, the sheriff would have the right to appear before the governor and show cause why he ought to be reinstated. We had a telegram from Governor Deneen informing us that on the following Wednesday and sheriff would appear before him demanding reinstatement.

[My husband,] M. [Ferdinand] Barnett spent some time urging representative men of our race to appear before the governor and fight the sheriff's reinstatement.

Colonel Frank Dennison and Robert Taylor had been down in that county hunting at the time of this occurrence, and they were reported as saying they had seen signals being wigwagged between the mob which was hunting "Frog" James and the sheriff who had him in charge. Colonel Dennison was asked to appear. He refused, saying that the whole episode was going to be a whitewash and he wasn't going to have anything to do with it. When he and others were reminded that it was their duty to fight the effort to reinstate the sheriff, they still refused.

This information was given us at the dinner table by Mr. Barnett, and he wound up his recital of his fruitless efforts that Saturday afternoon to get someone to appear by saying, "And so it would seem that you will have to go to Cairo and get the facts with which to confront the sheriff next Wednesday morning. And your train leaves at eight o'clock." I objected very strongly because I had already been accused by some of our men of jumping in ahead of them and doing work without giving them a chance.

It was not very convenient for me to be leaving home at that time, and for once I was quite willing to let them attend to the job. Mr. Barnett replied that I knew it was important that somebody gather the evidence as well as he did, but if I was not willing to go, there was nothing more to be said. He picked up the evening paper and I picked up my baby and took her upstairs to bed. As usual I not only sang her to sleep but put myself to sleep lying there beside her.

I was awakened by my oldest child, who said, "Mother, Pa says it is time to go." "Go where?" I said. He said, "To take the train to Cairo." I said, "I told your father downstairs that I was not going. I don't see why I should have to go and do the work that the others refuse." My boy was only ten years old. He and the other children had been present at the dinner table when their father told the story. He stood by the bedside a little while and then said, "Mother if you don't go nobody else will."

I looked at my child standing there by the bed reminding me of my duty, and I thought of that passage of Scripture which tells of the wisdom from the mouths of babes and sucklings. I thought if my child wanted me to go that I ought not to fall by the wayside, and I said, "Tell daddy it is too late to catch the train now, that I'll go in the morning. It is better for me to arrive in Cairo after nightfall anyway."

Next morning all four of my children accompanied my husband and me to the station and saw me start on the journey. They were intensely interested and for the first time were willing to see me leave home.

I reached Cairo after nightfall, and was driven to the home of the leading A.M.E. minister, just before he went into church for his evening service. I told him why I was there and asked if he could give me any help in getting the sentiment of the colored people and investigating facts. He said that they all believed that "Frog" James had committed that murder. I asked him if he had anything upon which to base that belief. "Well," he said, "he was a worthless sort of fellow, just about the kind of a man who would do a trick like that. Anyhow, all of the colored people believe that and many of us have written letters already to the governor asking the reinstatement of the sheriff."

I sprang to my feet and asked him if he realized what he had done in condoning the horrible lynching of a fellowman who was a member of his race. Did he not know that if they condoned the lynching of one man, the time might come when they would have to condone that of other men higher up, providing they were black?

I asked him if he could direct me to the home of some other colored persons; that I had been sent to see all of them, and it wouldn't be fair for me to accept reports from one man alone. He gave me the names of one or two others, and I withdrew. I had expected to stop at his home, but after he told me that I had no desire to do so. One of the men named was Will Taylor, a druggist, whom I had known in Chicago, and I asked to be directed to his place. The minister's wife went with me because it was dark.

Mr. Taylor greeted me very cordially and I told him what my mission was. He also secured me a stopping place with persons by the name of Lewis, whom I afterward found were teachers in the colored high schools, both the man and his wife. They welcomed me very cordially and listened to my story. I told them why I was there; they gave me a bed. The next morning Mrs. Lewis came and informed me that she had already telephoned Dr. Taylor that she was sorry she could not continue to keep me. I found afterward that after they heard the story they felt that discretion was the better part of valor.

Mr. Taylor and I spent the day talking with colored citizens and ended with a meeting that night. I was driven to the place where the body of the murdered girl had been found, where the Negro had been burned, and saw about twenty-five representative colored people of the town that day. . . .

The meeting was largely attended and in my statement to them I said I had come down to be their mouthpiece; that I correctly understood how hard it would be for those who lived there to take an active part in the movement to oust the sheriff; that we were willing to take the lead in the matter but they must give me the facts; that it would be endangering the lives of other colored people in Illinois if we did not take a stand against the all too frequent lynchings which were taking place.

I went on to say that I came because I knew that they knew of my work against lynching for fifteen years past and felt that they would talk more freely to me and trust me more fully than they would someone of whom they knew nothing. I wanted them to tell me if Mr. Frank Davis had used his great power to protect the victim of the mob; if he had at any time placed him behind bars of the country jail as the law required; and if he had sworn in any deputies to help protect his prisoner as he was obliged by law to do until such time as he could be tried by due process of law. Although the meeting lasted for two hours, and although most of those present and speaking were friends of Frank Davis, some of whom had been deputy sheriffs in his office, not one of them could honestly say that Frank Davis had put his prisoner in the county jail or had done anything to protect him. I therefore offered a resolution to the effect which was almost unanimously adopted. There was one single objection by the ubiquitous "Uncle Tom" Negro who seems always present. I begged the people, if they could do nothing to help the movement to punish Frank Davis for such glaring negligence of his duty, that they would do nothing to hinder us.

Next morning before taking the train I learned of a Baptist ministers' meeting that was being held there and decided to attend for the purpose of having them pass the same resolution. I was told that it would do no good to make the effort and that it would delay me until midnight getting into Springfield. But I went, got an opportunity to speak, offered the resolution, told of the men who had sent letters to the governor, showed how that would confuse his mind as to the attitude of the colored people on the subject, and stated clearly that all such action would mean that we would have other lynchings in Illinois whenever it suited the mob anywhere.

I asked the adoption of the resolution passed the night before. There was discussion pro and con, and finally the moderator arose and said, "Brethren, they say an honest confession is good for the soul. I, too, am one of those men who have written to the governor asking Frank Davis's reinstatement. I knew he was a friend of ours; that the man who had taken his place has turned out all Negro deputies and put in Democrats, and I was told that when the mob placed the rope around "Frog" James's neck the sheriff tried to prevent them and was knocked down for his pains. But now that the sister has shown us plainly the construction that would be placed upon that letter, I want her when she appears before the governor tomorrow to tell him that I take that letter back and hereby sign my name to this resolution." By this time the old man was shedding tears. Needless to say the resolution went through without any further objections.

Mr. Barnett had told me that he would prepare a brief based upon what had been gleaned from the daily press, which would be in the post office at Springfield when I got there Wednesday morning; that if I found any facts contrary to those mentioned I could easily make the correction. There had been no precedent for this procedure, but he assumed that the attorney general would be present to represent the people.

When I entered the room at ten o'clock that morning I looked around for some of my own race, thinking that perhaps they would journey to Springfield for the hearing, even though they had been unwilling to go to Cairo to get the facts. Not a Negro face was in evidence! On the other side of the room there was Frank Davis, and with him one of the biggest lawyers in southern Illinois, so I was afterward told, who was also a state senator.

There was the parish priest, the state's attorney of Alexander County, the United States land commissioner, and about half a dozen other representative white men who had journeyed from Cairo to give aid and comfort to Frank Davis in his fight for reinstatement.

The governor said that they had no precedent and that he would now hear the plea to be made by the sheriff; whereupon this big lawyer proceeded to present this petition for reinstatement and backed it up with letters and telegrams from Democrats and Republicans, bankers, lawyers, doctors, editors of both daily papers, and heads of women's clubs and of men's organizations. The whole of the white population of Cairo was evidently behind Frank Davis and his demand for reinstatement.

In addition to this there were read these letters from Negro ministers and colored politicians. Special emphasis was laid upon them. Just before reading one of them the state senator said, "Your Excellency, I have known the writer of this letter since I was a boy. He has such a standing for truth and veracity in the community that if he were to tell me that black was white I would believe him, and he, too, has written to ask that Frank Davis be reinstated." . . .

When the gentlemen had finished, Governor Deneen said, "I understand Mrs. Barnett is here to represent the colored people of Illinois." Not until that moment did I realize that the burden depended upon me. It so happened that Attorney A. M. Williams, a

Negro lawyer of Springfield, having heard that I was in town, came over to the Capitol to invite me to his home for dinner. Finding me by myself, he immediately camped by my side and remained with me all through the ordeal. I was indeed thankful for this help, since never before had I been confronted with a situation that called for legal knowledge.

I began by reading the brief which Mr. Barnett prepared in due legal form. I then launched out to tell of my investigation in Cairo. Before I had gotten very far the clock struck twelve, and Springfield being a country town, everything stopped so people could go home to dinner, which was served in the middle of the day. I did not go with Mr. Williams to his home but urged him to do so.

I went to his office and stayed there, getting the balance of my address in shape. At two o'clock he came for me and we went back to the Capitol. I resumed the statement of facts I had found—of the meeting held Monday night and of the resolution passed there which stated Frank Davis had not put his prisoner in the county jail or sworn in deputies to protect him although he knew there was talk of mob violence.

I was interrupted at this point by Mr. Davis's lawyer. "Who wrote that resolution?" he asked. . . . I said, "I wrote the resolution and presented it, but the audience adopted and passed it. It was done in the same way as the petition which you have presented here. Those petitions were signed by men, but they were typewritten and worded by somebody who was interested enough in Mr. Davis to place them where the men could reach them. But that is not all, Governor; I have here the signature of that leading Baptist minister who has been so highly praised to you. I went to his meeting yesterday and when I told him what a mistake it was to seem to condone the outrage on a human being by writing a letter asking for the reinstatement of a man who permitted it to be done, he rose and admitted he had sent the letter which has been read in your hearing, but having realized his mistake he wanted me to tell you that he endorsed the resolutions which I have here, and here is his name signed to them."

And then I wound up by saying, "Governor, the state of Illinois has had too many terrible lynchings within her borders within the last few years. If this man is sent back it will be an encouragement to those who resort to mob violence and will do so at any time, well knowing they will not be called to account for so doing. All the colored friends in Cairo are friends of Mr. Davis and they seem to feel that because his successor, a Democrat, has turned out all the Republican deputies, they owe their duty to the party to ask the return of a Republican sheriff. But not one of these, Mr. Davis's friends, would say that for one moment he had his prisoner in the county jail where the law demands that he should be placed or that he swore in a single deputy to help protect his life until he could be tried by law. It looked like encouragement to the mob to have the chief law officer in the county take that man up in the woods and keep him until the mob got big enough to come after him. I repeat, Governor, that if this man is reinstated, it will simply mean an increase of lynchings in the state of Illinois and an encouragement to mob violence."

When I had finished it was late in the afternoon, and the governor said that as he wanted to leave town next day he would suggest that both sides get together and agree upon a statement of fact. He asked that we return that evening about eight o'clock. The big lawyer was very unwilling to do this. He and his party expected to go through the form of presenting that petition and taking the afternoon train back to Cairo, arriving there in time for dinner.

Instead we had to have a night session which would necessitate their remaining over until the next day. He angrily tossed the petition across the table like a bone to a dog and insisted that there was nothing else to be considered. But the governor held firm, and I was quite willing to go home and get something to eat. I was quite surprised when the session adjourned that every one of those white men came over and shook my hand and congratulated me on what they called the wonderful speech I had made. Mr. Frank Davis himself shook hands with me and said, "I bear you no grudge for what you have done, Mrs. Barnett." The state's attorney of Alexander County wanted to know if I was not a lawyer. The United States land commissioner, a little old man, said, "Whether you are a lawyer or not you made the best speech of the day." It was he who told me that the state senator who had represented Mr. Davis, whose name I have forgotten, was the biggest lawyer in southern Illinois.

When we returned to the night session, there was all the difference in the world in the attitude of those white men. The state's attorney and the big lawyer had already drawn up what they called an agreed statement of fact and were waiting for my ratification of the same. When I picked up the pen and began to draw a line through some of the phrases which described the occurrence in Cairo, the state's attorney asked what I was doing.

I told him that although I was not a lawyer, I did know a statement of fact when I saw one, and that in the description of the things which had taken place on the day of "Frog" James's arrest, he had said that "the sheriff, fearing an outbreak by the mob, had taken 'Frog' to the railroad station." I had drawn a line through the words which said, "fearing an outbreak by the mob," because that was his opinion rather than a fact. His face grew red, but he let it ride.

By the time we had finished it was ten o'clock. The governor had been waiting in the room across the hall while we argued back and forth over this agreed statement of fact. He then suggested that it was too late to go on, and asked that we return next morning. This we did and when I walked up the Capitol steps next morning every one of those white men with whom I had been in battle the day before swept off his hat at my approach. The big lawyer said, "Mrs. Barnett, we have decided that if you are willing we won't make another argument over this matter but will submit it all for the governor's action." I replied that whatever my lawyer advised, that I would do, and turned to Mr. Williams, who was still with me.

After scanning the papers he, too, agreed to their suggestion. We went into the governor's office and submitted the case without further argument, bade each other adieu and left for our homes.

Mr. Williams said as we went down the steps, "Oh, the governor's going to send him back. I don't see how he can help it with such terrific pressure being brought to bear to have him to do so. But, by george, if I had time to dig up the law I would have furnished him so much of it that he wouldn't dare do so." I said, "We have done the best we could under the circumstances, and angels could do no more."

The following Tuesday morning Governor Deneen issued one of the finest state papers that emanated from him during his whole eight years in the Capitol. The summary of his proclamation was that Frank Davis could not be reinstated because he had not properly protected the prisoner within his keeping and that lynch law could have no place in Illinois.

That was in 1909, and from that day until the present there has been no lynching in the state. Every sheriff, whenever there seem to be any signs of the kind, immediately telegraphs the governor for troops. And to Governor Deneen belongs the credit.

Abigail Scott Duniway

~

ABIGAIL SCOTT DUNIWAY (1871–1912) traveled to Oregon on a covered wagon as a teenager and became the leading women's rights worker of the Pacific Northwest. She was founder and proprietor of the suffrage newspaper *The New Northwest*, and founder and president of the Oregon Equal Suffrage Association. In her autobiography, *Path Breaking*, she describes events that led her to the suffrage cause and her efforts on its behalf.

~

My labors on that farm became an added burden as our resources grew. I recall one day which, like hundreds of others, was occupied to the limit. After dishes were washed, beds made, rooms swept, and when dinner was over for the family and hired men; after the week's washing was finished and the churning done, and I was busy in an outside house picking ducks—for those were pioneer days, and even our pillows, like our stockings, were home-made—a man came up from the village to our woodpile, where my husband was at work, and asked him to become surety for a considerable sum, with interest at two per cent per month, to be compounded semi-annually until paid. The two men parleyed awhile and then went into the house. It dawned upon me suddenly, as I was picking a duck, that it would ruin us financially if those notes were signed. I tried hard to be silent, being a nonentity in law, but my hands trembled, my heart beat hard, and I laid the pinioned duck on its back and repaired to the

Duniway, Abigail Scott. *Path Breaking: An Autobiographical History of the Equal Suffrage Movement in Pacific Coast States.* 1914. Rpt., New York: Shocken Books, 1971, pp. 13–19, 37–43.

living room to investigate. My husband had already signed two notes, and was in the act of signing the third, when I leaned over his shoulder and said, tremulously: "My dear, are you quite certain about what you are doing?" The other fellow looked daggers at me, but said nothing, and my husband answered, as he signed the last note: "Mama, you needn't worry; you'll always be protected and provided for!" I wanted to say: "I guess I'll always earn all the protection I get," but I remembered that I was nothing but a woman; so I bit my lips to keep silent and rushed back to my work, where for several minutes, I fear that duck-flesh suffered, for I didn't pluck the feathers tenderly. But I cooled down after awhile, and to my credit be it said, I never alluded to the notes afterwards. But hard times came, crops failed, my butter and egg money all went to pay interest and taxes, and the months went on and on. A great flood swept away the warehouse on the bank of Yamhill River at holiday time, carrying off the year's harvest, and the unpaid notes, with accrued interest, compounded semi-annually at 2 per cent per month, all fell due at once.

One busy day, when I had added to my other duties several rapid hurries down the hillside to scare the coyotes away from the sheep, and just as dusk was coming on—my husband having been away from home all day—the sheriff came to the house and served summons on me for those notes! Now, observe that, when that obligation was made, I was my husband's silent partner—a legal nonentity—with no voice or power for self-protection under the sun; but, when penalty accrued, I was his legal representative. I took the warrant smilingly from the sheriff's hand, and said: "It is all right. Won't you walk in?" He excused himself and went to a neighbor's house, nearly a mile distant, and served a wife with another paper. I afterwards learned that the good wife had, as the sheriff expressed it, "blowed him up," and he said to her, as he turned away: "You'd better go and see Mrs. Duniway and learn a lesson in politeness."

When the hired man came into supper I was as entertaining as I knew how to be. I told them of some cute sayings of the children, and strove in many ways to conceal the fact that I had been sued. I had yet to learn that the right to sue and be sued was the inalienable right of an American citizen.

As the night came down my husband came home, and, after he had eaten his supper, and while he was playing with the children, the hired men having gone to their quarters, I confess I felt a little secret satisfaction when I served those papers on him. I had framed up a little "spiel," which I meant to practice on him when I should serve the papers, but he turned so pale and looked so care-worn I couldn't even say, "I told you so!"

The lawsuit was not alluded to again until the next morning, when my husband informed me that he was going to town after breakfast to get that trouble settled out of court. Just what sort of a deal he made I do not now remember, but it resulted in the sale of the farm for just about enough to pay those security notes and interest, leaving us in possession of a little piece of town property in Lafayette, where I had often said I wished we were poor enough so we might be able to live in such a place, that I might have a chance to keep a few boarders, or take in washing for a livelihood; then I thought I might not only make a living more easily, but might have control of a little money that I could call my own, with which to clothe my children properly.

We had hardly become settled in our new quarters when an accident with a runaway team befell my husband, which, though he lived for many years thereafter, incapacitated him for physical labor on a farm, and threw the financial, as well as domestic, responsibility of our family upon my almost unaided self. His serious accident aroused the keenest sympathies of my being. He had become so deeply depressed by reverses for which he blamed himself, that I endeavored in every way to encourage him in negotiations he was making for another farm, by opening a private school. But this accident upset all of our plans. Our cottage was a one and a half story frame building, with the upper part merely enclosed and a roofed. This enclosure I lined and ceiled with unbleached muslin; and by working at it outside of school and kitchen hours, I soon had a neat and comfortable dormitory for the accommodation of young lady boarders, whom I added to my burdened household. Finding hired help unattainable, as the marriage of girls in their early teens was at that time universal, and Chinese servants had not yet penetrated our village, I would arise from my bed at 3 o'-clock in Summer and 4 o'clock in Winter, to do a day's work before school time. Then, repairing to my school room I would teach the primer classes while resting at my desk. For two hours afterwards I would occupy the time with the older students, often hearing recitations from text books I had never studied, over which, so keyed to thought was I from sheer necessity, that I caught the inspiration of every problem as I came to it, and never stumbled over any lesson, or let my pupils see that it was new to me.

I would prepare the table for luncheon in the dining room before repairing to the school room; and, returning to lessons at 1 o'clock P.M., would resume school work until 4 o'clock, before taking up my household duties again in the home. And yet, notwithstanding all this effort, I led an easier life than I had known on a pioneer farm. My work was rest for both mind and body. Health improved and hope revived. The evenings were recreative, musical, intellectual and thoroughly enjoyable; but how I got through with all of this physical work, and kept ahead of my constantly improving classes, as the weeks and months and years went on, I do not know. I had never had an opportunity to study English grammar, higher arithmetic or algebra; but I never failed, as a teacher, to impart any required knowledge at any recitation. I could never even find time to look at any lesson until my classes were called. I would then call a student to the blackboard, where he or she would stand with chalk in hand till, after reading the problem for the first time myself, I would ask the pupil to state it according to formula. If the class had mastered the lesson, the rest was easy. But if, as sometimes happened, the solution was not comprehended at all, I had to think like lightning to catch the inspiration myself. So I would say: "Suppose we analyze it." Taking for example, articles in the room, such as the stove, doors, windows, sashes or panes, desks, seams in the floor, etc., and by grouping, analyzing and amalgamation, adapting such articles to the solution of the problem before us, we would all begin to see through it at once; and the pupil at the board would begin with a hurried, nervous movement, to transcribe his thoughts in characters, figures, letters or diagrams; and the lesson would be mastered in fine shape—no student imagining that I had been catching the inspiration of it myself as we went along.

The town of Albany had sprung up in the interior of the Willamette Valley, and we sold out our little possessions in Lafayette and moved to this wider field, where I again engaged in teaching until I thought I had money enough to go into trade. By the time I had moved my school house to Broadalbin street and converted it into a store, with counters, shelves and showcases, and had bought out a partner and was ready to start up with millinery and notions, I had left on hand, after paying expenses to Portland and return, just thirty dollars. . . .

Among the many incidents I recall, which led me into the Equal Suffrage movement and crowd upon my memory as I write, was one which calls for special mention, and ought not to be omitted here. I had grown dispirited over an accumulation of petty annoyances in the store, when a woman entered suddenly, and throwing back a heavy green berage veil, said: "Mrs. Duniway, I want you to go with me to the court house!" I replied rather curtly, I fear: "The court house is a place for men." The visitor, whose eyes were red with weeping, explained that the county court had refused to accept the terms of her annual settlement, as administratrix of her husband's estate. But her lawyer had told her to get some merchant to accompany her to the court house, to bear testimony to the manner of settling her accounts. "Can't you get some man to go with you?" I asked, with growing sympathy. "I have asked several, but they all say they are too busy," was her tearful response. A sudden impulse seized me, and, calling one of the girls from the work room to wait upon customers, I started with the widow to the court house, feeling half ashamed, as I walked the street, to meet any one who might guess my errand. The woman kept up a running conversation as we proceeded, her words often interrupted by sobs. "Only think!" she cried, in a broken voice, "my husband—if he had lived and I had died—could have spent every dollar we had earned in twenty years of married life, and nobody would have cared what became of my children. I wasn't supposed to have any children. My girls and I have sold butter, eggs, poultry, cord wood, vegetables, grain and hay—almost enough to pay taxes and meet all of our bills, but after I've earned the means to pay expenses I can't even buy a pair of shoestrings without being lectured by the court for my extravagance!" By this time I was so deeply interested that I shouldn't have cared if all the world knew I was going to the court house. I felt a good deal as the man must have felt "who whipped another man for saying his sister was cross-eyed." When arraigned for misconduct before the court he said: "Your Honor, my sister isn't cross-eyed. I haven't any sister. It was the principle of the thing that stirred me up!"

The court had adjourned for recess as I entered the room, and I felt much relieved, as I knew the officers and didn't feel afraid to meet them when off duty. The urbane judge, who was still occupying his revolving chair, leaned back and listened to my story. When I had finished, he put his thumbs in the armholes of his vest and said, with a patronizing air: "Of course, Mrs. Duniway, as you are a lady, you are not expected to understand the intricacies of the law." "But we are expected to know enough to foot the bills, though," I retorted, with more force than elegance. The widow's lawyer beckoned us to him and said, with a merry twinkle in his eye: "I guess there won't be any more trouble with the county court, or the commissioners this year." As we were returning to the store the widow said: "I have to pay that lawyer enough every year to meet all my taxes, if I wasn't compelled to administer on my husband's estate."

In relating this incident to my husband at night, I added: "One-half of the women are dolls, the rest of them are drudges, and we're all fools!" He placed his hand on my head, as I sat on the floor beside his couch, and said: "Don't you know it will never be any better for women until they have the right to vote?" "What good would that do?" I asked, as a new light began to break across my mental vision. "Can't you see," he said earnestly, "that women do half of the work of the world? And don't you know that if women were voters there would soon be law-makers among them? And don't you see that, as women do half the work of the world, besides bearing all the children, they ought to control fully half of the pay?" The light permeated my very marrow bones, filling me with such hope, courage and determination as no obstacle could conquer and nothing but death could overcome.

⌒

Early in the month of November, in the year 1870, shortly after many such practical experiences as related above, which led me to determine to remove from Albany to Portland, to begin the publication of my weekly newspaper, "The New Northwest," I met one day at the home of my estimable neighbor, the late Mrs. Martha J. Foster, and our mutual friend, Mrs. Martha A. Dalton, of Portland, to whom I announced my intention. My friends heartily agreed with my idea as to Equal Rights for Women, but expressed their doubts as to the financial success of the proposed newspaper enterprise. After much discussion and finding my determination to begin the work unshaken, the three of us met at my home and decided to form the nucleus of a State Equal Suffrage Association. . . .

The first number of "The New Northwest" was issued on the 5th of May, 1871. As I look backward over the receded years, and recall the incidents of this venture, in the management of which I had had no previous training, I cannot but wonder at my own audacity, which can be compared to the spirit of adventure which led the early pioneers to cross, or try to cross, the unknown plains, with helpless families in covered wagons, drawn by teams of oxen. It is true that I did not encounter the diseases and deaths of the desert . . . but I did encounter ridicule, ostracism and financial obstacles, over which I fain would draw the veil of forgetfulness.

Mary Cunningham Agee, founder and executive director of The Nurturing Network. *"You know this woman. She is your next door neighbor, your waitress, your colleague at work, the cashier at your favorite restaurant. She could even be your own daughter."* (Courtesy of Mary Cunningham Agee)

Clara Barton, Civil War nurse and first president of the American Red Cross. *"I remembered our prisons, crowded with starving men whom all the powers and pities of the world could not reach even with a bit of bread."* (Courtesy of the Library of Congress)

Mary McLeod Bethune, founder of Bethune-Cookman College. *"My total capital was a dollar and a half, but I talked him into trusting me until the end of the month for the rest."* (Courtesy of the Library of Congress)

Carrie Chapman Catt, president of the National American Woman Suffrage Association during the final campaign to enfranchise women. *"You know, and you know that we know, that it has been the aim of both dominant parties to postpone woman suffrage as long as possible."* (Courtesy of the Library of Congress)

Hillary Rodham Clinton, first lady and U.S. senator. *"We need to understand that there is no one formula for how women should lead their lives."* (Courtesy of the Library of Congress)

Dorothy Day, founder of the Catholic Worker Movement. *"There had been the physical struggle, the mortal combat almost, of giving birth to a child, and now there was coming the struggle for my own soul."* (Courtesy of the Library of Congress)

Amelia Earhart, aviator. *"So I excused myself and went to listen to a man's voice asking me whether I was interested in doing something dangerous in the air."* (Courtesy of the Library of Congress)

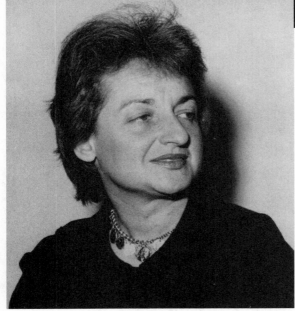

Betty Friedan, author of *The Feminine Mystique* and a founder of the National Organization for Women. *"I felt so guilty, somehow, that I hadn't done the big things everybody expected me to do with my brilliant Smith education— giving up the fellowship in psychology, getting fired from my newspaper job for being pregnant. . . . "* (Courtesy of the Library of Congress)

Ruth Bader Ginsburg, associate justice of the U.S. Supreme Court. *"Inherent differences between men and women, we have come to appreciate, remain cause for celebration, but not for denigration of the members of either sex or for artificial constraints on an individual's opportunity."* (Courtesy of the Supreme Court Historical Society)

Helen Keller, seated on the left, with her teacher and friend Anne Sullivan. *"The thought of going to college took root in my heart and became an earnest desire, which impelled me to enter into competition for a degree with seeing and hearing girls."* (Courtesy of the Library of Congress)

Liliuokalani, Queen of Hawaii. *"The first night of my imprisonment was the longest night I have ever passed in my life; it seemed as though the dawn of day would never come."* (Courtesy of the Library of Congress)

Lucretia Mott, a founder of the Philadelphia Female Anti-Slavery Society and an organizer of the Seneca Falls Convention. *"And although woman may not yet be so awakened to the consideration of the subjects as to be sensible of the blessing of entire freedom, she will, I doubt not, as she comes to reflect on the subject more and more, see herself in her true light."* (Courtesy of the Friends Historical Library, Swarthmore College)

Eleanor Roosevelt, first lady and U.S. delegate to the United Nations. *"It was not until I reached middle age that I had the courage to develop interests of my own, outside of my duties to family."* (Courtesy of the Library of Congress)

Carry A. Nation, America's most famous temperance leader. *"My father and mother warned me that the doctor was addicted to drink, but I had no idea of the curse of rum."* (Courtesy of the Library of Congress)

Margaret Sanger, birth control reformer and founder of what became Planned Parenthood Federation. *"Mrs. Sachs was in a coma and died within ten minutes. I folded her still hands across her breast, remembering how they had pleaded with me, begging so humbly for the knowledge which was her right."* (Courtesy of the Library of Congress)

Elizabeth Cady Stanton, founder of the organized women's rights movement in the United States. *"No words could express our astonishment on finding, a few days afterward, that what seemed to us so timely, so rational, and so sacred, should be a subject for sarcasm and ridicule to the entire press of the nation."* (Courtesy of the Library of Congress)

Frances E. Willard, president of the National Woman's Christian Temperance Union from 1879 to 1898. *"It is said that Napoleon was wont to consult his marshals and then do as he pleased, but I have found this method equally characteristic of ordinary mortals and certainly it was the one I followed in the greatest decision of my life."* (Courtesy of the Library of Congress)

While I did not regret meeting insults and misrepresentation on my own account, I did suffer deeply because of my budding family, who naturally resented the slander and downright abuse I suffered from ambitious editors, to all of whose attacks I replied in my own paper, in such a way as to bring to my defense the wiser comments of successful men, among whom I number many of our most prominent citizens of today; while among my detractors, I cannot recall a single one who has placed on record a single important deed redounding to his public or private credit.

Of the many men and women, who have honestly differed from me in the past, I have no word of censure. To my good brother, the late Mr. Harvey W. Scott, three years my junior, editor of the "Oregonian," then a rising journalist, universally honored in his later years, I owe a debt of lasting gratitude, for much assistance, editorial and otherwise, during the stormy years of my early efforts to secure a footing in my inexperienced attempts at journalism. . . . [A]lthough my brother did not editorially espouse my mission, as I believe he would have done if I had not been his sister, he many a time gladdened my heart by copying incidents of woman's hardships from my "New Northwest" into his own columns, thus indirectly championing, or at least commending, my initial efforts to secure Equal Rights for women.

To my faithful, invalid husband, the late Mr. Ben C. Duniway, but for whose sterling character as a man I could not have left our growing family in the home while I was away, struggling for a livelihood and the support of my newspaper . . . I owe undying gratitude.

To the 61,265 affirmative votes cast for the [state] Equal Suffrage Amendment, at the November election of 1912, and the more than an equal number of women, who rejoice with me over the culmination of my life's endeavors, I turn with words and thoughts of love and thankfulness. Many will live to see the beneficent results of their patriotism and foresight, long after I shall have joined the silent majority. Others may see their cherished ambitions fade, and will lay their failure to their discovery that all women cannot be made to vote or think according to their dictation, any more than all men can be so made, or led or driven.

Margaret Sanger

~

MARGARET SANGER (1879–1966), birth control reformer and founder of what ultimately became Planned Parenthood Federation, worked as a visiting nurse among New York City's poor during the second decade of the twentieth century. It was her experience with a young female patient, Sadie Sachs, that prompted Sanger to leave nursing and to work—in defiance of then-existing laws—to provide contraceptive information to women. In *Margaret Sanger: An Autobiography*, she remembers this patient.

~

During these years in New York trained nurses were in great demand. Few people wanted to enter hospitals; they were afraid they might be "practiced" upon, and consented to go only in desperate emergencies. Sentiment was especially vehement in the matter of having babies. A woman's own bedroom, no matter how inconveniently arranged, was the usual place for her lying-in. I was not sufficiently free from domestic duties to be a general nurse, but I could ordinarily manage obstetrical cases because I was notified far enough ahead to plan my schedule. And after serving my two weeks I could get home again.

Sometimes I was summoned to small apartments occupied by young clerks, insurance salesmen, or lawyers, just starting out, most of them under thirty and whose wives were having their first or second baby. They were always eager to know the best and latest method in infant care and feeding. In particular, Jewish

Sanger, Margaret. *Margaret Sanger: An Autobiography*. 1938. Rpt., New York: Cooper Square Press, 1999, pp. 86–92.

patients, whose lives centered around the family, welcomed advice and followed it implicity.

But more and more my calls began to come from the lower East Side, as though I were being magnetically drawn there by some force outside my control. I hated the wretchedness and hopelessness of the poor, and never experienced that satisfaction in working among them that so many noble women have found. My concern for my patients was now quite different from my earlier hospital attitude. I could see that much was wrong with them which did not appear in the physiological or medical diagnosis. A woman in childbirth was not merely a woman in childbirth. My expanded outlook included a view of her background, her potentialities as a human being, the kind of children she was bearing, and what was going to happen to them.

The wives of small shopkeepers were my most frequent cases, but I had carpenters, truck drivers, dishwashers, and pushcart vendors. I admired intensely the consideration most of these people had for their own. Money to pay doctor and nurse had been carefully saved months in advance—parents-in-law, grandfathers, grandmothers, all contributing.

As soon as the neighbors learned that a nurse was in the building they came in a friendly way to visit, often carrying fruit, jellies, or gefüllter fish made after a cherished recipe. It was infinitely pathetic to me that they, so poor themselves, should bring me food. Later they drifted in again with the excuse of getting the plate, and sat down for a nice talk; there was no hurry. Always back of the little gift was the question, "I am pregnant (or my daughter, or my sister is). Tell me something to keep from having another baby. We cannot afford another yet."

I tried to explain the only two methods I had ever heard of among the middle classes, both of which were invariably brushed aside as unacceptable. They were of no certain avail to the wife because they placed the burden of responsibility solely upon the husband—a burden which he seldom assumed. What she was seeking was self-protection she could herself use, and there was none.

Below this stratum of society was one in truly desperate circumstances. The men were sullen and unskilled, picking up odd jobs now and then, but more often unemployed, lounging in and out of the house at all hours of the day and night. The women seemed to slink on their way to market and were without neighborliness.

These submerged, untouched classes were beyond the scope of organized charity or religion. No labor union, no church, not even the Salvation Army reached them. They were apprehensive of everyone and rejected help of any kind, ordering all intruders to keep out; both birth and death they considered their own business. Social agents, who were just beginning to appear, were profoundly mistrusted because they pried into homes and lives, asking questions about wages, how many were in the family, had any of them ever been in jail. Often two or three had been there or were now under suspicion of prostitution, shoplifting, purse snatching, petty thievery, and, in consequence, passed furtively by the big blue uniforms on the corner.

The utmost depression came over me as I approached this surreptitious region. Below Fourteenth Street I seemed to be breathing a different air, to be in another world and country where the people had habits and customs alien to anything I had ever heard about.

There were then approximately ten thousand apartments in New York into which no sun ray penetrated directly; such windows as they had opened only on a narrow court from which rose fetid odors. It was seldom cleaned, though garbage and refuse often went down into it. All these dwellings were pervaded by the foul breath of poverty, that moldy, indefinable, indescribable smell which cannot be fumigated out, sickening to me but apparently unnoticed by those who lived there. When I set to work with antiseptics, their pungent sting, at least temporarily, obscured the stench.

I remember one confinement case to which I was called by the doctor of an insurance company. I climbed up the five flights and entered the airless rooms, but the baby had come with too great speed. A boy of ten had been the only assistant. Five flights was a log way; he had wrapped the placenta in a piece of newspaper and dropped it out the window into the court.

Many families took in "boarders," as they were termed, whose small contributions paid the rent. These derelicts, wanderers, alternately working and drinking, were crowded in with the children; a single room sometimes held as many as six sleepers. Little girls were accustomed to dressing and undressing in front of the men, and were often violated, occasionally by their own fathers or brothers, before they reached the age of puberty.

Pregnancy was a chronic condition among the women of this class. Suggestions as to what to do for a girl who was "in trouble" or a married woman who was "caught" passed from mouth to mouth—herb teas, turpentine, steaming, rolling downstairs, inserting slippery elm, knitting needles, shoe-hooks. When they had word of a new remedy they hurried to the drugstore, and if the clerk were inclined to be friendly he might say, "Oh, that won't help you, but here's something that may." The younger druggists usually refused to give advice because, if it were to be known, they would come under the law; midwives were even more fearful. The doomed women implored me to reveal the "secret" rich people had, offering to pay me extra to tell them; many really believed I was holding back information for money. They asked everybody and tried anything, but nothing did them any good. On Saturday nights I have seen groups of from fifty to one hundred with their shawls over their heads waiting outside the office of a five-dollar abortionist.

Each time I returned to this district, which was becoming a recurrent nightmare, I used to hear that Mrs. Cohen "had been carried to a hospital, but had never come back," or that Mrs. Kelly "had sent the children to a neighbor and had put her head into the gas oven." Day after day such tales were poured into my ears—a baby born dead, great relief—the death of an older child, sorrow but again relief of a sort—the story told a thousand times of death from abortion and children going into institutions. I shuddered with horror as I listened to the details and studied the reasons back of them—destitution linked with excessive childbearing. The waste of life seemed utterly senseless. One by one worried, sad, pensive, and aging faces marshaled themselves before me in my dreams, sometimes appealingly, sometimes accusingly.

These were not merely "unfortunate conditions among the poor" such as we read about. I knew the women personally. They were living, breathing, human beings, with hopes, fears, and aspirations like my own, yet their weary, misshapen bodies, "always ailing, never failing," were destined to be thrown on the scrap heap before they were thirty-five. I could not escape from the facts of their wretchedness; neither was I able to see any way out. My own cozy and comfortable family existence was becoming a reproach to me.

Then one stifling mid-July day of 1912 I was summoned to a Grand Street tenement. My patient was a small, slight Russian Jewess, about twenty-eight years old, of the special cast of feature to which suffering lends a madonna-like expression. The cramped three-room apartment was in a sorry state of turmoil. Jake Sachs, a truck driver scarcely older than his wife, had come home to find the three children crying and her unconscious from the effects of a self-induced abortion. He had called the nearest doctor, who in turn had sent for me. Jake's earnings were trifling, and most of them had gone to keep the none-too-strong children clean and properly fed. But his wife's ingenuity had helped them to save a little, and this he was glad to spend on a nurse rather than have her go to a hospital.

The doctor and I settled ourselves to the task of fighting the septicemia. Never had I worked so fast, never so concentratedly. The sultry days and nights were melted into a torpid inferno. It did not seem possible there could be such heat, and every bit of food, ice, and drugs had to be carried up three flights of stairs.

Jake was more kind and thoughtful than many of the husbands I had encountered. He loved his children, and had always helped his wife wash and dress them. He had brought water up and carried garbage down before he left in the morning, and did as much as he could for me while he anxiously watched her progress.

After a fortnight Mrs. Sachs' recovery was in sight. Neighbors, ordinarily fatalistic as to the results of abortion, were genuinely pleased that she had survived. She smiled wanly at all who came to see her and thanked them gently, but she could not respond to their hearty congratulations. She appeared to be more despondent and anxious than she should have been, and spent too much time in meditation.

At the end of three weeks, as I was preparing to leave the fragile patient to take up her difficult life once more, she finally voiced her fears, "Another baby will finish me, I suppose?"

"It's too early to talk about that," I temporized.

But when the doctor came to make his last call, I drew him aside. "Mrs. Sachs is terribly worried about having another baby."

"She well may be," replied the doctor, and then he stood before her and said, "Any more such capers, young woman, and there'll be no need to send for me."

"I know, doctor," she replied timidly, "but," and she hesitated as though it took all her courage to say it, "what can I do to prevent it?"

The doctor was a kindly man, and he had worked hard to save her, but such incidents had become so familiar to him that he had long since lost whatever delicacy he might once have had. He laughed good-naturedly. "You want to have your cake and eat it too, do you? Well, it can't be done."

Then picking up his hat and bag to depart he said, "Tell Jake to sleep on the roof."

I glanced quickly at Mrs. Sachs. Even through my sudden tears I could see stamped on her face an expression of absolute despair. We simply looked at each other, saying no word until he door had closed behind the doctor. Then she lifted her thin, blue-veined hands and clasped them beseechingly. "He can't understand. He's only a man. But you do, don't you? Please tell me the secret, and I'll never breathe it to a soul. *Please!*"

What was I to do? I could not speak the conventionally comforting phrases which would be of no comfort. Instead, I made her as physically easy as I could and promised to come back in a few days to talk with her again. A little later, when she slept, I tiptoed away.

Night after night the wistful image of Mrs. Sachs appeared before me. I made all sorts of excuses to myself for not going back. I was busy on other cases; I really did not know what to say to her or how to convince her of my own ignorance; I was helpless to avert such monstrous atrocities. Time rolled by and I did nothing.

The telephone rang one evening three months later, and Jake Sachs' agitated voice begged me to come at once; his wife was sick again and from the same cause. For a wild moment I thought of sending someone else, but actually, of course, I hurried into my uniform, caught up my bag, and started out. All the way I longed for a subway wreck, an explosion, anything to keep me from having to enter that home again. But nothing happened, even to delay me. I turned into the dingy doorway and climbed the familiar stairs once more. The children were there, young little things.

Mrs. Sachs was in a coma and died within ten minutes. I folded her still hands across her breast, remembering how they had pleaded with me, begging so humbly for the knowledge which was her right. I drew a sheet over her pallid face. Jake was sobbing, running his hands through his hair and pulling it out like an insane person. Over and over again he wailed, "My God! My God! My God!"

I left him pacing desperately back and forth, and for hours I myself walked and walked and walked through the hushed streets. When I finally arrived home and let myself quietly in, all the household was sleeping. I looked out my window and down upon the dimly lighted city. Its pains and griefs crowded in upon me, a moving picture rolled before my eyes with photographic clearness; women writhing in travail to bring forth little babies; the babies themselves naked and hungry, wrapped in newspapers to keep them from the cold; six-year-old children with pinched, pale, wrinkled faces, old in concentrated wretchedness, pushed into gray and fetid cellars, crouching on stone floors, their small scrawny hands scuttling through rags, making lamp shades, artificial flowers; white coffins, black coffins, coffins, coffins interminably passing in never-ending succession. The scenes piled one upon another on another. I could bear it no longer.

As I stood there the darkness faded. The sun came up and threw its reflection over the house tops. It was the dawn of a new day in my life also. The doubt and questioning, the experimenting and trying, were now to be put behind me. I knew I could not go back merely to keeping people alive.

I went to bed, knowing that no matter what it might cost, I was finished with palliatives and superficial cures; I was resolved to seek out the root of evil, to do something to change the destiny of mothers whose miseries were vast as the sky.

Carrie Chapman Catt

~

CARRIE CHAPMAN CATT (1859–1947), suffragist, feminist, and peace advocate, was president of the National American Woman Suffrage Association from 1900 to 1904 and from 1915 until 1920, when suffrage was won. The following selections depict the concluding years of the women's suffrage campaign.

~

[When Susan B. Anthony retired as president of the National American Woman Suffrage Association (NAWSA) in 1900, Carrie Chapman Catt was elected to succeed her. Accepting the position, Catt addressed the membership as follows.]

Good friends, I should hardly be human if I did not feel gratitude and appreciation for the confidence you have shown me; but

Anthony, Susan B., and Ida Husted Harper, eds. *History of Woman Suffrage*. Vol. 4, 1902. Rpt., Salem, NH: Ayer Company, 1985, p. 388 (comments upon her election as president of NAWSA).

Frost, Elizabeth, and Kathryn Cullen-DuPont. *Women's Suffrage in America: An Eyewitness History*. New York: Facts On File, 1992, pp. 311–313 (Catt's outline of her "Winning Plan") and pp. 335–336 (Catt's letter, Thanksgiving Day, 1920).

Catt, Carrie Chapman. "An Address to the Congress of the United States." New York: National Woman Suffrage Publishing Company, Inc., [1917?], pp. 18–21 ("Address to Congress").

I feel the honor of the position much less than its responsibility. I never was an aspirant for it. I consented only six weeks ago to stand. I was not willing to be the next president after Miss Anthony. I have known that there was a general loyalty to her which could not be given to any younger worker. Since Miss Anthony announced her intention to retire, there have been editorials in many leading papers expressing approval of her—but not of the cause. She has been much larger than our association. The papers have spoken of the new president as Miss Anthony's successor. Miss Anthony never will have a successor.

A president chosen from the younger generation is on a level with the association, and it might suffer in consequence of Miss Anthony's retirement if we did not still have her to counsel and advise us. I pledge you whatever ability God has given me, but I can not do this work alone. The cause has got beyond where one woman can do the whole. I shall not be its leader as Miss Anthony has been; I shall be only an officer of this association. I will do all I can, but I can not do it without the co-operation of each of you. The responsibility much overbalances the honor, and I hope you will all help me bear the burden.

[In 1916, Catt held a closed meeting of the Executive Board of NAWSA to set a strategy for what she hoped would be—and what indeed was—the final phase of the suffrage struggle. More than thirty-six state leaders of NAWSA, moved by Catt's passion and vision, signed a compact to "move on Congress with a will . . . prepared to give their lives and their fortunes for success." Catt's outline of what became known as "The Winning Plan" follows.]

When thirty-six state associations, or preferably more, enter into a solemn compact to get the [Federal] Amendment submitted by Congress and ratified by their respective legislatures; when they live up to their compact by running a red-hot, never ceasing campaign in their own states designed to create sentiment behind the political leaders of the states and to aim both these forces at the men in Congress as well as the legislatures, we *can* get the Amendment through, and ratified. We cannot do it by any other process. No such compact has ever been made, and no virile intention exists in the minds of the majority of the Association to back up a Washington lobby. Whether this is due to a prevailing belief that a lobby, assisted now and then by a bombardment of letters and telegrams, can pull the Amendment through, or to a lack of confidence in suffrage by the Federal route, or to sheer, unthinking carelessness, I am not prepared to say. I am inclined to believe that all three of these causes exist. . . .

This Convention must not adjourn should it sit until Christmas, until it creates a logical and sensible policy toward the Federal Amendment. . . . If it be decided that we *do* want enfranchisement by the Federal route, then at least thirty-six states must sign a compact to go after it with a will. . . .

National Boards must be selected hereafter for one chief qualification—the ability to lead the national fight. There should be a mobilization of at least thirty-six armies, and these armies should move under the direction of the national officers. They should be disciplined and obedient to the national officers in all matters concerning the national campaign. This great army with its thirty-six, and let us hope, forty-eight divisions, should move on Congress with precision, and a will. . . . More, those who enter on this task, should go prepared to give their lives and fortunes for success, and any pusillanimous coward among us who dares to call retreat, should be court-martialled. . . .

When a general is about to make an attack upon the enemy at a fortified point, he often begins to feint elsewhere in order to draw off attention and forces. If we decide to train up some states into preparedness for campaign, the best help which can be given them is to keep so much "suffrage noise" going all over the country that neither the enemy nor friends will discover where the real battle is. . . .

We should win, if it is possible to do so, a few more states before the Federal Amendment gets up to the legislatures. . . . A southern state should be selected and made ready for a campaign, and the solid front of the "anti" south broken as soon as possible.

Some break in the solid "anti" East should be made too. If New York wins in 1917 the backbone of the opposition will be largely bent if not broken . . .

By 1920, when the next national party platforms will be adopted, we should have won Iowa, South Dakota, North Dakota, Nebraska, New York, Maine and a southern state . . .

With these victories to our credit and the tremendous increase of momentum given the whole movement, we should be able to secure planks in all platforms favoring the Federal Amendment (if it has not passed before that time) and to secure its passage in the December term of the 1920 Congress.

It should then go to the legislatures of thirty-nine states which meet in 1921, and the remaining states would have the opportunity to ratify the amendment in 1922. If thirty-six states had ratified in these two years, the end of our struggle would come by April 1, 1922, six years hence. . . .

It will require, however, a constructive program of hard, aggressive work for six years, money to support it, and the cooperation of all suffragists. It will demand the elimination of the spirit of criticism, back-biting and narrow-minded clashing of personalities which is always common to a stagnant town, society or movement, and which is beginning to show itself in our midst. Success will depend less on the money we are able to command, than upon our combined ability to lift the campaign above this sordidness of mind, and to elevate it to the position of a crusade for human freedom.

~

[In 1917, Catt addressed Congress.]

[W]e know, and you know that we know, that it has been the aim of both dominant parties to postpone woman suffrage as long as possible. A few men in each party have always fought with us fearlessly, but the party machines have evaded, avoided, tricked and buffeted this question from Congress to Legislatures, from Legislatures to political conventions. I confess to you that many of us have a deep and abiding distrust of all existing political parties—they have tricked us so often and in such unscrupulous fashion that our doubts are natural. Some of you are leaders of those parties and all are members. Your parties we also know have a distrust and suspicion of new women voters. Let us counsel together. Woman suffrage is inevitable—you know it. The political parties will go on—we know it. Shall we then be enemies or friends? Can party leaders in twelve States really obtain the loyal support of women voters when those women know that the same party is ordering the defeat of amendments in States where campaigns are pending, or delaying action in Congress on the Federal Amendment? Gentlemen, we ask you to put yourselves in our places. What would you do? Would you keep on spending your money and your lives on a slow, laborious, clumsy State method, or would you use the votes you have won to complete your campaign on behalf of suffrage for all women in the nation? Would you be content to keep a standing army of women, told off for the special work of educating men in the meaning of democracy; would you raise and spend millions of dollars in the process; would you give up every other thing in life you hold dear in order to keep State campaigns going for another possible quarter of a century? Would you do this and see the women of other countries leaving you behind, or would you make "a hard pull, a long pull and a pull altogether" and finish the task at once? You know you would choose the latter. We make the same choice.

Do you realize that in no other country in the world with democratic tendencies is suffrage so completely denied as in a considerable number of our own States? There are 13 black States where no suffrage for women exists, and 14 others where suffrage for women is more limited than in many foreign countries.

Do you realize that no class of men in our own or in any other land have been compelled to ask their inferiors for the ballot?

Do you realize that when you ask women to take their cause to State referendum you compel them to do this; that you drive women of education, refinement, achievement, to beg men who cannot read for their political freedom?

Do you realize that such anomalies as a College President asking her janitor to give her a vote are overstraining the patience and driving women to desperation?

Do you realize that women in increasing numbers indignantly resent the long delay in their enfranchisement?

Your party platforms have pledged woman suffrage. Then why not be honest, frank friends of our cause, adopt it in reality as your own, make it a party program and "fight with us"? As a party measure—a measure of all parties—why not put the amendment through Congress and the Legislatures? We shall all be better friends, we shall have a happier nation, we women will be free to support loyally the part of our choice and we shall be far prouder of our history.

"There is one thing mightier than kings and armies"—aye, than Congresses and political parties—"the power of an idea when its time has come to move." The time for woman suffrage has come. The woman's hour has struck. If parties prefer to postpone action longer and thus do battle with this idea, they challenge the inevitable. The idea will not perish; the party which opposes it may. Every delay, every trick, every political dishonesty from now on will antagonize the women of the land more and more, and when the party or parties which have so delayed woman suffrage finally let it come, their sincerity will be doubted and their appeal to the new voters will be met with suspicion. This is the psychology of the situation. Can you afford the risk? Think it over.

We know you will meet opposition. There are a few "woman haters" left, a few "old males of the tribe," as Vance Thompson calls them, whose duty they believe it to be to keep women in the places they have carefully picked out for them. Treitschke, made world famous by war literature, said some years ago: "Germany, which knows all about Germany and France, knows far better what is good for Alsace-Lorraine than that miserable people can possibly know." A few American Treitschkes we have who know better than women what is good for them. There are women, too, with "slave souls" and "clinging vines" for backbones. There are female dolls and male dandies. But the world does not wait for such as these, nor does Liberty pause to heed the plaint of men and women with a grouch. She does not wait for those who have a special interest to serve, nor a selfish reason for depriving other people of freedom. Holding her torch aloft, Liberty is pointing the way onward and upward and saying to America, "Come."

To you the supporters of our cause, in Senate and House, and the number is large, the suffragists of the nation express their grateful thanks. This address is not meant for you. We are more truly appreciative of all you have done than any words can express. We ask you to make a last, hard fight for the amendment during the present session. Since last we asked a vote on this amendment your position has been fortified by the addition to suffrage territory of Great Britain, Canada and New York.

Some of you have been too indifferent to give more than casual attention to this question. It is worthy of your immediate consideration—a question big enough to engage the attention of our Allies in war time, is too big a question for you to neglect.

Some of you have grown old in party service. Are you willing that those who take your places by and by shall blame you for having failed to keep pace with the world and thus having lost for them a party advantage? Is there any real gain for you, for your party, for the nation by delay? Do you want to drive the progressive men and women out of your party?

Some of you hold to the doctrine of State's rights, as applying to woman suffrage. Adherence to that theory will keep the United States far behind all other democratic nations in action upon this question. *A theory which prevents a nation from keeping up with the trend of world progress cannot be justified.*

Gentlemen, we hereby petition you, our only designated representatives, to redress our grievances by the immediate passage of the Federal Suffrage Amendment and to use your influence to secure its ratification in your own state, in order that the women of our nation may be endowed with political freedom before the next presidential election, and that our nation may resume its world leadership in democracy.

Woman suffrage is coming—you know it. Will you, Honorable Senators and Members of the House of Representatives, help or hinder it?

∽

[The Nineteenth Amendment was ratified on August 26, 1920. On Thanksgiving Day of that year, Catt wrote this letter to her staff at the National American Woman Suffrage Association.]

Out here alone with my thoughts, I have kept Thanksgiving sacred to reflections upon the long trail behind us, and the triumph which was its inevitable conclusion. John Adams said long after the Revolution that only about one third of the people were for it, a third being against it, and the remaining third utterly indifferent. Perhaps this proportion applies to all movements. At least a third of the women were for our cause at the end. . . . As I look back over the years . . . I realize that the greatest thing in the long campaign for us was not its crowning victory, but the discipline it gave us all. . . . It was a great crusade, the world has seen none more wonderful. . . . My admiration, love and reverence go out to that band which fought and won a revolution . . . with congratulations that we were permitted to establish a new and good thing in the world.

Alice Paul

~

ALICE PAUL (1885–1977), suffragist and feminist, led the National Woman's Party during the last years of the suffrage struggle and was jailed, along with 167 of her followers, for picketing the White House. (The official charge was "obstructing a sidewalk.") Paul drafted the Equal Rights Amendment in 1923, three years after suffrage was won, and spent the rest of her life fighting to make it part of the U.S. Constitution. In 1972, the amendment, with wording slightly different than what Paul had proposed, was passed by congress. Paul died in 1977, hoping the Equal Rights Amendment would be ratified, but it failed in 1982. In this interview with Amelia Fry, Paul reviews the history of the Equal Rights Amendment and the legacy of women such as Susan B. Anthony.

~

Amelia Fry: Was this at your Seneca Falls meeting? You had another meeting at Seneca Falls like the original one [in July of 1923].

Alice Paul: No, that Seneca Falls meeting was just to commemorate Seneca Falls. It was the seventy-fifth anniversary.

Paul, Alice. *Conversations with Alice Paul: Woman Suffrage and the Equal Rights Amendment*, typescript of an oral history conducted in 1972 and 1973 by Amelia Fry, Regional Oral History Office, the Bancroft Library, University of California, Berkeley, 1976, pp. 265–272, 288–289, 512–513. Excerpts from *Conversations with Alice Paul* reprinted by permission of the Bancroft Library.

Fry: But you did submit an equal rights amendment wording.

Paul: Yes by that time I think I had gotten all my awful [suffrage campaign] bills [laughing] out of the way and paid. It is just amazing that you can have a—I always sympathize at the end of these Republican campaigns, Democrat campaigns, because I know that somebody is being left with these awful bills. Because you really would have thought, with wealthy women like Mrs. Belmont and so on that, while certainly one couldn't be too grateful for all she did after all they all sailed away on their own lives. Suffrage was won and now the thing is over. We certainly had a hard time then.

But I would end up, it seems to me, by saying that when the ratification was over, we celebrated by putting in the Capitol the statues of the great pioneers who in large measure had started the modern campaign at Seneca Falls [in 1848]. It was one of the really big things we did, because it was starting women to have a feeling of respect for women and by putting statues of women in the Capitol when it had always been a Capitol of men. Until Jeannette Rankin no woman was venturing into the—like you say venturing into the Cosmos Club. And that then when we had a convention on and presented the statue to the Capitol, the last thing that we did in the suffrage campaign was that we voted to go on. Elsie Hill was very gallant and courageous and took the leadership.

Well then by the end of two years had gone by, we sort of I guess [laughing] gathered up some more strength. And this was a really very wonderful meeting up at Seneca Falls. There we proposed not only would we work for equality but we would work for an equal rights amendment to the Constitution. And we started on that campaign. That's enough to finish up with.

Fry: And you did submit a wording of the amendment, which is in that issue of the *Suffragist* (or I guess, maybe it was called the *Equal Rights* by that time).

Paul: The amendment read—I made the speech, you know, presenting this [amendment]. Of course, by this time I had recovered enough strength [laughing] I think to feel convinced that we ought to go ahead with the campaign and we ought to do it in the form of another amendment to have *complete* emancipation as our goal. So the amendment that I proposed—and I said, "This is just a tentative proposal because we have asked a good many lawyers to work on the form and so on, and the wording doesn't make much difference if we agree on what we want." So I presented this:

"Men and women shall have equal rights throughout the United States and every place subject to its jurisdiction."

That said it all, and I said, "That's what we want, let's say what we want, and if they can find—"

That's when I started in to study law because I thought, "I can't do anything without knowing as much as the people who will be our opponents. I don't know anything whatsoever about law."

So I then went up and lived at the headquarters and early morning about six I went to the American University and enrolled in the law department, and I got my bachelor's degree in law.

And then I thought, "I really don't know much, I must say, still about law, as far as being able to cope with the people who say you can't have any such amendment as that." So you see we went around from person to person who was supposed to be a great authority. I went up myself to see Dean Pound at Harvard, who was supposed to be the greatest authority on constitutional law in the country, and Mrs. Lewis had her son work on it, and Elsie Hill met her husband when she and I went down to see him in the George Washington University law school to ask him to work on some kind of an amendment to the Constitution.

Fry: You mean, a man she later married?

Paul: Yes, her later husband. That's where she met him. Everybody drew up things, and we knew they wouldn't do. But I thought I wasn't very well-equipped to be making judgments on this subject, so then I went on and took a master's degree in law at the American University. And then I thought, "Still I really don't know very much about this—it is such a vast subject"—we had to study Roman law and all kinds of laws of all—things like that, quite a lot to do. So I then took the doctor of law. By that time I felt really I could talk to people on this subject, because I knew that they didn't know very much either. My feeling of complete ignorance they seemed pretty much to share.

So then the Judiciary Committee of the Senate paid no attention to us at all. We went to all the national conventions of the Republican party and the Democratic party that intervened, and the first hearing we had in 19—this is just for your *information* you know, not for this article—but 1923 was the first hearing on the subject of the new amendment, and the amendment was "Men and women shall have equal rights throughout the United States and every place subject to its jurisdiction."

Well, at that hearing—and this seems almost impossible to believe—all the women's organizations that came now with the votes in their hands so they counted for something (while before nobody paid much attention to us or to anybody else when we went to hearings because we were all voteless) now became a great power, even more power in the minds of the congressmen and the senators then they really had, because they didn't have back of themselves any united, strong group that would always stand together on this subject. But they got up and spoke and the congressmen certainly felt they had power then. All of them spoke I think *against* the Equal Rights Amendment. And if they didn't speak against us they remained silent. They didn't speak for us. So we were the only group that spoke for the Equal Rights Amendment when it was first put in. . . .

Our problem would not be the Senate and Congress and the President, because now we were voters and had this power; but it would be changing the thought of American women because more than half the country were now new voters, and if the new voters through their own organizations went up and said, "Please don't have a thing to do with this, we don't want women working at night, we don't want women standing up to work and we don't want women to lose their alimony and we don't want married women working when their husbands are working," and all these things that they said. (*You* know what they say.) Well, we said, "Now we have a wholly different task, which is to change the thought of American women, really.["]

So we started then to one convention after another after another and kept it up until this year. We are still keeping it up, the last one being the League of Women Voters and the one before that the AAUW [American Association of University Women]. I have told you all this, I think, before.

Fry: Well, yes, and I remember myself taking long lists of women's organizations to use with congressmen for you. By 1971 huge numbers had gotten behind the Amendment.

Paul: I know, but you see our task through these years was this monotonous one of getting these women to change their minds to make them see what this principle meant and so on. So that's what has taken, more or less, all these years to do.

Well now, we went to convention after convention of the political parties. It was in 1940—this is just in case you are interested, all for your own information.

Fry: This is marvelous, Alice, to give me a good overview of this.

Paul: Well, in 1940 for the first time we got in the Republican platform. Then in 1944 we got it in the Democratic one. That was a very hard-fought fight. Then we had it in both. Well, by that time Congress began to—

Fry: When did Republicans—?

Paul: 1940. 1944—Democrats. And that's when we finally began to work with Mrs. Emma Guffey Miller because she was so prominent in the Democratic party. She came in and joined us then and laid our fight before the Democratic National Convention to put it in the platform, and we got it in.

Well, then Congress began to pay more attention to us. It was in the political party platforms, and the Judiciary Committee of the Senate began seriously to consider the wording.

I remember going myself to—while I was not national chairman I went down whenever I could to try to help—I went in to see Senator Burton, I remember, from Ohio, who was on the Supreme Court later. At that time he was on the Senate Judiciary Committee. I went to talk about how it could be worded. I remember him saying, "Well, Senator Austin of Vermont, who is perhaps the most concerned man on the Judiciary Committee, and I have worked and worked and worked and we still cannot find the wording that we think will express what you want."

So this went on. We had asked Dean Pound, and the versions that everybody had given us we knew enough at least about law to know we didn't want it. A great deal of this responsibility fell on me because I was now beginning to know a little bit about law, you see. So I think it was in 1943 that finally we took a draft to—Mrs. Broy went with me; she didn't know very much about it but she was our political chairman so she went with me—to see Senator Austin. We handed him a draft, "Equality of rights under the law shall not be denied or abridged"—what we now have, you see, the one that is now through Congress. So he studied it for a time and then he said, "Well, I really think perhaps this is just exactly right. I don't see anything the matter with it. And I think it will probably give you just what we all have in mind. But I wouldn't want to do it without Senator [Joseph Christopher] O'Mahoney of Wyoming who, on the Democratic side, is the chief person working for this measure."

So Mrs. Broy and I then went up to Senator O'Mahoney's office. He was just departing for Wyoming where he lived, but he studied it and he said, "Well, you can go back and tell the senator that you just left that I will be, anyway, the second senator and I will support it, so you will have probably the man who is most concerned on the Republican side and the man who is the most concerned on the Democratic side." So we did.

Then we were asked to make sure that the women of the country who had already (in a few cases, not many, but a few organizations had) endorsed the old amendment, "Men and women shall have equal rights," these two men said, "We don't want to put this in and then find that the women won't stand back of us. So will you get the signature of the responsible person in every woman's organization that has endorsed the old amendment ('Men and women shall have equal rights') saying that they approve of the new amendment." So that's what we started and did.

We drew up a paper with the new proposed amendment addressed to the Senate Judiciary and called up each women's organization or had them come to see us, or in some form or other had them consider it, and we got a page of signatures of all these different women's groups. None of them knew enough to have any objection! Especially when we said we thought we could get the Senate Judiciary to support this. You see, the difference was, the old one said, "Men and women shall have equal rights throughout the United States and every place subject to its jurisdiction." They took the position that while they personally were for equal rights throughout the United States, they didn't think Congress had the right to interfere so much in the lives of *individual* people; they thought it ought to deal with the *government*; the *government* should not deny equal rights. So when we changed it to saying, "Equality of rights under the law shall not be denied or abridged *by the United States or any state* on account of sex," then they all signed, they all signed their approval of the new one.

Fry: That fixed that.

Paul: And so we went down to the Judiciary meeting the next time it was held and—I remember this so very vividly—I remember one of our members said, "It is so useless to do this. You know that Judiciary Committee; they will never do this. They won't listen to us. They won't even read it, they won't care, they don't care anything, they are just against us."

This was one of our officers from Virginia, a very fine member. And you know you are so pulled down by this defeatist attitude and discouragement. (Of course you have been through all that; you know what it is.) Anyway we did. And quite a group of maybe forty or fifty women assembled in the hall outside the Judiciary Committee, and I had the paper there, full of joy myself, with all these people saying, "You are just wasting your time. That committee will never care twopence about it, will never look at it; we can be sure of that."

So anyway I sent the guard in to tell the senator that I was out there, as he had asked, with the paper. He came out and took it in and presented it to the Committee. Senator O'Mahoney was there and gave his report as he had promised to give and the whole Committee voted—I think the whole Committee voted unanimously, but I am not absolutely positive about that—anyway the majority voted to report out this new version.

So from that time on we had this one that we now have before Congress, which is more limited because when it says, "shall not be denied or abridged by the *United States or by any state*" it is only a prohibition on the *government* of the country. An individual family, such as you and your husband, can have inequality with you the head of the family or he the head of the family or anything you want to do. It is not interfering with any private business or anything excepting where the government has some regulation on the subject, which I think is the right thing myself. So, from then on there was never any deviation, until this new thing that has now been sent on to all the states for ratification.

Now this campaign is a very different one from the other campaign because the other one concentrated on the President. Suffrage was something that we thought was sufficiently in existence because we already had a number of states where it was in existence, and there was not any conceivable reason why it should not become universal for our country. But this one, you couldn't possibly start out to put something in the Constitution that all—practically all—women of the country who were supposed to benefit from it were opposed to. And that is what we were confronted by, which was a very hard thing to be confronted by.

When you think of the long hold-out by the AAUW—imagine taking all these years, and this very great educator I told you about, M. Carey Thomas, coming down and succeeding in having AAUW's name at least deleted from the letter sent to every member of Congress saying we are opposed to the Equal Rights Amendment. (They wouldn't *support* us; they just agreed not to fight us.) See what we were up against was about unbelievable.

Fry: You were starting from scratch like Susan B. Anthony, I guess, did in the very early days of suffrage, or would it be even worse than that?

Paul: I think as far as law and government, the Amendment won't do away with all the innumerable phases of the subjection of women; but as far as *government*, it seems to me, it completes the emancipation of women as far as can see.

Now the thing that I think is before us next is to work with the women of other countries where we have almost all gotten the vote now and try to make the power of women so clear and recognized that we can really make the world according to the ideals of women as well as the ideals of men.

I don't think we can do it all alone in our country. We've got to do it with the women of all countries because so much is being done through the United Nations now and it increasingly will be. While I am not very keen on our meddling in other countries, still we seem to be involved to do it, so when we meddle, it will be, I think, essential to have the power of women guiding that meddling—if we can't keep them from meddling. . . .

I wish that perhaps now women could have a more respectful, if you had more respect for the campaign for the equality for women and for the women who took part in it. Because when I came along from England as just a young college student, I had never heard of the name of Elizabeth Cady Stanton, and only vaguely of the name of Susan B. Anthony. Just it was a name I knew I'd heard, but I didn't know anything about her.

And I only knew about Lucretia Mott because her painting was up in the head place of honor in the collection hall where we met every morning. All the students met and every day I looked up at Lucretia Mott, and we had a fellowship that was called the Lucretia Mott Fellowship. And that was because she was a Quaker, and *they* had preserved her name. But in the *woman* movement, I didn't know she had anything to do with the woman movement.

Fry: It's hard to think of you not knowing that at one time, Alice. *[Laughing.]*

Paul: But I meant, *nobody* knew it. *Nobody* who had just an ordinary college education had ever been told a thing about these or ever heard of it. And the woman movement wasn't enough developed so that people were talking about the generation before them. They were just tiny little groups of women meeting together, talking about how could they get a few signatures to a little petition and so on, when I went to these meetings.

So then I really think that by encouraging one of our members to start a [postage] stamp—a Susan B. Anthony stamp and things like that, and having pageants—we had one great pageant in Washington put on by Hazel McKaye on the life of Susan B. Anthony: this was the time that we were trying to get people to follow the old Amendment [ratify the nineteenth amendment]. We thought if we could identify it in any way in their minds with some heroic woman who had been outstanding, it would help.

Fry: Today they call that consciousness-raising—

Paul: Do they?

Fry: —Of women about women.

Paul: Is that so? I didn't know it. At all events it certainly has then we started having meetings every birthday of Susan B. Anthony in the capital, and birthdays of Lucretia Mott once in a while, Elizabeth Cady Stanton once in a while. And then we started having meetings, general meetings in the capital in Statuary Hall, for instance, on the death of Inez Milholland and we started out to make Inez Milholland known and revered. So that's one—I think when you think of this period, not only did it—as you can see very easily—in a very short time, change the feeling of people toward accepting an amendment to the Constitution. . . .

The other thing you asked me to tell you about when we got the tape, I think, was about the Susan B. Anthony desk.

Fry: Oh, yes. Do you have time to tell me about that tonight?

Paul: I have time to tell you about anything because this is my last chance, you see.

Fry: Well, all right, but you could tell me in the morning.

Paul: No, I'd rather tell you now.

Fry: You look so bright-eyed right now, you might as well go ahead.

Paul: I think in the morning, if you are going on a plane, you have a lot to do.

When the National American Woman Suffrage board, acting upon the request and suggestion of Miss Jane Addams, appointed Lucy Burns and myself as members of their congressional committee to go down to Washington and do what we could for the passage of the federal suffrage amendment, which Miss Anthony worked for so long, we had no office to begin with and no place from which to work. The first thing we did was to put a little notice in the newspapers saying that we were coming down to take up the work that Miss Anthony had laid down "[w]hen she had to give up going to Washington,["] and we were going to open an office and start a procession, if we were able, through the streets of Washington, to occur the day before the inauguration of the new President, Wilson.

When this notice was read by Miss Anthony's former secretary, named Rachael Brill Ezekiel, Mrs. Ezekiel telephoned to me that when Miss Anthony left Washington she expected to come back again but she did not because of her death. Mrs. Ezekiel was in possession of her desk that she had left behind. She said that, having read in the paper about our trying to go on with the work of Miss Anthony, she felt that she ought to turn the desk over to those who were going on with Miss Anthony's work. And so she had called me to say she had the desk, what should she do with it, would I like to have it?

I said, of course, we would like to have it; we had not yet even gotten an office, much less a desk. We were getting an office in this little basement on 1420 F Street, so she said she would have the desk brought down to us. And she did.

The desk arrived, and we opened our office with only one piece of furniture, the Susan B. Anthony desk. We continued to use this desk all through the suffrage campaign and all through the following campaign for complete equality for women, and it is still at the headquarters of the National Woman's Party in Washington. . . .

Dorothy Day

~

DOROTHY DAY (1897–1980), founder and head of the Catholic
Worker Movement, was motivated by conservative religious beliefs and by radical political instinct to live a life of voluntary
poverty and to perform "works of mercy and personalist action"
among the poor. Nothing in her early life suggested that she would
ultimately be proposed for sainthood by the Roman Catholic
Church, as she was in 1998 by John Cardinal O'Connor of New
York. Her conversion to Catholicism followed the birth in 1927 of
her daughter and necessitated, in her view, a separation from the
child's father, whom she loved but could not marry. Her conversion was painful in other ways as well, as she details in her autobiography, *The Long Loneliness*.

~

I was surprised that I found myself beginning to pray daily. I could
not get down on my knees, but I could pray while I was walking.
If I got down on my knees I thought, "Do I really believe? Whom
am I praying to?" A terrible doubt came over me, and a sense of
shame, and I wondered if I was praying because I was lonely, because I was unhappy.

But when I walked to the village for the mail, I found myself
praying again, holding in my pocket the rosary that Mary Gordon

gave me in New Orleans some years before. Maybe I did not say it correctly but I kept on saying it because it made me happy.

Then I thought suddenly, scornfully, "Here you are in a stupor of content. You are biological. Like a cow. Prayer with you is like the opiate of the people." And over and over again in my mind that phrase was repeated jeeringly, "Religion is the opiate of the people."

"But," I reasoned with myself, "I am praying because I am happy, not because I am unhappy. I did not turn to God in unhappiness, in grief, in despair—to get consolation, to get something from Him."

And encouraged that I was praying because I wanted to thank Him, I went on praying. No matter how dull the day, how long the walk seemed, if I felt sluggish at the beginning of the walk, the words I had been saying insinuated themselves into my heart before I had finished, so that on the trip back I neither prayed nor thought but was filled with exultation.

Along the beach I found it appropriate to say the *Te Deum*. When I worked about the house, I found myself addressing the Blessed Virgin and turning toward her statue.

It is so hard to say how this delight in prayer grew on me. The year before, I was saying as I planted seeds in the garden, "I *must* believe in these seeds, that they fall into the earth and grow into flowers and radishes and beans. It is a miracle to me because I do not understand it. Neither do naturalists understand it. The very fact that they use glib technical phrases does not make it any less of a miracle, and a miracle we all accept. Then why not accept God's mysteries?"

I began to go to Mass regularly on Sunday mornings.

. . . Forster was in the city all week, only coming out week ends. I finished the writing I was doing and felt at loose ends, thinking enviously of my friends going gaily about the city, about their work, with plenty of companionship.

The fact that I felt restless was a very good reason to stay on the beach and content myself with my life as a sybaritic anchorite. For how could I be a true anchorite with such luxuries as the morning paper, groceries delivered to the door, a beach to walk on, and the water to feast my eyes on? And then the fresh fish and clams, mushrooms, Jerusalem artichokes, such delicacies right at hand. I invited Lefty to supper and discussed with him the painting of the house. I read Dickens every evening.

In spite of my desire for a sociable week in town, in spite of a desire to pick up and flee from my solitude, I took joy in thinking of the idiocy of the pleasures I would indulge in if I were there. Cocktail parties, with prohibition drinks, dinners, the conversation or lack of it, dancing in a smoky crowded room when one might be walking on the beach, the dull, restless cogitations which come after dissipating one's energies—things which struck me with renewed force every time I spent days in the city. My virtuous resolutions to indulge in such pleasure no more were succeeded by a hideous depression when neither my new-found sense of religion, my family life, my work nor my surroundings were sufficient to console me. I thought of death and was overwhelmed by the terror and the blackness of both life and death. And I longed for a church near at hand where I could go and lift up my soul.

It was pleasant rowing about in the calm bay with Forster. The oyster boats were all out, and far on the horizon, off Sandy Hook, there was a four-masted vessel. I had the curious delusion that several huge holes had been stove in her side, through which you could see the blue sky. The other vessels seemed sailing in the air, quite indifferent to the horizon on which they should properly have been resting. Forster tried to explain to me scientific facts about mirages and atmospheric conditions, and, on the other hand, I pointed out to him how our senses lie to us.

But it was impossible to talk about religion or faith to him. A wall immediately separated us. The very love of nature, and the study of her secrets which was bringing me to faith, cut Forster off from religion.

I had known Forster a long time before we contracted our common-law relationship, and I have always felt that it was life with him that brought me natural happiness, that brought me to God.

His ardent love of creation brought me to the Creator of all things. But when I cried out to him, "How can there be no God, when there are all these beautiful things," he turned from me uneasily and complained that I was never satisfied. We loved each other so strongly that he wanted to remain in the love of the moment; he wanted me to rest in that love. He cried out against my attitude that there would be nothing left of that love without a faith.

I remembered the love story in Romain Rolland's *Jean Christophe*, the story of his friend and his engrossing marriage, and how those young people exhausted themselves in the intensity of their emotions.

I could not see that love between man and woman was incompatible with love of God. God is the Creator, and the very fact that we were begetting a child made me have a sense that we were made in the image and likeness of God, co-creators with him. I could not protest with Sasha about "that initial agony of having to live." Because I was grateful for love, I was grateful for life, and living with Forster made me appreciate it and even reverence it still more. He had introduced me to so much that was beautiful and good that I felt I owed to him too this renewed interest in the things of the spirit.

He had all the love of the English for the outdoors in all weather. He used to insist on walks no matter how cloudy or rainy the day, and this dragging me away from my books, from my lethargy, into the open, into the country, made me begin to breathe. If breath is life, then I was beginning to be full of it because of him. I was filling my lungs with it, walking on the beach, resting on the pier beside him while he fished, rowing with him in the calm bay, walking through fields and woods—a new experience entirely for me, one which brought me to life, and filled me with joy.

I had been passing through some years of fret and strife, beauty and ugliness—even some weeks of sadness and despair. There had been periods of intense joy but seldom had there been the quiet beauty and happiness I had now. I had thought all those years that I had freedom, but now I felt that I had never known real freedom nor even had knowledge of what freedom meant.

Now, just as in my childhood, I was enchained, tied to one spot, unable to pick up and travel from one part of the country to another, from one job to another. I was tied down because I was going to have a baby. No matter how much I might sometimes wish to flee from my quiet existence, I could not, nor would I be able to for several years. I had to accept my quiet and stillness, and accepting it, I rejoiced in it.

For a long time I had thought I could not bear a child, and the longing in my heart for a baby had been growing. My home, I felt, was not a home without one. The simple joys of the kitchen and garden and beach brought sadness with them because I felt myself unfruitful, barren. No matter how much one was loved or one loved, that love was lonely without a child. It was incomplete.

I will never forget my blissful joy when I was first sure that I was pregnant—I had wanted a baby all the first year we were together. . . . I remember . . . feeling so much in love, so settled, so secure that now I had found what I was looking for.

It did not last all through my pregnancy, that happiness. There were conflicts because Forster did not believe in bringing children into such a world as we lived in. He still was obsessed by the war. His fear of responsibility, his dislike of having the control of others, his extreme individualism made him feel that he of all men should not be a father.

Our child was born in March at the end of a harsh winter. In December I had come in from the country and taken an apartment in town. My sister came to stay with me, to help me over the last hard months. It was good to be there, close to friends, close to a church where I could pray. I read the *Imitation of Christ* a great deal during those months. I knew that I was going to have my child baptized, cost what it may. I knew that I was not going to have her floundering through many years as I had done, doubting and hesitating, undisciplined and amoral. I felt it was the greatest thing I could do for my child. For myself, I prayed for the gift of faith. I was sure, yet not sure. I postponed the day of decision.

A woman does not want to be alone at such a time. Even the most hardened, the most irreverent, is awed by the stupendous fact of creation. Becoming a Catholic would mean facing life alone and I clung to family life. It was hard to contemplate giving up a mate in order that my chid and I could become members of the Church. Forster would have nothing to do with religion or with me if I embraced it. So I waited.

Those last months of waiting I was too happy to know the unrest of indecision. The days were slow in passing, but week by week the time came nearer. I spent some time in writing, but for the most part I felt a great stillness. I was incapable of going to meetings, of seeing many people, of taking up the threads of my past life.

When the little one was born, my joy was so great that I sat up in bed in the hospital and wrote an article for the *New Masses* about my child, wanting to share my joy with the world. I was glad to write this joy for a worker's magazine because it was a joy all women knew, no matter what their grief at poverty, unemployment and class war. The article so appealed to my Marxist friends that the account was reprinted all over the world in workers' papers. Diego Rivera, when I met him some four years afterward in Mexico, greeted me as the author of it. And Mike Gold, who was at that time editor of the *New Masses*, said it had been printed in many Soviet newspapers and that I had rubles awaiting me in Moscow.

When Tamar Teresa—for that is what I named her—was six weeks old, we went back to the beach. It was April and, though it was still cold, it was definitely spring.

Every morning while she napped on the sunny porch, well swathed in soft woolen blankets, I went down to the beach and with the help of Lefty brought up driftwood, enough to last until next morning. Forster was home only week ends and then he chopped enough wood to last a few days. But when the wind was high and piercing it penetrated the house so that much wood was needed, and it was a pleasure to tramp up and down the beach in the bright sun and collect wood which smelled of seaweed, brine and tar. It was warmer outside than it was in the house, and on the porch Teresa was nicely sheltered. Sometimes in the afternoon I put her in her carriage and went out along the woods. . . .

Supper always was early and the baby comfortably tucked away before it was dark. Then, tired with all the activities that so rejoiced and filled my days, I sat in the dusk in a stupor of contentment.

Yet always those deep moments of happiness gave way to a feeling of struggle, of a long silent fight still to be gone through. There had been the physical struggle, the mortal combat almost, of giving birth to a child, and now there was coming the struggle for my own soul. Tamar would be baptized, and I knew the rending it would cause in human relations around me. I was to be torn and agonized again, and I was all for putting off the hard day. . . .

The day [Sacco and Vanzetti] died, the papers had headlines as large as those which proclaimed the outbreak of war. All the nation mourned. All the nation, I mean, that is made up of the poor, the worker, the trade unionist—those who felt most keenly the sense of solidarity—that very sense of solidarity which made me gradually understand the doctrine of the Mystical Body of Christ whereby we are the members one of another.

Forster was stricken over the tragedy. He had always been more an anarchist than anything else in his philosophy, and so was closer to these two men than to Communist friends. He did not eat for days. He sat around the house in a stupor of misery, sickened by the cruelty of life and men. He had always taken refuge in nature as being more kindly, more beautiful and peaceful than the world of men. Now he could not even escape through nature, as he tried to escape so many problems in life.

During the time he was home he spent days and even nights out in his boat fishing, so that for weeks I saw little of him. He stupefied himself in his passion for the water, sitting out on the bay in his boat. When he began to recover he submerged himself in maritime biology, collecting, reading only scientific books, and paying no attention to what went on around him. Only the baby interested him. She was his delight. Which made it, of course, the harder to contemplate the cruel blow I was going to strike him when I became a Catholic. We both suffered in body as well as in soul and mind. He would not talk about the faith and relapsed into a complete silence if I tried to bring up the subject. The point of my bringing it up was that I could not become a Catholic and continue living with him, because he was averse to any ceremony before officials of either Church or state. He was an anarchist and an atheist, and he did not intend to be a liar or a hypocrite. He was a creature of utter sincerity, and however illogical and bad-tempered about it all, I loved him. It was killing me to think of leaving him. . . .

I speak of the misery of leaving one love. But there was another love too, the life I had led in the radical movement. That very winter I was writing a series of articles, interviews with the workers, with the unemployed. I was working with the Anti-Imperialist League, a Communist affiliate, that was bringing aid and comfort to the enemy, General Sandino's forces in Nicaragua. I was just as much against capitalism and imperialism as ever, and here I was going over to the opposition, because of course the Church was lined up with property, with the wealthy, with the state, with capitalism, with all the forces of reaction. This I had been taught to think and this I still think to a great extent. "Too often," Cardinal Mundelein said, "has the Church lined up on the wrong side." "Christianity," Bakunin said, "is precisely the religion par excellence, because it exhibits, and manifests, to the fullest extent, the very nature and essence of every religious system, which is the impoverishment, enslavement, and annihilation of humanity for the benefit of divinity."

I certainly believed this, but I wanted to be poor, chaste and obedient. I wanted to die in order to live, to put off the old man and put on Christ. I loved, in other words, and like all women in love, I wanted to be united to my love. Why should not Forster be jealous? Any man who did not participate in this love would, of course, realize my infidelity, my adultery. In the eyes of God, any turning toward creatures to the exclusion of Him is adultery and so it is termed over and over again in Scripture.

I loved the Church for Christ made visible. Not for itself, because it was so often a scandal to me. Romano Guardini said the Church is the Cross on which Christ was crucified; one could not separate Christ from His Cross, and one must live in a state of permanent dissatisfaction with the Church.

The scandal of businesslike priests, of collective wealth, the lack of a sense of responsibility for the poor, the worker, the Negro, the Mexican, the Filipino, and even the oppression of these, and the consenting to the oppression of them by our industrialist-capitalist order—these made me feel often that priests were more like Cain than Abel. "Am I my brother's keeper?" they seemed to say in respect to the social order. There was plenty of charity but too little justice. And yet the priests were the dispensers of the Sacraments, bringing Christ to men, all enabling us to put on Christ and to achieve more nearly in the world a sense of peace and unity. "The worst enemies would be those of our own household," Christ had warned us.

We could not root out the tares without rooting out the wheat also. With all the knowledge I have gained these twenty-one years I have been a Catholic, I could write many a story of priests who were poor, chaste and obedient, who gave their lives daily for their fellows, but I am writing of how I felt at the time of my baptism.

Not long afterward a priest wanted me to write a story of my conversion, telling how the social teaching of the Church had led me to embrace Catholicism. But I knew nothing of the social teaching of the Church at that time. I had never heard of the encyclicals. I felt that the Church was the Church of the poor, that St. Patrick's had been built from the pennies of servant girls, that it cared for the emigrant, it established hospitals, orphanages, day nurseries, houses of the Good Shepherd, homes for the aged, but at the same time, I felt that it did not set its face against a social order which made so much charity in the present sense of the word necessary. I felt that charity was a word to choke over. Who wanted charity? And it was not just human pride but a strong sense of man's dignity and worth, and what was due to him in justice, that made me resent, rather than feel proud of so mighty a sum total of Catholic institutions. . . .

It was an age-old battle, the war of the classes, that stirred in me when I thought of the Sacco-Vanzetti case in Boston. Where were the Catholic voices crying out for these men? How I longed to make a synthesis reconciling body and soul, this world and the next, the teachings of Prince Peter Kropotkin and Prince Demetrius Gallitzin, who had become a missionary priest in rural Pennsylvania.

Where had been the priests to go out to such men as Francisco Ferrer in Spain, pursuing them as the Good Shepherd did His lost sheep, leaving the ninety and nine of their good parishioners, to seek out that which was lost, bind up that which was bruised. No wonder there was such a strong conflict going on in my mind and heart.

"Babe" Mildred Didrikson Zaharias

~

"BABE" MILDRED DIDRIKSON ZAHARIAS (1911–1956), one of America's most outstanding athletes, earned her life-long nickname from the high school teammates who enthusiastically and frequently compared her to Babe Ruth. An athlete who set American, Olympic, and world records in track and who once struck out Joe DiMaggio in an exhibition game, she excelled in every sport that she played. As cofounder of the Ladies Professional Golf Association, she helped to increase opportunities for professional sports competition among women. In her autobiography, *This Life I've Led*, she recalls training and competing in the early 1930s.

~

All my life I've always had the urge to do things better than anybody else. Even in school, if it was something like making up a current-events booklet, I'd want mine to be the best in the class. I remember once I turned one in with hand-drawn maps and everything, and my teacher, Mrs. Rummell, wrote on it, "Babe, your work is beautiful. A triple plus!"

My sister Lillie had to make a current-events booklet in her class too, and she hadn't got around to it. So we erased what Mrs. Rummell had written on my book, and Lillie took it to school.

She never got to hand it in. Her teacher was Mrs. Rummell's sister, and when Lillie walked up to the desk to turn in that book, the teacher said, "Lillie, I've already seen that one, and I think Babe did a wonderful job on it." . . .

Zaharias, Babe Didrikson. *This Life I've Led*. New York: A. S. Barnes and Company, Inc., 1955, pp. 43–54.

When I was in the grade school, both the junior-high and the high-school girls' basketball teams had to come over to Magnolia to practice. Today the Magnolia school is condemned. I went by there not long ago, and they had a big cyclone fence around what used to be our play yard. But in my day it was the newest and best. We had four outdoor basketball courts and a big gym inside.

When those high-school girls came over to our courts to practice, I was just dying to get in and play with them. I'd hang around and pester them. Finally they did let me in, and I made a few scores and everything. They said they wished I was old enough and in a higher grade, so I could play on their team.

In junior high school I made the basketball team, but when I got to Beaumont High they said I was too small. All of us Didrikson kids seemed to get our growth late. Even in the Olympics, when I was eighteen, I wasn't much over five feet tall, and weighed only 105 pounds.

I couldn't accept the idea that I wasn't good enough for the basketball team. I didn't think the girls who played on it were anything wonderful. I was determined to show everybody. To improve myself, I went to the coach of the boys' team, Lil Dimmitt. I said to myself, "The men know more about basketball than the women."

I'd use my study hours to go practice basketball. I'd show the teacher that I had my homework all done, and get excused from the study hall. I'd go where Coach Dimmitt was, and say, "Coach, how about watching me for a while?" I'd worry him to death with questions about how to pivot and shoot free throws and do this and that. He took the time to help me, because he could see I was interested.

. . . I saw him a few years ago at a dinner down in Texas. He could still remember how I used to get out there in a little T shirt and practice basketball. I'd be barefooted, because I didn't have any tennis shoes. He'd show me how to do different things, and encourage me, and I'd say, "Coach Dimmitt, tell those women I can play basketball!"

When the high school boys practiced, he'd tell me, "You sit down here and watch these boys play." I remember how I used to admire Raymond Alford—I met him again at that same dinner where I saw Coach Dimmitt. Raymond was the star athlete of the whole high school. He wasn't my boy friend or anything. I didn't have any boy friends then. I was just a fourteen-year-old kid, and I was too busy learning to dribble and pass and shoot baskets.

I was a junior before they finally gave me a chance on the Beaumont High girls' team. And I was the high scorer from the start. We went to different towns to play girls at other high schools, and we beat them all. I got my first newspaper write-up—a little item headed, BEAUMONT GIRL STARS IN BASKETBALL GAME. Then it was, BEAUMONT GIRL STARS AGAIN. I became all-city and all-state in basketball.

Down in Dallas, Col. M. J. McCombs saw those write-ups and decided to take a look at me. He's dead now. He was the boss of a department in an insurance firm, the Employers Casualty Company, and he also was director of the women's athletic program. He put in a lot of time on it after the regular office hours. He read about me scoring thirty and forty points in these high-school games, and he wanted to see if I was good enough to help their basketball team, which had finished second the year before in the women's national A.A.U. tournament.

He went to Houston one afternoon to watch us play the Houston Heights high-school girls. This was in February 1930. I wasn't sixteen yet. That Houston eights team was made up of big, tall girls, like the name of the school. I was still small, but I was fast, and I could run right around those girls. I scored something like twenty-six points in that game.

After the game Colonel McCombs came around and introduced himself, and asked if I'd like to play on a real big-time basketball team.

I said, "Boy, would I! Where?"

He said, "At the Employers Casualty Company in Dallas. We're getting ready to go into the nationals in March."

I told him that sounded great, and asked what I'd have to do. He said, "Well, see if you can arrange to get off from school, and get permission from your mother and dad to go."

"My dad's right here," I told him.

So Colonel McCombs spoke to Poppa, and Poppa said to me, "We'll have to talk this over with Momma. If you get up there in Dallas, that's a long way from home. You'd best talk to Momma about this."

Colonel McCombs drove us home to Beaumont in that big car of his. He had dinner with us—Norwegian meat balls and everything. He told Momma that he thought I could be a great basketball player, and that he'd like to have me on his team.

Momma and Poppa told Colonel McCombs that we'd think it over and let him know. After he'd gone, Momma said, "*Min Babe*, do you want to go way up to Dallas?"

I said, "Yeah, Momma, I want to go."

She turned to Poppa. "Oolie mon," she said—that was what her pronunciation of his name sounded like, "what do you think?"

He said, "I think it might be good for Babe."

There was a lot of talking. Momma thought I was too young to be making a trip like that, but Poppa said he'd travel along with me. Finally Momma said all right.

It was arranged that I should play out the season with the Employers Casualty Company, then come back to Beaumont and finish up at high school. The school let me take three weeks out there to play basketball because my marks were good. I had a B plus average, as I remember.

. . . Colonel McCombs met us with his car at the station. He had one of the basketball girls with him, Leona Thaxton. She was a big guard. We drove to the company's offices in the Interurban Building. I remember that we went to Room 327. That's where Colonel McCombs' department was. Practically all the basketball players worked there. I guess that was to make it easier to round them all up and take off when there was a basketball trip.

I'd never seen so many large girls—large feet, and large hands. They were really husky. That was a great era of women's athletics. Nowadays the big sports for women are tennis, fancy diving, swimming and golf. And those are the best sports for women— some of the others are really too strenuous for girls. But back there in the 'thirties they made a big thing out of sports like women's basketball.

Colonel McCombs introduced me to all the girls. One of them, Lalia Warren, said, "What position do you think you're going to play?"

So I got a little pepped up there, and I said, "What do *you* play?"

She said, "I'm the star forward."

I said, "Well, that's what I want to be." And that's how it worked out, too.

Colonel McCombs asked me what kind of office work I could do. I told him I knew typing and shorthand. I'd taken that in high school. I wanted to be an athlete, but didn't suppose then that I could make a living out of it, except maybe in physical education. I thought I might wind up being a secretary. I won a gold medal in school for hitting the best speed on the typewriter. I think it was eighty-six words a minute. I practiced by typing out "The Story of My Life." I was only fourteen or fifteen, and that story ran 42,000 words!

Anyway, Colonel McCombs asked if I could work a slide rule. I said, "No, but if it's numbers I can learn it quick." And they wound up assigning me to a job where I used a slide rule.

Then they had me pick out a basketball uniform for myself. I'd always had No. 7 in high school. I went through the extra uniforms, and there was No. 7 waiting for me. Everything seemed to be working to my pattern. The pants and shirt were too big for me, but I could sew them to fit all right. I just took the shirt in at the seams a little bit. And I tucked the pants in and made them fit skin tight, the way I liked my basketball pants. I was in great condition as a kid. There wasn't an ounce of fat on me.

I went right into a game that first night. We played the Sun Oil Company girls, the defending national champions, in a pre-tournament game. They had some pretty tough guards. They'd heard about me, and they weren't going to let this little kid from Beaumont do any shooting at all. They started hitting me that night, and they kept it up the whole season. If one guard fouled out against me, they'd send in another one.

But I broke away for my share of shots. We beat them that first night by a pretty good score. I was the high scorer. I got four or five points more than the whole Sun Oilers' team did. From that night on I had it made.

We went on to the national tournament, and met the Sun Oilers again. This time it was a close game. At that time when a player was fouled, you could choose anyone on your team to take the free throw. We had a free-throw specialist, but late in the game, when we got a foul shot, she and the other veteran players said to me, "Here, you take it."

So I stepped up to the line, not thinking about it especially, and missed the shot. It turned out that we lost the game by one point. I really felt bad about the whole thing, even though at the end of the tournament I was chosen for the women's All-American basketball team.

I was an All-American basketball player three years in a row. The second year, 1931, we stayed at the Lasson Hotel in Wichita, Kansas, during the national tournament. Our first night there we couldn't get on the court to practice until pretty late. When we got back to the hotel, I was in such a hurry to take my shower and get to bed that I began unlacing my basketball shoes in the elevator. I kicked my shoes off as I got in the door, and pulled my socks off and tossed them in the corner.

The next day I went out and set a record by scoring more than 100 points against some Sunday School team that wasn't very good. I was superstitious about things in sports then—I've gotten completely away from that since. For the rest of the tournament, I did everything the same as the first night. I'd untie my shoes in the elevator, kick them off as I came in the room, and throw my socks in the corner.

We went all the way through and won that national championship in 1931. We got to the finals the next year too, but lost by three points to Oklahoma Presbyterian College.

In the 1931 finals we beat a team called the Thurstons, of Wichita, 28–26. In the newspaper they ran this layout with pictures of the girls on our team. My picture was in the center, blown up way big. There were just little head shots of the others. Man, I just loved that! It was the first big publicity I'd ever had. I cut it out and sent it home to Momma. She always saved my clippings.

Anyhow, after the first national tournament back there in 1930 I went home to finish up at Beaumont High, then came back to Dallas in June to go to work permanently for the Employers Casualty Company.

I was getting $75 a month salary, and sending $45 of it home. I paid about $5 a month for a room. I wasn't spending anything on clothes. I had just the one pair of shoes, and the leather was beginning to curl. Sometimes a girl would give me one of her old dresses, and I'd cut it up and make a skirt out of it for myself.

I lived on Haines Street in the Oak Cliff section of Dallas. The basketball girls all lived in that neighborhood. We ate at the same place, Danny Williams' house. He was the assistant coach. His wife did the cooking, and she was a good cook. I can still remember her pies with graham cracker crust.

We paid 15 cents for breakfast and 35 cents for dinner. For lunch I always had toasted cupcakes and a coke down in the drugstore. The guy at the soda fountain would never charge me for my coke. He'd say, "How about another one, champ?" That made me feel good, because I wasn't any champ then.

Colonel McCombs would drive me to and from work, and any of the other girls that wanted to go, to save us carfare. One Saturday morning at the office early that first summer he said to me, "Babe, what are you doing to occupy yourself now that the basketball season's over?" I told him I wasn't doing anything much. He said, "Well, how would you like to go out to Lakeside Park with me this afternoon and watch a track meet?"

Here I'd been thinking about the Olympic Games since 1928, and yet I never had seen a track meet. So I went out there with him, and we stood around watching. I saw this stick lying on the ground, and I said, "What's that?" Colonel McCombs said, "It's a javelin. You throw it like a spear."

He went through the motions for me, and I picked it up and tried it. I got pretty good distance, but it was so heavy—it was a men's javelin—that I slapped my back with it as I threw it, and raised a welt. Four times I slapped myself on exactly the same spot. And that welt was really big.

Colonel McCombs took me around and explained some of the other events. He showed me the high jump and the hurdles and stuff like that. Those hurdles reminded me of all the hedge-jumping I'd done back home. I liked the looks of that event better than almost anything else.

By the time we left, Colonel McCombs was agreeing with me that it would be a good idea if Employers Casualty had a women's track and field team, so the girls would have some athletics during the summer. I'm sure that's what he'd had in mind all along. He said he'd take it up with Homer R. Mitchell, the president of the company.

I told him I was going to talk to Mr. Mitchell too. Monday morning I went in and made my pitch, and Mr. Mitchell said, "Babe, whatever you all want you can have."

So we all got together and started talking about this track team we were going to organize. One girl said, "I'm going to throw the javelin." Another said, "I'm going to throw the discus." Another girl thought she'd like to do the hurdles.

When it came around to me, I said, "Colonel, how many events are there in this track and field?" He said, "Why, Babe, I think there are about nine or ten."

I said, "Well, I'm going to do them all."

Everybody nearly died laughing. I talked like that in those days, and some people thought I was just popping off. But I was serious. I said it because I thought I could do it. And in one meet we had, competing for the Texas state championship against the Bowen Air Lines girls of Forth Worth, I entered all ten events and won eight of them.

I took the three weight throws—the shot put, the discuss and the javelin. I was first in both the broad jump and the high jump. I won the 100-yard dash and the 200-yard dash. In the 50-yard dash I was second. And I was on the losing team in the relay race.

I really worked hard at that track and field. I trained and trained and trained. I've been that way in every sport I've taken up. After dinner I'd go out in my tennis shoes and run. They had a hill on Haines Street that went down to a lake. I'd run all the way down there, and then I'd jog all the way back up. I'd jog my legs real high, and work my arms high, to get them in shape. Of course, they were already about as hard as they could be, but I thought they had to be better.

We had just a few days to get ready for our first meet. Our regular hour or two of practice in the afternoon wasn't enough to satisfy me. I'd go out to Lakeside Park at night and practice by myself until it got dark, which wasn't until nine or nine-thirty at that time of year. If there was good clear moonlight, I might keep going even longer.

The last night before that first track meet I went out and worked extra hard. I practiced my step timing for the broad jump and for the high jump. I put in about two hours at that, and then finished off by running the 440 yards. They'd told me to pace myself in that, but I was going to see if I couldn't sprint all the way.

Well, I just barely made it to the finish line. I fell face down on the grass. I was seeing stars. I must have laid there fifteen or twenty minutes before I could get up.

When I told Colonel McCombs about it the next morning, he said "What are you trying to do, kill yourself?" And he told me I should take it easier. But I think he admired me for working so hard.

I competed in my four events that afternoon, and I won all four. It was that last extra practice that did it, especially in the broad jumping and the high jump, where I had my steps down just right.

I eventually got to be pretty good at the high jump. I started out doing the old-style scissors jump. One afternoon I was working out, and I kept going higher and higher. Finally Colonel McCombs had the cross bar up to the women's world record. I believe it was five feet, three inches at that time.

He said, "Babe, tell you what. I'll buy you a chocolate soda if you can jump this."

I said, "Out of my way!" and sailed right over.

Amelia Earhart

～

AMELIA EARHART (1897–1937), famous as an aviator, was a dedicated supporter of women's rights. In the posthumously published *Last Flight*, she discusses her love of flying, her aspirations for women, and the dangers encountered prior to her final flight in 1937.

～

Pilots are always dreaming dreams.

My dream, of owning a multi-motored plane, probably first took form in May, 1935.

I was flying non-stop from Mexico City to New York. The straight line course, from Tampico to New Orleans, took me over about seven hundred miles of the Gulf of Mexico. There weren't many clouds, so for once what lay below was quit visible. It did seem a good deal of water.

Previously I'd been by air twice across the North Atlantic, and once from Hawaii to California. All three voyages were flown chiefly at night, with heavy clouds during most of the daylight hours. So in the combined six thousand miles or more of previous over-ocean flying it happened I'd seen next to nothing of ocean.

Given daylight and good visibility, the Gulf of Mexico looked large. And wet. One's imagination toyed with the thought of what would happen if the single engine of the Lockheed Vega should conk. Not that my faithful Wasp ever had failed me, or indeed, even protested mildly. But, at that, the very finest machinery *could* develop indigestion.

Earhart, Amelia. *Last Flight*. Arranged by George Palmer Putnam. New York: Harcourt, Brace and Company, Inc., 1937, pp. 3–18.

So, on that sunny morning out of sight of land, I promised my lovely red Vega I'd fly her across no more water. And I promised myself that any further over-ocean flying would be attempted in a plane with more than one motor, capable of keeping aloft with a single engine. Just in case.

Which, in a way, was for me the beginning of the world flight project. Where to find the tree on which costly airplanes grow, I did not know. But I did know the kind I wanted—an Electra Lockheed, big brother of my Vegas, with, of course, Wasp engines.

Such is the trusting simplicity of a pilot's mind, it seemed ordained that somehow the dream would materialize. Once the prize in hand, obviously there was one flight which I most wanted to attempt—a circumnavigation of the globe as near its waistline as could be.

Before writing about the preparation for that flight, and of the journey itself, it seems well to set down briefly the career, such as it is, of a girl who grew up to love flying—the who, when and why of this particular pilot.

At the age of ten I saw my first airplane. It was sitting in a slightly enclosed area at the Iowa State Fair in Des Moines. It was a thing of rusty wire and wood and looked not at all interesting. One of the grown-ups who happened to be around pointed it out to me and said: "Look, dear, it flies." I looked as directed but confess I was much more interested in an absurd hat made of an inverted peach-basket which I had just purchased for fifteen cents.

What psychoanalysts would make of this incident, in the light of subsequent behavior, I do not know. Today I loathe hats for more than a few minutes on the head and am sure I should pass by the niftiest creation if an airplane were anywhere around.

The next airplane which impinged upon my consciousness was about the time of the armistice. Again I found myself at a Fair, this time the great exposition held at Toronto in Canada. A young woman friend and I had gone to the Fair grounds to see an exhibition of stunt flying by one of the aces returned from the war. These men were the heroes of the hour. They were in demand at social teas, and to entertain crowds by giving stunting exhibitions. The airplanes they rode so gallantly to fame were as singular as they. For aviation in those days was very limited. About all a pilot could do was to joy-hop. That is (1) taking a few hardy passengers for short rides; (2) teaching even hardier students to fly; and (3) giving exhibitions.

The idea that airplanes could be transportation as today entered nobody's noggin.

My friend and I, in order to see the show, planted ourselves in the middle of a clearing. We watched a small plane turn and twist in the air, black against the sky excepting when the afternoon sun caught the scarlet of its wings. After fifteen or twenty minutes of stunting, the pilot began to dive at the crowd. Looking back as a pilot I think I understand why. He was bored. He had looped and rolled and spun and finished his little bag of tricks, and there was nothing left to do but watch the people on the ground running as he swooped close to them.

Pilots, in 1918, to relieve the monotony of never going anywhere, rolled their wheels on the top of moving freight trains; flew so low over boats that the terrified occupants lay flat on the deck; or they dived at crowds on the beach or at picnics. Today of course the Department of Commerce would ground a pilot for such antics.

I am sure the sight of two young women alone made a tempting target for the pilot. I am sure he said to himself, "Watch me make them scamper."

After a few attempts one did but the other stood her ground. I remember the mingled fear and pleasure which surged over me as I watched that small plane at the top of its earthward swoop. Commonsense told me if something went wrong with the mechanism, or if the pilot lost control, he, the airplane and I would be rolled up in a ball together. I did not understand it at the time but I believe that little red airplane said something to me as it swished by.

I worked in a hospital during the war. From that experience I decided that medicine interested me most. Whether or not medicine needed me I did not question. So I enrolled at Columbia University in New York and started in to do the peculiar things they do who would be physicians. I fed orange juice to mice and dissected cockroaches. I have never seen a cockroach since but I remember that the creature has an extraordinarily large brain.

However, I could not forget airplanes.

I went to California for a summer vacation and found air meets, as distinct from wartime exhibitions, just beginning. I went to every one and finally one day came a chance to ride. Frank Hawks took me on the first hop. He was then a barnstorming pilot on the west coast, unknown to the fame he later acquired. By the time I had got two or three hundred feet off the ground I knew I had to fly.

I think my mother realized before I did how much airplanes were beginning to mean to me, for she helped me buy the first one. It was second-hand, painted bright yellow, and one of the first light airplanes developed in this country. The motor was so rough that my feet went to sleep after more than a few minutes on the rudder bar. I had a system of lending the plane for demonstration so as not to be charged storage. Hangar rental would have annihilated my salary.

After a year my longest hop was from Long Beach to Pasadena, about 40 miles. Still I all but set off to cross the continent by air. The fact that I couldn't buy gasoline myself forced me to compromise and drive a car with Mother along. I am sure I wouldn't be here to tell the tale if I had carried out the original plan.

I did what flying I could afford in the next few years and then the "Friendship" came along. I was working in Denison House in Boston, one of America's oldest social settlements.

"Phone for you, Miss Earhart."

"Tell 'em I'm busy." At the moment I was the center of an eager swarm of Chinese and Syrian neighborhood children, piling in for games and classes.

"Says it's important."

So I excused myself and went to listen to a man's voice asking me whether I was interested in doing something dangerous in the air. At first I thought the conversation was a joke and said so. Several times before I had been approached by bootleggers who promised rich reward and no danger—"Absolutely no danger to you, Leddy."

The frank admission of risk stirred my curiosity. References were demanded and supplied. Good references. An appointment was arranged for that evening.

"Would you like to fly the Atlantic?"

My reply was a prompt "Yes"—provided the equipment was all right and the crew capable. Nine years ago flying oceans was less commonplace than today, and my own experience as a pilot was limited to a few hundred hours in small planes which work and finances permitted.

So I went to New York and met the man entrusted with the quaint commission of finding a woman wiling to fly the Atlantic. The candidate, I gathered, should be a flyer herself, with social graces, education, charm and, perchance, pulchritude.

His appraisal left me discomforted. Somehow this seeker for feminine perfection seemed unimpressed. Anyway, I showed my pilot's license (it happened to be the first granted an American woman by the F.A.I.) and inwardly prepared to start back for Boston.

But he felt that, having come so far, I might as well meet the representatives of Mrs. Frederick Guest, whose generosity was making the flight possible, and at whose insistence a woman was to be taken along. . . .

A few days later the verdict came. The flight actually would be made and I could go if I wished. Naturally I couldn't say "No." Who would refuse an invitation to such a shining adventure? . . .

I myself did no piloting on that trip. But I gained experience. In London I was introduced to Lady Mary Heath, the then very active Irish woman flyer. She had just made a record flight from London to Cape Town and I purchased the small plane she had used. It wore on its chest a number of medals given her at various stops she made on the long route.

After the pleasant accident of being the first woman to cross the Atlantic by air, I was launched into a life full of interest. Aviation offered such fun as crossing the continent in planes large and small, trying the whirling rotors of an autogiro, making record flights. With these activities came opportunity to know women everywhere who shared my conviction that there is so much women can do in the modern world and should be permitted to do irrespective of their sex. Probably my greatest satisfaction was to indicate by example now and then, that women can sometimes do things themselves if given the chance.

Here I should add that the "Friendship" flight brought me something even dearer than such opportunities. That Man-who-was-to-find-a-girl-to-fly-the-Atlantic, who found me and then managed the flight, was George Palmer Putnam. In 1931 we married. Mostly, my flying has been solo, but the preparation for it wasn't. Without my husband's help and encouragement I could not have attempted what I have. Ours has been a contented and reasonable partnership, he with his solo jobs and I with mine. But always with work and play together, conducted under a satisfactory system of dual control.

I was hardly home when I started off to fly the continent—my 1924 ambition four years late. Lady Heath's plane was very small. It had folding wings so that it actually could fit in a garage. I cranked the motor by standing behind the propeller and pulling it down with one hand. The plane was so light I could pick it up by the tail and drag it easily around the field.

At that time I was full of missionary zeal for the cause of aviation. I refused to wear the high-bred aviation togs of the moment. Instead I simply wore a dress or suit. I carried no chute and instead of a helmet used a close-fitting hat. I stepped into the airplane with as much nonchalance as I could muster, hoping that onlookers would be persuaded that flying was nothing more than an everyday occurrence. I refused even to wear goggles, obviously. However, I put them on as I taxied to the end of the field and wore them while flying, being sure to take them off shortly after I landed.

That was thoroughly informal flying. Pilots landed in pastures, race courses, even golf links where they were still enough of a novelty to be welcome.

In those days domestic animals scurried to the fancied protection of trees and barns when the flying monsters roared above them. Now along the airways there's not enough curiosity left for a self-respecting cow even to lift her head to see what goes on in the sky. She's just bored. Stories of that happy-go-lucky period should be put together in a saga to regale the scientific, precision flyers of tomorrow.

Nineteen-twenty-nine was the year of the women's derby from California to Cleveland, the first time a cross-country race had ever been sponsored for women alone. I felt I needed a new plane for this extraordinary sporting event. So I traded in the faithful little Avion for my first Lockheed Vega. It was a third-hand clunk but to me a heavenly chariot.

I crossed the continent again from New York to California to stop at the Lockheed factory. I thought possibly there might be a few adjustments necessary before I entered the race. There I met the great Wiley Post for the first time. Wiley Post had not then had his vision of stratosphere flying, and was simply a routine check pilot in the employ of the Lockheed company.

It fell to him to take my airplane up for test. Having circled the field once, he came down and proceeded to tell everyone within earshot that my lovely airplane was the foulest he had ever flown. Of course the worse he made the plane, the better pilot I became. The fact that I should have been able to herd such a hopeless piece of mechanism across the continent successfully was the one bright spot in the ensuing half hour.

Finally Lockheed officials were so impressed by my prowess (or so sorry for me) that they traded me a brand new plane. The clunk was never flown again. . . .

After the "Friendship" flight I did not immediately plan to fly the Atlantic alone. But later as I gained in experience and looked back over the years I decided that I had had enough to try to make it solo. Lockheed #2 was then about three years old. It had been completely reconditioned and a new and larger engine put in. By the spring of 1932 plane and pilot were ready.

Oddly, one of my clearest memories of the Atlantic solo concerns not the flight itself but my departure from home. On May 19th the weather outlook was so unpromising we had abandoned hope of getting off that day. So I had driven in to New York from our home in Westchester. Just before noon an urgent message caught up with me immediately to get in touch with Mr. Putnam at the Weather Bureau.

Our phone conversation was brief.

"It looks like the break we've waited for," he said. "Doc Kimball says this afternoon is fine to get to Newfoundland—St. John's anyway. And by tomorrow the Atlantic looks as good as you're likely to get it for some time." . . .

As fast as I dared—traffic cops being what they are—I drove the twenty-five miles to Rye. Five minutes was enough to pick up my things. Plus a lingering few more to drink in the beauty of a lovely treasured sight. Beside and below our bedroom windows were dogwood trees, their blossoms in luxuriant full flower, unbelievable bouquets of white and pink flecked with the sunshine of spring. Those sweet blooms smiled at me a radiant farewell. . . . That is a memory I have never forgotten.

Looking back, there are less cheering recollections of that night over the Atlantic. Of seeing, for instance, the flames lick through the exhaust collector ring and wondering, in a detached way, whether one would prefer drowning to incineration. Of the five hours of storm, during black midnight, when I kept right side up by instruments alone, buffeted about as I never was before. Of much beside, not the least the feeling of fine loneliness and of realization that the machine I rode was doing its best and required from me the best I had.

And one further fact of the flight, which I've not set down in words before. I carried a barograph, an instrument which records on a disc the course of the plane, its rate of ascent and descent, its levels of flight all co-ordinated with clocked time. My tell-tale disc could tell a tale. At one point it recorded an almost vertical drop of three thousand feet. It started at an altitude of something over 3000 feet, and ended—well, something above the water. That happened when the plane suddenly "iced up" and went into a spin. How long we spun I do not know. I do know that I tried my best to do exactly what one should do with a spinning plane, and regained flying control as the warmth of the lower altitude melted the ice. As we righted and held level again, through the blackness below I could see the white-caps too close for comfort.

All that was five full years ago, a long time to recall little things. So I wonder if Bernt Balchen remembers as I do the three words he said to me as I left Harbor Grace. They were: "Okeh. So-long. Good luck."

Jeannette Rankin

~

JEANNETTE RANKIN (1880–1973), suffragist, peace activist, and the first woman elected to serve in the United States House of Representatives, was also the only member of Congress to vote against entry into both World War I and World War II. In these oral histories conducted by Malca Chall and Hannah Josephson, Jeannette Rankin describes the events of 1917 through 1941.

~

From Malca Chall's Interview, June 8, 1972

Malca Chall: Let's start with your work for peace.

Yesterday you told me, and from what I've read it seems to be so, that when you voted, No against going into World War I, that upside the women's suffrage movement—the leaders.

Jeanette Rankin: Just a few of the leaders. Not the rest. Because, for instance, New York had a campaign for the vote and New York City never asked me to speak. Buffalo did, and I think there was quite a little discussion as to whether it was right to ask me, and Buffalo carried with a larger majority than New York.

Rankin, Jeannette. *Jeanette Rankin: Activist for World Peace, Women's Rights, and Democratic Government*, typescript of an oral history conducted in 1972 by Malca Chall and Hannah Josephson, Regional Oral History Office, the Bancroft Library, University of California, Berkeley, 1974, pp. 1–4, 7– 20, 212–15. Reprinted by permission of the Bancroft Library.

I didn't hurt the movement. . . . You see, they had a campaign on for woman's suffrage, and they carried, and Buffalo carried with a larger percentage than New York City. And they did have me at a very big meeting in Buffalo.

Chall: And this was after you had cast your No vote?

Rankin: The first thing I did.

Chall: That's right, so it would have to have been after.

Rankin: The first vote. Did you get it that there were fifty-five men voting with me?

Chall: Yes. Some of the authors of magazine articles written at that time seemed to feel that this might be an example of what women would do if they got into power—if they got the vote—as if they really weren't sure what your vote meant. You always felt, however, and still do, I guess, that women are the ones who are going to bring a stop to war if it's going to be done—

Rankin: I tell, whenever I have enough time to tell, that after I cast my vote against war, I read Benjamin Kidd's book on social evolution. Did you ever hear of Benjamin Kidd?

Chall: No.

Rankin : He was a philosopher at Cambridge, England, and he wrote this book at the turn of the century, which was an answer to what some people thought was the Darwin theory. And then in 1918 he wrote a book called *The Science of Power*, and at the first meeting of the women afterwards national or international, in America, there were five different people who spoke of that book and what it meant to them, and then we never heard of it again, and he died shortly after.

He brought off in this book that there was a difference between force and power. That force is something you use in the present—you cut down a tree, you build a bridge, you do something. That's force. But power—it's something you can use in the future, and that the greatest power in the world was the emotion of an idea. And he said that women, from their racial and physical and so forth, had a greater capacity to work for an ideal in the future. That it was the women who persuaded the men to stop the chase and wait for the crops to mature; and that seems to me to be recognized everywhere, with the beginning of agriculture and the beginning of the home. And he said that the woman waits nine months for the child, and then there's never—any one day that's more important than another in the future. They're always working for something in the future. They take care of the child, and when he goes to school, when he goes to college, when he marries, the grandchildren—women are always working for the future.

And I don't remember whether Kidd brought this up or not, but I've always thought that it's the same thing in men that changed civilization. The great leaders in thought and in change have been those who have been working for the future, and not the present—self-aggrandizement or anything of that kind. Martin Luther King and Gandhi in the present, and Jesus, and all the great religious leaders, make their appeal on the future.

Chall: So you think that it is not necessarily a man or a woman difference—

Rankin: There is a difference, and I say in my speeches, we have two hands, and they're not the same. And no one would think because they're not the same, you'd tie one behind your back. They work separately and they work together, and we need both men and women and they do work together. But modern civilization is tying women one hand behind her back and not allowing her expression. And as a result, they have to keep the other hand from progressing.

Men haven't got the freedom today that they had when the Constitution was written. The men in the West had a great deal of freedoms more than the men in the East who copied the traditions of Europe. You have to have the women because they're different, and *because* all of humanity needs freedom. Freedom isn't a sex thing; it's a human thing. And therefore both men and women have to have it. Men today haven't the freedom they had when I started working for women's suffrage.

In that time, men could go into their own business. They could follow farming and they could do this and that. Today, young men in college are not planning on individual development, as much as getting a job. They have someone else raise the money, and then they do the work. And men haven't the freedom because big business doesn't give it to them. And so men's jobs are dependent on having a nice mousy wife who doesn't do anything. And one of the greatest difficulties that the women's lib has to contend with is the fact that the women can't go any faster than the men. And this isn't because men want to hold them down. My most conspicuous illustration was that in birth control the experience of my sister, Edna Rankin McKinnon, who was a leader in the birth control movement. For instance, there was one woman they wanted to make president of a birth control organization. She was a perfect candidate for the job—she had intelligence, judgments and educations and her children were in college. Her husband worked in a big organization. They told him if she took that job, he'd lose his.

Chall: About when was this—in the 1920s?

Rankin: Oh, I don't know, I think later than that. That's just one illustration. When it was very definite. In campaigning in Montana, you found right along that the wife had to be still when her husband had a job. And they controlled workers in the same way. There was one candidate who was very near a dam. A big company—the Anaconda company had their people. And they told the people in that place that if there was one vote for that candidate that all of them would lose their jobs. . . .

Chall: Under whose auspices, between the wars, were you lobbying for peace?

Rankin: For the National Council for Prevention of War—Frederick J. Libby was the head.

Chall: Is that a pacifist organization?

Rankin: It's a council of organizations for the prevention of war. They were mostly Quakers.

Chall: Were you a paid lobbyist for them?

Rankin: I was a paid lobbyist in Washington, and when the Congress wasn't in session, they continued my salary to work in Georgia.

Chall: I see.

Rankin: I didn't do it all there; I did it other places too. . . .

Chall: In the period between the wars, particularly in the late 1930s, groups became involved in anti-war activities, like the America First Committee, some organizations that seemed committed to what others thought was a doctrine of fascism—the Communists were opposed to the war at one time. How did you work with all of these different groups?

Rankin: Oh all that fascism and that communism and all that was just the newspapers. They were devoted to peace—the people I worked with.

Chall: You didn't have any difficulty in working with Burton K. Wheeler [U.S. Senator from Montana, 1923–47].

Rankin: Oh he was a great pacifist.

Chall : He was basically a pacifist?

Rankin: Yes. We're still friends; I talked to him the other day.

Chall: And Lindbergh—?

Rankin: He was well known, and his father was a pacifist.

Chall: So you feel that the America First Committee was a—

Rankin: Loyal, brilliant organizations destroyed by Roosevelt. . . .

Chall: You worked on your own—you stayed with the National Council for—

Rankin: Oh no, I left the Council when the people were getting converted to Roosevelt's idea of war. The National Council wasn't as aggressive as it was before and I left them—

Chall: And then where did you go?

Rankin: I ran for Congress.

Chall: Now, the casting of your vote the second time against the war—was that as traumatic an experience for you as casting it the first time?

Rankin: No. Because I learned from the first one, and I didn't let anybody approach me. You see, I knew it was coming. I knew Roosevelt was trying, but I said on Saturday night (some people came to see me), I said I didn't think it was coming soon, because Roosevelt knows we're not prepared to go to war. And then it came right away. But I knew he was trying to get us in. And I wrote an article a year later, not an article—I wrote a speech, which I had in the *Congressional Record*, December 8, 1942, in which I said I was entitled to some questions about Pearl Harbor, and I brought out all the facts that I could gather at that time, which indicated that Roosevelt was deliberately trying to get us in the war, that it was a provoked attack.

Chall: There are people who think that, of course.

Rankin :   Oh, there are a great many now.

Chall: You were a well-known pacifist by 1940, so that your vote, while it created a great deal of furor, needn't have surprised anybody, except that I suppose people felt that we were attacked, and therefore all of our energies should go into fighting the war. But that wasn't where you stood.

Rankin: It was not. On Sunday Pearl Harbor was attacked; I had an engagement to speak in Detroit on Monday afternoon. I couldn't get hold of anyone at the Capitol, to find out what the program was going to be. I felt the only thing I could do was to start going to Detroit because it wasn't possible then to get there in such a short time.

So I took the train Sunday night, and I took a radio with me, and from the conversation on the radios after the train got started, I knew that the vote was coming the next day. So I got off at Pittsburgh and went back. So I was traveling all night, and when I got there and they said it was coming at 12 o'clock, I got into my car and left the office and left everything, and no one knew where I was. And no one could get after me; no one could bring any pressure on me, because I knew what I was going to do. And so it was very simple, at last.

The thing hasn't ever been brought up since—at the time it was mentioned—at the First World War vote, James Mann came to me afterwards and said, "If I had known you were going to vote against it, I might have had the courage." So, I decided then, that *never* would I wait to prepare a speech, that I'd speak out any time, and so when they read the resolution, I asked to have it referred to committee.

And I asked, and they wouldn't let me talk. They proved that we haven't free speech. The only free speech we have is the filibuster in the Senate, and that's about to be taken away. So, we have no free speech. You *can't* speak out with an audience in this country. That was the most important vote that we've ever taken. I think the First World War was at that time the most important. But to repeat the same mistake was a *terrible* mistake. . . .

I was attacked viciously after the First World War. But I wasn't attacked after the Second. And Raymond Clapper said in his column, before I left Washington that "Miss Rankin has written her footnote in history, and that's the last we'll hear of her." And never was I mentioned. When I introduced some questions on Pearl Harbor, there was one man (I've forgotten his name), who had been hired by Ford as a commentator, and he'd been a commentator in Washington. I always listened to him. Not that I agreed with him, but he was a good commentator. I mean, he was on the other side. He attacked me. And a man in California attacked me. And those are the only two that did. And I never can get the words of the man in California—he was an Englishman. But this man that had been hired by Ford—Ford received so many letters that he never rehired him. And I wrote to him and sent him a dime and asked for a copy.

Chall: And he sent it to you.

Rankin: [*Laughs.*] I've forgotten how he put it—But he lost his jobs because I had received a thousand letters saying they listened to the Ford commentators and they condemned him—

Chall: For his talking about you.

Rankin: I lost all those letters. I sent them to a man, and he never returned them, and I couldn't get them.

Chall: That's why it's better to put such material into a library, and say, "If you want them, come and read them."

Rankin: But no library would take them.

Chall: I guess that may have been true at one time, but it surely is not anymore.

Rankin: And I never was mentioned—which is a great relief.

Chall: Yes, you disappeared from the news, as it were.

Rankin: Absolutely. . . .

Chall: Well now in the period from, '30–'47, Mabel Vernon was the director of the Women's International League for Peace and Freedom—and then of the People's Mandate to End the War from '35–'47.

Rankin: They wouldn't have anything to do with me.

Chall: Why?

Rankin: They were for the Second World War.

Chall: So, what was their platform then, in term of the People's Mandate to End the War.

Rankin: They wanted peace and good will; they loved their mother. [*Laughs.*]

Chall: Do you think the Women's International League for Peace and Freedom was not a truly bona fide peace organization?

Rankin: No, they were silent plenty of times.

Chall: What about the women's International League for Peace and Freedom as it was organized immediately following the Nineteenth Amendment—

Rankin: It was before—

Chall: I had understood that it was a split-off from the Woman's Party.

Rankin: No. Miss Addams [Jane]—I've got some material here I can give you—Miss Addams worked in 1915. At that time, I was lobbying for peace in Washington. She called a meetings and then in 1919, the Women's International League was formed. And I was with Miss Addams and traveled with her and roomed with her part of the time on that trip. WILPF organized in

Zurich, Switzerland. I was one of a delegation of about fifteen (I don't know how many exactly) from the United States. All the great women of that period were in the groups and I was very much a junior member, if age was a criterion. I tried to draw parallels between the county-by-county methods of organization I had used in Montana to win suffrage and my own election to Congress, and I suggested that these same methods be applied to the peace movement. But—they never would take my advice on how to campaign and what to do. . . .

Chall: When you were in Congress, the House of Representatives passed the voting rights amendment. Did you play a part in this?

Rankin: Well certainly! Why ask me such a stupid question!

Chall: What did you do? According to an article I read, they were afraid you were going to pester the members of the House about women's suffrage, and according to the writer you didn't pester them.

Rankin: I worked, where it was worthwhile working.

Chall: You did go from man to man—

Rankin: No, of course not, you don't do that in Congress.

Chall: What did you do?

Rankin: Well, they had a women's suffrage committee—oh I hate to tell this! It makes me just burn! You'd think People would have more sense. How could I have gotten it through if I hadn't worked? And I didn't do the stupid things that they do.

Chall: I see, you had a different method. Were you working with Alice Paul?

Rankin: No. I was working with Congress! And I was working with myself. I commanded myself. When I made speeches and so on, I said what *I* wanted to say.

Chall: In the meantime, the other ladies were out doing their thing in Washington, holding vigils and marches and processions. Did you participate in this at all?

Rankin: No, I said it was a good thing. I always said some people work that way; I don't. And everything helps, but they helped by making those who were for it stronger for it, and not by converting people. I had lots of fun with them when they were there, because I didn't say anything against them. And someone wanted me to go to the prison to see them.

And one day, I had a little extra time, and I tried to find the prison, and I couldn't. And so, I called a very important woman—her brother—I've forgotten their names—her brother was a very noted doctor—and at that time appendectomies were very new and very important, and he was known everywhere for his skill at that—so I called her up (I think her name was Lewis, but I am not sure) and I said "I couldn't find the prison." And she said, "I don't know where it is. I've always gone in a Black Maria." [police car] [laughter] I finally found it and went up. . . .

Chall: In terms of your work in Congress, can you tell me, unless it's already been put down someplace, what you did for the suffrage movement while you were there?

Rankin: I clubbed them over the head with a good club, and then they were insensitive, and then they were *for* it. [wryly]

Chall: Yes, of course. All right, now what did you really do? How did you really operate?

Rankin: I operated as a Congressman. I was polite and sensitive, and I didn't do the wrong thing, and all the men had to do was to watch me. I didn't have to say anything.

James R. Mann was the leader of the Republicans. And the Republicans were almost equal to the Democrats. Every vote counted when the Democrats organized against women voting. So we were just as strong as the Democrats, if there was any difference. And then, the Democrats organized the House, and everyone—every chairmanship went to the Democrats. And there was a man as head of the women's suffrage committee; there'd always been a woman's suffrage committee. I heard the rumor going around that the men, the Republicans, were thinking of asking the Democrats to give me the chairmanship of the women's suffrage committee, and this was to be held on Monday.

On the Friday before, a man from Massachusetts, Joe Walsh, that I had been warned against before I went in—that he was violently opposed to woman's suffrage—so I always avoided him; I always sat in back of him in the Houses and I never made myself conspicuous. He came over to see so, and said I was going to speak in his district. I said I didn't know, that I had a manager and I didn't know where I was to speak. So, I was leaving for New York and the manager said he had this speaking engagement. So I went.

I began my speech by saying that they had a very able man from their district and I told all the good things he did, because he did do lots of good things, and praised him as much as I possibly could. But I said, "He has one fault and that's *your* fault. It's because you haven't converted him. He's against woman's suffrage!" And I said, "That's your fault." And went on and made my speech.

When I got back on Monday, this committee was meeting, and I went to it. And *I* didn't want to be chairman. I said it may cost us a vote or two from the Democrats. I said, "I don't want to be chairman." And this fellow, Joe Walsh, didn't want me to be chairman, and so he couldn't make a speech, because he couldn't say, "I don't believe in woman's suffrage." And he couldn't talk against what I was saying. And so he was all mixed up. [laughs] If I had said, "I want to be chairman," he would have talked against it, but then I said I didn't—So, when we got through, I wasn't to be chairman. He and I had agreed.

Well, the next day he came around to me, and it was the funniest thing I ever heard. He's trying to apologize for being nasty, when I hadn't accused him. And he'd gotten word from his district, and they said that I had said only nice thing about him. So, after that, we smiled and talked, but never about woman's suffrage.

Then when woman's suffrage was going to come out, I went to his office, and I said I wanted to ask a favor. I said, "I don't want you to do anything against your conscience. If you are against woman's suffrage I'm not going to ask you to vote for it. But I *am* going to ask you *not* to make a speech against it." I said, "Your speeches will convert them, and you're such a good speaker—" [laughs]. I've forgotten it all. "I don't want you to make a speech against it." He said, "Well what may he say?" I said, "You don't have to answer. Just leave the room." And he was helpful. He said, "I'm having difficulty voting against it." He didn't say what it was, and I didn't want to ask him.

When the vote came, we won by one vote, and they had a recapitulation, and when anyone came up that he thought might change his vote and be against it, he said, "If you change your vote, I'll change mine."

Chall: Oh my, he certainly did come around.

Rankin: That was real work!

Chall: You felt he was a key man in this—

Rankin: Oh he was. He didn't let anybody change their vote to go against it—

Chall: So he was honest. He was opposed to it, but he was honest about the vote.

Rankin: Well he thought his people weren't, I think.

Chall: He thought his people would vote against it?

Rankin: Yes, and they would have. He would have lost votes if he'd voted for it—in his district. But nobody knew but me what he had done. Some of the men that saw him and heard him told me. He didn't tell me. But they said he sat right there and when he thought they were going to change, he said, "If you change yours, I'll change mine."

Chall: He must have been sympathetic toward it eventually.

Rankin: He wasn't opposed. He hadn't talked with me, and I hadn't beat him over the head every time he came in the office.

But before the vote came, James R. Mann had said to me, "We'll put this over," and he asked about the suffragists and what they were doing, and I told him and he said, "Well you and I will put this over." Then he was ill, and he was in the hospital—very ill. And when the vote came out, two men, one on each side of him, guided him in, looking like death—he was so pale and so sick. And then when the vote came, his vote was needed. And the whole hall rose and applauded and cheered. They knew how hard it was for him to do it.

Chall: So you're saying in effect that you helped put over woman's suffrage by being a good female leader in Congress.

Rankin: No. I didn't do any female things—

Chall: No, but you were a good worker, you were a good Congressman, and that allowed them to realize that women could function with the votes and in Congress.

Rankin: Yes, I was a good Congressman. But I never worked any female stuff.

From Hannah Josephson's Interview, April 2–4, 1972

Josephson: Was he accurate—or did I read that in John Board—about your vote against World War I, that Wellington [Rankin's brother] tried to dissuade you from voting against the war because of the possibility that you might not be re-elected? You answered Wellington that you were not going to send any boys to be killed in order to be re-elected. Is that accurate?

Rankin: I don't remember saying that.

Josephson: I think John Board has something about that; I think he said that Wellington told him as much.

Rankin: He may have. But he did talk a lot with Wellington. That first vote was hard to explain because I had lobbied for woman's suffrage in Congress and I had talked to Congressmen and I had sat up in the gallery. The suffragists divided the members of Congress among different workers, and they gave me the South; I talked to these Southern Congressmen.

I think that had an influence on my coming South to live, because these men were not militarists, I mean they were not so opposed to woman's suffrage as they seemed. My feeling about peace, I think, was deeper than my feeling about suffrage, in a way. I never talked it, but you could sense it.

And the southern Congressmen were more against war than people realize. (For instance, this [Samuel] McReynolds of Tennessee—he was doing what Roosevelt wanted but he was for peace underneath.)

And I had sat in the gallery days and days and watched them vote. I'd seen men walking around on the floor that I had talked to who just weren't voting [on the first roll call]; they might vote on the second roll call, don't you know. They knew how it was coming out. They didn't change their vote, but for some reason or other they wouldn't vote on the first roll call.

Wellington and all the suffragists were begging me to vote for war, the suffragists because it would hurt suffrage if I didn't, and Wellington because as he said, "You're the most conspicuous woman and you're best known of any woman" at that time. And he said, "After the vote there'll be nothing." He wanted it for me purely; he didn't want the war. Oh, he was just as much of a pacifist at that time as I was. But he didn't want me to destroy myself.

Josephson: I don't think you did.

Rankin: I didn't and I didn't think I would. With all this pressure for four days, everyone was worn out. He said, "You just listen to the pacifists." I said, "I won't listen to the pacifists; I'll not listen to any of them, and I'll not vote until the very last moment. If I can see that I can vote for the war, I will."

So it wasn't that I didn't know what I was doing. . . .

Josephson: By the way, Eric Goldman, in his book, *Rendezvous With Destiny*, has an inaccuracy about your behavior. He claims that you wept or fainted or whatever when you cast your vote; that was not true, was it?

Rankin: No. You couldn't deny it when you'd wept for three days, you know. I couldn't say that. I never wept. And anyway, I didn't realize they'd make such a point of it, but that's all they talked about.

Claude Kitchen stood on the floor and the tears ran down his face and he wiped his eyes and he said, "It takes neither moral nor physical courage to declare a war for others to fight."

And they forgave him. But they insisted that I wept. I didn't have any tears by that time! I was just wept out when I cast my vote. A man named Don Drucker—he was very conspicuous in Holland; Holland made a great fuss over him. He was editor of the *Passaic News*. He was sitting next to me, and he has answered that tear thing in many letters. He wrote to Jack Kennedy, "I was sitting next to her and she did not weep."

Josephson: How did you feel in 1941 when you were the only one?

Rankin: I was mad.

Josephson: No tears then either?

Rankin: No. Someone said, "Why do you have to vote against this?" I said, "Because I can't bear to be a worm." [Laughter] I was so mad. A hundred men—I'm sure there were as many as a hundred men—that I had seen when I was lobbying, would say, "I'm just as much against war as you are." And I would answer that by saying, "Would you vote against a war resolution?" "I certainly would." And then they all forsook me.

The suffragists—I don't know how I could prove any of this, but Dorothy Detzer [of the Women's International League for Peace and Freedom], who was the secretary told some Congressmen that she didn't know how she would have voted if they'd come to her. . . .

The Quakers made the biggest fuss over me when I voted against the First World War, and they never wrote me a letter after the Second.

Josephson: You were really alone, then, weren't you?

Rankin: Absolutely.

Josephson: How did Wellington feel about your second vote? . . .

Rankin: I don't know; I never asked him.

Josephson: This time, you knew where you stood; you didn't need any advice, did you?

Rankin: Well, I wasn't going to put myself through that again and I wasn't going to put others through it—trying to persuade me and then my not doing it. I just went on my own.

Rachel Carson

~

RACHEL CARSON (1907–1964), biologist, conservationist, and writer, brought environmental awareness into the mainstream of American thought with her book *The Silent Spring* (1962). In this 1954 speech, she discusses the early years of her career and her hopes for the future of our planet.

~

I can remember no time, even in earliest childhood, when I didn't assume I was going to be a writer. I have no idea why. There were no writers in the family. I read a great deal almost from infancy, and I suppose I must have realized someone wrote the books, and thought it would be fun to make up stories, too.

Also, I can remember no time when I wasn't interested in the out-of-doors and the whole world of nature. Those interests, I know, I inherited from my mother and have always shared with her. I was rather a solitary child and spent a great deal of time in woods and beside streams, learning the birds and the insects and flowers.

There is another thing about my childhood that is interesting now, in the light of later happenings. I might have said, with Emily Dickinson:

Carson, Rachel. *Lost Woods: The Discovered Writing of Rachel Carson*. Linda Lear, ed. Boston: Beacon Press, 1998, pp. 148–163. Rachel Carson's writing © 1998 by Roger Allen Christie. Compilation, introduction, and text (other than Carson's writing) © 1998 by Linda Lear. Reprinted by permission of Frances Collin, Literary Agent.

I never saw a moor,
I never saw the sea;
Yet know I how the heather looks,
And what a wave must be.

For I never saw the ocean until I went from college to the marine laboratories at Woods Hole, on Cape Cod. Yet as a child I was fascinated by the thought of it. I dreamed about it and wondered what it would look like. I loved Swinburne and Masefield and all the other great sea poets.

I had my first prolonged contact with the sea at Woods Hole. I never tired of watching the tidal currents pouring through the Hole—that wonderful place of whirlpools and eddies and swiftly racing water. I loved to watch the waves breaking at Nobska Point after a storm. At Woods Hole, too, as a young biologist, I first discovered the rich scientific literature of the sea. But it is fair to say that my first impressions of the ocean were sensory and emotional, and that the intellectual response came later.

Before that meeting with the sea had been accomplished, however, I had a great decision to make. At least, I thought I had. I told you that I had always planned to be a writer; when I went to college, I thought the way to accomplish that was to major in English composition. Up to that time, despite my love for the world of nature, I'd had no training in biology. As a college sophomore, I was exposed to a fine introductory course in biology, and my allegiance began to waver. Perhaps I wanted to be a scientist. A year later the decision for science was made; the writing courses were abandoned. I had given up writing forever, I thought. It never occurred to me that I was merely getting something to write about. What surprises me now is that apparently it didn't occur to any of my advisors, either.

The merging of the two careers didn't begin until several years after I had left Johns Hopkins, where I had gone to do graduate work in zoology. Those were depression and post-depression years, and after a period of part-time teaching jobs, I supplemented them with another part-time assignment. The Bureau of Fisheries in Washington had undertaken to do a series of radio broadcasts. They were looking for someone to take over writing the scripts—someone who knew marine biology and who also could write. I happened in one morning when the chief of the biology division was feeling rather desperate—I think at that point he was having to write the scripts himself. He talked to me a few minutes and then said: "I've never seen a written word of yours, but I'm going to take a sporting chance."

That little job, which eventually led to a permanent appointment as a biologist, was in its way a turning point. One week I was told to produce something of a general sort about the sea. I set to work, but somehow the material rather took charge of the situation and turned into something that was, perhaps, unusual as a broadcast for the Commissioner of Fisheries. My chief read it and handed it back with a twinkle in his eye. "I don't think it will do," he said. "Better try again. But send this one to the *Atlantic*." Eventually I did, and the *Atlantic* accepted it. Since then I have told my chief of those days that he was really my first literary agent.

From those four *Atlantic* pages, titled "Undersea," everything else followed. Quincy Howe, then editor for Simon and Schuster, wrote to ask why I didn't do a book. So did Hendrik Willem van Loon. My mail had never contained anything so exciting as his first letter. It arrived in an envelope splashed with the green waves of a sea through which van Loon sharks and whales were poking inquiring snouts.

That was only the beginning of a wonderful correspondence, for it seemed Hendrik van Loon had always wanted to know what lay undersea, and he was determined I should tell the world in a book or books. His typing was amazing but his handwritten letters were almost illegible. Often he substituted a picture for a word, and that helped. After a few weeks of such correspondence, I spent a few days with the van Loons in their Connecticut home, during which I was properly introduced to my future publisher.

To a young and very tentative writer, it was a stimulating and wonderful thing to have the interest of this great man, so overwhelming in his person and his personality, but whose heart was pure gold. Through him, I had glimpses of a world that seemed exciting and fabulous, and I am sure his encouragement had a great deal to do with the fact that my first book, *Under the Sea-Wind*, was eventually published.

When that happened, however, on the eve of Pearl Harbor, the world received the event with superb indifference. The reviewers were kind, but that rush to the book store that is the author's dream never materialized. There was a Braille edition, a German translation, and use of various chapters in anthologies. That was all. I was busy with war work, and when I thought at all about writing, it was in terms of magazine pieces; I doubted that I would ever write another book. But I did, and ten years after *Under the Sea-Wind*, *The Sea Around Us* was published.

The fifteen years that I spent in fishery and wildlife conservation work with the Government have taken me into certain places where few other women have been. Perhaps you would like to hear about some of those.

While I was doing information work for Fish and Wildlife, the Service acquired a research vessel for work at sea, specifically on the famous fishing ground known as Georges Bank, that lies some 200 miles east of Boston and south of Nova Scotia. Some of the valuable commercial fishes are becoming scarce on the Bank, and the Service is trying to find the reason. The *Albatross III*, as this converted fishing trawler was called, operated out of Woods Hole, making repeated trips to Georges. She was making a census of the fish population; this was done by fishing according to a systematic plan over a selected series of stations. Of course, various scientific data on water temperatures and other matters were collected, too.

It was decided finally—and I might have had something to do with originating the idea—that perhaps I could do a better job of handling publications about the *Albatross* if I had been out on her. But there was one great obstacle. No woman had ever been on the

Albatross. Tradition is important in the Government, but fortunately I had conspirators who were willing to help me shatter precedent. But among my male colleagues who had to sign the papers, the thought of one woman on a ship with some fifty men was unthinkable. After much soul searching, it was decided that maybe *two* women would be all right, so I arranged with a friend, who was also a writer, to go with me. Marie [Rodell] thought she would write a piece about her experiences, and declared that her title would be: "I Was a Chaperone on a Fishing Boat." . . .

One of the most vivid impressions I carried away from the *Albatross* was the sight of the net coming up with its load of fish. The big fishing trawlers such as this one drag a cone-shaped net on the floor of the ocean, scraping up anything lying on the bottom or swimming just above it. This means not only fish but also crabs, sponges, starfish and other life of the sea floor. Much of the fishing was done in depths of about 100 fathoms, or 600 feet. After a half hour of trawling the big winches would begin to haul in the cables, winding them on steel drums as they came aboard. There is a marker on every hundred fathoms of cable, so one can tell when to expect the big net to come into view, still far down in the green depths.

I think that first glimpse of the net, a shapeless form, ghostly white, gave me a sense of sea depths that I never had before. As the net rises, coming into sharper focus, there is a stir of excitement even among the experienced fishermen. What has it brought up?

No two hauls are quite alike. The most interesting ones came from the deeper slopes. Georges Bank is like a small mountain resting on the floor of a surrounding deeper sea—most of the fishing is done on its flat plateaus, but sometimes the net is dragged down on the slopes near the mountain's base. Then it brings up larger fish from these depths. There is a strange effect, caused by the sudden change of pressure. Some of the fish become enormously distended and float helplessly on their backs. They drift out of the net as it nears the surface but they are quite unable to swim down.

Then one sees the slender shapes of sharks moving in to the kill. There was something very beautiful about those sharks to me—and when some of the men got out rifles and killed them for "sport" it really hurt me.

In those deep net hauls, too, there were often the large and grotesque goosefish or angler fish. The angler has a triangular shape, and its enormous mouth occupies most of the base of the triangle. It lives on the floor of the sea, preying on other fish. The anglers always seemed to have been doing a little fishing of their own as the net came up, and sometimes the tails of two or three large cod would be protruding from their mouths.

Sometimes at night we would go up on the deck to watch the fishing. Then the white splash of electric light on the lower deck was the only illumination in a world of darkness and water. It was a colorful sight, with the men in their yellow oilskins and their bright flannel shirts, all intensified and made somehow dramatic by the blackness that surrounded them.

There is something deeply impressive about the night sea as one experiences it from a small vessel far from land. When I stood on the afterdeck on those dark nights, on a tiny man-made island of wood and steel, dimly seeing the great shapes of waves that rolled about us, I think I was conscious as never before that ours is a water world, dominated by the immensity of the sea. . . .

From what I have told you, you will know that a large part of my life has been concerned with some of the beauties and mysteries of this earth about us, and with the even greater mysteries of the life that inhabits it. No one can dwell long among such subjects without thinking rather deep thoughts, without asking himself searching and often unanswerable questions, and without achieving a certain philosophy.

There is one quality that characterizes all of us who deal with the sciences of the earth and its life—we are never bored. We can't be. There is always something new to be investigated. Every mystery solved brings us to the threshold of a greater one. . . .

The pleasures, the values of contact with the natural world, are not reserved for the scientists. They are available to anyone who will place himself under the influence of a lonely mountain top—or the sea—or the stillness of a forest; or who will stop to think about so small a thing as the mystery of a growing seed.

I am not afraid of being thought a sentimentalist when I stand here tonight and tell you that I believe natural beauty has a necessary place in the spiritual development of any individual or any society. I believe that whenever we destroy beauty, or whenever we substitute something man-made and artificial for a natural feature of the earth, we have retarded some part of man's spiritual growth.

I believe this affinity of the human spirit for the earth and its beauties is deeply and logically rooted. As human beings, we are part of the whole stream of life. We have been human beings for perhaps a million years. But life itself—passes on something of itself to other life—that mysterious entity that moves and is aware of itself and its surroundings, and so is distinguished from rocks or senseless clay—[from which] life arose many hundreds of millions of years ago. Since then it has developed, struggled, adapted itself to its surroundings, evolved an infinite number of forms. But its living protoplasm is built of the same elements as air, water, and rock. To these the mysterious spark of life was added. Our origins are of the earth. And so there is in us a deeply seated response to the natural universe, which is part of our humanity.

Now why do I introduce such a subject tonight—a serious subject for a night when we are supposed to be having fun? First, because you have asked me to tell you something of myself—and I can't do that without telling you some of the things I believe in so intensely.

Also, I mention it because it is not often I have a chance to talk to a thousand women. I believe it is important for women to realize that the world of today threatens to destroy much of that beauty that has immense power to bring us a healing release from tension. Women have a greater intuitive understanding of such things. They want for their children not only physical health but mental and spiritual health as well. I bring these things to your attention tonight because I think your awareness of them will help, whether you are practicing journalists, or teachers, or librarians, or housewives and mothers.

What are these threats of which I speak? What is this destruction of beauty—this substitution of man-made ugliness—this trend toward a perilously artificial world? Unfortunately, that is a subject that could require a whole conference, extending over many days. So in the few minutes that I have to devote to it, I can only suggest the trend.

We see it in small ways in our own communities, and in larger ways in the community of the state of the nation. We see the destruction of beauty and the suppression of human individuality in hundreds of suburban real estate developments where the first act is to cut down all the trees and the next is to build an infinitude of little houses, each like its neighbor.

We see it in distressing form in the nation's capital, where I live. There in the heart of the city we have a small but beautiful woodland area—Rock Creek Park. It is a place where one can go, away from the noise of traffic and of man-made confusions, for a little interval of refreshing and restoring quiet—where one can hear the soft water sounds of a stream on its way to river and sea, where the wind flows through the trees, and a veery sings in the green twilight. Now they propose to run a six-lane arterial highway through the heart of that narrow woodland valley—destroying forever its true and immeasurable value to the city and the nation.

Those who place so great a value on a highway apparently do not think the thoughts of an editorial writer for the *New York Times* who said: "But a little lonesome space, where nature has her own way, where it is quiet enough at night to hear the patter of small paws on leaves and the murmuring of birds, can still be afforded. The gift of tranquillity, wherever found, is beyond price."

We see the destructive trend on a national scale in proposals to invade the national parks with commercial schemes such as the building of power dams. The parks were placed in trust for all the people, to preserve for them just such recreational and spiritual values as I have mentioned. Is it the right of this, our generation, in its selfish materialism, to destroy these things because we are blinded by the dollar sign? Beauty—and all the values the derive from beauty—are not measured and evaluated in terms of the dollar.

Years ago I discovered in the writings of the British naturalist Richard Jefferies a few lines that so impressed themselves upon my mind that I have never forgotten them. May I quote them for you now?

> The exceeding beauty of the earth, in her splendor of life, yields a new thought with every petal. The hours when the mind is absorbed by beauty are the only hours when we really live. All else is illusion, or mere endurance.

Those lines are, in a way, a statement of the creed I have lived by, for, as perhaps you have seen tonight, a preoccupation with the wonder and beauty of the earth has strongly influenced the course of my life.

Since *The Sea Around Us* was published, I have had the privilege of receiving many letters from people who, like myself, have been steadied and reassured by contemplating the long history of the earth and sea, and the deeper meanings of the world of nature. These letters have come from all sorts of people. There have been hairdressers and fishermen and musicians; there have been classical scholars and scientists. So many of them have said, in one phrasing or another: "We have been troubled about the world, and had almost lost faith in man; it helps to think about the long history of the earth, and of how life came to be. And when we think in terms of millions of years, we are not so impatient that our own problems be solved tomorrow."

In contemplating "the exceeding beauty of the earth" these people have found calmness and courage. For there is symbolic as well as actual beauty in the migration of birds, in the ebb and flow of the tides; in the folded bud ready for the spring. There is something infinitely healing in these repeated refrains of nature—the assurance that dawn comes after night, and spring after winter.

Mankind has gone very far into an artificial world of his own creation. He has sought to insulate himself, with steel and concrete, from the realities of earth and water. Perhaps he is intoxicated with his own power, as he goes farther and farther into experiments for the destruction of himself and his world. For this unhappy trend there is no single remedy—no panacea. But I believe that the more clearly we can focus our attention on the wonders and realities of the universe about us, the less taste we shall have for destruction.

Eleanor Roosevelt

~

ELEANOR ROOSEVELT (1884–1962), first lady, reformer, diplomat, and author, struggled until mid-life to overcome timidity and a tendency to defer to others. She succeeded in this endeavor and became internationally renowned for her advocacy of social justice and international cooperation. She wrote the following in 1959, following her seventy-fifth birthday.

~

In October of 1959 I reached my seventy-fifth birthday. It was a busy day, as most of mine are, with little time for introspection. Nonetheless, it was, in a way, a milestone, and I found myself looking back along the way I had come, trying to get a long-range view of the journey I had made and, if I could, to evaluate it. I wanted, if possible, to draw a kind of balance sheet, to formulate for myself the objectives I had had and to estimate how far I had achieved them.

This kind of introspection is one in which I rarely indulge. At times, of course, it is valuable in throwing light into dark places, but its danger is that one may easily tend to become self-absorbed in one's voyage of discovery and self-analysis.

People still ask me frequently how I planned my career and what over-all objective I had in mind. Actually I never planned a career, and what basic objective I had, for many years, was to grasp every opportunity to live and experience life as deeply, as fully, and as widely as I possibly could. It seemed to me stupid to have the gift of life and not use it to the utmost of one's ability.

I was not a gifted person but I was always deeply interested in every manifestation of life, good or bad. I never let slip an opportunity to increase my knowledge of people and conditions. Everything was grist to my mill: not only the things I saw but the people I met. Indeed, I could not express adequately the debt I owe to the friends who taught me so much about the world I live in. I had really only three assets: I was keenly interested, I accepted every challenge and every opportunity to learn more, and I had great energy and self-discipline.

As a result, I have never had to look for interests to fill my life. If you are interested, things come to you, they seem to gravitate your way without your lifting a hand. One thing leads to another and another, and as you gain in knowledge and in experience new opportunities open up before you.

Before my seventy-fifth birthday something else had happened that forced me to turn back and look at my past life rather than to look ahead, as I prefer doing. Dore Schary wrote *Sunrise at Campobello*, a play that dealt with my husband's serious illness and his spiritual victory over being crippled. I can remember still the evening when the dramatist read his play to me. And I can remember the strange experience of seeing it performed.

I have been asked countless times how I felt about seeing myself, my children, my husband portrayed on the stage. Did I feel a sense of recognition? Did I say, "But it wasn't like that at all?" Did I feel that my privacy as a woman had been invaded?

The truth is that I watched the play with complete detachment. It is true that when I closed my eyes Ralph Bellamy evoked the very quality and cadence of Franklin's voice and I seemed to hear him speak. But, for the rest, it seemed quite impersonal; it was a play, so far as I personally was concerned, about someone else.

I think if the average person tries to look back he will be unable to remember what he was like, or how he looked, or even, except for major matters, what he did when he was young. He can remember only what he felt. Even in the case of my children I felt that I was watching the actions of quite fictitious characters. One of the best-drawn characters in that play, by the way, was Louis Howe. True, he was less untidy than the Louis I had known, but the lines were excellent and the portrayal was true of the man.

No, it was not by seeing the character of "Eleanor Roosevelt" on the stage that I could come any closer to an analysis of the woman who had now reached seventy-five years of age.

Looking back, I could see that the over-all objective of which many people spoke to me had no existence. It seems hardly human that anyone can plan his life clearly from the beginning, making no allowances for a changing or developing character or for circumstances.

I am sure that my objectives, during those early years at least, were constantly changing. In the beginning, because I felt, as only a young girl can feel it, all the pain of being an ugly duckling, I was not only timid, I was afraid. Afraid of almost everything, I think: of mice, of the dark, of imaginary dangers, of my own inadequacy. My chief objective, as a girl, was to do my duty. This had been drilled into me as far back as I could remember. Not my duty as I saw it, but my duty as laid down for me by other people. I never occurred to me to revolt. Anyhow, my one overwhelming need in those days was to be approved, to be loved, and I did whatever was required of me, hoping it would bring me nearer to the approval and love I so much wanted.

As a young woman, my sense of duty remained as strict and rigid as it had been when I was a girl, but it had changed its focus. My husband and my children became the center of my life and their needs were my new duty. I am afraid now that I approached this new obligation much as I had my childhood duties. I was still timid, still afraid of doing something wrong, of making mistakes, of not living up to the standards required by my mother-in-law, of failing to do what was expected of me.

As a result, I was so hidebound by duty that I became too critical, too much of a disciplinarian. I was so concerned with bringing up my children properly that I was not wise enough just to love them. Now, looking back, I think I would rather spoil a child a little and have more fun out of it.

It was not until I reached middle age that I had the courage to develop interests of my own, outside of my duties to my family. In the beginning, it seems to me now, I had no goal beyond the interests themselves, in learning about people and conditions and the world outside our own United States. Almost at once I began to discover that interest leads to interest, knowledge leads to more knowledge, the capacity for understanding grows with the effort to understand.

From that time on, though I have had many problems, though I have known the grief and the loneliness that are the lot of most human beings, though I have had to make and still have to make endless adjustments, I have never been bored, never found the days long enough for the range of activities with which I wanted to fill them. And, having learned to stare down fear, I long ago reached the point where there is no living person whom I fear, and few challenges that I am not willing to face.

On that seventy-fifth birthday I knew that I had long since become aware of my over-all objective in life. It stemmed from those early impressions I had gathered when I saw war-torn Europe after World War I. I wanted, with all my heart, a peaceful world. And I knew it could never be achieved on a lasting basis without greater understanding between peoples. It is to these ends that I have, in the main, devoted the past years.

One curious thing is that I have always seen life personally; that is, my interest or sympathy or indignation is not aroused by an abstract cause but by the plight of a single person whom I have seen with my own eyes. It was the sight of a child dying of hunger that made the tragedy of hunger become of such overriding importance to me. Out of my response to an individual develops an awareness of a problem to the community, then to the country, and finally to the world. In each case my feeling of obligation to do something has stemmed from one individual and then widened and become applied to a broader area.

More and more, I think, people are coming to realize that what affects an individual affects mankind. To take an extreme example, one neglected case of smallpox can infect a whole community. This is equally true of the maladjusted child, who may wreak havoc in his neighborhood; of the impoverished, who become either economic burdens or social burdens and, in any case, are wasted as human beings. Abuses anywhere, however isolated they may appear, can end by becoming abuses everywhere.

I learned, too, while I was groping for more and more effective ways of trying to cope with community and national and world problems, that you can accomplish a great deal more if you care deeply about what is happening to other people than if you say in apathy or discouragement, "Oh, what can I do? What use is one person? I might as well not bother."

Actually I suppose the caring comes from being able to put yourself in the position of the other person. If you cannot imagine, "This might happen to me," you are able to say to yourself with indifference, "Who cares?"

I think that one of the reasons it is so difficult for us, as a people, to understand other areas of the world is that we cannot put ourselves imaginatively in their place. We have no famine. But if we were actually to see people dying of starvation we would care quite a bit. We would be able to think, "These could be my people."

Because of our rather extraordinary advantages, it is difficult for us to understand the other peoples of the world. We started with tremendous national resources. Our very isolation, in those early years, forced us to develop them. Many of the people who settled here had escaped from poverty and want and oppression and lack of opportunity. They wanted to forget their background and they soon did, because the difficulty of travel made it hard for them to go back and refresh their memories. So we grew out of the past and away from it. Now it would be valuable for us to remember the conditions of that Old World. It would help us to understand what the poorer countries need and want today.

And this, I suppose, indicates what has happened to me in seventy-five years. Though now as always it is through individuals that I see and understand human needs, I find that my over-all objectives go beyond individuals to the fate of mankind. It is within that larger framework that one must think today if mankind is to survive the threat that hangs, in a mushroom cloud, over it.

So I come to the larger objective, not mine, except as I am an American, but America's. It seems to me that America's objective today should be to try to make herself the best possible mirror of democracy that she can. The people of the world can see what happens here. They watch us to see what we are going to do and how well we can do it. We are giving them the only possible picture of democracy that we can: the picture as it works in actual practice. This is the only way other peoples can see for themselves how it works; and can determine for themselves whether this thing is good in itself, whether it is better than what they have, better than what other political and economic systems offer them.

Now, while we are a generous nation, giving with a free hand and with an open heart wherever there is need or suffering (that we can understand, at least), we have one weakness that, considering our political maturity as a nation, is rather immature. We continue to expect the world to be grateful to us and to love us. We are hurt and indignant when we do not receive gratitude and love.

Gratitude and love are not to be had for the asking; they are not to be bought. We should not want to think that they are for sale. What we should seek, rather than gratitude or love, is the respect of the world. This we can earn by enlightened justice. But it is rather naïve of us to think that when we are helping people our action is entirely unselfish. It is not. It is not unselfish when we vaccinate the public against smallpox. It is a precautionary measure, but nonetheless good in itself.

Other nations are quite aware that when we try to bolster up their economy and strengthen their governments and generally help them to succeed there is a certain amount of self-interest involved. They are inevitably going to be on the lookout to see what we want in return. Consciously we do not want anything, but unconsciously almost anything we do, as a nation or through the United Nations, is intended to benefit us or our cause, directly or indirectly. So there is no reason for demanding either gratitude or love.

Our obligation to the world is, primarily, our obligation to our own future. Obviously we cannot develop beyond a certain point unless the other nations develop too. When our natural resources peter out, we must seek them in other countries. We cannot have trade if we are the only solvent nation. We need not only areas from which to buy but areas to which we can sell, and we cannot have this in underdeveloped areas.

We must, as a nation, begin to realize that we are the leaders of the non-Communist world, that our interests at some point all touch the interests of the world, and they must be examined in the context of the interests of the world. This is the price of leadership.

We cannot, indeed, continue to function in a narrow orbit or in a self-enclosed system. We cannot weigh or evaluate even our domestic problems in their own context alone. We no longer have merely domestic issues. Perhaps the best illustration of this is the question I am asked everywhere in the world:

"We hear you Americans pay to keep land out of production because there is too much to eat. Is there no better way to use your ability to produce food than to get rid of it?"

This is a home question; it is literally of vital moment to the millions of starving in the world who look to us. I do not see how we can retain world leadership and yet continue to handle our problems as though they concerned us alone; they concern the world. We feel that a surplus of food is only an embarrassment. We solve it as though only we were concerned. But think of the hungry people and their bitterness as the food that could save their lives is plowed under. To say they think it highly unfair is to put it mildly.

We have never put our best brains to work in the ways we can produce to the maximum, give our farmers a better income, and still employ our surpluses in a way to solve the pressing needs of the world, without upsetting our economy or that of friendly nations who might fear we were giving food to markets they are accustomed to selling to.

We have a great variety of climate, we can grow almost anything we want. Canada can grow only wheat. There need be no clash of interests here.

How have we tried to "solve" matters up to now? We cut our acreage and store the surplus or dump it; we pay our farmers too little to give them an income on a par with that of industrial workers, so we have a dwindling farm population. No one has ever sat down and said, "This is a problem you *must* work out."

It is in ways like these, using our intelligence and our good will and our vast capacity to produce, that we can meet and overcome the Communist threat and prove that democracy has more to give the world.

All this seems like a far cry from my seventy-fifth birthday and yet I find that, as I have grown older, my personal objectives have long since blended into my public objectives. I have, of course, realized that I cannot continue indefinitely the strenuous life I now lead, the constant traveling from state to state, from country to country.

What, then? Then, I thought, even if I must relinquish much of my traveling, perhaps there is a way in which I can still reach people with things that it seems important for them to hear. The most practical way of doing this is through a radio or television program. My radio and television agent shook his head.

"You are too controversial a figure," he told me. "The sponsors would be afraid of you. Some of them feel so strongly about you that they believe the public would not buy any product on whose program you might appear."

I remembered then that some years earlier the head of the Red Cross had been afraid to accept a donation for fear that my participation would drive away other subscribers!

It is startling to realize that one is so deeply, fanatically disliked by a number of people. And yet, while I weigh as honestly as I can their grounds for disapproval, when I feel that I am right in what I do, it seems to me that I cannot afford, as a self-respecting individual, to refuse to do a thing merely because it will make me disliked or bring down a storm of criticism on my head. I often feel that too many Americans today tend to reject the thing, however right they believe it to be, that they want to do because they fear they will be unpopular or will find themselves standing alone instead of in the comfortable anonymity of the herd.

As a result, when I believe, after weighing the evidence, that what I am doing is right I go ahead and try as hard as I can to dismiss from my mind the attitude of those who are hostile. I don't see how else one can live.

One day my radio agent appeared, looking very much surprised, to say that he had had an offer for me to do television commercials for an organization that sold margarine.

"I know this isn't the kind of thing you had in mind," he pointed out, "but if a conservative firm feels that you can sell their product I think you should at least try it. It may break the ice for you."

I thought it over. I had to face the fact that I would be bitterly criticized for doing commercials. On the other hand, if this was a field I wanted to open up I ought at least to see whether I could do it, no matter how disagreeable the reaction of many people might be.

So at length I agreed. The only stipulation I made was that, outside of selling the product, I should be allowed to say one thing of my own that I thought had value. So I reminded the audience that there were hungry people in the world.

There were, of course, as many disagreeable comments as I had expected, but the program went all right and the sponsors discovered that, after all, I did not prevent people from buying their product!

This year (1960–61) I am going to introduce a program of refugee stories, as my participation in the Refugee Year work of the United Nations.

The purpose of this refugee organization, now headed by Mr. Lint, is to try to reduce the population of the refugee camps in Europe; to wipe them out if that is humanly possible. Ten years is too long for these people to have lived in camps, stateless and with no solution in sight for their problem. There are children who have never known any other life.

Actually a good deal has been accomplished. The number of refugees has been greatly reduced. Where they still remain in camps, an effort has been made to provide permanent housing and to find them jobs. A number of countries have accepted what is called "hard-core cases," those who are blind or have other disabilities. Of course, I am referring now only to the refugee camps in Europe. There are between 800,000 and a million refugees in the Near East and no one knows how many in Hong Kong and in China.

The refugees of the world are a constant and painful reminder of the breakdown of civilization through the stupidity of war. They are its permanent victims. No time in history has known anything like the number of stateless people who have existed or survived the rigors of the past thirty years.

When we closed the work of the United Nations Relief Association in the United Nations we set up the present Commission for Refugees with headquarters in Geneva. No money, however, was set aside for this. Its function is to see that these peple are given papers which will allow them to get work, to make life more possible for them, though they are still stateless.

Mr. Lint discovered that there were still many who needed financial help and he requested aid for a fund which he could use for this purpose. Every year he comes to the United States to get further funds to meet these needs.

In the American Association of the United Nations we were willed a considerable sum of money which was to be applied to alleviating the conditions of refugees. We had to set up a group to handle this, and, of course, we had to have the consent of the high commissioner to turn the money over to Mr. Lint for this purpose. Before long even this ugly scar of war may be healed.

Interspersed among my other activities, traveling and lecturing, work with the A.A.U.N., radio and television appearances, I continue to entertain a number of interesting people who visit Hyde Park from time to time, sometimes to leave flowers at my husband's grave or to visit the library, sometimes to come as guests to my cottage, either through arrangements made with the State Department or independently.

Perhaps the most confusing time was in September, 1959, when the visits of Princess Beatrice of Holland and Premier Khrushchev almost overlapped. The little princess came at the time of the Hudson-Champlain celebration. Like most foreign visitors she had been feted and had listened to speeches and had attended functions until she was exhausted.

When she reached my cottage she was very tired. There was an hour free before dinner, I told her, and she said wearily to her lady in waiting, "Please open my bed."

Young as she was, she had been living under the strictest protocol and had been entertained, for the most part, by much older people, dignified statesmen, and so forth.

There was, I assured her, going to be no protocol. I planned a buffet supper, with people waiting on themselves and seated at small tables, and my guests for her were some boys from Harvard and my granddaughter, who was about her own age.

Later my granddaughter told me of their conversation. The princess told them that she was going to college and how much she valued the time there. She had even regretted losing a month from college because of her trip to America. This was the last time in her life that she would be able to live naturally with other people.

She told them, too, what difficulties arose for young people in her position. There were so few people left whom they could marry.

She was a very gentle, simple person, very sweet and simply brought up.

On the morning of the day she left Mr. Khrushchev and his wife were to arrive on their first visit to the United States. The princess and her party—we had sixteen for breakfast—left at nine in the morning. We were to feed an unknown number of members of Mr. Khrushchev's party and tables were set up and ready for them, all managed by my faithful and capable couple.

Never, I think, have I seen anything like the number of state police who were called out by our anxious government to protect Mr. Khrushchev. When I reached the library, where I was to meet him, they were lined up, side by side, all the length of the driveway and parking place. When we returned to my cottage, the dirt road which leads from the highway to the house had men stationed every few feet all the way. They had even suggested the possibility of my trees hiding malefactors who could climb them to shoot at the Communist leader. But I put my foot down at having my trees destroyed.

Anyhow Mr. Khrushchev, his pleasant and simple wife, and his entourage arrived very late at the cottage, so late they had time for nothing but a glance around and a hasty bun, which Mr. Khrushchev snatched from a table to sustain him while they rushed back to New York for his speech at the United Nations.

No shots were fired, no unpleasantness of any kind occurred, and the piles of uneaten food were disposed of by the hordes of state police. It was all rather silly.

Before his arrival there had been much speculation about what Mr. Khrushchev would get out of his visit to the United States. I don't see how, in that hasty breathless fashion, any preconception could be altered. Perhaps if he had had any chance to speak to the farmers in Iowa at leisure, he could have obtained an effective, firsthand impression of the American people, of their independence, self-respect and self-reliance. But, being hurried along, he naturally could not be expected to get a very fair impression.

But even in that rushed, cursory visit, he must have realized that we are not ripe for revolution. He must have seen for himself that while we have great prosperity we are not entirely materialistic. At least, he *may* have seen these things. I don't know. I do think, however, that if foreign leaders could visit our country quietly and on their own, they would form a much sounder impression of it than through these exhausting official receptions, parades and endless speeches.

So an account of my seventy-fifth birthday ends, in spite of me, with a discussion of foreign affairs. There is such a big, muddled world, so much to be done, so much that *can* be done if we increase in depth of understanding, in learning to care, in thinking of hunger not as an abstraction but as one empty stomach, in having a hospitable mind, open like a window to currents of air and to light from all sides.

Ethel Barol Taylor

~

ETHEL BAROL TAYLOR (1916–) has been a long-time member of Women Strike for Peace, an organization founded to oppose the use of nuclear weapons and to urge peaceful solutions to international conflict. In this oral history conducted by Judith Porter Adams, Ethel Barol Taylor describes her life as a committed peace activist.

~

I was catapulted into the peace movement with the dropping of the bomb on Hiroshima. I was pretty apolitical up to that point. I used to get up in the morning and start polishing the furniture until I was polishing the polish. I thought, "There must be more to life than this."

I had a daughter, who was a small child at the time of the bombing of Hiroshima. When I read that the blast was so hot that in some circumstances it incinerated people and left just a shadow against a stone wall, creating instant fossils, I was numbed. I realized there were wars and there were wars, but this kind of war must never happen again.

There were others who felt as I did, and a few of us got together and talked. We formed a little group of women to study issues. I think even then, even though I was not political, I had this feeling that because women are not in positions of power and they have no role in policy-making, that maybe what we had to do was to make

Adams, Judith Porter. *Peacework: Oral Histories of Women Peace Activists*. Boston: Twayne Publishers, 1990, pp. 12–18. Excerpt from *Peacework: Oral Histories of Women Peace Activists,* by Judith Porter Adams, Twayne Publishers, 1990, copyright © 1991 by G. K. Hall & Co. Reprinted by permission of the Gale Group.

policy outside of government and demand of government that it listen to us.

A columnist once wrote a piece about me, and she called it "Rebel in White Gloves" because in the early days of Women Strike for Peace, women in the demonstrations, who were generally middle-class women, wore white gloves and hats. We used to do things like sit down and not move in the middle of the street, or whatever, but we would have our hats and white gloves on. I always thought that was a real protection until once we had an action, and hundreds of people went to Washington as a symbolic takeover of Congress. We walked and we came to a narrow street. The police said, "Cross this street and you get arrested." Well, I realized then that, what could they do? They're not going to electrocute me. They're not going to shoot me. It was much easier to cross that street than not to cross that street, so I crossed that street. Then we sat on the ground and waited to be arrested. We sat down, but we decided we weren't going to be yanked by our armpits, we were going to walk like ladies to the police van. We did. We got to the jail, and they opened the back door of the van. I looked out, and there was a five-foot drop to the ground. I waited for the policeman to help me down. The policeman came around and said, "Jump, sister." So I jumped into an entirely new world.

I didn't realize when I first got involved, when our government dropped the bomb on Hiroshima and Nagasaki, that this was going to be a lifetime commitment. I think if I had realized it I might have thought twice, because it's a terrible business to be in.

I think most of the pressures were because of the issues, not just because I was a woman—although there were those pressures too. You can really go nuts working for something and never have a success, never see enough change. Camus said, and I'm para-phrasing, that just because a thing is hopeless doesn't mean you don't get involved. That sounds gloomy. We have had some successes, but when I first got in, there were two bombs and they were both ours. Now there are 50,000 in the world. Someone once said, "Ethel, that's going to look lousy on your résumé." I think I developed an early anger that leaders had such contempt for the people they were supposed to be leading. That anger really has sustained me.

My anger is directed towards leaders who threaten the lives of children now and those yet unborn with their inhumane policy of nuclear weapons. We started because of children, because the scientists and doctors said that the strontium 90 and iodine 131 from the atomic tests would poison our children's milk and cause cancer. When we first organized we sent out a call throughout the streets with leaflets saying, "Take your children off milk." We sent our children's baby teeth to a lab in St. Louis to determine if strontium 90 was present. We were concerned about an epidemic, like polio before vaccines, except that polio is viral and these were man-made epidemics. Those who were then children now have children themselves.

My work in Women Strike for Peace sustains me. Outside of my family and my friends, WSP to me is the most important entity. It started out as a one-day action. We would meet every week around my dining room table to plan our "strike." There was a sugar bowl in the middle of the table for contributions toward the action. Some women stopped going to the hairdresser and did their own hair and put the money in the bowl. Some put birthday checks in. In one remarkable case, a woman who had very little money would occasionally give blood to the Red Cross and put the five dollars in the bowl. There was a wonderful outpouring of feeling and sisterhood. We were the harbingers of the women's movement—our weekly round table discussions were certainly consciousness raising. It was really an amazing experience. We never pledged solidarity, but we really were solid.

It was like an electric current running through the country with these women who decided that this couldn't just be a one-day action; it would have to go on. That has been our strength and weakness, to try to make a permanent organization out of a one-day action. WSP is more than an organization; it's a state of mind. I've never been part of a group—and I've been in a lot of them—where there was such a feeling of sisterhood. That is not to say that we don't sometimes get furious at each other.

In 1962 some WSP members were brought before the House Un-American Activities Committee [HUAC]. In order to show solidarity, many of us wrote to the chair of the committee asking for an opportunity to testify. The hearing was in 1962. It was pure theater. There is a wonderful cartoon about the HUAC hearings and WSP. There are these two guys sitting up at the HUAC table, and one of them says, "What are we against, women or peace?" They were against both. When some of us walked in, the guards were standing out in the hall outside the hearing room minding baby carriages and babies. We all carried red roses, and each time a woman would step down from testifying, we would present her with a bouquet, and we would applaud. The committee kept threatening to clear the room. They were in real trouble! They couldn't get out of the sessions, and they became more and more permissive because we were all so good-natured. The committee was just ridiculed away. It was a tremendous victory against the hearings.

When Dagmar Wilson was asked if there were Communists in WSP, she responded very pleasantly by saying something like, "We welcome everyone as long as they are for disarmament." That was quite a statement to make. I can't really speak for the women who faced the committee, and what the effect was on their lives, but it wasn't like the early McCarthy days, when people informed on others because they feared for their jobs—or the brave ones who refused to buckle under were ruined professionally. Then there was the real unadulterated fear and panic, because once you were blacklisted, that was it. But these were middle-class women whose jobs did not depend on whether or not they were cleared by this committee. I'm sure the HUAC experience for the women questioned was pretty scary, but the great difference was the tremendous, enthusiastic support they received publicly. We had a clipping service of all of the newspapers that covered the hearings. It was all "hats off to the ladies," as I remember.

In 1975 President Ford appointed a commission on CIA activities within the United States. We learned things that amazed us. We learned that the CIA paid women, mostly housewives, one hundred dollars a week to infiltrate WSP. We suspected it at the time, but we didn't know. These women were instructed by the CIA to attend meetings, to show an interest in the purpose of the organization, and to make modest financial contributions, but not to exercise any leadership. It was a perfect cover; that describes half our membership—they don't want leadership roles, and they don't give too much money. The CIA also opened our mail. When we learned this we immediately instituted a suit against the CIA; we sued for surveillance, infiltration, and for mail opening. The first two charges were dropped, but they settled out of court for mail opening and gave us five thousand dollars. It wasn't so much money, but what a sweet moral victory! We used part of the money for our campaign to abolish the CIA.

During the Vietnam War three of us went to Hanoi to discuss the transmission of mail and packages between the prisoners of war and their families. It was the most exciting event in my life because up until that point very few letters were getting through. The Vietnamese didn't consider our soldiers prisoners of war under the Geneva Convention, since war had never been declared. They considered them war criminals. Others had gone before us, such as the Berrigan brothers, and a couple of prisoners had been brought home. The Vietnamese said they would not deal with the subject of prisoners with the government, but only with the peace movement.

A couple who lived in my neighborhood had a son who was shot down in 1964, and my trip was in 1969. They didn't know if he was alive or dead. When they heard I was going they asked me to try to find out about him, and they gave me a letter for him. They were active in the National Organization of Families of POWs [prisoners of war]. They notified their group that I was going to Vietnam, and I was flooded with letters for delivery from all over the country—letters for sons, husbands, and so on. We brought all these letters with us. While I was in Vietnam I asked the Vietnamese women about the status of my neighbors' son. One of the women left the room and later came back with a letter from him. His parents were at that time in Thailand on what they called a sentimental journey, so they could get as close as they could to where their son might be. I sent them a cable, "John is alive and well and I have a letter for you." Get this—it was Christmas. I came home with over thirty letters. My husband and I sat down, and we called families all over the country to tell them their son or husband was alive and that I was sending them his letter.

When I got back I was nearly deluged by the press. I was having a press conference in my living room when the phone rang. My husband answered it, and he came back and said, "It's a colonel from the Pentagon." I spoke to him. He said, "Mrs. Taylor, I want to tell you that you and the two other women have done a most marvelous job that no one else could do. I would like to send two of my men down just to discuss it with you." I said, "That won't be necessary. I'm glad you appreciate it." That night the television news anchor opened his broadcast by saying, "Local woman cited by the Pentagon." A couple weeks later the FBI warned the families not to accept any mail from our committee; they accused us of being a Communist group. Would you believe that one family wouldn't accept mail that we brought from their son?

After my trip to Vietnam I was invited to speak at many service clubs—the Optimists, the Lions, the Rotary. At one event I went through my talk, and in the back during the question period, they started chanting "Hanoi Hannah." They were very disruptive. While the chanting was going on the chair was in the process of presenting me with a plaque for distinguished service. When I left I met two of the men outside the room who I knew were opposed to the war. I said, "Why didn't you defend me?" They evidently were afraid to. So I wrote a letter to the membership chair who had invited me. I said, "There was a breath of fascism at that meeting. Reverend so-and-so and Mr. so-and-so were afraid to stand up and defend me even though they agreed with me when I spoke to them outside." I got a letter back from him that said, "I asked them and they said they never spoke to you."

I spoke at a church where as soon as I was introduced everybody got up and walked out. The minister had warned me when I came in. He said, "You are in John Birch Society territory." Another time I spoke on Worldwide Peace Day. The chairwoman had said, "After the program is over, Mrs. Taylor will go to the back where you can greet her and speak to her." By the time I got through speaking. I saw the backs of everybody moving out. She escorted me to the back, and a woman ran over to me, put something in my hand, and ran out. When I got outside I read the note. It said, "Please call me." I called her. She wanted to know something about WSP but was afraid to ask me. I shouldn't have been so naive. But they invited me, and I expected them at least to be courteous. I didn't realize how deep the hate was for me and what I stood for, because I was a very public person. I learned later, through my FBI files, that the federal attorney here in Philadelphia and the FBI communicated for a long time about whether I should be brought before the grand jury for sedition because of my activities in draft resistance.

During the Vietnam War, we had no choice but to lessen considerably our involvement in our original cause, atmospheric testing, and turn our attention towards the war. When we got back to our original concern after the war, it was evident that the government had not lessened its commitment to accelerating the arms race. The war economy had really multiplied. Our membership also suffered losses after the war; there was a drop, a lull. The women's movement also drew women away who decided to go back to school, to go out in the workplace, to have a career, and so on.

I think the situation today is so frightening because people seem to have forgotten the war in Vietnam, and they so glibly talk about Central America and the Persian Gulf. The war in Vietnam was a holocaust for the Vietnamese people. When I was in Hanoi a woman said to me, "The American people must put so little value on human life." I said, "You know, that's very funny, because that's what everybody says about Asians." She said she could not understand how Americans explain to their children why their fathers died nine thousand miles away from home.

Women have proven that they can be a tremendous power in their neighborhoods. Participatory democracy is alive and growing—mothers and fathers get together and block a street until the city provides a stop sign to save the lives of their children. We've got to make the antiwar issue that kind of issue so that people will get together, not only because the arms race is a threat to their children, but because of the tremendous displacement of funds for bombs instead of funds for people.

I made it very clear to my children, when they could understand it, that this was my decision to give my time and life to peace work. It wasn't my decision for them. But they were sympathetic. My husband was very supportive too; it was he who convinced me to go to Hanoi. My son once said proudly to me, "You know, you're the only mother in the whole block who has ever gone to jail."

I'm tempted to say that women are more peace loving than men who are not in the movement, but then I think of women who have gained power, as of Prime Minister Thatcher, and the Falklands War in the 1980s, or I think of the screaming women who tried to prevent black children from entering a school in Arkansas during the civil rights movement, and the prolife women who scream, "Murderer!" outside family-planning clinics. I know it's a simplistic thing to say, but I think that women care; they have a very strong feeling for humanity. The bonds between women are stronger, perhaps, because women haven't gotten a fair shake; it unites women in a closer relationship than men, who generally are in power. At our meetings we dig into our experiences in order to create programs that might end war and bring peace and help our children. It seems like a womanly thing to do.

I think one of the amazing things about my own personal life is that on the day of that first protest, where we were challenged to cross the street, it was easier to do it than not to do it. The next time it was a natural thing to do. So many women in the movement did things that they never thought would be possible to do because of the deep feelings they had against war.

Here's a little story. I was appointed by President Carter to an International Year of the Woman conference. I was the only woman who represented a peace constituency—most of them were women's-issue-oriented. My job was to make peace a women's issue. After the conference the Carters had a reception for us at the White House in the East Room. WSP has bibs that we tied under our coats during protest marches; they say, "End the Arms Race, Not the Human Race." The other side says, "There is No Shelter from Nuclear War." I decided I was going to wear it under my coat and when Carter came to shake my hand, I'd reveal it.

To get to the reception we had to go through a subterranean passage. Everybody went through except me: when they came to me the security people said, "Just a moment." They got on the telephone, talking, talking. Then they said, "Okay, you can go too." I said, "Could you explain to me why everybody went through but when it came time for me to go through you had to make a telephone call?" He said, "There's a bad Ethel Taylor out there. I made these calls, and they figured that if the president appointed you, you can't be the bad Ethel Taylor." Little did they know!

We got up on the dais, and the president came down the aisle and stepped up on the dais. The press was all there. He started to go to each woman shaking hands. He came to me, and I opened my coat and showed the bib with the message. His smile got caught in his teeth. He didn't shake my hand. He went right past me. As soon as it happened, the secretary of commerce, who was a woman, and a group of women, jumped in front of me and blocked me off from the media. Somebody said they looked over, and they saw me standing there and thought of Joan of Arc.

People have to align themselves with their elected representatives, and the elected representatives have to know that you're there watching. If a group of people set themselves up as watch-dogs of a congressperson or a senator, I think it can have an effect. The letter writing which everybody is doing is a lifeline from the people to those who represent them.

I've survived by maintaining a sense of humor. It's better to laugh than to cry. I always got a tremendous amount of satisfaction and strength from the women with whom I worked. We can't always see immediate results from our work, but we have had an effect; we women have been dedicated and have made these issues ones that the government has to reckon with.

Anne Moody

〜

ANNE MOODY (1940–), author and activist in the civil rights movement during the early 1960s, was one of the students who took part in the sit-in at Woolworth's segregated lunch counter in 1963. She recalls the events in her autobiography, *Coming of Age in Mississippi*.

〜

During my senior year at Tougaloo, my family hadn't sent me one penny. I had only the small amount of money I had earned at Maple Hill. I couldn't afford to eat at school or live in the dorms, so I had gotten permission to move off campus. I had to prove that I could finish school, even if I had to go hungry every day. I knew Raymond and Miss Pearl were just waiting to see me drop out. But something happened to me as I got more and more involved in the Movement. It no longer seemed important to prove anything. I had found something outside myself that gave meaning to my life.

I had become very friendly with my social science professor, John Salter, who was in charge of NAACP activities on campus. All during the year, while the NAACP conducted a boycott of the downtown stores in Jackson, I had been one of Salter's most faithful canvassers and church speakers. During this last week of school, he told me that sit-in demonstrations were about to start in

Jackson and that he wanted me to be the spokesman for a team that would sit-in at Woolworth's lunch counter. The two other demonstrators would be classmates of mine, Memphis and Pearlena. Pearlena was a dedicated NAACP worker, but Memphis had not been very involved in the Movement on campus. It seemed that the organization had had a rough time finding students who were in a position to go to jail. I had nothing to lose one way or the other. Around ten o'clock the morning of the demonstrations, NAACP headquarters alerted the news services. As a result, the police department was also informed, but neither the policemen nor the newsmen knew exactly where or when the demonstrations would start. They stationed themselves along Capitol Street and waited.

To divert attention from the sit-in at Woolworth's, the picketing started at J.C. Penney's a good fifteen minutes before. The pickets were allowed to walk up and down in front of the store three or four times before they were arrested. At exactly 11 A.M., Pearlena, Memphis, and I entered Woolworth's from the rear entrance. We separated as soon as we stepped into the store, and made small purchases from various counters. Pearlena had given Memphis her watch. He was to let us know when it was 11:14. At 11:14 we were to join him near the lunch counter and at exactly 11:15 we were to take seats at it.

Seconds before 11:15 we were occupying three seats at the previously segregated Woolworth's lunch counter. In the beginning the waitresses seemed to ignore us, as if they really didn't know what was going on. Our waitress walked past us a couple of times before she noticed we had started to write our own orders down and realized we wanted service. She asked us what we wanted. We began to read to her from our order slips. She told us that we would be served at the back counter, which was for Negroes.

"We would like to be served here," I said.

The waitress started to repeat what she had said, then stopped in the middle of the sentence. She turned the lights out behind the counter, and she and the other waitresses almost ran to the back of the store, deserting all their white customers. I guess they thought that violence would start immediately after the whites at the counter realized what was going on. There were five or six other people at the counter. A couple of them just got up and walked away. A girl sitting next to me finished her banana split before leaving. A middle-aged white woman who had not yet been served rose from her seat and came over to us. "I'll like to stay here with you," she said, "but my husband is waiting."

The newsmen came in just as she was leaving. They must have discovered what was going on shortly after some of the people began to leave the store. One of the newsmen ran behind the woman who spoke to us and asked her to identify herself. She refused to give her name, but said she was a native of Vicksburg and a former resident of California. When asked why she had said what she had said to us, she replied, "I am in sympathy with the Negro movement." By this time a crowd of cameramen and reporters had gathered around us taking pictures and asking questions, such as Where were we from? Why did we sit-in? What organization sponsored it? Were we students? From what school? How were we classified?

I told them that we were all students at Tougaloo College, that we were represented by no particular organization, and that we planned to stay there even after the store closed. "All we want is service," was my reply to one of them. After they had finished probing for about twenty minutes, they were almost ready to leave.

At noon, students from a nearby white high school started pouring in to Woolworth's. When they first saw us they were sort of surprised. They didn't know how to react. A few started to heckle and the newsmen became interested again. Then the white students started chanting all kinds of anti-Negro slogans. We were called a little bit of everything. The rest of the seats except the three we were occupying had been roped off to prevent others from sitting down. A couple of the boys took one end of the rope and made it into a hangman's noose. Several attempts were made to put it around our necks. The crowds grew as more students and adults came in for lunch.

We kept our eyes straight forward and did not look at the crowd except for occasional glances to see what was going on. All of a sudden I saw a face I remembered—the drunkard from the bus station sit-in. My eyes lingered on him just long enough for us to recognize each other. Today he was drunk too, so I don't think he remembered where he had seen me before. He took out a knife, opened it, put it in his pocket, and then began to pace the floor. At this point, I told Memphis and Pearlena what was going on. Memphis suggested that we pray. We bowed our heads, and all hell broke loose. A man rushed forward, threw Memphis from his seat, and slapped my face. Then another man who worked in the store threw me against an adjoining counter.

Down on my knees on the floor, I saw Memphis lying near the lunch counter with blood running out of the corners of his mouth. As he tried to protect his face, the man who'd thrown him down kept kicking him against the head. If he had worn hard-soled shoes instead of sneakers, the first kick probably would have killed Memphis. Finally, a man dressed in plain clothes identified himself as a police officer and arrested Memphis and his attacker.

Pearlena had been thrown to the floor. She and I got back on our stools after Memphis was arrested. There were some white Tougaloo teachers in the crowd. They asked Pearlena and me if we wanted to leave. They said that things were getting too rough. We didn't know what to do. While we were trying to make up our minds, we were joined by Joan Trumpauer. Now there were three of us and we were integrated. The crowd began to chant, "Communists, Communists, Communists." Some old man in the crowd ordered the students to take us off the stools.

"Which one should I get first?" a big husky boy said.

"That white nigger," the old man said.

The boy lifted Joan from the counter by her waist and carried her out of the store. Simultaneously, I was snatched from my stool by two high school students. I was dragged about thirty feet toward the door by my hair when someone made them turn me loose. As I was getting up off the floor, I saw Joan coming back inside. We started back to the center of the counter to join Pearlena. Lois Chaffee, a white Tougaloo faculty member, was now sitting next to her. So Joan and I just climbed across the rope at the front end of the counter and sat down. There were now four of us, two whites and two Negroes, all women. The mob started smearing us with ketchup, mustard, sugar, pies, and everything on the counter. Soon Joan and I were joined by John Salter, but the moment he sat down he was hit on the jaw with what appeared to be brass knuckles. Blood gushed from his face and someone threw salt into the open wound. Ed King, Tougaloo's chaplain, rushed to him.

At the other end of the counter, Lois and Pearlena were joined by George Raymond, a CORE field worker and a student from Jackson State College. Then a Negro high school boy sat down next to me. The mob took spray paint from the counter and sprayed it on the new demonstrators. The high school student had on a white shirt; the word "nigger" was written on his back with red spray paint.

We sat there for three hours taking a beating when the manager decided to close the store because the mob had begun to go wild with stuff from other counters. He begged and begged everyone to leave. But even after fifteen minutes of begging, no one budged. They would not leave until we did. Then Dr. Beittel, the president of Tougaloo College, came running in. He said he had just heard what was happening.

About ninety policemen were standing outside the store; they had been watching the whole thing through the windows, but had not come in to stop the mob or do anything. President Beittel went outside and asked Captain Ray to come and escort us out. The captain refused, stating the manager had to invite him in before he could enter the premises, so Dr. Beittel himself brought us out. He had told the police that they had better protect us after we were outside the store. When we got outside, the policemen formed a single line that blocked the mob from us. However, they were allowed to throw at us everything they had collected. Within ten minutes, we were picked up by Reverend King in his station wagon and taken to the NAACP headquarters on Lynch Street.

After the sit-in, all I could think of was how sick Mississippi whites were. They believed so much in the segregated Southern way of life, they would kill to preserve it. I sat there in the NAACP office and thought of how many times they had killed when this way of life was threatened. I knew that the killing had just begun. "Many more will die before it is over with," I thought. Before the sit-in, I had always hated the whites in Mississippi. Now I knew it was impossible for me to hate sickness. The whites had a disease, an incurable disease in its final stage. What were our chances against such a disease? I thought of the students, the young Negroes who had just begun to protest, as young interns. When these young interns got older, I thought, they would be the best doctors in the world for social problems.

Before we were taken back to campus, I wanted to get my hair washed. It was stiff with dried mustard, ketchup and sugar. I stopped in at a beauty shop across the street from the NAACP office. I didn't have on any shoes because I had lost them when I was dragged across the floor at Woolworth's. My stockings were sticking to my legs from the mustard that had dried on them. The hairdresser took one look at me and said, "My land, you were in the sit-in, huh?"

"Yes," I answered. "Do you have time to wash my hair and style it?"

"Right away," she said, and she meant right away. There were three other ladies already waiting, but they seemed glad to let me go ahead of them. The hairdresser was real nice. She even took my stockings off and washed my legs while my hair was drying.

There was a mass rally that night at the Pearl Street Church in Jackson, and the place was packed. People were standing two abreast in the aisles. Before the speakers began, all the sit-inners walked out on the stage and were introduced by Medgar Evers. People stood and applauded for what seemed like thirty minutes or more. Medgar told the audience that this was just the beginning of such demonstrations. He asked them to pledge themselves to unite in a massive offensive against segregation in Jackson, and throughout the state. The rally ended with "We Shall Overcome" and sent home hundreds of determined people. It seemed as though Mississippi Negroes were about to get together at last.

Before I demonstrated, I had written Mama. She wrote me back a letter, begging me not to take part in the sit-in. She even sent ten dollars for bus fare to New Orleans. I didn't have one penny, so I kept the money. Mama's letter made me mad. I had to live my life as I saw fit. I had made that decision when I left home. But it hurt to have my family prove to me how scared they were. It hurt me more than anything else—I knew the whites had already started the threats and intimidations. I was the first Negro from my hometown who had openly demonstrated, worked with the NAACP, or anything. When Negroes threatened to do anything in Centreville, they were either shot like Samuel O'Quinn or run out of town, like Reverend Dupree.

I didn't answer Mama's letter. Even if I had written one, she wouldn't have received it before she saw the news on TV or heard it on the radio. I waited to hear from her again. And I waited to hear in the news that someone in Centreville had been murdered. If so, I knew it would be a member of my family.

On Wednesday, the day after the sit-in, demonstrations got off to a good start. Ten people picketed shortly after noon on Capitol Street, and were arrested. Another mass rally followed the demonstrations that night, where a six-man delegation of Negro ministers was chosen to meet Mayor Thompson the following Tuesday. They were to present to him a number of demands on behalf of Jackson Negroes. They were as follows:

1. Hiring of Negro policemen and school crossing guards
2. Removal of segregation signs from public facilities
3. Improvement of job opportunities for Negroes on city payrolls—Negro drivers of city garbage trucks, etc.
4. Encouraging public eating establishments to serve both whites and Negroes
5. Integration of public parks and libraries

6. The naming of a Negro to the City Parks and Recreation Committee
7. Integration of public schools
8. Forcing service stations to integrate rest rooms. . . .

During this period, civil rights workers who had become known to the Jackson police were often used to divert the cops' attention just before a demonstration. A few cops were always placed across the street from NAACP headquarters, since most of the demonstrations were organized there and would leave from that building. The "diverters" would get into cars and lead the cops off on a wild-goose chase. This would allow the real demonstrators to get downtown before they were noticed. One evening, a group of us took the cops for a tour of the park. After giving the demonstrators time enough to get to Capitol Street, we decided to go and watch the action. When we arrived there ourselves, we met Reverend King and a group of ministers. They told us they were going to stage a pray-in on the post office steps. "Come on, join us," Reverend King said. "I don't think we'll be arrested, because it's federal property." . . .

We entered the post office through the side entrance. . . . There were fourteen of us, seven whites and seven Negroes. We walked out front and stood and bowed our heads as the ministers began to pray. We are immediately interrupted by the appearance of Captain Ray. "We are asking you people to disperse. If you don't, you are under arrest," he said.

Most of us were not prepared to go to jail. Doris Erskine, a student for Jackson State, and I had to take over a workshop the following day. Some of the ministers were in charge of the mass rally that night. But if we had dispersed, we would have been torn to bits by the mob. The whites standing out there had murder in their eyes. They were ready to do us in and all fourteen of us knew that. We had no other choice but to be arrested. . . .

When Doris and I got to the cell where we would spend the next four days, we found a lot of our friends there. There were twelve girls altogether. The jail was segregated. I felt sorry for

Jeanette King, Lois Chaffee, and Joan Trumpauer. Just because they were white they were missing out on all the fun we planned to have. Here we were going to school together, sleeping in the same dorm, worshipping together, playing together, even demonstrating together. It all ended in jail. They were rushed off by themselves to some cell designated for whites.

Our cell didn't even have a curtain over the shower. Every time the cops heard the water running, they came running to peep. After the first time, we fixed them. We took chewing gum and toilet tissue and covered the opening in the door. They were afraid to take it down. I guess they thought it might have come out in the newspaper. Their wives wouldn't have liked that at all. Peep through a hole to see a bunch of nigger girls naked? No! No! They certainly wouldn't have liked that. All of the girls in my cell were college students. We had a lot to talk about, so we didn't get too bored. We made cards out of toilet tissue and played Gin Rummy almost all day. Some of us even learned new dance steps from each other.

There were a couple of girls in with us from Jackson State College. They were scared they would be expelled from school. Jackson State, like most of the state-supported Negro schools, was an Uncle Tom school. The students could be expelled for almost anything. When I found this out, I really appreciated Tougaloo.

The day we were arrested one of the Negro trusties sneaked us a newspaper. We discovered that over four hundred high school students had also been arrested. We were so glad we sang freedom songs for an hour or so. The jailer threatened to put us in solitary if we didn't stop. At first we didn't think he meant it, so we kept singing. He came back with two other cops and asked us to follow them. They marched us down the hall and showed us one of the solitary chambers. "If you don't stop that damn singing, I'm gonna throw all of you in here together," said the jailer. After that we didn't sing any more. We went back and finished reading the paper.

We got out of jail on Sunday to discover that everyone was talking about the high school students. All four hundred who were arrested had been taken to the fairgrounds and placed in a large open compound without beds or anything. It was said that they were getting sick like flies. Mothers were begging to have their children released, but the NAACP didn't have enough money to bail them all out.

The same day we went to jail for the pray-in, the students at Lanier High School had started singing freedom songs on their lunch hour. They got so carried away they ignored the bell when the break was over and just kept on singing. The principal of the high school did not know what to do, so he called the police and told them that the students were about to start a riot.

When the cops came, they brought the dogs. The students refused to go back to their classrooms when asked, so the cops turned the dogs loose on them. The students fought them off for a while. In fact, I was told that mothers who lived near the school had joined the students in fighting off the dogs. They had begun to throw bricks, rocks, and bottles. The next day the papers stated that ten or more cops suffered cuts or minor wounds. The papers didn't say it, but a lot of students were hurt, too, from dog bites and lumps on the head from billy clubs. Finally, one hundred and fifty cops were rushed to the scene and several students and adults were arrested.

The next day four hundred of the high school students from Lanier, Jim Hill, and Brinkley High schools gathered in a church on Farish Street, ready to go to jail. Willie Ludden, the NAACP youth leader, and some of the SNCC and CORE workers met with them, gave a brief workshop on nonviolent protective measures and led them into the streets. After marching about two blocks they were met by helmeted police officers and ordered to disperse. When they refused, they were arrested, herded into paddy wagons, canvas-covered trucks, and garbage trucks. Those moving too slowly were jabbed with rifle butts. Police dogs were there, but were not used. From the way everyone was describing the scene it sounded like Nazi Germany instead of Jackson, USA.

On Monday, I joined a group of high school students and several other college students who were trying to get arrested. Our intention was to be put in the fairgrounds with the high school students already there. The cops picked us up, but they didn't want to put us so-called professional agitators in with the high school students. We were weeded out, and taken back to the city jail.

I got out of jail two days later and found I had gotten another letter from Mama. She had written it Wednesday the twenty-ninth, after the Woolworth sit-in. The reason it had taken so long for me to get it was that it came by way of New Orleans. Mama sent it to Adline and had Adline mail it to me. In the letter she told me that the sheriff had stopped by and asked all kinds of questions about me the morning after the sit-in. She said she and Raymond told them that I had only been home once since I was in college, that I had practically cut off all my family connections when I ran away from home as a senior in high school. She said he said that he knew I had left home. "He should know," I thought, "because I had to get him to move my clothes for me when I left." She went on and on. She told me he said I must never come back there. If so he would not be responsible for what happened to me. "The whites are pretty upset about her doing these things," he told her. Mama told me not to write her again until she sent me word that it was O.K. She said that I would hear from her through Adline.

I also got a letter from Adline in the same envelope. She told me what Mama hadn't mentioned—that Junior had been cornered by a group of white boys and was about to be lynched, when one of his friends came along in a car and rescued him. Besides that, a group of white men had gone out and beaten up my old Uncle Buck. Adline said Mama told her they couldn't sleep, for fear of night riders. They were all scared to death. My sister ended the letter by cursing me out. She said I was trying to get every Negro in Centreville murdered.

I guess Mama didn't tell me these things because she was scared to. She probably thought I would have tried to do something crazy. Something like trying to get the organizations to move into Wilkinson County, or maybe coming home myself to see if they would kill me. She never did give me credit for having the least bit of sense. I knew there was nothing I could do. No organization was about to go to Wilkinson County. It was a little too tough for any of them. And I wasn't about to go there either. If they said they would kill me, I figured I'd better take their word for it.

Betty Friedan

~

BETTY FRIEDAN (1921–), author, feminist, and a founder of the
National Organization for Women, wrote the book that launched
the second wave of American feminism. Here, she recalls her decision to write *The Feminine Mystique*, which was published in 1963.

~

My book grew out of a Smith alumnae questionnaire I was asked
to do for our fifteenth college reunion in 1957. I felt so guilty, somehow, that I hadn't done the big things everybody expected me to do
with my brilliant Smith education—giving up the fellowship in
psychology, getting fired from my newspaper job for being pregnant, writing too many mundane, inane women's magazine articles. It wasn't just a shame at not living up to others' expectations
of me. It was also, I now believe, an existential guilt, which I have
to this day when I'm just coasting and not using my powers to
meet serious new challenges.

The reason I agreed to do the questionnaire was because of a
widely debated book that had just come out, *Modern Women: The
Lost Sex*, by Marynia Farnham and Ferdinand Lundberg, two
Freudian psychoanalysts who said something was terribly wrong
with American women—they'd had too much education and it
was keeping them from "adjusting to their role as women." A noise
of diffuse angst, discontent, anger was coming out of those ideal

suburbs where between the hours of 9:00 A.M. and 5:00 P.M. nothing stirred over three feet tall. If American suburban housewives weren't "happy" taking care of their children and running appliances other women only dreamed of, their education must be the problem.

Now, that made me really angry. I bought all that Freudian stuff about the role of women, of course. After all, hadn't I given up my big psychology fellowship, my newspaper "career" to be fulfilled as a wife and mother myself? But the concept that educating women had negative consequences for themselves and their families was going too far. I *valued* my Smith education, valued it a lot, even though I felt guilty about not using it very well. I knew my Smith classmates were doing great things in their own communities, and having a great time, as I was, fixing up their houses, getting their kids educated, though most of their husbands' careers were probably grander than my husband's. Surely, education made us *better* wives and mothers, as Adlai Stevenson had said in his commencement address to the Smith class of 1955:

> Women, especially educated women, have a unique opportunity to influence us, man and boy . . . [yet] once immersed in the very pressing and particular problems of domesticity, many women feel frustrated and far apart from the great issues and stirring debate for which their education has given them understanding and relish. Once they wrote poetry. Now it's the laundry list. Once they discussed art and philosophy until late into the night. Now they are so tired they fall asleep as soon as the dishes are finished. . . . They had hoped to play their part in the crises of the age. But what they do is wash the dishes.
>
> The point is that whether we talk of Africa, Islam or Asia, women never had it so good as you. In short, far from the vocation of marriage and motherhood leading you away from the great issues of our day, it brings you back to their very center and places upon you an infinitely deeper and more intimate responsibility than that borne by the majority of those who hit the headlines and make the news and live in such a turmoil of great issues

that they end by being totally unable to distinguish what issues are really great.

[Woman's political mission] to inspire in her home a vision of the meaning of life and freedom . . . to help her husband find values that will give purpose to his specialized daily chores . . . to teach her children the uniqueness of each individual human being. . . . This assignment for you, as wives and mothers, you can do in the living room with a baby in your lap or in the kitchen with a can opener in your hand. . . . I think there is much you can do about our crises in the humble role of housewife. I would wish you no better vocation than that.

I decided to use that Smith questionnaire to write a major magazine article refuting *Modern Women: The Lost Sex* and proving education didn't make American women frustrated in their role as women. Why couldn't we appreciate our true political part in the "crises of the age" as wife and mother? I pitched the idea to *Mc-Call's,* and they wanted it.

I spent an inordinate amount of time on that questionnaire. I asked two friends of mine, Mario Ingersoll Howell and Anne Mather Montero, to work on it with me. So Mario and Anne came out to Rockland County once and we met several times in the city and dreamed up open-ended questions as well as the usual ones. I realized later that we were putting into words questions that we had not asked ourselves out loud before. We included the following in our list of questions:

About "Your Marriage" we asked: Is your marriage truly satisfying? How does it compare with your expectation of marriage? How does it change with the years? To what extent do you talk to your husband about your deepest feelings? Do you believe the same things are important? How do you make major decisions (together, or which his, which yours)?

About "Your Sex Life": Is your sex life less important than it used to be? Getting better and better? At 35–37, do you feel almost over and done with sexuality? Or just beginning to feel the satisfaction of being a woman?

About "Your Children": Did you plan your children's births? Did you enjoy pregnancy? Were you depressed after birth? Did you fear childbirth? Exult in it? Take it in your stride? Did you breast-feed? How long? Did you try? Do, or did, you have problems with: Eating? Toilet training? Discipline? Do you have fun with your children? As a mother, do you usually feel: Harassed? Martyred? Contented? Do you try hard to be a good mother? Or just let it work itself out? Do you feel you are a good mother? Or guilty that you aren't?

About "Your Home": Does your home reflect your taste, your husband's, or what? How much time do you spend on housework? What major household appliances do you have? Do you put the milk bottle on the table? Use paper napkins? Are you a good cook? What part of housekeeping do you enjoy? Detest? Does your husband complain about your housekeeping? What does he do around the house? How is your home different from your home as a child?

About "Your Finances": Who manages the family finances, you or your husband? Do you worry about money? Live above your income?

About "The Other Part of Your Life": Did you have career ambitions? What? Are you pursuing it actively? Have you given it up? Or postponed until kids are older? If you work, is it mainly for the money? Or because you want to? Or both? What does it cost you to work? What is your arrangement for children and house while you work? Do you feel guilty about leaving the children? If you don't work, is it: From preference? Not qualified? Would feel guilty about kids? . . . If your main occupation is homemaker, do you find it totally fulfilling? Are you frustrated? Have you managed to find a satisfying interest outside your home? Do you find volunteer work as satisfying as professional? Please describe any "professional" volunteer work—over and above routine or occasional volunteer tasks.

We asked about "Your Intellectual Life": How many books have you read in the last year? Do you read a newspaper every day? What television programs do you watch regularly?

About "Your Political Life": Do you vote: Regularly? Occasionally? Straight Republican? . . . Democrat? Or cross party lines? Do you take any active part in party politics? Are your politics the same as your husband's? Have you ever taken a public stand or done anything about a controversial issue or unpopular cause in your community?

We asked about "Your Religious Life": Which church? How often do you go? Do you believe in a personal God? Or in religion as a system of human values and social ethics? Or does religion have no place in your life at all?

We asked about "Your Social Life": How do you spend most of your evenings during the week? Weekends? How much time do you spend alone? Enough? Do you feel your life is too fragmented? Do you feel that in most social situations you or others "never really say anything" except empty chitchat? Or is there real communication? Are there things you do because everybody else where you live does them, that do not reflect your own individual values? What do you do—little or big—because you or your family want to, that is *not* exactly "the thing to do" in your community?

And, finally, we asked about "You, Personal": How has your appearance changed? Clothes less important to you? More? Have you had psychotherapy? Your husband, or children? Do you feel you need it? In what ways have you changed inside, as a person, since college? What difficulties have you found in working out your role as a woman? What are the chief satisfactions of your life today? The chief frustrations? What do you think of as the best time in your life? How do you visualize your life after your children are grown? Are you doing anything about that now? What? Do you hate getting older?

We sent out the questionnaires and received two hundred responses. When the results were tabulated, I realized they raised more questions than they answered. The ones who seemed to value their education the most, who seemed the most zestful and healthy about their lives, were the ones who didn't *exactly* conform to "the role of women" in the sense that it was then being defined—wife, mother, housewife, living through husbands, children, home and so on. The ones who really seemed to be doing only that were either depressed or outright frustrated. But the ones with many other interests and activities—like the kind I couldn't quite stop doing myself—seemed to be *enjoying* their children, their homes, their marriages more. Maybe it wasn't education that was the problem, keeping American women from "adjusting to their role as women," but that narrow definition of "the role of women."

And, for sure, the noises then coming out from those idyllic suburbs belied the image of the happy, happy suburban housewife. The "woman problem," it was now being called. There were strange, undiagnosed diseases that sent those women to doctors, who somehow couldn't find a cause or cure for their "chronic fatigue syndromes."

When we went to the Smith reunion in June 1957 to report on our questionnaire, for the first time since we'd graduated I didn't feel uneasy with my former college classmates. They had expected such great things of me, looked up to me so, and here I was, "just a housewife" as almost all of them were now. But I was onto something, something I already sensed might be important.

That feeling was underscored when Eli Chinoy, professor of sociology at Smith, got in touch with me before the reunion and asked to see the questionnaire and its results. He also thought it might be important. . . .

The night after we presented our questionnaire results, to the great interest of the Smith class of '42, in our late thirties now, almost all of us married, mothers, housewives—and serious community leaders—and a few of us, despite everything, doing professional work, we got back late from drinks at Wiggins Tavern and found Hubbard House, where we were staying, locked. Did Smith still have a curfew? A few graduating seniors were also locked out and joined us, waiting for the janitor to come to the rescue. I started talking to those lovely young graduates. "What are the courses you get excited about now?" I asked them, remembering how in the heady intellectual excitement of my days at Smith, we would linger outside Hans Kohn's history class, or Otto Kraushaar's philosophy class, or Kutschnig's on government, arguing about communism, fascism, democracy, war and peace, capitalism and workers' exploitation, and the future. What were students arguing about in 1957? And those young women, in their white dresses and black robes—who had walked with their red roses through the ivy chain as we had not, in the foregone Ivy Day of World War II—looked at us as if we were aliens from another plant.

"We don't get excited about things like that," one explained. "I'm going to get married right after graduation. I spend every weekend with my fiancé. What I'm interested in is where we're going to live and his career. I want to have four children, and live somewhere where I can spend a lot of time ice-skating with them." Try as we might, we, who were reveling in being together again, in the college where we had acquired our taste for a life of the mind and a passionate commitment to politics, a sense of personal responsibility for our society, for making it better, and had gotten an authentic taste of what that might be like, running the student government, the college paper—try as we might, we couldn't get these fifties seniors to admit they had become interested in *anything*, at that great college, except their future husbands and children and suburban homes.

I sensed something strange going on here, juxtaposing these young ones' carefully *limited* dreams with the results of my own class's questionnaire. I didn't think Smith education could have deteriorated that much; a lot of the faculty that had inspired me was still there. And Eli and Helen and their friend Peter Rose were obviously superbly qualified in their own fields, inspiring teachers. It was as if something was making these girls defensive, inoculating them against the larger interests, dreams and passions really good higher education can lead to. Did lead to, with me and my classmates, even if we felt we weren't doing justice to it, living up to it, in our current suburban life. It was as if these young women weren't going to let themselves have those larger passions and trained abilities that might indeed be frustrated by suburban housewife life.

And so I went home and wrote my article for *McCall's*—"Are Women Wasting Their Time in College?"—suggesting maybe it wasn't higher education making American women frustrated in their role as women, but the current definition of the role of women. *McCall's* turned it down. (I learned later that the male editor of *McCall's* had been "shocked" at that article, though the women subeditors had tried to get it in. I'd never had that experience before.) Then the *Ladies' Home Journal* rewrote it to say the opposite of what I'd found, and I took the article back. I wouldn't let them mess with my findings that way. I'd never done that before either. And then Bob Stein at *Redbook* wrote my agent: "Betty has always done good work for us before. But she must be going off her rocker. Only the most neurotic housewife will identify with this."

Each time my article got turned down, I'd do more interviews. I interviewed doctors and counselors and did group interviews among my own suburban neighbors in Rockland County, in Westchester. And increasingly, I knew it wasn't just overeducated Smith graduates I was writing about.

It was on an April morning in 1959 that I listened to a mother of four, having coffee with four other mothers in a suburban development fifteen miles from New York, say in a tone of quiet desperation "'the problem.'" And suddenly I sensed that they all seemed to share the same problem. "I'm Jim's wife, and Janey's mother, a putter on of diapers and snowsuits, a server of meals, a Little League chauffeur. But who am I, as a person myself? It's like the world is going on without me." And I identified what I later called "the problem that has no name."

Women were being blamed for all kinds of "problems" then—their children's bedwetting, their husbands' ulcers, not cleaning the kitchen sink white enough, not pressing their husbands' shirts smooth enough, their own lack of orgasm. But the "problem" they kept bringing up and others always recognized had nothing to do with children, marriage, home, sex. And there was no name for it, in all the words being written by the experts, telling women how to catch a man and keep him, how to breastfeed children and han-

dle their toilet training, how to cope with sibling rivalry and ado-
lescent rebellion; how to buy a dishwasher, bake bread, cook gour-
met snails, and build a swimming pool, how to dress, look, and act
more feminine and make marriage more exciting. Truly feminine
women did not want careers, graduate degrees, political rights.
Educated, middle-class women were being taught to pity the neurotic, unfeminine, unhappy women who wanted to be poets or
physicists or presidents.

"If a woman had a problem in the 1950s and 1960s, she knew
that something must be wrong with her marriage, or with herself,"
I had written in the magazine article. "What kind of a woman was
she if she did not feel mysterious fulfillment waxing the kitchen
floor? She was so ashamed to admit her dissatisfaction that she
never knew how many women shared it."

On a bus, taking my kids into the city to go to the dentist, I
opened a letter from Marie Rodell, about yet another editor turning down my article, and I knew that editor was wrong. All those
editors were wrong. I'd wasted nearly a whole year on this article.
But I knew now I was really onto something. I also realized, suddenly, why all the editors had turned it down, why it never would
get printed in one of those big women's magazines. It wouldn't, because what I was finding out, from answers to the questionnaire—
from new interviews with my own suburban neighbors and other
real suburban housewives—and what I'd started to write in my article somehow threatened the firmament they stood on, the very
world the magazines were defining for women, the whole amor-
phous, vague, invisible miasma around "the role of women," "feminine fulfillment" as it was then defined by men and psychological
followers of Freud, and taken for granted by everyone as true.
Maybe it wasn't as true as it seemed. I hadn't yet called it "the feminine mystique," but, taking my kids to the dentist that day, I
stopped at a pay phone and called my agent and told her not to
send that article to any more magazines. I was going to write it as
a book.

Jessie Lopez De La Cruz

~

JESSIE LOPEZ DE LA CRUZ (1919–   ), a union organizer for United Farmworkers and a founder of National Land for People, joined Cesar Chavez in the effort to unionize migrant farm workers in the 1960s. In this oral history conducted by Ellen Cantarow, Jessie Lopez De La Cruz recalls the events of that decade.

~

[I]n one camp we were living at, the camp was at the edge of a cotton patch and the cotton needed to be thinned. We would start early. It was May. It got so hot, we would start around 6:30 A.M. and work for four or five hours, then walk home and eat and rest until about three-thirty in the afternoon when it cooled off. We would go back and work until we couldn't see. Then we'd get home and rest, visit, talk. Then I'd clean up the kitchen. I was doing the housework and working out in the fields and taking care of the kids. I had two children by this time.

Other times we would pick grapes. The sand is very hot. It gets up to about a hundred-eight, a hundred-ten degrees during the summer out in the fields. We wore tennis shoes to protect our feet from the hot sand. I'd get a pan and put it under the vine and cut the grapes. The grower wanted us to cut them, not pull them. You had to hold the grape bunches gently—not to crush the grapes—

Cantarow, Ellen, with Susan Gushee O'Malley and Sharon Hartman Strom. *Moving the Mountain: Women Working for Social Change.* New York: The Feminist Press at the City University of New York, 1980, pp. 119–121, 134–136, 138–145. Excerpts from *Moving the Mountain: Women Working for Social Change,* copyright © 1980 by Ellen Cantarow and the Feminist Press at the City University of New York.

in your hand, and you'd have to use your knife to cut off from the stem and place the grapes in a pan. After that pan was full, you would spread these grapes in a paper tray where the sun was shining. But I was using my knife this way, and kept on cutting and cutting toward me, and these knives have a hook on them, and the handle is kind of rounded. One day I came to a real hard one. The stem was drying so I had to use a lot of strength, and this knife gave me a big cut on my neck. It scared me! [My husband,] Arnold, said to just sit down and stay there. He washed the blood off. That was my first experience working out in the field after I married. . . .

Out in the fields there were never any restrooms. We had to go eight or ten hours without relief. If there wasn't brush or a little ditch, we were forced to wait until we got home! Just the women. The men didn't need to pull their clothes down. Later, when I worked for the Farmworkers, in a hearing I said, "I was working for Russell Giffen, the biggest grower in Huron. These big growers have a lot of money because we earned all that money for them. Because of our sweat and our labor that we put on the land. What they do instead of supplying restrooms and clean water where we can wash our hands, is put posts on the ground with a piece of gunny sack wound around them." That's where we went. And that things was moved along with us. It was just four stakes stuck in the ground, and then there was canvas or a piece of gunny sack around it. You would be working, and this restroom would be right there. The canvas didn't come up high enough in front for privacy. We made it a practice to go two at a time. One would stand outdoors and watch outside that nobody came along. And then the other would do the same for the one inside. Then we'd go back to work. . . .

[L]ate one night in 1962, there was a knock at the door and there were three men. One of them was Cesar Chavez. And the next thing I knew, they were sitting around our table talking about a union. I made coffee. Arnold had already told me about a union for the farmworkers. He was attending their meetings in Fresno, but I didn't. I'd either stay home or stay outside in the car. But then Cesar said, "The women have to be involved. They're the ones working out in the fields with their husbands. If you can take the women out to the fields, you can certainly take them to meetings." So I sat up straight and said to myself, "*That's* what I want!"

When I became involved with the union, I felt I had to get other women involved. Women have been behind men all the time, always. Just waiting to see what the men decide to do, and tell us what to do. In my sister-in-law and brother-in-law's families, the women do a lot of shouting and cussing and they get slapped around. But that's not standing up for what you believe in. It's just trying to boss and not knowing how. I'd hear them scolding their kids and fighting their husbands and I'd say, "Gosh! Why don't you go after the people that have you living like this? Why don't you go after the growers that have you tired from working out in the fields at low wages and keep us poor all the time? Let's go after them! *They're* the cause of our misery!" Then I would say we had to take part in the things going on around us. "Women can no longer be taken for granted—that we're just going to stay home and do the cooking and cleaning. It's way past the time when our husbands could say, 'You stay home! You have to take care of the children! You have to do as I say!'"

Then some women I spoke to started attending the union meetings, and later they were out on the picket lines.

I think I was made an organizer because in the first place I could relate to the farmworkers, being a lifelong farmworker. I was well-known in the small towns around Fresno. Wherever I went to speak to them, they listened. I told them about how we were excluded from the NLRB [National Labor Relations Board] in 1935, how we had no benefits, no minimum wage, nothing out in the fields—no restrooms, nothing. I would talk about how we were paid what the grower wanted to pay us, and how we couldn't set a price on our work. I explained that we could do something about these things by joining a union, by working together. I'd ask people how they felt about these many years they had been working out in the fields, how they had been treated. And then we'd all talk about it. They would say, "I was working for so-and-so, and when I complained about something that happened there, I was fired." I said, "Well! Do you think we should be putting up with this in this modern age? You know, we're not back in the twenties. We can stand up! We can talk back! It's not like when I was a little kid and my grandmother used to say, 'You have to especially respect the Anglos,' 'Yessir,' 'Yes, Ma'am!' That's over. This country is very rich, and we want a share of the money these growers make of our sweat and our work by exploiting us and our children!" I'd have my sign-up book and I'd say, "If anyone wants to become a member of the union, I can make you a member right now." And they'd agree!

So I found out that I could organize them and make members of them. Then I offered to help them, like taking them to the doctor's and translating for them, filling out papers that they needed to fill out, writing their letters for those that couldn't write. A lot of people confided in me. Through the letter-writing, I knew a lot of the problems they were having back home, and they knew they could trust me, that I wouldn't tell anyone else about what I had written or read. So that's why they came to me. . . .

It was very hard being a woman organizer. Many of our people my age and older were raised with the old customs in Mexico: where the husband rules, he is king of his house. The wife obeys, and the children, too. So when we first started it was very, very hard. Men gave us the most trouble—neighbors there in Parlier! They were for the union but they were not taking orders from women, they said. . . .

[Picketing] at White River Farms one morning very early, we were out there by the hundreds by the road, and [scabs] got down and started working out there in the grapes. We were asking them not to work, telling them that there was a strike going on. The grower had two guards at the entrance, and there was a helicopter above us. At other White River Farm ranches they had the sheriff, the county police, *everybody*. But there were pickets at three different ranches, and where we were picketing there wasn't anybody except these two guards. So I said, "Hey! What about the women getting together and let's rush 'em!" And they said, "Do you think we could do that?" And I said, "Of course we can! Let's go in there. Let's get 'em out of there any way we can." So about fifty of us rushed. We went under the vines. We had our banners, and you could see them bobbing up and down, up and down, and we'd go under those rows on our knees and roll over. When the scabs saw us coming they took off. All of them went and they got on the bus. The guards had guns that they would shoot, and something black like smoke or teargas would come out. That scared us, but we still kept on. After we saw all those workers get back on the buses, we went back. Instead of running this time, we rolled over and over all the way out. The vines are about four feet tall, and they have wire where you string up the vines. So you can't walk or run across one of these fences. You have to keep going under these wires. So I tripped, and rolled down about three or four rows before I got up. I rolled so they wouldn't get at me when they were shooting. When I got out there on the road they were getting these big, hard dirty clods and throwing them at us. And then the pickets started doing the same thing. When the first police car came, somebody broke the windshield. We don't know if it was the scabs or someone on the picket lines, but the picketers were blamed.

When we women ran into the fields, we knew we'd be arrested if they caught us. But we went in and we told the scabs, "If you're not coming out we're gonna pull you out!" Later I told Arnold, "See? See what women can do? We got all those men out there to come out!"

At another place, in Kern County, we were sprayed with pesticides. They would come out there with their sprayers and spray us on the picket lines. They have these big tanks that are pulled by a tractor with hoses attached, and they spray the trees with this. They are strong like a water hose, but wider. They get it started and spray the vines and the trees. When we were picketing, they came out there to spray the pickets. What could we do? We tried to get as far away as we could, and then we would come back. . . .

While I was working for the union, I learned about negotiating for a contract. In 1966, when we were negotiating for a contract with Christian Brothers, Delores Huerta [founder of United Farmworkers] asked me along. "I want you to learn this because eventually you might have to take over the negotiating of the contracts." I'd sit there at those meetings with the Christian Brothers, who were Catholic priests. Dolores and the ranch committee would argue, "You can't say we're asking for too much money, because just think, you have over fifty varieties of fine grapes that go into making the most expensive wines for the church and they sell at very high prices. So why can't these workers share some of the money that comes out of those grapes that they've harvested?" They would bargain back and forth this way. Then the ranch committee would caucus—we would walk out of that meeting room, and we'd drink water and discuss what we were going to say when we went back. We'd say, "They have to meet our demands." We were asking for protective clothing; that they supply the pans we picked the grapes in. We also asked for a smoke device for the tractors. We were on our knees working beside the tractors and we would feel dizzy, smelling all of the smoke from the exhaust pipe for hours. We also didn't have any water on the tractors. To get water we had to go with the tractor driver to where the water was, and then we'd lose time picking and lose money. We demanded that they supply each crew with a can of drinking water, so we could drink water right there when we were thirsty.

Our demands were met, but it was hard bargaining. At one point, one of the Christian Brothers' lawyers said, "Well, sister, it sounds to me like you're asking for the moon for these people." Dolores came back, "Brother, I'm not asking for the moon for the farmworkers. All we want is just a little ray of sunshine for them!" Oh, that sounded beautiful! . . .

The second year we had a contract I started working for Christian Brothers. The men were doing the pruning on the grape vines. After they did the pruning, the women's crew would come and tie the vines—that was something we got changed. We made them give pruning jobs to women.

I was made a steward on the women's crew. If there were any grievances, it was up to me to listen and then enforce the contract. For example, the first time we were paid when I started working, during the break the supervisor would come out there with our checks. It was our fifteen-minute break, which the contract gave us the right to. He always came then! We had to walk to the other end of the row, it took us about five minutes to get there, the rest of the fifteen to get our checks, and walk back, and we'd start working. This happened twice. The third time I said, "We're not going to go after our checks this time. They always come during our break and we don't get to rest." So when we saw the pickup coming with the men who had the checks I said, "Nobody move. You just sit here." I walked over to the pickup. I said to the man inside, "Mr. Rager, these women refuse to come out here on their break time. It's their time to rest. So we're asking you, if you must come during our rest period, you take the checks to these ladies." From that day on, every payday he would come to us. That was the sort of thing you had to do to enforce the contract.

I became involved in many of the activities in the community—school board meetings, city council meetings, everything that I could get into. For example, I began fighting for bilingual education in Parlier, went to a lot of meetings about it and spoke about it.

You see, when I was a nine-year-old child going to school, I couldn't speak English. I remember vividly one day all the children, mostly Chicanos, were lined up, and we had to stand before this lady all dressed in white, a health nurse. She told me to open my mouth and I just stared a her. She stuck a stick to push my tongue down, and I couldn't help it; I vomited all over her dress. Oh! I started crying, and the teacher came up and she kept saying, "I'm sorry. I'm sorry." Those words stuck to me; I even dreamed them.

Another time something else happened when I ran out of underwear! See, we were very poor, and when I ran out of underwear, grandmother tore open a pillow and used the red satin to make some drawers for me. I was ashamed; I didn't want nobody to see me. I was dressed very different from all the other children in the first place. My dresses were almost down to my ankles and they were gathered in the waist with a drawstring that my grandmother made me, and high boy's shoes and heavy black stockings.

When I got the red underwear, I was out there after school like a little monkey up on the swings and two Anglo girls about my age started teasing me: "Oh, she's got red panties! red panties!" and they tried to lift my dress up. By this time, I was off the swings and standing against the wall. When one of the older girls leaned over to pull my dress up, I lifted my knee and hit her nose and she started bleeding and crying. The teacher came over and she slapped me. But since I didn't know English, *I couldn't tell her, I couldn't explain what had happened.*

To top it off, being a migrant worker I changed schools about every three to four weeks. As soon as one crop was picked, we went on to the next one. I'd go to school for about a week or two, then I was transferred. Every time we transferred I had a pain in my stomach, I was shaking, scared to go to school.

This is why I began fighting for bilingual education. I didn't want what happened to me to happen to the little children in Parlier whose parents couldn't speak English.

Parlier is over eighty-five percent Chicano, yet during that time there were no Chicanos on the school board, on the police force, nowhere. Now it's changed; we fought to get a Chicano mayor and officials. . . .

Fresno County didn't give food stamps to the people—only surplus food. There were no vegetables, no meat, just staples like whole powdered milk, cheese, butter. At the migrant camp in Parlier, the people were there a month and a half before work started, and since they'd borrowed money to get to California, they didn't have any food. I'd drive them into Fresno to the welfare department and translate for them, and they'd get food, but half of it they didn't eat. We heard about other counties where they had food stamps to go to the store and buy meat and milk and fresh vegetables for the children. So we began talking about getting that in Fresno. Finally, we had Senate hearings at the Convention Center in Fresno. There were hundreds of people listening. A man I know comes to me and says, "Jessie, you're next." He'd been going to speak, but he said we wanted me to speak in his place. I started in Spanish, and the senators were looking at each other, you know, saying, "What's going on?" So then I said, "Now, for the benefit of those who can't speak Spanish, I'll translate. They tell us there's no money for food stamps for poor people. But if there is money enough to fight a war in Vietnam, and if there is money enough for Governor Reagan's wife to buy a three-thousand-dollar dress for the Inauguration Ball, there should be money enough to feed these people. The nutrition experts say surplus food is full of vitamins. I've taken a look at that food, this cornmeal, and I've seen them come up and down. But you know, we don't call them vitamins, we call them weevils!" Everybody began laughing and whistling and shouting. In the end, we finally got food stamps for the people in Fresno County.

Sometimes I'd just stop to think: what if our parents had done what we were doing now? My grandparents were poor. They were humble. They never learned to speak English. They felt God meant them to be poor. It was against their religion to fight. I remember there was a huge policeman named Marcos, when I was a child, who used to go around on a horse. My grandmother would say, "Here comes Marcos," and we just grew up thinking, "He's law and order." But during the strikes I stood up to them. They'd come up to arrest me and I'd say, "O.K., here I come if you want. Arrest me!"

"Jane"

⌒

"JANE" (1969–1973), the code name for the Abortion Counseling Service of Women's Liberation, was an underground group in Chicago. Women seeking abortions would call the current contact, always named "Jane," for a referral to an abortion provider. Eventually, the group's members began performing the abortions themselves. Jane disbanded in 1973, when the Supreme Court decision in *Roe v. Wade* legalized abortion. It is estimated that Jane's approximately 100 members performed about 11,000 abortions without any fatalities. Here, a member of Jane, under the pseudonym Laura Kaplan, tells her story.

⌒

During the four years before the Supreme Court's 1973 *Roe v. Wade* decision legalized abortion, thousands of women called Jane. Jane was the contact name for a group in Chicago officially known as The Abortion Counseling Service of Women's Liberation. Every week desperate women of every class, race and ethnicity telephoned Jane. They were women whose husbands or boyfriends forbade them to use contraceptives; women who had conceived on every method of contraception; women who had not used contraceptives. They were older women who thought they were no longer fertile; young girls who did not understand their reproductive physiology. They

Kaplan, Laura. *The Story of Jane: The Legendary Underground Feminist Abortion Service*. New York: Pantheon Books, 1995, pp. ix–xx. Excerpt from *The Story of Jane* by Laura Kaplan, copyright © 1995 by Laura Kaplan. Reprinted by permission of Pantheon Books, a division of Random House, Inc.

were women who could not care for a child and women who did not want a child. Some women agonized over the decision, while others had no doubts. Each one was making the best decision about motherhood that she could make at the time.

Organized in 1969, Jane initially counseled women and referred them to the underground for abortions. Other groups offering the same kind of crucial help took shape at this time throughout the country. But Jane evolved in a unique way. At first the women in Jane concentrated on screening abortionists, attempting to determine which ones were competent and reliable. But they quickly realized that as long as women were dependent on illegal practitioners, they would be virtually helpless. Jane determined to take control of the abortion process so that the women who turned to Jane could have control as well. Eventually, the group found a doctor who was willing to work closely with them. When they discovered that he was not, as he had claimed to be, a physician, the women in Jane took a bold step: "If he can do it, then we can do it, too." Soon Jane members learned from him the technical skills necessary to perform abortions.

As members of the women's liberation movement, the women in Jane viewed reproductive control as fundamental to womens' freedom. The power to act had to be in the hands of each woman. Her decision about an abortion needed to be underscored as an active choice about her life. And, since Jane wanted every woman to understand that in seeking an abortion she was taking control of her life, she had to feel in control of her abortion. Group members realized that the only way she could control her abortion was if they, Jane, controlled the entire process. This group concluded that women who cared about abortion should be the ones performing abortions.

None of the women who started Jane ever expected to perform abortions. What they intended was to meet what one member called "a crying need." That need gradually led them to radical actions. Their work was not based on a medical model, but on how they themselves wanted to be treated. When a woman came to Jane for an abortion, the experience she had was markedly different from what she encountered in standard medical settings. She was included. She was in control. Rather than being a passive recipient, a patient, she was expected to participate. Jane said, "We don't do this to you, but with you." By letting each woman know before-hand what to expect during the abortion and the recovery stage, and then talking with her step by step through the abortion itself, group members attempted to give each woman a sense of her own personal power in a situation in which most women felt powerless. Jane tried to create an environment in which women could take back their bodies, and by doing so, take back their lives. When I joined Jane, the group had managed to give women not only psy-chological control, but also freedom from the financial extortion that illegal abortionists subjected them to. Jane charged only the amount necessary to cover medical supplies and administrative expenses. And no woman was turned away because of her inabil-ity to pay.

Whenever individuals gain access to the tools and skills to affect the conditions of their own lives, they define empowerment. Our ac-tions, which we saw as potentially transforming for other women, changed us, too. By taking responsibility, we became responsible. Most of us grew stronger, more self-assured, confident in our own abilities. In picking up the tools of our own liberation, in our case medical instruments, we broke a powerful taboo. That act was ter-rifying, but it was also exhilarating. We ourselves felt exactly the same powerfulness that we wanted other women to feel. We came to understand that society's problems stemmed from imbalances in power, the power of one person over another, teacher over student, doctor over patient. The weight of the authority and the expert was inherent in the position, no matter who held it. Jane, through the group's practice, challenged institutionalized authority and tried to redress these imbalances of power.

But the politics of power, which we recognized so clearly in the larger society, were ironically mirrored in our own internal dynamics. While Jane succeeded in giving control to the women in need of abortions, the group was not as successful in sharing control among its own members. A hierarchy of knowledge developed—knowledge of medical technique, of crucial problems and critical decisions. Those who withheld the knowledge frequently justified their actions by citing the need for secrecy to protect the group from exposure. This was a valid argument in an era in which simply providing information about abortion was a criminal act. But necessary caution was not the only explanation. We discovered how difficult it was to resist reproducing those ordering structures which shape our society, even as we challenged many of their manifestations. Sometimes it seemed that our determination to empower the individual could find consistent expression only in our interactions with the women who turned to us for help. To them, we gave as much information as we could uncover about the workings of their bodies and what they could do to foster their own health.

Jane developed at a time when blind obedience to medical authority was the rule. There were no patient advocates or hospital ombudsmen, no such person as a health consumer. Few women understood their reproductive physiology or had any idea where to get the information they needed. The special knowledge doctors had was deliberately made inaccessible, couched in language incomprehensible to the lay person. We did not have a right to it.

It was only in late 1970 that *Our Bodies, Ourselves*, the first in a wave of self-help books, was published. Now many of us know that we can get the medical information we need in a library or bookstore, but this was unheard of twenty-five years ago. Still, finding health care that is not only adequate and affordable, but also respectful, is, for most of us, a continuing struggle.

In the late 1960s others outside the womens' liberation movement were working to change abortion laws. There were legal scholars and organizations like the Association for the Study of Abortion in New York; population control groups like ZPG (Zero Population Growth), and NARAL (then, The National Association for Repeal of Abortion Laws) that supported legislative change and challenged the constitutionality of laws in the courts. They directed their efforts at the established channels of institutionalized authority, but their gains were only modest until the women's liberation movement mobilized women across the country who accelerated the struggle with their anger.

Women's liberation groups organized speak-outs at which women testified to their own illegal abortions. They marched and demonstrated and disrupted legislative hearings on abortion that excluded women. They demanded that women, the true experts on abortion, be heard and recognized. They brought abortion out of the closet, where it had been shrouded in secrecy and shame.

But the women's liberation movement did more than place abortion in the realm of public discourse. It framed the issue, not in terms of privacy in sexual relations, and not in the neutral language of choice, but in terms of a woman's freedom to determine her own destiny as she defined it, not as others defined it. Abortion was a touchstone. If she did not have the right to control her own body, which included freedom from forced sterilizations and unnecessary hysterectomies, gains in other arenas were meaningless. These issues were addressed not only in political terms, but also in moral terms. To force a woman either to carry an unwanted pregnancy or to venture into a dangerous underground was considered morally indefensible. Women were dying because they were denied the ability to act on their own moral decisions.

While the public struggle was underway, every day women who tried to find abortions put their lives at risk. Their suffering could not be ignored. Women's groups and networks of the clergy organized to meet these women's immediate needs. Based on a moral imperative, Howard Moody, a Baptist minister, founded the first clergy group, the New York Clergy Consultation Service on Abortion. He encouraged clergymen throughout the country to set up similar networks to help women get safe abortions. These clergy groups, with the moral standing of organized religion, played a public role, announcing their work in the newspapers, framing the issue in moral terms and advocating for legislative change.

Both the clergy and women's liberation groups sought out competent abortionists, negotiated the price, raised money to pay for abortions and counseled thousands of distraught women. Not only did they help women but, by breaking the law, they also undermined it. They followed the tradition of the Underground Railroad which defied another immoral law, the Fugitive Slave Act, and helped to undermine the institution of chattel slavery. Like the scores of people who were part of the Underground Railroad, the stories of those who participated in these referral services are part of our hidden history. . . .

A few years ago I was asked to speak to a class of first-year teachers in a Master's of Education program. The professor hoped that Jane's example would help her students understand empowerment. After my talk we broke into discussion groups. I tried to describe to these young teachers the position women were in before the women's movement. The message that women received was that they were less intelligent, less capable, less valuable than men. They weren't the heroes. They were the ones rescued by heroes. The issues that directly affected women's lives were rarely framed by them, but rather by institutions and authorities dominated by men, such as legislatures and the church.

A young man in the group asked, seemingly astonished, "You mean the women's movement was about options for women and not about women becoming lawyers?"

I thought, is that what the younger generation thinks? . . .

For those of us who came of age in the 1960s, the arguments for our sexual freedom are still fresh. For those born after that time it may all seem like ancient history. But it was not until 1965 that the Supreme Court guaranteed even the right to acquire contraceptives, and then for married people only. Before that some states still had laws, stemming from Anthony Comstock's nineteenth-century "moral purity" campaign, prohibiting the sale and distribution of contraceptives. Not until 1972, less than a year before its decision in *Roe v. Wade*, did the Supreme Court in *Eisenstadt v. Baird* extend the right to contraception to single people. Before that, access to contraceptives for unmarried people varied from place to place, doctor to doctor. Some women bought cheap wedding rings at the Five and Dime to convince physicians that they were married. One woman I know went to her doctor for contraceptives just before her wedding. He told her to come back after the honeymoon.

For young women in the 1960s control of our bodies and control of our sexuality were central concerns. It was at a time when segments of society were breaking out of the cultural and political repression of the 1950s. The civil rights movement, the student and antiwar movements, challenged accepted norms and authority. Out of those upheavals the modern women's movement was born.

When I moved back to Chicago in 1971, two years after graduating from college, I knew I wanted to participate in the women's liberation movement, but abortion was not my primary interest. I had just moved from New York state which had, in 1970, enacted the most liberal abortion reform in the country, a law that legalized abortions by physicians up to twenty-four weeks of pregnancy. The legislative victory was high drama. Just as the vote tally was about to be announced, Assemblyman George Michaels, representing a heavily Catholic upstate district yet overwhelmed by his conscience, switched his vote from no to yes, dooming his political career. The bill passed by his vote. At the time I did not think about what it meant that one vote was all that protected women's lives, nor was I aware of the ongoing battle between reformers and radicals that the New York legislation had highlighted.

When New York's legislature debated legalizing abortion in 1969 and 1970, radical feminists passed out a copy of their ideal abortion law—a blank sheet of paper. They advocated repeal and repeal meant no laws on abortion. They argued that any reform, no matter how liberal, was a defeat since it maintained the State's right to legislate control over women's bodies. With that control codified, as in New York's liberal law, the door was open for further restrictions. These radicals could foresee a time when abortion was legal but relatively inaccessible, perhaps as inaccessible to most women as it had been before reform.

The Supreme Court's *Roe v. Wade* decision of 1973 stated that abortion in the first two trimesters of pregnancy was a medical decision to be made by a woman and her doctor. Four years later Congress passed the Hyde Amendment, which banned the use of federal Medicaid dollars for abortion. Only seventeen states continue to fund abortions for poor women. Eighty percent of counties in the United States have no abortion services. Half of medical schools do not teach doctors abortion techniques. Because of harassment and intimidation by anti-abortion forces, few doctors are willing to perform abortions. The Supreme Court's decision in *Webster v. Reproductive Health Services* (1989), a Missouri case, upheld a ban on the use of public funds and public hospitals for abortions and allowed a number of other restrictions that the Missouri statute included. Although the Webster decision did not overturn *Roe v. Wade*, as some had predicted it might, it was a signal that the Court would consider a variety of restrictions on abortion, state by state. Justice Harry Blackmun, who had written the *Roe v. Wade* decision, noted in his dissent in Webster that the future seemed ominous "and a chill wind blows." It seems that the radicals' prescient warnings have come true with a vengeance.

Those of us who remember what it was like before *Roe v. Wade* know that restricting abortion will not end it. For every woman, abortion as a decision is not a theoretical abstraction, but is rooted in the concrete conditions of her life. She will weigh her decision and then try to act on it. This is what women have always done, irrespective of the law or even of the risks to their own lives. In 1988 in Indiana, a state that requires parental notification, a teenager, Becky Bell, died from an illegal abortion because she felt she could not tell her parents she was pregnant. In Texas in 1977 Rosie Jimenez died from an illegal abortion because she could not afford a legal one. Newspapers still print accounts of the lengths to which women are driven in order to do what they feel they have to do.

For those of us who participated in the struggle for abortion the growing threats to a woman's right to control her own body are more than a chill wind blowing. In the public discourse the fetus has been elevated to an equal status with a living, breathing human being. More and more, women are viewed as the enemy of children, requiring the State's intervention to protect their developing children from them. But, in reality, women still conceive, nurture, give birth to and, in most cases, are the primary caregivers of children. Women are being reduced, once again, to the incubators of future generations with total responsibility but no power. That is the same oppressive view that the women's movement sought to challenge. It is not just abortion, but women's power to control their destinies that is at stake.

For feminists in the late 1960s the issues were clear. We were not bombarded with the false emotionalism of fetal images. The "unborn" were just that, not yet born, not yet human beings. The decision of when or whether to carry a child to term belonged to only one person, the pregnant woman. That very moral decision had to be hers. She was the one to bear the consequences. It was the basis of the freedom women were trying to gain. Abortion referral groups saw themselves as facilitating each woman's decision-making power.

I consider myself lucky that a friend's IUD failure led me to Jane. After her abortion she came to see me, excited and surprised that her illegal abortion had been not only medically safe, but a positive and educational experience. I had just moved back to Chicago and was looking for a way to participate in the movement. Here was a group that was doing something concrete that was also risky, daring and secret, all of which appealed to me. I decided to join.

The group I joined in the fall of 1971 had already evolved to the point at which the members were performing the abortions themselves. Jane was an established organization, with defined procedures and a track record. I started out as a counselor, then took on administrative and medical tasks and worked with the group until we folded in the spring of 1973 when the first legal abortion clinics opened.

Jane taught me about more than abortion or women's liberation. Its history presents a fascinating example of what happens when people organize to do something and how they are changed by the actions they take. Since my time with Jane, I have drawn on those experiences as a way to understand personal power. We in Jane were fortunate that we were able to create a project that met an immediate, critical need and, at the same time, put into practice our vision of how the world ought to be.

For me Jane was the most transforming project I have had the privilege to be part of. I could never pretend to be objective about it. . . .

Those of use who were members of Jane were remarkable only because we chose to act with women's needs as our guide. In doing so we transformed an illegal abortion from a dangerous, sordid experience into one that was life-affirming and powerful.

Gloria Steinem

⁓

GLORIA STEINEM (1934–), feminist, writer, editor, and publisher, founded *Ms.* magazine with Patricia Carbine in 1972. In this excerpt from *Outrageous Acts and Everyday Rebellions*, Steinem recalls the childhood she spent as her mother's caretaker and the sacrifice her mother made to provide for her daughter's college education.

⁓

For many years I . . . couldn't imagine my mother any way other than the person she had become before I was born. She was just a fact of life when I was growing up; someone to be worried about and cared for; an invalid who lay in bed with eyes closed and lips moving in occasional response to voices only she could hear; a woman to whom I brought an endless stream of toast and coffee, bologna sandwiches and dime pies, in a child's version of what meals should be. She was a loving, intelligent, terrorized woman who tried hard to clean our littered house whenever she emerged from her private world, but who could rarely be counted on to finish one task. In many ways, our roles were reversed: I was the mother and she was the child. Yet that didn't help her either, for she still worried about me with all the intensity of a frightened mother, plus the special fears that came from her own world full of threats and hostile voices.

Even then, I suppose I must have known that years before she was thirty-five and I was born, she had been a spirited,

Steinem, Gloria. *Outrageous Acts and Everyday Rebellions*, 2nd ed. New York: Henry Holt & Company, 1995, pp. 140–158. Excerpt from *Outrageous Acts and Everyday Rebellions* by Gloria Steinem, © 1983 by Gloria Steinem, © 1984 by East Toledo Productions, Inc., © 1995 by Gloria Steinem. Reprinted by permission of Henry Holt and Company, LLC.

adventurous young woman who struggled out of a working-class family and into college, who found work she loved and continued to do, even after she was married and my older sister was there to be cared for. Certainly, our immediate family and nearby relatives, of whom I was by far the youngest, must have remembered her life as a whole and functioning person. She was thirty before she gave up her own career to help my father run the Michigan summer resort that was the most practical of his many dreams, and she worked hard there as everything from bookkeeper to bar manager. The family must have watched this energetic, fun-loving, book-loving woman turn into someone who was afraid to be alone, who could not hang on to reality long enough to hold a job, and who could rarely concentrate enough to read a book.

Yet I don't remember any family speculation about the mystery of my mother's transformation. To the kind ones and those who liked her, this new Ruth was simply a sad event, perhaps a mental case, a family problem to be accepted and cared for until some natural process made her better. To the less kind or those who resented her earlier independence, she was a willful failure, someone who lived in a filthy house, a woman who simply refused to pull herself together. . . .

[E]xterior events were never suggested as reason enough for her problems. Giving up her own career was never cited as her personal parallel of the Depression. . . .

Even the explanation of mental illness seemed to contain more personal fault when applied to my mother. She had suffered her first "nervous breakdown," as she and everyone else called it, before I was born, when my sister was about five. It followed years of trying to take care of a baby, be the wife of a kind but financially irresponsible man with show-business dreams, and still keep her much-loved job as reporter and newspaper editor. After many months in a sanatorium, she was pronounced recovered. That is, she was able to take care of my sister again, to move away from the city and the job she loved, and to work with my father at the iso-

lated rural lake in Michigan he was trying to transform into a resort worthy of the big dance bands of the 1930s.

But she was never again completely without the spells of depression, anxiety, and visions into some other world that eventually were to turn her into the nonperson I remember. And she was
never again without a bottle of dark, acrid-smelling liquid she
called "Doc Howard's medicine," a solution of chloral hydrate that
I later learned was the main ingredient of "Micky Finns" or
"knockout drops," and that probably made my mother and her
doctor the pioneers of modern tranquilizers. . . .

But why was she never returned to that first sanatorium? Or to
help that might have come from other doctors? It's hard to say.
Partly, it was her own fear of returning to that pain. Partly, it was
too little money, and a family's not-unusual assumption that mental illness is an inevitable part of someone's personality. . . .

In retrospect, perhaps the biggest reason my mother was cared
for but not helped for twenty years was the simplest: her functioning was not that necessary to the world. Like women alcoholics
who drink in their kitchens while costly programs are constructed
for male executives who drink, or like homemakers subdued with
tranquilizers while male patients get therapy and personal attention instead, my mother was not an important worker. She was not
even the caretaker of a very young child, as she had been when she
was hospitalized the first time. My father had patiently brought
home the groceries and kept our odd household going until I was
eight or so and my sister went away to college. Two years later,
when wartime gas rationing closed his summer resort and he had
to travel to buy and sell in summer as well as winter, he said: How
can I travel and take care of your mother? How can I make a living? He was right. It was impossible to do both. I did not blame
him for leaving once I was old enough to be the bringer of meals
and answerer of my mother's questions. ("Has your sister been
killed in a car crash?" "Are there German soldiers outside?") I replaced my father, my mother was left with one more way of maintaining a sad status quo, and the world went on undisturbed.

That's why our lives, my mother's from forty-six to fifty-three, and my own from ten to seventeen, were spent alone together . . . .

[T]here were . . . times when she woke in the early winter dark, too frightened and disoriented to remember that I was at my usual after school job, and so called the police to find me. Humiliated in front of my friends by sirens and policemen, I would yell at her—and she would bow her head in fear and say, "I'm sorry, I'm sorry, I'm sorry," just as she had done so often when my otherwise-kind-hearted father had yelled at her in frustration. Perhaps the worst thing about suffering is that it finally hardens the hearts of those around it. . . .

But my ultimate protection was this: I was just passing through; I was a guest in the house; perhaps this wasn't my mother at all. Though I knew very well that I was her daughter, I sometimes imagined I had been adopted and that my real parents would find me, a fantasy I've since discovered is common. (If children wrote more and grown-ups less, perhaps being adopted might not be seen only as a fear, but also as a hope.) Certainly, I didn't mourn the wasted life of this woman who was scarcely older than I am now. I worried only about the times when she got worse.

Pity takes distance and a certainty of surviving. It was only after our house was bought for demolition by the church next door, and after my sister had performed the miracle of persuading my father to give me a carefree time before college by taking my mother with him to California for a year, that I could afford to think about the sadness of her life. Suddenly, I was far away in Washington, living with my sister who shared a house with several of her friends. While I finished high school and discovered to my surprise that my classmates felt sorry for me because my mother *wasn't* there, I also realized that my sister, at least in her early childhood, had known a very different person who lived inside our mother, an earlier Ruth.

She was a woman I met for the first time in a mental hospital near Baltimore, a humane place with gardens and trees where I visited her each weekend of the summer after my first year away in college. Fortunately, my sister hadn't been able to work and be our mother's caretaker, too. After my father's year was up, my sister had carefully researched hospitals, and found the courage to break the family chain of simply tolerating our mother's condition.

At first, this Ruth was the same abstracted, frightened woman I lived with all those years, now all the sadder for being approached through long hospital corridors and many locked doors. But gradually she began to talk about her past life, and to confide memories that doctors there must have been awakening. I began to meet a Ruth I had never known:

. . . A tall, spirited, auburn-haired high-school girl who loved basketball and reading; who tried to drive her uncle's Stanley Steamer when it was the first car in the neighborhood; who had a gift for gardening and who sometimes wore her father's overalls in defiance of convention; a girl with the courage to go to dances even though her church told her that music itself was sinful, and whose sense of adventure almost made up for feeling gawky and unpretty next to her daintier, dark-haired sister. . . .

. . . A good student at Oberlin College whose freethinking traditions she loved, where friends nicknamed her "Billy"; a student with a talent for both mathematics and poetry . . . ; a daughter who had to return to Toledo, live with her family, and go to a local university when her ambitious mother—who had scrimped and saved, ghostwritten a minister's sermons, and made her daughters' clothes in order to get them to college at all—ran out of money. At home, this Ruth became a part-time bookkeeper in a lingerie shop that catered to the very rich, commuting to classes and listening to her mother's harsh lectures on the security of becoming a teacher; but also a young woman who was still rebellious enough to fall in love with my father, the editor of their university newspaper, a funny and charming young man who was a terrible student, had no intention of graduating, put on all the campus dances, and was unacceptably Jewish.

I knew from family lore that my mother had married my father twice; once secretly, after he invited her to become the literary editor of the campus newspaper, and once a year later in a public ceremony, which some members of both families refused to attend because it was the "mixed marriage" of its day.

And I also knew that my mother had gone on to earn a teaching certificate. She had used it to scare away truant officers during the winters when, after my father closed the summer resort for the season, we lived in a house trailer and worked our way to Florida or California and back by buying and selling antiques.

But only during those increasingly adventurous weekend outings from the mental hospital in Baltimore—going shopping, to lunch, to the movies—did I realize that she had taught college calculus for a year in deference to her mother's insistence that she have teaching "to fall back on." And only then did I realize she had fallen in love with newspapers along with my father. After graduating from the university, she wrote a gossip column for a local tabloid, under the name "Duncan MacKenzie," since women weren't supposed to do such things. Soon after, she had earned a job as society reporter on one of Toledo's two big dailies. By the time my sister was four or so, she had worked her way up to the coveted position of Sunday editor.

It was a strange experience to look into those brown eyes I had seen so often and realize suddenly how much they were like my own. For the first time, I realized that she really was my mother.

I began to think about the many pressures that might have led up to her first nervous breakdown: leaving my sister whom she loved so much with a grandmother whose values my mother didn't share; trying to hold on to a job she loved but was being asked to leave by her husband; wanting very much to go with a woman friend to pursue their own dreams in New York but punishing herself for even the thought; falling in love with a co-worker at the newspaper who frightened her by being more sexually attractive, more supportive of her work than my father, and perhaps the man she should have married; and finally, nearly bleeding to death with a miscarriage because her own mother had little faith in doctors and refused to get help.

Did those months in the sanatorium brainwash her in some Freudian or very traditional way into making what were, for her, probably the wrong choices? I don't know. It almost doesn't matter. Without extraordinary support to the contrary, she was already convinced that divorce was unthinkable. A husband could not be left for another man, and certainly not for any reason as selfish as a career. A daughter could not be deprived of her father, and certainly not be uprooted and taken off to an uncertain future in New York. A bride was supposed to be virginal (not "shop-worn," as my euphemistic mother would have said), and if your husband turned out to be kind, but innocent of the possibility of a woman's pleasure, then just be thankful for his kindness. . . .

At the hospital and in later years when Ruth told me stories of her past, I used to say, "But why didn't you leave? Why didn't you take the job? Why didn't you marry the other man?" She would always insist it didn't matter, she was lucky to have my sister and me. If I pressed hard enough, she would add, "If I'd left you never would have been born."

I always thought but never had the courage to say: *But you might have been born instead.* . . .

It was the length of her illness that had made doctors pessimistic. In fact, they could not identify any serious mental problem and diagnosed her only as having "an anxiety neurosis": low self-esteem, a fear of being dependent, a terror of being alone, a constant worry about money. She also had spells of what now would be called agoraphobia, a problem almost entirely confined to dependent women: fear of going outside the house, and incapacitating anxiety attacks in unfamiliar or public places.

Would you say, I asked one of her doctors, that her spirit had been broken? "I guess that's as good a diagnosis as any," he said. "And it's hard to mend anything that's been broken for twenty years."

But once out of the hospital for good, she continued to show flashes of a different woman inside; one with a wry kind of humor, a sense of adventure, and a love of learning. Books on math, physics, and mysticism occupied a lot of her time. ("Religion," she used to say firmly, "begins in the laboratory.") When she visited me in New York during her sixties and seventies, she always told taxi drivers that she was eighty years old ("so they will tell me how young I look"), and convinced theater ticket sellers that she had difficulty in hearing long before she really did ("so they'll give us seats in the front row"). She made friends easily, with the vulnerability and charm of a person who feels entirely dependent on the approval of others. After one of her visits, every shopkeeper within blocks of my apartment would say, "Oh yes, I know your mother!" At home, she complained that people her own age were too old and stodgy for her. Many of her friends were far younger than she. It was as if she were making up for her own lost years. . . .

Part of the price she paid for this much health was forgetting. A single reminder of those bad years in Toledo was enough to plunge her into days of depression. There were times when this fact created loneliness for me, too. Only two of us had lived most of my childhood. Now, only one of us remembered. But there were also times in later years when, no matter how much I pleaded with reporters *not* to interview our friends and neighbors in Toledo, *not* to say that my mother had been hospitalized, they published things that hurt her very much, and sent her into another downhill slide. . . .

She was very proud of my being a published writer, and we generally shared the same values. After her death, I found a mother-daughter morals quiz I had written for a women's magazine. In her unmistakably shaky writing, she had recorded her own answers, her entirely accurate imagination of what my answers would be, and a score that concluded our differences were less than those "normal for women separated by twenty-odd years." Nonetheless, she was quite capable of putting a made-up name on her name tag when going to her conventional women's club where she feared our shared identity would bring controversy or even just questions. When I finally got up the nerve to tell her I was signing a 1972 petition of women who publicly said we had had abortions and demanded the repeal of laws that made them illegal and dangerous, her only reply was sharp and aimed to hurt back. "Every starlet says she's had an abortion," she said. "It's just a way of getting publicity." I knew she agreed that abortion should be a legal choice, but I also knew she would never forgive me for embarrassing her in public. . . .

When my mother died just before her eighty-second birthday in a hospital room where my sister and I were alternating the hours in which her heart wound slowly down to its last sounds, we were alone together for a few hours while my sister slept. My mother seemed bewildered by her surroundings, and by the tubes that invaded her body, but her consciousness cleared long enough for her to say: "I want to go home. Please take me home." Lying to her one last time, I said I would take her. "Okay, honey," she said. "I trust you." Those were her last understandable words. . . .

Her memorial service was in the Episcopalian church that she loved because it fed the poor, let the homeless sleep in its pews, had members of almost every race, and had been sued by the Episcopalian hierarchy for having a woman priest. Most of all, she loved the affection with which its members had welcomed her, visited her at home, and driven her to services. I think she would have liked the Quaker-style informality with which people rose to tell their memories of her. I know she would have loved the presence of many friends. It was to this church that she had donated some of her remaining Michigan property in the hope that it could be used as a multiracial camp, thus getting even with those neighbors who had snubbed my father for being Jewish.

I think she also would have been pleased with her obituary. It emphasized her brief career as one of the early women journalists, and asked for donations to Oberlin's scholarship fund so others could go to this college she loved so much but had to leave. . . .

I still don't understand why so many, many years passed before I saw my mother as a person, and before I understood that many of the forces in her life were patterns women share. Like a lot of daughters, I couldn't afford to admit that what had happened to my mother was not all personal or accidental. It would have meant admitting it could happen to me. . . .

[T]he world . . . missed a unique person named Ruth. Though she longed to live in New York and travel in Europe, she became a woman who was afraid to take a bus across town. Though she drove the first Stanley Steamer, she married a man who never let her drive at all.

I can only guess what she might have become. There are clues in her moments of spirit and humor.

After all the years of fear, she still came to Oberlin with me when I was giving a speech there. She remembered everything about its history as the first college to admit blacks as well as the first to admit women, and responded to students with the dignity of a professor, the accuracy of a journalist, and the charm that was all her own. . . .

My father was the Jewish half of the family, yet it was my mother who taught me to have pride in this tradition. It was she who encouraged me to listen to a radio play about a concentration camp when I was little. "You should know that this can happen," she said. Yet she did it just enough to teach, never enough to frighten.

It was she who introduced me to books and a respect for them, to poetry that she knew by heart, and to the idea that you could never criticize someone unless you "walked miles in their shoes."

It was she who sold that Toledo house, the only home she had, with the determination that the money be used to start me in college. She gave both her daughters the encouragement to leave home for the four years of independence she herself had never had.

After her death, my sister and I found a journal she had kept of her one cherished and belated trip to Europe. It was a trip she had described very little when she came home perhaps because she always deplored people who talked boringly about their personal

travels and showed slides. Nonetheless, she had written a narrative essay called "Grandma Goes to Europe." After all those years,
she still thought of herself as a writer. Yet she showed this long
journal to no one.

I miss her—but perhaps no more in death than I did in life.
Dying seems less sad than having lived too little. But at least
we're now asking questions about all the Ruths in all our family
mysteries.

If her song inspires that, I think she would be the first to say: It
was worth the singing.

Susan Brownmiller

~

SUSAN BROWNMILLER (1935–) wrote *Against Our Will: Men, Women and Rape*, a book that, when published in 1975, was influential in changing attitudes and laws regarding rape. In her memoir, *In Our Time: Memoir of a Revolution*, Brownmiller recalls the writing and publication of her landmark book.

~

Rape theory started for me in the fall of 1970 inside my consciousness-raising group, as part of a germination process that was taking place all over the country. Looking back, I can see that [the feminist group] Cell 16 in Boston was ahead of the curve as usual with its classes in self-defense and the essay on rape-murder, "More Slain Girls," in *No More Fun and Games*. Working independently in New York, Kate Millett, a pioneer in so many respects, had identified rape as a "weapon of the patriarchy" in *Sexual Politics*.

What was to become a major, sustained feminist campaign against sexual violence began percolating at the edges, where I think new ideas and great discoveries always begin. Street harassment, a relatively minor but pervasive piece of the sexual abuse continuum, drew the movement's first open confrontations.

Every woman in a big city lived with routine street harassment. You couldn't make your appointed rounds during a typical day without an incident of some kind or another, a catcall, "Oh, sweetheart, what I'd like to do to *you!*" from a truck driver, a murmured "Suck my dick" from an innocuous-looking fellow walking by in a business suit. And God forbid you had to pass a construction site when the guys were taking their break at lunchtime. Pam Kearon of THE FEMINISTS said it was like being under twenty-four-hour-a-day surveillance.

Many of us, made bold by our heightened consciousness, had developed individual strategies for coping with the harassment instead of scurrying by quickly with a lowered head as we had done in the past. Some women halted in their tracks and patiently tried to explain to the bewildered offender why an explicit sexual comment made by a stranger was so unpleasantly intrusive. My response had become a snarled "Fuck *you* up *your* ass," a hollow threat to be sure, and one that dangerously escalated the confrontation on a couple of occasions.

In 1970 the movement began to politicize street harassment with collective action. The Ogle-In was a popular tactic. A bunch of us would gather on a street corner and turn the tables on leering, lip-smacking men by giving them a taste of their own medicine. After the newspapers reported that a bunch of stock exchange employees had developed a "fun" morning ritual before work, gathering on the street to watch a particular secretary with large breasts emerge from the subway station, Karla Jay organized a retaliatory Ogle-In on Wall Street. She chose a March afternoon at lunchtime. It was incredibly liberating to reverse the wolf whistles, animal noises, and body-parts appraisals that customarily flowed in our direction. Wendy Roberts, a free-spirited hippie who called herself Wendy Wonderful, was my heroine that day. She sauntered up behind an unwitting passerby and grabbed his crotch. Oh, retribution! Los Angeles feminists struck in September with their Ogle-In during Girl-Watching Week, an official Chamber of Commerce promotion. Trailed by the local media, the women boy-watched at several locations in Century City. One activist wielded a tape measure: "Too small!" "Too skinny!" "Hey, fella, can you type, file, and make coffee?" The Los Angeles boy-watchers dubbed themselves Sisters Against Sexual Slavery, or SASS. . . .

Tuesday had become our appointed night for consciousness-raising. One of our new members was Diane Crothers, an impatient, visionary activist from the defunct Stanton-Anthony brigade. Diane more than anyone else kept us clued in to the nuances and tremors of the national movement. One evening she arrived with a copy of *It Ain't Me Babe* from San Francisco.

Earlier in the summer, the July 23, 1970 *Babe* had run an unsigned, tape-recorded account, "Anatomy of a Rape," by a young artist in Marin. Buoyed by the experience of going to her first women's meeting in Berkeley, the artist had waved off suggestions that she stay overnight, preferring to hitchhike home. Her first ride left her on Van Ness. Almost immediately two Vietnam vets in a truck pulled up. "Okay, now, we're not gonna hurt ya, we're just gonna take ya out and ball ya," one said as they approached the bridge. A couple of hours later they dumped her at a bus station. . . .

The September 4 *Babe* that Diane brought to our meeting carried a second rape story, news of a stunning retaliatory action. "Jack the Raper" was a report by a women's group calling itself, with all due bravado, the Contra Costa Anti-Rape Squad #14. A go-go dancer hired to perform at a bachelor party in Pinole had been roughed up by the groom's drunken friends, dragged into a bedroom, and raped by the sodden guest of honor. In a free-for-all, her gown was ripped, she was doused with wine, and her seventy-five-dollar dancing fee was stolen from her purse before her friends came to the rescue. The dancer, who considered herself a tough professional, filed a complaint that night with the Pinole police, but the district attorney in Richmond declined to prosecute under the boys-will-be-boys logic. He said it was the men's word against hers, even though a hospital test showed evidence of semen.

On the day of the wedding reception at the Stockton Inn, the Contra Costa Anti-Rape Squad plastered the guests' cars in the parking lot with a leaflet headlined "How Jack and His Friends Play When 'Their' Women Aren't Around." The flyer named names, including the groom's friends and the dismissive D.A., and ended with the words "Sounds ugly? Well, it is. It goes on all the time, one way or another. These pigs know the law won't touch them, they can always insist the woman is a liar or slut or crazy. We women are learning to see through that nonsense. We hope you learn to, too."

After we read this story in *It Ain't Me Babe*, Diane announced that rape was an important new feminist issue and proposed that we should begin to explore it through consciousness-raising. I wasn't convinced. The prevailing opinion, which I'd absorbed without question, held that rape was a murky, deviant crime any alert woman could avoid. Rape was political, I argued, only when it was "rape" in quotation marks, as the Old Left wrote it—the false accusation of white women against black men that lay behind some accounts of southern lynching. In fact, three years earlier I'd done a story about capital punishment and a Maryland interracial rape case for *Esquire* with no demonstrable sympathy for the victim. Our group [West Village–One] had been analyzing femininity for months, and I was finding the revelations very helpful. I did not want to switch gears and talk about rape.

The others definitely wanted to talk about rape. Sara Pines quietly offered to begin the process. Sara was married, a professional psychologist, and the calmest woman in our group. Fifteen years earlier, she told us, she had been hitchhiking back to her school after a weekend at Harvard. The young man who picked her up asked where she was headed, and then said he wanted to make a detour to pick up a friend.

"*Pick up a friend?*" I interrupted. "And warning bells didn't go off your head?"

"No, he seemed okay."

"In my hitchhiking days I'd never ride in a car with more than one man! I'd have gotten out right then."

"I trusted him," she said simply.

Sara was raped in a deserted park by the man and three of his buddies. "I was told to be quiet or I'd be buried there and no one would know," she recounted. The worst part of her ordeal had been at the police station. "Aww, who'd want to rape you?" an officer teased. Another said she was too calm to be credible—in his view she should have been crying hysterically. After several postponements there was a trial that Sara did not attend, and the men were given suspended sentences.

Listening to Sara Pines was the moment when I started to change my mind about rape. She was a trusting person; I wasn't. I had to accept that not every woman viewed the world with my suspicions and caution. After Susan Frankel and Lucille Iverson finished their accounts of lucky escapes from threatening situations, I proposed that New York Radical Feminists hold a conference on rape with research papers and panel discussions. The others argued that personal testimony in a public speak-out was the proper way to begin, the way abortion had been politicized by Redstockings the previous year. I doubted that we could find enough women willing to go public. Once again I was wrong.

West Village–One presented the two plans at the next general meeting of New York Radical Feminists. The bold idea of summoning women to gather in public to talk about rape, as authorities, to put an unashamed human face on a crime that was shrouded in rumors and whispers, or smarmy jokes, had never been attempted before, anywhere. In their wisdom the affiliated consciousness-raising groups of New York Radical Feminists voted to hold a speak-out on rape at the earliest possible opportunity, to be followed by a conference on rape three months later. We chose as our slogan "Rape Is a Political Crime Against Women."

The speak-out took place on Sunday afternoon, January 24, 1971, at St. Clement's, a tiny Episcopal church on West Forty-sixth Street that doubled as a home for off-off-Broadway productions. A one-page flyer, in Spanish on the reverse side, had been circulated to women's groups, inviting everyone who'd had an experience with rape to testify. Admission was free, cameras and tape recorders were banned, and men could attend only if they paid two dollars and were accompanied by a woman. My job was to take tickets at the door. I collected thirty dollars, which meant that fifteen men actually showed up. Or maybe it was sixty dollars and thirty men. I do know that more than three hundred women crammed into the small circular arena, arriving early to fill the seats above a multilevel stage set designed for a less memorable drama. Latecomers hugged the walls, hunkered down in the aisles. Somebody commandeered a wheelchair, a production prop, for the last seat in the house. The ten women who were prepared to testify arranged themselves as best they could on the dimly lit stage.

In the hush, they began speaking. I took notes, which I've saved to this day, but the drama was too intense for pen and paper. Sara Pines recounted her hitchhiking story. Alix Kates Shulman described the childhood ritual of "pantsing," getting caught by a gang of boys as she tried to run past a vacant lot near her home in Cleveland. (The incident appears in *Memoirs of an Ex-Prom Queen*, published the following year.)

A dark-haired woman told of her date with a medical resident, arranged with great expectations by his aunt and her mother. The future gynecologist assaulted her in his room at the hospital. "I was so hung up on propriety," she confessed, "that I went to dinner with him afterward as if nothing had happened. I didn't tell my mother, much less the police."

Another woman spoke of rape by her therapist—"Not a real doctor, a lay analyst," she said amid groans—who continued to charge her for the weekly sessions. "When I took sleeping pills to kill myself, he dropped me," she finished.

A gray-haired woman in her sixties told of being assaulted in her apartment after opening her door to a man who said he was delivering a package.

A modern dancer graphically described a street encounter that happened one evening as she returned home after a class. "He slammed me against the wall and clawed at my leotard. The leotard kept snapping back. This seemed to enrage him. Then I kicked him in his precious groin. The people on the street didn't help, and the police talked me out of pressing charges. They said, 'You did enough to the poor guy.'" . . .

In all, thirty women were inspired to speak out that afternoon, and their words were to reverberate far beyond the confines of the tiny church. So many varieties and aspects of rape had been revealed at St. Clement's. Sexual assault was a crime of power that crossed all lines of age, race, and class; women feared they would be killed; resistance was possible; the police were dismissive. All of us were reeling from the new knowledge. . . .

Plane for our next event, the Conference on Rape, took over the general meetings of New York Radical Feminists. . . .

I freely offered my advice on how the rape conference should be organized. We needed workshops on the psychology of the rapist, the psychology of the victim, rape and the law, rape in marriage, rape and sexuality, rape and the cultural climate, rape during wartime (we could discuss Vietnam). The more I talked, the more I saw that workshops by themselves could not produce the comprehensive research that an analysis of rape deserved and required. I realized that I'd begun outlining chapters for a book in my head, a book I very much wanted to write. . . .

On Monday morning I was in the office of literary agent Wendy Weil with a four-page proposal for a book on rape. Simon and Schuster, the first publisher Wendy approached, offered a contract for ten thousand dollars. In my naïveté I agreed to deliver the manuscript in one year. That seemed right to Jonathan Dolger, my laid-back editor.

I spent the next four years writing *Against Our Will* in the New York Public Library, where the card catalogue had more entries for rapeseed than for rape but the stacks held treasures that could be retrieved if I followed a dim trial of footnotes and trusted my instincts. The book surprised me as it grew. All reporters are sleuths, but few are privileged to start their work at the beginning of a great discovery. I was finding answers to questions that no one had ever asked before. Hot on the trial of an elusive case or a legal point, sometimes I'd leave the Forty-second Street library at closing time and dash to the law library at NYU to browse undisturbed for another few hours. Occasionally I suffered paroxysms of doubt. Was it legitimate to isolate rape in war? Could I find the precise moment in English law when rape evolved from a crime of property to a crime against a woman's body? Should I make fewer enemies and perhaps gain some friends by skirting the minefield of race and sex? Indeed, could I argue the premise that rape had a history without becoming the laughingstock of historians everywhere? . . .

While I worked in relative isolation, the rape crisis center movement continued to grow, with every new counseling-service hot line attracting its own local publicity. Operating from her NOW chapter in northern Virginia, Mary Ann Largen almost singlehandedly placed rape on NOW's national agenda. Jan BenDor in Ann Arbor, a founder of one of the earliest crisis centers, began advancing ideas for new state legislation. Her Michigan Women's Task Force on Rape descended on the capitol in Lansing to pioneer an overhaul of sexual assault statutes that had gone unchanged for 117 years.

BenDor's ideas helped me enormously. Antirape people in several states had begun to lobby for more realistic legislation, but the Michigan Women's Task Force was amazing. Earlier than most, they saw the need to eliminate the archaic and sexist evidentiary requirements in the criminal codes that virtually guaranteed few prosecutions and even fewer convictions. Two practical goals that activists in many states fought for were the abolition of a corroborating witness rule and a restriction on testimony regarding the victim's prior sexual history (now called the rape shield law). BenDor's group was among the first to propose extending the assault statues to cover rape in marriage. . . .

Against Our Will was published in October 1975. . . .

〜

[It] was a great moment for me. A powerful publisher was committed to turning a heavy, provocative treatise into a commercial best seller, feature writers and book reviewers were prepared to treat a feminist analysis of rape seriously, and public interest programming was getting good airtime on television and radio stations. Individual women, wherever they had a foothold, rose up to help the cause. Joni Evans, Simon and Schuster's director of subsidiary rights, alerted Lucy Rosenthal at the Book-of-the-Month Club, who took it upon herself to be my champion. The book became a main selection. All the general interest periodicals edited by men passed on prepublication excerpts, but *Mademoiselle, Glamour,* and *Family Circle* stepped into the breech, thanks to a determined feminist editor inside each house. . . .

～

Outraged criticism of *Against Our Will* started pouring in from the right and the left after the first positive wave of media attention. I should not have been surprised, since feminism overturns so many facets of conventional political wisdom, but I believed my arguments about male violence were so convincing, and my evidence for seeing the routine deployment of rape as a weapon of intimidation was so impressive, that thoughtful people would say "Aha!" and take it from there.

My first inkling that not everyone on the intellectual left was prepared to thank me for their enlightenment had come when an old acquaintance in publishing accosted me on the street. "You," he thundered, shaking involuntarily and wagging his finger, "have set back the cause of civil rights and civil liberties ten years."

New York's certified male intellectuals, the *New York Review of Books* and *Partisan Review* crowd, had been caught off guard by the tidal wave of feminist thinking. We upset their applecart, trampled with muddy boots on their tight little island of political certainty. Most male intellectuals reacted badly to feminism throughout its explosion, trying to ignore it and not give an inch. The two or three females in their midst . . . didn't dare risk their standing by identifying too openly—or identifying at all—with the feminist camp. They had fought too hard to be honorary men. . . .

The people who challenged my ideas most deeply were the women of the activist left. I must say I was unprepared for their concentrated assault. Several women, black and white, accused me of being a racist, a charge that still crops up from time to time. Nothing devastates me more.

When I wrote chapter 7, "A Question of Race," in *Against Our Will*, I knew I was challenging Old Left dogma. After describing the bitter legacy of rape in slavery, mob lynching by whites, and the discriminatory application of the death penalty to black men convicted of rape, I had explored the Communist Party's use of the interracial rape case, beginning with Scottsboro, as a dramatic symbol of American injustice. My point was that the left and those influenced by the left saw rape as a political cause only when they believed a white woman was falsely accusing a black man. Going further, I reserved my toughest comments for the story of Emmett Till, the fourteen-year-old youth lynched in Money, Mississippi, in 1955 for whistling at a white woman. I said that Till and the men who lynched him shared something in common: a perception of the white woman as the white man's property. For leftists with inflexible minds, this observation amounted to heresy. Some dogmatists willfully interpreted it to mean that I condoned the lynching. . . .

I toughed out the racism charges publicly in my usual dukes-up manner, but I grieved inside knowing that *Against Our Will* would never be read by a substantial number of radicals whose opinions were formed by the harmful attacks. . . .

⟿

By late 1976, a moment in time when *Against Our Will* was reaching bookstores in its paperback edition . . . four hundred rape crisis centers were in place around the country. Few of the centers, however, bore more than a faint resemblance to the original radical feminist model run by a volunteer collective of movement women. Professional social workers and psychologists had moved into the field, and even in cities where they hadn't, most of the centers had applied for and received federal funding, either through the LEAA (Law Enforcement Assistance Administration) or the NIMH (National Institute of Mental Health). The newly available public monies, a tribute to the antirape movement's success, acted to turn the centers into pure service and counseling organizations with paid staffs and conventional structures. With amazing speed, the rape crisis centers became *part* of the system, not a radical political force in opposition to the system. I witnessed the evolution first-hand while I was on the road with my book.

Changes in the law took place just as swiftly. In one year, 1975, thirty states overhauled their rape laws to make them more equi-table to victims. Between 1970, when the feminist movement first started to talk about rape, and 1979, when the militance had re-ceded, every state in the union went through a serious reevaluation of its rape codes and made significant adjustments. Hospital pro-cedures and police attitudes were transformed as well. The revolu-tion in thinking about rape was profound. I am very proud to have been part of it, along with thousands of others who did not write best-selling books.

Adrienne Rich

⁓

ADRIENNE RICH (1929–) is an award-winning poet who has never segregated political concerns from her art. Two poems follow: "A Woman Dead in Her Forties" (1974–1977) and "Mother-Right" (1977).

⁓

A Woman Dead in Her Forties

1.
Your breasts/   sliced-off   The scars
dimmed   as they would have to be
years later

All the women I grew up with are sitting
half-naked on rocks   in sun
we look at each other and
are not ashamed

and you too have taken off your blouse
but this was not what you wanted:

to show your scarred, deleted torso

I barely glance at you
as if my look could scald you
though I'm the one who loved you

I want to touch my fingers
to where your breasts had been
but we never did such things

You hadn't thought everyone
would look so perfect
unmutilated

you pull on
your blouse again: stern statement:

*There are things I will not share
with everyone*

2.
You send me back to share
my own scars   first of all
with myself

What did I hide from her
what have I denied her
what losses suffered

how in this ignorant body
did she hide

waiting for her release
till uncontrollable light began to pour

from every wound and suture
and all the sacred openings

3.
Wartime.   We sit on warm
weathered, softening grey boards

the ladder glimmers where you told me
the leeches swim

I smell the flame
of kerosene   the pine

boards where we sleep side by side
in narrow cots

the night-meadow exhaling
its darkness   calling

child into woman
child into woman
woman

4.
Most of our love from the age of nine
took the form of jokes and mute

loyalty: you fought a girl
who said she'd knock me down

we did each other's homework
wrote letters   kept in touch, untouching

lied about our lives: I wearing
the face of the proper marriage

you the face of the independent woman
We cleaved to each other across that space

fingering webs
of love and estrangement   till the day

the gynecologist touched your breast
and found a palpable hardness

5.
You played heroic, necessary
games with death

since in your neo-protestant tribe the void
was supposed not to exist

except as a fashionable concept
you had no traffic with

I wish you were here tonight   I want
to yell at you

Don't accept
Don't give in

But would I be meaning your brave
irreproachable life, you dean of women, or

your unfair, unfashionable, unforgivable
woman's death?

6.
You are every woman I ever loved
and disavowed

a bloody incandescent chord strung out
across years, tracts of space

How can I reconcile this passion
with our modesty

your calvinist heritage
my girlhood frozen into forms

how can I go on this mission
without you

you, who might have told me
everything you feel is true?

7.
Time after time in dreams you rise
reproachful

once from a wheelchair pushed by your father
across a lethal expressway

Of all my dead it's you
who come to me unfinished

You left me amber beads
strung with turquoise from an Egyptian grave

I wear them wondering
How am I true to you?

I'm half-afraid to write poetry
for you   who never read it much

and I'm left laboring
with the secrets and the silence

In plain language: I never told you how I loved you
we never talked at your deathbed of your death

8.
One autumn evening in a train
catching the diamond-flash of sunset

in puddles along the Hudson
I thought: *I understand*

life and death now, the choices
I didn't know your choice

or how by then you had no choice
how the body tells the truth in its rush of cells

Most of our love took the form
of mute loyalty

we never spoke at your deathbed of your death

but from here on
I want more crazy mourning, more howl, more keening

We stayed mute and disloyal
because we were afraid

I would have touched my fingers
to where your breasts had been
but we never did such things

—1974–1977

Mother-Right

(For M. H.)
Woman and child   running
in a field   A man planted
on the horizon

Two hands   one long, slim   one
small, starlike   clasped
in the razor wind

Her hair cut short for faster travel
the child's curls grazing his shoulders
the hawk-winged cloud   over their heads

The man is walking boundaries
measuring   He believes in what is his
the grass   the waters underneath   the air

the air   through which child and mother
are running   the boy singing
the woman   eyes sharpened in the light
heart stumbling making   for the open

—1977

Phyllis Schlafly

~

PHYLLIS SCHLAFLY (1924–), president of the Eagle Forum, syndicated radio show host, and newspaper columnist, founded Stop ERA and successfully led the fight to defeat the Equal Rights Amendment. In this speech, delivered on March 27, 1979, in Orlando, Florida, she explains her opposition to the Amendment.

~

Good morning friends. The subject assigned today is, indeed, an important one: the women's movement and family life. It is important that we first of all define the term. I would not agree that there is just *the* women's movement. In order to make sure we know what we are talking about, I will first of all describe what I think could be more appropriately called the women's liberation movement. It could be defined as the movement of women who have, in a general way, been working for the Equal Rights Amendment.

This movement was born in the mid-1960s with the publication of Betty Friedan's book *The Feminine Mystique*. This movement accomplished the task of getting the Equal Rights Amendment through Congress in 1972. It reached its peak in November 1977 in Houston at the National Conference of the Commission on International Women's Year. Since that date, it's no longer a nebulous

Torricelli, Robert, and Andrew Carroll. *In Our Own Words: Extraordinary Speeches of the American Century.* New York: Kodansha America, Inc., 1999, pp. 330–335 (with a correction to that text provided by Ms. Schlafly). Phyllis Schlafly's 1979 speech, reprinted by permission of Phyllis Schlafly.

thing. It is a very precise movement that can be definitely defined with particular people and particular goals.

Participating in that Houston Conference were all the leaders of the women's liberation movement. These included the head of the National Organization for Women (NOW), the head of the Women's Political Caucus, the head of ERAmerica (the lobbying group for the ERA), the head of the Gay Task Force, the person who put the ERA through the Senate, the person who put ERA though the House, Gloria Steinem, and Bella Abzug was the chairman. These were all presidential appointees, and they gathered in Houston. They had $5 million of federal funds and they passed twenty-five resolutions, which represent the goals of the women's liberation movement.

The four "hot button" issues, the term used by *Newsweek* magazine—their most important goals—were ratification of the Equal Rights Amendment, government-funded abortion, lesbian privileges to be recognized with the same dignity as husbands and wives and with the right to teach in schools, and massive, universal, federal child care, which *Time* magazine estimated would cost us an additional $25 billion a year. There were other resolutions, too, but the four "hot button" issues were admitted by everybody—the media plus both sides—as being the main ones.

These are the goals and those are the personalities of the women's liberation movement in our country today. It is my belief, based on working with this movement for quite a number of years, that the movement is having an adverse effect on family life, that it is a major cause of divorce today, and that it is highly detrimental to our country and to our families. . . .

For a woman to function effectively in the family, it is necessary for her to believe in the worth of her position, to have a certain amount of self-esteem, to believe that her task as wife and mother is worthy, is honorable, is useful, and is fulfilling. The fundamental attitude by the women's liberation movement takes all that away from women. I have listened to thousands of their speeches, and basically those speeches inculcate in woman a negative attitude toward life, toward the family, toward their country, and most of all toward themselves. It was best summed up in an advertisement developed by the principal women's liberation organization, the National Organization for Women. It was run as a spot announcement on many television stations and as ads in many magazines and newspapers. This advertisement shows a darling, curly-headed child. The caption under the picture is: "This normal, healthy child was born with a handicap. It was born female."

Think about that. That is the starting assumption of the woman's liberation movement: That somebody—it isn't clear who, God or the establishment or a conspiracy of male chauvinist pigs—has dealt women a foul blow by making them female; that it is up to society to remedy these centuries of oppression, of bondage, even of slavery. Women are told that they are not even persons in our society. They are told that they are second-class citizens. I have given speeches where women have been picketing up and down outside, wearing placards saying, "I am a second-class citizen." I feel so sorry for women who are deliberating inculcating this inferiority complex. Women are not second-class citizens in our society. Whatever women may have been hundreds of years ago, in other lands, or in other countries, that is not the condition of women in our country today.

The thesis of the speeches that women's liberation movement speakers are giving runs basically like this: "Sister, when you wake up in the morning, the cards are stacked against you. You won't get a job, and if you get one, it won't be a good one. You'll never be paid what you're really worth. You won't be promoted as you deserve to be. You simply will never get a fair break in our society. And if you get married, your husband will treat you like a servant, like a chattel"—that's one of their favorite words—"and life is nothing but a bunch of dirty diapers and dirty dishes."

It's no wonder that women have problems when they listen to that line. The women's liberation movement literature is the greatest put-down of women that anything could possibly be. It's difficult to pick yourself up off the floor after you have listened to those tirades about how women are kept in bondage and enslaved, and how the home is a cage or a prison from which women must be liberated. This line creates a natural hostility between men and women. No longer are men people with whom we work in harmony. Men are the enemy who must make it up to us for these centuries of injustice.

Whatever lowly status women may endure in other lands, that is not the situation of American women. It is also true that nobody in this world who wakes up in the morning with a chip on your shoulder, whether it is man or woman, is going to have a happy or fulfilling life, or get ahead in this world.

This is not to say that there aren't any problems. The world is full of problems. I don't know anybody who doesn't have problems. Women face all kinds of problems: husbands out of a job, handicapped children, senile parents, or not enough money. The world is full of problems. But you don't solve your problems by waking up in the morning with a chip on your shoulder, believing and telling yourself hour after hour that you've been oppressed, and that it is up to somebody to remedy years of injustice.

After having flattened women by spreading this negative attitude, the women's liberation movement then comes along and offers its solution. The solution can be best described as the "new narcissism." You remember the story of Narcissus: the Greek youth who fell in love with his own image in the reflecting pool and finally died of unrequited desire.

The women's liberation movement teaches women this fundamental approach to life: "Seek your own self-fulfillment over every other value." It's a free country for those who choose to establish their scale of values that way. Some women make that choice, and they are free to do so if that is what they want. But I simply have to tell women that *that* attitude, that choice of goals, is not compatible with a happy marriage. It is *not* compatible with a successful family life and it is *not* compatible with motherhood.

In order to live in harmony in family life, with a man who's been brought up in another environment, you have to make social compromises, and most of us think that marriage is worth the price.

Motherhood must be a self-sacrificing role, a role of dedication and service. The mother must be able to subordinate her self-fulfillment and her desire for a career to the well-being of her children so that she can answer her child's call any hour of the day or night. This is what marriage and motherhood are all about, and it is not compatible with the dogmas of the women's liberation movement.

The women's liberation movement preaches that the greatest oppression of women is that women get pregnant and men don't get pregnant, and so women must be relieved of this oppression! The second greatest oppression of women, according to the liberation movement, is that society expects mothers to look after their babies, that society reduces women to this menial, tedious, tiresome, confining, repetitious chore of looking after babies.

Well, I suppose it's all in your point of view. Many of us believe that the ability to participate in the creation of human life is the great gift that God gave to women. The task of taking care of babies, despite its tedious drudgery, is better than most of the jobs of the world. Women should find out how exhausting most of the rest of the jobs of the world are. Besides, a mother has something to show for her efforts after twenty years: You've got a living, breathing human being, a good citizen, a wonderful human being you've given to this world.

But the women's movement is causing wives with relatively good families to walk out. Women's lib is a dogma that is especially contagious among women in their forties and fifties after their children are in school. Wives who "catch" the disease of women's liberation are walking out on marriage—not because of the traditional problems in marriage such as alcohol, or money, or adultery, but just to seek their own self-fulfillment.

I speak almost every week on college campuses and I see these abandoned teenagers. Young women come up to me and say, "My mother has left. What can you say to my mother, who has brought up four children and now thinks her whole life is wasted?" The women who "catch" women's liberation are walking out. It makes no difference whether they're northern and eastern liberal homes or southern and western conservative homes. Once they get this message, they go out into emptiness, abandoning their families.

This women's liberation dogma is also very contagious among young college women. They have bought a large part of it. The biggest thing that hits you on the college campuses today is that the educated young women of our nation are rejecting marriage and motherhood. Most important, they're rejecting motherhood. They're saying that if they have a baby, they don't want it to interfere with their careers. I have young men coming to me now saying that they want to marry a young woman, but she tells them very frankly, "If we have a baby, I'm not going to let that baby interfere with my career. I see nothing the matter with putting the baby in some child-care facility at the age of three or four weeks." Remember, this is not a matter of need. These are not hungry people. These are a class of women who expect to have degrees but they don't want that baby to interfere with their careers. Of course, my answer to those young men is, "Forget her." A woman who is unwilling to take care of her own baby is a pathetic sight, and there's nothing in marriage for a man to have a relationship like that. This is what the women's liberation movement is doing to the young women of our nation. . . .

There *is* another women's movement. You don't hear much about it, but I believe it is more powerful. It is the Positive Woman's Movement: the woman who knows who she is. The Positive Woman is not searching for her identity. She knows God made her, she knows why she's here, and she has her scale of values in order. This movement was born in 1972 when some of us realized we had to protect ourselves against the takeaway of the legal rights of the homemaker that was embodied in the Equal Rights Amendment. This movement showed itself at the marvelous Pro-Family Rally in Houston in 1977 where 15,000 people came at their own expense—not like the other one where people came at the taxpayers' expense. Our movement of Positive Women came of age on March 22, 1979 in Washington, D.C., when we celebrated, at a marvelous dinner in Washington, the expiration of the seven years that was set as the time period for ratification of the Equal Rights Amendment. . . .

Our Positive Women are not seeking their own self-fulfillment as the highest value, as the women's liberation movement tries to teach women. Our Positive Women are dedicated to service, to faith and trust in God, to the family, and to this great country that we have been fortunate enough to live in. We are not seeking to get our bit at the price of taking benefits away from others, as the woman's liberation movement is doing. We have taken on these great odds, believing, as we are told in II Chronicles, "Be not afraid, nor dismayed by reason of the great multitude, for the battle is not yours but God's."

We have fought the greatest political forces that anybody has ever fought in our country in this century. We have won, with God's help, because we are Positive Women. We don't wake up in the morning mad at anybody. We have women who are talented, articulate, capable. We have lady legislators and successful career women. We have some who are solely successful career women, others who are wives and mothers but who are also successful in an auxiliary career. The great thing about woman's role is that she can have different careers at different times in her life. But our Positive Women have their scale of values in order: no matter what they may seek for their own self-fulfillment, they know that the family is more important.

Our women are, I believe, the greatest positive force in our country today. We believe that we can do great things. Now that we move into the more positive phase of our activity, we will work for the restoration of the family unit, which is coming apart at the seams in many areas. We want to show women how, in this great country, women can do whatever they want to have all kinds of exciting lives. But for a woman to be a successful wife and mother, during that period of her life, marriage and motherhood must come first over selfish values.

In conclusion, I share with you the comment attributed to a French writer who traveled our country in another century and wrote many commentaries which are still studied in our schools. When he came to the conclusion of his travels, Alexis de Tocqueville wrote, "I sought for the greatness and genius of America in her commodious harbors and ample rivers, but it was not there. I sought for the greatness of America in her fertile lands and boundless prairies, but it was not there. It was not until I went into the churches of America and found her pulpits aflame with righteousness that I understood the secret of her genius and her power. America is great because America is good, and if America ever ceases to be good, she will cease to be great." The Positive Women of America are pledging themselves to do our part to make sure that America continues to be good.

Merle Woo

~

MERLE WOO (1941–   ), a socialist feminist activist, educator, and writer, is a leader in Radical Women and the Freedom Socialist Party. She wrote the following "Letter to Ma" in January 1980.

~

Dear Ma,

I was depressed over Christmas, and when New Year's rolled around, do you know what one of my resolves was? Not to come by and see you as much anymore. I had to ask myself why I get so down when I'm with you, my mother, who has focused so much of her life on me, who has endured so much; one who I am proud of and respect so deeply for simply surviving.

I suppose that one of the main reasons is that when I leave your house, your pretty little round white table in the dinette where we sit while you drink tea (with only three specks of Jasmine) and I smoke and drink coffee, I am down because I believe there are chasms between us. When you say, "I support you, honey, in everything you do except . . . except . . ." I know you mean except my speaking out and writing of my anger at all those things that have caused those chasms. When you say I shouldn't be so ashamed of Daddy, former gambler, retired clerk of a "gook suey" store, because of the time when I was six and saw him humiliated on Grant

Morega, Cherrie, and Gloria Anzaldua, eds. *This Bridge Called My Back: Writings by Radical Women of Color.* New York: Kitchen Table: Women of Color Press, 1983, pp. 140–146. "Letter to Ma," reprinted by permission of Merle Woo.

Avenue by two white cops, I know you haven't even been listening to me when I have repeatedly said that I am not ashamed of him, not you, not who we are. When you ask, "Are you so angry because you are unhappy?" I know that we are not talking to each other. Not with understanding, although many words have passed between us, many hours, many afternoons at that round table with Daddy out in the front room watching television, and drifting out every once in a while to say "Still talking?" and getting more peanuts that are so bad for his health.

We talk and we talk and I feel frustrated by your censorship. I know it is unintentional and unconscious. But whatever I have told you about the classes I was teaching, or the stories I was working on, you've always forgotten within a month. Maybe you can't listen—because maybe when you look in my eyes, you will, as you've always done, sense more than what we're actually saying, and that makes you fearful. Do you see your repressed anger manifested in me? What doors would groan wide open if you heard my words with complete understanding? Are you afraid that your daughter is breaking out of our shackles, and into total anarchy? That your daughter has turned into a crazy woman who advocates not only equality for Third World people, for women, but for gays as well? Please don't shudder, Ma, when I speak of homosexuality. Until we can all present ourselves to the world in our completeness, as fully and beautifully as we see ourselves naked in our bedrooms, we are not free.

After what seems like hours of talking, I realize it is not talking at all, but the filling up of time with sounds that say, "I am your daughter, you are my mother, and we are keeping each other company, and that is enough." But it is not enough because my life has been formed by your life. Together we have lived one hundred and eleven years in this country as yellow women, and it is not enough to enunciate words and words and words and then to have them only mean that we have been keeping each other company. I desperately want you to understand me and my work, Ma, to know what I am doing! When you distort what I say, like thinking I am against all "caucasians" or that I am ashamed of Dad, then I feel anger and more frustration and want to slash out, not at you, but at those external forces which keep us apart. What deepens the chasms between us are our different reactions to those forces. Yours has been one of silence, self-denial, self-effacement; you believing it is your fault that you never fully experienced self-pride and free-dom of choice. But listen, Ma, only with a deliberate consciousness is my reaction different from yours.

When I look at you, there are images: images of you as a little ten-year-old Korean girl, begin sent alone from Shanghai to the United States, in steerage with only one skimpy little dress, being sick and lonely on Angel Island for three months; then growing up in a "Home" run by white missionary women. Scrubbing floors on your hands and knees, hauling coal in heavy metal buckets up three flights of stairs, tending to the younger children, putting hot bricks on your cheeks to deaden the pain from the terrible toothaches you always had. Working all your life as maid, waitress, salesclerk, office worker, mother. But throughout there is an image of you as strong and courageous, and persevering: climbing out of windows to escape from the Home, then later, from an abusive first husband. There is so much more to these images than I can say, but I think you know what I mean. Escaping out of windows offered only temporary respites; surviving is an everyday chore. You gave me, physically, what you never had, but there was a spiritual, emo-tional legacy you passed down which was reinforced by society: self-contempt because of our race, our sex, our sexuality. For deeply ingrained in me, Ma, there has been that strong, compulsive force to sink into self-contempt, passivity, and despair. I am sure that my fifteen years of alcohol abuse have not been forgotten by either of us, nor my suicidal depressions.

Now, I know you are going to think that I hate and despise you for your self-hatred, for your isolation. But I don't. Because in spite of your withdrawal, in spite of your loneliness, you have not only survived, but been beside me in the worst of times when your com-pany meant everything in the world to me. I just need more than that now, Ma. I have taken and taken from you in terms of needing you to mother me, to be by my side, and I need, now, to take from you two more things: understanding and support for who I am now and my work.

We are Asian American women and the reaction to our identity is what causes the chasms instead of connections. But do you realize, Ma, that I could never have reacted the way I have if you had not provided for me the opportunity to be free of the binds that have held you down, and to be in the process of self-affirmation? Because of your life, because of the physical security you have given me: my education, my full stomach, my clothed and starched back, my piano and dancing lessons—all those gifts you never received—I saw myself as having worth; now I begin to love myself more, see our potential, and fight for just that kind of social change that will affirm me, my race, my sex, my heritage. And while I affirm myself, Ma, I affirm you.

Today, I am satisfied to call myself either an Asian American Feminist or Yellow Feminist. The two terms are inseparable because race and sex are an integral part of me. This means that I am working with others to realize pride in culture and women and heritage (the heritage that is the exploited yellow immigrant: Daddy and you). Being a Yellow Feminist means being a community activist and a humanist. It does not mean "separatism," either by cutting myself off from non-Asians or men. It does not mean retaining the same power structure and substituting women in positions of control held by men. It does mean fighting the whites and the men who abuse us, straight-jacket us and tape our mouths; it means changing the economic class system and psychological forces (sexism, racism, and homophobia) that really hurt all of us. And I do this, not in isolation, but in the community.

We no longer can afford to stand back and watch while an insatiable elite ravages and devours resources which are enough for all of us. The obstacles are so huge and overwhelming that often I do become cynical and want to give up. And if I were struggling alone, I know I would never even attempt to put into action what I believe in my heart, that (and this is primarily because of you, Ma) Yellow Women are strong and have the potential to be powerful and effective leaders.

I can hear you asking now, "Well, what do you mean by 'social change and leadership'? And how are you going to go about it?" To begin with we must wipe out the circumstances that keep us down in silence and self-effacement. Right now, my techniques are education and writing. Yellow Feminist means being a core for change, and that core means having the belief in our potential as human beings. I will work with anyone, support anyone, who shares my sensibility, my objectives. But there are barriers to unity: white women who are racist, and Asian American men who are sexist. My very being declares that those two groups do not share my complete sensibility. I would be fragmented, mutilated, if I did not fight against racism and sexism together.

And this is when the pain of the struggle hits home. How many white women have taken on the responsibility to educate themselves about Third World people, their history, their culture? How many white women really think about the stereotypes they retain as truth about women of color? But the perpetuation of dehumanizing stereotypes is really very helpful for whites; they use them to justify their giving us the lowest wages and all the work they don't want to perform. Ma, how can we believe things are changing when as a nurse's aide during World War II, you were given only the tasks of changing the bed linen, removing bed pans, taking urine samples, and then only three years ago as a retired volunteer worker in a local hospital, white women gave themselves desk jobs and gave you, at sixty-nine, the same work you did in 1943? Today you speak more fondly of being a nurse's aid during World War II and how proud you are of the fact that the Red Cross showed its appreciation for your service by giving you a diploma. Still in 1980, the injustices continue. I can give you so many examples of groups which are "feminist" in which women of color were given the usual least important tasks, the shitwork, and given no say in how that group is to be run. Needless to say, those Third World women, like you, dropped out, quit.

Working in writing and teaching, I have seen how white women condescend to Third World women because they reason that because of our oppression, which they know nothing about, we are behind them and their "progressive ideas" in the struggle for freedom. They don't even look at history! At the facts! How we as Asian American women have always been fighting for more than mere survival, but were never acknowledged because we were in our communities, invisible, but not inaccessible.

And I get so tired of being the instant resource for information on Asian American women. Being the token representative, going from class to class, group to group, bleeding for white women so they can have an easy answer—and then, and this is what really gets to me—they usually leave to never continue their education about us on their own.

To the racist white female professor who says, "If I have to watch everything I say I wouldn't say anything," I want to say, "Then get out of teaching."

To the white female poet who says, "Well, frankly, I believe that politics and poetry don't necessarily have to go together," I say, "Your little taste of white privilege has deluded you into thinking that you don't have to fight against sexism in this society. You are talking to me from your own isolation and your own racism. If you feel that you don't have to fight for me, that you don't have to speak out against capitalism, the exploitation of human and natural resources, then you in your silence, your inability to make connections, are siding with a system that will eventually get you, after it has gotten me. And if you think that's not a political stance, you're more than simply deluded, you're crazy!"

This is the same white voice that says, "I am writing about and looking for themes that are 'universal.'" Well, most of the time when "universal" is used, it is just a euphemism for "white": white themes, white significance, white culture. And denying minority groups their rightful place and time in U.S. history is simply racist.

Yes, Ma, I am mad. I carry the anger from my own experience and the anger you couldn't afford to express, and even that is often misinterpreted no matter how hard I try to be clear about my position. A white woman in my class said to me a couple of months ago, "I feel that Third World women hate me and that *they* are being racists; I'm being stereotyped, and I've never been part of the ruling class." I replied, "Please try to understand. Know our history. Know the racism of whites, how deep it goes. Know that we are becoming ever more intolerant of those people who let their ignorance be their excuse for their complacency, their liberalism, when this country (this world!) is going to hell in a handbasket. Try to understand that our distrust is from experience, and that our distrust is power*less*. Racism is an essential part of the status quo, power*ful*, and continues to keep us down. It is a rule taught to all of us from birth. Is it no wonder that we fear there are no exceptions?"

And as if the grief we go through working with white women weren't enough; so close to home, in our community, and so very painful, is the lack of support we get from some of our Asian American brothers. Here is a quote from a rather prominent male writer ranting on about a Yellow "sister":

> . . . I can only believe that such blatant sucking off of the identity
> is the work of a Chinese American woman, another Jade Snow
> Wong Pochahontas yellow. Pussywhipped again. Oh, damn,
> pussywhipped again.

Chinese American woman: "another Jade Snow Wong Pochahontas yellow." According to him, Chinese American women sold out—are contemptuous of their culture, pathetically strain all their lives to be white, hate Asian American men, and so marry white men (the John Smiths)—or just like Pochahontas: we rescue white men while betraying our fathers; then marry white men, get baptized, and go to dear old England to become curiosities of the civilized world. Whew! Now, that's an indictment! (Of all women of color.) Some of the male writers in the Asian American community seem never to support us. They always expect us to support them, and you know what? We almost always do. Anti-Yellow men? Are they kidding? We go to their readings, buy and read and comment on their books, and try to keep up a dialogue. And they accuse us of betrayal, are resentful because we do readings together as Women, and so often do not come to our performances. And all the while we hurt because we are rejected by our brothers. The Pochahontas image used by a Chinese American man points out a tragic truth: the white man and his ideology are still over us and between us. These men of color, with clear vision, fight the racism in white society, but have bought the white male definition of "masculinity": men only should take on the leadership in the community because the qualities of "originality, daring, physical courage, and creativity" are "traditionally masculine."*

Some Asian men don't seem to understand that by supporting Third World women and fighting sexism, they are helping themselves as well. I understand all too clearly how dehumanized Dad was in this country. To be a Chinese man in America is to be a victim of both racism and sexism. He was made to feel he was without strength, identity, and purpose. He was made to feel soft and weak, whose only job was to serve whites. Yes, Ma, at one time I was ashamed of him because I thought he was "womanly." When those two white cops said, "Hey, fat boy, where's our meat?" he left me standing there on Grant Avenue while he hurried over to his store to get it; they kept complaining, never satisfied, "That piece isn't good enough. What's the matter with you, fat boy? Don't you have respect? Don't wrap that meat in newspapers either; use the good stuff over there." I didn't know that he spent a year and half on Angel Island; that we could never have our right names; that he lived in constant fear of being deported; that, like you, he worked two full-time jobs most of his life; that he was mocked and ridiculed because he speaks "broken English." And Ma, I was so ashamed after that experience when I was only six years old that I never held his hand again.

*AHEEEEE! An Anthology of Asian American Writers, editors Frank Chin, Jeffrey Paul Chan, Lawson Fusao Inada, Shawn Wong (Howard University Press, 1974).

Today, as I write to you of all these memories, I feel even more deeply hurt when I realize how many people, how so many people, because of racism and sexism, fail to see what power we sacrifice by not joining hands.

But not all white women are racist, and not all Asian American men are sexist. And we choose to trust them, love and work with them. And there are visible changes. Real tangible, positive changes. The changes I love to see are those changes within ourselves.

Your grandchildren, my children, Emily and Paul. That makes three generations. Emily loves herself. Always has. There are shades of self-doubt but much less than in you or me. She says exactly what she thinks, most of the time, either in praise or in criticism of herself or others. And at sixteen she goes after whatever she wants, usually center stage. She trusts and loves people, regardless of race or sex (but, of course, she's cautious), loves her community and works in it, speaks up against racism and sexism at school. Did you know that she got Zora Neale Hurston and Alice Walker on her reading list for a Southern Writers class when there were only white authors? That she insisted on changing a script done by an Asian American man when she saw that the depiction of the character she was playing was sexist? That she went to a California State House Conference to speak out for Third World students' needs?

And what about her little brother, Paul? Twelve years old. And remember, Ma? At one of our Saturday Night Family Dinners, how he lectured Ronnie (his uncle, yet!) about how he was a male chauvinist? Paul told me once how he knew he had to fight to be Asian American, and later he added that if it weren't for Emily and me, he wouldn't have to think about feminist stuff too. He says he can hardly enjoy a movie or TV program anymore because of the sexism. Or comic books. And he is very much aware of the different treatment he gets from adults: "You have to do everything right," he said to Emily, "and I can get away with almost anything."

Emily and Paul give us hope, Ma. Because they are proud of who they are, and they care so much about our culture and history.

Emily was the first to write your biography because she knows how crucial it is to get our stories in writing.

Ma, I wish I knew the histories of the women in our family before you. I bet that would be quite a story. But that may be just as well, because I can say that *you* started something. Maybe you feel ambivalent or doubtful about it, but you did. Actually, you should be proud of what you've begun. I am. If my reaction to being a Yellow Woman is different than yours was, please know that that is not a judgment on you, a criticism or a denial of you, your worth. I have always supported you, and as the years pass, I think I begin to understand you more and more.

In the last few years, I have realized the value of Homework: I have studied the history of our people in this country. I cannot tell you how proud I am to be a Chinese/Korean American Woman. We have such a proud heritage, such a courageous tradition. I want to tell everyone about that, all the particulars that are left out in the schools. And the full awareness of being a woman makes me want to sing. And I do sing with other Asian Americans and women, Ma, anyone who will sing with me.

I feel now that I can begin to put our lives in a larger framework. Ma, a larger framework! The outlines for us are time and blood, but today there is breadth possible through making connections with others involved in community struggle. In loving ourselves for who we are—American women of color—we can make a vision for the future where we are free to fulfill our human potential. This new framework will not support repression, hatred, exploitation and isolation, but will be a human and beautiful framework, created in a community, bonded not by color, sex or class, but by love and the common goal for the liberation of mind, heart, and spirit.

Ma, today, you are as beautiful and pure to me as the picture I have of you, as a little girl, under my dresser-glass.

I love you,
Merle

Geraldine Ferraro

~

GERALDINE FERRARO (1935–), Walter F. Mondale's running mate in 1984, was the first American woman to receive the nomination of a major political party for vice president. The following is her acceptance speech before the Democratic National Convention.

~

Ladies and gentlemen of the convention—ladies and gentlemen of the convention—ladies and gentlemen of the convention, my name is Geraldine Ferraro, I stand before you to proclaim tonight: America is a land where dreams can come true for all of us.

As I stand before the American people and think of the honor this great convention has bestowed upon me, I recall the words of Dr. Martin Luther King Jr., who made America stronger by making America more free.

He said: "Occasionally in life there are moment which cannot be completely explained by words. Their meaning can only be articulated by the inaudible language of the heart."

Tonight is such a moment for me. My heart is filled with pride.

My fellow citizens, I proudly accept your nomination for Vice President of the United States.

And—you're wonderful. And—And—And I am proud to run with a man who will be one of the great Presidents of this century, Walter F. Mondale.

New York Times, July 20, 1984, I 14:1.

Tonight the daughter of a woman whose highest goal was a future for her children talks to our nation's oldest party about a future for us all.

Tonight, the daughter of working Americans tells all Americans that the future is within our reach—if we're willing to reach for it.

Tonight, the daughter of an immigrant from Italy has been chosen—has been chosen to run for [Vice] President in the new land my father came to love.

Our faith that we can shape a better future is what the American dream is all about. The promise of our country is that the rules are fair. If you work hard and play by the rules, you can earn your share of America's blessings.

Those are the beliefs I learned from my parents. And those are the values I taught my students as a teacher in the public schools of New York City.

At night, I went to law school. I became an Assistant District Attorney, and I put my share of criminals behind bars. I believe: If you obey the law, you should be protected. But if you break the law, you must pay for your crime.

When I first ran for Congress, all the political experts said a Democrat could not win in my home district in Queens. I put my faith in the people and the values that we shared. Together, we proved the political experts wrong.

In this campaign, Fritz Mondale and I have put our faith in the people. And we are going to prove the experts wrong again.

We are going to win. We are going to win, because Americans across this country believe in the same basic dream.

Last week, I visited Elmore, Minn., the small town where—Yay Elmore!—the small town where Fritz Mondale was raised. And soon Fritz and Joan will visit our family in Queens.

Nine hundred people live in Elmore. In Queens there are 2,000 people on one block. You would think we'd be different, but we're not.

Children walk to school in Elmore past grain elevators; in Queens, they pass by subways stops. But, no matter where they live, their future depends on education—and their parents are willing to do their part to make those schools as good as they can be.

In Elmore, there are family farms; in Queens, small businesses. But the men and women who run them all take pride in supporting their families through hard work and initiative.

On the Fourth of July in Elmore, they hang flags out on Main Street; in Queens, they fly them over Grand Avenue. But all of us love our country, and stand ready to defend the freedom that it represents.

Americans want to live by the same set of rules. But under this Administration, the rules are rigged against too many of our people.

It isn't right that every year, the share of taxes paid by individual citizens is going up, while the share paid by large corporations is getting smaller and smaller. The rules say: Everyone in our society should contribute their fair share.

It isn't right that this year Ronald Reagan will hand the American people a bill for interest on the national debt larger than the entire cost of the Federal Government under John F. Kennedy.

Our parents left us a growing economy. The rules say: We must not leave our kids a mountain of debt.

It isn't right that a woman should get paid 59 cents on the dollar for the same work as a man. If you play by the rules, you deserve a fair day's pay for a fair day's work.

It isn't right that if trends continue, by the year 2000 nearly all of the poor people in America will be women and children. The rules—the rules of a decent society say, when you distribute sacrifice in times of austerity, you don't put women and children first.

It isn't right that young people today fear they won't get the Social Security they paid for, and that older Americans fear they will lose what they have already earned. Social Security is a contract between the last generation and the next, and the rules say: You don't break contracts. We are going to keep faith with older Americans.

We hammered out a fair compromise in the Congress to save Social Security. Every group sacrificed to keep the system sound. It is time Ronald Reagan stopped scaring our senior citizens.

It isn't right that young couples question whether to bring children into a world of 50,000 nuclear warheads.

That isn't the vision for which Americans have struggled for more than two centuries. And our future doesn't have to be that way. Change is in the air, just as surely as when John Kennedy beckoned America to a New Frontier; when Sally Ride rocketed into space; and when Reverend Jesse Jackson ran for the office of President of the United States.

By choosing a woman to run for our nation's second highest office, you send a powerful signal to all Americans. There are no doors we cannot unlock. We will place no limit on achievement.

If we can do this, we can do anything.

Tonight, we reclaim our dream. We're going to make the rules of American life work fairly for all Americans again.

To an Administration that would have us debate all over again whether the Voting Rights Act should be renewed and whether segregated schools should be tax exempt, we say, Mr. President: Those debates are over. On the issue of civil rights voting rights and affirmative action for minorities, we must not go backwards. We must and we will move forward to open the doors of opportunity.

To those who understand that our country cannot prosper unless we draw on the talents of all Americans, we say: We will pass the equal rights amendment. The issue is not what America can do for women, but what women can do for America.

To the Americans who will lead our country into the 21st century, we say: We will not have a Supreme Court that turns the clock back to the 19th century. To those concerned about the strength of American and family values as I am I say we are going to restore those values; love, caring, partnership by including and not excluding those whose beliefs differ from our own because our own faith is strong we will fight to preserve the freedom of faith for others.

To those working Americans who fear that banks, utilities, and large special interests have a lock on the White House we say: Join us; let's elect a people's President; and let's have a government by and for the American people again.

To an Administration that would savage student loads in education at the dawn of a new technological age, we say: You fit the classic definition of a cynic: You know the price of everything, but the value of nothing.

To our students and their parents, we say: We will insist on the highest standards of excellence because the jobs of the future require skilled minds.

To young Americans who may be called to our country's service, we say: We know your generation will proudly answer our country's call, as each generation before you.

This past year we remembered the bravery and sacrifice of Americans at Normandy. And we finally paid tribute, as we should have done years ago, to that unknown soldier who represents all the brave young Americans who died in Vietnam.

Let no one doubt we will defend America's security and the cause of freedom around the world. But we want a President who tells us what America is fighting for, not just what we are fighting against. We want a President who will defend human rights—not just where it is convenient—but wherever freedom is at risk—from Chile to Afghanistan from Poland to South Africa. To those who would want this Administration's confusion in the Middle East as it is tilted first toward one and then another of Israel's long-time enemies and wonder will America stand by her friends and sister democracies? We say America knows who her friends are in the Middle East and around the world. America will stand with Israel always.

Finally, we want a President who will keep America strong, but use that strength to keep America, and the world, at peace. A nuclear freeze is not a slogan: it is a tool for survival in the nuclear age. If we leave our children nothing else, let us leave them this earth as we found it—whole and green and full of life.

I know in my heart that Walter Mondale will be that President.

A wise man once said, "Every one of us is given the gift of life, and what a strange gift it is. If it is preserved jealously and selfishly, it impoverishes and saddens. But if it is spent for others, it enriches and beautifies."

My fellow Americans: We can debate policies and programs. But in the end what separates the two parties in this election campaign is whether we use the gift of life—for others or only ourselves.

Tonight, my husband, John, and our three children are in this hall with me. To my daughters, Donna and Laura, and my son, John Jr., I say: My mother did not break faith with me and I will not break faith with you. To all the children of America, I say: The generation before ours kept faith with us, and like them, we will pass on to you a stronger, more just America.

Thank you very much.

Wilma Mankiller

~

WILMA MANKILLER (1945–) was the first woman to serve as principal chief of the Cherokee Nation or, indeed, of any major Native American tribe. In her autobiography, *Mankiller: A Chief and Her People*, she recalls her work on behalf of her people and their election of her to serve as their chief.

~

I honestly believed I could not possibly get elected. I realized that I had successfully developed and managed tribal programs and had much experience . . . but I simply could not picture myself in high tribal office. I told Chief Swimmer I was honored that he had chosen me, but my answer was a polite no. I had to decline.

But almost immediately after I gave him my answer, I started to think about what was transpiring around me. I then gave Chief Swimmer's offer more thought. I went out among some of our rural communities in eastern Oklahoma where we were facilitating development projects. In one small community, I came upon three of our people living in an abandoned bus without any roof. Their few extra clothes were hanging on a line. They had few other possessions. It was a very sad scene. It burned into my mind.

I knew this was not an isolated situation. Many Cherokees were forced to put up with poor housing, rising medical costs, and educational deficits. I realized I was being given an opportunity to create change for Cherokee families such as those living in the old bus. I knew that if I did not act, I would no longer have any right to talk about or criticize the people who held tribal offices.

The visit to that small community had a major impact on me. I drove straight to Ross Swimmer's home. I told him I had reconsidered, and I would run for election as deputy chief in the 1983 election. I quite my job with the Cherokee Nation so there would be no conflict of interest, and I filed for office.

From the start, I figured most people would be bothered about my ideas on grass-roots democracy and the fact that I had a fairly extensive activist background. I adhered to a different political philosophy than many people living in the area. But I was wrong. No one challenged me on those issues, not once. Instead, I was challenged mostly because of one fact—I am female. The election became an issue of gender. It was one of the first times I had ever really encountered overt sexism. I recalled that my first real experience with sexism had occurred in California. I had once slugged a boss during a Christmas party in San Francisco when he came up behind me and tried to kiss me. He did not fire me, but I do believe he got the message that I did not want to be mauled. The memory of that time came back to me during the 1983 campaign.

I heard all sorts of things—some people claimed that my running for office was an affront to God. Others said having a female run our tribe would make the Cherokees the laughing stock of the tribal world. I heard it all. Every time I was given yet another silly reason why I should not help run our government, I was certain that I had made the correct decision.

The reaction to my candidacy stunned me. It was a very low time in my life, but I would not be swayed. I figured the best tactic was to ignore my opponents. I remembered a saying I had once read on the back of a tea box. It said something like this—if you argue with a fool, someone passing by will not be able to tell who is the fool and who is not. I did not wish to be taken for a fool.

I built my run for office on a positive and cheerful foundation to counter the incredible hostility and great opposition I encountered. To say that the campaign was heated would be the understatement of all times. Most of the negative acts did not originate with my opponents for office, but with those who did not want a woman in office. I even had foes *within* the Swimmer-Mankiller team. Toward the end of the campaign, some of them openly supported one of my opponents.

Occasionally, the actions of those who were out to stop my election were violent. I received hate mail, including several death threats. After one evening rally, I returned to my car and discovered that all four tires had been slashed. On other occasions, there were threatening messages over the telephone. Once I picked up my ringing telephone and heard the sound of a rifle bolt being slammed shut on the other end of the line.

I also had a chilling experience while riding in a parade. I was waving and laughing and smiling at the crowd along the street when I spied someone in the back of the crowd. I saw a young man, and he had his hand cocked and his fingers pointed at me as if he were holding a pistol. Then he drew his hand back, firing an imaginary gun. I never even blinked. I just calmly looked away. The parade continued. No matter how disturbing those incidents were, the scare tactics did not work. One consolation was that the people in Bell and other rural Cherokee communities where I had worked were very supportive.

My two opponents for office were J. B. Dreadfulwater, a popular gospel singer and former member of the tribal council, and Agnes Cowan, the first woman to serve on the tribal council. She was older than I was, and already established in our tribal government. They were worthy opponents who liked to criticize me for having no experience in tribal politics. . . .

I think my opponents ignored the fact that I had a great deal of experience as a community organizer. I had learned a long time ago, at the Indian Center in San Francisco, how to reach large groups of people and bring them together. That is just what I did. I went door to door and campaigned. I attended every event and rally. I kept encountering opposition as a female candidate, but I did not use it as an issue in my campaign. Gradually, I saw some changes, but they were very few and far between.

Finally, election day arrived. When the ballots had been counted, Ross Swimmer was reelected, to his third term. I beat out Dreadfulwater in that first election, but had to face Cowan in a July runoff. In a tough battle, I defeated her and was able to claim ultimate victory. It was truly a moment to remember forever. The people of my tribe had selected me to serve as the first woman deputy chief in Cherokee history. I took office on August 14, 1983. As one of my supporters put it, at long last a daughter of the people had been chosen for high tribal office. . . .

My two years as deputy chief proved to be difficult—very difficult. I had inherited many people on Ross Swimmer's staff, and would not have my own people aboard for some time to come. Although Swimmer had chosen me as deputy and had stuck with me through the tough campaign, there were major differences between us. He was a Republican banker with a very conservative viewpoint, and I was a Democratic social worker and community planner who had organized and worked for Indian civil and treaty rights. . . .

I stayed very busy as a deputy chief, helping to govern an Indian nation spread over fourteen counties in northeastern Oklahoma. Despite our differences, Swimmer and I shared an absolute commitment to the rebuilding and revitalizing of our rural communities. As deputy chief, I helped to supervise the daily operations of the tribe. Those included more than forty tribally operated programs ranging from health clinics to day care, elderly assistance to water projects, Head Start classes to housing construction.

Then in September of 1985—just a little more than two years after I took office—there was more sudden change to deal with. Chief Swimmer was asked to go to Washington to head the BIA [Bureau of Indian Affairs] when he was nominated by President

Ronald Reagan to serve as assistant secretary of the interior for Indian affairs. To assume the top Indian affairs post in the federal government . . . was an offer that Swimmer, then forty-one, did not want to refuse. . . .

I had to serve the balance of Ross Swimmer's term—from 1985 to 1987—without any real mandate from the people.

Swimmer's presidential nomination was ultimately confirmed by the United States Senate, and on December 5, 1985, I was sworn in as principal chief of the Cherokee Nation in a private ceremony. Formal ceremonies were held on December 14 at the tribal headquarters. Right before I took the oath of office, Ross Swimmer called me to offer his best.

Memories of my public inauguration will stay with me as long as I live. It was not the happiest of occasions. Swimmer had had little time to prepare me for all the complex issues we were facing. His staff members and many other people felt that the Cherokee National would crash and burn with a woman in charge. I was very wary. I knew full well what was ahead.

For the ceremony, I wore a dark suit and white blouse. There was snow on the ground, but the sky was clear and blue and cloudless. So many people came to me with hugs and smiles and good wishes. There were tears of happiness. I recall sitting behind the chief's desk for the first time for an official photo, and someone in the office said, "You look very natural sitting there. It's very becoming."

The council chamber was packed. There were many photographers, reporters, and guests. At the proper time, I stepped forward and placed my hand on a Bible. I raised my other hand to take the oath of office. It is a very straightforward pledge:

"I, Wilma P. Mankiller, do solemnly swear, or affirm, that I will faithfully execute the duties of Principal Chief of the Cherokee National. And will, to the best of my abilities, preserve, protect, and defend the Constitutions of the Cherokee Nation and the United States of America. I swear, or affirm, further that I will do everything within my power to promote the culture, heritage, and tradition of the Cherokee Nation."

Thunderous applause followed when I finished the oath and stepped up to the podium. As the crowd became still, the sound of camera shutters clicking continued until I spoke. I thanked everyone in attendance, and all of my friends, family, and supporters. I spoke of the deep honor of assuming the position of chief. I complimented Ross Swimmer for his leadership, and I talked of the many tasks before me. . . .

By the time I took the oath of office, my eldest daughter, Felicia, had married, and I had my first grandchild, Aaron Swake. I was a forty-year-old grandmother, as well as the first woman to serve as chief of a major tribe. I told the reporters, who seemed to materialize from out of nowhere, that the only people who were really worried about my serving as chief were members of my family. That was because all of them knew very well how much time I tended to devote to my job. My daughters were, of course, concerned about my health. But my little grandson thought it was great that his grandma was the chief. . . .

One thing that I never tried to become as chief was "one of the boys," nor am I a "good ol' girl." I never will be. That goes against my grain. I do know how to be political and to get the job done, but I do not believe that one must sacrifice one's principles. Gradually, I noticed changes within the tribe and especially within the council.

Rural development was, and still remains, a high priority on my list of goals. For me, the rewards came from attempting to break the circle of poverty. My feeling is that the Cherokee people, by and large, are incredibly tenacious. We have survived so many major political and social upheavals, yet we have kept the Cherokee government alive. I feel confident that we will march into the twenty-first century on our own terms.

We are staffed with professionals—educators, physicians, attorneys, business leaders. Already, in the 1800s, we fought many of our wars with lawsuits, and it was in the courts where many of our battles were won. Today, we are helping to erase the stereotypes created by media and by western films of the drunken Indian on a horse, chasing wagon trains across the prairie. I suppose some people still think that all native people live in tepees and wear tribal garb every day. They do not realize that many of us wear business suits and drive station wagons. The beauty of society today is that young Cherokee men and women can pursue any professional fields they want and remain true to traditional values. It all comes back to our heritage and our roots. It is so vital that we retain that sense of culture, history, and tribal identity.

We also are returning the balance to the role of women in our tribe. Prior to my becoming chief, young Cherokee girls never thought they might be able to grow up and become chief themselves. That has definitely changed. From the start of my administration, the impact on the younger women of the Cherokee Nation was noticeable. I feel certain that more women will assume leadership roles in tribal communities.

In 1992, I attended a meeting in the Midwest. My keynote presentation had been well publicized in the region. After my presentation, a native man told me he had an important message for me. He told me he was an Oneida, and one of the prophecies he had heard was that this time period is the time of the women—a time for women to take on a more important role in society. He described this as "the time of the butterfly."

When I read recently of Judge Ruth Bader Ginsburg's nomination to the Supreme Court, Hillary Rodham Clinton's work on health-care reform, the appointment of Ada Deer as assistant secretary of the interior in charge of the BIA, and the election of a female Canadian prime minister, I smiled and thought about the prophecy of the anonymous Oneida man who had driven all day to pass along his message to me. . . .

In 1987, after I had fulfilled the balance of Ross Swimmer's term as chief, I made the decision to run on my own and to win a four-year term of office. It was not an easy decision. I knew the campaign would be most difficult. I talked to my family and to my people. I spent long hours discussing the issues with Charlie Soap, whom I had married in 1986. Charlie had contracted with private foundations to continue development work with low-income native community projects. His counsel to me was excellent. He encouraged me to run. So did many other people.

But there were others who were opposed to my continuing as chief. Even some of my friends and advisers told me they believed the Cherokee people would accept me only as deputy, not as an elected principal chief. Some of those people came to our home at Mankiller Flats. I would look out the window and see them coming down the dirt road to tell me that I should give up any idea of running for chief. Finally, I told Charlie that if one more family came down that road and told me not to run, I was going to run for sure. That is just what happened.

I made my official announcement in early 1987, calling for a "positive, forward-thinking campaign." . . .

I drew three opponents in the race for principal chief. I had to face Dave Whitekiller, a postal assistant from the small community of Cookson and a former councilman; William McKee, deputy administrator at W. W. Hastings Indian Hospital, in Tahlequah; and Perry Wheeler, a former deputy chief and a funeral home director from Sallisaw, in Sequoyah County.

From the beginning, the best description of the campaign came from someone on the council, who said there was an "undercurrent of viciousness." I ignored things that were going on around me. I did the same thing I had always done—went out to the communities and talked to as many of the Cherokee people as possible about the issues. I tried to answer all their questions. My critics claimed that I had failed to properly manage and direct the Cherokee Nation, which was obviously false. Our revenue for 1986 was up $6 million, higher than it had ever been to that point. I was not about to lose focus by warring with my opponents.

The election eliminated all the candidates except for Perry Wheeler and me. None of us had received more than 50 percent of the votes. I had polled 45 percent to Wheeler's 29 percent. We had to face each other in a July runoff. My supporters worked very hard during those last few weeks. Charlie was one of my main champions. On my behalf, Charlie visited many rural homes where

English is a second language to remind the people that prior to the intrusion of white men, women had played key roles in our government. He asked our people to not turn their backs on their past or their future.

Charlie's help was especially important because I was stricken with my old nemesis, kidney problems, during the final weeks of the campaign. Finally, just before the election, I had to be hospitalized in Tulsa, but the physicians never determined the exact location of the infection and could not bring it under control. The lengthy infection and hospitalization would nearly cost me not only the election but also my life, since it brought on extensive and irreversible kidney damage. From that point forward, I was repeatedly hospitalized for kidney and urinary-tract infections, until I underwent surgery and had a kidney transplant in 1990.

Wheeler, an unsuccessful candidate for the chief's job against Ross Swimmer in 1983, tried to make my hospitalization a major issue. He waged a vigorous and negative runoff campaign. He publicly stated that I had never been truthful about my health. . . .

When all the ballots from thirty-four precincts plus the absentee votes were tallied, the woman who supposedly knew nothing about politics was declared the winner. The night of the runoff election, we went to the Tulsa Powwow, where my daughter Gina was being honored. In a photograph taken that evening, Charlie, Gina, Felicia, and I look very tired and worn, as if we had just been through a battle. Later that night, we returned to Tahlequah to check on the election results. When the votes of the local precincts were counted, it appeared that I had won easily. Everyone around me was celebrating, but I was concerned about the absentee votes. Once that vote was included, I allowed myself to celebrate.

At last, the Cherokee Nation had elected its first woman as principal chief—the first woman chief of a major Native American tribe. . . .

At long last, I had the mandate I had wanted. I had been chosen as principal chief of the Cherokee Nation by my own people. It was a sweet victory. Finally, I felt the question of gender had been put to rest. Today, if anyone asks members of our tribe if it really matters if the chief is male or female, the majority will reply that gender has no bearing on leadership.

Because I have risen to the office of chief, some people erroneously conclude that the role of native women has changed in *every* tribe. That is not so. People jump to that conclusion because they do not really understand native people. There is no universal "Indian language." All of us have our own distinct languages and cultures. In the African-American community, people can rally around a single leader, as they did for a while around Dr. Martin Luther King, Jr. Because Native Americans have our own languages, cultures, art forms, and social systems, our tribes are radically different from one another. Many tribal groups do not have women in titled positions, but in the great majority of those groups, there is some degree of balance and harmony in the roles of men and women. Among the Lakota, there is a very well known saying that "a nation is not defeated until the hearts of the women are on the ground." . . .

In the instance of the Cherokees, we are fortunate to have many strong women. I have attained a leadership position because I am willing to take risks, but at the same time, I am trying to teach other women, both Cherokees and others, to take risks also. I hope more women will gradually emerge in leadership positions. When I ran for deputy chief in 1983, I quit my job and spent every dollar of my personal savings . . . to pay for campaign expenses. Friends describe me as someone who likes to dance along the edge of the roof. I try to encourage young women to be willing to take risks, to stand up for the things they believe in, and to step up and accept the challenge of serving in leadership roles. . . .

If I am to be remembered, I want it to be because I am fortunate enough to have become my tribe's first female chief. But I also want to be remembered for emphasizing the fact that we have indigenous solutions to our problems. Cherokee values, especially those of helping one another and of our interconnections with the land, can be used to address contemporary issues.

During those first few years of serving as chief, I began to feel an immense responsibility. I would think to myself that if I did not make it to this meeting or to that session, it would reflect poorly on all women. I felt that not only my credibility but also the credibility of any woman who might follow me was on the line.

Gradually, I relaxed. As my comfort level with my position as chief increased with each passing day, I found myself able to accomplish even more for the Cherokee people. . . .

Mary Cunningham Agee

~

MARY CUNNINGHAM AGEE (1951–) is the founder and executive director of the Nurturing Network, a nationwide organization that provides practical help for women facing unwanted pregnancies. The organization tries to provide enough support to enable a woman to continue her pregnancy without sacrifice to her own future. In this essay, originally written for inclusion in the anthology *Why I Am Still a Catholic* (1998), she explores her religious faith and the work of the Nurturing Network. (The loss of privacy she refers to occurred when her promotion to vice president at the Bendix Corp. was attributed to her relationship with company chairman William Agee, whom she later married. She left Bendix and was hired by Joseph Seagram & Sons for the same position.)

~

Why Am I Still a Catholic?

Two words embedded in this seemingly simple and certainly direct question caught my attention from the first moment it was posed to me for consideration: "I" and "still." Both made me uncomfortable from the outset for it was quite clear that they would demand something far more revealing from any thoughtful respondent than the relatively safe inquiry, "Why would anyone become a Catholic?

Agee, Mary Cunningham. "The Catholic Church: His Way, Truth, and Life," n.d., photocopy provided by Mary Cunningham Agee, pp. 1–3, 5–7, 10–17, 19. Excerpts from "The Catholic Church: His Way, Truth, and Life," reprinted by permission of Mary Cunningham Agee.

The word "I" would deny permission for the more comfortable stance of a detached theologian or logical thinker offering one more well-reasoned apologetic about Catholicism. Instead, any meaningful reply would have to take on a distinctly personal tone. No answer could avoid providing a testimony of faith, and with it, an intimate look into the very nature of that which is most precious to me, that which defines my very being: my religious commitment.

As if the prospect of exposing such private and vulnerable thoughts in a decidedly public forum were not enough reason to back away from this invitation, the word "still" conjured up two additional concerns: First, the word left no room for discourse in anything but the *present* tense. Gone would be any hope of relying upon the childhood nostalgia that we lifelong or "cradle" Catholics are so fond of using to cover up the gaps in our less than rigorous spiritual formation. No permission would be granted to escape into an historical context where vague reasons could be excused due to the passage of time. No, this answer would have to measure up against the stark reality that a mature convert must face when asked to make a religious commitment here and now. I couldn't help but wonder if my answer would hold up—not so much to the scrutiny of an audience of readers out there—but to the inescapable and far more critical audience in here.

Also, the word "still" in the title made me uncomfortable, and, frankly, still does. It appears to arise from the same kind of misguided assumptions about individual freedom that have fueled the so-called "pro-choice" movement in this country for over two decades. For the past twelve years I have expended every ounce of my professional energy to expose the faulty reasoning and outright lies that lurk beneath the deceptive rhetoric of this euphemistically named movement. And yet, the allure of "choice" has pressed on, compromising the emotional lives of 25 million mothers and the physical lives of a generation of children.

To suggest that I have a "choice" not to "still" remain Catholic—despite knowing that the practice of my religious faith will directly impact my chance at eternal life, is disturbingly analogous to suggesting that a mother might exercise her "choice" not to "still" remain pregnant—despite knowing that the practice of her nurturing love will directly impact her unborn child's chance at physical life. The exercise of both choices requires either a callous disregard or tragic ignorance about the inherent inferiority of one option over the other.

Granted, some Catholics do choose not to remain Catholic and some mothers do choose not to remain pregnant and so, in this sense, the question has a legitimate right to be asked. But I would be less than forthright, if I did not at least express my view that questions of choice that gloss over or ignore the distinct inequality of two alternatives should be identified as such right up front.

If overcoming the hurdles imposed by the wording of the title question seemed challenging, it proved to be only a minor feat when compared to one additional obstacle that had to be conquered: Fear. At best, this emotion may have been rooted in an honest humility about the imperfections of my own faith journey not to mention the limitations of my skills as a communicator. At worst, it was rooted in a form of vanity that felt justified in shrinking away from any public exposure that could invite ridicule or criticism. I rationalized that I had already been through enough of both, thanks in no small measure to a media that prefers entertainment to facts and finds nothing wrong with turning someone's life into a cartoon-like tabloid—especially if her values don't happen to mesh with those prevalent in secular editorial circles. Whenever this admission of fear tweaked my conscience, I could always fall back on the seemingly excessive demands on my time as a wife who takes her vocation seriously, as a mother of two young children whom I still try to home school during several months of the year and as a managing director of a growing nationwide charity that is as good at saving human lives as any I have found.

How true it is that Satan tries to engage us at our point of greatest weakness! But even his promptings could not drown out the bold directive I heard clearly articulated on the evening of my decision whether to write this chapter. In the utterly uncompromising voice of our nine-year-old son and from a supposedly random page of our family Bible came back the ultimate reminder from Our Lord Himself. "So everyone who acknowledges Me before men, I will also acknowledge before My Father in heaven; but whoever denies Me before men, I will also deny before My Father in heaven" (Matthew 10:32–33). . . .

Enough said: I'm convinced and I'm writing. Why am I still Catholic? . . .

It should be acknowledged that any topic as profound as this presents a special challenge. It is not at all unlike my trying to respond in finite words to the question posed by one of our children, "Why do you still love me?" On the one hand, I know that my reply, no matter how eloquent, is bound to fall short of capturing the depth of my full emotional commitment. Even the most lucid answer is in danger of sounding hollow, superficial or even insincere. On the other hand, not to respond at all presents a far greater risk of sounding unclear, uncertain or even unconvinced. It is against this delicate backdrop and upon this fragile canvas that I will now try to paint a picture of my spiritual life and love as a Catholic.

I have often thought that the most unambiguous and comprehensive words Jesus Christ ever said about Himself were, "I am the *Way*, the *Truth* and the *Life*" (John 14:6). I find that these three words provide the most meaningful structure for me to shape my response to the title question:

First, I choose to still be Catholic because I *love the Truth*. Jesus Christ *is* the Truth. We know this because He said so. As the Truth, He is incapable of deceit in anything He says or does. One of His greatest deeds was the creation of His Church. Having assumed our human nature, He understood that we would need His ongoing, living Presence in our lives. And so, He gave His first priests, the apostles, the Holy Eucharist and asked us to recognize Him in the breaking of the bread and the drinking of the wine (Mt 26:26–28, Mark 14:22–24). Since He promised to be with us for all eternity (Mt 28:20), it is my privilege and duty to continue to seek and find Him in His Church no matter how difficult this may seem at times. Just as I love the Truth, I love His Presence in His Church and would never knowingly choose to be separated from Him.

Second, I choose to still be Catholic because I *need to follow the Way*. Jesus told us that He *is* the Way. His Way is the way to salvation. This is my ultimate goal in life and the true purpose for which I was created. My task is to grow in love for His Truth and work diligently to obey His commands which light and guide the Way to eternal Life. Jesus asked us to "Pick up our cross and follow Him" (Luke 9:23), and promised that those who did so would find salvation (Luke 9:24). When he said, "If you love me, obey my commandments" (John 14:15), He linked love to obedience. And when He said, "If anyone keep my word, he will never see death" (John 8:51), He linked obedience to eternal Life. Since the grace needed to overcome my many weaknesses and to be obedient is given through the sacraments of His Church, I choose to participate as fully as possible in the Life of the Church.

Third, I choose to still be Catholic because, in the words of the Mosaic Law, I *choose Life*. Jesus said that He *is* Life. He was sent by our Creator, His Father, so that "we might have new Life and have it more abundantly" (Rom 6:4). He gave us Himself in the ultimate act of sacrifice on the Cross in order to "free us from sin and death" (Rom 6:23). He anticipated our need for forgiveness, communion and spiritual fortification and so He asked us to partake of His instruments of grace, the sacraments of His Church. He connected a Life of holiness with salvation (Mt 5:20) and salvation with participation in the sacraments: "Whoever eats my flesh and drinks my blood will have eternal life and I will raise him up on the last day" (John 6:54). Therefore, I would not deliberately choose to separate myself from the Source of all Life by denying my soul the vital nourishment of the Church's grace-filled sacraments.

Frankly, as I review these thoughts about the reasons for my religious commitment as a Catholic, it all seems much more reasonable than I would have expected. I feel obliged to admit that there is a far greater part of me than these three logical explanations would suggest. I practice my faith in much the same way as I practice the art of loving—without the need for words of rational support. . . .

The Call to Personal Responsibility

The very essence of Christian morality can be summed up in one word: *"responsibility"*; that is, *response-ability*, and I'm not about to shirk it. I believe that my very salvation depends upon my *ability* to *respond* "with all my heart and all my soul" (Deut 10:12) to both God and my neighbor. . . .

Social scientists have determined that three conditions need to be met in order for a person to feel a strong sense of personal responsibility. First, the person must feel a sense of *importance* and even *urgency* about the need to perform this task; Second, the individual must believe that the task is *do-able*; and Third, a person must feel *uniquely qualified* to perform the task at hand. As I reflect upon the Catholic Church's pressing need for renewal, I must confess to reluctantly answering "yes" to all three. . . .

Given both its divine origin and the living presence of Christ within the Church, it should be obvious why I consider the task of helping and healing the Church to be "important." Given the gravity and intensity of the threats being mounted against Her today, it should also be clear why I consider this task to be "urgent." And given any number of scriptural passages that remind us "in God all things are possible" (Mt 19:26), it should come as no surprise that I believe the task is "doable."

But it is the third criterion for assuming personal responsibility that almost caused me to stumble. Most of us with even just a modicum of humility would be hard-pressed to describe ourselves as "uniquely qualified" to assist in the ongoing formation of the Life of the Church. And yet, the scriptural passages that refer to *each of us* as being "called by name" and putting to good use the many "varieties of gifts" of the Spirit (1 Cor 12:4) cannot be ignored. Even just a quick reading of the warning that was given in the parable about the rich man who hoarded his gifts (James 5:1–7) is chilling enough to make me think twice before "passing the buck" to someone "more qualified." And there is always that familiar passage indelibly etched upon my conscience from a childhood marked by frequent lapses in everything from piano practice to homework studies to household chores: "To whom much has been given, much will be expected" (Luke 19:26). I interpret each of these scriptural passages as being important reminders not to undervalue or underutilize the unique array of gifts that each of us has been given.

On an even more personal note and still well within the bounds of considering this third criteria for personal responsibility, I believe that there are three unique gifts that have, in particular, shaped my identity and my willingness to "stand up and be counted" whenever the Church or any of Her members is in need of support. I can discern their catalyzing influence at the very heart of all that I do. Right now I'm wondering if they actually make me "qualified" as much as they surely make me "unique," but for the sake of this discussion, I am inclined to think it may be both.

Paradoxically enough, as I force myself to analyze these very special "gifts," I discover that each initially came wrapped in the riveting anguish of human tragedy. Each would demand that I learn an invaluable lesson: to convert a life-altering loss into a Life-saving gain. Each would require me to put into full practice the spiritual survival skills of faith, hope and love if I were to overcome the temptations that await anyone who has known profound grief: despair, self-pity and anger. Upon reflection, only a most loving God intimately in tune with the precise needs of my individual soul could have pinpointed the perfect time and circumstances for each of these "gifts" to be presented: At age five, I lost my father; at age thirty, I lost my privacy; at age thirty-three, I lost my first child.

I believe that it was in these moments of extreme brokenness that I managed to discover the singularity of purpose and clarity of mission that might otherwise have eluded me for longer than I care to speculate. How painfully true it seems to be that we easily-distracted human beings can only hear the call to holiness when the cluttered paths of our busy, self-indulgent lives are laid bare, when we finally fall humbly upon our knees. I know, because I have spent a lot more time in that position than I would ever have freely chosen. And yet, like the vine that has been sharply pruned or the metal that has been forged and tested by fire, I can now give thanks.

I believe that each of these potentially devastating events has, by the grace of God, been converted into the "leaven" in the bread of my life. Through the invitation to let go of my human father, I received the gift of compassionate love for any child who feels abandoned. I was also given a far more intimate relationship with my Heavenly Father Who kept His promise not "to leave me orphaned" (Jer 49:11) and never seemed to tire of reminding me of my "belovedness" as a "child of God." Through the invitation to relinquish the safety of my privacy, I received the gift of compassionate love for those brave souls throughout history who have been "persecuted for the sake of righteousness" (Mt 5:10). I was also given a stronger resolve to loosen my grip on the vain pursuits of power, fame and fortune. Through the invitation to release the life of my first child, Angela Grace, I received the gift of compassionate love for every mother who has ever lost a child in any manner or form. I was also given a more genuine desire to learn the single-minded devotion of Abraham who was willing even to sacrifice the life of his only son, Isaac.

The Catholic faith was not designed by its Founder to be a tidy set of doctrines that could be neatly practiced alone in the safety of one's private relationship with Almighty God. It is a generous religion that demands authentic expression in practical and loving service to others. Its Founder was not mincing words when He warned, "Anyone who says that he loves God and hates his neighbor is a liar" (1 John 2:4) and "Whoever says he is in the light, and yet hates his brother is still in the darkness" (1 John 2:9). He could hardly have been more clear when He said, "As long as you did it for the least of these, you did it for Me" (Mt 25:40). This is why we find included in the same Great Commandment that demands an absolute love of God, an equally stringent requirement of an unconditional love of one's neighbor. Christ left no room for confusion. His was not a Church that would look with favor on anyone who would hope to achieve salvation by just "looking out for number one."

For me, this call to loving action has taken a very specific and concrete form. It is my small but determined attempt to "light a candle rather than to curse the darkness" of the "culture of death" in which we find ourselves living. My "Little Drummer Girl" response to the second part of Jesus' Great Commandment is called The Nurturing Network.

My Personal Response to This Call to Action: The Nurturing Network

The idea of The Nurturing Network did not come to me in a dream, but in the nightmare of a mid-trimester miscarriage, when the emptiness makes you want to cry out, "Why me, God, why me?" In my anguish, I was initiated into a sorority of loss, listening in the darkness for the cry of a child whom I would never be able to hold or comfort. As I put away the empty crib and folded the handmade baby blanket, I began to comprehend the vivid truth in what Bishop Fulton Sheen had said so often, "There could never have been an Easter Sunday without there first being a Good Friday."

In meditating over this truth, I'd like to believe that it was the Holy Spirit who whispered to my broken heart the possibility that *the life of many could be born out of the death of one.* If I could feel that much pain and loss over a child I wanted, how must other women feel when they are coerced by circumstances or family members to surrender the life of their child to abortion? How deep must be their grief, anger and guilt. How cruel that "choice" must seem to those who feel they have *no other* choice. I knew I was being given a rare glimpse into the injured hearts of so many women whose babies are aborted: "I felt alone, violated." "My child was taken from me. My little child, not a 'fetus,' not 'tissue,' not 'membrane,' but a baby. My baby!" The personal "call by name" to be my sisters' keeper came over a decade ago and with it was born an organization that to date has saved over 8,000 children's lives and provided a hope-filled solution to each of their mothers. I structured this grassroots organization with the all-consuming hope that one day we would live in a society that no longer required our services. My prayer was that we would someday literally "be put out of business" by compassion and love: Love of a parent so strong that it might withstand the onslaught of a thing called shame; love of a mate or boyfriend so binding in fidelity that it would not instantly check out; love of a community so Christ-like that it would not cast the first stone of judgment but transform that stone into the bread of Life.

After some of our ten- and twelve-hour days at the Network, I find myself asking, "Is love too much to ask? Is there room for love to slip in between the pronouns of me, myself and I in a self-indulgent society that shuns moral absolutes and where nothing is considered wrong as long as you don't get caught?" I find it difficult to answer these questions just as a relief doctor in Bosnia, Sarajevo or Rwanda finds little time to ponder the arguments for a just war. For there are literally hundreds of thousands of women in our midst who are in immediate, desperate need of our practical life-saving compassion.

I know, because I hear their mothers' broken voices on our telephone lifeline. I listen to their stories of abandonment and betrayal and discover not only the most obvious culprit, the father of the baby, at the heart of their struggle, but you and me. I believe that we are accomplices in these desperate, hopeless decisions every time we turn a deaf ear to Our Lord's command to "Love one another as I have loved you" (John 13:34).

I believe that if we are "for life," we have a moral obligation to provide the means to support and sustain it. As I reflect upon the underlying weakness or flaw in the pro-life movement in America at this time, I have to admit that it may have much more to do with the Christian community's lukewarm and inconsistent response to this vital issue than with the deliberate efforts of pragmatic politicians or a Godless media. Despite almost two million abortions each year, Christ's call to action is still too often met with a series of lame excuses, conditional promises and allegedly higher priorities.

If there were just one moment in my many years of professional experience at The Nurturing Network that I would try to bring into sharper focus for those who think they can just "sit on the sidelines" of this culture-defining issue, it would be that charged instant when I hear a mother's heart lament, *"If only I had known."*

In case you are about to dismiss this contemporary Mary Magdalene, let me clarify a few facts about who she really is. Our practical research has debunked the false assumption that the majority of those experiencing abortion are uneducated young teens from disadvantaged backgrounds. Rather, we have found that the most likely candidate for this procedure is an unmarried, middle class woman between the ages of 20 and 26, who has earned at least a high school diploma. You know this woman. She is your next door neighbor, your waitress, your colleague at work, the cashier at your favorite restaurant. She could even be your own daughter. These are women you encounter everyday and yet, their scars are hidden—some with band-aids called denial, others with armored rhetoric called "reproductive freedom."

The facts are that there are four basic influences that weight heavily in all abortion decisions: The father of the baby, frightened and confused, issues a personally devastating ultimatum, "Either me or the baby." The family, embarrassed and disappointed, issues an emotionally crippling ultimatum, "Either your family or the baby." The peer group, well-intentioned by misinformed, issues a socially-charged ultimatum, "Either your social standing or the baby." And finally, the employer, blinded by "bottom line" pragmatism, issues an economically threatening ultimatum, "Either your career or the baby."

Of course, none of these ultimatums has anything to do with "freedom of choice." All have to do with unfair, seemingly impossible tradeoffs. This is why The Nurturing Network was formed—to give a woman a positive alternative, one which recognizes her unique values, needs and circumstances. Our Network of 22,000 volunteer members is made up of doctors, counselors, educators, employers and nurturing families from every state in this nation and from fourteen foreign countries. These contemporary "Simons of Cyrene" empower a mother to nurture her baby's life—while making the most of hers as well. Our volunteers devote their time, talent and treasure not to removing an option but to creating one, not to debating the merits of one alternative over another but to making sure that no woman feels she has been left without the choice to give birth.

During the twelve years that I have had the privilege of working face to face and heart to heart with these living "profiles in courage," I have learned a well-kept secret that I believe could fatally undermine the "pro-choice" movement if ever fully exposed. The simple truth is that most abortions do *not* occur as a result of "free choice" but because women in crisis feel they have *no other* choice. My informal research with hundreds of women who have experienced prior abortions reveals that over 90% of these mothers would have chosen a positive, life-saving alternative *if only it had been made available to them.*

And, as if the moral absolute to protect and nurture all life were not enough, our clients have shown us time and time again that an unwanted pregnancy does not have to mean an unwanted baby. There is an obvious correlation between how much practical compassionate support we are willing to give women with crisis pregnancies and how many healthy infants will be available for the hundreds of thousands of potential parents wishing to adopt. But unless we are willing to offer the emotional, social and financial support needed by women facing this kind of pregnancy, we cannot legitimately express either condemnation or surprise when we discover that they have chosen a less hopeful solution.

You could say that The Nurturing Network was my "Field of Dreams" with that recurring and haunting voice that said, "Build it, and they will come." Indeed they have. And they continue to come. For our Network is no longer a dream but a powerful reality to the women and children of this country, a reality that is only a toll-free phone call away: 1-800-TNN-4MOM. This compassionate outreach is my living testimony to the daily miracles that can occur when each of us takes to heart the Divine Carpenter of Nazareth's plea to "Feed My lambs" (John 21:15). . . .

It is crystal clear to me that the Catholic Church with Her abundant gifts of grace is the only hope I have of approaching my day of judgment with any confidence at all. And maybe, just maybe, as I lay my earthly burdens down, a few familiar faces will be there waiting in the wings. As I turn to hear the Almighty's verdict, I might catch a grateful wink here or a knowing nod there for having played some small part that helped to nudge them on their way. I pray that with the help of my Holy Mother Church, I will hear the words from the Father Himself, "Well done! My good and faithful servant."

Margarethe Cammermeyer

~

MARGARETHE CAMMERMEYER (1942–) in 1992 became the highest-ranking military official discharged for homosexuality. In her memoir, *Serving in Silence*, she recalls her service to her country, her love for a woman, and her military trial.

~

Boundaries between people are crucial. Military officer, nurse, teacher—each occupation requires a particular type of behavior and demeanor. I believe that achievement in these fields comes not just from skill and dedication, but also from respecting the boundaries of each role.

That means simple things: I'm not a friend to my patients or to soldiers under my command. I show respect for rank. Personal matters are not discussed or disclosed except with friends. Caring for others—my sons, patients, troops—requires a focus on others' needs and feelings, not my own.

These separations of roles are necessary. But what is also necessary is a place where they can all come together. A place where what *I* feel is permitted. For all the gifts in my life, I never had that place. I never knew it was even possible to have.

Until I met Diane. . . .

No one listens like Diane. No one I have ever known. Hers is a receptivity that's intelligent, compassionate, and amused. Her

Cammermeyer, Margarethe, with Chris Fisher. *Serving in Silence*. New York: Viking Penguin, 1994, pp. 211–212, 218–220, 235–236, 273–276. Excerpt from *Serving in Silence*, by Margarethe Cammermeyer, copyright © 1994 by Margarethe Cammermeyer. Reprinted by permission of Viking Penguin, a division of Penguin Putnam, Inc.

heart is light, her laughter warm and ready. It's laughter that is never mean or petty, but embraces, loves, values. The laughter of an artist and teacher who inquires into the mysteries of religion with the same intensity she gives to a succession of Scottie dogs.

I'd never known what it means to be understood by one person. It is that simple. It is no different from what every other person in the world wants: to be special to one other person.

Meeting Diane and experiencing the rightness of being with her made me realize I am a lesbian. Finally being able to acknowledge that gave me the last, connecting piece to the puzzle of my identity.

It was a puzzle I'd tried and failed to solve since my adolescence. Not understanding—or not accepting—my sexual orientation was like looking at myself through a faulty lens. If something didn't feel right, I couldn't find the reason because I couldn't see myself clearly. I attributed my social discomfort in school to various sources. I was shy because I was Norwegian, I didn't fit in because I was too tall, I didn't want to date because my clothes weren't fashionable—but none of those explanations was entirely right. My on-and-off reclusiveness in college seemed to have no cause at all.

I so wanted to fit in. I wanted to be accepted, to be like all the women in the movies I saw, like the heroines in the books I read, like the classmates I knew, like my mother, whom I loved. I tried to play the role of a woman they played: a woman who desires a man. But I really didn't.

But when I acknowledged I am a lesbian, I could look back and see clearly for the first time. All my life I had recoiled at being intimate with a man, but I believed that I could change those feelings with time. I enjoyed working with my male colleagues, I had affection for male friends like Doug and cared for Harvey. But when I dated and when I married, not only was I not attracted to my male partners, I felt physically violated whenever I was kissed or touched by them. Despite trying, wanting to be an accommodating wife, I withdrew physically whenever possible. Being sexual with a man felt like a violation. It wasn't Harvey's fault. It wasn't any man's fault. Some unchangeable part of myself felt that sex with a man was an invasion and I resented it. Over fifteen years of marriage, those feelings only got stronger. At the age of forty-six, I finally had to face the fact that being straight wasn't a choice I had.

Yet, when I left my marriage, all I knew about my identity was contained in a negative statement: Being in a relationship with a man is not who I am. When a friend wanted to fix me up with an eligible man, I said no. My friend assumed that as an older, divorced woman, I was going to stay single and unattached for the duration and was not looking for another relationship. I wasn't asked to explain my lack of interest in dating, so I didn't. But silently I tried to understand my disinterest in men. I read books and studied scientific reports. I learned that the medical profession does not consider homosexuality to be a mental illness, and many scientists believe it is genetically determined.

I didn't want to have a relationship with a man. I accepted that in the years after my divorce. But I didn't want to be with a woman, either. I feared being a member of a despised and stigmatized minority. And there was something more. Like the world around me, I was homophobic—fearful of those who are labeled gays and lesbians. In my ignorance, I had only negative images of them: they were taunted, beaten up, fired from jobs, rejected by friends and families. I didn't want to be part of that group.

My homophobia was also unconscious. Just recently, a former colleague told me that when we served together in Vietnam I mentioned that I thought some of the women on my high-school softball team had been lesbians and that I didn't approve. I was very surprised by his memory. First, because it's hard to acknowledge my own intolerance and prejudice, and second, because I have no memory at all of saying or feeling such a thing.

Only once from the time of my divorce until I met Diane did I let down my armor. In San Francisco, I began to care for a person. I avoided thinking this special feeling linked me to an ostracized minority by telling myself that this person "just happens to be a woman." That relationship never evolved but the memory of new kinds of feelings remained.

After that, as much as I might have liked to, I couldn't be as naïve as I was in my youth. And I couldn't deny my suspicions that I might be homosexual. But my own homophobia continued to hold that self-knowledge in a kind of intellectual prison. I wondered if I was a homosexual, but I banished any feelings that might go with the concept. Also, I never said or thought the word "lesbian." "Lesbian" was too personal. It had ownership—and I wasn't ready for ownership. I could only use the term "homosexual"—it locked the feelings in a theoretical trap, keeping them impersonal, like the word itself.

Over the next couple of years, I focused on my military and professional work and my sons. But when I met Diane, I realized how lonely I'd been. I cared for her, and I realized that this caring was more than friendship. It was love. For the first time in my life I felt: I can talk to this person. We discuss things. We have feelings for each other. We express those feelings easily, and I don't try to keep my distance as I always had done with men. One of the things that most surprised me was that my feelings came not from attraction but from an emotional connectedness. For the first time, I experienced completely fulfilling love. . . .

It wasn't until the following November, seven months after my statement to Agent Troutman, that the military responded. It was during the monthly drill weekend. I was called to a meeting with the Washington National Guard Chief of Staff, Colonel Dines, and Colonel Koss, the man who had hired me as state Chief Nurse. Also there was Lieutenant Colonel Ryan, the legal adviser for the Guard.

It was a formal and courteous session. They explained that the DIS had contacted the Department of the Army concerning my disclosure of my sexual orientation. There was an adverse report based on my own statement, and as a result, my security clearance was going to be withdrawn and my federal recognition was under consideration for withdrawal. Translated, that military language meant the Army was going to kick me out.

With those words, my world collapsed. The Army was actually thinking of discharging me? It made no sense. I could continue to serve and contribute with the same energy and success I had shown for the past twenty-four years. Nothing had changed. Why couldn't they see that? But like my fellow officers around the table, I kept my thoughts to myself. These men, my colleagues, were transmitting information from their superiors. I did not feel animosity toward them. And for their part, they treated me with respect. Like them, I showed no emotion. We were all good soldiers. . . .

Colonel Dines outlined the next steps I could expect in the process. Once I was officially notified of my hearing date, I would have ninety days to respond to the impending separation action. . . .

⌒

Finally, it was time to give my final statement. I had spent a long time preparing what I would tell this jury of my military peers. I stood up and faced the board again. But my prepared statement left my mind and my heart spoke.

"Thirty years ago," I began, "when I joined the military, I had a dream of one day being in a position of becoming Chief Nurse of the Army Nurse Corps. And so as part of that process, I began both preparing educationally in the military and in my civilian world. I applied for top-secret clearance, and knew, I think, at a subconscious level that there might be some questions and it may be an awkward time because I had come to understand a little bit more about myself in terms of my sexual identity, and yet felt so strongly that this was what I'm supposed to do with my life that I applied for the top-secret clearance, willing to take whatever chance came my way.

"And when the time came whether or not to disclose to the investigator, I told the truth. It seemed like that was the very premise of everything I stood for in my entire life and career. And because of previous experiences that I'd had in the military and changes that I had seen in the course of my own career, I believed in it as an organization that could deal with the individual and look in terms of the human component and contribution that someone could make to the service.

"In October of 1989 I was called to the chief of staff's office and told that my federal recognition was being considered for withdrawal. My world dropped out, and I was very—I don't know why I should have been surprised, but I was. And I felt very hurt in some ways because by this time I had more than twenty-three years in the military and had served well, both here, on active duty in Vietnam, and in the Army Reserves and now in the National Guard, and felt abandoned and very alone. At the time I believed very strongly that I had something to contribute to the military. And for the past twenty-six months have continued to serve with every bit of the effort and energy I had beforehand.

"And when the time came now to decide whether or not to resign or retire, I felt that this was one of the decisions I had to make in my life. A crossroad. Do I back down or do I stand up for what I truly believe is my right as a human being, which is to be acknowledged as a human being. My professional career, my abilities, my contributions have nothing to do with my sexual orientation.

"Throughout my career and throughout the world there are times when change can be made only by someone stepping forth, being willing perhaps to expose themselves and their vulnerability so that others become aware of the fact that there are differences in the world. So that people will understand these differences are okay and don't affect our ability to be part of an organization or to make a contribution.

"And so, I choose to be here. To sit before you and my family, and be vulnerable in hopes that perhaps it can influence making a change and allowing us to serve as we have in the past and will continue to do in the future.

"I appreciate your presence, your attendance, your attentiveness, and I thank you very much."

The two days of testimony was over, and the board began its deliberations. . . .

After about an hour, we were told the decision had been reached, and we all reentered the hearing room. The board president, Colonel Patsy Thompson, got up.

"Would you stand, Margarethe," she said.

I rose and faced her, knowing that my uniform was flawless. And knowing that it made no difference.

Colonel Thompson then read the following statement on behalf of the board:

"I truly believe that you are one of the great Americans, Margarethe. And I've admired you for a long time and the work that you've done and all that you've done for the Army National Guard. When I was Chief Nurse, I said many times, I'm really glad that we have Margarethe Cammermeyer or Grethe Cammermeyer in the Guard. She's doing such an outstanding job. We're really fortunate that she came to us. And I really meant that. And I still do mean that.

"And we're really proud of you and all of your accomplishments, and I say that from the Army National Guard Nurse Corps perspective. And I think that one of the things that I read in your record pretty well sums it up. It really touched me. One young nurse summed it up when she said, 'It was a rare privilege to work under you during your tenure as Chief Nurse. I waited a long time in the trenches for your kind of nurse to come along. You were an inspiration for us all.' Another nurse wrote that you 'provided me with an excellent role model. She was one of the few members of the unit hierarchy who knew anything about being an officer. She has provided consistent positive guidance for those who cared enough to listen. Her ability to lead and inspire others was obvious, even to me, a person who did not know whether or not she was even going to stay in the military as a career.' But through your inspiration, that person did stay in and reached great heights, and those are just a few of the people that you've touched in your thirty years of military career.

"It's my sad duty to read what I'm going to read for you at this time, so I will proceed with that." Her voice caught. She stopped for a second.

"Colonel Cammermeyer has proved to be a great asset to both the active and reserve component, the medical profession as a whole. She has consistently provided superb leadership and has many outstanding accomplishments to her credit, both military and civilian. Notwithstanding, the board finds that Colonel Margarethe Cammermeyer is a homosexual as defined in AR 135–175 and as evidenced by her statement to DIS Agent Brent B. Troutman on 28 April 1989, and her admission under oath to this board that she is a lesbian, and statements made under oath to this board by five character witnesses. We recommend that Colonel Cammermeyer's federal recognition be withdrawn. In the event that subsequent action results in discharge from the USAR, an honorable discharge certificate should be awarded. We are aware that the DOD [Department of Defense] policy on homosexuality is currently under review. If the review results in change, these recommendations should be reexamined."

Colonel Thompson sat back down. And with that the board adjourned.

My military career was over.

Alice Walker

~

ALICE WALKER (1944–), a Pulitzer Prize–winning author, has worked to end female genital mutilation. In the first selection she explores the creation of her stories; in the second, the impact she hopes her work will have in the world at large.

~

Writing *The Color Purple*

I don't always know where the germ of a story comes from, but with *The Color Purple* I knew right away. I was hiking through the woods with my sister, Ruth, talking about a lovers' triangle of which we both knew. She said: "And you know, one day The Wife asked The Other Woman for a pair of her drawers." Instantly the missing piece of the story I was mentally writing—about two women who felt married to the same man—fell into place. And for months—through illnesses, divorce, several moves, travel abroad, all kinds of heartaches and revelations—I carried my sister's comment delicately balanced in the center of the novel's construction I was building in my head.

Walker, Alice. *In Search of Our Mothers' Gardens: Womanist Prose.* New York: Harcourt Brace Jovanovich, 1984, pp. 355–360 ("Writing *The Color Purple*"). Excerpt from "Writing *The Color Purple*" copyright © 1982 by Alice Walker. Reprinted by permission of Harcourt, Inc.

Walker, Alice, and Pratibha Parmer. *Warrior Marks.* New York: Harcourt Brace and Company, 1993, pp. 21–25. Excerpt from *Warrior Marks: Female Genital Mutilation and the Sexual Blinding of Women,* copyright © 1993 by Alice Walker and Pratibha Parmer. Reprinted by permission of Harcourt, Inc.

I also knew *The Color Purple* would be a historical novel, and thinking of this made me chuckle. In an interview, discussing my work, a black male critic said he'd heard I might write a historical novel someday, and went on to say, in effect: Heaven protect us from it. The chuckle was because, womanlike (he would say), my "history" starts not with the taking of lands, or the births, battles, and deaths of Great Men, but with one woman asking another for her underwear. Oh, well, I thought, one function of critics is to be appalled by such behavior. But what woman (or sensuous man) could avoid being intrigued? As for me, I thought of little else for a year.

When I was sure the characters of my new novel were trying to form (or, as I invariably thought of it, trying to contact me, to speak *through* me), I began to make plans to leave New York. Three months earlier I had bought a tiny house on a quiet Brooklyn street, assuming—because my desk overlooked the street and a maple tree in the yard, representing garden and view—I would be able to write. I was not.

New York, whose people I love for their grace under almost continual unpredictable adversity, was a place the people in *The Color Purple* refused even to visit. The moment any of them started to form—on the subway, a dark street, and especially in the shadow of very tall buildings—they would start to complain.

"What is all this tall shit anyway?" they would say.

I disposed of the house, stored my furniture, packed my suitcases, and flew alone to San Francisco (it was my daughter's year to be with her father), where all the people in the novel promptly fell silent—I think, in awe. Not merely of the city's beauty, but of what they picked up about earthquakes.

"It's pretty," they muttered, "but us ain't lost nothing in no place that has earthquakes."

They also didn't like seeing buses, cars, or other people whenever they attempted to look out. "Us don't want to be seeing none of this," they said. "It make us can't think."

That was when I knew for sure these were country people. So my lover* and I started driving around the state looking for a country house to rent. Luckily I had found (with the help of friends) a fairly inexpensive place in the city. This too had been a decision forced by my characters. As long as there was any question about whether I could support them in the fashion they desired (basically in undisturbed silence) they declined to come out. Eventually we found a place in northern California we could afford and that my characters liked. And no wonder: it looked a lot like the town in Georgia most of them were from, only it was more beautiful and the local swimming hole was not segregated. It also bore a slight resemblance to the African village in which one of them, Nettie, was a missionary.

Seeing the sheep, the cattle, and the goats, smelling the apples and the hay, one of my characters, Celie, began, haltingly, to speak.

But there was still a problem.

Since I had quit my editing job at *Ms.* and my Guggenheim Fellowship was running out, and my royalties did not quite cover expenses, and—let's face it—because it gives me a charge to see people who appreciate my work, historical novels or not, I was accepting invitations to speak. Sometimes on the long plane rides Celie or Shug would break through with a wonderful line or two (for instance, Celie said once that a self-pitying sick person she went to visit was "laying up in the bed trying to look dead"). But even these vanished—if I didn't jot them down—by the time my contact with the audience was done.

What to do?

Celie and Shug answered without hesitation: Give up all this travel. Give up all this talk. What is all this travel and talk shit anyway? So, I gave it up for a year. Whenever I was invited to speak I explained I was taking a year off for Silence. (I also wore an imaginary bracelet on my left arm that spelled the word.) Everyone said, Sure, they understood.

---

*Ironically and unfortunately, "lover" is considered a pejorative by some people. In its original meaning, "someone who loves" (could be a lover of music, a lover of dance, a lover of a person . . .), it is useful, strong and accurate—and the meaning I intend here.

I was terrified.

Where was the money for our support coming from? My only steady income was a three-hundred-dollar-a-month retainer from *Ms.* for being a long-distance editor. But even that was too much distraction for my characters.

Tell them you can't do anything for the magazine, said Celie and Shug. (You guessed it, the women of the drawers.) Tell them you'll have to think about them later. So, I did. *Ms.* was unperturbed. Supportive as ever (they continued the retainer). Which was nice.

Then I sold a book of stories. After taxes, inflation, and my agent's fee of ten percent, I would still have enough for a frugal, no-frills year. And so, I bought some beautiful blue-and-red-and-purple fabric, and some funky old secondhand furniture (and accepted donations of old odds and ends from friends), and a quilt pattern my mama swore was easy, and I headed for the hills.

There were days and weeks and even months when nothing happened. Nothing whatsoever. I worked on my quilt, took long walks with my lover, lay on an island we discovered in the middle of the river and dabbled my fingers in the water. I swam, explored the redwood forests all around us, lay out in the meadow, picked apples, talked (yes, or course) to trees. My quilt began to grow. And, of course, everything was happening. Celie and Shug and Albert were getting to know each other, coming to trust my determination to serve their entry (sometimes I felt *re*-entry) into the world to the best of my ability, and what is more—and felt so wonderful—we began to love one another. And, what is even more, to feel immense thankfulness for our mutual good luck.

Just as summer was ending, one or more of my characters—Celie, Shug, Albert, Sofia, or Harpo—would come for a visit. We would sit wherever I was sitting, and talk. They were very obliging, engaging, and jolly. They were, of course, at the end of their story but were telling it to me from the beginning. Things that made me sad often made them laugh. Oh, we got through that; don't pull such a long face, they'd say. Or, You think Reagan's bad, you ought've seen some of the rednecks us come up under. The days passed in a blaze of happiness.

Then school started, and it was time for my daughter to stay with me—for two years.

Could I handle it?

Shug said, right out, that she didn't know. (Well, her mother raised *her* children.) Nobody else said anything. (At this point in the novel, Celie didn't even know where *her* children were.) They just quieted down, didn't visit as much, and took a firm Well, let's us wait and see attitude.

My daughter arrived. Smart, sensitive, cheerful, at school most of the day, but quick with tea and sympathy on her return. My characters adored her. They saw she spoke her mind in no uncertain terms and would fight back when attacked. When she came home from school one day with bruises but said, You should see the other guy, Celie (raped by her stepfather as a child and somewhat fearful of life) began to reappraise her own condition. Rebecca gave her courage (which she *always* gives me)—and Celie grew to like her so much she would wait until three-thirty to visit me. So, just when Rebecca would arrive home needing her mother and a hug, there'd be Celie, trying to give her both. Fortunately I was able to bring Celie's own children back to her (a unique power of novelists), though it took thirty years and a good bit of foreign travel. But this proved to be the largest single problem in writing the exact novel I wanted to write between about ten-thirty and three.

I had planned to give myself five years to write *The Color Purple* (teaching, speaking, or selling apples, as I ran out of money). But, on the very day my daughter left for camp, less than a year after I started writing, I wrote the last page.

And what did I do that for?

It was like losing everybody I loved at once. First Rebecca (to whom everyone surged forth on the last page to say goodbye), then Celie, Shug, Nettie, and Albert. Mary Agnes, Harpo, and Sofia. Eleanor Jane. Adam and Tashi Omatangu. Olivia. Mercifully, my quilt and my lover remained.

I threw myself in his arms and cried.

Remarks of Alice Walker upon
Receiving the Radcliffe Medal on June 5, 1992

For many years now, I have studied, have thought about, the mother who collaborates with the destroyer of daughters. The mother who betrays.

In my recently published book, the novel *Possessing the Secret of Joy*, I explore the life of a daughter so betrayed. A daughter whose culture demands the literal destruction of the most crucial external sign of her womanhood: her vulva itself.

This is a brief excerpt from the novel, an exchange between Tashi, the genitally mutilated woman from Africa, and Raye, her African-American psychiatrist:

As for the thing that was done to me . . . or for me, I said. And stopped. Because Raye had raised her eyebrows, quizzically.

The initiation . . .

Still she looked at me in the same questioning way.

The female initiation, I said. Into womanhood.

Oh? she said. But looked still as if she didn't understand.

Circumcision, I whispered.

Pardon? she said, in a normal tone of voice that seemed loud in the quiet room.

I felt as if I had handed her a small and precious pearl and she had promptly bitten into it and declared it a fake.

What exactly is this procedure? she asked, briskly.

I was reminded of a quality in African-American women that I did not like at all. A bluntness. A going to the heart of the matter even if it gave everyone concerned a heart attack. Rarely did black women in America exhibit the graceful subtlety of the African woman. Had slavery given them this? Suddenly a story involving Raye popped into my mind: I saw her clearly as she would have been in the nineteenth century, the eighteenth, the seventeenth, the sixteenth, the fifteenth . . . Her hands on her hips, her breasts thrust out. She is very black, as black as I am. "Listen, cracker," she is saying, "did you sell my child or not?" The "cracker" whines, "But listen, Louella, it was my child too!" The minute he turns his back, she picks up a huge boulder, exactly like the one that is in my throat, and . . . But I drag myself back from this scene.

Don't you have my file? I asked, annoyed. I was sure The Old Man sent it before he died. On the other hand, this was a question he'd never asked me. I'd said "circumcision" to him and he'd seemed completely satisfied; as if he knew exactly what was implied. Now I wondered; had he understood?

I have your file, said Raye, tapping its bulging gray cover with a silver-painted nail and ignoring my attitude. I am ignorant about this practice, though, and would like to learn about it from you. She paused, glanced into the folder. For instance, something I've always wondered is whether the exact same thing is done to every woman. Or is there variation? Your sister . . . Dura's clitoris was excised, but was something else done too, that made it more likely that she would bleed to death?

Her tone was now clinical. It relaxed me. I breathed deeply and sought the necessary and familiar distance from myself. I did not get as far away as usual, however.

Always different, I would think, I said, exhaling breath, because women are all different. Yet always the same, because women's bodies are all the same. But this was not precisely true. In my reading I had discovered there were at least three forms of circumcision. Some cultures demanded excision of only the clitoris, others insisted on a thorough scraping away of the entire genital area. A sigh escaped me as I thought of explaining this.

A slight frown came between Raye's large, clear eyes.

I realize it is hard for you to talk about this, she said. Perhaps we shouldn't push.

But I am already pushing, and the boulder rolls off my tongue, completely crushing the old familiar faraway voice I'd always used to tell this tale, a voice that had hardly seemed connected to me.

It was only after I came to America, I said, that I even knew what was supposed to be down there.

Down there?

Yes. My own body was a mystery to me, as was the female body, beyond the function of the breasts, to almost everyone I knew. From prison

Our Leader said we must keep ourselves clean and pure as we had been since time immemorial—by cutting out unclean parts of our bodies. Everyone knew that if a woman was not circumcised her unclean parts would grow so long they'd soon touch her thighs; she'd become masculine and arouse herself. No man could enter her because her own erection would be in his way.

You believed this?

Everyone believed it, even though no one had ever seen it. No one living in our village anyway. And yet the elders, particularly, acted as if everyone had witnessed this evil, and not nearly a long enough time ago.

But you knew this had not happened to you?

But perhaps it had, I said. Certainly to all my friends who'd been circumcised, my uncircumcised vagina was thought of as a monstrosity. They laughed at me. Jeered at me for having a tail. I think they meant my labia majora. After all, none of them had vaginal lips; none of them had a clitoris; they had no idea what these things looked like; to them I was bound to look odd. There were a few other girls who had not been circumcised. The girls who had been would sometimes actually run from us, as if we were demons. Laughing, though. Always laughing.

And yet it is from this time, before circumcision, that you remember pleasure?

When I was little I used to stroke myself, which was taboo. And then, when I was older, and before we married, Adam and I used to make love in the fields. Which was also taboo. Doing it in the fields, I mean. And because we practiced cunnilingus.

Did you experience orgasm?

Always.

And yet you willingly gave this up in order to . . . Raye was frowning in disbelief.

I completed the sentence for her: To be accepted as a real woman by the Olinka people; to stop the jeering.

An estimated ninety to one hundred million women in African, Asian, and Middle Eastern countries have been genitally mutilated, causing unimaginable physical pain and psychological suffering. And though one is struck by the complicity of the mothers, themselves victims, as of the fathers, the brothers, and the lovers, even the complicity of the grandparents, one must finally acknowledge, as Hanny Lightfoot-Klein does in the title of her book about genital mutilation in Africa [*Prisoners of Ritual*] that those who practice it are, generally speaking, kept ignorant of its real dangers—the breakdown of the spirit and the body and the spread of disease—and are themselves prisoners of ritual.

I wrote my novel as a duty to my conscience as an educated African-AmerIndian woman. To write a book such as this, about a woman such as Tashi, about a subject such as genital mutilation, is in fact, as far as I am concerned, the reason for my education. Writing it worked my every nerve, as we say in African-American culture about those areas of struggle that pull from us every ounce of creative energy and pull away from us every last shred of illusion. I know only one thing about the "success" of my effort. I believe with all my heart that there is at least one little baby girl born somewhere on the planet today who will not know the pain of genital mutilation because of my work. And that in this one instance, at least, the pen will prove mightier than the circumciser's knife. Her little beloved face will be the light that shines on me.

Ruth Bader Ginsburg

⁓

RUTH BADER GINSBURG (1933–) was a member of the legal team that finally persuaded the Supreme Court that women were protected under the Fourteenth Amendment. That decision in *Reed v. Reed* (1971) formed the basis for other women's rights victories before the Supreme Court, including five cases argued by Ginsburg between 1973 and 1978. President Jimmy Carter appointed her to serve on the U.S. Court of Appeals for the District of Columbia Circuit in 1980. When President Bill Clinton appointed her to serve as an associate justice of the U.S. Supreme Court in 1993, she became only the second woman to serve on that court. (Sandra Day O'Connor, appointed by President Ronald Reagan in 1981, was the first.) The following are Ginsburg's remarks upon her Supreme Court nomination and an excerpt from her majority opinion in *United States v. Commonwealth of Virginia* (1996).

⁓

Ruth Bader Ginsburg's Remarks upon
Her Nomination to the U.S. Supreme Court

Mr. President, I am grateful beyond measure for the confidence you have placed in me, and I will strive with all that I have to live up to your expectations in making this appointment.

New York Times, June 15, 1993, A 24:1 (Ginsburg's remarks upon her nomination).

Cullen-DuPont, Kathryn. *Encyclopedia of Women's History in America*, 2nd ed. New York: Facts on File, 2000, pp. 367–371 (excerpt from *United States v. Commonwealth of Virginia*).

I appreciate, too, the special caring of Senator Daniel Patrick Moynihan, the more so because I do not actually know the Senator. I was born and brought up in New York, the state Senator Moynihan represents, and he was the very first person to call with good wishes when President Carter nominated me in 1980 to serve on the U.S. Court of Appeals for the District of Columbia Circuit. Senator Moynihan has offered the same encouragement on this occasion.

May I introduce at this happy moment three people very special to me: my husband, Martin B. Ginsburg, my son-in-law, George T. Spera Jr., and my son, James Steven Ginsburg.

The announcement the President just made is significant, I believe, because it contributes to the end of the days when women, at least half the talent pool in our society, appear in high places only as one-at-a-time performers. Recall that when President Carter took office in 1976, no woman ever served on the Supreme Court, and only one woman, Shirley Hufstedler of California, then served at the next Federal court level, the United States Court of Appeals.

Today Justice Sandra Day O'Connor graces the Supreme Court bench, and close to 25 women serve at the Federal Court of Appeals level, two as chief judges. I am confident that more will soon join them. That seems to me inevitable, given the change in law school enrollment.

My law school class in the late 1950's numbered over 500. That class included less than 10 women. As the President said, not a law firm in the entire city of New York bid for my employment as a lawyer when I earned my degree. Today few law schools have female enrollment under 40 percent, and several have reached or passed the 50 percent mark. And thanks to Title VII, no entry doors are barred.

My daughter, Jane, reminded me a few hours ago in a good-luck call from Australia of a sign of the change we have had the good fortune to experience. In her high school yearbook on her graduation in 1973, the listing for Jane Ginsburg under "ambition" was "to see her mother appointed to the Supreme Court." The next line read, "If necessary, Jane will appoint her." Jane is so pleased, Mr. President, that you did it instead, and her brother, James, is, too.

I expect to be asked in some detail about my views of the work of a good judge on a High Court bench. This afternoon is not the moment for extended remarks on that subject, but I might state a few prime guides.

Chief Justice Rehnquist offered one I keep in the front of my mind: a judge is bound to decide each case fairly in a court with the relevant facts and the applicable law even when the decision is not, as he put it, what the home crowd wants.

Next, I know no better summary than the one Justice O'Connor recently provided drawn from a paper by New York University Law School Prof. Bert Neuborne. The remarks concern the enduring influence of Justice Oliver Wendell Holmes. They read: "When a modern constitutional judge is confronted with a hard case, Holmes is at her side with three gentle reminders: first, intellectual honesty about the available policy choices; second, disciplined self-restraint in respecting the majority's policy choice; and third, principled commitment to defense of individual autonomy even in the face of majority action." To that I can only say, "Amen."

I am indebted to so many for this extraordinary chance and challenge: to a revived women's movement in the 1970's that opened doors for people like me, to the civil rights movement of the 1960's from which the women's movement drew inspiration, to my teaching colleagues at Rutgers and Columbia and for 13 years my D.C. Circuit colleagues who shaped and heightened my appreciation of the value of collegiality.

Most closely, I have been aided by my life partner, Martin D. Ginsburg, who has been, since our teen-age years, my best friend and biggest booster, by my mother-in-law, Evelyn Ginsburg, the most supportive parent a person could have, and by a daughter and son with the tastes to appreciate that Daddy cooks ever so much better than Mommy and so phased me out of the kitchen at a relatively early age.

Finally, I know Hillary Rodham Clinton has encouraged and supported the President's decision to utilize the skills and talents of all the people of the United States. I did not, until today, know

RUTH BADER GINSBURG ⌢ 577

Mrs. Clinton, but I hasten to add that I am not the first member of my family to stand close to her. There is another I love dearly to whom the First Lady is already an old friend. My wonderful granddaughter, Clara witnessed this super, unposed photograph taken last October when Mrs. Clinton visited the nursery school in New York and led the little ones in "The Toothbrush Song." The small person right in front is Clara.

I have a last thank-you. It is to my mother, Celia Amster Bader, the bravest and strongest person I have known, who was taken from me much too soon. I pray that I may be all that she would have been had she lived in an age when women could aspire and achieve and daughters are cherished as much as sons. I look forward to stimulating weeks this summer and, if I am confirmed, to working at a neighboring court to the best of my ability for the advancement of the law in the service of society. Thank you.

From *United States v. Commonwealth of Virginia*

[The Supreme Court's decision in *United States v. Commonwealth of Virginia* required the country's last two publicly funded all-male colleges to admit women or forgo further state funding. The colleges in question—the Virginia Military Institute and the Citadel— both decided to admit women. What follows is an excerpt from Ruth Bader Ginsburg's majority opinion.]

In 1971, for the first time in our Nation's history, this Court ruled in favor of a woman who complained that her State had denied her the equal protection of its laws. *Reed v. Reed*, 404 U.S. 71, 73 (holding unconstitutional Idaho Code prescription that, among "'several persons claiming and equally entitled to administer [a decedent's estate], males must be preferred to females'"). Since *Reed*, the Court has repeatedly recognized that neither federal nor state government acts compatibly with the equal protection principle when a law or official policy denies to women, simply because they are women, full citizenship stature—equal opportunity to aspire, achieve, participate in and contribute to society based on their individual talents and capacities. . . .

Without equating gender classifications, for all purposes, to classifications based on race or national origin, . . . the Court, in post-*Reed* decisions, has carefully inspected official action that closes a door or denies opportunity to women (or to men). . . . To summarize the Court's current directions for cases of official classification based on gender: Focusing on the differential treatment or denial of opportunity for which relief is sought, the reviewing court must determine whether the proffered justification is "exceedingly persuasive." The burden of justification is demanding and it rests entirely on the State. See *Mississippi Univ. for Women*, 458 U.S., at 724. The State must show "at least that the [challenged] classification serves 'important governmental objectives and that the discriminatory means employed' are 'substantially related to the achievement of those objectives.'" Ibid. (quoting *Wengler v. Druggists Mutual Ins. Co.*, 446 U.S. 142, 150 (1980)). The justification must be genuine, not hypothesized or invented post hoc in response to litigation. And it must not rely on overbroad generalizations about the different talents, capacities, or preferences of males and females. See *Weinberger v. Wiesenfeld*, 420 U.S. 626, 643, 648 (1975); *Califano v. Goldfarb*, 430 U.S. 199, 223–224 (1977) (Stevens, J., concurring in judgment).

The heightened review standard our precedent establishes does not make sex a proscribed classification. Supposed "inherent differences" are no longer accepted as a ground for race or national origin classifications. See *Loving v. Virginia*, 388 U.S. 1 (1967). Physical differences between men and women, however, are enduring: "[T]he two sexes are not fungible; a community made up exclusively of one [sex] is different from a community composed of both." *Ballard v. United States*, 329 U.S. 187, 193 (1946).

"Inherent differences" between men and women, we have come to appreciate, remain cause for celebration, but not for denigration of the members of either sex or for artificial constraints on an individual's opportunity. Sex classifications may be used to compensate women "for particular economic disabilities [they have] suffered," *Califano v. Webster*, 420 U.S. 313, 320 (1977) (per curiam), to "promot[e] equal employment opportunity," see *California Federal Sav. & Loan Assn. v. Guerra*, 479 U.S. 272, 289 (1987), to advance full development of the talent and capacities of our Nation's people. [n.7] But such classifications may not be used, as they once were, see *Goesaert*, 335 U.S., at 467, to create or perpetuate the legal, social, and economic inferiority of women.

Measuring the record in this case against the review standard just described, we conclude that Virginia has shown no "exceedingly persuasive justification" for excluding all women from the citizen soldier training afforded by VMI. We therefore affirm the Fourth Circuit's initial judgment, which held that Virginia had violated the Fourteenth Amendment's Equal Protection Clause. Because the remedy proffered by Virginia—the Mary Baldwin VWIL program—does not cure the constitutional violation, i.e., it does not provide equal opportunity, we reverse the Fourth Circuit's final judgment in the case.

. . . Virginia . . . asserts two justifications in defense of VMI's exclusion of women. First, the Commonwealth contends, "single sex education provides important educational benefits," . . . and the option of single sex education contributes to "diversity in educational approaches" . . . Second, the Commonwealth argues, "the unique VMI method of character development and leadership training," the school's adversative approach, would have to be modified were VMI to admit women. Id., at 33–36. We consider these two justifications in turn.

Single sex education affords pedagogical benefits to at least some students, Virginia emphasizes, and that reality is uncontested in this litigation . . . Similarly, it is not disputed that diversity among public educational institutions can serve the pubic good. But Virginia has not shown that VMI was established, or has been maintained, with a view to diversifying, by its categorical exclusion of women, educational opportunities within the State.

Mississippi Univ. for Women is immediately in point. There the State asserted, in justification of its exclusion of men from a nursing school, that it was engaging in "educational affirmative action" by "compensat[ing] for discrimination against women." 458 U.S., at 727. Undertaking a "searching analysis," id., at 728, the Court found no close resemblance between "the alleged objective" and "the actual purpose underlying the discriminatory classification," id., at 730. Pursuing a similar inquiry here, we reach the same conclusion. . . .

. . . [W]e find no persuasive evidence in this record that VMI's male only admission policy "is in furtherance of a state policy of 'diversity.'" See 976 F. 2d, at 899. . . . A purpose genuinely to advance an array of educational options, as the Court of Appeals recognized, is not served by VMI's historic and constant plan—a plan to "affor[d] a unique educational benefit only to males." Ibid. However "liberally" this plan serves the State's sons, it makes no provision whatever for her daughters. That is not equal protection.

Virginia next argues that VMI's adversative method of training provides educational benefits that cannot be made available, unmodified, to women. Alterations to accommodate women would necessarily be "radical," so "drastic," Virginia asserts, as to transform, indeed "destroy," VMI's program. . . . Neither sex would be favored by the transformation, Virginia maintains: Men would be deprived of the unique opportunity currently available to them; women would not gain that opportunity because their participation would "eliminat[e] the very aspects of [the] program that distinguish [VMI] from . . . other institutions of higher education in Virginia." . . .

. . . [I]t is uncontested that women's admission would require accommodations, primarily in arranging housing assignments and physical training programs for female cadets. . . . It is also undisputed, however, that "the VMI methodology could be used to educate women." 852 F. Supp., at 481. . . . The parties, furthermore, agree that "some women can meet the physical standards [VMI] now impose[s] on men." 976 F. 2d, at 896. In sum, as the Court of

Appeals stated, "neither the goal of producing citizen soldiers," VMI's raison d'être, "nor VMI's implementing methodology is inherently unsuitable to women." Id., at 899.

In support of its initial judgment for Virginia, a judgment rejecting all equal protection objections presented by the United States, the District Court made "findings" on "gender based developmental differences." 766 F. Supp., at 1434–1435. These "findings" restate the opinions of Virginia's expert witnesses, opinions about typically male or typically female "tendencies." Id., at 1434. For example, "[m]ales tend to need an atmosphere of adversativeness," while "[f]emales tend to thrive in a cooperative atmosphere." Ibid. . . .

The United States does not challenge any expert witness estimation on average capacities or preferences of men and women. Instead, the United States emphasizes that time and again since this Court's turning point decision in *Reed v. Reed*, 404 U.S. 71 (1971), we have cautioned reviewing courts to take a "hard look" at generalizations or "tendencies" of the kind pressed by Virginia, and relied upon by the District Court. . . . State actors controlling gates to opportunity, we have instructed, may not exclude qualified individuals based on "fixed notions concerning the roles and abilities of males and females." . . .

It may be assumed, for purposes of this decision, that most women would not choose VMI's adversative method. . . . The issue, however, is not whether "women—or men—should be forced to attend VMI"; rather, the question is whether the State can constitutionally deny to women who have the will and capacity, the training and attendant opportunities that VMI uniquely affords. . . .

The notion that admission of women would downgrade VMI's stature, destroy the adversative system and, with it, even the school, is a judgment hardly proved, a prediction hardly different from other "self-fulfilling prophec[ies]," see *Mississippi Univ. for Women*, 458 U.S., at 730, once routinely used to deny rights or opportunities. When women first sought admission to the bar and access to legal education, concerns of the same order were expressed. . . .

Medical faculties similarly resisted men and women as partners in the study of medicine. . . .

Women's successful entry into the federal military academies, and their participation in the Nation's military forces, indicate that Virginia's fears for the future of VMI may not be solidly grounded. . . .

Virginia and VMI trained their argument on "means" rather than "end," and thus misperceived our precedent. Single sex eduction at VMI serves an "important governmental objective," they maintained, and exclusion of women is not only "substantially related," it is essential to that objective. By this notably circular argument, the "straightforward" test *Mississippi Univ. for Women* described, see 458 U.S., at 724–745, was bent and bowed.

The State's misunderstanding and, in turn, the District Court's, is apparent from VMI's mission: to produce "citizen soldiers," individuals "'imbued with love of learning, confident in the functions and attitudes of leadership, possessing a high sense of public service, advocates of the American democracy and free enterprise system, and ready . . . to defend their country in time of national peril.'" 766 F. Supp., at 1425 (quoting Mission Study Committee of the VMI Board of Visitors, Report, May 16, 1986).

Surely that goal is great enough to accommodate women, who today count as citizens in our American democracy equal in stature to men. Just as surely, the State's great goal is not substantially advanced by women's categorical exclusion, in total disregard of their individual merit, from the State's premier "citizen soldier" corps. Virginia, in sum, "has fallen far short of establishing the 'exceedingly persuasive justification,'" *Mississippi Univ. for Women*, 458 U.S., at 731, that must be the solid base for any gender defined classification.

In the second phase of the litigation, Virginia presented its remedial plan—maintain VMI as a male-only college and create VWIL as a separate program for women. The plan met [with] approval.

Virginia chose not to eliminate, but to leave untouched, VMI's exclusionary policy. For women only, however, Virginia proposed a separate program, different in kind from VMI and unequal in tangible and intangible facilities. . . .

Virginia maintains that . . . methodological differences are "justified pedagogically," based on "important differences between men and women in learning and developmental needs," "psychological and sociological differences" Virginia describes as "real" and "not stereotypes."

As earlier stated, generalizations about "the way women are," estimates of what is appropriate for most women, no longer justify denying opportunity to women whose talent and capacity place them outside the average description. Notably, Virginia never asserted that VMI's method of education suits most men. It is also revealing that Virginia accounted for its failure to make the VWIL experience "the entirely militaristic experience of VMI" on the ground that VWIL "is planned for women who do not necessarily expect to pursue military careers." 852 F. Supp., at 478. By that reasoning, VMI's "entirely militaristic" program would be inappropriate for men in general or as a group, for "[o]nly about 15% of VMI cadets enter career military service." See 766 F. Supp., at 1432.

In contrast to the generalizations about women on which Virginia rests, we note again these dispositive realities: VMI's "implementing methodology" is not "inherently unsuitable to women," 976 F. 2d, at 899; "some women . . . do well under [the] adversative model," 766 F. Supp., at 1434 (internal quotation marks omitted); "some women, at least, would want to attend [VMI] if they had the opportunity," id., at 1414; "some women are capable of all of the individual activities required of VMI cadets," id., at 1412, and "can meet the physical standards [VMI] now impose[s] on men," 976 F. 2d, at 896. It is on behalf of these women that the United States has instituted this suit, and it is for them that a remedy must be crafted, a remedy that will end their exclusion from a state supplied educational opportunity for which they are fit, a decree that will "bar like discrimination in the future." *Louisiana*, 380 U.S., at 154.

In myriad respects other than military training, VWIL does not qualify as VMI's equal. VWIL's student body, faculty, course offerings, and facilities hardly match VMI's. Nor can the VWIL graduate anticipate the benefits associated with VMI's 157-year history, the school's prestige, and its influential alumni network.

Virginia, in sum, while maintaining VMI for men only, has failed to provide any "comparable single gender women's institution." Id., at 1241. Instead, the Commonwealth has created a VWIL program fairly appraised as a "pale shadow" of VMI in terms of the range of curricular choices and faculty stature, funding, prestige, alumni support and influence. See id., at 1250 (Phillips, J., dissenting).

Virginia's VWIL solution is reminiscent of the remedy Texas proposed 50 years ago, in response to a state trial court's 1946 ruling that, given the equal protection guarantee, African Americans could not be denied a legal education at a state facility. See *Sweatt v. Painter*, 339 U.S. 629 (1950). Reluctant to admit African Americans to its flagship University of Texas Law School, the State set up a separate school for Herman Sweatt and other black law students. Id., at 632. As originally opened, the new school had no independent faculty or library, and it lacked accreditation. Id., at 633. Nevertheless, the state trial and appellate courts were satisfied that the new school offered Sweatt opportunities for the study of law "substantially equivalent to those offered by the State to white students at the University of Texas." Id., at 632 (internal quotation marks omitted).

Before this Court considered the case, the new school had gained "a faculty of five full time professors; a student body of 23; a library of some 16,500 volumes serviced by a full time staff; a practice court and legal aid association; and one alumnus who ha[d] become a member of the Texas Bar." Id., at 633. This Court contrasted resources at the new school with those at the school from which Sweatt had been excluded. The University of Texas Law School had a full time faculty of 16, a student body of 850, a library containing over 65,000 volumes, scholarship funds, a law review, and moot court facilities. Id., at 632–633.

More important than the tangible features, the Court emphasized, are "those qualities which are incapable of objective measurement but which make for greatness" in a school, including "reputation of the faculty, experience of the administration, position and influence of the alumni, standing in the community, traditions and prestige." Id., at 634. Facing the marked differences reported in the Sweatt opinion, the Court unanimously ruled that Texas had not shown "substantial equality in the [separate] educational opportunities" the State offered. Id., at 633. Accordingly, the Court held, the Equal Protection Clause required Texas to admit African Americans to the University of Texas Law School. Id., at 636. In line with Sweatt, we rule here that Virginia has not shown substantial equality in the separate educational opportunities the State supports at VWIL and VMI.

When Virginia tendered its VWIL plan, the Fourth Circuit did not inquire whether the proposed remedy, approved by the District Court, placed women denied the VMI advantage in "the position they would have occupied in the absence of [discrimination]." . . .

The Fourth Circuit plainly erred. . . . Valuable as VWIL may prove for students who seek the program offered, Virginia's remedy affords no cure at all for the opportunities and advantages withheld from women who want a VMI education and can make the grade. . . . In sum, Virginia's remedy does not match the constitutional violation; the State has shown no "exceedingly persuasive justification" for withholding from women qualified for the experience premier training of the kind VMI affords.

VMI . . . offers an educational opportunity no other Virginia institution provides, and the school's "prestige"—associated with its success in developing "citizen soldiers"—is unequaled. Virginia has closed this facility to its daughters and, instead, has devised for them a "parallel program," with a faculty less impressively credentialed and less well paid, more limited course offerings, fewer opportunities for military training and for scientific specialization. Cf. Sweatt, 339 U.S., at 633. VMI, beyond question, "possesses to a far greater degree" than the VWIL program "those qualities which are incapable of objective measurement but which make for greatness in a . . . school," including "position and influence of the alumni, standing in the community, traditions and prestige," Id., at 634. Women seeking and fit for a VMI quality education cannot be offered anything less, under the State's obligation to afford them genuinely equal protection.

A prime part of the history of our Constitution, historian Richard Morris recounted, is the story of the extension of constitutional rights and protections to people once ignored or excluded. [n. 21] VMI's story continued as our comprehension of "We the People" expanded. See supra, at 29, n. 16. There is no reason to believe that the admission of women capable of all the activities required of VMI cadets would destroy the Institute rather than enhance its capacity to serve the "more perfect Union."

For the reasons stated, the initial judgment of the Court of Appeals, 976 F. 2d 890 (CA4 1992), is affirmed, the final judgment of the Court of Appeals, 44 F. 3d 1229 (CA4 1995), is reversed, and the case is remanded for further proceedings consistent with this opinion.

It is so ordered.

Hillary Rodham Clinton

~

HILLARY RODHAM CLINTON (1947–) was twice named one of the "One Hundred Most Influential Lawyers in America" by the *National Law Journal* prior to her husband's election as president of the United States. As first lady, she maintained an office in the White House's west wing and was widely—and controversially—viewed as wielding political influence within Bill Clinton's administration. In November 2000, she became the first sitting first lady to win elective office when she was elected to represent New York State in the U.S. Senate. The following are her remarks at the United Nation's Fourth International Conference on Women, which took place in Beijing, China, in 1995.

~

First Lady Hillary Rodham Clinton Remarks to the United Nations Fourth World Conference on Women

Distinguished delegates and guests, I would like to thank the Secretary General of the United Nations for inviting me to be part of

Clinton, Hillary Rodham. "Remarks to the United Nations Fourth World Conference on Women, Beijing, China, September 5, 1995." Available online: http://clinton3.nara.gov/WH/EOP/First_Lady/html/China/plenary.html.

———. "Remarks to the NGO Forum, Huairou, China, September 6, 1995." Available online: http://clinton3.nara.gov/WH/EOP/First_Lady/html/China/ngo.html.

this important United Nations Fourth World Conference on Women. This is truly a celebration—a celebration of the contributions women make in every aspect of life: in the home, on the job, in the community, as mothers, wives, sisters, daughters, learners, workers, citizens and leaders.

It is also a coming together, much the way women come together every day in every country.

We come together in fields and in factories. In village markets and supermarkets. In living rooms and board rooms.

Whether it is while playing with our children in the park, or washing clothes in a river, or taking a break at the office water cooler, we come together and talk about our aspirations and concerns. And time and again, our talk turns to our children and our families.

However different we may appear, there is far more that unites us than divides us. We share a common future. And we are here to find common ground so that we may help bring new dignity and respect to women and girls all over the world—and in so doing, bring new strength and stability to families as well.

By gathering in Beijing, we are focusing world attention on issues that matter most in the lives of women and their families: access to education, health care, jobs, and credit, the chance to enjoy basic legal and human rights and to participate fully in the political life of their countries.

There are some who question the reason for this conference. Let them listen to the voices of women in their homes, neighborhoods, and workplaces.

There are some who wonder whether the lives of women and girls matter to economic and political progress around the globe. . . . Let them look at the women gathered here and at Hairou [site of the Non-Governmental Organizations forum] . . . the homemakers, nurses, teachers, lawyers, policymakers, and women who run their own businesses.

It is conferences like this that compel governments and peoples everywhere to listen, look and face the world's most pressing problems.

Wasn't it after the women's conference in Nairobi ten years ago that the world focused for the first time on the crisis of domestic violence?

Earlier today, I participated in a World Health Organization forum. In that forum we talked about ways that where government officials, NGOs, and individual citizens are working on ways to address the health problems of women and girls.

Tomorrow, I will attend a gathering of the United Nations Development Fund for Women. There, the discussion will focus on local—and highly successful—programs that give hard-working women access to credit so they can improve their own lives and the lives of their families.

What we are learning around the world is that, if women are healthy and educated, their families will flourish. If women are free from violence, their families will flourish. If women have a chance to work and earn as full and equal partners in society, their families will flourish.

And when families flourish, communities and nations will flourish.

That is why every woman, every man, every child, every family, and every nation on our planet does have a stake in the discussion that takes place here.

Over the past 25 years, I have worked persistently on issues relating to women, children and families. Over the past two-and-a-half years, I have had the opportunity to learn more about the challenges facing women in my own country and around the world.

I have met new mothers in Indonesia, who come together regularly in their village to discuss nutrition, family planning, and baby care.

I have met working parents in Denmark who talk about the comfort they feel in knowing that their children can be cared for in creative, safe, and nurturing after-school centers.

I have met women in South Africa who helped lead the struggle to end apartheid and are now helping build a new democracy.

I have met with the leading women of my own hemisphere who are working every day to promote literacy and better health care for the children in their countries.

I have met women in India and Bangladesh who are taking out small loans to buy milk cows, rickshaws, thread and other materials to create a livelihood for themselves and their families.

I have met doctors and nurses in Belarus and Ukraine who are trying to keep children alive in the aftermath of Chernobyl.

The great challenge of this conference is to give voice to women everywhere whose experiences go unnoticed, whose words go unheard.

Women comprise more than half the world's population. Women are 70% of the world's poor, and two-thirds of those who are not taught to read and write.

Women are the primary caretakers for most of the world's children and elderly. Yet much of the work we do is not valued—not by economists, not by historians, not by popular culture, not by government leaders.

At this very moment, as we sit here, women around the world are giving birth, raising children, cooking meals, washing clothes, cleaning houses, planting crops, working on assembly lines, running companies, and running countries.

Women also are dying from diseases that should have been prevented or treated; they are watching their children succumb to malnutrition caused by poverty and economic deprivation; they are being denied the right to go to school by their own fathers and brothers; they are being forced into prostitution, and they are being barred from the bank lending office and banned from the ballot box.

Those of us who have the opportunity to be here have the responsibility to speak for those who could not.

As an American, I want to speak up for women in my own country—women who are raising children on the minimum wage, women who can't afford health care or child care, women whose lives are threatened by violence, including violence in their own homes.

I want to speak up for mothers who are fighting for good schools, safe neighborhoods, clean air and clean airwaves. . . .

. . . for older women, some of them widows, who have raised their families and now find that their skills and life experiences are not valued in the workplace . . . for women who are working all night as nurses, hotel clerks, and fast food chefs so that they can be at home during the day with their kids . . . and for women everywhere who simply don't have time to do everything they are called upon to do each day.

Speaking to you today, I speak for them, just as each of us speaks for women around the world who are denied the chance to go to school, or see a doctor, or own property, or have a say about the direction of their lives, simply because they are women.

The truth is that most women around the world work both inside and outside the home, usually by necessity.

We need to understand that there is no one formula for how women should lead their lives.

That is why we must respect the choices that each woman makes for herself and her family. Every woman deserves the chance to realize her God-given potential.

We also must recognize that women will never gain full dignity until their human rights are respected and protected.

Our goals for this conference, to strengthen families and societies by empowering women to take greater control over their own destinies, cannot be fully achieved unless all governments—here and around the world—accept their responsibility to protect and promote internationally recognized human rights.

The international community has long acknowledged—and recently affirmed at Vienna—that both women and men are entitled to a range of protections and personal freedoms, from the right of personal security to the right to determine freely the number and spacing of the children they bear.

No one should be forced to remain silent for fear of religious or political persecution, arrest, abuse or torture.

Tragically, women are most often the ones whose human rights are violated.

Even in the late 20th century, the rape of women continues to be used as an instrument of armed conflict. Woman and children make up a large majority of the world's refugees. And when women are excluded from the political process, they become even more vulnerable to abuse.

I believe that, on the eve of a new millennium, it is time to break our silence. It is time for us to say here in Beijing, and the world to hear, that it is no longer acceptable to discuss women's rights as separate from human rights.

These abuses have continued because, for too long, the history of women has been a history of silence. Even today, there are those who are trying to silence our words.

The voices of this conference and of the women at Hairou must be heard loud and clear:

It is a violation of human rights when babies are denied food, or drowned, or suffocated, or their spines broken, simply because they are born girls.

It is a violation of human rights when women and girls are sold into the slavery of prostitution.

It is a violation of human rights when women are doused with gasoline, set on fire and burned to death because their marriage dowries are deemed too small.

It is a violation of human rights when individual women are raped in their own communities and when thousands of women are subjected to rape as a tactic or prize of war.

It is a violation of human rights when a leading cause of death worldwide among women ages 14 to 44 is the violence they are subjected to in their own homes by their own relatives.

It is a violation of human rights when young girls are brutalized by the painful and degrading practice of genital mutilation.

It is a violation of human rights when women are denied the right to plan their own families, and that includes being forced to have abortions or being sterilized against their will.

If there is one message that echoes forth from this conference, let it be that human rights are women's rights. . . . And women's rights are human rights, once and for all.

Let us not forget that among those rights are the right to speak freely. And the right to be heard.

Women must enjoy the right to participate fully in the social and political lives of their countries if we want freedom and democracy to thrive and endure.

It is indefensible that many women in non-governmental organizations who wished to participate in this conference have not been able to attend—or have been prohibited from fully taking part.

Let me be clear. Freedom means the right of people to assemble, organize, and debate openly. It means respecting the views of those who may disagree with the views of their governments.

Remarks to the Non-Governmental Organizations Forum

. . . As I said yesterday, the faces of the women who are here mirror the faces of the millions and millions who are not. It is our responsibility, those of us who have been able to attend this Conference and this NGO Forum, to make sure that the voices that go unheard will be heard. This Conference is about making sure that women, their children, their families, have the opportunities for health care and education, for jobs and political participation, for lives free of violence, for basic legal protections, and yes, for internationally recognized human rights no matter where they are or where they live.

Time and time again we have seen that it is NGOs who are responsible for making progress in any society. Some of us never knew we were NGOs twenty and twenty-five and thirty years ago. That was not even a phrase that any of us had ever heard. We were people working together on behalf of all of those rights which we care about and hold dear. But when one looks at the progress that has been made throughout the world, it is clear that it is the NGOs who have charted real advances for women and children. It is the NGOs who have pressured governments and have led governments down the path to economic, social, and political progress, often in the face of overwhelming hostility. Again, NGOs have persevered, just as you have by coming here and staying here and participating in this Forum. What will be important as we end the Forum and the Conference at the end of this week is that it will be NGOs who will hold governments to the commitments that they make. And it is important that the final Platform for Action that is adopted to be distilled down into words that every woman, no matter where she lives, or how much education she has, can understand. I think we should want every woman, no matter where she is, to believe that there are women all over the world who care about her health, who want her children to be educated, who want her to have the dignity and respect that she deserves to have.

When I think of the faces that I have seen in my own country, when I think of the women who did not have health care because they cannot afford it in the United States of America, when I think particularly of a woman I met in New Orleans, Louisiana, who told me that because she did not have enough money she was told by physicians there in our country, that they would not do anything about the lump in her breast, but would merely wait and watch, because if she had insurance she would have been sent to a surgeon. I think about the woman I met in a village outside Lahore, Pakistan, who had ten children, five boys and five girls, and was struggling as hard as she could to make sure her girls were educated and wanted help to get that job done. I think of the faces of the beautiful women I met at SEWA, the Self-Employed Women's Association in India. All of them had walked miles and miles, some of them for twelve and fifteen hours to get to our meeting together, and I listened as they stood up and told me what it had meant that for the first time in their lives, they were having a little money of their own. They could buy their own vegetable carts. They could buy their own thread and materials so that they could make income for themselves and their families.

I think of the women in the village in Bangladesh, a village of untouchables, I think of how those women who were Hindus invited to their village for my visit women from the neighboring village who were Moslems. I think of how those women sat together under a lean-to. Hindus and Moslems together in one of the poorest countries of the world, but so many of those women telling me what their lives had been changed . . . because they had become borrowers that were now part of the Grameen Bank micro-enterprise effort. I think particularly of the play that their children put on for me to see, a play in which the children acted out the refusal by a family to let a girl child go to school. And then further down the road from that village, I stood and watched families coming to receive food supplements in return for keeping their girl children in school.

Those are the kinds of women and experiences that happen throughout the world, whether one talks about my country or any country. Women are looking for the support and encouragement they need to do what they can for their own lives and the lives of their children and the lives of their families. The only way this Conference will make a difference to these women is if the results of the Conference are taken and distilled down into one page perhaps, which states basic principles that you and I would perhaps debate and understand but may not be easily communicated.

If that is done, then to carry that message into every corner of the world so there can be sharing of experiences. When I came home from Bangladesh, I visited in Denver, Colorado, a program that is modeled on the Grameen Bank, helping American women who are welfare recipients get the dignity and the skills that they need to take care of themselves and their children.

So despite all of the difficulties and frustrations you have faced in coming here and being here, you are here not only on behalf of yourselves, but on behalf of millions and millions of women whose lives can be changed for the better. If you resolve along with all of us, to leave this place and do what we can together to make the changes that will give respect and dignity to every woman.

I know that today at the women's conference there is a special celebration of girls. The theme is: "Investing in Today's Girls, Tomorrow's Women, and the Future." We know that much of what we do, we are doing not for ourselves, but we are doing for our daughters, our nieces, our granddaughters. We are doing it because we have the hope that the changes we work for will take root and flower in their lives. When I was privileged to be in New Delhi, India, I met a young woman who I think spoke for many, many women, and someone asked me yesterday at the Conference if I had a copy of the poem which this young woman wrote. And I said that I did and she asked if I could read it today, and I said that I would. Because this was a poem about breaking the silence, the silence that afflicts too many women's lives, the silence that keeps women from expressing themselves freely, from being full participants even in the lives of their own families. This poem written by a young woman, I think, is particularly appropriate since we are celebrating today the future of girls. Let me read it to you:

"Too many women in too many countries speak the same language of silence. My grandmother was always silent, always agreed. Only her husband had the positive right, or so it was said, to speak and to be heard. They say it is different now.

"After all, I am always vocal, and my grandmother thinks I talk too much. But sometimes I wonder. When a woman gives her love as m[o]st do generously, it is accepted. When a woman shares her thoughts as some women do graciously, it is allowed. When a Woman fights for power as all women would like to, quietly or loudly, it is questioned. And yet, there must be freedom if we are to speak. And yes, there must be power if we are to be heard. And when we have both freedom and power, let us not be misunderstood. We seek only to give words to those who cannot speak—too many women in too many countries. I seek only to forget my grandmother's silence."

That is the kind of feeling that literally millions and millions of women feel every day. And much of what we are doing here at this Forum and at this Conference is to give words to break the silence and then to act. When I was at Copenhagen for the Summit on Social Development, I was pleased to announce that the United States would make an effort to enhance educational opportunities for girls so that they could attend school in Africa, Asia, and Latin America. Today that effort, funded with United States' dollars, is being organized in countries throughout those continents by NGOs.

There are so many ways we can work together. There are so many things that must be done. And let me just end with a postcard that I received from a woman who, with many, many others, wrote me her feelings and thoughts about this Conference. I don't know this woman, but she wrote to tell me that she wanted me to carry this card to Beijing. And she went on to say, "Be assured of many prayers for the success of the Conference, to better conditions for women and children throughout the world."

She put on this card a prayer and the prayer was written in many languages. It's a prayer that applies and can be said by many, if not all the world's religions. And I want to end with that because I think that in many respects what we are attempting to do requires the kind of faith and commitment that this prayer represents:

"Oh God, creator of the heavens and the earth, we pray for all who gather in Beijing [and I would add Huairou as well] bless them, help them and us to see one another through eyes enlightened by understanding and compassion. Release us from prejudice so we can receive the stories of our sisters with respect and attention. Open our ears to the cries of a suffering world and the healing melodies of peace. Empower us to be instruments in bringing about your justice and equality everywhere."

That is my prayer as well, and with my thanks to all of you I believe we can take the results of this Forum and this Conference and begin to translate them into action that will count, in the lives of girls and women who will have never heard of what we have done here, [but] whose lives can be changed because of what you have done coming here.

Thank you all very much.

Eileen Collins

~

EILEEN COLLINS (1956–) was the first woman to pilot a U.S. space shuttle and the first women to command a mission into space. In this interview with Kathryn Cullen-DuPont, Collins discusses her experiences in space, her appreciation of earlier groundbreaking women, and her hopes for the next generation.

~

An Interview
with Eileen Collins

Kathryn Cullen-DuPont: I understand that you grew up in difficult financial circumstances in public housing, and that you worked to pay for your own flying lessons and to put yourself through community college before attending Syracuse University on an ROTC scholarship. What would you like to say to youngsters struggling now, kids with large dreams and limited resources?

Eileen Collins: Well, there are many opportunities to reach your goals, and in this country, if there's something you want to do, you should be able to do that. Barring some kind of serious medical problem, you should be able to achieve your goals, because there are avenues to help you overcome things like financial difficulties. Now, in my case, I made the effort to research things like government grants, government loans, other loans, scholarships—all kinds of tuition assistance—and I wasn't ashamed to take advantage of that. *[Laughter.]* And I also looked into the military, which provided

Collins, Eileen. Telephone interview with Kathryn Cullen-DuPont, May 17, 2001.

598

a tremendous opportunity for me, first of all by giving me a full scholarship for the last two years of college. And then, when I actually went on active duty, they delayed my—you're not required to pay back on your college loans for three years, you get a legal delay in your tuition loan payments. So, you know, the military may not be for everyone, but those are some of the things I would recommend for getting through college. That four-year degree really does a lot for you in opening up certain job opportunities that normally would not be available if you didn't have the degree.

Cullen-DuPont: Now, as a young woman having saved up for your own flying lessons, is it true that the door flew open on your first solo flight? What was that like and what did you do about it? *[Laughter.]*

Collins: That's true. Now, right now, looking back, *it is not a big deal at all*. If you wear your seat belt, you should be just fine. *[Laughter, Cullen-DuPont.]* But what happened to me was, you know, you're on your first solo flight, or even your second or third or any solo flight when you're a student. You're very focused on what you're doing and what could go wrong and you're the only one in there. No one's going to help you. When that happened, you feel just—the noise level goes up, there's a big rush of air, you look straight down, you see the ground, so it really gets your attention. And I just—well, I think I'm going to shut the door. And I did. And I just pressed on. But believe me, it got my attention. *[Laughter.]* There was a certain rush of air that came out of my lungs when that happened.

Cullen-DuPont: And nothing about that was enough to deter you from just moving on. *[Laughter.]*

Collins: Well, no, I think I learned something about myself. I learned that when, you know, you're—what's the word I'm looking for—when you're on your own and—I mean the potential for panic is there—and I didn't. So I think I learned that I was able to make decisions and take the proper actions in an unusual situation that I hadn't planned for. I learned that about myself. I mean, these things can happen to you even if you're not flying. You're driving a car, or you find yourself in a situation where your house is on fire or you observe a car wreck. And what are you going to do. You can run into these situations in your everyday life and I think you learn something about yourself. You know, are you the kind of person who's going to try to provide assistance in an emergency. And I think I learned that, yes, I can overcome things that happen to me and probably learned that I can operate in a flying environment even under unusual circumstances.

Cullen-DuPont: And can you tell me what it was that most appealed to you about becoming an astronaut? What made you make the decision to—

Collins: Well, I would say I really believe two reasons and you've got to put the two reasons together. I really believe that there's a place for people to explore space, there's a reason why people should explore, and we've pretty much explored most of the earth's surface—not quite under the sea totally, there's still a lot of exploration left under the sea—but there's a lot of exploration left in space, and there's a lot we need to learn about ourselves and the universe that we live in. And even as a child, I was fascinated with just exploring—space exploration—so, take that, in conjunction with the fact that my career is that of a pilot and even as a child I was interested in flying—flying not only for the space program, but flying airplanes, flying military airplanes—and I was able to take those two interests of mine together in the job of an astronaut.

Cullen-DuPont: How wonderful for you that opportunities opened for women.

Collins: That's true. There's so many things that you do as an astronaut. There's just a tremendous variety of things that are expected out of you: doing simulations, whether it's ascents or entries or rendezvous, flying the T-38, flying the shuttle training aircraft, making speeches, helping people in the program make decisions on operational and planning items, plus flying in space. And I think it—one nice thing about this job is you feel like you are in a position where you can really have an input, where you can really make a difference.

Cullen-DuPont: There are a lot of firsts in your career, even from the very beginning: one of four women in a class of 320 during pilot training, first female flight instructor at the Vance Air Force Base, second woman pilot to attend the Air Force Test Pilot School at Edwards Air Force Base. Was this lonely, exhilarating, or something else entirely?

Collins: I would say probably none of those. I was never lonely. Never. Exhilarating—eh, maybe once in a while. What was the other one?

Cullen-DuPont: Something else entirely. Your choice. *[Laughter.]* Just what was it like. . . .

Collins: I was very matter of fact about the whole thing. And I think that's the reason I was able to get through it without any problems, really. I mean, I couldn't even name a problem that I had. I wasn't looking for problems, I wasn't trying to feel different or look different. I pretty much tried to blend in. I focused on my job, because if you focus on other things like what do people think about the women pilots, and you worry about that stuff, you're just going to waste energy. So I would say, really, nothing. I was very matter of fact, very focused on my job, I loved to fly, I got along with the guys really well. I made it a point to get to know their wives—for the guys who were married, get to know their wives so they didn't kind of wonder who's this—you know, back in those days, it was like, well "Who's this woman working with my husband."

Cullen-DuPont: Right. My dad was a firefighter. I remember the wives' perspective when that began to open up and go coed and there was just this panic of, "But you all sleep there at night."

Collins: Yeah. Well, you know, nowadays it's not—it's accepted, but back then, when it was something new, there was all this mystery behind it. So I did make it a point to get to know the wives of the guys that I worked with and, you know, I wanted to make sure that they knew I was there because I wanted to fly. And, you know, I didn't say that, I just got to be friends with them and they got to know me and then I think that was probably enough.

But, really, I can't say much about it. Once in a while it was distracting because they'd come by and they'd say "Oh, we need a woman to do"—somebody else would say, "we need a woman to do this or we need a woman to do that."

Cullen-DuPont: It wasn't getting coffee, was it? *[Laughter.]*

Collins: No, no, it was more like, well, we've got a general officer coming on base and we ought to have him meet the women students. It was kind of along those lines. But there wasn't a whole lot of it. I think they took pretty good care of us as far as, let's lay off the women students and just let them work on their training. But occasionally these things would happen and it really wasn't that bad because it was not that often. So I wish I had something dramatic I could tell you about that, but I think it was just fine. To be honest, I loved what I was doing, and in many cases it was stressful and it was hard and I would just go home and study, and study, and study, and think through the flight that I was going to be doing the next day and make sure that I was prepared for that.

Cullen-DuPont: What is it like to see our planet from space?

Collins: You could probably say exhilarating for that. *[Laughter.]*

Cullen-DuPont: *[Laughter]* So that's the exhilarating experience.

Collins: Yes. It's really an experience that I wish everyone could have. It's a very human experience. It's the kind of thing that can change your attitude about the way you look at everyday life. And I combine that with being in microgravity and floating. You can put your face up against the window and stretch out your arms and legs and be in a position where your face—where you can't see anything inside the shuttle but all you can see is the ground below you, and it actually feels like you're flying over the surface of the earth.

Cullen-DuPont: Wow.

Collins: And you're floating. I mean, you can just imagine, it's a pretty—I'd say, pretty human experience, because you're thinking about the people that are down on the earth, and yet you're also looking at the landscape, which in some cases is just clouds. If it's maybe just a stormy season or in the winter in the northern hemisphere, it's cloudy. [Laughter.] My February flight was quite boring when it came to looking at the earth. But I also flew in May and July and those were flights where I could see a lot of the surface of the earth and I would say that what jumps out at you is the blue of seas and lakes. And the tan of the desert really jumps out at you. The Middle East is the most beautiful part of the earth because you're looking down at Egypt, Sinai Peninsula, Syria, Iran, Iraq—light brown, tan—and then you've got the Mediterranean Sea, the Red Sea, the Persian Gulf, very blue, reflections from the sun, and it's just a striking contrast. And also you think about the people living down there now, and you think about the history of the people who lived there many, many years ago, back to the biblical times. Now, Australia's also very striking, because Australia is mostly desert with ocean around it, and there's coral reefs on the eastern side of Australia. Just beautiful. But the other things you think about—and sometimes this doesn't happen until afterward, but you'll think about how thin the atmosphere is. You can see—when the sun's setting just right, you can see how thin the atmosphere is. And it's really only—the breathable atmosphere only goes up about two to three miles. I mean, two or three miles is—some people drive that to work every day. That's pretty thin atmosphere. And then the atmosphere that you can fly in, in a conventional airplane, goes up only about six miles on the average. So the atmosphere is very thin. And you think about—everybody shares that air. And when you see a thunderstorm, when you see fires going on like in the Amazon—there's always fires going on in South America, *lots* of them. And you think about, if you see a volcano erupt—all that debris or waste product goes into the atmosphere, and it goes everywhere. We share the air. We also share the pollution. And the national borders—obviously you don't see those from space, but in space you can see that even though there may be political lines between the countries you really share the natural resources. You share the benefits of the natural resources as well as the waste products. You know, things like jungles, for example, are good for the air, but the jungles—you look at pictures taken from Sky Lab and compare them to pictures taken from the shuttle—you can see how the jungles have been wasted away by people cutting them down and burning them. You can see that from space and it's really kind of scary. But the feeling that you get is that you really want to take care of the earth.

Cullen-DuPont: Can you describe what it's like to pilot the space shuttle?

Collins: Well . . . I view the space shuttle as really three different things. On launch, it's a rocket. On orbit, it's a space craft. And on entry, it's an airplane. And the pilots can fly the shuttle through all three of those phases. Now, on launch, we don't normally fly, it's under autopilot, computer control, but it could be flown. If you had to, you could take over manually. And in flying, the pilot would make an input into the stick. The message goes to the computer—what does the pilot want to do, go up, down, right, left, in, out, speed up, slow down, whatever. The message goes to the computer and the computer selects what to do. Now, on the launch, it would gimbal the engines or move the engines right to left, up or down. On orbit, it would send a message to the jets—we have 44 jets—and the computer would pick which jets would fire to fly the way the pilot wants to go. On entry, we can do the same thing to the control stick, but the computer would send messages to the control services, up to what's now an airplane. So it flies differently—the shuttle flies differently in those three phases and you have to actually know what you're doing. I would say the shuttle flies nicely and predictably but it requires—I don't want to say a lot of training—it requires a certain amount of training so the pilot will understand why it's different from airplanes that he or she has flown in the past. For example, on landing the shuttle's very sensitive in the pitch access, the up and down access, and it could be possible to over control because it is so sensitive. It flies like a fighter airplane. But in the roll access, the right/left, turning right, turning left, it flies like an airliner. It's a little more sluggish. So it's kind of hard to describe how the shuttle flies, because it flies so differently in the three different phases of flight, but the important thing I would have to say is that pilots have to be very highly trained so they can predict what's going to happen and they know what input to make.

Cullen-DuPont: As pilot, you were second only to the shuttle commander. When you became shuttle commander yourself in 1999, how large was the added responsibility?

Collins: In my opinion, there is a difference between flying as a pilot versus flying as a commander. The commander has the added responsibility—he has the responsibility for the overall conduct of the flight while in orbit, definitely safety in the mission and the success of the mission. And also, taking care of the crew, and making sure that the crew members' needs are met, whether they're, you know, personal or mission-related requirements. Now, before the flight, the commander also has a major input into the planning process, and usually when something new is happening on the flight, almost every flight they're doing something new, the crew needs to make their input to the planning process to make sure that everything is planned ahead of time. You don't go up in orbit and say, "Well I think I'll do it this way." So we make inputs to our management on the operations side and the planning side as to how we'd like to see things done and, you know, it's a big team effort. The crew doesn't decide how to do it and just go off and do it. We make an input and then the team gets together and looks at everybody's input, and we all kind of make a decision on how it's going to be done. And I think the system works pretty well. But yes, there is a difference. The pilot is a crew member who makes his input to the commander, but the commander is usually the final authority as to what the crew input is.

Cullen-DuPont: And bears the responsibility for the way that goes?

Collins: Oh yes. If something goes wrong you've got to answer for it, so we try to anticipate all possible things that could go wrong. And that's probably my biggest concern. You know, when I go off to fly, I think, did we think of everything? What did we forget? You just hope that there wasn't anything that you—like failure modes or there's something that could happen on the flight that someone didn't predict. That's kind of my biggest concern. Because if we know about an issue or a potential problem beforehand, it usually gets plenty of attention and you have a plan. But you worry about the ones you think you didn't think about.

Cullen-DuPont: You've carried women's history memorabilia into space. Can you tell me a bit about this and about your appreciation of the women who've gone before you?

Collins: Yes, definitely. We go all the way back to the Wright brothers' day, I guess. Women flew and it wasn't something that was expected out of women, so it made—they flew because they loved to fly, and it's nice to have that history behind you, that there were women who flew because they loved to fly and made great contributions. Some of the things that I flew: Bobbie Trout is a famous aviator from years ago—I flew her pilot's license on my first flight [into space], and actually it's interesting that it was signed by Orville Wright. *[Laughter.]*

Cullen-DuPont: Really!

Collins: Yeah—we thought, "We better take care of this, we don't want to ruin it!" But I also flew a scarf that belonged to Amelia Earhart on my first flight, and I think that a scarf of hers had flown before, that one of the women had taken it up, but I don't remember who took it up or what flight. But I did fly a scarf that belonged to her. I flew some items that belonged to the Mercury 13 women—women who had gone through the medical testing for the Mercury program but never actually got a chance to fly because NASA decided they wanted to fly test pilots, military test pilots, and there were no women flying in the military back in those days, so. . . .

Cullen-DuPont: But I understand they acquitted themselves very well during the testing process, right?

Collins: Oh, yes. There was nothing that would have excluded them, and there was one gal—her name was Jerrie Cobb, and she—actually, I've flown something for her also. . . . I also flew items for the Women Airforce Service Pilots, the WASPS. They flew during World War II here in the United States to ferry aircraft. I also flew an item for the Women's Military Memorial, which is in Washington, and it was just a small little pin. I flew it for General Wilma Vaught. She was the moving force behind getting that memorial approved and built in Washington. But that's for all military women, not just for pilots. They made a contribution, all these women did really great jobs, and you know, one barrier after another has fallen as the decades have gone by, and the reason that the barriers have come down is because the system, which is primarily male, would look up and say, "Hey, these women can really do the job, so why should we restrict them." So I always make it a point to acknowledge the women who flew before me, and were in the military before me, because their contributions have allowed my generation to have the opportunities that we have, and if they had not done the things that they did, I don't think women would have these opportunities today.

Cullen-DuPont: I absolutely agree with you on that. In closing, can you tell me about your dreams for your own daughter, and all of our daughters growing up in America?

Collins: Yes. Freedom. We take freedom for granted. And I'll tell you, if we ever have it taken away from us, we will be a fighting country. *[Laughter.]* Because I think, you know, this country was built on that—other things are important, but freedom is very important. So for my daughter and for other children, both girls and boys, if they grow up to choose the things they want to do with their career, the jobs they would like to have, the opportunities are out there. I don't ever want to tell my daughter, "You have to go into this area." I want her to make her own decisions, and that's where the opportunities come in. Take advantage of the opportunities that are there. So I would like to see the younger generation have opportunities presented to them. I don't think they should take them for granted, I think they should go out and look for the opportunities and make use of them, and then make the decision as to what they want to do with their life. Because I think if you make your own decision on what you want to do, you're going to be more motivated to contribute. . . . I try to tell young people that they have these great opportunities and they have the freedom to choose their career and to not take that for granted.

Cullen-DuPont: Well, I thank you very much for the interview. . . . Goodbye, now.

Collins: Okay, good luck. Bye-bye.

Bibliography

~

Adams, Judith Porter. *Peacework: Oral Histories of Women Peace Activists.* Boston: Twayne Publishers, 1990.

Addams, Jane. *Twenty Years at Hull House.* 1910. Rpt., New York: NAL Penguin, 1981.

Agee, Mary Cunningham. "The Catholic Church: His Way, Truth, and Life," full text of essay, n.d. Photocopy provided by Mary Cunningham Agee.

Andrews, William L. *Classic American Autobiographies.* New York: Penguin Books, 1992.

Anthony, Susan B., and Ida Husted Harper, eds. *History of Woman Suffrage.* Vol. 4 (1902). Rpt., Salem, NH: Ayer Company, 1985.

Baron, Robert C. *Soul of America: Documenting Our Past, 1492–1974.* Golden, CO: Fulcrum, Inc., 1989.

Barton, Clara. *The Red Cross: A History of This Remarkable Movement in the Interest of Humanity.* Washington, D.C.: American National Red Cross, 1898.

Beecher, Catharine E. *The True Remedy for the Wrongs of Woman.* Boston: Phillips, Sampson, and Company, 1851.

Beecher, Catharine E., and Harriet Beecher Stowe. *The American Woman's Home.* New York: J. B. Ford & Co., 1869.

Bethune, Mary McLeod. "Faith That Moved a Dump Heap," *Who* magazine, vol. 1, no. 3, June 1941.

Blackwell, Alice Stone. *Lucy Stone: Pioneer of Woman's Rights.* Boston: Little, Brown, and Company, 1930.

Blackwell, Elizabeth. *Pioneer Work in Opening the Medical Profession to Women.* Hastings, U.K.: K. Barry, 1895.

Boydston, Jeanne, Mary Kelly, and Anne Margolis. *The Limits of Sisterhood: The Beecher Sisters on Women's Rights and Woman's Sphere.* Chapel Hill: University of North Carolina Press, 1988.

Brownmiller, Susan. *In Our Time: Memoir of a Revolution.* New York: Dial Press, 1999.

Cammermeyer, Margarethe, with Chris Fisher. *Serving in Silence.* New York: Viking Penguin, 1994.

Cantarow, Ellen, with Susan Gushee O'Malley and Sharon Hartman Strom. *Moving the Mountain: Women Working for Social Change.* New York: The Feminist Press at the City University of New York, 1980.

Carson, Rachel. *Lost Woods: The Discovered Writing of Rachel Carson.* Linda Lear, ed. Boston: Beacon Press, 1998.

Catt, Carrie Chapman. "An Address to the Congress of the United States." New York: National Woman Suffrage Publishing Company, Inc., [1917?].

Clinton, Hillary Rodham. "Remarks to the United Nations Fourth World Conference on Women, Beijing, China, September 5, 1995." Available online: http://clinton3.nara.gov/WH/EOP/First_Lady/html/China/plenary.html.

———. "Remarks to the NGO Forum, Huairou, China, September 6, 1995." Available online: http://clinton3.nara.gov/WH/EOP/First_Lady/html/China/ngo.html.

Collins, Eileen. Telephone interview with Kathryn Cullen-DuPont, May 17, 2001.

Cooper, Anna J. *A Voice from the South by a Black Woman of the South.* 1892. Rpt., New York: Negro Universities Press, 1969.

Cullen-DuPont, Kathryn. *Encyclopedia of Women's History in America,* 2nd ed. New York: Facts On File, 2000.

Day, Dorothy. *The Long Loneliness: The Autobiography of Dorothy Day.* New York: Harper & Row Publishers, Inc., 1952.

Duniway, Abigail Scott. *Path Breaking: An Autobiographical History of the Equal Suffrage Movement in Pacific Coast States.* 1914. Rpt., New York: Schocken Books, 1971.

Earhart, Amelia. *Last Flight.* Arranged by George Palmer Putnam. New York: Harcourt, Brace and Company, Inc., 1937.

Flynn, Elizabeth Gurley. *The Rebel Girl.* New York: International Publishers, 1973.

Friedan, Betty. *Life So Far: A Memoir.* New York: Simon & Schuster, 2000.

Frost, Elizabeth, and Kathryn Cullen-DuPont. *Women's Suffrage in America: An Eyewitness History.* New York: Facts On File, 1992.

Fuller, Margaret. *The Essential Margaret Fuller.* Jeffrey Steele, ed. New Brunswick, NJ: Rutgers University Press, 1992.

Gilbert, Sandra M., and Susan Gubar. *The Norton Anthology of Literature by Women: The Tradition in English.* New York: W. W. Norton, 1985.

Goldman, Emma. *Living My Life.* 2 vols. 1931. Rpt., New York: Dover Publications, 1970.

Hall, David D. *The Antinomian Controversy, 1636–1638: A Documentary History.* Durham: Duke University Press, 1990.

Harper, Frances Ellen Watkins. *Poems on Miscellaneous Subjects.* Philadelphia: Merrihew and Thompson, 1857.

Harper, Ida Husted, ed. *History of Woman Suffrage.* Vols. 5 and 6 (1922). Rpt., Salem, NH: Ayer Company, 1985.

Jones, Mary Harris. *Autobiography of Mother Jones.* Mary Field Parton, ed. Chicago: Charles H. Kerr & Company, 1925.

Kaplan, Laura. *The Story of Jane: The Legendary Underground Feminist Abortion Service.* New York: Pantheon Books, 1995.

Keller, Helen. *The Story of My Life.* 1902. Rpt., New York: Penguin Books USA, 1988.

Liliuokalani. *Hawaii's Story By Hawaii's Queen.* 1898. Rpt., Honolulu, HI: Mutual Publishing, 1990.

Lyon, Mary. *The Inception of Mount Holyoke College; portions of letters written by Mary Lyon between 1831 and 1837.* Springfield, MA: Springfield Printing and Binding Co. [n.d.]

Mankiller, Wilma, and Michael Wallis. *Mankiller: A Chief and Her People.* New York: St. Martin's Press, 1993.

Moody, Anne. *Coming of Age in Mississippi.* 1968. Rpt., New York: Dell Publishing, 1976.

Morega, Cherrie, and Gloria Anzaldua, eds. *This Bridge Called My Back: Writings by Radical Women of Color.* New York: Kitchen Table: Women of Color Press, 1983.

Mott, Lucretia. *Lucretia Mott: Her Complete Speeches and Sermons.* Dana Greene, ed. New York: The Edwin Mellen Press, 1980.

Nation, Carry A. *The Use and Need of the Life of Carry A. Nation.* Topeka, KS: F. M. Steves & Sons, 1909.

New York Times. July 20, 1984, and June 15, 1993.

Paul, Alice. *Conversations with Alice Paul: Woman Suffrage and the Equal Rights Amendment*, typescript of an oral history conducted in 1972, 1973 by Amelia Fry, Regional Oral History Office, the Bancroft Library, University of California, Berkeley, 1976.

Packard, Mrs. E. P. W. *Marital Power Exemplified in Mrs. Packard's Trial and Self-Defense from the Charge of Insanity; Three Years' Imprisonment for Religious Belief, by the Arbitrary Will of a Husband with an Appeal to the Government to so Change the Laws as to Protect the Rights of Married Women.* Hartford: Published by the Authoress, 1866.

Rankin, Jeannette. *Activist for World Peace, Women's Rights, and Democratic Government*, typescript of an oral history conducted in 1972 by Malca Chall and Hannah Josephson, Regional Oral History Office, the Bancroft Library, University of California, Berkeley, 1974.

Rich, Adrienne. *The Dream of a Common Language: Poems 1974–1977*. New York: W. W. Norton and Company, 1978.

Rogers, Katharine M. *Early American Women Writers: From Anne Bradstreet to Louisa May Alcott, 1650–1895*. New York: Meridian, 1991.

Roosevelt, Eleanor. *The Autobiography of Eleanor Roosevelt*. 1961. Rpt., New York: Da Capo Press, 1992.

Rossi, Alice S. *The Feminist Papers: From Adams to de Beauvoir*. Boston: Northeastern University Press, 1988.

Ryan, Kevin and Marilyn. *Why I Am Still a Catholic*. New York: Riverhead Books, 1998.

Sanger, Margaret. *An Autobiography*. 1938. Rpt., New York: Cooper Square Press, 1999.

Shaw, Anna Howard. *Anna Howard Shaw: The Story of a Pioneer*. 1915. Rpt., Cleveland, OH: The Pilgrim Press, 1994.

Stanton, Elizabeth Cady. *Eighty Years and More: Reminiscences, 1815–1897*. 1898. Rpt., New York: Schocken Books, 1971.

Stanton, Elizabeth Cady, Susan B. Anthony, and Matilda Joslyn Gage, eds. *History of Woman Suffrage*. Vol. 1 (1881), vol. 2 (1882), vol. 3 (1886). Rpt., Salem, NH: Ayer Company, 1985.

Steinem, Gloria. *Outrageous Acts and Everyday Rebellions*, 2nd ed. New York: Henry Holt and Company, 1995.

Sterling, Dorothy. *We Are Your Sisters: Black Women in the Nineteenth Century*. New York: W. W. Norton & Company, 1984.

Stewart, Maria W. *Maria W. Stewart, America's First Black Woman Political Writer: Essays and Speeches.* Marilyn Richardson, ed. Bloomington and Indianapolis: Indiana University Press, 1987.

Still, William. *The Underground Railroad.* 1872. Rpt., New York: Arno Press, 1968.

Tarbell, Ida M. *All in the Day's Work.* New York: Macmillan Company, 1939.

Torricelli, Robert, and Andrew Carroll. *In Our Own Words: Extraordinary Speeches of the American Century.* New York: Kodansha America, Inc., 1999.

Truth, Sojourner. *Narrative of Sojourner Truth.* Written for Sojourner Truth by Olive Gilbert, 1850. Rpt., New York: Penguin Books, 1998.

Wald, Lillian. *The House on Henry Street.* 1915. Rpt., New Brunswick, NJ: Transaction Publishers, 1991.

Walker, Alice. *In Search of Our Mothers' Gardens: Womanist Prose.* New York: Harcourt Brace Jovanovich, 1984.

Walker, Alice, and Pratibha Parmer. *Warrior Marks.* New York: Harcourt Brace and Company, 1993.

Weld, Theodore Dwight, Angelina Grimké Weld, and Sarah Grimké. *Letters of Theodore Dwight Weld, Angelina Grimke Weld and Sarah Weld, 1822–1844.* 2 vols. Gilbert H. Barnes and Dwight L. Dumond, eds. New York: D. Appleton-Century Company, Inc., 1934.

Wells-Barnett, Ida B. *Crusade for Justice: The Autobiography of Ida B. Wells.* Alfreda M. Duster, ed. Chicago: University of Chicago Press, 1970.

Willard, Frances E. *Glimpses of Fifty Years: The Autobiography of an American Woman.* Chicago: Women's Temperance Publication Association, 1889.

Woodhull, Victoria. "The Beecher-Tilton Scandal: A Complete History of the Case, From November 1872 to the Present Time, with Mrs. Woodhull's Statement, as published in *Woodhull & Claflin's Weekly,* November 2, 1872." New York: F. A. Bancker, 1874.

Zaharias, Babe Didrikson. *This Life I've Led.* New York: A. S. Barnes and Company, Inc., 1955.

Sources and Permissions

~

Every effort has been made to seek out and obtain permissions from the copyright holders of the pieces selected for inclusion in American Women Activists' Writings. *Grateful acknowledgment is made for permission to reprint the following:*

Mary McLeod Bethune: excerpt from "Faith That Moved a Dump Heap." Reprinted by permission of the Sophia Smith Collection, Smith College, Northampton, Massachusetts.

Elizabeth Gurley Flynn: excerpt from *The Rebel Girl*. Reprinted by permission of International Publishers Co., New York.

Ida B. Wells-Barnett: excerpt from *Crusade for Justice*. Reprinted by permission of the University of Chicago Press.

Alice Paul: excerpt from *Conversations with Alice Paul: Woman Suffrage and the Equal Rights Amendment,* typescript of an oral history conducted in 1972, 1973 by Amelia Fry, Regional Oral History Office, the Bancroft Library, University of California, Berkeley. Reprinted by permission of the Bancroft Library.

Dorothy Day: excerpt from *The Long Loneliness* by Dorothy Day, copyright © 1952 by Harper & Row Publishers, Inc. Copyright renewed © 1980 by Tamar Teresa Hennessy. Reprinted by permission of HarperCollins Publishers, Inc.

Jeannette Rankin: excerpt from *Jeannette Rankin: Activist for World Peace, Women's Rights, and Democratic Government,* typescript of an oral history conducted in 1972 by Malca Chall and Hannah Josephson, Regional Oral History Office, the Bancroft Library, University of California, Berkeley. Reprinted by permission of the Bancroft Library.

Rachel Carson: Rachel Carson's writing © 1998 by Roger Allen Christie. Compilation, introduction, and text (other than Carson's

About the Editor

~

KATHRYN CULLEN-DUPONT is the author of *The Encyclopedia of Women's History in America* and *Elizabeth Cady Stanton and Women's Liberty*; co-author of *Women's Suffrage in America* and *Women's Rights on Trial*; contributor to *Academic American Encyclopedia*; permanent consultant for Grolier's *New Book of Knowledge* encyclopedia; and frequent guest lecturer at educational institutions. She lives in Brooklyn, New York, where she is at work on a novel.

OTHER COOPER SQUARE PRESS TITLES OF INTEREST

MARGARET SANGER
An Autobiography
New introduction by Kathryn Cullen-DuPont
516 pp., 1 b/w photo
0-8154-1015-8
$17.95

JUST FOR A THRILL
Lil Hardin Armstrong, First Lady of Jazz
James L. Dickerson
248 pp., 15 b/w photos
0-8154-1195-2
$28.95 cl.

MY ARCTIC JOURNAL
A Year among Ice-Fields and Eskimos
Josephine Peary
Foreword by Robert E. Peary
New introduction by Robert M. Bryce
280 pp., 67 b/w illustrations, maps, & diagrams
0-8154-1198-7
$18.95

KATHERINE MANSFIELD
A Darker View
Jeffrey Meyers
With a new introduction
344 pp., 29 b/w photos
0-8154-1197-9
$18.95

THE DESERT AND THE SOWN
The Syrian Adventures of the Female Lawrence of Arabia
Gertrude Bell
New introduction by Rosemary O'Brien
368 pp., 162 b/w photos
0-8154-1135-9
$19.95

ROE V. WADE
**The Untold Story of the Landmark Supreme Court Decision
That Made Abortion Legal
Updated Edition**
Marian Faux
404 pp., 15 b/w photos
0-8154-1093-X
$19.95

WITH THE ARMIES OF THE TSAR
A Nurse at the Russian Front, 1914–1918
Florence Farmborough
352 pp., 48 b/w photos, 4 maps
0-8154-1090-5
$19.95

GEORGE ELIOT
The Last Victorian
Kathryn Hughes
416 pp., 33 b/w illustrations
0-8154-1121-9
$19.95

GRANITE AND RAINBOW
The Hidden Life of Virginia Woolf
Mitchell Leaska
536 pp., 23 b/w photos
0-8154-1047-6
$18.95

MY STORY
Marilyn Monroe
Co-authored by Ben Hecht
New introduction by Andrea Dworkin
176 pp., 14 b/w & 4 color photos
0-8154-1102-2
$22.95 cl.

MARILYN MONROE
The Biography
Donald Spoto
752 pp., 50 b/w photos
0-8154-1183-9
$24.95

BLUE ANGEL
The Life of Marlene Dietrich
Donald Spoto
376 pp., 57 b/w photos
0-8154-1061-1
$18.95

DREAMGIRL & SUPREME FAITH
My Life as a Supreme
Updated Edition
Mary Wilson
732 pp., 150 b/w photos, 15 color photos
0-8154-1000-X
$19.95

FAITHFULL
An Autobiography
Marianne Faithfull with David Dalton
320 pp., 32 b/w photos
0-8154-1046-8
$16.95

ROCK SHE WROTE
Women Write About Rock, Pop, and Rap
Edited by Evelyn McDonnell & Ann Powers
496 pp.
0-8154-1018-2
$16.95

BACKSTAGE PASSES
Life on the Wild Side with David Bowie
Angela Bowie with Patrick Carr
368 pp., 36 b/w photos
0-8154-1001-8
$17.95

CLARA BOW
Runnin' Wild
David Stenn
With a new filmography
368 pp., 27 b/w photos
0-8154-1025-5
$21.95

LOVE AFFAIR
A Memoir of Jackson Pollock
Ruth Kligman
With a new introduction
224 pp., 3 b/w photos
0-8154-1009-3
$16.95

THE GREENWICH VILLAGE READER
Fiction, Poetry, and Reminiscences, 1872–2002
Edited by June Skinner Sawyers
800 pp., 1 b/w map
0-8154-1148-0
$35.00 cl.

Available at bookstores; or call 1-800-462-6420

 **Cooper Square Press**

150 Fifth Avenue
Suite 817
New York, NY 10011